OSS Essentials

Support System Solutions for Service Providers

Kornel Terplan

Wiley Computer Publishing

John Wiley & Sons, Inc.

NEW YORK · CHICHESTER · WEINHEIM · BRISBANE · SINGAPORE · TORONTO

Publisher: Robert Ipsen

Editor: Margaret Hendrey

Assistant Editor: Adaobi Obi

Managing Editor: Micheline Frederick

Text Design & Composition: North Market Street Graphics

This book is printed on acid-free paper. ∞

Published by John Wiley & Sons, Inc.

Published simultaneously in Canada.

This publication is designed to provide accurate and authoritative information in regard to the subject matter covered. It is sold with the understanding that the publisher is not engaged in professional services. If professional advice or other expert assistance is required, the services of a competent professional person should be sought.

Library of Congress Cataloging-in-Publication Data
Terplan, Kornel.
   OSS essentials : support system solutions for service providers / Kornel Terplan.
      p.   cm.
   "Wiley Computer Publishing."
   Includes bibliographical references and index.
   ISBN 0-471-39240-5 (pbk. : alk. paper)
   1. Computer networks—Management.   2. Internet service providers.
3. Computer technical support—Data processing.   4. Support services
(Management)—Data processing.   I. Title: Operations Support Systems essentials.
   II. Title.
TK5105.5 .T473 2001
004.67'8—dc21
                                                                00-068495

Printed in the United States of America.
10 9 8 7 6 5 4 3 2 1

Dedicated with love and affection to my daughters Krisztina and Kornelia

–KT

CONTENTS

Three principal information sources helped me to write this book. Being a member of the Telemanagement Forum, I have utilized the basic ideas of the Operations Map that helps to group business processes of service providers into fulfillment, assurance, and billing processes. I have also used tutorials and white papers from TeleStrategies Inc., a leading institution in the area of OSS strategies, products, interoperability, and integration. This information source was extremely helpful in judging the principal applicability of certain concepts, such as CORBA, EIS, and EAI. And finally, I have utilized my consulting experiences with AT&T, Unisource, France Telecom, German Telekom, Telcel, and Hungarian Telecom over the last 15 years. During this period of time, I have worked with subject-matter experts in practically all business areas of service providers. Dear friends, a very special thank you to everybody I have worked with during this period.

I would like to thank to Jozsef Wiener for brainstorming sessions; Karl Whitelock for his input on OSS trends and service portfolios; Matthew Lucas for his sharing rating and billing views; Endre Sara from Goldmann Sachs for preevaluating support systems; and Katalin Lanc for preparing the artwork for this publication.

Special thanks are due to Margaret Hendrey, Editor; Adaobi Obi, Assistant Editor; and Micheline Frederick, Managing Editor. They were extremely helpful in every phase of this production.

The telecommunications industry is transitioning from a circuit switched to a packet switched infrastructure. This technology paradigm change, combined with deregulation and privatization, challenges the existing support, documentation, and management systems currently in use with service providers. The broadening use of Internet technology by the majority of service providers is forcing them to reengineer, simplify, and unify their business processes. Success from these changes relies on the awareness that everybody is part of the supply value chain, consisting of customers, suppliers, manufacturers, and service providers. The principal goal of this book is to target the three high-priority success factors for service providers: business processes, support tools, and human resources.

After classifying service providers, Chapter 1 explores the market drivers in the telecommunications industry. Each of the principal drivers, such as growth, network complexity, communications convergence, and customer orientation are addressed individually. The service delivery cycle emphasizes the continuity of executing business processes that encompass service fulfillment, service assurance, and billing. Successful operations cannot be guaranteed without support, documentation, and management tools. The status, expectations, and trends of these tools are briefly discussed. Despite the continuous automation trends of processes, human resources remain the focal point of visions, decision making, and service creation, and they continue to deal with unexpected events and situations. Chapter 1 closes with a discussion of the strategic benefits of support systems.

Service portfolios are the key differentiators between service providers. In each offer, the service is on top of the physical infrastructure that represents wireline, wireless, and Internet technology. The products of service providers are a combination of physical and logical overlays, as introduced in Chapter 2. Service portfolios are grouped into wireline voice and data, wireless and mobile services, and video, cable, and integrated services. IP-based services are handled separately and independently from the fact that they may share physical resources with other non-IP services. Innovative services are also briefly discussed; some that might be very interesting targets for service providers include content management, Web hosting, application services provisioning—all new areas with very high potential profit margins. Chapter 2 also includes a complete list of basic principles that significantly impact products and services creation. These principles should be addressed by all kinds of service providers.

The focus of Chapter 3 is on the management protocols that enable communication between various managing and agent entities. Two major groups are addressed: (1) the traditional telecommunication protocols offering stability, robustness, and predictability at the price of higher development, implementation, and operating expenses, and (2) the enterprise protocols offering easy installation, low overhead, and acceptable performance at the price of lower predictability and security. Telecommunication Management Network (TMN) plays a strategic role for service providers; its layers are used throughout the book as a baselining instrument for assigning business processes and support tools. The Web-based management protocols and concepts that implement CIM/XML may revolutionarily change the operations of many support, documentation, and management systems. In this industry, XML is going to standardize the information content to be exchanged between systems; CORBA, DCOM, or other middleware solutions will actually execute the information exchange. Directories may play a key role to serve as repositories of all relevant information for customers, services, policies, and so on. Standardization, unification, and simplification of information exchange between support, documentation, and management systems should be a high priority for service providers.

Chapter 4 is devoted to customer-facing business processes of service providers. They include customer care, sales, problem handling, customer QoS management, customer relationship management, call rating and discounting, billing, and professional services. Each process flow is presented graphically; input and output information is detailed, and the sources and destinations are also clearly identified. Each principal function of the business process is described in necessary depth. When appropriate, practical examples are given. Also, the impacts of the paradigm change toward Internet technology are addressed.

Flow-through provisioning is the principal target in Chapter 5. All business processes of order processing and provisioning, including inventory management, service creation and deployment, service order processing, service activation, service problem resolution, service quality management, and security management are described in some depth. As in Chapter 4, each process flow is presented graphically, input and output information is detailed, and the sources and destinations are clearly identified. The principal functions of the business process presented in Chapter 5 are described in depth as necessary and practical examples are given. Again, the impacts of the paradigm change toward Internet technology are also addressed.

Chapter 6 deals with network operational processes such as fault management, network maintenance and restoration, performance monitoring, data collection, and data management. Each process flow is presented graphically, input and output information is detailed, and the sources and destinations are clearly identified. The principal functions of the business process that are introduced in Chapter 6 are described in necessary depth and when appropriate, practical examples are given. Again, the impacts of the paradigm change toward Internet technology are also addressed. Special emphasis is put on enabling technologies that help to increase the efficiency of network operations. These enabling technologies include mediation, data warehousing, and the use of SS7 as a tool for signaling and call data collection.

The second critical success factor is represented by support, documentation, and management systems. After briefly introducing the suppliers of tools, Chapter 7 offers a broad scope of product examples available on the market for service providers today. Management frameworks are discussed first, followed by the most widely used management applications. Best-of-suite products are introduced for customer care and billing, order processing and provisioning, and network operations. These solution examples are followed by the first implementation experiences of eOSS solutions. Service providers are very interested in integrating their support, documentation, and management systems. In order to help with this integration, the last segment of this chapter is devoted to integration concepts and engines.

The third critical success factor for service providers is people. Chapter 8 uses a very simple organizational structure to represent the generic service provider. Both building and maintaining the support organization are addressed in some depth. In order to help service providers streamline job profiles, examples are given for the responsibilities, job contacts, and qualifying experiences for selected jobs. This chapter also recommends optimal assignments of subject-matter experts to business processes and support tools. People expenses are always high in operations; head count estimates are given to various sizes of networks, represented by the number of managed objects. Finally, enabling technologies supporting workforce management are briefly outlined; they include document, knowledge, and workflow management.

Chapter 9 is devoted to estimate trends in the telecommunications industry, including technologies and support tools. Telco in the box summarizes the requirements for a compact, simplified set of business processes supported by various databases (such as customer, inventory, and portfolio) and by enabling technologies. Particular attention is paid in this chapter to emerging eOSS technologies addressing the need to provision, manage, and bill in near-real-time for IP-based services. This segment of the book helps service providers to reposition themselves in the ever changing digital economy and new ecoSystems environments.

Operations, Business, and Marketing Support Systems

1.1 Introduction

The telecommunications industry shows both evolutionary and revolutionary signs. Evolution is seen with incumbent carriers; revolutionary attributes are visible with new entrants. The technology itself shows a mixture of wireline, wireless, and Internet Protocol (IP) services supporting all principal communication forms such as voice, data, and video.

1.2 Status, Definitions, and Markets of Operations, Business, and Marketing Support Systems

Operations support systems (OSSs), business support systems (BSSs), and marketing support systems (MSSs) represent a very complex, but increasingly significant, segment of the communication industry. OSS, BSS, and MSS software enable the support, administration, and management from day-to-day operations to traffic trending, capacity planning, and forecasting of communication network services providers. Customer care, billing, provisioning, order processing, and network operational management are all functions implemented via OSSs, BSSs, and MSSs. Until recently, there was little opportunity for direct investments in this important telecommunications segment. Increasingly, however, service providers, both incumbent and new, have come to view these systems as critical service-differentiating assets. As a result, there is a growing number of public and private companies expected to benefit from the strategic importance of these support systems. The three principal support systems are referred to as 3SS in this book.

Besides traditional support systems, documentation and management systems are also extremely important. In some circumstances, they are considered part of network operational management. Documentation systems of telecommunications providers represent a very high value; both technical information and customer data are expected to be maintained. Relational and object-oriented databases are used with a migration toward Geographic Information Systems (GIS). Management systems are in charge of monitoring and administering network elements (routers, switches, mobile stations, nodes, etc.) and transmission routes for both backbone and access networks. Usually, they are heterogeneous systems, provided by manufacturers. If not differentiated otherwise, support systems also represent documentation and management systems.

1.2.1 Classification of Service Providers

Due to the opportunities given by deregulation in many countries, there are a number of new entrants in the telecommunications services industry. Product and service portfolios need some fine tuning in most cases because customers are faced with overlapping offers from various service providers. Service creation and provisioning are becoming more dynamic, and provider-customer interconnections are getting simpler by using Internet technology.

Telecommunications services providers can be grouped as follows:

ASP (applications service provider). Emerging service provider who must combine application, systems, and network management. Service level expectations are extremely high; the whole business of a customer may rely on this provider.

CAP (competitive access provider). Facilities-based or non–facilities-based; is similar to the ILEC, but has carefully selected local loops for high-profit commercial customers.

CLEC (competitive local-exchange carrier). Smaller, flexible provider who owns little or no telecommunications facilities (facilityless). By offering excellent customer care and new services, they try to build the support structure step-by-step. Their support systems are state-of-the-art, lightweight, and less expensive to operate. In certain cases, they use service bureaus for billing and provisioning.

CSP (cable service provider). Emerging service providers with offers for access networks. They still face technological challenges, which can be overcome. Support systems are practically nonexistent. In terms of support systems, they buy instead of build; occasionally, they use service bureaus for billing and provisioning.

CSP (content service provider). Emerging service providers who concentrate on the value, quality, and timeliness of content in eCommerce environments. They strongly cooperate with ISPs and ASPs.

ESP (enterprise service provider). Emerging service provider from the enterprise environment. They offer services for a limited user community with similar attributes to the provider. They use and customize their existing support systems that may not scale well.

ICP (integrated communications provider). Emerging provider with integrated services offer, concentrating on next generation, high-speed data and wireless services, in particular for profitable business users. Their acceptance in the market space is expected to be high. In terms of support systems, they buy instead of build; occasionally, they use service bureaus for billing and provisioning. They take advantage of the fact that intranet, extranet, virtual private networks, eCommerce, and multimedia applications require more bandwidth than is available over traditional circuit-switched voice networks.

IEX (interexchange carrier). Primarily responsible for long-distance services with stepwise penetration of the local-exchange area. They can be both incumbent and competitive providers with the result of the need for very heterogeneous support systems.

ILEC (incumbent local-exchange carrier). Strong provider who owns a considerable amount of telecommunications facilities and doesn't want to give away this position easily. Most likely, has a number of legacy support systems with little interoperability and integration in use. The result is high operating costs.

ISP (Internet service provider). Wide variety of sizes of these providers. Their main goal is to provide Internet access to business and private customers. Major challenges include peering to each other and to other carriers, managing quality, and offering acceptable performance.

NSP (network service provider). They are responsible for providing a highly reliable networking infrastructure, consisting of equipment and facilities. Their responsibilities are usually limited to the physical network, but element management systems are usually included in their offers.

PTT (Post, Telegraph, and Telephone). Strong provider who owns a considerable amount of telecommunications facilities and doesn't want to give away this position easily. Most likely, has a number of legacy support systems with little interoperability and integration in use. The result is high operating costs. It represents service providers prior to liberalization of telecommunications services.

WSP (wireless service provider). Carrier who provides cellular, personal, and mobile communications services.

1.2.2 Industry Issues of Support Systems

Service providers have been collecting experiences with 3SSs for a long period of time, in particular in ILEC and PTT environments. But, due to limited markets, the critical messages have never reached the right vendors or the public. Now, markets are growing for existing solutions, and completely new markets are opening for next generation support systems that support eCommerce. Industry issues of OSSs, BSSs, and MSSs are:

Convergence and telecom consolidation. It accelerates the use of advanced support systems. Consolidation of carriers across multiple end markets creates advantages for support systems targeting multiple end markets. It increases the complexity of telecom networks and the demand for the integration of support systems.

Developing support systems markets. Growth is dominated by new carrier adoptions and incumbent upgrades. Developing markets, such as data solutions, local number portability, and carrier interconnection, are likely to justify the next wave of support systems spendings.

Emergence of complex, multiplatform environments. Reliability and scalability of large centralized systems remain excellent. Service providers incorporate a multiplatform strategy augmenting existing investments in legacy solutions with newer technologies targeted at profitable customer market sectors.

Emphasis on telecom systems integration. Complex multiplatform, multivendor telecom networks require substantial systems integration for interoperability. With multiple client server and legacy support systems in place, integration capabilities of vendors are in high demand.

Growth of support systems is tied to share-shift among telecom end markets and carriers. The strongest near-term growth has been achieved by vendors targeting the fast-growing telecom end markets, emerging local-exchange carriers (LECs), and wireless carriers.

Outsourcing. Ongoing structural changes in the telecom industry will place new requirements on support systems. In order to concentrate on customer management, some back-office functions may be outsourced to service bureaus. These service bureaus might use support systems from the same vendors, but they use them in a shared fashion among multiple service providers.

Product-based vendor-driven solutions. Carriers increasingly demand solutions rather than raw technology and development kits for custom-developed support systems solutions. The advent of technology standards encourages the use of best-of-breed vendor solutions.

Upgrade cycles in support systems. As a result of global deregulation, carrier competition is driving the demand for new, more efficient back-office solutions. In addition to reducing operating expenses, advanced support systems improve time-to-market and often facilitate the introduction of new, revenue-producing solutions.

1.3 Market Drivers for Support Systems

The market is changing very rapidly. Support systems should be positioned well and should meet providers' expectations in a timely fashion. Principal market drivers are addressed in this segment.

1.3.1 Growth of the Global Telecommunications Market

Explosive telecom expansion driven by internal growth and acquisition is forcing telecommunications providers to assess the productivity of their current support systems. Growth and acquisition mean that the number of subscribers grows for existing services; new services are provisioned on existing infrastructures; and completely new services on new infrastructures are deployed or acquired. Several support system vendors have striven to capitalize on this opportunity with solutions that reduce complexity. These vendors do not usually replace existing systems, but add functionality to accommodate new services, such as

- Internet, intranets, and extranet
- Special data services on top of voice networks
- Wireless services
- Cable and video services
- Voice and fax services on top of IP
- Storage area networks
- Web hosting
- Content management
- Support of ASPs
- eCommerce services

Adding functionality and interoperability with each other opens new business opportunities for 3SS vendors.

1.3.2 Increasing Network Complexity

As a result of customer expectations, the time-to-market of new services is extremely short. Incumbent and new telecommunications services providers do not have the time to build anew, but instead combine existing and new infrastructures, such as copper, fiber, and wireless. They are deploying new services on the basis of a mixture of infrastructures as an overlay. These services use emerged and emerging technologies, such as

- Emerged technologies [voice networks, Integrated Services Digital Network (ISDN), circuit switching, packet switching, message switching, frame relay, Fast Ethernet, Fast Token Ring, and Fiber Distributed Data Interface/Copper Distributed Data Interface (FDDI/CDDI)]
- Emerging technologies [Asynchronous Transfer Mode (ATM), mobile and wireless, SMDS, SONET/SDH, cable, xDSL, and Broadband ISDN (B-ISDN)]

Each of these technologies has its own support system solutions. The only elements in a public switched telephone network (PSTN) that should be managed are the switches themselves. On average, the ratio of managed elements to subscriber lines is around 1 : 10,000. The advent of distributed, software-based switching and transmission created a large number of additional managed elements, about one for every 500 subscriber lines. Moreover, multiple elements per subscriber in digital loop carrier systems, digital cellular networks, or hybrid fiber-coax systems may cause an explosion in terms of managed elements. As a result, the size of configuration databases and the number of event messages generated by more intelligent network elements have grown exponentially over approximately the last 20 years.

Growth in the number of network elements has been accompanied by an increase in the complexity of items to be managed. SONET/SDH, ATM, and digital wireless are highly complex, with a high degree of interdependence among network elements. This, in turn, makes service activation and fault isolation a challenge, especially as the number of service providers increases. As networks shift from lower-speed, dedicated-rate, and inflexible services to mobile, fully configurable, bandwidth-on-demand, and high-speed services, support systems must adapt to this new situation.

1.3.3 Emerging Standards for Telecommunications Providers

When services are offered in combination, support systems should be modified, reengineered, and connected to each other. This opens new business opportunities for support systems vendors.

The introduction of standards for support systems is accelerating the demand for third-party support systems. Legacy systems are primarily proprietary systems not integrated across functional areas. Service providers depend upon custom development by internal development staff and outside integrators to connect various support systems. The introduction of technology standards, such as Telecommunication Management Network (TMN), Distributed Common Object Model (DCOM), Common Object Request Broker Architecture (CORBA), Telecommunication Information Network Architecture (TINA), and Web-Based Enterprise Management (WBEM), have begun to gain critical support by new support systems vendors.

Telecommunication Management Network (TMN) is a special network in its own right that is implemented to help manage the telecommunication network of the service provider. As such, it interfaces to one or more individual networks at several points in order to exchange information. It is logically separate from the networks it manages, and may be physically separate as well. However, TMN may use parts of the telecommunication networks for its own communications.

Telecommunication Management Network is an extension of the Open Systems Interconnection (OSI) standardization process. It attempts to standardize some of the functionality and many of the interfaces of the managed networks. When fully implemented, the result will be a higher level of integration. TMN is usually described by three architectures:

1. The functional architecture describes the appropriate distribution of functionality within TMN, appropriate in the sense of allowing for the creation of function blocks from which a TMN of any complexity can be implemented. The definition of function blocks and reference points between them leads to the requirements for the TMN-recommended interface specifications.

2. The information architecture, based on an object-oriented approach, gives the rationale for the application of OSI systems management principles to the TMN principles. The OSI systems management principles are mapped onto the TMN principles, and where necessary, are expanded to fit the TMN environment.

3. The physical architecture describes interfaces that can actually be implemented together with examples of physical components that make up the TMN.

Telecommunication Management Network distributes management responsibilities into several layers, such as business management layer (BML), service management layer (SML), network management layer (NML), element management layer (EML), and into the actual network element layer (NEL).

Distributed Common Object Model (DCOM) is the heart of Microsoft's ActiveOSS suite. Basically, DCOM is an integration framework infrastructure designed to facilitate communication between software components operating on the same host or with DCOM on multiple-networked hosts. It was originally developed to create interoperability between components. ActiveOSS acts as a centralized management and translation point for an OSS network. Conceptually, applications ride on top of the framework, but communicate through it. Distributed Common Object Model abstracts various application interfaces into objects, basically mapping the functions of the application into a common model that can be stored in a database. The common model allows the various applications to communicate in a uniform manner within the framework or across multiple-networked frameworks.

By abstracting interfaces into software objects, applications theoretically can be upgraded and/or changed without affecting surrounding systems because integration is based upon independent software components that communicate, not applications that are heavily modified to fit together one-to-one. In this sense, upgrading an application means mapping a new interface into the framework, or modifying an existing one. The framework needs to work with the interface, but doesn't need to affect details of the application. The framework is intended to create uniformity among application services without any modifications to source code. Application services are built into and managed by the framework. The overall architecture also incorporates the Smart TMN business process model and related work by TINA.

Common Object Request Broker Architecture (CORBA) is a generic communication framework to connect various network management applications. The object request broker (ORB) is the coordinator between distributed objects. The broker receives messages, inquiries, and results from objects, and routes them to the right destination. If the objects are in a heterogeneous environment, multiple brokers are required. They will talk to each other in the future by a new protocol based on Transmission Control Protocol/Internet Protocol (TCP/IP). There is no information model available; no operations are predefined for objects. But an object does exist containing all the necessary interfaces to the object request broker. For the description, the Interface Definition Language (IDL) is being used. There are no detailed management information bases (MIBs) for objects because open management architecture (OMA) is not management specific.

The functional model consists of the Object Services Architecture. It delivers the framework for defining objects, services, and functions. Examples of services are instantiation, naming, storing objects' attributes, and the distribution/receipt of events and notification. Common Object Request Broker Architecture (CORBA) services and facilities represent more generic services; they are expected to occur in multiple applications or they are used in specific applications. The driving force beyond designing common facilities for systems management is the X/Open Systems Management Working Group. The Managed Set Service, defined by this group, encourages grouping of objects in accordance with their management needs, resulting in easier administration. In the future, more services are expected to be defined; the next is an Event Management Service that expands the present Object Event Service by a flexible mechanism of event filtering.

Telecommunications Information Networking Architecture (TINA) is based on the concept that call processing in networks, and its control and management, are separated from each other. TINA is actually a concept integrator from intelligent network (IN), TMN, open distributed processing (ODP) from ISO and CORBA from object management group (OMG). The core is OSI-based network management, expanded by the layered structure of TMN. But the emphasis with TINA is not on the management of network elements, but on the network and services layers. TINA is going to be standardized by a consortium consisting of telecommunications suppliers and computer and software vendors.

Web-Based Enterprise Management (WBEM) is a joint initiative of many manufacturers led by Compaq, Microsoft, and Cisco. The initial announcement called for defining the following specifications:

■ *HyperMedia Management Schema (HMMS).* An extensible data description for representing the managed environment that was to be further defined by the Desktop Management Task Force (DMTF).

■ *HyperMedia Object Manager (HMOM).* Data model consolidating management data from different sources; a C++ reference implementation and specification, defined by Microsoft and Compaq, to be placed in the public domain.

■ *HyperMedia Management Protocol (HMMP).* A communication protocol embodying HMMS, running over HTTP, and with interfaces to SNMP and DMI.

■ *Common Information Model (CIM).* It is the basis of the information exchange between various management applications.

Web-Based Enterprise Management (WBEM) is helpful to unify and simplify network management. The combination of CIM and eXtensible Markup Language (XML) is going to set the basics of a new standard that significantly facilitates the interoperability between various support, documentation, and management systems. In many cases, they will be embedded into middleware solutions. CIM and XML are enablers for management intranets that represent an easy entry of integrating various support systems.

The implementation of standard gateways enables interaction between newer client/server solutions with existing legacy systems and eases interoperability among all support systems. In particular, TMN may help to streamline support systems' processes and to position support systems.

1.3.4 Deregulation and Privatization

Telecommunications service competition began in the 1980s in the United States led by MCI with 3SSs playing a key role. The AT&T divestiture in 1984 marked a major breakthrough. The second significant milestone was the Telecom Act of 1996. As telecom deregulation continues, with Regional Bell Operating Companies (RBOCs) actively pursuing the long-distance market and long-distance carriers moving into local services, major 3SS reengineering efforts are expected.

Under the pressure of the European Commission (EC), Europe is in the process of deregulation and privatization. It is a much slower process than in the United States because multiple countries are involved with their own agendas. Interoperability of support systems is more difficult than in the United States; at the same time, it offers opportunities for support systems vendors. It is assumed that Asia/Pacific, South America, Eastern Europe, and Africa will follow this deregulation and privatization trend.

Competition is everywhere: long-distance, local exchange, ISP, cable, and wireless. In many cases, 3SSs are the differentiators. The best support systems opportunities are seen with CLECs. Support systems' requirements vary substantially from carrier to carrier. As a result, CLEC 3SS strategies are ranging from internal development to outsourcing to systems integrators and to third-party software/service providers. CLECs could be small or midsize; they may or may not own facilities. In all cases, they must interoperate with ILECs by opening the support systems to permit access by CLECs in various phases of provisioning, order processing, and service activation. Key issues are:

- *Local Number Portability (LNP).* It allows customers to retain their telephone numbers even if they change service providers. It is not only the telephone number that is important; customers also typically want to retain access to advanced features they have come to expect from an intelligent network.

- *Extranets connecting support systems of ILECs and CLECs.* ILECs are required to provide access to information on five classes of support systems. They are pre-ordering, ordering, provisioning, repair, and maintenance. This is now the principal focus of local and access service providers.

- *Directory services.* Real-time service processing requires additional customer-related data. The expanded directory role includes end-user authorization and authentication. It also includes the real-time allocation of network resources according to a user's class of service and other policy-based variables. Directory enabled networks (DENs) promise to increase momentum for directory services by bringing physical infrastructure under the directory umbrella and tackling the standardization of directory information.

Incumbent service providers have turned to advanced support systems to differentiate their long-distance or local-exchange services from each other. After a substantial investment in custom systems in recent years, many incumbents have begun to focus on upgrading select support systems with best-of-breed technologies. Many of them try to augment older systems to add more flexibility while sustaining traditional levels of performance and reliability. This creates additional complexity and requires that new management solutions designed for advanced equipment also work with older technologies.

As a result, umbrella types of support systems are in demand, opening new opportunities for vendors of support systems with integration capabilities. To remain competitive, incumbent carriers need to deliver an increasingly larger number of new products and services. This has created a mixture of equipment, software, and services within many carriers.

Innovation and reengineering on behalf of the incumbent carriers show a trend toward:

Better customer care. Based on call detail record (CDR) and other resource utilization–related data, unsophisticated customer analysis can be accomplished. It includes discovering trends in customer behavior, traffic patterns, reasons for frauds, and also service-related items.

Convergent billing. The customer may expect to receive one bill for all services, such as voice, data, video, and Internet. The minimal requirement is to receive multiple bills with electronic staples.

Rapid provisioning of new services. Based on additional support systems, provisioning can be expedited by better interfaces and more accurate data.

Service differentiation. Still using the same infrastructures, new services can be created and deployed. By carefully defining the value-added nature, they may be considered by customers as differentiators.

Offering new services, such as Internet access, xDSL, VPN, and VoIP. Also, incumbent service providers are expected to react rapidly to new communication needs, including offering Internet access for reasonable money, the deployment of xDSL, digital subscriber line, virtual private networks (VPNs), and voice over IPs (VoIP).

In each of these cases, either the deployment of new support systems or the customization of existing 3SSs is required. In both cases, additional market opportunities open for support systems vendors.

1.3.5 Communication Convergence

Advanced technology, coupled with deregulation, is driving communications convergence. Customers prefer to get all types of services, such as long-distance and local voice, data/Internet, cable/video, and wireless access from the same service provider. Voice is expected to support both local and long-distance, requiring the capability to play a LEC and IEX role at the same time. Data is gaining importance for both local and long-distance, and usually does include Internet access. Data is supposed to reach voice volumes within 5 years, requiring the total rebuild of circuit-switching technology. Cable is expected to accommodate voice and data in addition to video. Wireless includes all kinds of mobile services and satellites supporting voice, video, and data.

Deregulation meant to encourage competition through the proliferation of new entrants. Looking to gain share, carriers are entering each other's markets, blurring traditional lines between services, geographic coverage, and communication platforms. Aggressive new carriers have moved rapidly to establish nationwide service networks, consolidating local, long-distance, Internet, wireless, and cable services under one umbrella. Incumbent carriers are trailing this way of convergence. The United States shows an excellent example of this convergence; the big convergence carriers cover most end markets. But they still leave room for hundreds of point products, mostly best-of-breed telecommunications products and services. Communication convergence necessitates the deployment of next generation support systems. Relying upon advanced technologies, client/server or Web-based support systems enable convergence carriers to offer their customers higher total value through new, innovative products and services, superior customer service, and customized pricing and billing. At the same time, support systems guarantee profitability by increasing effectiveness of processes by automation of all routine processes and by supervising quality of service metrics.

1.3.6 Customer Orientation

Competition is driving telecommunications service providers to emphasize customer management. Driven by global competition, carriers are likely to focus on improving the total value of their services—quality, support, and price—as a means to retain customers. Many of these improvements will come from advanced support systems. Besides improving the customer interface (e.g., offering Web access), granular data available with new support systems can be utilized to retain key customers and reduce the amount of customer churn. Over the long range, further differentiation is expected. High-margin customers may receive special treatment, average customers just average services—similar to other industries.

Customer network management (CNM) incorporates a class of support systems that enable end users to securely view, troubleshoot, reconfigure, and generate reports on their subscribed telecommunication services. CNM provides strategic links to the customer and allows service providers to further differentiate their offerings. Support systems' vendors are expected to offer the following:

- *Performance.* Extraction of the information from the network without slowing overall network operations.

- *Customization.* Packaging information so that customers can receive an appropriate level of detail in a way they can understand.

- *Security.* Delivery of the information to the customer in a cost-effective and secure manner, so that customers see only relevant information about their portion of the network.

It is expected that Web technology is used to deliver this service. CNM represents a modest source of incremental growth for 3SS suppliers.

Certain support systems services can also be outsourced. The customers may not be aware where the 3SS services come from. Today's outsourced solutions are with service bureaus. They may outsource all or part of the carrier's support systems. In the latter case, the vendor relies upon remote access to the carrier's existing solution to deliver incremental functionality. For most emerging carriers, the benefits of outsourcing outweigh the negatives. The application services provider (ASP) model may gain momentum here.

1.3.7 ASP Model

There is an industry trend that shows a number of of companies teaming up in an attempt to meet the market demand for streamline OSS applications.

OSS APSs pull together applications rather than create their own, and more companies are entering this space. Their success depends on their value to the network service providers and on how their solutions integrate across each OSS application.

BusinessNow from NetworkOSS is a good example of an ASP model. Its applications suite includes components in interconnections, billing, customer care, sales force automation, trouble administration, provisioning, activation, and network management. An unbiased collection of OSS applications from a number of suppliers enables NetworkOSS to form partnerships with its customers.

The present suite consists of the following products:

- Cygent Inc. provides its eBusiness support systems (eBSS) to streamline each step in the demand chain through an integrated Internet storefront that supports one-to-one marketing, online shopping and ordering, bill presentment and payment, as well as customer self-care.

- Daleen offers solutions that include eCare for Internet self-care and partner management, billing via BillPlex, and SwitchFlow for service activation.

- DSET offers a suite of electronic bonding gateways for customers that need to interconnect their OSSs with their trading partners to exchange information and share network capabilities.

- OpenCon adds its product portfolio to support billing mediation. It is a data mediation engine that interfaces new protocols, such as CORBA and IDL, with legacy protocols, such as TL1.

- Vitria Technology Inc. contributes with its eBusiness platform, called Business-Ware, which automates business processes across an extended enterprise.

- Portal Software, Inc. offers Infranet, which helps with customer care and billing to build and deploy new business models, support subscriber growth, and develop new business opportunities for service providers who take advantage of ASP capabilities.

- Various systems integrators, including BusinessEdge Solutions, Cap Gemini, Ernst & Young, and DataMat, help with targeted customization of the OSS package.

The buy or build dilemma for service providers enters a third dimension with ASPs. The jury is still out as to whether OSS ASPs have the staying power to become successful.

1.4 The Service Delivery Cycle

The telecommunications industry today is experiencing a number of changes and challenges. Deregulation, new services, new technologies, reengineering business processes, mergers, and acquisitions are just a few that demand attention. Also, multiple concepts such as service differentiation, quality of service, time-to-market, customer care, return on investment, and total cost of ownership request attention on behalf of business managers of service providers. Quality of processes, automation of processes, and integration of support and management tools may mean the difference between business success and failure.

Business processes may be organized in several ways, such as

- Customer care, service development, order processing, provisioning, network and systems management, and billing
- Fulfillment, service assurance, and billing processes

These processes are in continuous change and development. The information exchange is the glue between individual processes and their functions. Fully integrated structures are based on workflow concepts. The implementation and maintenance of workflow concepts require a phased approach from manual over mechanical toward integrated and fully automated solutions.

Figure 1.1 shows a simplified view of principal business processes and some of their key functions. Basically, this illustration emphasizes all potential layers between the customer and the physical networking infrastructure. The glue between customers and the infrastructure is represented by order processing and provisioning, and the central repository, called the data warehouse.

Table 1.1 defines the most important functions of the processes introduced in Figure 1.1.

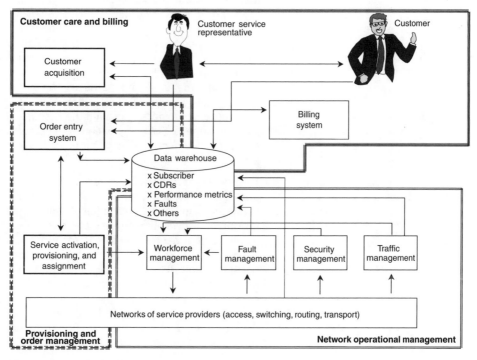

Figure 1.1 Principal support processes.

Table 1.1 Principal Processes and Functions

PRINCIPAL PROCESSES	SHORT DESCRIPTION OF PRINCIPAL PROCESSES
Customer Care and Billing Processes	
The customer interface management process	This process may be a distinct process or may be performed as part of the individual customer-care processes on an individual service or cross-service basis. These are the processes of directly interacting with customers and translating customer requests and inquiries into appropriate events, such as the creation of an order or trouble ticket or the adjustment of a bill. This process logs customer contacts, directs inquiries to the appropriate party, and tracks the status to completion. In those cases where customers are given direct access to service management systems, this process assures consistency of image across systems, and security to prevent a customer from harming its network or those of other customers. The aim is to provide meaningful and timely customer contact experiences as frequently as the customer requires.
The sales process	This process encompasses learning about the needs of each customer, and educating the customer about the communications services that are available to meet those needs. It includes working to create a match between the customer's expectations and the service provider's ability to deliver. Depending on the service provider process, it can be purely selling or can include various levels of support. The sales process may include preorder work and interfaces. The aim is to sell the correct service to suit the customer's need and to set appropriate expectations with the customer. Service-level agreement (SLA) negotiation, request for proposal (RFP) management, and negotiation are led from this process.
The problem handling process	This process is responsible to receive service complaints from customers, resolve them to the customer's satisfaction, and provide meaningful status on repair or restoration activity. This process is also responsible to be aware of any service-affecting problems, including notifying customers in the event of a disruption—whether reported by the customer or not. This proactive management also includes planned maintenance outages. The aim is to have the largest percentage of problems proactively identified and communicated to the customer, to provide meaningful status, and to resolve in the shortest time frame.

Table 1.1 *(Continued)*

PRINCIPAL PROCESSES	SHORT DESCRIPTION OF PRINCIPAL PROCESSES
The customer QoS management process	This process encompasses monitoring, managing, and reporting quality of service (QoS) as defined in service descriptions, SLAs, and other service-related documents. It includes network performance, but also performance across all service parameters (e.g., orders completed on time). Outputs of this process are standard (predefined) and exception reports, including but not limited to dashboards, performance of a service against an SLA, reports of any developing capacity problems, reports of customer usage patterns, etc. In addition, this process responds to performance inquiries from the customer. For SLA violations, the process supports notifying problem handling and for QoS violations, notifying service quality management. The aim is to provide effective monitoring. Monitoring and reporting must provide service provider (SP) management and customers meaningful and timely performance information across the parameters of the services provided. The aim is also to manage service levels that meet specific SLA commitments and standard service commitments.
The call rating and discounting process	The rating and discounting process encompasses the following functional areas ■ Applying the correct rating rules to usage data on a customer-by-customer basis, as required ■ Applying any discounts agreed to as part of the ordering process ■ Applying promotional discounts and charges ■ Applying outage credits ■ Applying rebates due because SLAs were not met ■ Resolving unidentified usage The aim is to correctly rate usage and to correctly apply discounts, promotions, and credits. Flat-rate accounting with IP-based services will not survive. In order to implement usage-based accounting, multiple data sources should be considered that include security servers, routers, applications, and all other components that have something to do with IP packets. This process determines the rates depending on the application and resource. In many cases, this process is embedded into mediation solutions.

Continues

Table 1.1 Principal Processes and Functions *(Continued)*

PRINCIPAL PROCESSES	SHORT DESCRIPTION OF PRINCIPAL PROCESSES
The invoicing and collection process	This process encompasses sending invoices to customers, processing their payments, and performing payment collections. In addition, this process handles customer inquiries about bills and is responsible to resolve billing problems to the customer's satisfaction. The aim is to provide a correct bill and, if there is a billing problem, resolve it quickly with appropriate status to the customer. An additional aim is to collect monies due to the service provider in a professional and customer-supportive manner. Some providers offer invoicing and collections functions for other providers as a service.
The consulting and supporting process	This process strives to reach a high level of collaboration between providers and customers. This collaboration includes establishing a special team of consultants for the customer, arranging periodic status and planning meetings, and clearly defining the interfaces between provider and customer.
Order Processing and Provisioning Processes	
The inventory management process	This process encompasses physical equipment and the administration of this equipment. The process is involved in the installation and acceptance of equipment, with the physical configuration of the network, but also with handling of spare parts and the repair process. Software upgrades are also a responsibility of this process. Implementing IP-based services, the number of managed objects is going to grow. Physical assets also include servers, access servers, gateways, gatekeepers, routers, and new connections. These components are identified by site, ports, and type. They are connected to each other during the provisioning process. Logical asset management includes domains, addresses, and other identification alternatives. Critical success factors are completeness of data, actuality of data, synchronization between multiple databases, and aligning assets between inventory databases and the actual network.

Table 1.1 *(Continued)*

PRINCIPAL PROCESSES	SHORT DESCRIPTION OF PRINCIPAL PROCESSES
The service creation, planning, and development process	This process is expected to be periodically executed. Triggers may come from customers or from the marketing departments of telecommunications providers. This process encompasses the following functional areas ■ Designing technical capability to meet specified market need at desired cost ■ Ensuring that the service (product) can be properly installed, monitored, controlled, and billed ■ Initiating appropriate process and methods modifications, as well as initiating changes to levels of operations personnel and training required ■ Initiating any modifications to the underlying network or information systems to support the requirements ■ Performing preservice testing that the technical capability works and that the operational support process and systems function properly ■ Ensuring that sufficient capacity is available to meet forecasted sales ■ Developing IP-based services. There is a shift toward applications. The difference can be clearly seen when e-mail and videoconferencing are compared with managed lines and ISDN. The trend is without any doubt toward software-based definition of new services with the result of very high change rates in networking infrastructures.
The network planning and development process	This process encompasses development and acceptance of strategy, description of standard network configurations for operational use, and definition of rules for network planning, installation, and maintenance. It is about the planning of boundary nodes, routes, and capacity. Considering IP-based services, multiple alternatives for the implementation are available. It depends on the technologies IP can collaborate with. Popular solutions are ■ IP over ATM ■ IP over frame relay ■ IP over SONET/SDH

Continues

Table 1.1 Principal Processes and Functions *(Continued)*

PRINCIPAL PROCESSES	SHORT DESCRIPTION OF PRINCIPAL PROCESSES
	After the topology of the networks has been determined, physical and logical connections are expected to be provisioned. Also, backup and reserve capacity is provisioned; this way, future customer demands can be met more rapidly than before.
	Special modeling tools are very useful to predict future performance under various load conditions. These tools utilize *what-if* scenarios to emulate performance under various load conditions. These tools depend today on the protocols used. Many providers work with multiple tools; there are practically different tools for each service. This process is also responsible to select and decide about measurability of SLA metrics.
	This process also deals with designing the network capability to meet a specified service need at the desired cost and for ensuring that the network can be properly installed, monitored, controlled, and billed. The process is also responsible for ensuring that enough network capacity will be available to meet the forecasted demand and supporting cases of nonforecasted demand. Based on the required network capacity, orders are issued to suppliers or other network operators and site preparation and installation orders are issued to the network inventory management or to a third-party network constructor. A design of the logical network configuration is provided to the network provisioning process.
The network provisioning process	This process encompasses the configuration of the network to ensure that network capacity is ready for provisioning of services. It carries out network provisioning as required to fulfill specific service requests and configuration changes to address network problems. The process must assign and administer identifiers for provisioned resources and make them available to other processes. Note that the routine provisioning of specific instances of a customer service—in particular, simple services such as Plain Old Telephone Service (POTS)—may not normally involve network provisioning, but may be handled directly by service provisioning from a preconfigured set.
	Provisioning IP-based services involves a large number of nodes and servers that are completely unknown in a voice environment. Provisioning requires experienced subject matter experts.

Table 1.1 *(Continued)*

PRINCIPAL PROCESSES	SHORT DESCRIPTION OF PRINCIPAL PROCESSES
	Provisioning volumes of today can be managed. Future requests must be satisfied by automated provisioning procedures, leaving just unusual provisioning requests to human operators. Workflow is considered the glue to connect multiple processes to each other.
The service ordering process	The service ordering process includes all the functions of accepting a customer's order for service, tracking the progress of the order, and notifying the customer when the order is complete. Orders can include new, change, and disconnect orders for all or part of a customer's service, as well as cancellations and modifications to orders. Preorder activity that can be tracked is included in this process. The development of an order plan may be necessary when service installation is to be phased in, and the need for preliminary feasibility requests and/or pricing estimates may be part of this process when certain services are ordered. The aim is to order the service the customer requested, support changes when necessary, and keep the customer informed with meaningful progress of the order, including its successful completion.
The service configuration process	This process encompasses the installation and/or configuration of services for specific customers, including the installation/configuration of customer premises equipment. It also supports the reconfiguration of service (either due to customer demand or problem resolution) after the initial service installation. The aim is to correctly provide service configuration within the time frame required to meet ever decreasing intervals. Offering IP-based services, additional functions must be considered. In particular, firewalls, application services such as e-mail, Web hosting, and their configurations are important. Also the setting of parameters to support QoS and SLA requirements is important. The more that can be automated, the better service providers do in the competitive market.
The security management process	Due to factors such as opening networks, connecting partners, and using a public domain such as the Internet, security risks increase considerably. Virtual private networks (VPNs) are one of the possible answers to combining existing infrastructure with acceptable protection. Security expectations may be different in various industries, but the generic security management procedures are identical or at least very similar. Security management enables

Continues

Table 1.1 Principal Processes and Functions *(Continued)*

PRINCIPAL PROCESSES	SHORT DESCRIPTION OF PRINCIPAL PROCESSES
	intranet managers to protect sensitive information by limiting access to Web servers and network devices by users both inside and outside of enterprises and notifying the security manager of attempted or actual violations of security.
	Security management is in charge of protecting all systems solutions. This process includes a planning and controlling function. In particular, three basic threats are considered: (1) loss of availability of services, (2) loss of integrity, and (3) loss of privacy.
Network Operational Management Processes	
The service problem resolution process	This process encompasses isolating the root cause of service-affecting and non–service-affecting failures and acting to resolve them. Typically, failures reported to this process affect multiple customers. Actions may include immediate reconfiguration or other corrective actions. Longer-term modifications to the service design or to the network components associated with the service may also be required. The aim is to understand the causes impacting service performance and to implement immediate fixes or initiate quality improvement efforts.
The service quality management process	This process supports monitoring service or product quality on a service class basis in order to determine whether ■ Service levels are being met consistently ■ There are any general problems with the service or product ■ The sale and use of the service is tracking to forecasts This process also encompasses taking appropriate action to keep service levels within agreed targets for each service class and to either keep ahead of demand or alert the sales process to slow sales. The aim is toward effective service-specific monitoring and to provide management and customers meaningful and timely performance information across the parameters of the specific service. The aim is also to manage service levels to meet SLA commitments and standard commitments for the specific service. There have been quality metrics for voice services for a long time. For IP-based services, the term *quality* is relatively new. The whole philosophy behind IP-based services is to offer best-effort quality depending on the

Table 1.1 *(Continued)*

PRINCIPAL PROCESSES	SHORT DESCRIPTION OF PRINCIPAL PROCESSES
	capacity constraints of networking infrastructures—but there are no guarantees even for that. This level of quality cannot be tolerated by business users. There are two alternatives with IP-based services: ■ Integrated Services (IntServ): This alternative supports RSVP and, as a result, bandwidth is guaranteed for application network ingress and egress points. ■ Differentiated Services (DiffServ): This alternative analyzes the type of service (ToS) header of IPv4 and assigns priorities depending on the ToS entries. Priority setting in IP nodes is controlled by policy-based networking.
The network maintenance and restoration process	This process encompasses maintaining the operational quality of the network in accordance with required network performance goals. Network maintenance activities can be preventative—such as scheduled routine maintenance—or corrective. Corrective maintenance can be in response to faults or to indications that problems may be developing (proactive). This process responds to problems, initiates tests, does analysis to determine the cause and impact of problems, and notifies service management of possible effects on quality. The process issues requests for corrective actions. Supervisory functions should be extended for IP-based services. In most cases, distributed monitoring capabilities must be implemented. Voice networks use Transaction Language 1 (TL1), Common Management Information Protocol (CMIP), and TMN as the basis of supervising status and resource utilization. The IP world brings Simple Network Management Protocol (SNMP) and Remote Monitoring (RMON) into the supervisory scenario. Powerful filters and correlation engines are required for the reduction of the total amount of data generated by the supervisory function.
The data collection and data management process	This process encompasses the collection of usage data and events for the purpose of network performance and traffic analysis. This data may also be an input to billing (rating and discounting) processes at the service management layer, depending on the service and its architecture.

Continues

Table 1.1 Principal Processes and Functions *(Continued)*

PRINCIPAL PROCESSES	SHORT DESCRIPTION OF PRINCIPAL PROCESSES
	The process must provide sufficient and relevant information to verify compliance/noncompliance to SLAs. The SLAs themselves are not known at the NML. The process must provide sufficient usage information for rating and billing.
	This process must ensure that the network performance goals are tracked, and that notification is provided when they are not met (threshold exceeded, performance degradation). This also includes thresholds and specific requirements for billing. This includes information on capacity, utilization, traffic, and usage collection. In some cases, changes in traffic conditions may trigger changes to the network for the purpose of traffic control. Reduced levels of network capacity can result in requests to network planning for more resources.
	In voice environments, switches and central office (CO) switches are the principal sources of data. Mediation devices collect data, process them, and distribute them to the rating and billing processes. The variety of data sources in IP environments is much higher. Routers, security servers, and firewalls may serve as data sources. Also, higher protocol layers, such as the application layer (e.g., use of RMON2 probes), may serve as data sources. All other processes are provided with raw data by this process. It is mandatory to have powerful and efficient database or data-warehousing solutions.

Most processes and functions represent a cycle starting with the evaluation of customer expectations and requirements, followed by product portfolio decisions. This result is the creation of new products or changes in the existing product portfolio. After receiving customer orders, the functions of order management and provisioning, such as order processing, service configuration, and service installation, take over. Service assurance is responsible for stable operations within the limits of service level agreements (SLAs). Finally, utilized services and resources are billed to customers. Billing records for both voice and IP data can also be utilized for customer analysis in order to recognize usage trends and future customer expectations. As part of the service assurance process, utilization thresholds are continuously supervised; if needed, resource changes and extensions are initiated. Figure 1.2 displays this never-ending cycle of business processes and their functions of providers.

Below these business processes, there are many support, documentation, and management systems; most of them are legacy applications, some of them are best-of-breed, and just a few of them are integrated with each other.

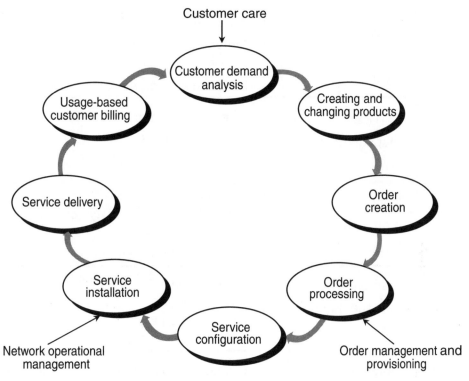

Figure 1.2   Service delivery cycle.

1.5 Support, Documentation, and Management Systems

The technology offers a variety of systems at various layers of the communication hierarchy. Telecommunications providers prefer the use of layers of TMN. Tools can be allocated to these layers in accordance with Figure 1.3.

This figure not only concentrates on support systems, management tools, and documentation solutions, but also includes decision support systems, planning tools, reporting software for QoS and service quality, end-to-end monitoring applications, and element-level system monitoring and configuration systems.

Tools are segmented by products such as voice, data, cable, wireless, and video. Every product has separate support systems, most likely also separate documentation systems, and eventually shared management systems. Sharing is possible at the low infrastructure layer due to the fact that multiple products may share the same infrastructure. In such cases, management systems offer management solutions for the physical components only; network- and service-layer alarm consolidation and management is very rare.

Business management layer	Business support systems Marketing support systems Planning tools Decision support systems
Service management layer	Operations support systems Service assurance tools Service management tools
Network management layer	Operations support systems Network management systems Network monitors Documentation systems
Element management layer	Element management systems System monitors Configuration systems Documentation systems
Network element layer	Configuration systems System monitors

Figure 1.3 TMN layers and tools.

In terms of support systems, Figure 1.4 shows the most likely solutions with telecommunications providers. Various agents are executing tasks downloaded and supervised by support systems. But the fact is that practically each product/service requires a separate support system. Large ILECs and CLECs operate a no-longer controllable number of support systems. Integration is on demand. Connecting support systems to each other could be the first step by using application programming interfaces (APIs), but bilateral information exchange cannot be the ultimate solution for various reasons:

- Too many individual interfaces
- High sensitivity against changes in individual support systems
- Difficult migration steps toward a more universal information exchange model

Object-oriented technology (OOT) is emerging and becoming more accepted by telecommunications providers. Its augmentation with a standards-based distributed object environment infrastructure can provide carrier-grade capabilities that can help

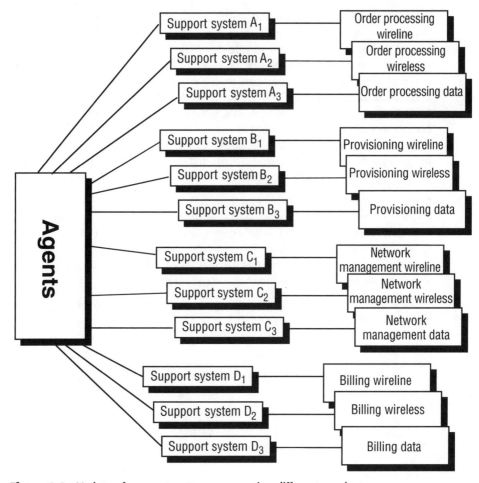

Figure 1.4 Variety of support systems supporting different products.

with the integration of support, documentation, and management systems. Using this technology, an ORB takes over the central control of information exchange between various tools. The result is that each tool must support just one interface to the ORB.

The primary goals of CORBA within the TMN architecture model include

- Separation of interface from implementation
- Platform and language independence
- Interoperability
- Location transparency

With an IDL that permits object interfaces to have definition independent of the object's implementation, CORBA becomes a very powerful tool. For example, legacy and TMN Q3 interfaces can remain intact and more easily interface to the data via standard and interoperable CORBA objects. CORBA-compliant client objects can be bound to servers statically or dynamically. Static binding is used when the client knows the server interface at compile time. The IDL compiler generates language-specific object definitions that link the client to the server. Clients that need to discover an object at run time and construct a request dynamically can use the Dynamic Invocation Interface (DII). An interface repository that is defined as a function of CORBA supports the DII. By accessing information in the interface repository, a client can retrieve all of the information necessary about an object's interface to construct and issue a request at run time. Requests can originate from many different languages, hardware platforms, and distributed object environments, including Orbix from Iona, Active/DCOM from Microsoft, or even downloadable Java applets.

Common Object Request Broker Architecture (CORBA) supplies a methodology to create a seamless TMN of legacy and new technology support systems that can pass information easily through the data communication network (DCN). CORBA also enables support for the Web by supporting both the Java and ActiveX models directly. Figure 1.5 shows this arrangement. The ORB is the glue for legacy and new support, documentation, and management systems.

Shallow integration may also be implemented. In this case, each legacy and new system is provided with universal Web access. Universal browsers gain access to each support, documentation, and management system, and work with data provided by

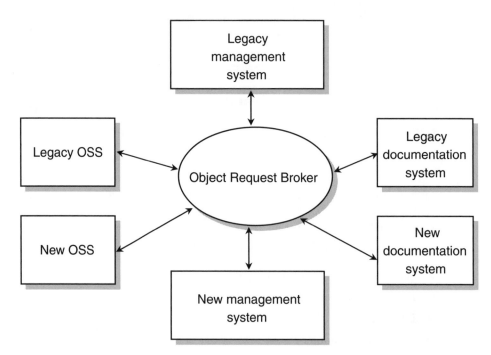

Figure 1.5 Role of object request brokers in unifying information exchange between legacy and new systems.

the system. In these cases, no changes are required to the internal structures of systems. If data is expected to be exchanged between systems, solutions migrate to the XML format. There are many issues open with this approach; its popularity is derived from easy implementation and maintenance.

Internet Inter-ORB Protocol (IIOP) is a key part of the CORBA standard. IIOP is an accepted standard for open/distributed communication between objects over the Internet. In order to interoperate with CORBA objects implemented on top of a commercial ORB, an application needs only to understand IIOP. This means that the overhead associated with higher-level ORB functionality can be avoided. Defined to reside within this operating environment, IIOP code is smaller and tighter than the commercial ORB. With IIOP implemented, devices are able to embed the ability to communicate with distributed objects running on traditional hardware, thus enabling products, including personal digital assistants (PDA) and PCs, to be attached to a web of objects running on the Internet.

In conjunction with the release of the IIOP standard, vendors of real-time operating systems have bundled these solutions with their operating systems, eliminating the need to integrate the software. As smaller devices become available to attach to the Internet, and vendors provide diverse environments to run these devices, IIOP will enable seamless connectivity. Applications domains including wireless technologies will also be able to take advantage of the IIOP availability.

Internet Inter-ORB Protocol (IIOP) ORBs must be able to connect to devices that utilize Java, Microsoft Visual Basic, C++, and ActiveX. As with the more traditional ORBs, IDL must be available in each of the required systems.

The telecommunications industry will ultimately be able to extend CORBA from their management infrastructure to the customer premise. This would serve two functions:

1. It would enable an end-to-end view of their network to the new intelligent devices beyond the network edge.
2. It would move service availability further into the customer domain.

For example, as mobile devices, intelligent devices, and consumer electronics are connected to the Web, service providers are extending their management domain to the customer premise.

More details on CORBA and mediation ORBs are covered in Chapter 3.

1.6 Organizational Structure of the Average Provider

It is very difficult to create an organizational model that fits all providers. But there are certain attributes that can be identified with each provider. With a few exceptions, the following organizational units can be discovered with telecommunications providers (see Figure 1.6):

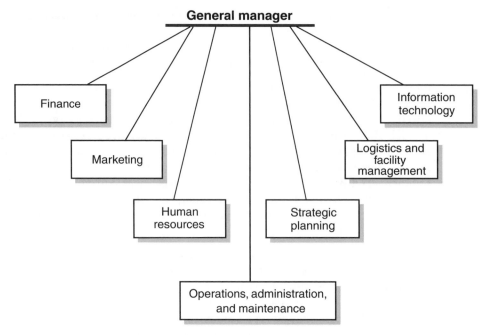

Figure 1.6 Organizational structure of an average telecommunications provider.

- Finance (enterprise resource management, revenue assurance, fraud management, credit analysis, etc.)

- Marketing (customer care, customer relationship management, products/services portfolio management, sales, order processing, billing, etc.)

- Human resources (salary accounting, administration, recruiting, training, career management, etc.)

- Logistics and facility management (order management, physical inventory, asset management, logistics, transport, energy management, security management, investments, purchase, etc.)

- Strategic planning (new technology, design, development, infrastructure optimization, etc.)

- Operations, administration, and maintenance (provisioning, deployment, change management, service configuration, maintenance, tests, monitoring, quality and service assurance, support systems, documentation systems, management systems, etc.)

- Information technology (application management, vendor management, software purchase, intranet, documents management, e-mail, groupware, knowledge management, Internet access, etc.)

This list of functions and responsibilities is not complete. At this stage, they are only examples. More detailed analysis is provided in Chapter 8.

How an information technology (IT) organization responds to the challenges of the competitive environment may become the key differentiator for the provider. Within this IT environment, network and IT managers continually struggle to find methods to cope with

- Shrinking headcounts
- Controlling tight operational budgets
- Increasing needs for new applications and services
- Deploying new network technologies into an already stressed environment
- Integrating and automating complex support, documentation, and network management systems
- Balancing resources between developing new applications and customizing purchased applications
- Upgrading skill sets of subject matter experts to capitalize on new information technologies
- Managing and reimplementing knowledge
- Balancing and optimizing use of systems and networking infrastructures for internal use
- Helping to establish extranets with customers

Lean management requires the clear allocation of processes, functions, and human resources to the TMN layers. This kind of allocation is not always obvious. Figure 1.7 gives a high-level example of allocation using the seven typical organizational units.

1.7 Strategic Benefits of Advanced Support Systems

Once deployed, advanced support systems offer the following strategic benefits:

- *Improved operating efficiencies in data, inventory, and network management.* It is expected that the management of various objects such as equipment, applications, databases, and so on is more integrated, and requires less human resources to manage.
- *Reduced support and maintenance costs associated with legacy systems.* Due to more automation and interconnection, the support and maintenance expenses are decreasing.
- *Shorter product development cycles.* Products and services can be created, tested, and deployed faster due to advanced technology used in support systems.

		Information technology	Human resources
Business management layer	Strategic planning and marketing		
Service management layer	Marketing Operations, administration, and maintenance Strategic planning		
Network management layer	Logistics and facility management Operations, administration, and maintenance		
Element management layer	Operations, administration, and maintenance		
Network element layer	Operations, administration, and maintenance		

Figure 1.7 Allocation of organizational units to TMN layers.

- *Speedier deployment of new services and pricing schemes.* Processes are connected to each other. Rapid service provisioning in combination with pricing guarantees rapid deployment.

- *Flexibility to modifying pricing and marketing schemes.* Due to interconnected processes, changes can be deployed very quickly. Even modeling and simulating resource utilization scenarios are easy to implement.

- *New synergistic products and convergent services.* BSS applications' bonding is very helpful to support convergent services. This bonding integrates OSSs, BSSs, MSSs, documentation, and management systems.

- *Strategic marketing to target and acquire profitable business customers.* Due to rich information on customers and their traffic generation patterns, marketing strategies can be customized.

- *Superior customer management to establish customer loyalty.* The significant improvement of customer care will help to avoid customer churn and to sell value-added communication services to loyal customers.

1.8 Summary

In order to position support systems and their vendors, future trends of support systems should be estimated. In other words, the dynamic of principal market drivers should be analyzed in depth. Table 1.2 summarizes the present goals and future targets from the perspective of incumbent carriers, emerging carriers, customers, equipment vendors, vendors of support systems, and system integrators.

In order to match the rich service offerings of new entrants, ILECs have implemented multiple upgrade strategies, including modifications by internal staffs, custom development by external system integrators, and integrating third-party products. Most likely, they won't completely replace their existing support systems. Several incumbent carriers are incorporating best-of-breed solutions with their legacy systems. This trend opens great opportunities for point support systems and for professional services.

Deregulation of the LEC market has stimulated and still stimulates significant demand for CLEC support systems. Most of them start from scratch and invite all types of support systems vendors with point and integrated products. Larger CLECs with custom-designed in-house solutions are enhancing these to accommodate new services and technologies—they show some similarities with incumbent providers. Replacement of these support systems is not expected soon. But back-office operational efficiency is expected to improve. In particular, network operational management solutions are in demand.

CLECs may want to outsource support systems services. They have started to evaluate the benefits of outsourcing their back-office services entirely. Outsourcing would eliminate the need for the carrier to invest scarce research and development dollars in support systems, allocating spending to their networks and/or customer management systems. Essentially, it allows CLECs to focus on their core business.

Lesser-known CLECs either purchase or license point products from third parties, or take advantage of service bureaus. It is highly unlikely that these CLECs are interested in in-house development and maintenance. Support systems vendors can sell to these CLECs directly or to service bureaus that may share their products between multiple CLECs.

Carrier interconnection opens excellent opportunities for support systems vendors. The unbundling of local-exchange elements for resale requires that resellers of local-exchange services provide electronic links to incumbent carriers for ordering, service activation, troubleshooting, and billing. Present support systems do not have these interconnect features. There is a significant opportunity for incremental support systems sales by emerged and also by new vendors. Specialized vendors for LNP will play a significant role during the next 10 years. The best-of-breed solutions are expected to offer provider portability, location portability, and also service portability.

Telecom industry consolidation creates new requirements of support systems, but the need is situation specific. It is difficult to estimate the time frames of reengineering or

Table 1.2 Goals and Targets

STAKEHOLDERS	GOALS	FUTURE TARGETS
Incumbent Service Providers (ILECs, PTTs, IXCs, NSPs, CAPs, and Global Carriers)		
	Rapid introduction of new services	Less internal development
	Cost reduction	More use of systems integrators
	Customer retention	More packaged software of support systems
	Multivendor management	Pervasive interconnection of support systems
	Convergent ordering	Self-care with support systems
	Up-to-date asset management	
Emerging Service Providers (CLECs, ISPs, ASPs, and Wireless)		
	Build network capacity	Minimal internal development
	Customer acquisition	Fully automated processes
	Improve service quality	More packaged software for support systems
	Offer new, differentiated services	Fewer service bureaus
		Strong interconnections between support systems
	Add facilities	Self-care with support systems
	More carrier-to-carrier applications	
	Offer IXC services	
	Support of micropayments and prepaid services	
Customers (End Users)		
	Increase service reliability	Self-provisioning
	Lower transport costs	Custom QoS reporting
	Faster service provider responsiveness	Flexible billing formats

Table 1.2 *(Continued)*

STAKEHOLDERS	GOALS	FUTURE TARGETS
	Customer network management	Electronic bill presentment and payment
		Usage-based accounting
Equipment Vendors		
	Sell more equipment (best of breed or best of suite)	Outsource element management systems to vendors of support systems
		Use of open interfaces
		Develop solutions for eCommerce
Vendors of Support Systems		
	Sell more software	Full-line offerings of support systems
	Sell more professional services	Target ILEC legacy support systems replacement
		Acquire other vendors of support systems
		Compete with system integrators
System Integrators		
	Sell consulting, custom programming, and integration services	Acquire vendors of support systems
		Conduct many projects
		Consolidate products

consolidating support systems of the consolidated telecommunication providers. Consolidated carriers are likely to work to fully integrate multiple platforms (customer care and billing, provisioning and order processing, network operational management), to create synergies in products and markets, and to reduce costs. Vendors of support systems with system integration capabilities are in demand. Support systems will mirror trends in the telecommunications industry; full-service vendors could emerge to serve convergence carriers.

CHAPTER 2

Portfolio of Products and Services

2.1 Introduction

Service providers are expected to continuously evaluate their service portfolios and their existing networking engines. There are basically two layers in the simplified portfolio

- Infrastructure
- Services

Figure 2.1 shows this layered architecture. The networking infrastructure consists of wireline, wireless, and Internet Protocol (IP) structures.

Products and services may follow the infrastructure components, but in a more advanced step, a combination of infrastructure components is required to create, deploy, and maintain products and services.

Important issues from the perspective of service providers are:

- What is the perceived quality of my network?
- Is the network keeping pace with the growth of subscribers?
- Where do I need to invest?
- How much do I need to invest?
- How can I get more revenue out of existing services?
- How can I reduce operating costs?

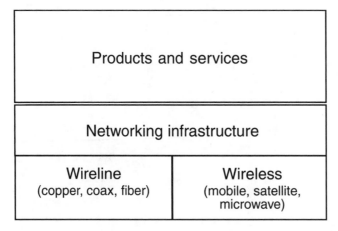

Figure 2.1 Products, services, and infrastructure.

- How do I know if a problem is just a solitary abnormality or a building problem?
- How can I reduce customer churn?
- How can I predict future capital expenditures?
- How can I get system usage information to improve marketing and sales?

The position of service providers can be clearly identified in a typical value chain (Figure 2.2). Besides traditional wireline and wireless voice and data services, integrated services such as asynchronous transfer mode (ATM), personal communications services (PCS), and digital subscriber line (xDSL) are also targeted by many providers.

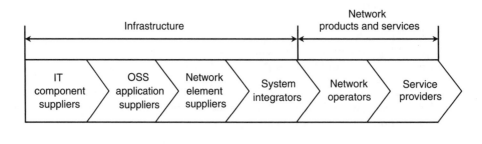

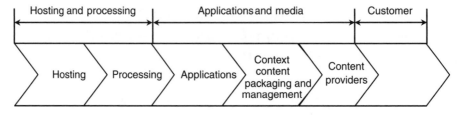

Figure 2.2 Value chain of products and services.

Due to the Internet Protocol (IP) revolution, completely new areas open opportunities for service providers, such as hosting content, processing content, operating applications, and even media services. This type of service mixture requires a revolutionary conduct of business, called eCommerce, NetEconomy, or NewEconomy. Complex service offers require unprecedented collaboration of service providers and customers.

2.2 Challenges to Products and Infrastructures

Service providers are continuously confronted with technological challenges. In particular, innovations in the infrastructure layer can impact the products and services. This segment addresses both types of challenges.

2.2.1 Challenges on Principal Products

Prices alone did not shake the fundamentals of the telecommunications industry. Traditional products in the voice and data areas carried a significant profit of which the carriers could have given discounts. But traditional products are also being challenged and or replaced by less expensive and newer products, which undermines the core business of incumbent service providers.

The traditional voice portfolio represents a massive revenue stream. Several competitive and alternative carriers are targeting voice services; in fact, few new entrants rule out the possibility of offering voice services to both business and residential segments. Consequently, the voice portfolio is attacked from several directions and in diverse ways, including

- Internet telephony
- Mobile as voice substitute
- Integrated voice and data solutions
- Low-price Plain Old Telephone Service (POTS) and voice over virtual private networks (VPNs)

All of these factors will have some impact on voice services in the future. The strongest impact, however, will be reinventing POTS. The combination of radical price reduction combined with customer-needs–driven pricing schemes and packages will be the biggest driver of change in telecommunications.

Mobile substitution will generate churn and reduce fixed-line traffic. The impact of mobile is based on the assumption that mobile penetration will exceed that of wireline. An increasing number of minutes will migrate to mobile networks, which will drive voice-related revenue growth, while fixed-line revenue growth will mainly stem from Internet usage. In any case, wireline service providers must be aware that as much as 20 percent of voice minutes could be lost to mobile networks.

Another large change driver is integrated voice and data. High-speed corporate networks, VPNs, and private branch exchange (PBX) trunking are operating today and the process will further accelerate. According to industry analysts, some 10 percent of voice traffic may migrate onto data networks.

Voice over IP has been gaining a lot of attention, but its impact is less than expected. As public switched telephone network (PSTN) prices are declining, the voice over IP's (VoIP) value proposition is dwindling rapidly. The primary cost advantage of Internet telephony will decrease as access and settlement charges converge to cost, which is today's trend driven by competition.

In terms of costs, VoIP is not less expensive than PSTN, due to expensive gateway technologies and other technical reasons. Carrier class or even corporate quality of service (QoS) levels are hard to meet for alternative operators without large international capacity, which is still expensive. In addition to cost concerns, quality and technical features of VoIP are lower than those of PSTN. VoIP and PSTN processes will level off and the products will converge.

This convergence will be driven not by low-grade Internet voice, but by broadband platforms, such as xDSL, which support all features of current PSTN. Voice services are going to be bundled with other products with the result that the relative price of voice is further lowered.

In summary, the traditional voice business will decline due to these factors. Although it will remain significant in terms of volume, it will not be a profit driver in 5 years. Service providers must focus on new areas to offset the inevitable fall of revenues and profit margins.

Data communications products drive telecommunication growth in all developed markets. This growth will outpace voice traffic. In addition to growth, it will also change significantly. The challenge of IP technology will have the largest and most visible impact on data services in the near future. IP optimizes data communications. It is cost effective, it was designed to support data communications, and corporate software applications and networks have been migrated to IP. This means that the current revenue stream of leased lines faces tough competition. All-IP networks are optimized to provide IP VPNs, which are cost-effective substitutes for leased lines. VPNs are less expensive to operate and manage, easier to implement, and offer functionality for customers. Their use is also less expensive, so it is easy to conclude that VPNs will grow significantly in the near future.

From the service providers' perspective, time division multiplexing (TDM)–based leased lines will be obsolete as soon as QoS IP VPNs are implemented. The process of replacing leased lines may be slowed down by the customers' hesitation to implement changes in business-critical networks and applications, but process advantages and additional features will generate churn in the not-too-distant future.

VPNs and mobile data solutions of the future are going to replace TDM-based data communications products only gradually. Independent from this fact, it is expected that leased line prices and pricing models will get closer to those of VPNs. It means distance-independent and bandwidth-based pricing, and lower rates, altogether. Data communications revenues will grow, but if incumbent service providers do not move fast enough to update and replace aging portfolios by IP-based VPNs and high-speed solutions, they will miss the opportunity and the increase will be captured by new entrants, Internet service providers (ISPs), and applications service providers (ASPs).

Mobile data is emerging, and mobile service providers regard it as an excellent opportunity to take business away from traditional operators. Even if mobile will be able to carry broadband with next generation systems, its bandwidth will still be physically limited by the availability of frequencies, compared to fixed-line solutions. Therefore, mobile data will have relatively limited impact on corporate data communications, but will be an adequate vehicle to carry narrowband incidental data and Internet access. Industry analysts predict that 30 percent of Internet usage will flow through mobile devices within the next 5 years, which is a significant enough amount for wireline service providers to pay more attention. Mobile data will have its role in the ISP business, so wireline carriers are recommended to identify synergies between wireless and wireline Internet solutions.

2.2.2 Challenges on Infrastructures

Basically, communication networks consist of two principal components:

1. Access networks.
2. Transport networks.

In dealing with particular services and support functions, more detailed partitioning—depending on the technologies in use—is required. In both segments of networks, various technologies of wireline (e.g., copper, coax, and fiber) and of wireless (e.g., mobile, satellite, and microware) may be implemented and maintained.

New entrants are challenging the efficiencies of incumbent networks and are introducing new infrastructure technologies, which can be superior in terms of capacity, scalability, and costs over old infrastructures. The core business is the voice service, but the role of data communication is increasing. Still, the networks that primarily support voice and data services are separated.

Traditional voice networks offer circuit-switched technology where users receive 64-Kbps channels that can provide 3.1 kHz uncompressed voice bandwidth. This technology allows cheap user terminals and makes possible data communications on the switched lines by means of modems that convert the digital data information to analog signals. The digital-analog conversion reduces the available bandwidth so 64 Kbps cannot be reached. The Integrated Services Digital Network (ISDN) was developed to eliminate the digital-analog conversion and provide direct digital access to the network that can be used for both voice and data transmission. The bottleneck is that a 64-Kbps data transmission rate is not sufficient for data transmission requirements.

The data networks developed separately from voice networks. X.25 provided a reliable narrowband packet-switched technology. Due to the developments of transmission networks, such robustness is no longer feasible. Therefore, new technologies such as frame relay and ATM are going to replace packet switching. The other type of data networks is built on leased lines. The increasing growth of data communications replaced the original analog leased lines with digital ones, and managing these networks became the challenge. Today's QoS-sensitive networks are using managed line services to interconnect them. Leased lines have made possible the integration of voice and data traffic to reduce overall costs.

It is obvious that the PSTN/ISDN network as access network cannot serve the Internet in the future due to bandwidth limitations. The continuous packet switched technology is forced to a narrowband switched technology, which hardly can coexist. In addition, new access networks are required to provide broadband continuous access, which is a prerequisite for high-speed Internet usage.

Leased lines are not economical for service providers. Instead, a shared backbone usage would be preferred, which can decrease the network costs and, in turn, prices. Consequently, due to Internet and data communications, the existing technologies become obsolete. A new IP-based technology is arising that shows very rapid development and aims not only to serve the Internet and data communications, but to replace the whole existing technology and integrate the different platforms to a single multiservice environment.

The new players are in position to implement the newest technology and serve the new demands. The incumbent operators have to restructure their networks. They will utilize as many existing elements as possible. They will free up and reuse expensive network resources to increase network capacity and economically serve the new demand.

There are specific challenges toward transport and access networks. The growth of data traffic will also produce significant changes in the transport network. Today, the transport network of several incumbent service providers is based on SONET/SDH. The voice and data networks share this network, which relies on the optical cable network that is a key asset for telecommunications service providers. The optical cable network, however, is saturated in some directions. The introduction of Dense Wavelength Division Multiplexing (DWDM) will free up resources to increase the network capacity. With the help of DWDM, multiple optical signals can be transmitted over a single optical fiber. This means better utilization of optics, but other cost advantages can be reached using new optical amplifiers. According to current calculations, DWDM offers cheaper costs than the ordinary SONET/SDH. IP-based technologies, ATM and xDSL, are able to utilize optical transmission and integrate all communication forms. Upgrades of the transport network are absolutely necessary for all principal service providers.

Access networks consist today of twisted copper cables maintained by the service providers. This type of access network is able to support the initial demands of IP using 56-Kbps modem connections, but this bandwidth is not suitable for quality applications. There is a need to provide better quality by ISDN or xDSL technologies. Additional revenues may be generated by broadband access services. The acceleration of deploying ISDN technology may be considered a temporary solution. Hence, it cannot avoid the PSTN exchanges, and it is not capable of providing cost-effective always-on IP connectivity. Emerging new IP applications need more than 2×64 Kbps bandwidth. Even so, ISDN will serve Internet and telephony needs to a wide range of customer segments in the next few years. Although the targeted deployment of xDSL broadband technologies is a must, ISDN should not be regarded as a technology without a future.

The existing twisted copper pairs can be reused by first-generation xDSL technology, usually asymmetric digital subscriber line (ADSL). ADSL is able to provide asymmetric high-speed IP connections and is capable of supporting ISDN or PSTN as well. The IP traffic bypasses the PSTN exchanges so there is no limit for always-on IP connections and available bandwidth is 2 to 6 Mbps downstream and 0.2 to 0.6 Mbps upstream, which supports various new applications including high-quality video streaming. It is mainly used for residential users, but until the new xDSL technologies arrive, it serves some business needs as well.

Optical access networks are also developing rapidly and provide the highest access bandwidth. Due to the high costs, hybrid optical-copper networks are built that easily fulfill the requirements of new xDSL technologies on the last copper mile. New competitors of incumbent service providers bring other alternative solutions to market using community antenna TV (CATV) technology. This technology offers similar features like asynchronous digital subscriber line (ADSL). Fixed radio networks like point-to-multipoint microsystems offer the most cost-effective solution on low-penetration areas supporting ISDN and data transmission up to 2 Mbps. There will be satellite systems with global coverage offering high-speed downstream communications up to 2 Mbps. And finally, mobile networks aim to replace the role of fixed networks. Their access capabilities are limited today, but third-generation systems will offer sufficient bandwidth for at least voice and data access services. Mobile data usage is low today due to slow connections and variable radio connections causing unexpected outages. The introduction of Wireless Application Protocol (WAP) further extends data usage and mobile networks' role in the rapidly growing data business. New technologies are emerging that will significantly increase the available bandwidth. General packet radio service (GPRS) offers up to 115 Kbps transfer rate and supports always-on IP connectivity. GPRS is followed by enhanced data rates for global evolution (EDGE) and universal mobile telecommunications system (UMTS) with much higher data-transfer rates.

Currently, the PSTN/ISDN network is an independent, stand-alone network. With the growth of Internet demand and traffic, it serves the Internet as an access network. In other words, long data sessions are supported by an access network that has been optimized and sized for short voice calls. It can be done while Internet penetration is low, but it will lead to network congestion if the penetration increases. In order to rectify this problem, exchange and routing vendors are trying to integrate the access servers with the exchanges. This solution seems to be a temporary one, hence the xDSL technology is developed to bypass the exchanges completely. Incumbent service providers will have to do more than implement temporary solutions to carry increased traffic volumes; xDSL technology might be the answer to the increasing data traffic in access networks. There is no doubt that the current PSTN/ISDN infrastructure must be reconstructed to match transfer capabilities in the transport network. According to industry experts, the switching function will be done by ATM or IP with special labeling. Such a solution would solve the existing congestion problems. In the long run, the bandwidth issues cannot be solved by using temporary solutions, so alternative infrastructure will ultimately replace PSTN/ISDN-based solutions.

2.3 Basic Principles of Product and Service Creation

The majority of emerged and emerging technologies has got a few basic foundation principles. These foundation principles will be addressed in this segment. The basics for this segment can be found in more detail in (BLAC94), (TERP98), and (MORR2000).

2.3.1 Connection-Oriented and Connectionless Communications

Communication systems that employ the concepts of circuits and virtual circuits are said to be connection-oriented. Such systems maintain information about the users, such as their addresses and their ongoing QoS needs. Often, this type of system uses state tables that contain rules governing the manner in which the user interacts with the network. While these state tables clarify the procedures between the user and the communication network, they do add overhead to the communication process.

In contrast, communication systems that do not employ circuits and virtual circuits are said to be connectionless systems. They are also known as datagram networks and are widely used throughout the industry. The principal difference between connection-oriented and connectionless operation is that connectionless protocols do not establish a virtual circuit for the end-user communication process. Instead, traffic is presented to the service provider in a somewhat ad hoc fashion. Handshaking arrangements and mutual confirmations are minimal and perhaps nonexistent. The network service access points and the network switching points maintain no ongoing knowledge about the traffic between the two end users. State tables as seen with connection-oriented solutions are not maintained. Therefore, datagram services provide no a priori knowledge of user traffic, and they provide no ongoing, current knowledge of the user traffic, but they introduce less overhead.

2.3.2 Use of Physical and Virtual Circuits

End users operating terminals, computers, and client equipment communicate with each other through a communication channel called the physical circuit. These physical circuits are also known by other names such as channels, links, lines, and trunks. Physical circuits can be configured wherein two users communicate directly with each other through one circuit, and no one uses this circuit except these two users. They can operate this circuit in half-duplex or full-duplex. This circuit is dedicated to the users. This concept is still widely used in simple networks without serious bandwidth limitations.

In more complex networks, circuits are shared with more than one user pair. Within a network, the physical circuits are terminated at intermediate points at machines that provide relay services on another circuit. These machines are known by such names as switches, routers, bridges, and gateways. They are responsible for relaying the traffic between the communicating users. Since many communication channels have the capacity to support more than one user session, the network device, such as the switch, router, or multiplexer, is responsible for sending and receiving multiple user traffic to and from a circuit.

In an ideal arrangement, a user is not aware that the physical circuits are being shared by other users. Indeed, the circuit provider attempts to make this sharing operation transparent to all users. Moreover, in the ideal situation, the user thinks that the circuit directly connects only the two communicating parties. However, it is likely that the physical circuit is being shared by other users.

The term *virtual circuit* is used to describe a shared circuit wherein the sharing is not known to the circuit users. The term was derived from computer architectures in which an end user perceives that a computer has more memory than actually exists. This other, additional virtual memory is actually stored on an external storage device.

There are three types of virtual circuits:

Permanent Virtual Circuit (PVC). A virtual circuit may be provisioned to the user on a continuous basis. In this case, the user has the service of the network anytime. A PVC is established by creating entries in tables in the network nodes' databases. These entries contain a unique identifier of the user payload, which is known by various names, such as a logical channel number (LCN), virtual circuit identifier (VCI), or virtual path identifier (VPI). Network features such as throughput, delay, security, and performance indicators are also provisioned before the user starts operations. If different types of services are desired, and if different destination endpoints must be reached, then the user must submit a different PVC identifier with the appropriate user payload to the network. This PVC is provisioned to the different endpoint, and perhaps with different services.

Switched Virtual Circuit (SVC). A switched virtual circuit (SVC) is not preprovisioned. When a user wishes to obtain network services to communicate with another user, it must submit a connection request packet to the network. It must provide the address of the receiver, and it must also contain the virtual circuit number that is to be used during the session. SVCs entail some delay during the setup phase, but they are flexible in that they allow the user to dynamically select the receiving party and the negotiation of networking parameters on a call-by-call basis.

SemiPermanent Virtual Circuit (SPVC). With this approach, a user is preprovisioned, as in a regular PVC. Like a PVC, the network node contains information about the communicating parties and the type of services desired. But these types of virtual circuits do not guarantee that the users will obtain their level of requested service. In case of congested networks, users could be denied the service. In a more likely scenario, the continuation of a service is denied because the user has violated some rules of the communications. Examples are higher bandwidth demand and higher data rates than agreed with the supplier.

Dense wave division multiplexing (DWDM) is very helpful to utilize physical optical channels by using laser technology for provisioning a large number of virtual circuits for communicating parties.

2.3.3 Switching Technologies

Voice, video, and data signals are relayed in a network from one user to another through switches. This section provides an overview of the prevalent switching technologies.

Circuit switching provides a direct connection between two networking components. Thus, the communicating partners can utilize the facility as they see it—within bandwidth and tariff limitations. Many telephone networks use circuit switching systems. Circuit switching provides clear channels; error checking, session establishment, frame flow control, frame formatting, selection of codes, and protocols are the responsibility of the users. Today, the traffic between communicating parties is usually stored in fast queues in the switch and switched on to an appropriate output line with TDM techniques. This technique is known as circuit emulation switching (CES). The properties of circuit switching include

- Direct connection end-to-end
- No intermediate storage unless CES used
- Few value-added functions
- TDM (modern systems) to emulate circuit switching

Message switching was the dominant switching technology during the last 2 decades. This technology is still widely used in certain applications, such as e-mail, but it is not employed in a backbone network. The switch is usually a specialized computer that is responsible for accepting traffic from attached terminals and computers. It examines the address in the header of the message and switches the traffic to the receiving station. Due to the low number of switching computers, this technology suffers from backup problems, performance bottlenecks, and lost messages due to congestion. The properties of message switching include

- Use of store-end-forward technology
- Disk serves as buffers
- Extensive value-added functions
- Star topology due to expense of switches

Innovations may be observed here as well. Instant messaging speeds up the information exchange between communicating parties. Depending on the technology, wireless data opportunities may also be included, such as short message service (SMS).

Packet switching relays small pieces of user information to the destination nodes. Packet switching has become the prevalent switching technology of data communications networks. It is used in such diverse systems as PBXs, local area networks (LANs), and even with multiplexers. Each packet only occupies a transmission line for the duration of the transmission; the lines are usually fully shared with other applications. This is an ideal technology for bursty traffic. Modern packet switching systems are designed to carry continuous, high-volume traffic as well as asynchronous, low-volume traffic, and each user is given an adequate bandwidth to meet service level expectations.

The concepts of packet and cell switching are similar; each attempts to process the traffic in memory as quickly as possible. However, cell switching is using much smaller protocol data units (PDUs) relative to packet switching. The PDU size is fixed with cell switching and may vary with packet switching. The properties of packet switching include

- Hold-and-forward technology
- Random-access memory (RAM) serves as buffers
- Extensive value-added functions for packet, but not many for cells

Switching will remain one of the dominant technologies in the telecommunications industry. Packet switching utilizes the infrastructure much better. This is the main reason for successful implementations of IP-based services. Service providers are expected to reevaluate their products and services offers that are still predominantly circuit switched. The transition is a long process because existing investments must be protected. Hybrid solutions are likely; for example, multiple protocol label switching (MPLS) tries to operate packet switching via circuit-switched routes.

2.3.4 Routing Technologies

There are two techniques to route traffic within and between networks: source routing and non-source routing. The majority of emerging technologies use non-source routing.

Source routing derives its name from the fact that the transmitting device—the source—dictates the route of the PDU through a network or networks. The source places the addresses of the *hops* in the PDU. The hops are actually routers representing the internetworking units. Such an approach means that the internetworking units need not perform address maintenance, but they simply use an address in the PDU to determine the destination.

In contrast, non-source routing requires that the interconnecting devices make decisions about the route. They don't rely on the PDU to contain information about the route. Non-source routing is usually associated with bridges and is quite prevalent in LANs. Most of the emerging technologies implement this approach with the use of a VCI. This label is used by the network nodes to determine where to route the traffic.

The manner in which a network stores its routing information varies. Typically, routing information is stored in a software table called a directory. This table contains a list of destination nodes. These destination nodes are identifiers with some type of network address. Along with the network address (or some type of label, such as a VCI), there is an entry describing how the router is to relay the traffic. In most implementations, this entry simply lists the next node that is to receive the traffic in order to relay it to its destination.

Small networks typically provide a full routing table at each routing node. For large networks, full directories require too many entries and are expensive to maintain. In addition, the exchange of routing table information can impact the available bandwidth for user payload. These networks are usually subdivided into areas called domains. Directories of routing information are kept separately in domains. Broadcast networks contain no routing directories. Their approach is to send the traffic to all destinations.

Network routing control is usually categorized as centralized or distributed. The centralized solution is using a network control center to determine the routing of the packets. The packet switches are limited in their functions. Central control is vulnerable; a backup is absolutely necessary, which increases operating expenses. Distributed solutions require more intelligent switches, but they provide a more resilient solution. Each router makes its own routing decisions without regard to a centralized control center. Distributed routing is more complex, but its advantages over the centralized approach have made it the preferred routing method in most communications networks.

2.3.5 Multiplexing Technologies

Most of the emerged and emerging technologies use some form of multiplexing. Multiplexers accept lower-speed voice or data signals from terminals, telephones, PCs, and user applications and combine them into one higher-speed stream for transmission efficiency. A receiving multiplexer demultiplexes and converts the combined stream into the original lower-speed signals. There are various multiplexing techniques.

Frequency Division Multiplexing

Frequency division multiplexing (FDM) divides the transmission frequency range into channels. The channels are lower-frequency bands, each of them capable of carrying communication traffic such as voice, data, or video. FDM is widely used in telephone systems, radio systems, and cable television applications. It is also used in microwave and satellite carrier systems. FDM decreases the total bandwidth available to each user, but even the narrower bandwidth is usually sufficient to the users' applications. Isolating the bands from each other costs some bandwidth, but the simultaneous use outweighs this disadvantage.

Time Division Multiplexing

Time division multiplexing (TDM) provides the full bandwidth to the user or application but divides the channel into time slots. Each user or application is given a slot, and the slots are rotated among the attached devices. The TDM multiplexer cyclically scans the input signals from the entry points. TDMs are working digitally. The slots are preassigned to users and applications. In case of no traffic at the entry points, the slots remain empty. This approach works well for constant-bit-rate applications, but leads to wasted capacity for variable-bit-rate applications.

Statistical Time Division Multiplexing

This approach allocates the time slots to each port on a statistical time division multiplex (STDM). Consequently, idle terminal time does not waste the capacity of the bandwidth. It is not unusual for two to five times as much traffic to be accommodated on lines using STDMs in comparison to a TDM solution. This approach can accommodate bursty traffic very well, but performs not very well with continuous, nonbursty traffic.

Wavelength Division Multiplexing

Wavelength division multiplexing (WDM) is the optical equivalent of FDM. Initial WDM systems were only two to four channels. Lasers operating at different frequencies are used in the same fiber, thereby deriving multiple communications channels from one physical path. Dense wave division multiplexing (DWDM) goes one step further to utilize the same physical infrastructure. In this case, up to 32 channels may be supported. Hyperdense and ultradense WDM (UDWDM) systems with channel densities of 40 and up and capacities of 400 Gbit/s are becoming available. Service providers are upgrading a few fibers on a route and then upgrading the others over the next few years.

2.3.6 Addressing and Identification Schemes

In order for user traffic to be sent to the proper destination, it must be associated with an identifier of the destination. Usually, there are two techniques in use. An explicit address has a location associated with it. It may not refer to a specific geographical location but rather to a name of a network or a device attached to a network. For example, the Internet Protocol (IP) address has a structure that permits the identification of a network, a subnetwork attached to the network, and a host device attached to the subnetwork. The ITU-T X.121 address has a structure that identifies the country, a network within that country, and a device within the network. Other entries are used with these addresses to identify protocols and applications running on the networks. Explicit addresses are used by switches, routers, and bridges as an entry into routing tables. These routing tables contain information about how to route the traffic to the destination nodes.

Another identifying scheme is known by the term of *label,* although other terms may be more widely used. Those terms are logical channel number (LCN) or virtual circuit identifier (VCI). A label contains no information about network identifiers or physical locations. It is simply a value that is assigned to a user's traffic that identifies each data unit of that user's traffic. Almost all connectionless systems use explicit addresses, and the destination and source addresses must be provided with every PDU in order for it to be routed to the proper destination.

Dynamic Host Configuration Protocol (DHCP) helps to distribute and maintain IP addresses dynamically. The great benefit is that ISP can more economically manage a given range of IP addresses. The disadvantage is that monitoring transactions on the basis of IP addresses is impossible. In such cases, the Universal Resource Locator (URL) is needed in addition.

2.3.7 Local Number Portability

The Telecommunication Act of 1996 is having a major impact on the U.S. telecommunications industry. One area of impact that is being considered by everyone is local number portability (LNP). For LNP, the Federal Communications Commission (FCC) requires the local-exchange carriers (LEC) of the nation to allow customers to keep their telephone numbers if they switch local carriers. The LECs must continue to maintain the quality of service and network reliability that the customer always received. The rules require that all LECs begin a phased deployment of a long-term service provider portability solution.

Wireless carriers are also affected by LNP. They have to be able to complete calls to a ported wireline number. Full portability between wireless and wireline including roaming capabilities in the United States is targeted for 2002. Advanced intelligent network (AIN) is a logical technology to help service providers meet this mandate. Many providers are looking to AIN LNP solutions because of the feasibility that AIN provides without the burden of costly network additions.

2.3.8 Control and Congestion Management

It is very important in communication networks to control the traffic at the ingress and egress points—also called service access points (SAPs)—of the network. The operation by which user traffic is controlled by the network is called *flow control*. Flow control should assure that traffic does not saturate the network or exceed the network's capacity. Thus, flow control is used to manage congestion.

There are three flow control alternatives with emerged and emerging technologies:

1. *Explicit flow control.* This technique limits how much user traffic can enter the network. If the network issues an explicit flow control message to the user, the user has no choice but to stop sending traffic or to reduce traffic. Traffic can be sent again after the network has notified the user about the release of the limitations.

2. *Implicit flow control.* This technique does not restrict the flow absolutely. Rather, it recommends that the user reduce or stop traffic it is sending to the network if network capacity situations require a limitation. Typically, the implicit flow control message is a warning to the user that the user is violating its service level agreement with the internal or external supplier—the network is congested. In any case, if the user continues to send traffic, it risks having traffic discarded by the network.

3. *No flow control.* Flow control may also be established by not controlling the flow at all. Generally, an absence of flow control means that the network can discard any traffic that is creating problems. While this approach certainly provides superior congestion management from the standpoint of the network, it may not meet the performance expectations of the users.

2.3.9 Signaling System 7

Signaling System 7 (SS7) is the prevalent signaling system of telephone networks for setting up and clearing calls and furnishing different services such as the use of toll-free numbers. SS7 defines the procedures for the set-up, ongoing management, and clearing of a call between telephone users. It performs these functions by exchanging telephone control messages between the SS7 components that support the customers' connections.

The SS7 signaling data link is a full duplex, digital transmission channel operating at 64 Kbps. Occasionally, an analog link can also be used. The SS7 link operates on both terrestrial and satellite links. The actual digital signals on the link are derived from PCM multiplexing equipment, or from equipment that employs a frame structure. The link must be dedicated to SS7. In accordance with clear channel signaling, no other transmission can be transferred with these signaling messages.

Figure 2.3 shows a typical SS7 topology. The subscriber lines are connected to the SS7 network through the service switching points (SSPs). The purpose of the SSPs is to receive the signals from the customer premises equipment (CPE) and perform call processing on behalf of the user. SSPs are implemented at switching centers. They serve as the source and destination for SS7 messages. SSPs initiate SS7 messages either to

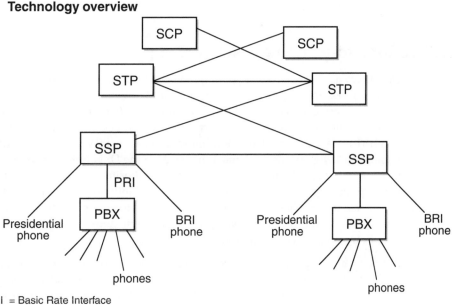

Technology overview

BRI = Basic Rate Interface
PRI = Primary Rate Interface
PBX = private branch exchange
SSP = service switching points
STP = signaling transfer point
SCP = service control point

Figure 2.3 Topology of an SS7 network.

another SSP or to a signaling transfer point (STP). STPs are expected to translate the SS7 messages and to route those messages between network nodes and databases. The STPs are switches that relay messages between SSPs, STPs, and services control points (SCPs). Their principal functions are very similar to the tasks of Layer 3 in the OSI model.

The SCPs contain software and databases for the management of the call. The SS7 components mentioned previously can be implemented as discrete entities or in an integrated fashion. SS7 has multiple ayers that show high conformance to the Open Systems Interconnection (OSI) layers. In particular, Layer 3 plays an important management role. The functional modules execute the following functions

- Message routing
- Message distribution
- Signaling traffic management
- Signaling link management
- Signaling route management

SS7 has been a significant success in the telecommunications industry. It is implemented in public telephone networks by practically all carriers throughout the world. In addition, features of SS7 have found their way into other systems such as global system for mobile communications (GSM) and satellite signaling. SS7 is operating with emerging technologies as well.

2.3.10 Directory Enabled Networking

Directory enabled networking (DEN) is a specification to save information about network devices, applications, and users in central directories. DEN addresses the integration of application and user-level directory information with network control and management, building on open Internet standards such as LDAPv2 and Web-Based Enterprise Management/Common Information Model (WBEM/CIM). The CIM initiative is being extended to meet the needs of the DEN initiative. In the future, management applications will have access to authoritative information on the relationships among network elements, services, and individuals, so that preferences, privileges, and profiles can be enforced according to enterprise policies (with personal customization), and so that policies governing network applications can make use of directory-based information.

A *network directory* is a logically centralized repository of infrequently changing data that is used to manage a network environment. A *directory* is a special-purpose database that contains information about the various devices, entities, and resources available on a network. It is optimized for high-volume read-access, but only handles low-volume write-access well. Standard features of full-blown database management systems (DBMSs) like transaction rollback are completely missing. The directory service may run on a single machine, or it is distributed across multiple machines for fault tolerance. In the latter case, replication maintains a consistent name space and provides the same view of the data regardless of from where the client tries to access the directory. The directory may contain any possible information (device configuration parameters, user profiles, application profiles, etc.) related to managed network objects (switches, routers, printers, servers, hosts, applications, users, etc.). Lightweight Directory Access Protocol (LDAP) is frequently used as the dominant directory access protocol. It is designed for thin clients and to run well over Transmission Control Protocol/Internet Protocol (TCP/IP) connections.

As the number and type of network devices, applications, and users increases, large corporate networks are increasingly complex to manage. Configuring and supervising managed objects is becoming very complex, error prone, and time consuming. Employment of directory technology in network management helps to provide a scaleable device configuration management. The idea is to maintain device configuration–related data centrally and update from there all the devices when changes are required.

Functional entities of DEN are the following (see Figure 2.4):

Directory server. Directory with LDAP-based access that stores network device configuration data in DEN-schema format.

Network device. Hosts, routers, switches, and so on, with a built-in LDAP client that queries the directory server for device configuration data.

Network management host. Possibly remote management terminal to change and maintain the network device configuration data stored in the directory. It includes a graphical tool, which presents the configuration data in a user-friendly form. Configuration data are stored in the abstract format of a DEN-schema.

Network devices

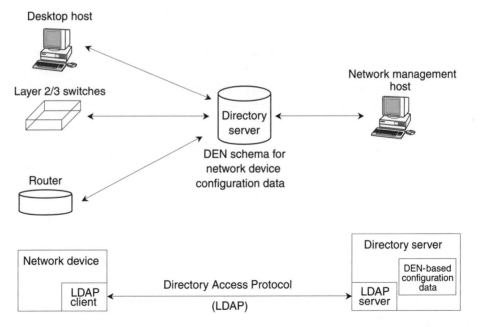

Figure 2.4 Principles of directory enabled networks.

The most important DEN features include:

- Employment of directory technology allows for centralized network device configuration management.
- In the DEN approach, any network entity must be able to access directory information.
- Any network entity must have an LDAPv3 interface.
- When connected to the network, a device automatically retrieves its configuration files and parameters from a corresponding directory server via LDAP.
- The directory acts as the central repository for device configuration data. It contains information on such diverse entities as hosts, routers, switches, applications, and users.
- The DEN information model and schema provide a standardized way to represent such diverse information in object-oriented format. They allow existing special-purpose directories, such as Domain Name Service (DNS) and Dynamic Host Configuration Protocol (DHCP), to merge into a single directory with a consistent data structure.
- Changes in the directory by network managers are pushed automatically to network devices.

The DEN information model can be defined as follows:

> DEN is an information model that is an abstraction of knowledge. It structures the knowledge about users, applications, and network devices, and how they interact into multiple knowledge domains to enable different people to use it. The structure is driven by object-oriented modeling.

The information model consists of three parts:

1. Six base-class hierarchies that form the basic framework that represents network elements and services.
2. An extensible schema based on inheritance and aggregation for modeling application-specific properties and information.
3. Simple mechanisms for establishing relationships among object instances.

The primary purpose of DEN is to separate the specification and representation of network elements and services from implementation details. A secondary purpose is to provide an extensible framework to represent vendor-specific functionality and implementation mechanisms by vendor-specific subclasses.

Figure 2.5 shows the base classes of DEN.

Directory enabled network (DEN) takes over base classes from both X.500 and CIM. In addition, new DEN classes expand the overall scope of classes. The following new concepts are defined by DEN:

- *Policy.* Rule instructing a network node on how to manage requests for network resources.

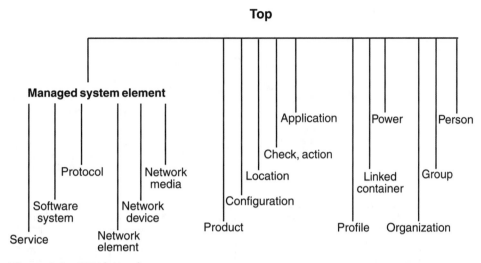

Figure 2.5 DEN base classes.

- *Profile.* Template of attributes and behaviors that describe an object or a set of objects.

- *Network media.* Associating the particular media of a given interface with services that are running on it.

- *Linked container.* Container class implementing a forward link.

- *Network device.* Not an actual class, but rather the abstraction of changes made to existing CIM classes to realize the physical characteristics of network devices.

2.3.11 Policy-Based Networking

The overall aim is to achieve business objective–controlled usage of network resources. Policy-based networking (PBN) is a technical concept to achieve this goal. Figure 2.6 shows the components and roles of PBN. The roles are

Information storage. A number of different back-end data stores (directory server, time server, certificate server, etc.) provide replicated data throughout the network that serve as input for policy decisions by the policy interpreter.

Policy requester. A policy request is triggered when a network device (e.g., host) issues a request to access network resources. The possibly transparent request trigger could be the launch of an application, a dial-in to a remote access server port, traffic across an Ethernet interface, or the start of a routed flow. Detection of the trigger may not always require the deployment of special software.

Policy interpreter. It weighs the resource request caught by the trigger against a corresponding policy. Policies define what resources a given resource consumer can

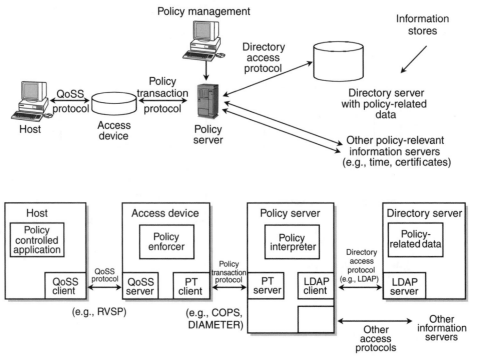

Figure 2.6 Policy-based networking.

use in the context of a given scenario. Technically speaking, a policy is a rule that instructs a network node how to manage requests for network resources. It is essentially a mechanism for encoding business objectives concerning the proper use of scarce resources. As a response to a policy request, the interpreter formulates a policy lease, which is a set of instructions for the policy requester detailing how to react to the network resource request. The lease may be cached on the requester but expires after a configurable amount of time to keep the policy data in the information storage in sync with the policies in actual use.

Policy enforcer. Enforcement is the role performed by a network device to ensure that the policy lease is realized. Enforcement of policy decisions is carried out by the specific hardware/software features residing in the device, such as packet filtering, bandwidth reservation, traffic prioritization, multiple forwarding queues, and so on. Actual policy enforcement requires detailed, low-level hardware/software know-how of network devices such as routers, switches, and others.

Policy manager. The policy manager provides a high-level user interface for operator input, translates this input into the proper schema for storage in the directory server, and pushes it out to the directory for storage.

Standard bodies are working on the roles for a policy-based environment. The proposed policy framework defines a policy decision point (PDP) and a policy enforcement point (PEP). The PDP makes decisions based on policies it retrieves from sources such as the policy repository and authentication servers. The PEP enforces the policy established by the PDP. The PEP contains an element called the local PDP, which allows certain policy decisions to be made at the PEP. The framework also provides guidelines for components such as a policy information base (PIB), a core policy schema, a policy architecture, policy functions, policy definitions, and policy storage and retrieval mechanisms. Another element of this model is the Policy Framework Definition Language (PFDL), which defines a device- and vendor-independent method of encoding policy descriptions in a portable fashion. It enables communication among heterogeneous policy-enabled devices through which the policy framework can be executed.

Common open policy service (COPS) addresses how policy information is communicated between servers and clients on a network. This query-response–based protocol transmits information between a policy server and its clients, which are policy-aware devices such as switches. The potential benefit of COPS is that it will create more efficient communication between policy servers and policy-aware devices, and increase interoperability among different vendors' systems.

2.3.12 Multi Protocol Label Switching

Multi protocol label switching (MPLS) is a technology that can address ever increasing network requirements. MPLS forwards information through networks by distributing and exploiting short identification markings called labels in packets. Use of the labels lets MPLS forward traffic without examining a packet's IP header, except when it is entering or exiting MPLS.

The benefits of MPLS include improved network scalability, QoS, and traffic engineering. MPLS QoS supports sensitive data such as video by incorporating mechanisms that can provide such traffic with preferential treatment. MPLS traffic engineering allows the manipulation of data flow across networks, so that new services can be offered. Using this technology benefits network operations by combining the advantages of circuit and packet switching. Figure 2.7 shows a simple example for MPLS (GIAC00).

MPLS presents a simple way to forward information through networks by installing and then examining short, fixed-length ID markings called labels in packets. By relying on labels to forward information, MPLS usually doesn't use a packet's IP header unless it is entering or leaving MPLS. Because labels reduce dependency on IP data, new and larger network designs become possible.

MPLS-enabled devices—called MPLS nodes or label switch routers (LSR)—process labels at Layer 2. Therefore, slower network devices may work more rapidly when enabled for MPLS. In some scenarios, the MPLS label can be directly integrated with other Layer 2 protocol headers. Because MPLS nodes can find integrated labels more rapidly than IP data or regular MPLS labels, network performance may be further improved.

As a packet arrives on the MPLS node, its label is compared to an onboard database called the label information base (LIB). The LIB contains a table that is used to add a label to a packet, or change and/or remove the existing label while determining the outgoing interface to which the data will be sent. After consulting the LIB, the MPLS

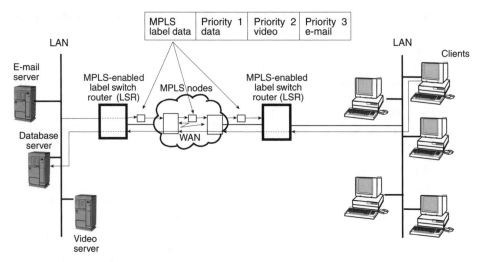

Figure 2.7 Operational example for MPLS.

1. Each MPLS node informs upstream nodes which label they should apply to packets that will be heading to a downstream destination. A label switched path is created when multiple nodes have information about the same destination.

2. When a packet gets to an MPLS node, its label is compared to information in its database, which tells the node where to send the packet. Efficiency is gained by the node tying multiple incoming labels to the same outgoing label information.

node forwards the packet toward its destination. The LIB can simplify by tying many incoming labels to the same outgoing label information, providing a new type of integrated summary routing. When a set of MPLS nodes have information in their LIBs related to the same destination, a label switched path (LSP) has been created. LSPs may be built automatically by the Label Distribution Protocol (LDP) or other protocols. In the simplest form of LPD, each MPLS node informs upstream nodes which label they should apply to packets that are heading to a destination downstream. Label distribution is normally based on well-known routing protocols. MPLS nodes use a routing protocol and the inherent benefits of these protocols like fault tolerance. Specific solutions can expand these capabilities. Considering the increasing expectations of networks, the benefits provided by MPLS make it a promising technology. MPLS can enhance network scalability and performance while providing advanced services in a simple package.

2.3.13 Quality of Service

QoS is a key factor for the success of IP-based products and services.

Basic QoS Alternatives

Best effort service. This is basic connectivity with no guarantees. Although best effort service is the lack of QoS, it provides customers with a reference point on the nondistinct end of the spectrum. Also, best effort is suitable for a wide range of networked applications such as general file transfers or e-mail.

Differentiated service. Some traffic is treated better than the rest—faster handling, more bandwidth on average, lower loss rate on average. This is a statistical preference, not a hard and fast guarantee. With proper engineering, including edge policing, differentiated service can provide expedited handling appropriate for a wide class of applications, including lower delay for mission-critical applications, packet voice applications, and so on. Typically, differentiated service is associated with grouping traffic into a small number of classes, with each class receiving a particular QoS in the network. DiffServ is using the type of service (ToS) field in IPv4 header as a QoS signaling mechanism, and it aims to provide definitions appropriate for aggregated flows for any level of aggregation.

Guaranteed service. An absolute reservation of network resources for specific traffic. It usually concentrates on bandwidth, which implies reservation of buffer space along with the appropriate queuing disciplines, to ensure that specific traffic gets a specific service level. Bandwidth is typically used as a proxy for the other QoS attributes (delay, jitter) as the widest audience most easily understands it. Typically, guaranteed service is associated with a fine level of traffic classification, often down to the level of individual traffic flows, which means that particular flows have network resources reserved for them so that required guarantees can be met. However, this does not have to be the case, as aggregated flows may receive guaranteed service.

QoS Signaling

Signaling is a form of communication. It provides a way for an end station or network element to signal certain requests to a neighbor. For example, an IP network can use part of the IP packet header to request special handling of priority or time-sensitive traffic. QoS signaling is useful for coordinating the traffic handling techniques and has a key role in configuring successful end-to-end QoS service across networks.

True end-to-end QoS requires that every element in the network path—switch, router, firewall, host, client, and so on—deliver its part of QoS, and it all must be coordinated with QoS signaling. However, the challenge is finding a robust QoS signaling solution that can operate end-to-end over heterogeneous infrastructures.

IP Precedence

IP precedence utilizes the three precedence bits in the IPv4 header's ToS field to specify class of service for each packet. Traffic can be partitioned in up to six classes of service using IP precedence (two others are reserved for internal network use). The queuing technologies throughout the network can then use this signal to provide the appropriate expedited handling. Features such as policy-based routing and computer-assisted retrieval (CAR) can be used to set precedence based on extended access-list classification. This allows considerable flexibility for precedence assignment, including assignment by application or user, or by destination and source subnet, and so on. Typically, this functionality is deployed as close to the edge of the network or administrative domain as possible, so that each subsequent network element can provide service based on the determined policy. IP precedence can also be set in the host or network client, and this signaling can be used optionally; however, this can be overridden by policy within the network. IP precedence enables service classes to be established using existing network queuing mechanisms [for example, weighted fair queuing (WFQ) or weighted random early detection (WRED)] with no changes to existing applications or complicated network requirements.

Figure 2.8 shows the DiffServ field in IPv4 and IPv6 packets. Remarks to the use of this field are as follows:

- The DiffServ field is carried in the headers of all IP packets traveling inside a specific DiffServ domain.

- It selects the packet forwarding behavior at each DiffServ-aware device, in other words, the type of DiffServ service the packet receives.

- Selection is done through the bit pattern of the DiffServ codepoint (DSCP) in the DiffServ field.

- The DSCP provides implicit, in-band QoS signaling in contrast to the explicit, outband approach of IntServ/RSVP.

- The DiffServ field supersedes the IPv4 type of service (ToS) octet and the IPv6 traffic class octet.

- A DiffServ-aware device must map a DSCP to a per hop behavior (PHB) via a configurable lookup table. Configuration of the lookup table in the DiffServ device can be accomplished via DEN/PBN.

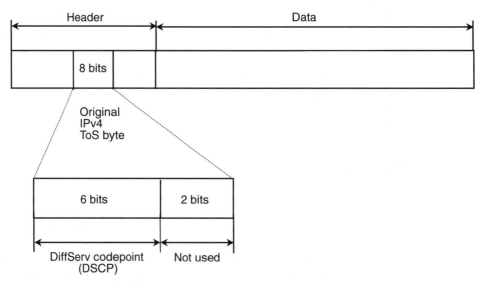

Figure 2.8 DiffServ field in IP packets.

- PHBs in the lookup table can be either standardized or experimental.
- A few DSCP values have permanently fixed mappings for backward compatibility.
- Different DSCPs may select the same PHB, allowing for flow aggregation and reduction of forwarding queues in network devices.

A DiffServ domain is a set of contiguous DiffServ devices, with common service provisioning and a set of PHB groups on all devices. A domain must have at least one ingress and one egress device. It may support a common, but local, set of PHBs. DiffServ devices can be ingress, internal, and egress device types. A DiffServ device supports one or more PHBs, reflecting how packets are handled internally and/or forwarded. A PHB is the description of an externally observable forwarding behavior at a device (e.g., loss, jitter, delay, drop properties). PHB groups express the idea of PHBs that work together based on a shared constraint such as sharing a queue or resource. PHB is selected by a DSCP in the packet to be forwarded.

Resource Reservation Protocol

Resource Reservation Protocol (RSVP) is a protocol for allowing an application to dynamically reserve network bandwidth. RSVP enables applications to request a specific QoS for a data flow. Using this protocol, network managers can take advantage of the benefits of RSVP in the network, even for non-RSVP-enabled applications and hosts. It is currently the only standard signaling protocol designed to guarantee network bandwidth from end-to-end IP networks. Hosts and routers use RSVP to deliver QoS requests to the routers along the paths of the data stream and to maintain routers and host states to provide the requested service, usually bandwidth and latency. RSVP uses a mean data rate, the largest amount of data the router will keep in queue, and minimum QoS to determine bandwidth reservation.

Using WFQ, RSVP can deliver integrated services guaranteed service. Using WRED, it can deliver a controlled load service. WFQ continues to provide its advantageous handling of nonreserved traffic by expediting interactive traffic and fairly sharing the remaining bandwidth between high-bandwidth flows. WRED provides its commensurate advantages for non-RSVP flow traffic. RSVP can be deployed in existing networks with a software upgrade.

2.3.14 Web Switching

As Web sites grow in complexity and size, they can be distributed across multiple data centers to improve scalability, provide site-level redundancy, guarantee content availability, and optimize Web response time. When deployed properly, each data center can handle Web traffic for a local subnet of the total client population without requiring that all requests be dispatched to a central site for fulfillment.

This approach, however, requires version control and synchronization of content across multiple servers to ensure that content is kept up-to-date. It also requires that a single domain name is used and shared by all data centers, despite the fact that these data centers are likely to be distributed geographically on servers having different IP addresses. Domain names shield users from having to be aware of the physical locations of data centers and content. They also allow new data centers, servers, and content to be added without disrupting network operations. For example, links in Web pages that refer to a particular site require no modification as additional data centers and servers hosting that content are added.

When multiple data centers exist, the most optimal data center should be selected automatically and seamlessly based on the proximity of the client to the data center, network path accessibility, requested content availability, and candidate server loading at the data center. This added intelligence could improve both content availability and Web site performance to users.

Web switching represents a new generation of networking specifically designed to address the unique requirements of Web traffic. Web switches are smart, equipped with sophisticated URL load balancing capabilities. Network address translation (NAT), embedded DNS intelligence, and the use of complex policies can manage and speed Web traffic flows. Web switches are able to optimize Web traffic because they use URLs in addition to IP addresses to make switching decisions. URLs provide a ubiquitous method to identify content across the Internet. Since a URL identifies only the content requested, it does not dictate where the content should be found. So instead of viewing the IP address associated with the URL as the network address where the content or service is located, this address points to the virtual IP address (VIP) of the Web switch, which functions as a cache or content traffic manager. The result—a consistently positive performance experience for Web site users.

Current load balancing solutions, including Layer 4 switches, route incoming packets based on the destination IP address or the combination of destination IP address, protocol ID, and transport port number. This can be problematic in a Web environment. To a Layer 4 load balancer, all of these Web applications appear to be using TCP port 80 (this is the typical port for HTTP), making them indistinguishable from one another. Therefore, a Common Gateway Interface (CGI) request looks no different from a Web-enabled SAP application or streaming audio request, even though all of these requests have very different QoS requirements.

In contrast, Web switches use URLs to route incoming TCP or User Datagram Protocol (UDP) flows to target servers. By looking deep into the HTTP payload down to the URL and cookie, a Web switch knows what content is being requested. With this knowledge, both user-defined and/or preset policies determine which flow security rules are enforced, which content is allowed or denied, and which QoS requirements are needed for specific content or even users. This provides flexibility in defining policies for traffic prioritization—enabling tiered services and ensuring service level agreements (SLAs) are met. Further, the ability to use cookies enables sticky connections and user authentication—two very critical requirements for eCommerce.

Web switches support this additional workload via a highly scaleable multiprocessor framework that evaluates policy only at flow (session) setup. Once a flow is set up, all subsequent packets within that flow are cut through at wire speed via high-speed forwarding application specific integrated circuit (ASICs) on a per-port basis. This approach of "flow setup once, switch all other packets" enables the complex classification of traffic at the URL level while achieving the price and performance of typical switches.

As the VIP address for a Web site, Web switches intercept all traffic destined for that site. This permits them to track content requests and to predict hot content before servers become overwhelmed. Web switches dynamically replicate hot content to a Web cache and bring the cache into the load balancing rotation, ensuring a continually positive user experience in the event of a flash crowd. In addition, since a Web switch tracks which servers have delivered specific content, new requests for that content can be sent directly to them, resulting in improved server cache coherency and performance.

Web switching also enables virtual Web sites, where one or more geographically dispersed data centers appears as one domain name. Users enter a URL and the Web switch determines which Web server or cache is best able to handle the specific request at that moment, based on a number of criteria. These include

- Proximity of the user to a server
- The server's current condition
- The condition of the network path
- Which content has been requested

Typically, the closest server to the user is best, but Web switches can use HTTP redirects to fulfill content requests from a server halfway around the world, offering a powerful backup system should a local server fail or overload.

These next generation Web switches were created from the ground up to handle the unique requirements of Web traffic. Creating a content-aware Web site infrastructure provides a high degree of scalability since content can be placed where it makes the most sense, not just at the data center. And Web switches offer the only viable solution for eCommerce because of their unique ability to provide sticky connections based on cookies. Web switching enables Web hosters, online and content service providers, and enterprises to deliver next generation eCommerce and business-critical Web site services.

Web switching works the following way:

Step 1. User makes a content request by typing a URL into a browser.

Step 2. Web switch with virtual IP (VIP) of the requested URL intercepts the request.

Step 3. Web switch spoofs TCP connect back to client and examines packet URLs.

Step 4. Simultaneously, the Web switch examines HTTP header and URL and compares to current content rules to select the best server or cache to satisfy request.

Step 5. A flow is created between the switch and the optimal server and snaps together the flow from the client to the switch.

Step 6. A flow control block is created in the port ASIC and all subsequent packets are forwarded without intervention by the switch controllers.

Web switching offers a combined solution consisting of some attributes of load balancers, Web caches, and traffic shapers. But the best results may be accomplished by combining each of the four different concepts.

High-availability server load balancing helps Web sites tolerate failures. To protect against a complete site outage, global server load balancing (GSLB) can transparently direct customers to other Web sites. Further, GSLB helps provide customers with faster Web response times by directing them to the nearest site. Typically, GSLB works within the framework of DNS to direct customers to the best site. When a customer requests a page, the browser must first find the IP address for the Web site. The browser goes to the local DNS server that is provided by the ISP or network administrator, which finds the authoritative DNS server for the Web site. A DNS server is considered authoritative for a particular zone if it is designated by their domain's network administrator.

When a DNS lookup request is received by the authoritative DNS server, it replies with one or more IP addresses for the requested Web site. Basic load balancing is accomplished by having the authoritative DNS server perform round-robin on a list of Web site IP addresses. The authoritative DNS server has no knowledge of site availability or the load on sites. It does not understand whether a customer is closer to one site or another in terms of Internet response time. At a high level, GSLB involves two tasks interoperating within the DNS framework to provide an intelligent DNS response, and selects the best site. A Web switch provides GSLB within a DNS framework in any of the following ways:

- The Web switch acts as the authoritative DNS server for a specified domain.

- The Web switch acts as a forward proxy to an existing DNS server. A virtual IP address on the Web switch is registered as the authoritative DNS server. The Web switch load balances all DNS traffic to the real DNS servers. The Web switch also modifies replies from the DNS servers, picks the best site, and forwards it to the client—useful if customers have one or more DNS servers and would like to load-balance DNS traffic for scalability, yet provide GSLB at the same time.

- The Web switch acts as a transparent DNS server proxy. When the Web switch is deployed in the DNS server traffic path, it intercepts responses from the authoritative DNS server to select the best site—useful if the customer doesn't want to disrupt the DNS configuration or if the authoritative DNS server is not under control of the customer.

Web switches use information about sites to determine the best site for each customer and provide an appropriate response. Web switches use several metrics to determine the best site. They

- Perform site health checks to determine if it is up and running

- Examine site load conditions to ensure the site is capable of accommodating new customer requests

- Measure the proximity (Internet response time) from the customer to each site and direct customers to the site with the best response time

- Use static preferences to direct certain branch-office customers to a specific data center

Because the local DNS server caches the response from the authoritative DNS server, Web switches also set the time-to-live parameter to a user-configurable value. This ensures the freshness of DNS server response data. To provide redundancy for the authoritative DNS server, multiple authoritative DNS servers can be deployed.

2.4 Products and Services Portfolio

Service providers are continuously reviewing their products and services portfolios. It is expected to be a very well-coordinated effort between research, design, capacity planning, and marketing. Customer needs, portfolios of the competition, and the company's own technological prerequisites should find a common denominator. Usually, there is no clear picture or documentation about available products, services, or available infrastructure capacity. In certain cases, sales representatives sign special agreements with their customers without checking the availability and maintainability of the service. Launching new services leads to tension between marketing, operations, administration, and maintenance, leaving the customer sometimes unattended. This segment introduces basic services for wireline, wireless, and IP that support all three principal communications forms—voice, data, and video.

2.4.1 Wireline Voice Services

The customer connects through the telephone system into the central office (CO), local exchange, or end office. In generic terms, we can talk about switching offices. There are thousands of these offices in each country. Connection is provided to the switching office through a pair of wires or four wires called the local loop or subscriber loop, respectively.

The connections between the switching centers are hierarchically arranged. In the United States and Canada, there are toll centers, primary centers, sectional centers, and regional centers. The use of direct or indirect connections between offices with tandem trunks or other tandem switching systems depends on several factors: distances between offices, the traffic volume between offices, and the potential for sharing facilities among the customers within the geographical area. In the case of intermediate traffic volumes or longer distances, the telephone system generally establishes a combination of direct and tandem lengths.

The connections are built around high-usage or high-volume trunks, which carry the bulk of the traffic. High-usage trunks are established when the volume of calls requires and justifies the installation of high-capacity channels between two offices. Consequently, trunk configurations vary depending on traffic volume between centers. The system attempts to switch the call down into the hierarchy, across the hierarchy, or up into the hierarchy. Routing the call usually entails more intermediate switching, thereby increasing the connection delay.

Voice-oriented applications use the telephone network. In addition, many data communication systems use the telephone network for data transmission. The process is workable, but does not offer the highest quality. The majority of telephone local loops have been designed and sized to carry human speech signals and not digital data. Speech signals show the well-known analog waveform characteristics. But server and client devices are digital devices, and they require complex and expensive conversion systems. These differences will become insignificant when digitized and compressed voice transmission is going to be used. Basic services in every case include call control, authentication, security, billing, and bandwidth management. The expansion of services in voice networks is continuous. There are multiple opportunities to increase the intelligence toward subscribers.

Virtual private networks (VPNs) offer an alternative to corporate networks. Corporate networks operate private lines. VPN offers a private numbering plan to be determined by the customer. The telecommunications provider may offer multiple VPNs on the basis of a powerful physical network. The customer does not see the other VPN customers or details from the physical backbone. As part of customer network management, the provider may open a window into the VPN for the customer.

Intelligent networks (INs) are based on the concept that certain events are received and evaluated by the service switching points (SSPs) in telephone networks. The results are forwarded to the service control points (SCPs) that are intelligent processors and capable of making immediate decisions. There is an international capability set to be accepted and followed by providers. This set is the basis for generic and specified services. Some of the services are

- Abbreviated dialing
- Call holdup
- Account card calling
- Automatic alternative billing
- Call forwarding (unconditional, do-not-disturb, time limit)
- Call distribution
- Conference calling (three-way up to n-way)
- Credit card calling
- Mass calling
- Televoting
- Wake-up
- Repeated wake-up calls
- User defined routing
- Call limitations (international, long-distance, value-added services)

The prerequisite is that the SCPs are able to process a very large number of events within a very short period of time. There is also an IN service, called virtual private network, with the goal of networking subscribers on the basis of specific performance attributes. The basis is a private numbering plan (PNP) that is independent from the public numbering plans. Subscribers reach each other via the PNP call-in number, also called the on-net connection, that may include special routing of calls. In order to reach numbers in public networks, called off-net connection, a centrally located peering point is available. Off-net calling is supported for authorized on-net users only.

There is an alternative to the PBX-based networking of subscribers. In particular, for a logically connected subscriber of the same enterprise with limited geography, Centrex services could be a cost-effective solution. All the known service attributes, known for individually managed PBXs, are offered from the location of the service providers. Management responsibilities for PBXs are replaced for some administration functions on behalf of subscribers for concentrators and multiplexers. Usually, there are multiple alternatives to connect subscribers to the center, including copper- and fiber-based connections. This is usually transparent to the subscriber. Service attributes include

- Call pick-up
- Call transfer
- Call forwarding
- Limitation of incoming calls
- Limitation of outgoing calls
- Audio conference
- Hunting groups and line hunting
- Do-not-disturb
- Short codes calling plans
- Call holding
- Hot line
- Wake-up and repeated wake-up calls

When multiple Centrex centers are involved in this service, the service is called wide area Centrex.

Conventional Centrex services require a carrier to wire a separate copper loop to each subscriber's phone, connected to a switch at the Centrex office. If a business is served by more than a single central office, then each office must be configured to support the business's Centrex environment. Porting the Centrex service to IP would make its capabilities available regardless of a subscriber's location and also cut down on the expenses associated with offering this service. It would require customers to merge their voice and data traffic onto a single conduit, a complex and time-consuming move still being evaluated and resisted by most information technology (IT) managers.

Advanced intelligent networks (AINs) add additional capabilities and independence to the switching systems. It enables a service provider to introduce new services rapidly, provide easy service customization, establish vendor independence, and create open interfaces. AIN technology uses the embedded base of stored program-controlled switching systems and the SS7 network. This technology also allows for the separation of service-specific functions from other network resources. This feature reduces the dependency on switching system vendors for software development and delivery schedules. Service providers have more freedom and flexibility to create and customize services. The SCP contains programmable service-independent capabilities or service logic that are under the control of service providers. It also contains service-specific data that allows service providers and their customers to customize services. IN is expected to meet individual customer needs. AIN meets expectations of generic customer needs. The service logic is controlled by the provider. By loading different service logics into the SCPs, a wide range of service portfolios can be sent through trials, sized, and finally offered to customers. Open interfaces help to establish communication between the service logic of various SCP suppliers.

Examples of intelligent services are

- Green numbers, such as 800-, 900-, and XXX-numbers based on a range of three-digit trigger capability
- Local call paid (difference is paid by the called party)
- Information services for a fee
- Identification of fraudulent calls
- Abbreviated dialing beyond central office boundaries
- Disaster recovery service
- Televoting and teledialog
- Directory services
- Unified, enhanced, and integrated messaging services
- Area number calling service
- Virtual PBX or IP Centrex services
- Various individual call routing services that are the result of AIN customization

Computer-telephone integration (CTI) technology takes many forms, from the simplest dial-the-phone from the PC to sophisticated links between computers and telephone systems in call center environments. Essentially, this technology describes any link between a computer and phone, enabling such functions as unified messaging, or having a single PC-based interface for all voice, e-mail, and fax messages. On the high end, a call center could receive incoming calls, identify callers either through caller identification or by asking them to touch-tone an account number. The interest for this technology is great, but it would need more corporate investments.

Automatic call distribution (ACD) is a simple, well-known service for customer help desks. ACD assigns incoming calls to agents on the basis of the agents' present workload. Calls can be distributed and assigned over wide areas. It can be combined with interactive voice response (IVR) to help streamline incoming calls. The first level is usually a voice computer, guiding callers to select the right options. The IVR dialog is logged and forwarded to the agent, who then continues the dialog with the caller. Both parties may use databases and Internet pages and services while talking to each other. Call centers are equipped with multiple system and network elements as shown in Figure 2.9 (AUST00).

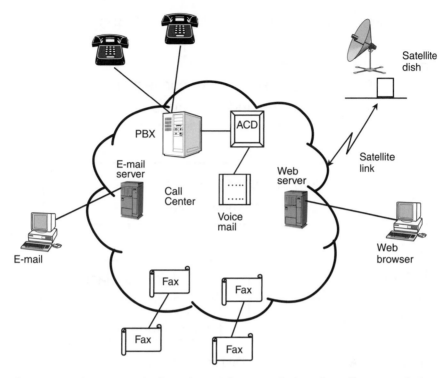

Figure 2.9 Computer-telephone integration as a platform for call-center solutions.

A VPN can support additional value-added services in the area of mail and messaging. Besides voice and fax mailboxes, offered by practically all service providers, unified messaging has gained attention recently. Figure 2.10 shows the architecture of such a service. The in- and outgoing messages include voice, fax, e-mail, SMS, and X.400. The server is in charge of formatting these message forms and also offers a common storage area of graphical and voice interfaces for the subscriber.

Service providers are starting to offer enhanced fax services as well. These services include (1) Mailbox, which provides secure fax mailbox access from any location; (2) Never-Busy Fax, which is a transparent service that stores faxes for later delivery; (3) Fax-on-Demand which allows businesses to create a library of faxable documents that customers can access and download; and (4) Fax Broadcast which delivers a document to a large number of locations with just one transmission.

2.4.2 Wireline Data Services

All wireline data services are using the existing infrastructure, consisting of the access and transport network. Due to infrastructure limitations, the service offers may also be limited.

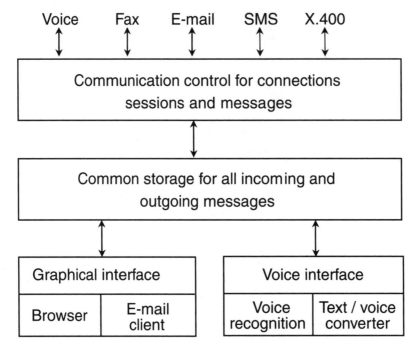

Figure 2.10 Architecture of the unified messaging service.

Clear Channels and Managed Leased-Lines-Based Services

The basis of these services is usually a very powerful digital network, consisting of SDH/SONET rings. Using various multiplexing technologies, physical media can be optimally utilized.

The T1/E1 carrier systems are high-capacity networks designed for the digital transmission of voice, data, and video. The original implementations digitized voice signals in order to take advantage of the benefits of digital technology. The term T1 was devised by the telephone companies to describe a specific type of carrier equipment. Today it is used to define a general carrier system, a data rate, and various multiplexing and framing conventions. A more concise term is DS1, which describes a multiplexed digital signal carried by the T carrier. Typical rates are

DS1 T1 1.544 Mbps

DS2 T2 6.312 Mbps

DS3 T3 44.736 Mbps

DS4 T4 274.176 Mbps

Europe and Japan use different throughput rates, but that does not change the basic characteristics of this technology.

Today, the majority of offerings digitize the voice signal through pulse code modulation (PCM), or adaptive differential pulse code modulation (ADPCM). Whatever the encoding technique, once the analog images are translated to digital bit streams, then many T1 systems are able to time division multiplex voice and data together in 24 user slots (30 in Europe) within each frame.

Different communications forms can use one digital pipe for transmission. Data transmissions are terminated through an STDM, which then uses the TDM to concentrate the traffic across the transmission line through a channel service unit (CSU). Other equipment, such as data service unit (DSU), can be used or the DSU and CSU may be combined as well.

The bandwidth of the channel or pipe can be divided into various T1 subrates. For example, a video system could utilize a 768 Kbps bandwidth, the STDM in turn could multiplex various data rates up to a 56 Kbps rate, and perhaps a CAD/CAM operation could utilize 128 Kbps of the bandwidth.

T/E-based carrier systems have been serving the industry well, but they are quite limited in their management capabilities, and they provide very little support for customers for the provisioning of services. In the early days, the use of bandwidth control headers for network management was not encouraged due to the limited transmission capacity of the facilities to accommodate this overhead traffic. Today, the prevailing idea is to exploit the high capacity of optical fibers and the processors, and allocate a greater amount of bandwidth to support control, maintenance, and management.

There are many opportunities to introduce additional services on the basis of clear channels. Examples are

- Telex
- Teletex
- Telefax
- E-mail
- Voice mail
- Teleconferencing
- Videotext
- Electronic Data Interchange (EDI)

Some of these services are losing their importance (e.g., telex, teletext, and videotext); others are gaining importance (e.g., various forms of mails, messaging, teleconferencing, and EDI).

The bandwidth requirements are constantly increasing. Service providers are expected to provision high-bandwidth services, measured in OC rates, including

OC-3	156 Mbps
OC-12	622 Mbps
OC-48	2.5 Gbps
OC-192	10 Gbps

Message Switching Services

E-mail has become such a critical part of how many people communicate that it needs special attention. E-mail is as popular as surfing the Internet. Adding voice and video to e-mail represents the next step in evolution. Some service providers are now able to deliver e-mail that contains embedded links to additional voice and video components of the message. The additional components are then sent to the user by streaming technology that uses the service provider's computers to do the majority of the required processing and then ships only the resulting images to be displayed using the end user's Web browser application. The challenge is to avoid disappointing end users with poor application performance that causes them to revert to standard text-only messages.

E-mail is fairly pervasive, fast, and relatively free. One of the next logical steps is to make it secure. Currently, the majority of financial and legal communications occur using either paper or the somewhat dated Electronic Data Interchange (EDI) systems. The problem with existing e-mail is that it can be easily faked. Internet security has five key requirements: access control, authentication, privacy, integrity, and nonrepudiation. Current secure e-mail solutions use a public key infrastructure (PKI). It is a set of security services that can be used to provide security over public networks.

The role of X.400 is still important for standardizing e-mail services. The message transfer service module resides in the core. Around this module, the message transfer agents represent various messaging applications, such as interfaces to known e-mail messaging systems, to EDI, to interpersonal messaging system (IPMS), and to voice messaging applications. The message store (MS) is the storage space for all messages. User agents represent users and applications. X.400 is for generic use; many times it is part of the portfolio of service providers.

In the future, it is expected that an additional service called instant messaging (IM) is going to be implemented. Once confined to the domain of consumer communications, IM is rapidly penetrating the corporate network, bringing with it new resource requirements. On the plus side, it offers timely communication, for instance when a project with many participants from various locations must be completed quickly. On the negative side, the inclusion of large files, as well as voice and video capabilities, can consume a lot of bandwidth.

Unified messaging (UM) is a superset of IM. It consolidates voice mail, faxes, and e-mail for convenient retrieval from a single source. Some UM approaches, however, involve a significant initial investment, recurring costs, scalability limitations, and interoperability issues. Service providers are actually in this business. The rising quality and quantity of UM products and services give enterprise network managers a rich choice of solutions.

Packet Switching Services

The idea of the X.25 interface was to define rules about how a public packet data network would handle users' traffic and accommodate various quality of service (QoS) features—called X.25 facilities—that were requested by the user. X.25 was designed to provide strict flow control on users' traffic and to provide substantial management services, such as sequencing and acknowledgment of traffic. Since its introduction in 1974, the standard has been expanded to include many options, services, and facilities, and several of the newer OSI protocols and service definitions operate with X.25. Unlike T1/E1, X.25 uses STDM techniques and is designed as a transport system for data.

The role and placement of X.25 is not always well understood. X.25 is not a packet switching specification. It is a packet network interface specification. X.25 does not specify operations within the network. X.25 is not aware whether the network is using adaptive or fixed-directory routing, or whether the internal operations of the network are connection-oriented or connectionless. X.25 defines the procedures for the exchange of data between a user device [data terminating equipment (DTE)] and the network [data communications equipment (DCE)].

X.25 provides two options to establish and maintain communications between the user devices and the network:

1. Permanent virtual circuits (PVC).
2. Switched virtual call (SVC).

A sending PVC user is assured of obtaining a connection to the receiving user and of obtaining the required services of the network to support the user-to-user session. X.25 requires that a PVC be established before a session can begin. Consequently, an agreement must be reached by the two users and the network administration before the PVC is allocated. Among other things, agreement must be made about the reservation of logical channel numbers for the PVC session and the establishment of facilities. An SVC requires that the originating user device transmits a call request packet to the network to start the connection operation. In turn, the network node relays this packet to the remote network node, which sends an incoming call packet to the called user device. If this receiving DTE chooses to acknowledge and accept the call, it transmits to the network a call accepted packet. The network then transports this packet to the requesting DTE in the form of a call connected packet. To terminate a session, a clear request packet is sent by either DTE. It is received as a clear indication packet and confirmed by the clear confirm packet.

X.25 also provides QoS options to the user. These options are called facilities. These facilities are preprovisioned for PVCs or are provided during the call establishment phase of the SVC hookup. The user is allowed to obtain features such as call redirections, security features for closed user groups, throughput, networking delays, reverse charge, reverse charge prevention, and a wide variety of other useful application support operations.

X.25-based public and private packet switching networks are widely used. The technology is old. It was designed to support user traffic on error-prone, low-quality networks, with the assumption that most user devices were unintelligent. Moreover, X.25 was designed to operate on physical interfaces that are also old and slow, such as RS-232 and V.28.

Despite these facts, X.25 usage continues to grow throughout the world for the following reasons:

- The technology is well understood.
- It is available in off-the-shelf products.
- There are extensive performance conformance tests available.
- It is cost effective for bursty, slow-speed applications.

Value-added services include

- Closed user group
- Use of permanent virtual circuits
- Implementation of reverse charging as an option

Frame Relay Services

The purpose of a frame relay network is to provide an end user with a high-speed VPN capable of supporting applications with large bit-rate transmission requirements. It gives a user T1/E1 access rates at a lower cost than can be obtained by leasing comparable T1/E1 lines. It is actually a virtually meshed network.

The design of frame relay networks is based on the fact that data transmission systems today are experiencing far fewer errors and problems than they did decades ago. During that period, protocols were developed and implemented to cope with error-prone transmission circuits. However, with the increased use of optical fibers, protocols that expend resources to deal with errors become less important. Frame relay takes advantage of this improved reliability by eliminating many of the now unnecessary error checking and correction, editing, and retransmission features that have been part of many data networks for almost 2 decades. This technology has been working for many years. It represents a scaled-down version of link access procedure D (LAPD). The flexibility of assigning bandwidth on-demand is somewhat new. Frame relay is one of the alternatives of fast packet switching.

Optimal applications with bursty data need occasional high-bandwidth requirements. Typical applications include

- LAN interconnections
- Transmitting graphics and x-rays
- Large database transfers
- CAD/CAM transfers
- Medium-quality, still-image video transmissions
- Connectionless data transfer
- Connection-oriented data transfer
- Voice transmission in first testing phase
- Value-added services (including voice over frame relay and fax over frame relay)

Fiber/Copper Distributed Data Interface Services

Fiber Distributed Data Interface (FDDI) was developed to support high-capacity LANs. To obtain this goal, the original FDDI specifications stipulated the use of optical fiber as the transport media, although it is now available on twisted pair cable (CDDI). FDDI has been deployed in many corporations to serve as a high-speed backbone network for other LANs, such as Ethernet and Token Ring.

Basically, the standard operates with 100 Mbps rate. Dual rings are provided for the LAN, so the full speed is actually 200 Mbps, although the second ring is used typically as a backup to the primary ring. In practice, most installations have not been able to utilize the full bandwidth of FDDI. The standard defines multimode optical fiber, although single-mode optical fiber can be used as well.

FDDI was designed to make transmission faster on an optical fiber transport. Due to the high-capacity 100-Mbps technology, FDDI has a tenfold increase over the widely used Ethernet, and a substantial increase over Token Ring. FDDI can also extend the distance of LAN interconnectivity. It permits the network topology to extend up to 200 km (14 miles). FDDI II, which is able to incorporate voice, is not getting enough industry interest. FDDI is actually not a new technology. But internetworked FDDIs offer new alternatives in metropolitan areas, competing with other technologies, such as frame relay and switched multimedia data service (SMDS). Any application on a LAN is optimal for this service: FDDI for data; FDDI II for voice and data.

High-Speed LANs-Based Services

Fast Ethernet is an umbrella for many technologies that increase the bandwidth of present implementations.

Full-Duplex LANs

The throughput can be increased when transmission is supported in both directions simultaneously. In most cases, cabling does not need to be changed at all. If two cable pairs are available between stations and the hubs, full-duplex operation can be supported with the result of doubling the potential throughput. It is a tactical solution for network managers, but very helpful in heavily loaded segments. In particular, server-hub connections can benefit from this solution. This migration needs adapter cards, hub boards, and bridge parts supporting full-duplex operations. But the implementation may include full-duplex Fast Ethernet, full-duplex FDDI, and also full-duplex Token Ring. Using fiber, two separate cables are necessary, each supporting unidirectional transmission. The higher speed does not cause emission problems because the individual cables are operated at the "old" speed. They are altogether just better utilized.

100BaseT

100BaseT supports 100 Mbps of bandwidth using existing Ethernet media access control (MAC) sublayers operating at 100 Mbps instead of 10 Mbps. Cabling supported in the first release of this standard includes four-pair Category-3 unshielded twisted pair, two-pair Category-5 unshielded twisted pair, two-pair shielded twisted pair, and multimode fiber.

Standard bodies are easy to modify carrier sense multiple access with collision detection (CSMA/CD), and to keep and increase its efficiency at higher speeds. Cabling is star-supported by centrally located repeater hubs. But the number of hubs is limited to two between any end-user devices. Due to the length of the collision window and as a result of the round-trip delay, the distance of 100BaseT is limited to 210 meter and to 100 meters between hubs and end-user devices. The majority of market leaders are supporting this technology. This technology, however, does not offer a breakthrough; it is a combination of shared media and a not-too-efficient access method.

100 VG AnyLAN

100 VG AnyLAN supports Ethernet and Token Ring frame formats at 100 Mbps. It operates over four-pair Category-3 unshielded twisted pair, two-pair shielded twisted pair, and multimode fiber. The physical topology is star; stations are connected to the central hub of the segments. The hub hosts the polling authority, allowing the implementation of demand priority access schemes. The hub polls each station whether they want to send or not. Usually, polling is implemented in a sequential order, but stations and applications may receive higher priorities by changing the polling table. Hubs function as repeaters; as an additional feature, they can also support security schemes by filtering incoming and outgoing packets by source and destination addresses.

The AnyLAN indicates that the hub—intelligency is assumed—supports both Ethernet and Token Ring. The limitation of distance is again approximately 100 meters between hubs and end-user devices. Due to using demand priorities, the utilization levels are expected to be higher than in the case of 100BaseT with CSMA/CD. The support on behalf of manufacturers is still very limited.

Local area network (LAN) switching may also be implemented to provide the full LAN bandwidth to the communicating partners. The next step is gigabit Ethernet that uses the same protocols while boosting transmission speeds to a billion bits per second. It will first serve as backbone, interconnecting multiple switches. This technology will provide an upgrade path for applications with above-average bandwidth demand.

Ethernets based on the CSMA/CD technology are limited to transmission rates below 100 Mbps. Higher transmission rates may be reached by switching technologies. These new switching technologies are using supplementary protocols for increasing efficiency. Gigabit Ethernet provides 1 Gbps bandwidth for campus networks with the simplicity of Ethernet at a lower cost than other technologies of comparable speed. It is an ideal backbone interconnect technology for use between 10 and 100BaseT switches, as a connection to high-performance servers, and as an upgrade path for future high-end desktop computers requiring more bandwidth than 100BaseT can offer. Although gigabit Ethernet is primarily an enterprise LAN technology, several service providers—most of them Internet service providers—have begun evaluating this technology for use in local and metropolitan areas of their networks. Gigabit Ethernet can connect network equipment, such as servers, routers, and switches, within a service provider's point of presence (POP) at high speeds and reasonable costs.

High-Speed Data Transfer Services

There are a few standards for this type of service. It has been considered a very local service between computers and their peripheries. High Performance Parallel Interface (HPPI) has offered the first standard offering a short distance (25 meters) at a throughput rate of 800 Mbps. Also, ATM could be considered here in the OC-12 version with 622 Mbps. Gigabit Ethernet promises more in the future, but current test results can confirm the OC-12 throughput range only. The efficiency of the technologies depends also on the packet sizes they are using and supporting. This is still an emerging area with a number of open issues. Service providers are interested in offering these services primarily to ASPs and also for storage area networks. Super HPPI, also called gigabytes system network (GSN), offers 6,400 Mbps and flow control. It is considered the fastest data network in use.

Audio Broadcasting Services

Voice and data channels may be utilized to transmit entertainment audio and video. Service providers have been offering such services for a variety of customers. The quality and prices are very different. Service alternatives are

- Voice channel with 4 kHz bandwidth for the transmission of speech and speech-type transmissions

- Analog/digital narrowband (0.05 to 7 kHz) low-quality audio service

- Analog/digital middleband (0.05 to 10 kHz) middle-quality audio service

- Mono-stereo quality bandwidth (0.04 to 15 kHz) audio service that can be implemented on a 2 Mbps communication line

- Hi-fi quality service (20 Hz to 20 kHz) provisioned on multiple 2 Mbps communication lines

2.4.3 Wireless and Mobile Services

The currently offered commercial wireless services can be classified based on two criteria: mobility support and technology. The mobility classification is strongly related to the coverage of the corresponding system, for example, the higher the speed of the mobile user, the larger the coverage of the system.

Paging Services

Paging, traditionally a one-way receive-only service, utilizing, for example, the FLEX protocol, has recently been offered as a full two-way service through the ReFLEX paging protocol. Significant growth rates are expected with paging.

Radio paging is a nonspeech, one-way—from base station to traveler—personal, selective, calling system with alert and without message or with defined message, such as numeric or alphanumeric. A person wishing to send a message contacts the PSTN operator and delivers the message. After a queuing delay, a system operator forwards the message to the traveler by radio repeater (FM broadcasting transmitter, VHF or UGF dedicated transmitter, satellite, cellular radio system). After receiving the message, a traveler's pager stores the message into its memory and either emits alerting tones or displays the message on demand.

Cordless Services

These are systems to be used with simple low-power portable stations operating within a short range of a base station and providing access to fixed public or private networks. There are four main applications, namely:

1. Residential (at home, for Plain Old Telephone Service) (POTS).

2. Public access (in public places and crowded areas, also called telepoint).

3. Wireless private automatic branch exchanges (WPABX) (providing cordless access in the office environment).

4. Emerging applications like radio access for local loop.

Cordless Telephony

Two communication forms are supported by cordless telephony (CT2):

Voice. The CT2 technology operates on time division multiplexing (TDM) concepts that support a speech rate of 32 Kbps using ADPCM for speech encoding. Using a common air interface (CAI) standard, multiple service providers can communicate with each other.

Data. Four types of services have been defined. These services operate on ISDN B channels at 32 Kbps in a circuit mode environment. These services are

- Asynchronous services for full-duplex operations

- Transparent synchronous services for full-duplex channels

- Conventional X.25 services

- Conventional ITU-T group fax service

Digital European Cordless Telecommunication (DECT)

Both voice and data communications are supported by DECT. For data transmissions, the IEEE 802 standards are utilized. Professional (or private) mobile radio covers a large variety of land mobile radio systems designed for professional users. This includes small local systems as well as regional or national networks, and open systems (with a commercial service) or closed systems (dedicated to particular private users). In conventional systems, each radio channel is permanently allocated to a given fleet of users (generally for low-density systems). In trunked systems, radio resources are shared among users and allocated on a per-call or per-transaction basis.

Cellular Services

There are no international standards in this area with the result that different countries have been following different implementation paths. There is some hope that the third-generation systems will find a common denominator.

Cellular refers to public land mobile radio networks for generally wide areas, for example, national coverage to be used with medium- or high-power vehicular mobiles or portable stations and for providing mobile access to the public switched telephone network. The network implementation exhibits a cellular architecture that enables frequency reuse in nonadjacent cells.

Cellular systems operate with higher power than do the cordless personal communications systems. Therefore, cellular systems can communicate within large cells with a radius in the kilometer range. In contrast, cordless cellular communication cells are quite small, usually in the order of 100 meters.

Cellular will continue to be a preferred medium for the consumer and business market. Personal communications services (PCS) will emerge as a driver for wireless. Telecommunications providers will use PCS to help reduce cellular churn, joining the customers closer to the vendor by providing end-to-end service. Wireless data connectivity, driven by lighter and smaller equipment capable of being carried by humans as well as in vehicles, will drive wireless connectivity requirements deeper and further into the network infrastructure.

The technology is not new, but implementation takes some time. Cordless systems are undergoing rapid technological changes. Different protocols and standards are used.

First-Generation Cellular Systems

The early cellular systems are based on analog FM. Advanced mobile phone service (AMPS) in the United States and total access communications system (TACS) in Europe are examples of these solutions. First-generation systems provide supervisory signaling during voice transmission to verify proper connection between the base station and the mobile terminal. This is achieved by sending tones at frequencies above the audio bands. In addition, a wideband signaling capability is provided (e.g., for use during handoffs) by means of the blank-and-burst technique, in which bursts of data are sent for short durations while speech is muted. During a call, the base station makes signal-strength measurements of its own mobiles. Also, a receiver is used to monitor signal strength of users in other cells. Based on the measurements forwarded by the base station, the control station makes decisions about call handoffs whenever needed. First-generation services are lacking international standardization. They are usually incompatible with each other due to different channel spacing and frequency band of operations.

Second-Generation Cellular Systems

The modulation format is digital rather than analog with this second generation. This offers considerable flexibility in handling the information signals, allowing the use of error control coding, source coding, and compression. There are basically two different types of solutions:

Code division multiple access (CDMA)-based systems. IS-95 takes advantage of spread spectrum modulation to guarantee reliable communication in the presence of interference and multipath. The particular interference rejection properties allow the use of the same frequency band everywhere throughout the system, so that user channel separation is achieved by the appropriate use of quasi-orthogonal spreading sequences. A key requirement for this technology is for all signals to reach the receiver with the same power, as power imbalances may greatly impact quality. For this purpose, power control is to be used in the mobile-to-base direction, to compensate for the channel attenuation. As in other systems, paging and random-access channels are present. The broadcast channels are used by the base stations to transmit a pilot signal, which is then used by the mobiles as a power control reference and also as a coherent reference for signal detection. A synchronization channel is also provided, which aids the acquisition phase as a timing reference.

Time division multiple access (TDMA)-based systems. GSM is subdividing each radio channel of 270 Kbps into eight users' channels to carry the conversations. Its very efficient coding scheme offers good quality in a digitized environment. The various base stations are interconnected through a backbone network, which also includes mobile switching centers and their databases. To manage a complex network with a variety of features, GSM supporters have chosen to rely on some already defined procedures and interfaces, possibly with some adaptation for the mobile environment. GSM is using SS7, originally defined for signaling in wireline ISDN.

Third-Generation Cellular Systems

The future promises to bring third-generation systems. Although the precise definition of a third-generation system is not unique, it is generally envisioned that it will (1) support multimedia communications, (2) integrate services that are provided today by separate networks, and (3) incorporate new features commensurate with the anytime, anywhere functionality.

Personal Communication System Services

Even though PCS systems are expected to provide a variety of services and therefore may be considered third-generation wireless cellular systems, they are mainly based on the current second-generation cellular technology, and so are somewhat between second and third generation. These systems are also referred to as low-tier and differ from cellular systems (high-tier) in that they envision smaller cells and reduced power levels. Also, they focus mainly on handheld devices with limited mobility and aim to provide a rich variety of services.

Key features of PCS will be easy-to-use high-functionality terminals and the personal dimension, which involves essentially two principal ideas:

1. A personal telephone number, where people will have their own number at which it will be possible to reach them at any time and regardless of their geographical location. It means that telephone numbers will correspond to persons instead of to a fixed installation.

2. Personalization through user profiles. Subscribers will be able to build their own set of preferences so that the network will deal with traffic addressed to or origi-

nating from them in an appropriately customized manner. Service may include call forwarding, call blocking, voice mail, paging, billing options, or others.

Future extensions will include QoS-related metrics into the service portfolio for PCS. PCS is an extension and integration of existing and future wireless and wired communication networking features and capabilities allowing communication with a person, regardless of his or her location.

Special Voice Services

Special services are emerging. A few examples are listed below.

Global positioning system (GPS). Service to accurately determine the three-dimensional position, velocity, and acceleration worldwide. It is based on spread-spectrum signals of satellite-based communication.

Mobile satellite systems (MSS). Provide wide-range coverage throughout the globe by portable equipment. Examples include Iridium (Motorola) and Teledesic (Microsoft/McCaw).

Universal personal telecommunication (UPT). Enables access to telecommunication services while allowing personal mobility. Each UPT user participates in a user-defined set of subscribed services and initiates and receives calls on the basis of a unique, personal, network-transparent UPT number across multiple networks at any terminal, fixed or mobile, irrespective of geographical location, limited only by terminal and network capabilities and restrictions imposed by the network operator.

Future public land mobile telecommunications systems (FPLMTS). Provide telecommunications services to mobile or stationary users by means of one or more radio links. This mobility will be unrestricted in terms of location within the radio coverage area. It will extend the telecommunication services of the fixed network to those users over wide geographic areas, subject to constraints imposed by spectrum allocation and radio propagation and, in addition, will support a range of services particular to mobile radio systems.

Wireless Data Services

Wireless data service providers are starting to shift their focus from vertical to horizontal applications. In the past, wireless data applications have been traditionally targeted at the public safety and utility markets. Newer applications and services are targeting members of the financial community, such as bankers, analysts, and traders, by providing real-time access to stock information. One of the key success factors for entering horizontal business markets will depend on each service provider's ability to create appealing service bundles. Future standards will unify different technologies.

Cellular Digital Packet Data (CDPD) Service

Cellular digital packet data (CDPD) uses the existing cellular network for the sole purpose of moving *bursty data,* or data that is transmitted back and forth only occasionally and in quick, short spurts. CDPD is being rapidly deployed by cellular providers, first of all in the United States. CDPD is TCP/IP implemented over cellular networks. It is well suited for certain types of transmission, especially short file transfers. CDPD is limited by two factors:

1. Services are available in selected markets.

2. Its bandwidth is currently limited and impacted even further down when voice traffic is high. Throughput rates targeting 56 Kbps are under consideration.

Service providers are offering utilities the ability to read customer's meters automatically via wireless data transmission using CDPD technology. The service would allow utilities to read meters and monitor energy flows among other services automatically from a central location, skipping the need to send personnel to customer locations. This service offers utility companies an advantage in a deregulated market because they can offer their customers a better picture of their usage patterns and then offer them a special deal to keep them from switching to other utility providers.

General Packet Radio System (GPRS) Service

The first step of significant throughput increases is GPRS. It offers up to 115 Kbps transfer rate and makes possible always-on IP connections. The GRPS is the initial step of GSM data solutions and does not require modifications in the GSM radio systems, so the implementation is straightforward.

Enhanced Data Rates for Global Evolution (EDGE) Service

The next step of mobile data evolution is EDGE. This service is able to provide even faster air interfaces. EDGE is not considered the ultimate solution because it requires expensive radio system modifications, and the implementation of the target third-generation mobile networks is too close to return the investment. Support data transfer rates are in the area of 384 Kbps.

Universal Mobile Telecommunications System (UMTS) Service

The third-generation standardized solution, called UMTS offers much higher packet data rates based on new, highly spectrum-efficient, coding schemes. Commercial deployment is expected in 2002. UMTS provides high bit rates, which can position the technology as a direct competitor of wireline offerings. Service offers are

- Vehicular transfer rates: 144 Kbps
- Pedestrian transfer rates: 384 Kbps
- Indoor transfer rates: 2 Mbps

   The fix network developments and the UMTS developments carry identical elements so the integration of fix and mobile core networks can be relatively trouble free and even unavoidable for service providers who offer and operate both services.

VSAT-Based and Direct Broadcast Services

There are three principal service alternatives with very small aperture satellite systems (VSATs):

1. *Interactive.* Includes packet-switched data and compressed voice by using different equipment.

2. *Broadcast.* Used to distribute data for the access reach of the VSAT by supporting usually synchronous and asynchronous data sources.

3. *Managed fixed connections for PPP-independent communication.* This service can be provisioned for different data transmission rates and for various QoS options.

Direct broadcast satellite (DBS) services support two areas: entertainment and data. The data service serves corporate customers with occasional and regular broadcast as well as residential customers. One possible use of the data service is software distribution. Internet access is also offered by this service as

- Direct delivery of text files at 12 Mbps
- Multimedia at 3 Mbps
- Internet access at 400 Kbps

This service is asymmetrical: Customers send information requests to the service provider via telephone lines and receive data via the satellite. VSATs are used for corporate broadcasts of data, including price updates for products. They operate between 14 Kbps and 64 Kbps.

Microwave Services

This service supports point-to-point data communication. It is protocol-independent, bit transparent service. It can be provisioned for different data transfer rates and QoS parameters.

Point-to-Multipoint (P–MP) Service

This service is related to wireless local loop (WLL) and expected to serve small and medium businesses or households in rural areas. Operators need licenses for radio frequencies to offer this service. Usually, this service is for data communications; sometimes, operators must provide voice services as well.

Distribution Services

A variety of broadband wireless providers has already introduced services that use multichannel multipoint distribution service (MMDS) and local multipoint distribution service (LMDS). MMDS service providers have been around for awhile as LMDS providers are emerging. MMDS offers a broader coverage, while LMDS offers greater capacity. Current service offerings use either the public network or a cable modem for the return path.

MMDS can, for instance, deliver 68 video channels, 32 music options, and near-on-demand with 40 channels of a pay-per-view basis.

LMDS can be used to offer many services such as business-oriented services like wire speed LAN Interconnect and fractional and full T1, teleworking at 10 Mbps, virtually as fast as being in the office. In addition, Internet access in the Mbps range, multiple broadcast video channels, and third phone lines at home or in the office are offered.

For the Internet to be a viable real-time audio/video medium, it needs a method for serving a community of users. IP multicast is a suite of tools that addresses the bandwidth cost, availability, and service-quality problems facing real-time, large-scale Webcasting.

Rather than duplicating data, multicast sends the same information just once to multiple users. When a listener requests a stream, the Internet routers find the closest node that has the signal and replicates it, making the model scaleable. IP multicast can run over just about any network that can carry IP, including ATM, frame relay, dial-up, and even satellite links. Originally developed in the late 1980s, it is now supported by virtually all major internetworking vendors, and its implementation and usage is picking up speed.

Reliability is a challenge with multicast because it is not necessarily a bidirectional path from the server to support retransmission of lost packets. A string of lost packets could create enough return traffic to negate multicast bandwidth savings. For this reason, TCP/IP cannot be used. Among the transport protocols developed for IP multicast, Real Time Protocol (RTP) and Real Time Control Protocol (RTCP) are the main ones for real-time multimedia delivery. RTP adds to each packet header the timing information necessary for data sequencing and synchronization. It does not provide mechanisms to ensure timely delivery or provide QoS guarantees; it does not guarantee delivery, nor does it assume that the underlying network is reliable.

Uninterrupted audio requires a reliable transport layer; nevertheless, existing basic concealment techniques such as frequency domain repetition combined with packet interleaving work reasonably well if packet loss is minimal and occasional departures from perfection can be tolerated. One approach is to use FEC (forward error correction). Adding some redundant data improves performance considerably; combined with interleaving, this can be a good strategy, but it requires more bandwidth for a given quality level. This can be a challenge on low-speed connections.

Reliable multicast can be used to increase the performance of many applications that deliver information or live events to large numbers of users, such as financial data or video streaming. Reliable multicast creates higher-value application services for IP-based networks. According to a study conducted by the IP Multicast Initiative (IPMI), over 50 percent of information systems/technology (IS/IT) managers stated that IP multicast had created new business opportunities for their companies, and these numbers are likely to grow.

Multicast intersects with QoS, especially in the domain of multimedia and collaboration tools. Use of multicast technology to distribute the same signal to many destinations without replicating the stream multiple times is a boon to network efficiency, but can complicate the QoS problem. For example, different clients may have different bandwidth requirements, or different users may have different privileges with respect to accessing premium bandwidth. The already complex QoS policy space becomes truly awesome when overlaid with the technical complexities of multicast distribution.

Some examples for successfully using multicast include:

- Data replication is handled in parallel, rather than serially.

- Financial transaction and news can be broadcast to multiple destinations simultaneously.

- Inventory reconciliation requests can be transmitted to all distribution centers at once.

- Distance-learning video/audio streams are efficiently transmitted.

Successful multicasting assumes that networking resources—equipment and facilities—are available for the duration of multicasting.

2.4.4 Integrated Services

This segment focuses on those services that support multiple communication forms. In the near future, this convergence will become the dominating form of service portfolios.

Integrated Services Digital Network (ISDN)

The initial purpose of ISDN was to provide a digital interface between a user and a network node for the transport of digitized voice and data images. It is now designed to support a wide range of services. Basically, all communication forms can be supported by ISDN. It has been implemented as an evolutionary technology by way of the telephone-based integrated digital network. Many digital techniques seen with T1 and E1 are used in ISDN. It includes signaling rates, transmission codes, and physical plugs.

For ISDN, there are two important terms: functional groupings and reference points. Functional groupings are a set of capabilities needed in an ISDN user-access interface. Specific functions within a functional grouping may be performed by multiple pieces of equipment or software. Reference points are the interfaces dividing the functional groupings. Usually, a reference point corresponds to a physical interface between pieces of equipment. Figure 2.11 shows a typical structure of ISDN including all the reference points. The reference points labeled R, S, T, and U are logical interfaces between the functional groupings, which can be either a terminal type 1 (TE1), a terminal type 2 (TE2), or a network termination (NT1, NT2) grouping. The reference points help to define the responsibilities in communications networking based on ISDN.

Between terminal equipment and an NT2-type ISDN node, the basic rate is used. The basic rate includes 2 B channels, each with 64 Kbps, and 1 D channel with 16 Kbps bandwidth. The primary rate is different in the United States and Europe. In the United States, 23 B channels and 1 D channel build the primary rate; Europe uses 31 B channels and 1 D channel for the primary rate. The corresponding throughput rates are exactly the rates as with T1 and E1.

ISDN cannot be considered successful based on the performance since its inception in the early 1980s. In North America, the progress has been much slower than in Europe because of the lack of cohesive implementation politics. This situation has changed in the past few years. RBOCs and Bellcore are aggressively implementing ISDN and

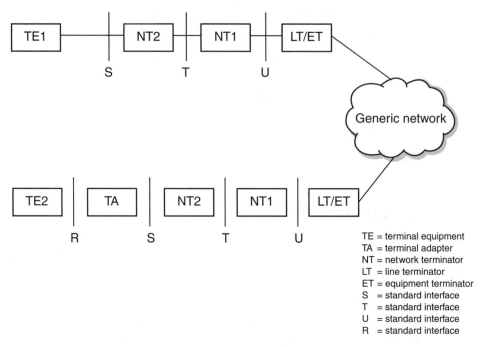

Figure 2.11 Typical topology of ISDN networks.

preparing themselves for B-ISDN. Most European countries have implemented ISDN; there is a cooperation between countries to promote Euro-ISDN. ISDN can be judged successful in another way. It has helped to implement the LAPD and the Q.931 messaging protocol. These two protocols can be found throughout the communications industry.

The technology is also useful for remote access to a data network. Telephone companies that market it well can win at ISDN, as well as those companies that can produce reasonably priced, easy-to-use customer-access equipment. Its potential, however, is in competition with high-speed modems and with much higher capacity options such as digital subscriber loop and transmission of data via the broadband cable television network.

Service offers are

- ISDN carrier services
  - 64 Kbps carrier service
  - Voice carrier service
  - 3.1 kHz audio carrier service
- ISDN teleservices
  - Phone teleservice
  - Group 4 fax teleservice

- 7 kHz phone teleservice
- Picture phone teleservice
- ISDN value-added services
  - Call identification services:
    - Direct dial-in
    - Multiple subscriber number
    - Calling line identification presentation
    - Calling line identification restriction
    - Connected line identification presentation
    - Connected line identification restriction
    - Malicious call identification
    - Subaddressing
    - Call forwarding services
    - Call forwarding busy
    - Call forwarding no reply
    - Call forwarding unconditional
    - Line hunting
  - Call establishment services:
    - Call waiting
    - Call hold
    - Terminal portability
    - Tariffing services
    - User-to-user signaling services
- ISDN applications
  - PBX-based customized applications
  - File transfer applications
  - Database applications
  - Audio applications
  - Credit authorization applications
  - Video teleconferencing
  - Internet access

Asynchronous Transfer Mode (ATM)

The purpose of asynchronous transfer mode (ATM) is to provide a high-speed, low-delay, multiplexing and switching network to support any type of user traffic, such as voice, data, or video applications. ATM is one of four fast relay services. ATM segments and multiplexes user traffic into small, fixed-length units called cells. The cell is 53 octets, with 5 octets reserved for the cell header. Each cell is identified with virtual circuit identifiers that are contained in the cell header. An ATM network uses these identifiers to relay the traffic through high-speed switches from the sending customer premises equipment (CPE) to the receiving CPE.

ATM provides limited error-detection operations. It provides no retransmission services, and few operations are performed on the small header. The intention of this approach—small cells with minimal services performed—is to implement a network that is fast enough to support multimegabit transfer rates.

ATM is a new technology. ATM is supposed to be the foundation for providing the convergence, multiplexing, and switching operations. ATM resides on top of the physical layer. Practically all kinds of applications can be supported. It is a multimedia technology. All applications supported by frame relay and SMDS can be supported by ATM, too.

In general, services are based on

- Constant bit rate (CBR) for video, file transfer, and voice applications
- Variable bit rate (VBR) for data transactions, some voice and video applications

Typical service alternatives are

- High-speed line connection service
- Layer 3 switching (routing) service
- Layer 2 switching (bridging) service
- ATM bearer, cell relay service

Inverse multiplexing for ATM (IMA) is a specification for provisioning multiple ATM circuits in T1 increments. IMA was created to bridge the bandwidth gap between T1 and T3. Using IMA, several low-cost T1 lines can be used to aggregate the bandwidth and distribute ATM traffic across physical circuits.

Digital Subscriber Line Access Services

The enabling technology is digital subscriber line (xDSL), a scheme that allows mixing data, voice, and video over phone lines. There are, however, different types of DSL to choose from, each suited for different applications. All DSL technologies run on existing copper phone lines and use special and sophisticated modulation to increase transmission rates (ABER97).

Asymmetric digital subscriber line (ADSL) is the most publicized of the DSL schemes and is commonly used as an ideal transport for linking branch offices and telecommuters in need of high-speed intranet and Internet access. The word asymmetric refers to the fact that it allows more bandwidth downstream (to the consumer) than upstream (from the consumer). Downstream, ADSL supports speeds of 1.5 to 8 Mbps, depending on the line quality, distance, and wire gauge. Upstream rates range between 16 and 640 Kbps, again depending on line quality, distance, and wire gauge.

For up to 18,000 feet, ADSL can move data at T1 using standard 24-gauge wire. At distances of 12,000 feet or less, the maximum speed is 8 Mbps.

ADSL delivers a couple of other principal benefits. First, ADSL equipment is installed at carriers' central offices, which offloads overburdened voice switches by moving data traffic off the public switched telephone network and onto data networks—a critical problem stemming from Internet use. Second, the power for ADSL is sent by the carrier over the copper wire with the result that the line works even when local power fails. This is an advantage over ISDN, which requires a local power supply and thus a separate phone line for comparable service guarantees. The third benefit is again over ISDN. ADSL furnishes three information channels—two for data and one for voice. Thus, data performance is not impacted by voice calls. Rollout plans are very aggressive with this service. Its widespread availability is expected through the end of this decade.

Rate-adaptive digital subscriber line (RADSL) has the same transmission limits as ADSL. But as its name suggests, it adjusts transmission speed according to the length and quality of the local line. Connection speed is established when the line syncs up or is set by a signal from the central office. RADSL devices poll the line before transmitting: Standards bodies are deciding if products will constantly scan the line speed. RADSL applications are the same as ADSL and include Internet, intranets, video-on-demand, database access, remote LAN access, and lifeline phone services.

High bit rate digital subscriber line (HDSL) technology is symmetric, meaning that it furnishes the same amount of bandwidth both upstream and downstream. The most mature of the xDSL approaches, HDSL has already been implemented in the telco feeder plant (the lines that extend from central office to remote nodes) and also in campus environments. Because of its speed—T1 over two twisted pairs of wiring, and E1 over three—telcos commonly deploy HDSL as an alternative to T1/E1 with repeaters. At 15,000 feet, HDSL operating distance is shorter than ADSL, but carriers can install signal repeaters to extend its useful range (typically by 3,000 to 4,000 feet). Its reliance on two or three wire pairs makes it ideal for connecting PBXs, interexchange carrier point of presence (POPs), Internet servers, and campus networks. In addition, carriers are starting to offer HDSL for digital traffic in the local loop, between two telecommunication central offices and customer premises. HDSL's symmetry makes this an attractive option for high-bandwidth services like multimedia, but availability is still very limited.

Single-line digital subscriber line (SDSL) is essentially the same as HDSL with two exceptions: It uses a single wire pair and has a maximum operating range of 10,000 feet. Since it is symmetric and needs only one twisted pair, SDSL is suitable for applications like video teleconferencing or collaborative computing with identical downstream and upstream speeds. Standards for SDSL are still under development.

Very high bit rate digital subscriber line (VDSL) is the fastest DSL technology. It delivers downstream rates of 13 to 52 Mbps and upstream rates of 1.5 to 2.3 Mbps over a single wire pair. But, the maximum operating distance is only 1,000 to 4,000 feet. In addition to supporting the same applications as ADSL, VDSL, with its additional bandwidth, could potentially enable carriers to deliver high-definition television (HDTV). VDSL is still in the definition stage.

A number of critical issues must be resolved before DSL technologies achieve widespread commercial deployment. Standards are still under development. Modulation techniques, such as carrierless amplitude phase (CAP) and discrete multitone (DMT), have been separated by standards bodies. Some other problems include interoperability, security, eliminating interference with ham radio signals, and lowering power systems requirements from the present 8 to 12 Watts down to 2 to 3 Watts. A nontechnical but important factor will be how well carriers can translate the successes they realize in their xDSL technology trials to market trials and then to commercial deployments.

Voice/Fax over xDSL Services

Regulators allow line sharing between voice and data for access networks. This fact drives incumbent service providers to utilize their infrastructure to offer both voice and data services. Also, competitive pricing may accelerate the provisioning of these services. It is economical for small and midsize businesses and for large enterprise telecommuters. Service providers can offer multiple phone and data lines—consolidated into one DSL pipe—at prices that undercut current pricing schemes. Another reason for a promising future is that competitive local-exchange carriers (CLECs) can attack the incumbent local-exchange carrier (ILEC) customer base by integrated service offers. Not only data, but also voice, may play a key role for revenue streams of CLECs in the future. The following factors will decide the success of this service (ALLE00)

- Network management
- Customer premises equipment
- Selection of service providers
- Service level agreements
- Billing customers for the service
- Future uses of the pipe

Business Video and Multimedia Services

Service providers are very interested in offering high-quality video-based digital communication services for business as well as entertainment applications. Digital methods deployment may be considered for supporting digital TV as an alternative to other distribution approaches, such as terrestrial broadcast, satellite broadcast, and cable TV distribution. There is general interest to distribute information via the Internet, by way of intranets and extranets. Service providers want to become part of desktop business video applications requiring value-added services in addition to providing the communication facilities and equipment. Both wireline and wireless video services are targets for service providers.

In general, emerging digital video applications can be classified in the following categories (MINO00)

- Corporate or institutional video transmission (both classical and H.323- or SIP-based solutions)
- Stored digital video for multimedia applications
- Entertainment video (including video broadcast and postproduction distribution)

Business video takes the form of desktop-based conferencing, multimedia, video-based training, reception of digitized broadcast video on the PC, and imaging-based document management. A few services are identified in this segment that might be of interest as part of service portfolios.

Videoconferencing Service

The following elements impact network connection options for videoconferencing services currently supported

- Point-to-point connection
- Bridging (i.e., point-to-multipoint, multipoint-to-multipoint)
- Inverse mixing (i.e., one video channel obtained via multiple network connections)

In existing networks, the provisioning of point-to-point connections is the network managers' responsibility. Bridging and inverse mixing are the roles of the customer's equipment with current videoconferencing service. New services, particularly ATM, can be utilized to place some of this responsibility into the network. LANs will become a major enabling technology for desktop videoconferencing. A growing number of projects are being developed for the LAN; however, the issue about network capacity and QoS on a legacy LAN remains.

Videoconferencing offers many benefits for corporations and individuals by saving travel expenses and an employee's time. Important pieces must be in place for videoconferencing to be successful, including rising demand from multinational corporations, improvements in technology, solidification of key standards, and proliferation of standards-compliant video-enabled products from principal suppliers like Microsoft or Intel. Key issues for service providers are

- Reliability of technical equipment
- Availability at many service access points (SAPs)
- Performance
- Quality
- Ease of use

IP multicasting can be considered by service providers for supporting this service. It is able to provide multipoint H.323 videoconferencing. IP multicasting can save customers bandwidth on packet networks because the information needs to be transmitted only once over a given link, with routers replicating information as required. One challenge associated with multicasting is that it imposes a significant communications load on the processor at each endpoint, since each endpoint must send information to every other endpoint. This means that IP multicasting is not currently scaleable for large videoconferences.

Multimedia Service

Multimedia, as a general field, is a technology that fully utilizes computers to store, manipulate, and display information in various formats, such as video, graphics, audio, and text. It has been enabled by the synergetic confluence of the PC, the television, and the optical storage media. Broad communication channels are another key technical driver. This service may incorporate the following applications: presentation development, distance learning, online magazines, telemedicine, kiosks, and computer-based training.

Digital Versatile Disk (DVD) technology is entering the market at the commercial and consumer level. It is the next generation optical disk technology able to hold video, audio, and computer data. It targets home entertainment, computers, and business information with a single digital format, eventually replacing audio CDs, videotape, laser disk, CD-ROM, and video game cartridges.

Digital Television Services

There are two competing standards for digital television: one promoted by the United States Advanced Television Systems Committee and the other by the European Digital Video Broadcasting Group. Digital television offers an almost unlimited potential to broadcast video, audio, and data to end users.

Video-on-Demand Services

The combination of digital storing capabilities with affordable bandwidth enables service providers to offer video on demand. Using powerful compression techniques for efficient streaming, bandwidth demand may be kept as low as possible. These services can be offered for both business and private users. Billing can be based on the content value, instead of resource utilization.

Streaming Media

Streaming media is maturing into an effective, viable, and potentially profitable business tool. Service providers should consider their content delivery network (CDNs) to be utilized for streaming media.

Simply downloading files doesn't work well for video and audio, even though throughput capabilities are improving. It is still time-consuming to download and further distribute audio and video files. The basic technology for streaming is relatively inexpensive. The content provider must digitize the content and set up a media server specific to the clients. Costs of streaming media servers are reasonable.

Until recently, streaming on the Internet found limited business applications. Restricted bandwidth made video unstable, and poor reliability resulted in missing video frames or dropouts in audio.

It is changing now due to rapid improvements in transmission quality. Sales and marketing are probably the leading business applications for streaming media. However, other rapidly growing business uses will include corporate communications, training, and customer support.

Service providers with streaming media products and services face three basic issues to be solved:

- Delivery to ensure good quality distribution, also across ISP peering points, by using edge caching and application multicast.

- Performance monitoring to continuously supervise QoS and to indicate and initiate rectifications in real time as needed.

- Content management by making the content searchable and navigable using metadata that indexes it.

The infrastructure is being rapidly deployed by service providers to deliver streaming content over the Internet or intranets reliably and at acceptable speeds. More and more businesses are taking advantage of these new opportunities. At the same time, service providers may generate revenue, and they may retain their customers by offering good quality service at a reasonable price.

2.4.5 Cable-Based Services

Cable service providers can enter the competition for voice and data services. Depending on the country, there are millions of households and businesses with cable television connections. In the majority of cases, cable television is a distribution channel supporting one-way communication only. But, using cable modems, channels could be provided for two-way communications, allowing consumers to send back data or use the cable for phone conversations.

- The equipment at the transmission site generates television signals and houses switches that route phone calls and monitor the network.

- Parallel fiber optic lines spread out over the area. If a line is out, traffic moves almost instantly to another route.

- Electronic nodes convert signals for transmission via coax cables. One node can serve between 500 and 1,000 homes, approximately.

- Coaxial cable runs into a box on the side of the home. Electronics in the box split signals, sending phone traffic over regular phone lines, television signals over cable lines to the television set.

- Phone service could work on the current wiring. Television could be interactive, allowing signals to flow back up the cable line. PCs could also be connected through a cable modem, which transmits information up to 1,000 times faster than phone lines.

Turning cable television systems into local phone networks will be not easy or cheap. Plans are ambitious to compete with local service providers. A basic cable system starts out as copper coax that carry signals in a line from the head-end—where TV signals are generated—to each consumer. Signals go one way; in case of cable cuts or other damages, all the consumers from that point are out of service.

But a system designed to handle phone calls and interactive TV looks much different. The main trunks of the network are set up in interconnecting rings of fiber-optic lines, which carry thousands of times more information than a copper line. If a line is cut, traffic moves to another ring in a microsecond, and practically no one loses service. Because phone calls are two-way, a phone-cable system must be two-way and contain the sophisticated switches that send calls to the right places.

About 40 percent of today's cable TV systems are still copper. The other 60 percent have some fiber in their trunk lines, but most of them need upgraded. Just a few are set up in rings and have switches.

Power could cause another problem. Telephone lines have just enough electricity running through them to power the phone and the network, independent of the power grid. If a storm knocks out the main electrical grid, most of the time the phone still works. Cable lines don't carry power. If electricity goes out, so does cable and so would a phone hooked to an unpowered cable network. Cable lines, however, are able to carry power. But adding power from a node over the coaxial cable could add noise. There is a debate today in the industry about whether to get power from the cable-phone network, or use another solution, like attaching backup batteries to the sides of households.

Once the pieces of the network come together, cable companies will face other issues. One is number portability—the ability to let consumers keep their phone numbers even if they change phone service from the local phone company to the cable company. Right now, if somebody changes carriers, the number must be changed. State or federal regulation is expected to change that. Cable-phone systems will also have to prove to a skeptical public that they can be as reliable as current phone systems, which almost never break down. Cable systems have to overcome a reputation for frequent disconnections.

From a technology standpoint, the competition in the high-speed data services market will initially be between a dedicated architecture and a shared architecture. ISDN and other dedicated solutions, like xDSLs and cable-LAN services, require infrastructure upgrades, and that means significant investments on the part of service providers. Also, while most performance comparisons focus on peak bandwidth, other aspects of network usage, such as customer density and average session time, can also affect cost and quality of service.

The type of upgrade needed to deliver high-speed data over cable networks should be fairly obvious: Cable television transmission is typically one way, but a data and phone network must permit two-way traffic. Limited forms of data service are possible by using the telephone line as a return route, but this is not a long-term solution. Some cable networks have already migrated to a hybrid fiber-coax infrastructure, but many operators are still immersed in the upgrading process. Once the networks are tailored for two-way traffic, broadband LAN technology will be incorporated so that digital data can be transmitted over a separate channel. Most of the vendors that supply technology to cable operators will use an Ethernet-like approach, where the consumer's computer will have to be fitted with a network interface card and a cable modem for accessing the cable LAN. Access speed will depend on the peak rate of the cable modem and the volume of traffic on the cable LAN. Subscribers will likely experience connection speeds that vary according to such factors as usage.

Cable LANs will operate full duplex with two channels, each channel sending data in a different direction. For customers using Internet or intranet applications, one of these channels would connect to an Internet or intranet POP router, which would then forward data packets from all users on the neighborhood LAN to and from all other systems on the Internet or on intranets. The other channel would receive data from the Internet or intranet service. Cable LANs are unlike ISDN-based services in that they furnish full-time connections, rather than switched or dial-up links. The obvious advantage is that it eliminates the need for dedicated transmission and switching resources. Users can access the cable LAN when needed, and only the cable network makes use of the Internet or intranet POP.

A shared cable LAN requires only a single connection to the Internet or intranet provider. With ISDN, the lines of many individually served subscribers have to be multiplexed and concentrated, and the number of subscribers online at any given time is limited by the number of connections between the provider and the telecommunication network.

In terms of geographical coverage, cable LANs can be quite large. At the beginning, they are intended to be implemented for residential broadband services. The future target is, however, corporate internetworking. Currently, there are no standards governing the transmission of data over cable LANs, but that has not slowed down equipment suppliers. They bring proprietary products to the market as rapidly as possible.

The cable modem, which is used to connect the consumer's PC with a coax drop linked to the two-way, broadband cable LAN, is specifically designed for high-speed data communications. When the modem is in operation, cable television programming is still available. But the return path that the cable modem uses is limited and must be shared among all digital services, including interactive television, video on demand, telephony, videoconferencing, and data services. One problem with cable modem is the immaturity of existing devices. The majority of manufacturers are targeting peak bandwidth between 128 Kbps and 30 Mbps.

Competing with cable technology are primarily ISDN and emerging technologies, such as ADSL, RADSL, HDSL, SDSL, and VDSL. They all use existing wires to corporations and residential customers. Because ISDN delivers both voice and data, it makes use of circuit-switching and packet switching technology. For high-speed data services, the local telephone plant must be upgraded so that two-way digital transmission—over the existing copper pairs that ISDN also relies upon—is possible. In addition, ISDN-capable digital switches must be installed at the telecommunications central office. ISDN may offer faster data transmission than analog modems, but the dial-up access model is still the same. From the data transmission perspective, this is an inefficient approach because circuit switching requires the service provider to dedicate resources to a customer at all times. In other words, it is inconsistent with the bursty nature of data services. The result is wasted bandwidth.

Implementing an ISDN network could end up being more costly than deploying cable LANs. In telecommunications networks, for example, an assessment of the incremental costs of providing ISDN Internet or intranet access includes the cost of initializing a subscriber's ISDN circuit at the central office; the cost of multiplexers, concentrators, and terminal servers; and possibly the cost of T1 lines from the service provider to the Internet or intranet provider.

Cable-LAN access might prove to be less expensive for data and online services. It is assumed that cable television providers are facing less financial risks than telecommunications providers when deploying data services. Lower costs translate into consumer savings. The cost per bit of peak bandwidth (ROGE95) in providing Internet or intranet access is significantly lower for hybrid fiber-coax networks than it is for ISDN—about 60 cents for a 4 Mbps residential service as opposed to $16 for a 128 Kbps service. Shared fiber-coax networks also compete well against dedicated ISDN on average bandwidth and peak bandwidth. A 4 Mbps residential cable service, for example, can provide the same average bandwidth and about 32 times the peak bandwidth of a 128 Kbps ISDN service for 40 percent less money.

While deployment costs for both technologies continue to decline, ISDN deployment still runs several hundred dollars more per subscriber than cable-LAN deployment. This difference, in addition to the higher performance of cable LANs, will be an important factor as Internet, intranet, and online service access become commodity products. However, the cable-LAN approach and the cable services industry have their shortcomings, too. Cable-LAN modems and access products are still proprietary, so when an operator selects a vendor, it is likely to remain locked in. Also, shared networks function properly only when subscribers' usage habits are well known. The more subscribers deviate from an assumed usage profile, the more performance is likely to deteriorate. Big changes in usage could impact the cost of providing acceptable service levels over neighborhood cable LANs.

Finally, the cable industry itself is in many countries greatly fragmented. This inhibits coordinated efforts, which are vital to the rapid deployment of services. Although telecommunications providers are in competition against each other, they will work better as a group if they act quickly in deploying the resources needed to make ISDN universally available.

In order to avoid these bottlenecks and other fault- and performance-related problems, cable services providers need a powerful management solution. It requires a complete rethinking of presently-used solutions. The management solution should address high volumes of events, alarms, and messages, fail-safe operations, traffic control and management, quality assurance of services, and collection of accounting data.

2.4.6 IP-Based Products and Services

The basic model for IP networks assumes a clear split between service and transport layers. All service logic for user services rests in application programs running on hosts connected to the IP networks. The hosts are not central network entities like the service control points in the PSTN but only connected to the edges of the network. The IP model expects the network to provide some means of basic transport. The networking part of applications can follow either the client/server model (e.g., WWW) or a peer-to-peer model (e.g., PC-to-PC direct VoIP with MS NetMeeting). Common to both models is that all service logic resides on the hosts. With the split of transport and applications, the code for applications can

- Use an existing application layer protocol, such as HTTP, SMTP, FTP
- Define their own application protocol
- Use no intermediate protocol

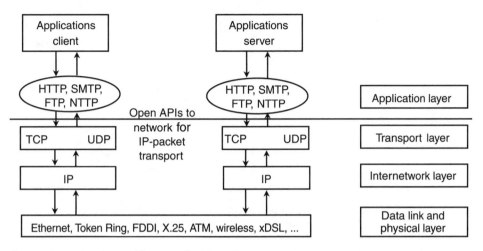

Figure 2.12 Service architecture for IP environments.

to access the transport protocols TCP or UDP of the transport layer. The network provides basic byters transfer only. QoS, VPN, mobility, IPSec, and so on, are considered value-added features of transport. Figure 2.12 shows the service architecture for IP environments.

In the classical value chain of telecommunications networks, the provisioning of services is closely tied to know-how and control over central network entities like local exchanges or SCPs. Telecommunications services are usually highly integrated into the corresponding hardware. Hence, only the supplier of the equipment or the operator of the telecommunications network can create and provide services. The value chain is closed, simple, and short. With the advent of IP-based services, creation of applications and new services is no longer limited to a few suppliers of networking equipment. This decoupling of networking equipment from the creation and provision of applications and services causes the formerly closed and simple value chain to open up and develop a more complex structure. Figure 2.13 shows this new structure.

Each link of the value chain will be addressed by a new generation of specified, highly competitive suppliers. The number of suppliers is growing significantly.

IP over Everything

For 2 decades, the telecommunications industry has been searching for a platform that offers convergence. First, ISDN, then B-ISDN based on ATM, were seen as providing this platform. Sometimes, we call B-ISDN broadband networking. Technologically, ISDN and B-ISDN are very different from each other.

The stable future model of B-ISDN should be reassessed for the following reasons:

■ The mix of traffic types is different from that which the architects of B-ISDN envisioned and is different for different classes of operators. Network traffic today

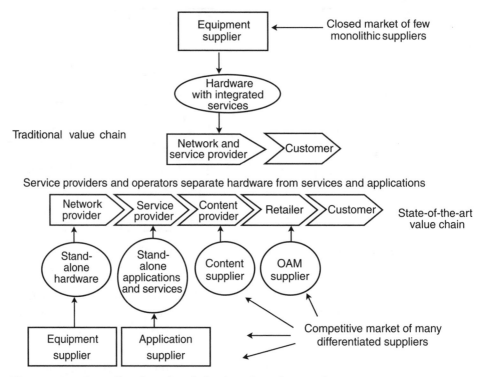

Figure 2.13 Extending the value chains in IP-based networks.

and in the near future includes a great deal of voice (as predicted), but there is little video, and the growth in data traffic is overwhelmingly in a single format—IP packets.

■ Alternative network architecture approaches are emerging, some of which offer better economics and performance. There are many alternative possible architectures for designing a network. One can build a network infrastructure that does not require a discrete network element for each layer of the ISO stack, thereby saving money and reducing complexity. Indeed, vendors are now introducing, and carriers evaluating, products that collapse layers of the ISO model, such as IP over SONET/SDH and IP/ATM hybrids.

■ Carriers are facing new, competitive pressures to reduce their capital and operating costs. With the advent of competition and the demise of rate-of-return regulation, incumbent carriers have become much more cost conscious and more concerned with finding efficient ways of delivering services. Different carriers have different needs, and may benefit from different network architectures.

As a result, both incumbent carriers and newcomers are beginning to reassess the B-ISDN model.

In order to evaluate alternatives, Figure 2.14 displays a layered architecture with six technological alternatives. These technological alternatives in the figure are:

1. *IP + ATM + SDH/SONET = B-ISDN.* Traditional approach, which has got the most supporting network elements and their element managers.

2. *ATM transport.* It includes both SDH/SONET-less ATM transport and ATM/SDH/SONET hybrids.

3. *Switched routing.* ATM/IP hybrids.

4. *IP over SDH/SONET.* Point-to-Point Protocol (PPP) or HDLC-framed IP mapped to SDH/SONET.

5. *Optical IP.* Transport of PPP or HDLC-framed IP over WDM with fast photonic restoration.

6. *Use of enhanced frame relay.* Substitution of ATM by frame relay in any of the approaches 1, 2, or 3.

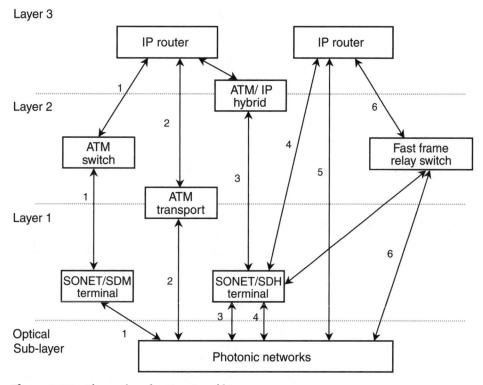

Figure 2.14 Alternatives for IP networking.

IP-Based Applications

GROUPS	APPLICATIONS
Personal communication	VoIP, FoIP
	e-mail, WWW, news
	Universal messaging
	Chatrooms
	Mediation
Telecommuting	Remote access service
	Virtual remote office
	Application sharing
Multicast Services	TV/radio over IP
	Conferencing
eCommerce	Business-to-business (B2B)
	Business-to-consumer (B2C)
	Direct delivery
Entertainment	Online gaming
	Online gambling
	MoD, VoD
Education	Distance learning
	Computer-based training
	Multimedia encyclopedia

Internet Access Services

Temporary access services are PSTN, ISDN, packet switching, and xDSL. Permanent access services are cable and managed lines.

Voice over IP Services

Communicating via packet data networks, such as IP, ATM, and frame relay, has become a preferred strategy for both corporate and public network planners. Experts are predicting that data traffic will soon exceed telephone traffic. At the same time, more and more companies are seeing the value of transporting voice over IP networks to reduce telephone and facsimile costs and to set the stage for advanced multimedia applications. Providing high-quality telephony over IP networks is one of the key steps in the convergence of voice, fax, video, and data communications services. Voice over IP has now been proven feasible; the race is on to adopt standards, design terminals and gateways, and begin the rollout of services on a global scale. The present technical difficulties of transporting voice and the complexities of building commercial products are challenges many companies face today. Adding voice to packet networks requires an understanding of how to deal with system level challenges, such as

- Interoperability
- Packet loss
- Delays
- Density
- Scalability
- Reliability

The Internet and corporate intranets must soon be voice-enabled if they are to make the vision of one-stop networking a reality.

The public telephone network and the equipment that makes it possible are taken for granted in most parts of the world. Availability of a telephone and access to national and international voice networks is considered an essential in modern society—telephones are even expected to work when the electric power is off.

Service providers are facing a paradigm shift beginning to occur because more and more communications are in digital form and transported via packet networks. Since data traffic is growing much faster than telephone traffic, there has been considerable interest in transporting voice over data networks as opposed to the more traditional data over voice networks.

In particular, VoIP (voice over IP) has become attractive given the low-cost, flat-rate pricing of the public Internet. In fact, good quality telephony over IP has now become one of the keys leading to the convergence of the voice, video, and data communications industries. The feasibility of carrying voice and call signaling messages over the Internet or intranets has already been demonstrated, but delivering high-quality commercial products, establishing public services, and convincing users to buy into the vision are just beginning.

VoIP can be defined as the ability to make telephone calls and send faxes (FoIP) over IP-based data networks with a suitable quality of service (QoS) and a much superior cost/benefit. Equipment producers see VoIP/FoIP as a new opportunity to innovate and compete. The challenge for them is turning this vision into reality by quickly developing new VoIP-enabled equipment. For Internet service providers, the possibility of introducing usage-based pricing and increasing their traffic volumes is very attractive. Users are seeking new types of integrated voice/data applications as well as cost benefits.

Successfully delivering voice over packet networks presents a tremendous opportunity; however, implementing the products is not as straightforward as it may first appear. Product development challenges such as ensuring interoperability, scalability, and cost-effectiveness are discussed as well. The types of applications that will both drive the market and benefit the most from the convergence of voice and data will be identified.

Typical Services, Applications, and Benefits

Voice communication will certainly remain the basic form of interaction for businesses and private homes. It cannot be replaced or even dramatically changed. The immediate goal for VoIP/FoIP service providers is to reproduce existing telephone capabilities at a significantly lower total cost of ownership and to offer a technically competitive alternative to the PSTN. It is the combination of VoIP with point-of-service applications that shows great promise for the longer term.

The first measure of success for VoIP will be cost savings for long-distance calls as long as there are no additional constraints imposed on the end user. For example, callers should not be required to use a microphone on a PC. VoIP provides a competitive threat to the providers of traditional telephone services that, at the very least, will stimulate improvements in cost and function throughout the industry. Figure 2.15 illustrates one scenario for how telephony and facsimile can be implemented using an IP network.

This design would also apply if other types of packet networks were being used. VoIP could be applied to almost any voice communications requirement, ranging from a simple interoffice intercom to complex multipoint teleconferencing/shared screen environments. The quality of voice reproduction to be provided could also be tailored according to the application. Customer calls may need higher quality than internal corporate calls. Hence, VoIP equipment must have the flexibility to cater to a wide range of configurations and environments and the ability to blend traditional telephony with VoIP. Current configuration alternatives are shown in Figure 2.16.

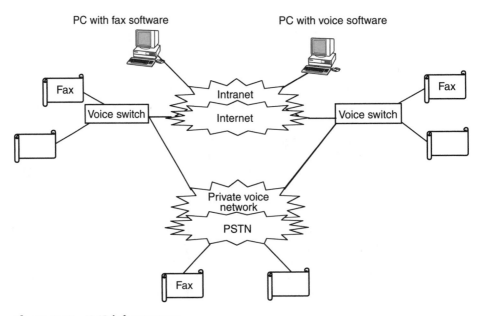

Figure 2.15 VoIP infrastructure.

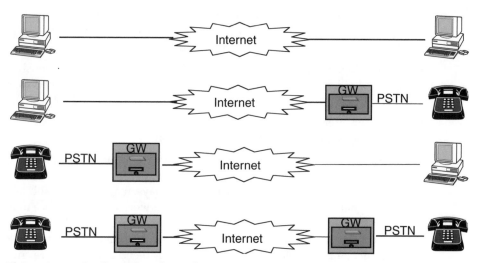

Figure 2.16 Configuration alternatives.

Some of the more important applications are listed following. It is a very dynamic list because applications are being continuously added.

PSTN gateways. Interconnection of the Internet and intranets to the PSTN can be accomplished using a gateway, either integrated into the PBX (iPBX) or provided as a separate device. A PC-based telephone, for example, would have access to the public network by calling a gateway at a point close to the destination. Thereby, long-distance charges can be minimized.

Internet-aware telephones. Ordinary wired and wireless telephones can be enhanced to serve as an Internet or intranet access device as well as providing normal telephony. Directory services, for example, could be accessed over the Internet or intranet by submitting a name and receiving a voice or text reply.

Interoffice trunking over the corporate intranet. Replacement of tie trunks between company-owned PBXs using an intranet link would provide economies of scale and help to consolidate network facilities.

Remote access from a branch or home office. A small or home office could gain access to corporate voice, data, and facsimile services using the company's intranet. This may be useful for home-based agents working in a call center, for example.

Voice calls from a mobile PC via the Internet or intranets. Calls to the office can be achieved using a multimedia PC that is connected via the Internet. One example would be using the Internet or intranets to call from a hotel instead of using expensive hotel telephones. This could be ideal for submitting or retrieving voice messages.

Internet call center access. Access to call center facilities via the Internet or intranets is emerging as a valuable adjunct to electronic commerce applications. Internet call centers would enable a customer who has questions about a product being offered over the Internet or intranets to access customer service agents online. This application is also called "surf and call" or "click and call." Another VoIP application for call centers is the interconnection of multiple call centers.

Team browsing. During the conversation with visitors, the agent can push Web pages and video clips to visitors to help them select the most appropriate product. Other clips can be pushed to them while waiting for offers and confirmations.

Video teleconferencing. This application can be utilized for multiple developers working on geographically distributed locations.

Real-time facsimile transmission. Facsimile services normally use dial-up PSTN connections, at speeds up to 14.4 Kbps, between pairs of compatible fax machines. Transmission quality is affected by network delays, machine compatibility, and analog signal quality. To operate over packet networks, a fax interface unit must convert the data to packet form, handle the conversion of signaling and control protocols, and ensure complete delivery of the scan data in the correct order. For this particular application, packet loss and end-to-end delay are more critical than in voice applications.

Store and forward voice services. Voice messages could be prepared locally, using a telephone and delivered to an integrated voice/data mailbox using Internet or intranet services.

The goal for developers is relatively simple—add telephone calling capabilities—both voice transfer and signaling—to IP-based networks and interconnect these to the public telephone network and to private voice networks in such a way as to maintain current voice quality standards and preserve the features everyone expects from the telephone.

Voice and telephone calling can be viewed as one of many applications for an IP network, with software being used to support the application and interface to the network. The emergence of VoIP is a direct result of the advances that were made in hardware and software technologies in the 1990s.

The software functionality required for voice-to-packet conversion are:

Voice processing module. Prepares voice samples for transmission over the packet network. This software is typically run on a digital signal processor (DSP).

Call processing (signaling) module. Serves as a signaling gateway, allowing calls to be established across the packet network. This software supports E&M (wink, delay, and immediate), loop, or ground start FXS and FXO.

Packet processing module. Processes voice and signaling packets, adding the appropriate transport headers prior to submitting the packets to the IP network. Signaling information is converted from telephony protocols to the packet signaling protocol.

Network management module. Provides management agent functionality, allowing remote fault, accounting, and configuration management to be performed from standard management systems. It could include ancillary services such as support for security features, access to dialing directories, and remote-access support.

Figure 2.17 shows these modules in an oversimplified structure.

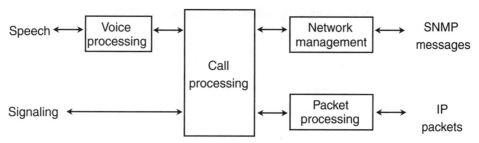

Figure 2.17 Gateway functions.

The following functions are supported by software:

PCM interface. Receives samples from the telephony (PCM) interface and forwards them to the appropriate VoIP software module for processing, and vice versa. The PCM interface performs continuous phase resampling of output samples to the analog interface.

Echo cancellation unit. Performs echo cancellation on sampled, full-duplex voice port signals in accordance with the ITU G.165 or G.168 standard. Since round-trip delay for VoIP is always greater than 50 ms, echo cancellation is a requirement. Operational parameters may be programmable.

Voice activity/idle noise detector. Suppresses packet transmission when voice signals are not present and hence saves additional bandwidth. If no activity is detected for a period of time, the voice encoder output will not be transported across the network. Noise levels are also measured and reported to the destination so that comfort noise can be inserted into the call.

Tone detector. Detects the reception of DTMF (Dial tone multifrequency) tones and discriminates between voice and facsimile signals. These can be used to invoke the appropriate voice processing functions (i.e., the decoding and packetizing of facsimile information or the compression of voice).

Generator. Generates DTMF tones and call progress tones under command of the operating system.

Facsimile processing module. Provides a facsimile relay function by demodulating the PCM data, extracting the relevant information, and packing the scan data into packets.

Packet voice protocol module. Encapsulates the compressed voice and fax data for transmission over the data network. Each packet includes a sequence number that allows the received packets to be delivered in the correct order. This also allows silence intervals to be reproduced properly and lost packets to be detected.

Voice playout module. Buffers at the destination the packets that are received and forwards them to the voice codes for playout. This module provides an adaptive jitter buffer and a measurement mechanism that allows buffer sizes to be adapted to the performance of the network.

The Call Processing (Signaling) Subsystem

This subsystem detects the presence of a new call and collects addressing information. Various telephony signaling standards must be supported. A number of functions must be performed if full telephony calling is to be supported:

- The interface to the telephone network must be monitored to collect incoming commands and responses.

- The signaling protocols (e.g., E&M) must be terminated and the information must be extracted.

- The signaling information must be mapped into a format that can be used to establish a session across the packet network.

- Telephone numbers (E.164 dial addresses) must be converted into IP addresses with the potential need for an external reference to a directory service. Two approaches to dialing are being used: single stage (dial the destination number and use automatic route selection functions) and two stages (dial the VoIP gateway number, then dial the real destination).

- The gatekeeper is doing the actual translation, and is also responsible for routing calls between gateways.

Packet Processing Subsystem

The packet processing module, which processes voice and signaling packets, adds the appropriate transport headers prior to submitting the packets to the IP network. Signaling information is concerted from telephony protocols to the packet signaling protocol.

The software used in VoIP devices must be supported by a real-time operating environment and provided with the ability to communicate among the modules and with the external world. Development time, testing, and risk can be minimized through the use of embedded software. The objective should always be to develop new ways to optimize the use of standard protocol software, not to reinvent basic functions that require extensive testing for standards compliance and product interoperability.

The deployment of a VoIP infrastructure for public use involves much more than simply adding compression functions to an IP network. Anyone must be able to call anyone else, regardless of location and form of network attachment (telephone, wireless phone, PC, or other device). Everyone must believe the service is as good as the traditional telephone network. Long-term costs—as opposed to simply avoiding regulatory costs—must make the investments in the infrastructure worthwhile. Any new approach to telephony will naturally be compared to the incumbent and must be seen as being no worse, implying that management, security, and reliability functions are included.

Figure 2.18 is a refinement of Figure 2.15 that includes placement of the VoIP gateway and system level support functions integral to the high-quality VoIP solution. The gateway is shown in this figure as a separate component, but it could be integrated into the voice switch (PBX or CO switch) or into an IP switch.

Some of the management functions that are required for VoIP system solutions include

- Fault management
- Accounting and billing

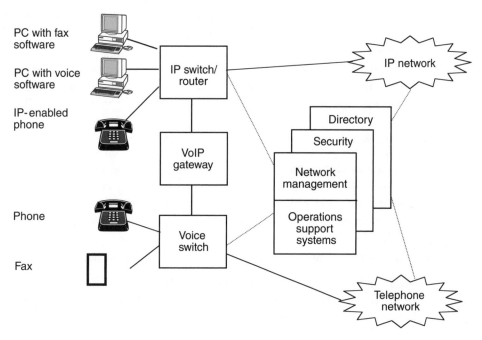

Figure 2.18 A combined PSTN/VoIP system.

- Configuration management
- Addressing and directories
- Authentication and encryption

Implementation of full-scale VoIP systems must provide the following attributes:

Interoperability. In a public networking environment, different products will need to interwork if any-to-any communications is to be possible. Using common software that has been tested for conformance to all applicable standards—such as for compression—can significantly reduce the cost of product development. Interconnection of VoIP to the PSTN also involves meeting the specific standards for telephone network access.

Reliability. The VoIP network, whether by design or through management, should be fault tolerant with only a very small likelihood of complete failure. In particular, the gateway between the telephone and VoIP systems needs to be highly reliable.

Availability. Sufficient capacity must be available in the VoIP system and its gateways to minimize the likelihood of call blocking and mid-call disconnects. This will be especially important when the network is shared with data traffic that may cause congestion. Mechanisms for admission control should be available for both the voice and data traffic, with prioritization policies set.

Scalability. There is potential for extremely high growth rates in VoIP systems, especially if they prove the equal of the PSTN at much lower cost. VoIP systems must be flexible enough to grow to very large user populations, to allow a mix of public and private services and to adapt to local regulations. The need for large numbers of addressable points may force the use of improved Internet protocols such as IPv6.

Accessibility. Telephone systems assume that any telephone can call any other telephone and allow conferencing of multiple telephones across wide geographic areas. This is driven by functions that map between telephone numbers and other types of packet network addresses, specifically IP addresses. There must, of course, exist gateways that allow every device to be reached.

Visibility. Many are claiming significant economic advantages due to the implementation of VoIP. These are often based on flat-rate prices for Internet services, the fact that services such as the Internet 911 are not required, and that there is no regulatory prohibition against interconnection of telephone systems with IP systems. Also assumed is that higher performance compression will not be used in the telephone network to reduce costs. If circumstances change, the motivation for VoIP purely for cost avoidance reasons will change also.

In addition, two more metrics may be considered for embedded gateway solutions:

Speeds and feeds. Most gateways link to the PBX via channeled T1/E1 or ISDN Primary Rate Interfaces (PRIs) and Basic Rate Interfaces (BRIs). But not all PBXs can handle T1s and ISDN; companies with these devices might want to look into products that come with analog interfaces.

Port counts. The number will vary, depending on vendor and product. For instance, gateways based on PC servers will top out at 96 ports—because they have got 4 slots, each can handle one 24-port T1 card. The number of ports is also equal to the number of simultaneous calls a gateway can make, since each port comes with its own digital signal processor (DSP).

IP Virtual Private Networks

IP VPNs are another form of virtual private networks (VPNs). They provide an alternative to leased line connections. IP VPNs provide an inexpensive way to extend the corporate network to telecommuters, home workers, day-extenders, remote offices, and business partners. They are implemented through tunneling, in which the data to be transmitted and header information are encapsulated inside standard IP packets, usually after encryption and sometimes after compression.

There are four principal application areas for IP VPNs:

1. Connecting remote sites to wide area networks (WANs).
2. Connecting remote users to networks.
3. Connecting business partners via extranets.
4. Connecting remote users to systems.

By supporting these application areas, IP VPNs provide

■ Network managers with reduced-cost means for increasing the effective span of the corporate network

- Network users with a convenient and secure means to remotely access their corporate network

- Corporations with a convenient, secure method for communicating with business partners

- Service providers with a great opportunity to grow their businesses by providing substantial incremental bandwidth with value-added services

The trend with many customers and service providers is to add more users, more bandwidth, more partners, and more applications. Based on user expectations, three changes emerge. First, customers are willing to expand their IP VPNs and consider them as a production tool to satisfy their users. They increase the bandwidth. Second, extranets are the next application wave for IP VPNs, and a large number of businesses will be opening up their networks to business partners and customers. Third, some IP VPN users will be taking the first cautious steps toward network convergence by enabling IP voice and video over their IP VPNs. All of these expectations assume scalability of IP VPNs-based services.

Figure 2.19 shows the tunnels in the Internet or intranets supporting the information exchange between the corporate VPN server and telecommuters, mobile workers, and remote offices.

Although many enterprise network and service provider managers realize that they need IP VPNs, they may not realize that they can vary in implementation, convenience, cost, and manageability. Furthermore, the division of IP VPN responsibilities between the enterprise network staff and the service provider ranges from completely in-house to totally outsourced. IP VPNs may be offered as a special customized service by service providers for supporting data, voice, and video.

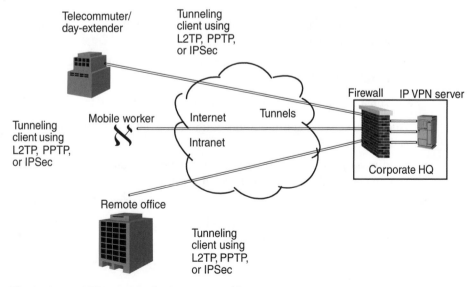

Figure 2.19 VPNs across the Internet and intranets.

Service providers can take many different approaches to their IP VPN offerings. Some selected IP VPN offerings include the following:

- Sell basic Internet access and bandwidth; the enterprise customer handles all IP VPN products and operations.

- Sell business-quality Internet or IP network services; the enterprise customer handles all IP VPN products and operations.

- Sell compulsory IP VPNs embedded in POP equipment.

- Offer IP VPN hardware and software bundled with VPN bandwidth and services.

- Design the customer's IP VPN solution.

- Operate the total IP VPN solution for the customer, including design, equipment installation and service, help desk, and billing support.

2.4.7 Customer Network Management Service

Customer network management lets corporate users of communication services view and alter their segments of a provider's network. Once such a standardized and open interface is in use, both service provider and corporate users benefit.

The advantages for the service providers are their ability to

- Keep network loads to a minimum, despite the inexact nature of traffic prediction

- Provide customers safe access to pertinent OSS and network data, from port assignments to billing and account details

- Isolate individual customer domains without revealing details of the carrier network configuration

- Accomplish even the most complex mapping by gathering values from across the network or among OSSs

- Establish customer network domains with full assurance that customers can make only authorized changes

The advantages for corporate users are their capacity to

- Alter data network configurations without the delays of paperwork or telephone calls

- Produce any level of report, from performance on a single switch to comprehensive management overviews of account histories

- Manage faults dynamically, reducing the need for carrier intervention

- Streamline troubleshooting with easily generated reports and automatic fixes, even in multicarrier environments

- Integrate to the carrier network whether or not current end-user management systems are robust

In order to avoid redundancy and inconsistencies, state-of-the-art CNM solutions request a very tight connection between the management architectures and products of the provider and the corporation.

There are a number of ways in which a CNM system could integrate or fail to integrate customer systems. The first alternative is no integration at all. The provider's CNM system could continue as an independent stand-alone system that provides a convenient point of access to services such as PBX management. Beyond that, the provider could supply customers with a standard interface that encapsulates a particular combination of protocols, information models, and behaviors such as a CNM agent and MIB. This will be the integration point for the management applications at the customer premises. But this will still cause problems if different providers define different interfaces with different information/object models for similar services. At the next level, integration could be achieved via a common graphical interface at the user interface level. The provider would provide a Windows or Motif CNM application that runs alongside the customer's management application on its net management platform. In some cases, the provider would furnish applications as part of the CNM system that uses a private provider CNM agent MIB on the provider side. This is really an extension of the previous approach: The provider offers more of the application functionality to the customer.

In order to enhance efficiency and simplification at the same time, the network management platform of the corporation should be connected to a very intelligent agent on behalf of the provider. This agent unifies and coordinates the work of multiple managers that are responsible for business applications, service, network, and element management. It is also responsible to synchronize data files, databases, and MIBs.

Figure 2.20 shows an integrated structure. There are two connections between the systems: one at the physical level and one at the network management level.

This high level of integration is expected to be reached in multiple phases. Telecommunications providers are on the move to select, customize, and deploy powerful management frameworks that will play the role of the intelligent agent.

CNM represents the first step of outsourcing. Outsourcing may include all FCAPS functions or just parts of them. Recently, firewall management services are gaining importance. Many management service providers (MSP) emerge with specific portfolios. They may offer their services alone or in combination with other service providers, such as ISPs, ASPs, and NSPs.

2.4.8 Innovative Services

Figure 2.2, on page 36, shows the actual, simplified value chain. Innovative service created and offered by service providers may fall into the categories hosting, processing, applications, and media.

Hosting and processing enable Web presence and interactivity on the Internet. They are typically provided by ISPs and NextGen service providers who are active in IP services. It mainly includes hosting Web server infrastructures and content and Web-

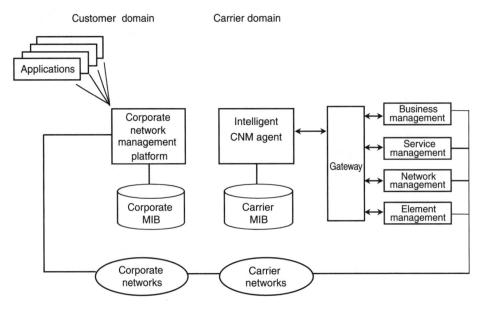

Figure 2.20 Customer network management.

enabled transaction software and hardware that allow the execution of online transactions. It is an infrastructure-type activity, although it is characterized by added value and a significant amount of additional services. Service offer alternatives are

- Web hosting, keeping content on Web server farms and offering access to it with good performance
- Value-added Web hosting, adding content and database maintenance and Webmaster services
- Data hosting, offering storage area networks
- Data management services, including search machines
- Public key infrastructure services, including trust center functions
- Centralized Web transaction services
- Web community and Internet account management
- Transaction authentication services

The typical customers of these services are businesses. While large businesses earlier deployed their own Web infrastructure in-house, now they also realize the efficiencies of lower complexity and economies of scale, which are given by professional service providers. This customer base can easily extend in the future. The key differentiator will be the service level and complexity of services offered to customers. Hosting and value-added hosting emerges as a volume business. Large data centers with server farms, load balancers, and traffic shapers combined with high availability and excellent performance will take business away from smaller service providers with lower availability and limited Internet access capability. Most service providers are inexperienced in this area.

Content delivery management is taking off and service providers are well positioned to earn revenues in this area. Content delivery management helps content owners provide seamless and fast Web site access for customers by

- Large-scale caching
- Distribution of Web server farms
- Complex Internet routing services on managed network segments

All these aspects help to deliver reasonable performance. Processing is an increasingly important revenue generation opportunity as traditional infrastructure business is shrinking. Transaction, therefore processing, which is the infrastructure and software enabler of transactions, is believed to grow to become the single most important revenue input of the Internet value chain. Processing by no means is related to the core business of service providers, but it is important for eCommerce service offers. Services can be created by the IT organization of service providers in collaboration with systems integrators.

2.4.9 Electronic Marketplaces

Volume projections may give a false impression of the future importance of eCommerce. More important than volume, from a business-to-business perspective, is value. Today's volume projections only hint at the value the Internet will provide in the years to come as an enabling technology for eBusiness. And the best mechanism to unlock that value is the Web-based electronic marketplace, which aligns buyers and sellers in product (or industry) focused Internet marketplaces for the exchange of goods and services.

Online markets, also known as B2B marketplaces, are commerce sites on the public Internet that allow large communities of buyers and suppliers to meet and trade with each other. They present ideal structures for commercial exchange, achieving new levels of market efficiency by tightening and automating the relationship between suppliers and buyers. They allow participants to access various mechanisms to buy and sell almost anything, from services to direct materials. Ultimately, all businesses will buy from, sell on, host, or be marginalized by a marketplace. For organizations committed to participating in the future of online business, B2B marketplaces offer an excellent entry point into the new economy. As eCommerce becomes more central to the operations of mainline companies, a diversity of marketplaces will arise in every industry sector.

There are always three components of eCommerce: sell-side storefront, buy-side eProcurement, and B2B marketplace.

Principal attributes of sell-side storefronts:

- Primary model used in current B2C scenarios.
- Single seller, typically a distributor, constructs a Web storefront to many consumers.

- Unless a single distributor can aggregate all the suppliers in a given industry, the buyer remains responsible for comparison shopping between stores.

- Expensive for buyer; does not meet the needs of corporate procurement organizations.

Principal attributes of buy-side eProcurement:

- Buy-side applications generally consist of a browser-based self-service front end to ERP and legacy purchasing systems.

- Corporate procurement aggregates many supplier catalogs into a single "universal" catalog and allows end-user requisitioning from the desktop, facilitating standard procurement for the organization and cutting down on maverick purchasing.

- Purchases made through this system are linked to the back-office ERP or accounting system, cutting time and expense from the transaction and avoiding potential bookkeeping errors.

- Model yields reduced transaction costs but not lower purchase costs; no impact on size of supplier base, no enablement of dynamic trade. Buying organizations must set up and maintain catalogs for each of their suppliers; too costly and technically demanding for most medium and small-sized businesses.

Principal attributes of B2B marketplaces:

- Latest evolution of B2B eCommerce, enabling a many-to-many relationship between buyers and suppliers.

- Buyers and suppliers leverage economies of scale in their trading relationships and access a more liquid marketplace.

- Sellers find buyers for their goods and services, buyers find suppliers with goods and services to sell.

- Many-to-many liquidity allows the use of dynamic pricing models such as auctions and exchanges, further improving the economic efficiency of the market.

Service providers can team up with experts on both sell and buy sides and offer electronic marketplaces to their customers. In this case, portal and catalog suppliers on the buy-side, and auction providers on the sell-side should be configured and connected by a commerce services network (CSN).

As the new trading hubs, marketplaces must enable certain processes and enterprise trading requirements. They should accommodate existing procurement processes and buyer-supplier interactions, and offer full interoperability with other markets. Marketplace requirements include:

- *Procurement processes.* Procurement professionals configure a virtual procurement system within B2B marketplaces. This replicates the buyers' unique procurement process down to individual permissions, rules, and workflow, allowing the procurement organization to control the overall buying process while distributing the buying task to end users.

- *Buyer-supplier relationships.* Before moving to a marketplace, most buyers and suppliers will have existing relationships that must be reflected in the marketplace. Suppliers can configure the system to reflect prenegotiated discounts for certain buyers, which will be automatically applied when those buyers access the marketplace. This many-to-many marketplace combines the advantages of both sell-side and buy-side models, but since it is hosted, avoids setup and maintenance costs for the participants. Significantly, this can allow access by the smaller organizations that would not otherwise have the resources to trade online. Both buyers and suppliers gain the advantage of a much broader trading community, and both sides can enjoy the benefits of a streamlined trading process.

- *Interoperable marketplaces.* One of the key factors in building a successful B2B marketplace is to focus on meeting all the buying needs of the target user. These needs may go beyond the specialist capabilities of any single marketplace, so to cater to broader buying requirements, marketplaces may link to each other, effectively extending the product range without giving up control of the buyer. The ability of marketplaces to interoperate extends the idea of liquidity and network effect by joining more buyers with more suppliers, but does not sacrifice the ability of each marketplace to be highly specific to the supply-chain node or target buyer group it serves.

Market makers are the keys to these new B2B eCommerce relationships, catalyzing the growth of the B2B economy by leveraging their domain expertise, customer relationships, and supply chain strength to support the growth of B2B marketplaces. In return for delivering value, market makers stand poised to earn substantial rewards by sharing in the returns achieved by buyers and suppliers.

The early stage of marketplace development focuses on establishing enough basic capability and buyer liquidity to make the market competitive. In nearly all cases, markets start out with a narrow range of products and services and target either a product category or a buyer group. As they grow, they must expand from this sharp focus to support a broader base of buyers and suppliers.

Commerce services networks (CSN) connect the sell and buy sides together. It is owned by the market maker. Besides the absolutely necessary physical infrastructure, basic services can be combined into a more generic offer. Such services are most likely in the portfolio of telecommunications service providers or OSS application services providers. Examples of such services (provided by Ariba) are

- Directory and interoperability services
- Payment and financial services
- Sourcing services for goods using reserve auctions
- Liquidation services
- Content services
- Transaction services
- Information services
- Logistics services

In most cases, launching, deploying, and managing electronic marketplaces is a joint venture of many service providers supported by powerful investors.

The application and media element of the value chain creates and translates traditional and digital content into a Web-ready format and creates the actual interface between the digital product and the customer. This service is targeting an end-to-end process that covers creation, manufacturing, delivery, and presentation of content to customers. This is believed to be the most promising business opportunity of the Internet. It carries the highest growth potential, but at the same time the highest risks, too. Telecommunications service providers, IT companies, media enterprises, retail chains, and several other industries are competing for revenues.

Service offers are:

- Application services to be provided by service providers, integrating IT, software, system integration, telecommunication, and consulting skills.

- Content authoring, auditing, deployment, and maintenance combined with bandwidth management, server-load management, and traffic management, supporting generic, corporate, and specialized niche portals, and B2B and B2C operations.

- Content creation targeting videos, movies, audio, photo archives, encyclopedic articles, analyst reports, financial evaluation, and many others. Music and written material combined with broadband access to support multimedia can be delivered over the Internet.

2.4.10 mCommerce

PC-based mCommerce has gained massive commercial support around the world. But WAP phones, PDAs, and other handheld computing devices are rapidly transforming the IT landscape and providing new opportunities for vendors. The next generation of eCommerce will exploit these wireless technologies to support mobile eCommerce (mCommerce). The growth of the Internet and wireless connectivity creates the possibility of accessing applications and information, and conducting business from almost anywhere, with wireless coverage. Wireless commerce is being driven by the move to a completely digital spectrum, with the convergence of wireless devices, mobile phones, and PDAs, and with mobile data and Internet services. These new developments are eliminating the distinction between computing and telephony.

The principal driving force for mCommerce is the predicted size of the future mobile marketplace. Internet-enabled mobile devices will be the most common method of accessing the Internet. There is, however, another reason for this massive interest. The large telecommunications vendors need to drive growth in the sector because the market for conventional voice calls is likely to reach saturation. Also, the mobile phone vendors need a reason for people to replace their current phones. These vendor drives are key factors for mCommerce deployment.

The success of mCommerce will depend on four critical requirements: availability, reliability, performance, and security.

The timeline of deployment is difficult to predict. In the short-term (twelve months), nonintensive tasks such as banking, eBay-type transactions, stock trading, and so on, will be frequently carried out using wireless data. The next to gain importance will be image transmissions: insurance photographs, medical images, aviation data, and so on. The key midterm development will be the integration of global positioning and mobile technology. This will promote the next wave of mCommerce applications, most likely within a two-to-four year time frame.

As consumers gain increasing access to data and information, eCommerce and eBusiness strategists will have to rethink and redesign their processes. For example, eCommerce on the Internet relies heavily on advertising as a revenue stream to compensate losses. This reliance will be significantly reduced on the mobile Internet because of high call charges and limited graphical capabilities.

The job of organizing, managing, and targeting Web content for delivery to wireless devices and transactions for different market segments will become much more challenging. Issues include design for mobile touch points, mobile interactive marketing, and different languages. Heavy investments in dynamic content management and configuration tools will be required to meet these needs, including rapid and real-time data mining for direct marketing to a mobile, transactive customer base. The considerable financial requirements for deploying successful mCommerce strategies mean that growth will stimulate alliances among large telecommunications service providers, financial services providers, and content providers.

These innovative service areas must be seriously investigated by service providers. In other traditional areas, the profit margins are narrowing; in the IP area, they have to face other competition. Continued success requires innovative minds that conduct business differently. It means more collaboration with customers, mergers, acquisitions, investment into smaller companies that may be acquired later, and flexibility in service creation, fulfillment, and quality assurance.

Another Internet-based service is immersive photography, which allows customers to use PCs to navigate around a digitized 360-degree photo. This technology is targeted towards Internet retailers who want to give their customers a wraparound view of their goods: high-end real estate agents, travel agents, cruise lines, and destination marketers.

2.5 Summary

This chapter summarized most of the basic disciplines needed to create, deploy, and maintain products and services. Each service provider owns a product portfolio that is unfortunately not always visible to customers, or even to the company's own marketing and sales organization. This chapter tried to bring order into the portfolio by offering a clear service classification for principal service segments, such as wireline, wireless, and IP. A lack of clarity regarding the services available to customers will result in tensions between contractually agreed upon and practically achievable service levels. Portfolio opportunities are almost limitless. Its maintenance needs careful attention on behalf of service providers. The worst that may happen to service providers is that each business unit maintains its own product and service portfolio. Synchronization is nonexistent, manual updates are rare, customers are confused, and SLA cannot be met by operations and maintenance. Product and service portfolios of the future are expected to be flexible; changes and creation can be done easily; a number of functions can be executed by customers. All this is possible because the underlying network infrastructure is changing as well. Both incumbent and new service providers can take advantage of the revolutionary changes in IP technology offering IP over everything and everything over IP, and all at the same time.

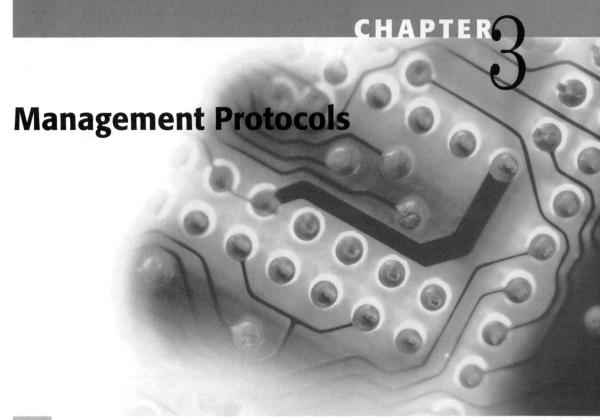

CHAPTER 3

Management Protocols

3.1 Introduction

Protocols always represent an agreement between the communicating parties. In the area of network management, management/agent relationships have frequently been implemented. Figure 3.1 shows this relationship. The agent side may be rendered hierarchical by implementing subagents in specific devices. Depending on the nature of the management protocol, either the manager or the agent starts the dialog. There are always exceptions for high-priority networking events.

In the case of Common Management Implementation Protocol (CMIP), eventing techniques are used. Assuming that the agents are intelligent enough to capture, interpret, filter, and process events, they will notify the manager about alarming conditions. Of course, the manager is allowed to interrupt and send inquiry-type messages to the agents.

In case of Simple Network Management Protocol (SNMP), the manager polls the agents periodically. The agents respond by sending lots of information on device status and performance. Usually, the agents wait for the poll unless unusual events occur in the network. For such events, special traps can be defined and implemented.

It is extremely difficult for service providers to find the common denominator for management protocols. In most cases, they select a layered architecture following the TMN recommendations from International Telecommunications Union (ITU). In this case, they tolerate various protocols at the element management layer, streamlining them into one or a few protocols at the network management layer. On top of this

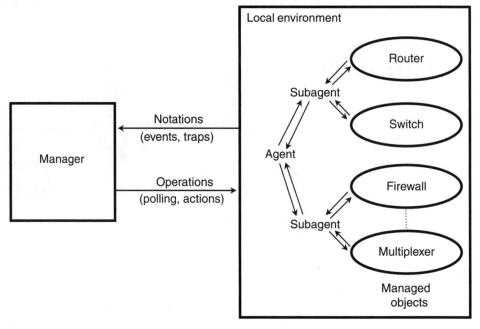

Figure 3.1 Communication paths between manager, agents, subagents, and managed objects.

layer, an umbrella or a so-called management framework may be implemented that would further aggregate and consolidate events, messages, and alarms for the service management layer. Special business applications may run on the framework to support the business management layer.

Figure 3.2 shows such an arrangement with various protocols in lower layers (FINE00).

After collection, mediation, and translation into objects, object relations are defined using various schemas. Finally, these object relationships, together with actual status values, are presented to service quality–oriented internal and external customers. Also, other applications may be connected to the framework using middleware solutions.

The protocols indicated in Figure 3.2 are discussed in more depth throughout this chapter.

3.2 Telecommunications-Oriented Management Protocols

In the field of management protocols, service providers are looking for robust and secure protocols with good scalability. They also want a stable structure and hierarchy of protocol stacks. In the past, service providers patiently waited for the results of

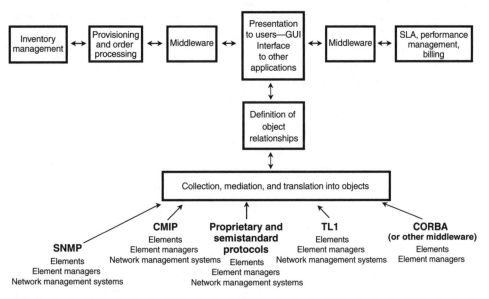

Figure 3.2 Layered integration architecture.

very long standardization processes. This segment concentrates on solutions and recommendations that may be useful to service providers. It does not mean, however, that other protocols from the enterprise world cannot find their place in complex management architectures.

3.2.1 Basics of Telecommunication Management Network

Telecommunication Management Network (TMN) is a special network in its own right that is implemented to help manage the telecommunication network of the service providers. As such, it interfaces to one or more individual networks at several points in order to exchange information. It is logically separate from the networks it manages, and it may be physically separate as well. However, TMN may use parts of the telecommunication networks for its own communications.

The TMN effort is chartered by the International Telecommunications Union Telecommunications Standardization Sector (ITU-TS). Development began in 1988 and has concentrated primarily on the overall architecture, using the synchronous digital hierarchy (the international version of the North American synchronous optical network, or SONET) technology as a target. However, the TMN techniques are applicable to a broad range of technologies and services.

TMN is an extension of the OSI standardization process. It attempts to standardize some of the functionality and many of the interfaces of the managed networks. When fully implemented, the result will be a higher level of integration. TMN is usually described by three architectures:

1. *The functional architecture* describes the appropriate distribution of functionality within TMN—appropriate in the sense of allowing for the creation of function blocks from which a TMN of any complexity can be implemented. The definition of function blocks and reference points between them leads to the requirements for the TMN-recommended interface specifications.

2. *The information architecture,* based on an object-oriented approach, gives the rationale for the application of OSI systems management principles to the TMN principles. The OSI systems management principles are mapped onto the TMN principles and, where necessary, are expanded to fit the TMN environment.

3. *The physical architecture* describes interfaces that can actually be implemented as well as examples of physical components that make up the TMN.

The management functions are grouped into the five functional areas identified as part of the OSI model:

1. Fault management (alarm surveillance, testing, trouble administration).

2. Configuration management (provisioning, rating).

3. Performance management (monitoring the quality of service, traffic control).

4. Security management (managing access and authentication).

5. Accounting management (rating and billing).

The management requirements that helped shape the TMN specifications include planning, provisioning, installing, maintaining, operating, and administering communications networks and services.

The TMN specifications use standard CMIP application services wherever appropriate. However, one of the key concepts of the TMN specifications is the introduction of *technology-independent* management, which is based on an abstract view of the managed network elements. Through this abstract view and a single communications interface, diverse equipment can be managed. Thus, TMN-managed networks can consist of both TMN-conforming and nonconforming devices.

The TMN specifications define an intended direction, with many details to be determined. The published TMN specifications address the overall architecture, the generic information model, the management services, the management functions, the management and transmission protocols, and an alarm surveillance function. Next, the TMN working groups will focus on the service layer, traffic (i.e., congestion), and network-level management.

The relatively slow pace of TMN specification development has not prevented companies from recognizing the benefits of the TMN approach to management. The Tele-Management Forum is incorporating TMN into its specifications, and many companies are beginning to build, or specify, management systems and components that comply with the TMN principles.

Management systems that comply with the TMN principles reduce costs and improve services for the following reasons (REED95):

■ Standard interfaces and objects make it possible to rapidly and economically deploy new services.

- Distributed management intelligence minimizes management reaction time to network events.

- Mediation makes it possible to handle similar devices in an identical manner, leading to more generic operations systems and vendor independence.

- Mediation makes it possible to manage and transparently upgrade the existing device inventory.

- Distributed management functions increase scalability.

- Distributed management functions isolate and contain network faults.

- Distributed management functions reduce network management traffic and the load on operations systems.

Many of the benefits that accrue from the TMN principles are due directly to its distributed architecture and to its mediation function.

The TMN architecture addresses communications networks and services as collections of cooperating systems. By managing individual systems, TMN has a coordinated effect on the network.

This coordination can be illustrated through a simple example. Within an enterprise, one operations system may deal with the network element inventory, another may deal with traffic planning, and several element managers may deal with network elements of various types. When a customer requires a circuit of specific bandwidth and quality of service, all of these systems must be coordinated to meet the customer's needs. The TMN architecture not only facilitates this effort, it allows for this function to be distributed among several systems. This distribution has a side effect of allowing a TMN-based system to scale to handle global networks by enabling the workload to be spread across multiple systems.

This ability to subdivide and distribute the total management effort requires clear definition of the functions, the interfaces, and the information model. These topics are defined in the TMN specifications and are outlined in the following sections.

The TMN architecture identifies specific functions and their interfaces. These functions are what allow a TMN to perform its management activities. The TMN architecture provides flexibility in building a management system by allowing certain functions to be combined within a physical entity. The following function blocks, along with their typical methods of physical realization, are defined within the TMN specifications (REED95).

Operations Systems Functions

The operations systems function (OSF) monitors, coordinates, and controls the TMN entities. It is a TMN-compliant management system or set of management applications. The system has to make it possible to perform general activities, such as management of performance, faults, configuration, accounting, and security. In addition, specific capabilities for planning of operations, administration, maintenance, and provisioning of communications networks and systems should be available. These capabilities are realized in an operations system. The operations system can be implemented in many different ways. One possibility is a descending abstraction (e.g., business, service, and network) wherein the overall business needs of the enterprise are met by coordinating the underlying services. In turn, the individual services are realized through coordinating the network resources.

Workstation Function

The workstation function (WSF) provides the TMN information to the user. This typically consists of things such as access control, topological map display, and graphical interfaces. These functions are realized in a workstation.

Mediation Function

The mediation function (MF) acts on information passing between an OSF and a network element function (NEF) or Q adapter function (QAF) to ensure the data the mediation function (MF) emits comply with the needs and capabilities of the receiver. MFs can store, adapt, filter, threshold, and condense information. The MFs provide the abstract view necessary to treat dissimilar elements in a similar manner. MFs may also provide local management to their associated NEFs (in other words, the MF may include an element manager). The MF function is realized in a mediation device. Mediation can be implemented as a hierarchy of cascaded devices by using standard interfaces. The cascading of mediation devices and the various interconnections to network elements provide a TMN with a great deal of flexibility. This also allows for future design of new equipment to support a greater level of processing within the network element—without the need to redesign an existing TMN.

Q Adapter Function

This connects non-TMN–compliant NEFs to the TMN environment and is realized in a Q adapter. A *Q adapter* allows legacy devices (i.e., those that do not support the TMN management protocols, including SNMP devices) to be accommodated within a TMN. A Q adapter typically performs interface conversion functions (i.e., it acts as a proxy). The network element function (NEF) is realized in the network elements themselves. They can present a TMN-compliant or noncompliant interface. This would include such things as physical elements (switches), logical elements (virtual circuit connections), and services (operations systems software applications). Figure 3.3 illustrates the functions within a TMN environment. The portions that are outside the TMN environment are not subject to standardization. For example, the human-interface portion of the workstation function is not specified in the TMN standard.

Within the TMN specification are well-defined reference points to identify the characteristics of the interfaces between the function blocks. The reference points identify the information that passes between the function blocks. The function blocks exchange information using the data communications function (DCF). The DCF may perform routing, relaying, and internetworking actions at Open Systems Interconnection (OSI) Layers 1 to 3 (i.e., physical, data link, and network layers) or their equivalents. These functions are performed in the data communications network. Figure 3.4 also shows the reference points (F, G, M, Qx, Q3, X) that have been defined by the

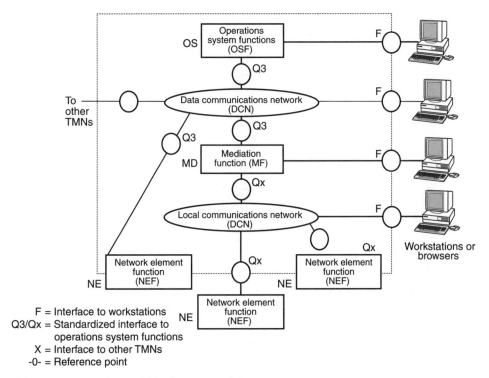

Figure 3.3 Functions within the TMN architecture.

TMN specification. These reference points are characterized by the information that is shared between their endpoints. The reference points are further explained as follows (REED95):

- F is the interface between a workstation and an operations system and a mediation device.

- G is the interface between a workstation and a human user. The specification of this interface is outside the scope of TMN.

- M is the interface between a Q adapter and a non-TMN–compliant network element. This interface, which is not specified by the TMN effort, is actually one of the most important, as today's networks consist primarily of devices that do not comply with the TMN standard.

- Qx is the interface between a Q adapter and a mediation device, a TMN-compliant element and a mediation device, or two mediation devices.

- Q3 is the interface between a TMN-compliant element and an operations system, a Q adapter and a mediation device, a mediation device and an operations system, or two operations systems.

- X is the interface between operations systems in different TMNs. The operations system outside the X interface may be part of a TMN or a non-TMN environment. This interface may require increased security over the level required by the Q interfaces. In addition, access limitations may also be imposed.

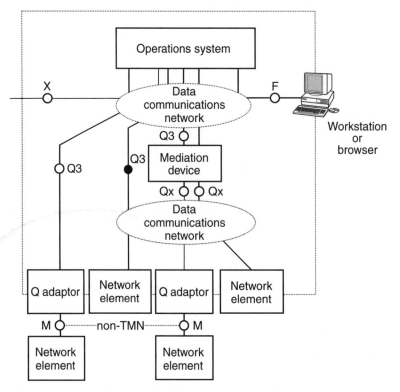

Figure 3.4 Sample TMN physical architecture and interfaces.

Currently, only the Q3 interface has been specified in any detail. The definition includes its management protocol (CMIP), alarm surveillance capabilities, and operations on the generic model used to describe the network. Alarm surveillance is a set of functions that enables the monitoring and interrogation of the network about alarm-related events or conditions.

The information model presents an abstraction of the management aspects of network resources and the related support management activities. This model consists of the management protocol object classes required to manage a TMN. Information about these objects is exchanged across the TMN-standard interfaces.

The TMN specifications provide a generic information model that is technology-independent. This independence allows management of diverse equipment in a common manner through an abstract view of the network elements. This concept is vital for TMN to achieve its goals. The generic information model also serves as a basis for defining technology-specific object classes. The resulting specific object classes support a technology-independent view while enabling more precise management. For example, there might be a TMN definition of a switch that could be used to perform common management activities, such as provisioning or performance gathering. In addition, this generic switch definition could be extended to cover the peculiarities of a particular vendor's switch. The extended definition could be used for such specialized activities as controlling the execution of diagnostic routines. TMN generic modeling techniques can be used by a resource provider or management system provider to define its own objects.

The TMN specification contains an information model that is common to managed communications networks. This model can be used to generically define the resources, actions, and events that exist in a network.

The TMN architecture provides excellent visualization of network and service management solutions.

The visualization technology may be used to support various regional network management systems. On top of these network management systems, service-oriented messages, events, and alarms may be extracted and displayed in various service centers, such as IP Center and Platinum Customer Service Center. Additional applications may be applied to support the BML.

3.2.2 Common Management Information Protocol

TMN protocols include OSI protocols such as CMIP and FTMP, ISDN, and Signaling System 7 protocols. They are organized into protocol suites, or profiles, for specific TMN interfaces. Functions and protocols that support TMN services include the following

- Traffic management
- Customer management
- Switching management
- Management of transport networks
- Management of intelligent networks
- Tariffing and changing

The primary protocol is Common Management Information Protocol (CMIP). The estimated overhead scares away both vendors and users, with the exception of the telecommunication industry, where separate channels can be used for management. CMIP is event-driven, assuming processing capabilities at the agent level. Once fault and performance thresholds are exceeded, the manager is alarmed by the agent. This is similar to SNMP traps.

Open Systems Interconnection network management follows an object-oriented model; physical and logical real resources are managed through abstractions known as managed objects (MOs). Management systems also need managed objects that do not represent anything but exist for the needs of the management systems itself. MOs are handled by applications in agent roles and are accessed by applications in manager roles in order to implement management policies. The global collection of management information is consolidated in management information bases (MIBs); each agent handles a part of it in its management information tree. Information in the manager-agent interactions is conveyed through the management service/protocol CMIS and CMIP. In this context, agent, managed system, and managed node are synonymous; manager, managing application, and management stations are synonymous as well. CMIP is part of the OSI management framework. Its elements are as follows:

- CMIS/CMIP defines the services provided to management applications and the protocol providing the information exchange capability.
- Systems management functions specify all the functions to be supported by management.
- Management information model defines the MIB.
- Layer management defines management information, service, and functions to specific layers.

Based on the seven-layer model, network management applications are implemented in Layer 7. Layers 1 through 6 contribute to network management by offering the standard services to carry network management–related information. Figure 3.5 shows the structure for the application layer. In particular, four system management application entities (SMAE) are very useful.

For generic use   Association control service element (ACSE)

                      Remote operations service element (ROSE)

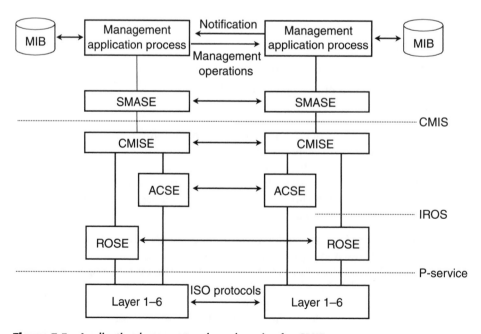

Figure 3.5 Application layer protocols and service for CMIP.

For specific use   Common management information service element
(CMISE)

System management application service element (SMASE)

Communication services in the OSI management model are provided by the common management information services (CMIS). The service is realized through CMIP over a full or lightweight OSI stack. In the OSI world, two mappings are defined:

1. A service over a full OSI stack (CMIP).

2. A connectionless one over logical link control 1 (LLC1)(CMOL).

In the Internet world, there is a third mapping to provide the service over TCP/UDP using a lightweight presentation protocol (CMOT). CMOT and CMIP applications are portable on each other's stack with the same API, but will not work over CMOL.

Figure 3.6 shows the complete structure of CMISEs and SMFs. The overall goal is to support typical network management functions, such as fault, configuration, performance, security, and accounting management. SMFs or a group of SMFs support specific management functions. For the communication between entities, CMISE is used. Each of the service elements is defined in Table 3.1. Further details can be found in TERP96.

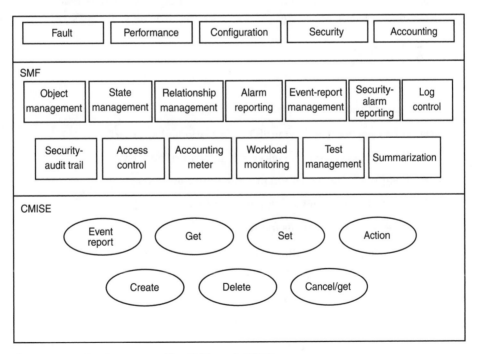

Figure 3.6 FCAPS supported by SMFs and CMISE.

Table 3.1 Definition of Service Elements

SERVICE	TYPE	DEFINITION
Management Notification Service		
M-event-report	Confirmed/unconfirmed	Reports on an event to a peer CMISE service user
Management Operations Service		
M-get	Confirmed	Requests retrieval of information from peer CMISE user
M-set	Confirmed/unconfirmed	Requests modification of information from peer CMISE user
M-action	Confirmed/unconfirmed	Requests that peer CMISE user perform some action
M-create	Confirmed	Requests that peer CMISE user create an instance of a managed object
M-delete	Confirmed	Requests that peer CMISE user delete an instance of a managed object
M-cancel-get	Confirmed	Requests that peer CMISE user cancel outstanding invocation of M-get service

The strengths of CMIP include the following:

■ It has a general and extensible object-oriented approach.

■ It has support from the telecommunications industry.

■ It supports manager-to-manager communications.

■ It supports a framework for automation.

Weaknesses of CMIP are as follows:

■ It is complex and multilayered.

■ High overhead is the price of many confirmations.

■ Few CMIP-based management systems are shipping.

■ Few CMIP-based agents are in use.

CMIP assumes the use of the OSI stack for exchanging CMIP protocol data units. In Layer 7, there are also other applications that may be combined with CMIP.

3.2.3 Telecommunication Information Network Architecture

TINA has evolved from two predecessors: IN and TMN. As a service architecture, TINA has inherited the concept of network support for telecommunication service from intelligent network (IN). As a management architecture, TINA has inherited the concept of distributed, object-oriented representation of network resources from TMN. As its design methodology, TINA has adopted open distributed processing (ODP) principles and has also developed its own specification languages for the description of information and computational viewpoints.

The TINA management architecture has many facets. It is a set of common goals, principles, and concepts covering the management of services, resources, and parts of the distributed processing environment (DPE). Due to its broad nature, management is one of the most challenging areas in TINA. The design goals on the management architecture are as follows:

- *Object-oriented and distributed.* TINA management architecture takes advantage of the distributed processing environment, which offers a natural distributed object-oriented environment for both resource and service management. It builds on the object-oriented and distributed approaches of TMN and open distributed management architecture (ODMA).

- *Service-oriented.* TINA uses a more goal-driven design approach rather than a resource-driven one. In particular, the service management should guarantee quality of service as an integrated part of the service.

- *Dynamic and flexible.* The service-oriented nature of TINA requires that resources need to be more dynamically assigned or configured, to support the flexibility required by TINA services.

- *Integrated.* Management is an integral part of service provision, inherent in the various TINA layers.

Conceptually, TINA can be decomposed into the following areas:

- *Partitioning.* It represents layering and domain concepts. TINA is partitioned into three layers: service, resource, and DPE (Figure 3.7). The management architecture is likewise partitioned into service, resource, and DPE management. It also supports the concept of domain and the management of domains.

- *Functions.* These include the typical areas of fault, configuration, accounting, performance, and security management (FCAPS). To support the FCAPS integrity of a service session, constructs such as management context and service transaction are provided.

- *Computations.* The computation supports for management needs are mostly offered by DPE, extended by TINA-specific event management and grouping concepts.

- *Life cycle.* The category of life-cycle issues includes service life-cycle management and customer management.

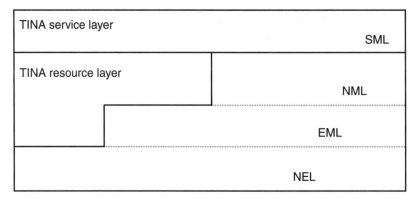

Figure 3.7 TINA and TMN service layers.

Some significant differences between TINA and TMN include the following:

- *Session concept.* TINA is session-oriented (i.e., many of the constructs and service components are dynamically bounded within the lifetime of service sessions). As a consequence, many of service management activities are also service session-oriented, which is in clear contrast to TMN.

- *Separation between information and computational viewpoints.* By adopting ODP principles, TINA maintains clearer separation between information and computational viewpoints than does TMN. In TMN, managed objects (MOs) correspond to an information viewpoint, and a computational viewpoint is represented by manager-agent roles and associated interfaces known as Q, X, and F interfaces. In terms of information to computational mappings, therefore, many-to-one mapping is dominant in TMN. In TINA, information objects can be mapped more freely to computational objects. For example, one information object may be mapped to one computational object (*one-to-one mapping*) or to a collection of computational objects (*one-to-many mapping*).

- *Different computational model.* In TMN, GDMO and CMIP in effect define the computational viewpoint of TMN systems. In TINA, CORBA-based DPE provides its computational viewpoint. Computational objects in TINA are described in CORBA IDL and TINA ODL, an extended version of CORBA IDL that allows multiple interface objects.

- *Different engineering model.* The preceding differences in computational models result in different engineering platforms. Usually, TMN systems are CMIP-based, whereas TINA systems are CORBA-based.

Interoperability between TMN and TINA is of serious practical concern. Interoperability and migration issues are expected to be addressed by various vendors in the near future.

3.2.4 Transaction Language 1

Today, TL1 is the most widely used protocol in connecting operations support systems. It is based on two simple concepts: (1) that the interface should be readable to humans as well as computers and (2) that the identification of the data be carried along with the value of the data as information is transferred between support systems. This powerful approach allows support systems that don't need all the data elements in one set of an information block to still use the interface and uncouple the support systems where designers want them uncoupled.

The interface can be changed between support systems by adding a data element, and any other support system using that data block won't have to be modified, because part of the protocol is to ignore any data item that it does not recognize. This Bellcore/Telcordia standard was defined in 1984 and is called Transaction Language 1. It was adopted to manage most parts of the telephone network. TL1 protocols have been easier to build than those of CMIP. They can be mapped into object mediators.

New support systems will likely be built around object libraries with Java to provide the way for running distributed architectures. It is relatively easy to integrate dispersed applications via Java on the Web. Work is under way to build an Internet version of CORBA, which is called Internet Inter-ORB Protocol (IIOP). Until Java tools and platforms are industrial strength, developers need to rely on the earlier TL1 protocols and CORBA solutions. But newer interfaces should rely on Java for administration of their configurations so that changes can be carried to the resident protocol code through the Internet or through intra- or extranets.

3.2.5 Wireless Application Protocol

Wireless Application Protocol (WAP), an application environment and associated set of protocols, is being developed to deliver Internet content to mobile devices. The key components of WAP are the microbrowser and the WAP gateway. In order to receive WAP content, a mobile device, be it a phone or other equipment, must be equipped with a microbrowser, which is a downscaled Web browser designed to work within the confines of small displays. The WAP gateway handles communications between the mobile device and requested Internet sites. Figure 3.8 shows this typical arrangement (POWE00).

WAP is a global industry standard for bringing together wireless telephony with Internet content and services regardless of wireless network architecture or device types. Because WAP is designed to work with any type of underlying wireless network architecture, it frees providers and customers to concentrate on the wireless application itself—without having to worry about whether applications are portable. WAP provides something similar to the well-known TCP/IP protocol stack used on the Internet and in corporate intranets. The difference is that the WAP protocol stack is specifically designed to accommodate the special challenges of wireless networking. Table 3.2 shows the WAP protocol stack (POWE00).

A WAP gateway server is located between the wireless service provider's network on one side and the public Internet or corporate intranet on the other. Gateways can be located within the firewalls of service providers, corporations, or both. In addition to taking care of various housekeeping functions, the WAP server handles the interface between the two sets of network protocols: WAP and TCP/IP.

A cell phone equipped with a HDML/WML microbrowser calls a cellular network and is routed to the Internet content by the WAP gateway

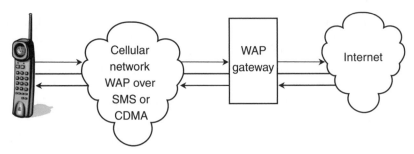

Figure 3.8 The role of microbrowsers and WAP gateways.

The WAP computing model is simply standard Web programming with a WAP gateway in the middle of the request/response cycle. A cell phone or other wireless terminal requests a given URL; the WAP gateway server decodes and decompresses this, then sends it on to the appropriate Web server as an ordinary HTTP request. The process is then repeated, in reverse, on the response side of the cycle. The WAP gateway can be located either within the wireless network of the service provider or, for security reasons, in an enterprise environment. The HTTP server can respond with HTML- or XML-based content. However, the WAE layer of WAP specifies an alternative markup language designed for use with thin wireless clients. If standard HTML or XML is served in response to the HTTP request, it falls to the WAP gateway server or to an additional layer of middleware to implement some form of content translation before the request can be relayed back to the WAP client.

The WAP gateway is the mobile provider's link between the Internet and the mobile network. When a WAP device requests information using WAP Session Protocol (WSP), the WAP gateway uses TCP/IP to communicate to the specified Internet site, pulls down the content, converts it, and hands it over to the mobile network for

Table 3.2 The WAP Protocol Stack

LAYERS	EXPLANATION
Application layer	Wireless Application Environment (WAE)
Session layer	Wireless Session Protocol (WSP)
Transaction layer	Wireless Transaction Protocol (WTP)
Security layer	Wireless Transport Layer Security (WTLS)
Transport layer	Wireless Datagram Protocol (WDP)
Network layer	Wireless bearers (SMS, USSD, CSD, CDMA, iDEN, CDPD)

transmission to the end user. Data compaction is necessary because mobile networks cannot yet handle massive data streams. WAP content is delivered using WAP Datagram Protocol (WDP), which is designed to send messages over any available bearer channel, including everything from short message service (SMS) to cellular digital packet data (CDPD) and a host of other mobile, packet data technologies. Basically, if a mobile network has a bearer channel for data delivery, WAP can be deployed on that network. WAP is also designed to be air interface–independent and operate over global system for mobile communications (GSM), time division multiple access (TDMA), code division multiple access (CDMA), and most other digital mobile protocols supported in all parts of the world in various networks.

Though WAP is intended to allow customers to create personalized, mobile Web portals, there are very few concrete examples for this functionality. In order to support this functionality, mobile providers must enhance their provisioning systems to support WAP. Generally, the mobile provider preprovisions all of the WAP-enabled phones/customers on its network into its provisioning system. The network then asks customers if they want to activate service. When a customer answers positively, he or she will be enabled by an existing over-the-air provisioning capability, and the WAP gateway and billing platform must be activated. Generally, the WAP gateway and the provisioning system communicate with each other using an FTP text file, often in batch mode and not yet in real-time. Service delivery delays cannot yet be avoided.

In summary, the WAP standard includes:

- Specification for a server-centric scripting language called WMLScript, support for which is gradually being implemented on the latest WAP-enabled cell phones.
- Voice-based user interfaces written in Voice eXtensible Markup Language (VXML).
- Location-specific applications that take full advantage of the global positioning system.
- Support for mobile teleconferencing.

Standards like WAP and the new XHTML specification (which lays the basis for a convergence between WML and HTML) should keep the networking site simple. In-house Web developers will have to learn some new development tools and APIs to support this convergence in practical applications.

Bluetooth is the official name of a specification that has become a very rapidly growing technology standard. It is a specification for wireless technologies, a global standard that lets devices communicate with each other using a secure radio frequency. Bluetooth-enabled portable computers, mobile phones, office equipment, household appliances, and other devices can communicate at short ranges without cables. They communicate securely, inexpensively, at a high data throughput, and without line-of-sight requirements. The Bluetooth device is a small, low-powered radio on a chip that communicates with other Bluetooth-enabled products. On this basis, piconets can be designed and implemented. Within a piconet, services can be offered to mobile users without the normal configuration requirements. Future work will concentrate on antenna design and power management.

3.3 Middleware Solutions

Due to the heavy online load on universal servers in telecommunication service providers' environments, the distribution of load between various types of servers (application, database, mailing, etc.) was unavoidable. Middleware technology is helpful to increase communication efficiency of the collaboration of various servers. Large work orders may be broken down into smaller ones. The coordination between those work orders is the primary task of standardized *middleware,* which can be defined as a software layer above the operating system and communication protocol layers but below the application layer that helps to simplify and unify the communication between various systems.

The goals of telecommunication services providers with middleware can be summarized as follows:

- Collaboration of operational, documentation, and management systems
- Concentration on business processes and their support data instead of on technical interface details
- Collaboration of different and partially distributed platforms
- Reduction of the number of different synchronous and asynchronous middleware solutions
- Full consideration of the selected middleware in future applications
- Use of middleware within the same business applications if a distributed implementation is preferred
- Separation of operations of middleware from business applications

When should middleware solutions be used in a telecommunication environment? The following list summarizes some of the criteria:

- When multiple applications intend to use services and data from other applications
- When a new application wants to use existing services, data, or even databases of other applications
- When an application wants to use many different databases
- When an application is implemented in a distributed manner (parallel processing, use of optimal subtasks, multiple geographical domains)
- When existing application components should become part of new applications

The benefits of using middleware solutions are as follows:

- Development time for new applications is reduced.
- Interface customization remains hidden to application designers.

- There is scalability at application level.

- Interfaces are controllable and can be monitored.

- There are fewer problems with integrating new application components.

Traditional middleware solutions include the following cases:

Remote procedure call. This is a typical way of distributing applications. Programs can call each other, transport data, and execute procedures. The interprogram communication remains hidden to users. It is independent of platforms. It supports synchronous processing.

Message processing. Instead of direct calls, information is exchanged by means of messages. It can successfully support distributed architectures. This technique supports both synchronous and asynchronous applications. It is very effective because message queues can be emptied depending on resource availability and utilization.

Transaction processing. This is real-time oriented and requires the fulfillment of at least two criteria: (1) Integrity of the execution should be guaranteed using commit or, in case of problems, rollback; and (2) There's a need to handle a large number of communication connections using transaction monitors.

New middleware solutions concentrate on the use of object-oriented technologies. This middleware solution implements a client/server connection between objects. It is well suited for heterogeneous environments. The physical implementation of the server and clients is very flexible. The broker is the central controlling instance that interprets requests and forwards them to the right destination. This internal decision making remains hidden to users. The most important object-oriented solutions include CORBA, Enterprise JavaBeans, and COM+.

3.3.1 Common Object Request Broker Architecture

Open management architecture (OMA) permits the cooperation of distributed objects independently from their locations. OMA has not been designed and structured only for network management. It is a general-purpose standard. In particular, it helps to design and implement distributed applications. This architecture has gained interest because the OMA technology is going to be used increasingly for end-user devices.

CORBA is a generic communication framework that connects various network management applications.

The organizational model is using a peer-to-peer approach, which means that communicating objects are equivalent in their importance. Figure 3.9 shows this architecture.

The communication model is based on Common Object Request Broker Architecture (CORBA). The object request broker is the coordinator between distributed objects. The broker receives messages, inquiries, and results from objects and routes them to the right destination. If the objects are in a heterogeneous environment, multiple brokers are required. They will talk to each other in the future via a new protocol based on TCP/IP. There is no information model available; no operations are predefined for

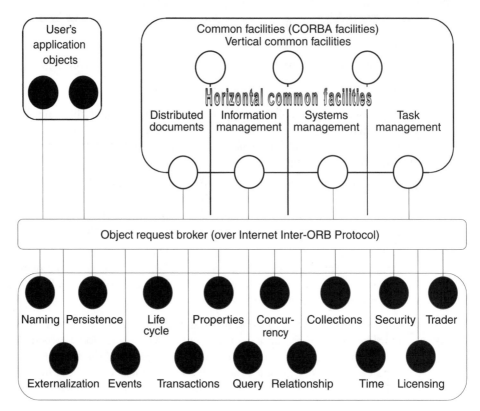

Figure 3.9 CORBA architecture.

objects. But an object does exist containing all the necessary interfaces to the object request broker. For the description, the Interface Definition Language (IDL) is being used. There are no detailed MIBs for objects because OMA is not management-specific.

The functional model consists of the Object Services Architecture. It delivers the framework for defining objects, services, and functions. Examples for services are instantiation, naming, storing objects' attributes, and the distribution/receipt of events and notification. CORBA services and facilities represent more generic services; they are expected to occur in multiple applications or they are used in specific applications. The driving force behind designing common facilities for systems management is the X/Open Systems Management Working Group. The Managed Set Service defined by this group encourages grouping of objects in accordance with their management needs, resulting in easier administration. In the future, more services are expected to be defined; the next one is an Event Management Service that expands the present Object Event Service through the flexible mechanism of event filtering.

To provide object-oriented (OO) connectivity of operations support systems requires a new and flexible approach. OMG with its CORBA specification can help fulfill this critical need.

CORBA separates the application from the connectivity interface, making it much easier and more economical to design, implement, and maintain complex environments. The ORB technology is the network glue to bind it together. Coupled with MOM, OO analysis and design tools, and off-the-shelf transactional gateways to legacy environments, service providers find it more cost-effective to implement automated, integrated, and interoperable solutions. CORBA's well-defined architecture provides an opportunity to interconnect management systems that are different in their management interfaces. IDL permits object interfaces to be defined independently of an object's implementation. After defining an interface in IDL, the interface definition is used as input to an IDL compiler, which produces target language classes. Application servers use these classes to implement the CORBA-compliant services. Client applications use the generated classes to connect to distributed CORBA objects instantiated within application servers. Diverse analysis and design tools support IDL. Development languages such as C++, Java, SmallTalk, Visual basic, PowerBuilder, and Forte are all supported by CORBA. It provides an environment that allows easy and flexible interconnection of applications and services.

CORBA allows for the sharing of network and corporate data through the use of object request brokers (ORBs). CORBA objects will be constructed using IDL in the incumbent development environment. This allows legacy systems to continue to provide their network services and evolve at their own pace, while enhanced services can be provided by newer operations support systems at other locations in the network. IIOP applications and services, developed by customers and third-party developers, can interoperate without proprietary development or internal implementation details. No specific ORB requirements exist other than support for IIOP and IDL.

One of the core strengths of CORBA is its reference model (Figure 3.9):

- The *object request broker* (ORB) enables objects to transparently make and receive requests and responses without regard to the location or execution environment. It is the foundation for building applications from distributed objects and for interoperability between applications in heterogeneous and homogeneous environments.

- *Object services* are collections of services that support basic functions for using and implementing distributed objects. Services are necessary to construct any distributed application and are always independent of application domains.

- *Common facilities*, also known as *components* or *frameworks*, are collections of services that many applications may share, but that are not as fundamental as object services.

- *Applications objects* are products of a single vendor or in-house development group that control their interfaces. Application objects correspond to the traditional notion of applications, so they are not standardized by OMG. Instead, they constitute the uppermost layer of the OSI Reference Model.

As TMN evolves, it may be required to transport legacy as well as object requests over the same data communication network (DCN). For example, the network topology may contain proprietary-based mediation devices as well as CORBA-compliant ORBs. The CORBA-compliant ORBs could potentially be used to develop mediation services—so-called mediation ORBs. These services would offer the advantages provided by the OMG specifications. As larger OSSs evolve, interfaces will need to be provided for legacy-type communications that are TL1-based and for object-oriented connections (e.g., ORBs). The mediation service will interface to the DCN, split the legacy messages from the object requests, and separately feed them to the appropriate OSS interface.

There are specific tools required to build the components using CORBA. The basic tools of the CORBA solution are the IDL and the tools supporting IDL to specific language mappings. These tools are enablers for building the required objects to interface to support systems. The OMG has defined the network-side interface of the ORB, allowing IDL to be mapped to various languages, including C, C++, Java, ActiveX, OLE, SmallTalk, COBOL, and ADA. CORBA-compliant ORBs are currently available to run on Unix, on Windows, and on Windows NT.

3.3.2 Enterprise JavaBeans

Sun was interested in creating a hardware- and software-independent language that would not need to be compiled for use in Web applications, which needed programming tools for browsers to create and run applications. Sun created a machine pseudocode—in other words, a virtual machine. Organizations could use their own implementations of this language. In parallel, Sun introduced Java, which is a very advanced object-oriented programming language and development tool. After organizations created their own machine-dependent virtual machines, Java programs could run on these machines.

Each architecture and operating system contains services that are not specified by Java. This results, for example, in ActiveX of Microsoft using Java without being able to run on Unix. In order to avoid legal problems, the original standard has been extended.

Java programs are slow on machines with code interpretation. In order to improve performance, JavaScript has been created, which provides browsers with Java source code. It has helped to show visualization examples and prototypes very rapidly, because Java is friendly enough to support such services.

Similar programs have been provided for Web servers as well. These programs are called Java *servlets*. In order to support them, a new Web server model was introduced that was responsible for the server-related services.

Reusability is an important factor in design and development. JavaBeans defines a framework of software design. It also supports framework-dependent service integration. Sun is trying to control this standard very carefully. In the case of JavaBeans, networking is very well supported.

Enterprise JavaBeans is intended for mainframe environments. It offers a solution for large software systems, such as event management, combined with excellent scalability. This model is being supported by software design tools. But confidence in this technology has been seriously undermined by performance differences between C and Java (to the disadvantage of Java). This performance difference has now been reduced to 10 to 30 percent, and Java trades this difference against user-friendliness. Java supporters include IBM, Sun-Netscape Alliance, BEA, Oracle, Inprise, Iona, Fujitsu, Sybase Gemstone, and Persistence.

The most important EJB object types are *entity beans* (long-term object types such as customers with data stored and maintained in a database) and *session beans* (short-range types such as executing a business process).

It is expected that EJB will incorporate the most important CORBA attributes within the next few years. Its success depends on the power and performance of Java. It uses an interpreter with advantages and disadvantages. For industrial use, it needs very complex fine-tuning.

3.3.3 The Communications Object Model (COM+)

This is not Java-based, but offers the same or at least comparable functionality to Java. It is coupled to Windows 2000. The benefits are as follows:

- COM+ is an existing product, not an emerging standard; after one year of heavy testing, it is available.

- It uses well-proven tools such as COM/DCOM, which has been extended by Microsoft Transaction Server (MTS).

- It is well scalable; its performance is expected to be close to leading transaction monitors, such as Tuxedo.

- Broad support is offered by Microsoft; it is expected that a number of development toolkits will be provided by third-party vendors.

- It is language-independent as long as Microsoft is supporting the language.

- The cost is low for Windows 2000 users.

The disadvantages are as follows:

- It is limited to Microsoft environments.

- Applications are not currently available, but are expected from a large number of third-party suppliers.

DCOM is the heart of Microsoft's ActiveOSS product suite. Basically, DCOM is an integration infrastructure designed to facilitate communication between software components operating on the same host or with DCOM on multiple networked hosts. It was originally developed to create interoperability between components. It is the most widely deployed component object model. ActiveOSS acts as a centralized management and translation point for an OSS network. Conceptually, applications ride on top of the framework, but they communicate through it. DCOM abstracts various application interfaces into objects, basically mapping the functions of the application into a common model that can be stored in a database. The common model allows the various applications to communicate in a uniform manner within the framework or across multiple networked frameworks.

Web-Based Solutions

Two facts impact the future use of middleware:

- The use of thick clients is getting very expensive in business environments. The total cost of ownership is getting too high. The trend is to use thin clients and to delegate the processing tasks to middleware servers.

- Bandwidth limitations are disappearing, which enables thin clients to get the necessary amount of data for viewing purposes. Universal browsers will have the presentation responsibility, which will be standardized on XML.

3.4 Enterprise-Oriented Management Protocols

This group of protocols is easier to understand, implement, and maintain. The first implementations were in enterprise environments. Because device manufacturers support these protocols, they in turn penetrate the infrastructures of service providers. They are of growing importance for supporting customer network management and eBusiness.

3.4.1 SNMPv1, SNMPv2, and SNMPv3

In the SNMP environment, the manager can obtain information (Figure 3.10) from the agent by polling managed objects periodically. Agents can transmit unsolicited event messages, called *traps,* to the manager. The management data exchanged between managers and agents is called the *management information base* (MIB). Data definitions that are outlined in structured management information (SMI) must be understood by managers and agents.

The manager is a software program residing within the management station. The manager has the ability to query agents using various SNMP commands. The management station is also in charge of interpreting MIB data, constructing views of the systems and networks, compressing data, and maintaining data in relational or object-oriented databases. A traditional SNMP manager is shown in Figure 3.11 (STAL99).

Figure 3.12 shows typical functions that are not only valid for managers, but also for managed agents (i.e., the typical functional blocks of SNMP agents).

In a traditional manager, the SNMP engine contains a dispatcher, a message processing subsystem, and a security subsystem. The dispatcher is a simple traffic manager. For outgoing PDUs, the dispatcher accepts PDUs from applications and performs the following functions. For each PDU, the dispatcher determines the type of message processing required (which may be different for SNMP versions 1, 2, and 3) and passes the PDU on to the appropriate message processing module in the message processing subsystem. Subsequently, the message processing subsystem returns a message containing that PDU, including the appropriate message headers. The dis-

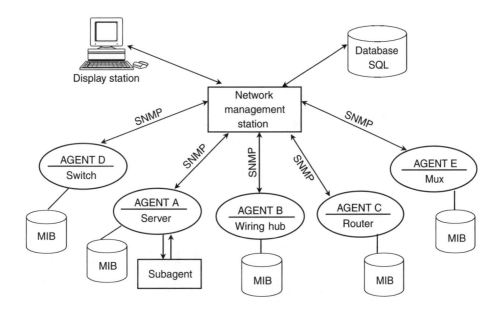

MIB: Management information base
SNMP: Simple Network Management Protocol

Figure 3.10 Structure of SNMP-based management services.

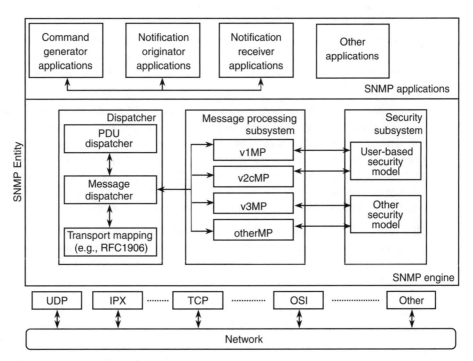

Figure 3.11 Traditional SNMP manager.

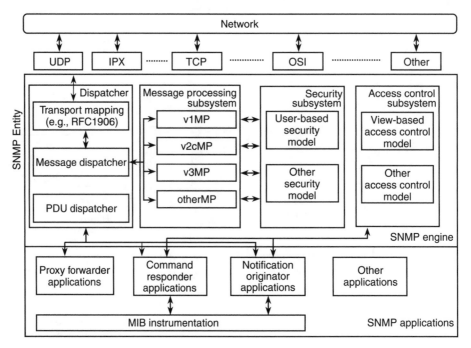

Figure 3.12 Traditional SNMP agent.

patcher then maps this message onto a transport layer for transmission. For incoming messages, the dispatcher accepts messages from the transport layer and performs the following functions. The dispatcher routes each message to the appropriate message processing module. Subsequently, the message processing subsystem returns the PDU contained in the message. The dispatcher then passes this PDU to the appropriate application.

The message processing subsystem accepts outgoing PDUs from the dispatcher and prepares these for transmission by wrapping them in the appropriate message header and returning them to the dispatcher. It also accepts incoming messages from the dispatcher, processes each message header, and returns the enclosed PDU to the dispatcher. An implementation of the message processing subsystem may support a single message format corresponding to a single version of SNMP, or it may contain a number of modules, each supporting a different version of SNMP.

The security subsystem performs authentication and encryption functions. Each outgoing message is passed to the security subsystem from the message processing subsystem. Depending on the services required, the security subsystem may encrypt the enclosed PDU, and it may generate an authentication code and insert it into the message header. The processed message is then returned to the message processing subsystem. Similarly, each incoming message is passed to the security subsystem from the message processing subsystem. If required, the security subsystem checks the authentication code and performs decryption. An implementation of the security subsystem may support one or more distinct security models.

The SNMP engine for a traditional agent has all the components found in the SNMP engine for a traditional manager, plus an access control subsystem. This subsystem provides services to control access to MIBs for the reading and setting of management objects. These services are performed on the basis of the contents of PDUs. An implementation of the security subsystem may support one or more distinct access control models. The security-related functions are organized into two separate subsystems: security and access control. This is an excellent example of modular design, because the two subsystems perform quite distinct functions; therefore it makes sense to allow standardization of these two areas to proceed independently. The security subsystem is concerned with privacy and authentication and operates on SNMP messages. The access control subsystem is concerned with authorized access to management information and operates on SNMP PDUs.

For both SNMP managers and agents, a number of components constitute the management functions. These components are listed in Table 3.3 (STAL99).

In terms of MIBs, there are continuing changes. In addition to standard MIBs, such as MIB I and II (Table 3.4), the IETF has defined a number of adjunct MIBs covering hosts, routers, bridges, hubs, repeaters, FDDI networks, AppleTalk networks, frame relay networks, switches, ATM nodes, mobile components, and applications.

In terms of SNMP, the following trends are expected. SNMP agent-level support will be provided by even a greater number of vendors. SNMP manager-level support will be provided by only a few leading vendors in the form of several widely accepted platforms. Management platforms provide basic services, leaving customization to vendors and users.

Wider use of intelligent agents is also expected. Intelligent agents are capable of responding to a manager's request for information and performing certain manager-like functions, including testing for thresholds, filtering, and processing management data. Intelligent agents enable localized polling and filtering on servers, workstations, and hubs, for example. Thus, these agents reduce polling overhead and management data traffic, forwarding only the most critical alerts and processed data to the SNMP manager.

RMON MIB will help to bridge the gap between the limited services provided by management platforms and the rich sets of data and statistics provided by traffic monitors and analyzers.

The strengths of SNMP include the following:

- Agents are widely implemented.
- It's simple to implement.
- Agent-level overhead is minimal.
- Polling approach is good for LAN-based managed object.
- It is robust and extensible.
- It offers the best direct manager-agent interface.
- SNMP met a critical need; it was available and implementable at the right time.

Table 3.3 Components of the SNMP Entity

Dispatcher	Allows for concurrent support of multiple versions of SNMP messages in the SNMP engine. It is responsible for (1) accepting PDUs from applications for transmission over the network and delivering incoming PDUs to applications; (2) passing outgoing PDUs to the message processing subsystem to prepare as messages and passing incoming messages to the message processing subsystem to extract the incoming PDUs; (3) sending and receiving SNMP messages over the network.
Message processing subsystem	Responsible for preparing messages to send and for extracting data from received messages.
Security subsystem	Provides security services such as the authentication and privacy of messages. This subsystem potentially contains multiple security models.
Access control subsystem	Provides a set of authorization services that an application can use for checking access rights. Access control can be invoked for retrieval or modification request operations and for notification generation operations.
Command generator	Initiates SNMP Get, GetNext, GetBulk, and/or Set request PDUs and processes the response to a request that it has generated.
Command responder	Receives SNMP Get, GetNext, GetBulk, and/or Set request PDUs destined for the local system, as indicated by the fact that the context EngineID in the received request is equal to that of the local engine through which the request was received. The command responder application will perform the appropriate protocol operation, using access control, and will generate a response message to be sent to the request's originator.
Notification originator	Monitors a system for particular events or conditions and generates Trap and/or Inform messages based on these events or conditions. A notification originator must have a mechanism for determining where to send messages and which SNMP version and security parameters to use when sending messages.
Notification receiver	Listens for notification messages and generates response messages when a message containing an Inform PDU is received.
Proxy forwarder	Forwards SNMP messages. Implementation of a proxy forwarder application is optional.

Table 3.4   MIB II Structure

11 CATEGORIES OF MANAGEMENT (2) SUBTREE	INFORMATION IN THE CATEGORY
System (1)	Network device operating system
Interfaces (2)	Network interface–specific
Address translation (3)	Address mappings
IP (4)	Internet protocol–specific
ICMP (5)	Internet control message protocol–specific
TCP (6)	Transmission protocol–specific
UDP (7)	User datagram protocol–specific
EGP (8)	Exterior gateway protocol–specific
CMOT (9)	Common management information services on TCP–specific
Transmission (10)	Transmission protocol–specific
SNMP (11)	SNMP-specific

Weaknesses of SNMP include the following:

■ It's too simple and does not scale well.

■ There's no object-oriented data view.

■ Unique semantics make integration with other approaches difficult.

■ It has high communication overhead due to polling—in particular, for WAN-based management objects.

■ It has many implementation-specific (private MIB) extensions.

■ It has no standard control definition.

■ Small agent (one agent per device) may be inappropriate for systems management.

SNMP is being continuously improved and extended. SNMPv2 addresses many of the shortcomings of version 1. SNMPv2 can support either a highly centralized management strategy or a distributed one. In the latter case, some systems operate as both manager and agent. In its agent role, such a system will accept commands from a superior manager; these commands may deal with access of information stored locally at the intermediate manager or may require the intermediate manager to provide summary information about subagents. The principal enhancements to SNMPv1 provided by version 2 fall into the following categories (STAL99):

■ Structure of management information is being expanded in several ways. The macro used to define object types has been expanded to include several new data types and to enhance the documentation associated with an object. Noticeable is the change that a new convention has been provided for creating and deleting conceptual rows in a table. The origin of this capability is RMON.

- Transport mappings help to use different protocol stacks to transport the SNMP information, including User Datagram Protocol, OSI connectionless-mode protocol, Novell internetwork (IPX) protocol, and AppleTalk.

- Protocol operations with the most noticeable changes include two new PDUs. The GetBulkRequest PDU enables the manager to efficiently retrieve large blocks of data. In particular, it is powerful in retrieving multiple rows in a table. The Inform-Request PDU enables one manager to send trap-type information to another.

- MIB extensions contain basic traffic information about the operation of SNMPv2; this is identical to SNMP MIB II. The SNMPv2 MIB also contains other information related to the configuration of SNMPv2 manager to agent.

- Manager-to-manager capability is specified in a special MIB, called M2M. It provides functionality similar to the RMON MIB. In this case, the M2M MIB may be used to allow an intermediate manager to function as a remote monitor of network media traffic. Reporting is also supported. Two major groups, alarm and event groups, are supported.

- SNMPv2 security includes a wrapper containing authentication and privacy information as a header to PDUs.

The SNMPv2 framework is derived from the SNMP framework. The evolution from SNMP to SNMPv2 is intended to be seamless. The easiest way to accomplish this is to upgrade the manager to support SNMPv2 in a way that allows the coexistence of SNMPv2 managers, SNMPv2 agents, and SNMP agents. In order to map commands mutually into the target protocol, proxy agents are used (STAL99). The actual implementation of the proxy agent depends on the vendor; it could be implemented into the agent or into the manager.

The key new feature of SNMPv3 is better security. The design goals for version 3 can be summarized as follows (STAL99):

- Use of existing work, for which there is implementation experience and some consensus regarding its value. As a result, the SNMP architecture and SNMPv3 security features rely heavily on SNMPv2u and SNMPv2*.

- Address the need for secure "Set request" messages over real-world networks, which is the most important deficiency of SNMPv1 and SNMPv2.

- Design a modular architecture that will (1) allow implementation over a wide range of operational environments, some of which need minimal, inexpensive functionality and some of which may support additional features for managing large networks; (2) make it possible to move portions of the architecture forward in the standards track even if consensus has not been reached on all pieces; (3) accommodate alternative security models.

- Keep SNMP as simple as possible despite the many necessary and useful extensions.

Based on these design goals, developers have made the following design decisions (STAL99):

1. *Architecture.* An architecture should be defined that identifies the conceptual boundaries between the documents. Subsystems should be defined that describe the abstract services provided by specific portions of an SNMP framework. Abstract service interfaces, as described by service primitives, define the abstract boundaries between documents and the abstract services that are provided by the conceptual subsystems of an SNMP framework.

2. *Self-contained documents.* Elements of procedure plus the MIB objects that are needed for processing for a specific portion of an SNMP framework should be defined in the same document and, as much as possible, should not be referenced in other documents. This allows pieces to be designed and documented as independent and self-contained parts, which is consistent with the general SNMP MIB module approach. As portions of SNMP change over time, the documents describing other portions of SNMP are not directly impacted. This modularity allows, for example, security models, authentication and privacy mechanisms, and message formats to be upgraded and supplemented as the need arises. The self-contained documents can move along the standards track on different timelines.

3. *Remote configuration.* The security and access control subsystems add a whole new set of SNMP configuration parameters. The security subsystem also requires frequent changes of secrets at the various SNMP entities. To make this deployable in a large operational environment, these SNMP parameters must be able to be remotely configured.

4. *Controlled complexity.* It is recognized that producers of simple managed devices want to keep the resources used by SNMP to a minimum. At the same time, there is a need for more complex configurations that can spend more resources for SNMP and thus provide more functionality. The design tries to keep the competing requirements of these two environments in balance and allows the more complex environment to logically extend the simple environment.

5. *Threats.* The security models in the security subsystem should protect against the principal threats, such as modification of information, masquerade, message stream modification, and disclosure. They do not need to protect against denial of service and traffic analysis.

SNMPv3 is secure against the following threats:

1. *Modification of information.* An entity could alter an in-transit message generated by an authorized entity to effect unauthorized management operations, including the setting of object values. The essence of this threat is that an unauthorized entity could change any management parameter, including those related to configuration, operations, and accounting.

2. *Masquerade.* Management operations that are not authorized for some entity may be attempted by that entity by assuming the identity of an authorized entity.

3. *Message stream modification.* SNMP is designed to operate over a connectionless transport protocol. There is a threat that SNMP messages could be reordered, delayed, duplicated, or replayed to effect unauthorized management operations. For example, a message to reboot a device could be copied and replayed later.

4. *Disclosure.* An entity could observe exchanges between a manager and an agent and thereby learn the values of managed objects and learn of notifiable events. For example, the observation of a set command that changes passwords would enable an attacker to learn the new passwords.

But SNMPv3 is not intended to secure against the following two threats:

1. *Denial of service.* An attacker may prevent exchanges between a manager and an agent.

2. *Traffic analysis.* An attacker may observe the general pattern of traffic between managers and agents.

SNMPv3 is still in its initial implementation phase. If fully implemented, the power of SNMP will be significantly improved.

3.4.2 RMON1 and RMON2

The Remote MONitoring (RMON) MIB will help to bridge the gap between the limited services provided by management platforms and the rich sets of data and statistics provided by traffic monitors and analyzers. RMON defines the next generation of network monitoring with more comprehensive network fault diagnosis, planning, and performance-tuning features than any current monitoring solution. The design goals for RMON are as follows (STAL99):

1. *Offline operation.* In order to reduce overhead of communication links, it may be necessary to limit or halt polling of a monitor by the manager. In general, the monitor should collect fault, performance, and configuration information continuously, even if it is not being polled by a manager. The monitor simply continues to accumulate statistics that may be retrieved by the manager at a later time. The monitor may also attempt to notify the manager if an exceptional event occurs.

2. *Preemptive monitoring.* If the monitor has sufficient resources and the process is not disruptive, the monitor can continuously run diagnostics and log performance. In the event of a failure somewhere in the network, the monitor may be able to notify the manager and provide useful information for diagnosing the failure.

3. *Problem detection and reporting.* Preemptive monitoring involves an active probing of the network and the consumption of network resources to check for error and exception conditions. Alternatively, the monitor can passively—without polling—recognize certain error conditions and other conditions (e.g., congestion, collisions) on the basis of the traffic that it observes. The monitor can be configured to continuously check for such conditions. When one of these conditions occurs, the monitor can log the condition and notify the manager.

4. *Value-added data.* The network monitor can perform analyses specific to the data collected on its subnetworks, thus relieving the manager of this responsibility. The monitor can, for instance, observe which station generates the most traffic or errors in network segments. This type of information is not otherwise accessible to the manager who is not directly attached to the segment.

5. *Multiple managers.* An internetworking configuration may have more than one manager in order to achieve reliability, perform different functions, and provide management capability to different units within an organization. The monitor can be configured to deal with more than one manager concurrently.

Table 3.5 summarizes the RMON MIB groups for Ethernet segments. Table 3.6 defines the RMON MIB groups for Token Ring segments. At the present time, there are just a few monitors that can measure both types of segments using the same probe.

RMON is very rich in features, and there is the very real risk of overloading the monitor, the communication links, and the manager when all the details are recorded, processed, and reported. The preferred solution is to do as much of the analysis as possible locally, at the monitor, and send just the aggregated data to the manager. This assumes powerful monitors. In other applications, monitors may be reprogrammed during operations by the managers. This is very useful when diagnosing

Table 3.5 RMON MIB Groups for Ethernet

Statistics group	Features a table that tracks about 20 different characteristics of traffic on the Ethernet LAN segment, including total octets and packets, oversized packets, and errors.
History group	Allows a manager to establish the frequency and duration of traffic-observation intervals, called *buckets.* The agent can then record the characteristics of traffic according to these bucket intervals.
Alarm group	Permits the user to establish the criteria and thresholds that will prompt the agent to issue alarms.
Host group	Organizes traffic statistics by each LAN node based on time intervals set by the manager.
HostTopN group	Allows the user to set up ordered lists and reports based on the highest statistics generated via the host group.
Matrix group	Maintains two tables of traffic statistics based on pairs of communicating nodes; one is organized by sending node addresses, the other by receiving node addresses.
Filter group	Allows a manager to define, by channel, particular characteristics of packets. A filter might instruct the agent, for example, to record packets with a value that indicates they contain DECnet messages.
Packet capture group	This group works with the filter group and lets the manager specify the memory resources to be used for recording packets that meet the filter criteria.
Event group	Allows the manager to specify a set of parameters or conditions to be observed by the agent. Whenever these parameters or conditions occur, the agent will record an event into a log.

Table 3.6   RMON MIB Groups for Token Ring

Statistics group	This group includes packets, octets, broadcasts, dropped packets, soft errors, and packet distribution statistics. Statistics are at two levels: MAC for the protocol level and LLC statistics to measure traffic flow.
History group	Long-term historical data for segment trend analysis. Histories include both MAC and LLC statistics.
Host group	Collects information on each host discovered on the segment.
HostTopN group	Provides sorted statistics that allow reduction of network overhead by looking at only the most active hosts on each segment.
Matrix group	Reports on traffic errors between any host pair for correlating conversations on the most active nodes.
Ring station group	Collects general ring information and specific information for each station. General information includes ring state (normal, beacon, claim token, purge); active monitor; and number of active stations. Ring station information includes a variety of error counters, station status, insertion time, and last enter/exit time.
Ring station order	Maps station MAC addresses to their order in the ring.
Source routing statistics	In source-routing bridges, information is provided on the number of frames and octets transmitted to and from the local ring. Other data include broadcasts per route and frame counter per hop.
Alarm group	Reports changes in network characteristics based on thresholds for any or all MIBs. This allows RMON to be used as a proactive tool.
Event group	Logging of events on the basis of thresholds. Events may be used to initiate functions such as data capture or instance counts to isolate specific segments of the network.
Filter group	Definitions of packet matches for selective information capture. These include logical operations (AND, OR, NOT) so network events can be specified for data capture, alarms, and statistics.
Packet capture group	Stores packets that match filtering specifications.

problems. Even if the manager can define specific RMON requests, it is still necessary to be aware of the trade-offs involved. A complex filter will allow the monitor to capture and report a limited amount of data, thus avoiding overhead on the network. However, complex filters consume processing power at the monitor; if too many filters are implemented, the monitor will become overloaded. This is particularly true if the network segments are busy, which is probably the time when measurements are most valuable.

Figure 3.13 shows the RMON probes in the segments. RMON probes can be implemented in three different ways:

1. Probe as a stand-alone monitor.
2. Probe as a module of hubs, routers, and switches.
3. Probe as a software module in Unix, NT operating systems, or in PC workstations.

RMON probes are extremely helpful for collecting data on Web site accesses and activities. In large networks, all the three implementative forms can be observed next to each other. But, vendors of probes are expected to work together. Standards are continuously improved to offer even more functionality in capturing and processing Web sites–relevant data.

The existing and widely used RMON version is basically a MAC standard. It does not give LAN managers visibility into conversations across the network or connectivity between various network segments. The extended standard is targeting the network layer and higher. It will give visibility across the enterprise. With remote access and distributed workgroups, there is substantial intersegment traffic. The following functionalities are included

- Protocol distribution
- Address mapping
- Network layer host table
- Network layer matrix table

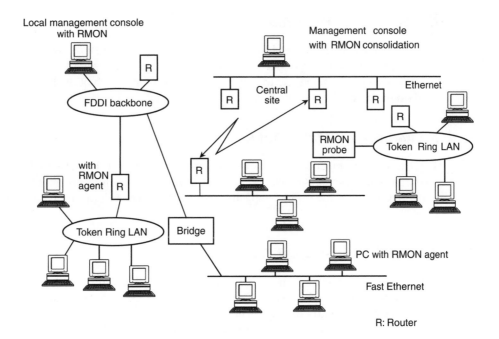

Figure 3.13 RMON probes in LAN segments.

- Application layer host table
- Application layer matrix table
- User history collection table
- Protocol configuration

Protocol Distribution and Protocol Directory Table

The issue here was how to provide a mechanism that would support the large number of protocols running on any one network. Current implementations of RMON employ a protocol filter that analyzes only the essential protocols. RMON2, however, will employ a protocol directory system that allows RMON2 applications to define which protocols an agent will employ. The protocol directory table will specify the various protocols an RMON2 probe can interpret.

Address Mapping

This feature matches each network address with a specific port to which the hosts are attached and also identifies traffic-generating nodes/hosts by MAC, Token Ring, or Ethernet addresses. It helps identify specific patterns of network traffic and is useful in node discovery and network topology configurations. In addition, the address translation feature adds duplicate IP address detection, resolving a common trouble spot with network routers and virtual LANs.

Network Layer Host Table

This tracks packets, errors, and bytes for each host according to a network layer protocol. It permits decoding of packets based on their network layer address, in essence permitting network managers to look beyond the router at each of the hosts configured on the network.

Network Layer Matrix Table

This tracks the number of packets sent between a pair of hosts by network layer protocol. The network manager can identify network problems quicker using this matrix table, which shows the protocol-specific traffic between communicating pairs of systems.

Application Layer Host Table

This tracks packets, errors, and bytes by host on an application-specific basis (e.g., Lotus Notes, e-mail, Web). Both the application layer host table and matrix table trace packet activity of a particular application. This feature can be used by network managers to charge users on the basis of how much network bandwidth was used by their applications.

Application Layer Matrix Table

Tracks packet activity between pairs of hosts by application (e.g., pairs of hosts exchanging Internet information).

Probe Configuration

Currently, vendors offer a variety of proprietary means for configuring and controlling their respective probes. This complicates interoperability. The probe configuration specification, based on the Aspen MIB, defines standard parameters for remotely configuring probes—parameters such as network address, SNMP error trap destinations, modern communications with probes, serial line information, and downloading of data to probes. It provides enhanced interoperability between probes by specifying standard parameters for operations, permitting one vendor's RMON application to remotely configure another vendor's RMON probe.

User History Collection Group

The RMON2 history group polls, filters, and stores statistics based on user-defined variables, thus creating a log of the data for use as a historical tracking tool. This is in contrast to RMON1, where historical data is gathered on a predefined set of statistics.

After implementation, more and more complete information will be available for performance analysis and capacity planning.

3.4.3 Desktop Management Interface

Basically, SNMP may be utilized to manage systems assuming system components accommodate SNMP agents. But there are as yet no MIBs that describe principal indicators for management purposes. An important emerging standard for desktop management is the Desktop Management Interface (DMI). The Desktop Management Task Force (DMTF) defined the DMI to accomplish the following goals:

- Enable and facilitate desktop, local, and network management
- Solve software overlap and storage problems
- Create a standard method for management of hardware and software components using Management Information Formats (MIFs)
- Provide a common interface for managing desktop computers and their components
- Provide a simple method to describe, access, and manage desktop components

The scope of management under DMTF includes CPUs, I/Os, motherboards, video cards, network interface cards, faxes, modems, mass storage devices, printers, and applications. Figure 3.14 shows the structure of this standard. There is a clear separation between the managed components, or component interfaces (CIs), and the services offered for management, or management interfaces (MIs). The commands are similar to SNMP, but they are not identical.

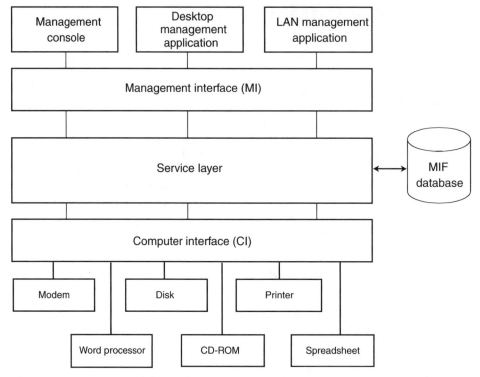

Figure 3.14 Structure of the Desktop Management Interface.

3.5 Agent Technologies

Intelligent agents play a key role in advanced management structures. Web-based systems and network management are heavily using agents in both WBEM and Java concepts. Java applets may even be considered mobile agents. An *agent* is a self-contained software element responsible for performing part of a programmatic process. Therefore it contains some level of intelligence, ranging from simple predefined rules to self-learning artificial intelligence interference machines. It typically acts on behalf of a user or a process, enabling task automation. Agents operate rather autonomously—they are often event- or time-triggered—and may communicate with the user, system resources, and other agents as required to perform their task. Moreover, more advanced agents may cooperate with other agents to carry out tasks beyond the capability of a single agent. Finally, as transportable or even active objects, they may move from one system to another to access remote resources or to meet or cooperate with other agents. Agents may be characterized by intelligence, communications, operations, cooperation, and mobility.

Intelligent agents may be classified as follows (MEGA97)

■ Single-agent systems

- Local agents (personal assistant, advisory assistant)
- Networked agents (personal assistant, smart mailboxes, retrieval agents, process automation)
- Multiagent systems
  - Distributed artificial intelligence–based agents (distributed problem solving)
  - Mobile agents (telecommunications, network management, electronic markets)

In single-agent systems, an agent performs a task on behalf of a user or some process. While performing its task, the agent may communicate with the user as well as with local or remote system resources, but it will never communicate with other agents. In contrast, the agents in a multiagent system may extensively cooperate with each other to achieve their individual goals. Of course, in those systems, agents may also interact with users and system resources.

Mobile agents are primarily for large networks with many intelligent systems. Agents may get different policy-driven tasks from the management platform or from users. The same platform may incorporate a Web server. Agents asynchronously perform tasks in different components. Performance can be good because agents are tuned to the tasks. But mobility causes communication overhead. The final decision depends on the interaction patterns and the size of the agent.

The following deployment alternatives may be considered for mobile agents (DETE95):

1. *Asynchronous and cooperative processing of tasks.* The possibility of delegating specific tasks by means of mobile agents to one specific node or even multiple nodes allows for highly dynamic and parallel computations. In particular, this supports disconnected operation of tasks and weak client computers.

2. *Customization and configuration of services.* In the light of an electronic marketplace, agent technology can provide new services instantly by either customization or (re)configuration of existing services. In this case, agents act as service adapters and could be easily installed.

3. *Instant service usage and active trading.* Mobile agents can travel to potential customers, providing spontaneous access to new services. This feature, enabling easy distribution of service clients, can be exploited to perform active trading.

4. *Decentralization of management.* Mobile agents can decrease pressure on centralized network management if necessary. Also, network bandwidth needs can be reduced by delegating specific management tasks from the central operation to dispersed management agents. Mobile agents representing management scripts enable both *temporal distribution* (over time) and *spatial distribution* (over different network nodes) of management activities.

5. *Intelligent communications.* Agents provide the basis for advanced communications. They support the configuration of a user's communications environment, where they perform control of incoming and outgoing communications on behalf of the end user. This includes communications screening, intelligent adoption of services to network access arrangements and end-user devices, and advanced service internetworking and integration.

6. *Information retrieval and support of dynamic information types.* Mobile agents provide an effective means for retrieving information and services within a distributed environment and support for dynamic information types within e-mail and advanced networked information systems.

The manager-agent relationship is significant in managing systems and networks. The manager can delegate certain management tasks to agents. That actually happens with element management systems, with manager of managers, and with platform-driven solutions. Delegation means that the manager downloads/pushes scripts to the agents. It could be JavaScript. The distribution software in use can be different. Distribution protocols are not relevant in this respect. The tasks remain the same for the agents until the next version is downloaded. The execution of operations follows prescheduled or delayed decision rules set by the manager. Mobile management applications represent an extension of the preceding scenario. In this case, the manager generates a mobile agent that performs specific management tasks autonomously and purposefully, directed at specific agents, in order to collect status information, deploy changes, download scripts, and so on. In a coordinated way, the visiting sequence of mobile agents can be set up by their managers.

The use of mobile agents is not in contradiction to Web-based management. Mobile agents execute tasks in management agents that can be accessed by universal Web browsers. In another approach, it can be said that mobile agents collect, process, and prepare information to be distributed by Web tools.

Traditionally, the Web-based management model is using the *pull* technique to view, review, select, and download information. It requests that members of the management team periodically use their browser to access Web servers. The result is that important events and status changes may remain unobserved. Other Web-based management activities, such as configuration management, distribution of reports, and preventive maintenance, are not impacted because people initiate these activities. Selected or *smart* push may help to distribute high-priority messages to selected users. The prerequisite is that events, alarms, and status changes are detected, interpreted, correlated, and, depending on their impacts, sent or referred to the right persons. Code books or expert rules can help with the first steps, push products with the second. Figure 3.15 shows the basics of this push solution. If the selection criteria are carefully chosen and message lengths are kept short, pushing will not cause any serious bottlenecks in the access networks.

3.6 Web Technology for Telecommunications Providers

The Internet is an existing network used by millions of people every single day. At the same time, the Internet is a generic term for a bundle of technologies available under the Internet umbrella. The Internet shares a number of similarities with the global phone system. Whoever is a subscriber can be reached by dialing the correct country code, area code, and individual phone number. In the case of the Internet, visitors who type in the correct Universal Resource Locator can access the necessary

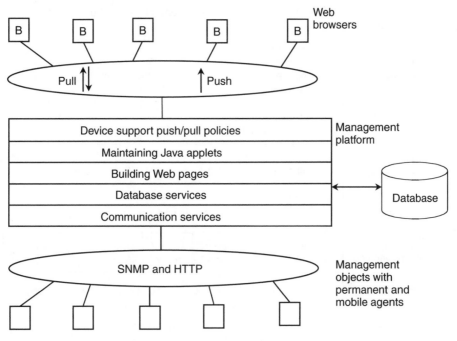

Figure 3.15 Selective push technology.

information. Even the billing process shares similarities: The longer you remain connected, the higher the bill.

Ownership is not as clear with the Internet as with public phone systems. There are multiple owners of the Internet physical backbone, but they are hidden from users. Administration and management are becoming more important as the number of subscribers explodes. A single administration issue—address management—causes a lot of headaches. Country institutions are coordinated by an independent U.S.-based company. Basically, the Internet can support multiple communication forms, such as voice, data, and video. The predominant form is still data.

3.6.1 Introduction into Internet Technologies

Internet users today use a small but powerful set of applications. The most widely used applications are e-mail, World Wide Web (WWW) content browsing, and file transfer services. These services are provided by high-powered servers within the network and the software that implements these applications (e.g., Web page hosting and mail forwarding). Figure 3.16 shows the typical layers of the communication architecture.

Application support services (e.g., Domain Name Service, which converts the widely seen host names like www.company.com into IP addresses) and authorization ser-

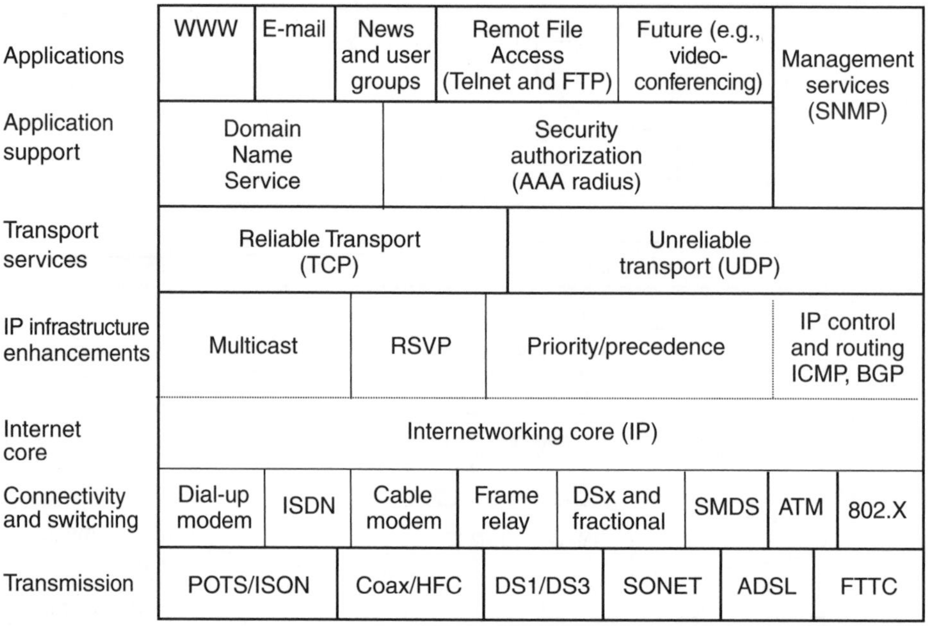

Applications	WWW	E-mail	News and user groups	Remot File Access (Telnet and FTP)	Future (e.g., video-conferencing)	Management services (SNMP)
Application support	Domain Name Service		Security authorization (AAA radius)			
Transport services	Reliable Transport (TCP)			Unreliable transport (UDP)		
IP infrastructure enhancements	Multicast		RSVP	Priority/precedence		IP control and routing ICMP, BGP
Internet core	Internetworking core (IP)					
Connectivity and switching	Dial-up modem	ISDN	Cable modem	Frame relay	DSx and fractional	SMDS / ATM / 802.X
Transmission	POTS/ISON		Coax/HFC	DS1/DS3	SONET	ADSL / FTTC

Figure 3.16 Typical layers of the communication architecture for Internet technologies.

vices provide support across applications. There are also software applications running on network servers. Transport services provide the option for reliable transport of information (error detection and retransmissions) or simple unacknowledged transfer. These services may operate end-to-end (e.g., in the case of file transfers, between an end user and a remote Internet server). In such cases, the network doesn't get involved at the transport level. In other cases (e.g., when the user is accessing a Web server internal to the network), the transport service is provided by the network, by UDP, or by TCP. IP infrastructure enhancements provide differentiated services at the IP router level. These emerging capabilities of and extensions to the current IP features will become key to future applications on the Internet (e.g., RSVP is providing reserved bandwidth to enable Internet telephony and videoconferencing). Based on this technology, in particular IP, all types of networks and their services could be standardized.

This standardization is a threat to proprietary networking architectures (e.g., SNA from IBM). In order to support both proprietary and standardized networks, gateways are being deployed to interconnect them with each other. It is very tempting to consider the Internet as the central switching point of corporate networking. But performance and security considerations drive corporate network managers to use privately owned Internet-like networking segments, called *intranets.*

Intranets are internal company networks that are using Internet technology. In particular, Web technology is used for information distribution (e.g., unifying company documentation, posting internal hiring procedures, etc.) and Web protocols for internal information transfer. The backbone of intranets is IP based on Layer 3. If interconnection is required to other networks (e.g., to SNA or to other companies), then firewalls are deployed to protect the company-owned intranet. Firewalls are actually filters; certain packets without the necessary authorization code cannot pass through the firewall.

If partnerships are the targets, networking equipment of partnering companies can be interconnected. In such cases, the connected intranets are called *extranets.* These require much lighter firewalls. Typical applications are between car manufacturers and their suppliers, between airlines in alliance, between airlines and travel agencies, between service providers to complement local, long-distance, and international services, and between service providers and their customers.

The Internet can be utilized as part of intranets and extranets. Virtual private networks are now offering this by securing channels that are part of the Internet, to be used by communicating parties in intra- and extranets. Several technical solutions are based on either Layer 2 or Layer 3 technologies.

Web browsers have become widely popular because they all share understanding of a simple media type—HTML formatting language. HTML is easy to understand and can be written by hand or generated from other text formats by translators. HTML is actually a simple document type of the Standard Generalized Markup Language (SGML).

HTML is simpler than other document languages in that it is not programmable. As a result, the descriptive capabilities of HTML are limited to low-level constructs, such as emphasis or indented lists. However, because HTML parsers are rather forgiving of HTML coding violations, many Web pages contain coding mistakes used purposely to achieve particular layout effects on popular browsers.

HTML is optimized for display rather than printing or storage. HTML has no notion of pages, which makes formatted printing difficult.

HTML has serious limitations. HTML does not provide the flexibility Web publishers need to create home pages. HTML pages are static, and dynamic updates are not really supported. Attributes, flexibility, and dynamics are absolutely necessary to successfully implement Web technology for network and systems management. Formerly, most technologies added interactivity to pages by using server-based CGI programs, Java applets, browser plug-ins, ActiveX controls, and scripting languages, which had little to do with HTML. But now, with dynamic HTML, new client-side technologies, combined with scripting languages like JavaScript, may solve many of HTML's problems.

DHTML extends the current set of HTML elements (and a few other elements such as style sheet properties) by allowing them to be accessed and modified by scripting languages. Dynamic features, which make pages come alive with movement and interactivity, can be added by exposing tags to scripts written in a language like JavaScript or VBScript (POWE97).

The tags are accessed through the document object model (DOM). The DOM describes each document as a collection of individual objects such as images, paragraphs, and forms down to individual characters. The DOM of DHTML can be complex, but does not always require a lot of work (POWE97). Developers may use the object model to find an image on a page and replace it with another when a user rolls a cursor over it. Such rollovers, or animated buttons, are common. DHTML also can animate a page by moving objects around, build an expanding tree structure to navigate a site, or create a complex application like a database front end.

The common denominator is expected to be the DOM. DOM is the basis for DHTML. It is a platform- and language-neutral interface that will allow programs and scripts to dynamically access and update the content, structure, and style of documents.

DOM has been accepted by both leading suppliers, Microsoft and Netscape. Their DOM implementation is very similar, with differences involving other features like positioning, dynamic fonts, and multimedia controls. Aside from extras like dynamic fonts and multimedia controls, the core ideas of Netscape and Microsoft are similar. With support for CSS and absolute positioning, advanced layout can be made to work under each browser. With DHTML and absolute positioning, it is possible to create sophisticated multimedia applications that can avoid frequent dialogs with the Web server. But building DHTML-based pages is still programming. Including dynamic elements in a page is a major step away from a static page paradigm and into the idea of Web pages as programs.

The DOM sets out the methods by which Web developers can access elements of HTML and XML documents to manipulate page elements and create dynamic effects, and it serves as the key enabling technology for dynamic HTML. There are three principal areas of XML applications:

1. High-end publishing, which views XML and SGML (Standard Generalized Markup Language) as highly structured document language.

2. Use of the extensible nature of XML by Web developers to create application-specific markup tags.

3. Use of XML as a data exchange format for distributed Web applications.

With XML and DHTML, it is relatively easy to share the user interface and information on the Web.

XML can help to eliminate the major limitations of HTML. XML can help Web search, foster interindustry communication, and enable a new form of distributed Web-based applications. But XML does not solve everything, and it does not make HTML obsolete.

Both HTML and XML are subsets of SGML, but XML could define HTML as a document type definition (DTD) of its own. They meet again only with regard to dynamic HTML, in which both require the use of DOM.

While the core syntax of XML is fairly well defined, there are many other areas that need addressing. XML provides no presentation services. Another technology must be deployed to present XML data within a Web browser. Eventual use of a style sheet language like CSS or the eXtensible Style Language (XSL) seems likely. Many users implement HTML as the presentation language for XML. To support presentation, Java applets may be downloaded to present even complex data forms. XML mirrors

SGML in that it lacks linking capabilities. To eliminate this weakness, the eXtensible Linking Language (XLL) is being added to XML. In addition, in order to support scripting capabilities, there is also a need to connect XML with DOM.

Without presentation, scripting, and linking, XML is limited to being simply a data format. But there are applications defined as *vertical* for supporting specific industries or *horizontal* for generic use. Microsoft has defined Channel Definition Format (CDF) to push content to selected targets. Open Software Description (OSD) has been defined in XML to support software installation procedures. Synchronized Multimedia Integration Language (SMIL) is used to define multimedia presentations for Web delivery. Also metalanguages, such as Resource Definition Framework (RDF), will be defined in the future.

XML involves a simple premise—describing data elements and their properties in plain text and providing a hierarchical framework for representing structured data for any domain and in a language that allows for the transmission of this encoded information across any interface. XML is optimized for data exchange:

- XMP enhances a communication provider's ability to expand its trading partner Web, as XML easily transforms to the data exchange requirements of multiple parties. By using XML, a communication provider has greater opportunities to interpret and process information with partners and across systems.

- An OSS XML architecture is easy to incorporate into an overall solution architecture since its translatable nature does not mandate a delivery method. In this way, it also addresses a fundamental business problem of which delivery vehicle to use as the landscape of downstream partner systems evolves.

- XML is easy to use and tool-enabled, so users of XML are not required to go to great lengths to find developers schooled in XML. Additionally, XML is applicable across multiple computing platforms, laying the groundwork for a provider to develop seamless integration throughout the enterprise.

XML can provide solutions to B2B problems. As service providers fight for good positions and competitive advantages in the changing communications marketplace, more emphasis is placed on how customer and partner relationships are managed. XML, and its integration into the fiber of providers' businesses, is allowing certain companies to pull away from their competitors.

Based on XML, there are more additions that may be considered important for eCommerce. Simple Object Access Protocol (SOAP) is a communication protocol to support access to individual projects in the Internet. It is using XML syntax in order to send text-based commands over the Internet. HTTP is used for the transport of these commands.

Universal Description Discovery and Integration (UDDI) is a recommendation for a new standard in eCommerce. It is using XML and SOAP as underlying tools. If implemented, various alternatives are offered to customers, similar to phone book entries. White pages contain names, mail and Web addresses, and phone numbers; yellow pages can then focus more on branch-specific attributes. But, in eCommerce, the so-called green pages take over the leading role by offering mutual direct links between businesses. These links are essential to access systems and applications of the partners. UDDI, originally developed by IBM, Microsoft, and Ariba, has enjoyed wide industry support from the very beginning.

But there remain a few areas where more work is needed, including standardizing many accompanying technologies such as XSL and XML schemas. Even more important, different industries need to standardize XML schemas for B2B transactions to better facilitate integration. Though this amount of work is significant, many organizations are dedicated to ensuring that it is completed. They have realized that there is no future in being an island in an interconnected business world.

The challenges facing XML are significant. The specifications of associated technologies such as style sheets and linking are not yet complete. XML style sheets based on DSSSL will most likely compete against CSS. The linking model of XML is more advanced than HTML, but it is incomplete and too complex. The interaction between XML and DOM needs further clarification.

Industry analysts assume that XML will be used together with HTML. HTML is widely used and is getting more powerful with CSS and DOM. XML may add formality and extensibility. Formality allows for guaranteed structure, exchange, and machine readability, which are difficult though not impossible with HTML. Extensibility means the opportunity to create specialized languages for specific applications. Such languages may have significant power within particular intranets or in the area of managing networks and systems.

Microsoft has rapidly implemented its XML Data Reduced (XDR) schema, which may be on its way to becoming a de facto standard. Industry groups designing their own DTDs or schemas are increasing in number significantly.

In order to carry out business processes, many transaction units must be assembled in real time. These units are usually maintained in directories. Directories are being enabled to operate across corporate boundaries, pointing users to services wherever they exist. To accomplish this work, directories need to be able to speak a common language. Directory Services Markup Language (DSML) is the emerging standard that expresses directory content in XML.

Directories typically store and manage information about each user in an enterprise—including names, addresses, phone numbers, and access rights. Directories are increasingly storing metadata about available Web services, what they do, what they require for inputs, how to execute them, what the results will be, who wrote them, and how to pay for them. Combined with the power of XML, this information enables whole new classes of individually tailored applications for eCommerce.

Applications consume DSML documents as they would use XML because DSML is a subset of XML. Applications can transmit DSML documents to other DSML-enabled applications on the Internet. This process effectively extends the Lightweight Directory Access Protocol (LDAP) across firewalls to any Internet transport protocol, such as HTTP, FTP, and SMTP. This is a major benefit for business-to-business commercial processes. Standard tags defined by DSML include object class, entry, attribute, and name in referring to well-established directory analogs.

LDAP, other directories, and vendor APIs will remain in place, and directories will continue to operate in their traditional manner. But new business-to-business eCommerce capabilities are available.

3.6.2 TCP/IP and HTTP

Since HTTP runs on top of TCP, TCP's behavior as a Web transport protocol deserves careful study. TCP provides some inherent flow control via end-to-end acknowledgments and TCP window size adjustments between two application endpoints. This mechanism allows applications to detect packet losses due to varying network conditions and rate-adapts automatically. However, this built-in flow control mechanism was designed originally for long-lived flows over very-low-bandwidth, long-haul pipes. In that scenario, the number of unacknowledged packets traveling through the pipe at any instant in time is small. This limits the number of packets that may have to be present in the case of packet loss. In situations where TCP packets travel through higher-speed links or over longer-delay end-to-end paths, the number of unacknowledged packets becomes large and TCP becomes more susceptible to expensive packet loss recovery. This problem is exacerbated by TCP's congestion avoidance mechanisms, which can result in oscillation between congested and uncongested conditions on busy links. TCP also exhibits behavior that is commonly referred to as *greedy source.* For long-lived flows, TCP will continue to grow the number of unacknowledged bytes outstanding (or window size) until it occupies all the bandwidth available in the connection. This process is called *slow start* and can take several round-trip times to complete. The bandwidth that the flow will consume is limited only by the speed of the lowest-speed link in the path of the connection with other flows sharing the pipe.

TCP cannot distinguish between congestion caused by a sudden traffic burst at the edge and that caused by true network congestion at the core of the Internet. Instead, it simply assumes the latter in all cases. To deal with burst-related congestion at the edge for short-lived flows, the best strategy is for the networking device at the edge (i.e., between the Web farm and the Internet) to allocate enough buffers to cope with them. For these flows, allocating additional buffers during a burst has the effect of smoothing out the packet processing load for the switch without the side effect of overallocating buffers at the expense of other active flows. The explanation for this is as follows: If a flow is short-lived, its net buffer requirements will peak only for a brief transient moment. If flows can be classified according to size, bandwidth, and type, it is possible to allocate buffer, switch, and uplink bandwidth resources accordingly.

Most TCP buffers will not cure all TCP problems, however. For long-lived flows, fairness issues and suspectibility to packet loss recovery must be carefully considered. In early ATM switches and in routers, the same conclusion was reached (i.e., throwing buffers at it does not solve the problem).

Rate-shaping techniques, in which a networking device in the data path intercepts TCP acknowledgments and alters their pacing and advertised window size, show promise, but these techniques suffer scaling limitations when deployed at the termination point for large numbers of flows (i.e., at the uplink for a large Web site). This is due to the requirement to maintain state information in the networking device for each flow. In addition, these techniques provide very little benefit for typical, short-lived Web flows. These flows are often just completing slow start around the time the flow terminates. Hence, window management techniques never have an opportunity to kick in. Obviously, these techniques apply only to TCP traffic. Although more research is required, these techniques appear most useful at a slow-speed WAN demarcation point such as might be found between an enterprise network and the Internet, where it may be useful to rate-limit long-lived flows. In the Web farm, the most useful technique for managing WAN and switch resources is to ensure that sufficient bandwidth and buffers are available to support the lowest-speed bottleneck link in the flow path. Admission control procedures can ensure that sufficient local switch, buffer, and bandwidth resources are available for admitted flows.

HTTP is the protocol used for access and retrieval of Web pages. As such, it is widely viewed as the core Web protocol. It is an application-level protocol used almost exclusively with TCP. The client, typically a Web browser, asks the Web server for some information via a "Get request." The information exchanged by HTTP can be any data type and is not limited to HTML.

HTTP usage has already surpassed that of older Internet access and retrieval mechanisms such as File Transfer Protocol (FTP), telnet, and gopher. However, these older services often coexist with and are supported by HTTP-based Web browsers.

HTTP is a simple protocol; its clients and servers are said to be *stateless* because they do not have to remember anything beyond the transfer of a single document. However, HTTP's simplicity results in inefficiency. For a typical HTML page, the client first retrieves the HTML page itself, then discovers that there are potentially dozens of images contained within the page and issues a separate HTTP request for each. Each HTTP request requires a separate TCP connection. HTTP pages are not real time. To retrieve new network status, the user must call up the Web page again. HTTP/Web is good for monitoring only one device at a time. This is the reason why Java is considered necessary for continuous monitoring.

To overcome this multistep process, typical Web browsers may open several TCP connections at once. However, this practice may overload slower-speed communication links. HTTP is a textual protocol (all headers are transferred as mostly ASCII text), which simplifies the writing of simple browsers.

HTTP needs significant performance improvements. This improvement will come in multiple steps. HTTP 1.0 is the basic link between Web browsers and Web servers. HTTP 1.1 will eliminate some major shortcomings of version 1.0, and Next Generation (NG) will guarantee that systems can communicate with each other without limitations and can exchange self-describing data.

HTTP 1.0 misuses TCP/IP by creating new connections constantly, resulting in overloaded communications links and deteriorating performance at high session numbers. Version 1.1 improves network performance and reduces congestion by offering a more controllable caching model, including the ability to specify what is cacheable, how long to keep files in cache, and when to revalidate files. HTTP 1.0 assigns domain names to individual Internet addresses. This means that large servers hosting many Web sites require many Internet addresses, which results in high administration overhead. HTTP 1.1 allows a single server to support hundreds of Web sites with a single Internet address. HTTP-NG will support applications using new data types (e.g., all multimedia file types in use today). These are data types, such as the eXtensible Markup Language (XML). XML data files include instructions on how the content is organized, so the receiver can accept the data without problems. The HTTP-NG packet will contain information explaining the format of the packet content, allowing Web servers to extend new types of content without requiring a client update.

3.6.3 WBEM

In July 1996, five major vendors announced an initiative to define de facto standards for Web-based Enterprise Management (WBEM). This effort, spearheaded by Microsoft, Compaq, Cisco, BMC, and Intel, was publicly endorsed by over 50 other vendors as well. The initial announcement called for defining the following specifications:

HyperMedia Management Schema (HMMS). An extensible data description for representing the managed environment that was to be further defined by the Desktop Management Task Force (DMTF).

HyperMedia Object Manager (HMOM). Data model consolidating management data from different sources; a C++ reference implementation and specification defined by Microsoft and Compaq to be placed in the public domain.

HyperMedia Management Protocol (HMMP). A communication protocol embodying HMMS, running over HTTP, and with interfaces to SNMP and DMI.

SunSoft has also announced a programming environment for developing Web-based network and systems management software. This environment, called Solstice Workshop, consists of a Java Management API (JaMAPI), a small footprint database, and a Java programming environment. Solstice Workshop's big drawing card is its extensibility and the popularity of Java's write-once-run-anywhere appeal. JaMAPI requires Java, whereas HMMP/HMMS/HMOM specifies HTML/HTTP, although Java is not specifically excluded.

Among these two efforts, the WBEM is certainly the broadest in scope, addressing not only protocol issues, but also data modeling and extensible data description as well. While JaMAPI includes object class definitions, it does not go as far as data description.

The complete solution is envisioned in Figure 3.17, which includes both major directions of webification.

The initial euphoria over WBEM and JaMAPI is starting to wear off, and it is time for doing the hard work of pounding out specifications and, more important, building products. Customer demand will push Web-based management to its limits, but disillusionment is sure to set in over the next few months if a lack a progress becomes obvious on the standards front. Several emerging products have been developed with

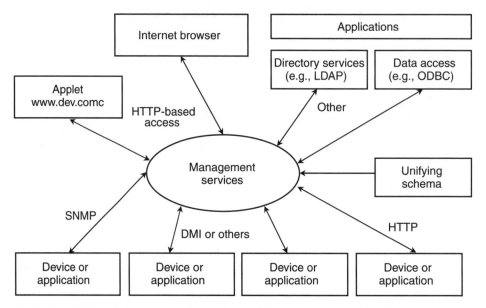

Figure 3.17 Use of the object manager to coordinate management services.

an eye for supporting current and future standards, and these bring to market a practical approach to take advantage of Web-based management.

3.6.4 Common Information Model

The DMTF has developed a Common Information Model (CIM) to take advantage of object-based management tools and provide a common way to describe and share management information enterprisewide. Using HMMS as an input, the new model can be populated by DMI 2.0 and other management data suppliers, including SNMP and CMIP, and implemented in multiple object-based execution models such as JaMAPI, CORBA, and HMM. CIM will enable applications from different developers on different platforms to describe and share management data, so users have interoperable management tools that span applications, systems, and networks (including the Internet).

CIM is a conceptual information model for describing management that is not bound to a particular implementation. This allows for the interchange of management information between management systems and applications. This can be either agent-to-manager or manager-to-manager communications, which provides for distributed system management.

In a fully CIM-compliant world, it should be possible to build applications such as service-level-agreement tracking applications using management data from a variety of sources and different management systems such as TME, OpenView, ManageWise, and SMS. The management data would be collected, stored, and analyzed using a common format (CIM) while allowing property extensions to provide a value-added dimension.

There are two parts to CIM: the CIM specification and the CIM schema.

The CIM specification describes the language, naming, metaschema, and mapping techniques for other management models such as SNMP MIBs and DMTF MIFs. The *metaschema* is a formal definition of the model, stating the terms, usage, and semantics used to express the model. The elements of the metaschema are classes, properties, and methods. The metaschema also supports indications and associations as types of classes and references as types of properties.

The CIM schema provides the actual model descriptions. The CIM schema supplies a set of classes with properties and associations that provide a well-understood conceptual framework within which it is possible to organize the available information about the managed environment.

Figure 3.18 shows the architecture of CIM.

The CIM schema itself is structured into three distinct layers:

1. *Core schema.* An information model that captures notions applicable to all areas of management.

2. *Common schema.* An information model that captures notions common to particular management areas but independent of a particular technology or implementation. The common areas are systems, applications, databases, networks, and devices. The information model is specific enough to provide a basis for the development of management applications. This schema provides a set of base classes for extension into the area of technology-specific schemas. The four com-

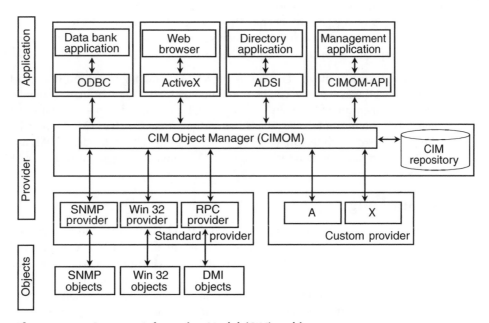

Figure 3.18 Common Information Model (CIM) architecture.

mon schemas currently in use are (1) systems, (2) applications, (3) networks (LAN), and (4) devices.

3. *Extension schemas.* Represent technology-specific extensions of the common schema. These schemas are specific to environments such as operating systems (e.g., Unix or Microsoft Windows).

More schemas are planned for definition in the areas of directory-enabled networks (DENs), service-level agreements (SLAs), and distributed application transaction measurement (DATM). Others will follow.

The formal definition of the CIM schema is expressed in a managed object file (MOF), which is an ASCII file that can be used as input into an MOF editor or compiler for use in an application.

The Unified Modeling Language (UML) is used to portray the structure of the schemas. Techniques to develop UML (VISIO) files from MOF files are being developed.

This is the first time in this industry that a common method of describing management information has been agreed to and followed up by implementation. Other efforts have failed because of the lack of industry support. Because the model is implementation-independent, it does not provide sufficient information for product development. It is the specific product areas—applications, systems, networks, databases, and devices—and their product-specific extensions that produced workable solutions.

Status of current CIM-related projects: The CIM TDC is defining rules and categories for an information model that provides a common way to describe and share management information enterprisewide. The group will define a metaschema or basic modeling language; a core schema, the base set of classes specific to systems, networks, and applications; and a common schema, a base set of platform-neutral, domain-specific extensions of core schema.

CIM will take advantage of emerging object-based management technologies to ensure that the new model can be populated by DMI and other management data suppliers, including SNMP and CMIP. The CIM is being designed to enable implementations in multiple, object-based execution models such as Common Object Request Broker Architecture (CORBA) and Common Object Model (COM) and in object-based management technologies such as Java Management API (JaMAPI).

3.6.5 Other Languages

Besides the popular languages, such as HTML, DHTML, XML, and JavaScripts, two other open source code scripting languages are gaining acceptance among Web site developers. The widespread use of Perl and TCL is attributable to the fact that they can act as a software integration platform, holding together the different elements of the site. Scripting languages are a collection of a few simple commands that are very easy to read and understand. Scripting languages are also distinguished by the fact that they are interpreted each time they execute. In contrast, the more traditional languages, such as C and C++, are compiled languages and are compiled at prior execution just once. Interpreted languages may impact the overall performance because interpretation happens during execution. Interpreted languages are good for development, however. Developers can create code and test-drive it rapidly, trying out their changes almost as fast as they can make them. C programmers try to make as many changes as they can before submitting their changed code to compilation.

The key target areas of these two scripting languages are as follows (BOBR98):

PERL

- *Text scanning.* Perl is optimized to scan text files, extract information, and print reports based on that information.

- *CGI scripts.* Perl is the most common language for developing applications that make use of Common Gateway Interface scripts on a Web server.

- *C replacement.* Many of the functions developers built with the C programming language can be done on a Web site by using Perl.

TCL

- *Embedded language.* TCL is a command language that can be embedded in common Web site applications.

- *Toolkit.* TCL comes with the TK toolkit, which makes it easy to build windowing interfaces in Web applications.

- *Components.* TCL commands can call components from inside applications, integrating Java, C, C++, and other components that can't otherwise talk to each other.

In the case of Perl, many of the language connections to outside sources of data and application logic already have been written and are available as free, open source code. TCL is a command language meant to issue commands to devices on a network. It can be embedded in the programs of other languages, thus providing a command structure to control varied hardware and software elements.

In addition, the scripting languages have been loosely defined regarding how they view the data and procedural logic with which they may work. This makes them actually very flexible and more useful for systems management than a strongly typed language such as Java. When Java is asked to deal with data from a source it does not recognize, it returns an error message and refuses to accept the data. Perl, on the other hand, tries to hook up to everything that it can on particular systems.

Both Perl and TCL are successful. Their roles must be seen as complementary, not competitive, to other Web site development languages.

3.7 Lightweight Directory Access Protocol (LDAP)

Directory services are fast becoming the key to the enterprise, allowing applications to locate the resources they need and enabling network managers to authenticate end users. Corporate network experts need to be aware about what LDAP is capable of, where it is headed, and what it was never intended to do.

LDAP was intended to offer a low-cost PC-based front end for accessing X.500 directories. Due to high overhead and acceptance delays of X.500, LDAP has emerged to fill the gap, somehow expanding its role. It rapidly became the solution of choice for all types of directory services applications on IP networks. LDAP applications can be loosely grouped into three categories: (1) those that locate network users and resources, (2) those that manage them, and (3) those that authenticate and secure them. Network managers who want to put the protocol to work need to go into detail, coming to terms with standard components and features. This protocol can save companies time and money. It can help network managers keep pace with the rising demand for directory services. New applications appear almost every day. But there are limits to what a protocol can do for distributed computing. It cannot store all the types of information needed by network applications. Knowing the difference between LDAP facts and fiction is the only way to avoid potential pitfalls.

3.7.1 Attributes of LDAP

The current specification comprises eight features and functions (HOWE99):

1. *Information model.* Organized according to collections of attributes and values, known as *entries,* this model defines what kinds of data can be stored and how that data behaves. For example, a directory entry representing a person named Jim Fox might have an attribute called sn (surname) with a value Fox. The information model, inherited almost unchanged from X.500, is extensible: Almost any kind of new information can be added to a directory.

2. *LDAP schema.* It defines the actual data elements that can be stored in a particular server and how they relate to real-world objects. Collections of values and attributes—representing objects such as countries, organizations, people, and groups of people—are defined in the standard, and individual servers can define new schema elements as well.

3. *Naming model.* It specifies how information is organized and referenced. LDAP names are hierarchical; individual names are composed of attributes and values from the corresponding entry. The top entry typically represents a domain name, company, state, or organization. Entries for subdomain, branch offices, or department come next, often followed by common name entries for individuals. Like the LDAP information model, the naming model derives directly from X.500. Unlike X.500, LDAP does not constrain the format of the namespace; it allows a variety of flexible schemes.

4. *Security model.* It spells out how information is secured against unauthorized access. Extensible authentication allows clients and servers to prove their identity to one another. Confidentiality and integrity also can be implemented, safeguarding the privacy of information and protecting against active attacks like connection hijacking.

5. *LDAP functional model.* It determines how clients access and update information in an LDAP directory, as well as how data can be manipulated. LDAP offers nine basic functional operations: add, delete, modify, bind, unbind, search, compare, modify distinguished name, and abandon. Add, delete, and modify govern

changes to directory entries. Bind and unbind enable and terminate the exchange of authentication information between LDAP clients and server, granting or denying end users access to specific directories. Search locates specific users or services in the directory tree. Compare allows client applications to test the accuracy of specific values or information using entries in the LDAP directory. Modify distinguished name makes it possible to change the name of an entry. Abandon allows a client application to tell the directory server to drop an operation in progress.

6. *LDAP protocol.* It defines how all the preceding models and functions map onto TCP/IP. The protocol specifies the interaction between clients and servers and determines how LDAP requests and responses are formed. For example, the LDAP protocol stipulates that each request is carried in a common message format and that entries contained in response to a search request are transported in separate messages, thus allowing the streaming of large result sets.

7. *Application program interface (API).* It details how software programs access the directory, supplying a standard set of function calls and definitions. This API is widely used on major development platforms running C, C++, Java, JavaScript, and Perl.

8. *LDAP data interchange format (LDIF).* It provides a simple text format for representing entries and changes to those entries. The ability helps synchronize LDAP directories. LDIF and the LDAP API, along with scripting tools like Perl, make it easy to write automated tools that update directories.

LDAP directories and operating systems are melding to create intelligent environments that can locate network resources automatically. Examples are as follows:

- Active Directory and Windows NT (Microsoft)
- HP-Unix and LDAP (Hewlett-Packard)
- Sun Solaris and LDAP (Sun Microsystems)
- Irix and LDAP (Silicon Graphics)
- Digital Unix and LDAP (Compaq)

In this new role as operating system add-on, LDAP furnishes a way to locate printers, file servers, and other network devices and services. LDAP makes these services standard, more accessible, and in many cases more powerful and flexible. LDAP is also starting to play a critical role in network management, where it can be a great help to network administrators. Without LDAP, managers and administrators have to maintain duplicate user information in many specific and separate directories across the network. With LDAP, it is possible to centralize this information in a single directory accessed by all applications (Figure 3.19). Of course, replacing key legacy applications with LDAP-enabled ones takes time, but big changes are already under way.

LDAP also has an important role to play in tighter security, with the directory acting as gatekeeper and deciding who has access to what. In this capacity, LDAP performs two critical jobs. First, it serves as an authentication database. Second, once the identity of a user has been established, it controls access to resources, applications, and services using stored policies and other information. LDAP also permits corporate

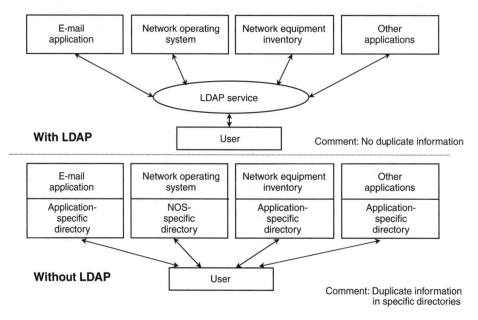

Figure 3.19 Directory centralization with LDAP.

network managers to use their directories to implement public key infrastructure (PKI) security. From the user's point of view, LDAP provides the directory in which certificates of other users are found, enabling secure communication. From the administrator's point of view, LDAP directories are the way in which certificates can be centrally deployed and managed.

3.7.2 Limitations of LDAP

LDAP has three major limitations. First, the protocol cannot and will not make relational databases redundant. It lacks the heavy update, transaction processing, and reporting capabilities of these products. Nor does it offer two-phase commits, true relational structure, or a relational query language like SQL. Using LDAP to implement an airline reservation system would be a serious mistake. Second, it is not reasonable to expect LDAP to serve as a file system. Its information model is based on simple pairing of attributes and values. Thus, it is not well suited to binary large object data that is managed by typical file systems. It is also not optimized for write performance and is unable to furnish byte-range access to values—both critical features of a file system. Finally, it does not have the locking semantics needed to read- and write-protect files. Third, LDAP is not a stand-in for DNS, which may well be the world's largest distributed database. Although LDAP's abilities are more or less a superset of DNS's—whose biggest job is translating names like home.netscape.com into IP addresses—there is a very good argument for not penetrating tasks of DNS; DNS is working fine. Also, LDAP cannot contend with the connectionless transport over which DNS usually runs. Ultimately, LDAP may have a role in managing and augmenting the information found in DNS. For example, it could link contact information to host information, but it cannot take the place of the DNS database itself.

In summary, LDAP has its place among the successful network management tools.

The Directory Interoperability Forum (DIF) is helpful in developing directory schemas for service providers (e.g., defining the directory objects and attributes necessary to provision and activate services and establish policies). Based on these schemas, developers can create applications that streamline service management for service providers.

3.8 Summary

There are multiple standards for network management. All of them have advantages and disadvantages and, of course, different application and implementation areas. Telecommunications suppliers and customers will have to live with multiple standards. The question becomes one of how these standards can seamlessly interoperate. There are basically three alternatives:

1. *Management gateway.* The interoperability is realized by a special system responsible for translating management information and management protocols. Looking at the practical realization of such a gateway, it is important to target the use of OMA for both OSI- and Internet-based management. Many existing object specifications for management could be taken over by the OMA-based management.

2. *Platforms with multiple architectures.* The interoperability is realized by a multilingual platform that understands multiple protocols. Protocol conversion is not necessary. Management information can be interpreted and transformed by the platform or by applications. Different architectures are supported simultaneously, but without deep integration.

3. *Agent with multiple architectures.* The interoperability is realized at the agent level. In this case, the management agent understands multiple protocols and languages. It requires some intelligence for the agent. If selected, agent software must be implemented in many, practically in all, networking components. This number is considerably higher than in the case of management platforms.

There is a new group—Joint X/Open TeleManagement Forum Inter-Domain Management Group—that addresses in particular the interoperability between OSI-management, Internet-management, and OMG-OMA. This type of work takes a lot of time. In the meantime, practical solutions are absolutely necessary. In most cases, gateways deliver the quickest solutions. One such solution with management gateways is shown in Figure 3.20. CORBA plays an important role in both gateways, related to OSI-CMIP and Internet-SNMP.

Standardization is absolutely necessary to ensure interoperability of various components of communication systems. This chapter has laid down the basics. Management frameworks and platforms may support some of the standards, but there is no product supporting all of them.

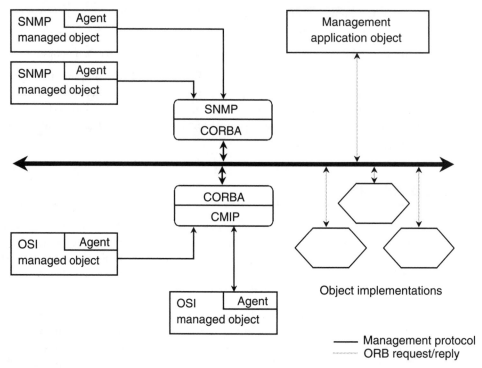

Figure 3.20 Using an object request broker to connect multiple management protocols.

Open database connectivity (ODBC) is an application programming interface (API) that allows a programmer to abstract a program from a database. When writing code to a database, the user usually has to add code that talks to a particular database-using language. If the user wants his program to talk to an Access, Fox, and Oracle database, he should code the program with three different database languages. This can cause some problems.

When programming to interact with ODBC, the user only needs to talk the ODBC language (a combination of ODBC API function calls and the SQL language). The ODBC manager will outline how to contend with the type of database the user is targeting. Regardless of the database the user is using, all of the calls will be to the ODBC API. All that the users need to do is to install an ODBC driver that is specific to the type of database the users will be using.

In summary, information will be consistent in DEN directories and in CIM management systems.

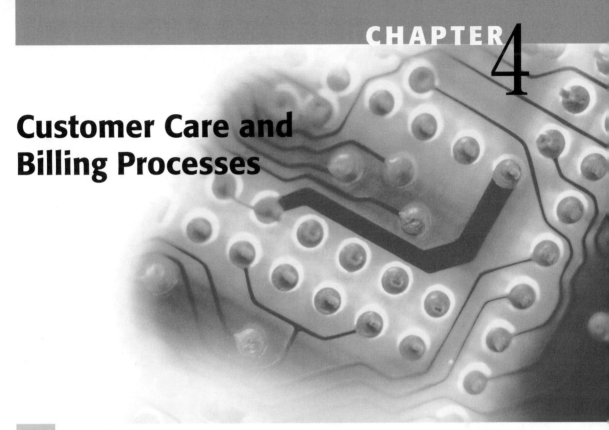

CHAPTER 4

Customer Care and Billing Processes

4.1 Introduction

Customer care is a typical front-office function, because the service provider is facing its customers. It could be a face-to-face contact or eCommerce contact; common to both is that the customer gets responses, information, and explanations in real time. Billing is a typical back-office function in its traditional sense; recent changes toward electronic bill presentation and payment, however, have transitioned this function to the front office as well.

Figure 4.1 shows a typical sequence of activities to generate a bill that has flat-rate elements (one-time installation, monthly recurring), usage charges, and possible SLA adjustments. Service providers may also choose to apply discounts or rebates for outages and/or SLA breaches to a specific customer's bill, according to service type, by promotion, by customer relationship, or according to its policy or customer contract.

When a service is supplied by a combination of different providers, usage and/or other billing data may be aggregated by the main service provider from input by secondary service providers and one bill presented to the customer. This is a trend, but it depends on service provider billing strategy, customer preference, the actual service arrangement provided, and/or service provider process capability and policy.

Information exchanges are numbered as follows:

1. Network usage data.

2. Aggregated usage data.

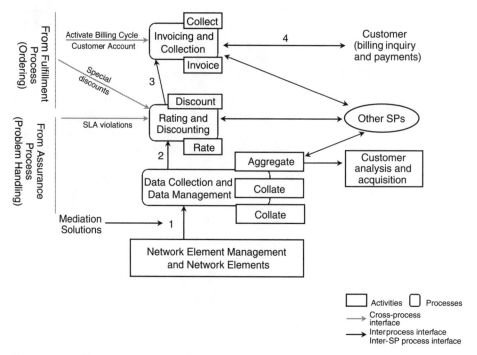

Figure 4.1 Billing process example.

3. Summarized bill content.

4. Bill generation.

In subsequent sections, each process will be described in terms of its tasks and input and output connections, along with its internal and external processes and activities.

The billing process does not stand alone. It has links and interfaces to the service fulfillment and service assurance processes.

Customer care processes have been basically reactive processes. But the extreme pressures of cost and customer demand for more control and more proactive service support are driving service providers to offer this support through automation.

Internet and intranet access from universal browsers now facilitates excellent interactive support, including giving the customer the ability to see and act on service performance. On path 1 in Figure 4.1 additional mediation solutions may be inserted. Mediated data can also be used for the purposes of customer analysis and customer acquisition.

Customer interface management helps to streamline the information exchange between provider processes and customers. Each process may have a direct interface with customers, but central interface management seems to be the better solution.

4.2 Customer Care

The telecommunications industry is characterized by a very high rate of change. Be it regulatory-driven, technology-driven, or customer-driven change, telecommunications companies are racing forward in this new and explosive area with a combination of boldness and uncertainty—bold in their resolve to meet and beat their competition, and yet uncertain of ways to entice and embrace their customers. Winners in this race must increase their focus on the customer. To do so successfully, companies are compelled to find the proper blend of external influences (customers and competition) and internal capabilities (organization, process, and information technology). But many companies, while transporting data and voice at the speed of light, are moving in slow motion in their quest to become more customer focused.

It is not enough to provide basic telephony service—customers are demanding much more. Unfortunately, many telecommunications providers are promising a vision they are not currently capable of fulfilling. The challenges of integrating local, long distance, wireless, messaging, Internet, interactive media, and other such services are overwhelming the industry. In an attempt to meet these challenges, service providers concentrate on a few immediate elements: customers, competition, organization, process, and information technology (HERO96). The value and quality of customer care can be judged using these five dimensions.

Table 4.1 shows the attributes of the infancy and maturity stages. Surveys are recommended for finding the actual position of a particular telecommunications provider. Incumbent telecommunications providers have traditionally focused on one element; most often that is market share. Typically, those with significant market share have seen revenues and stock prices rise over time. However, while most marketing efforts in the competitive sectors of the industry—such as long distance and cellular—have focused on attracting customers, there has been little or no attention to retaining them. In the short run, stock prices are largely unaffected by retention efforts. As a result, the only time a customer feels important is during the acquisition process; once the chase is over, so is the attention. It should come as no surprise that consumers feel little loyalty to their providers.

Customer-based management (HERO96) shifts a business's perspective from a short-term focus based on quarterly results to a longer-term emphasis built on lifetime customer relationships. These relationships are created by balancing business value and customer value, rather than being driven by market share objectives and existing product capabilities. Deeper and more lasting strength can be realized by understanding and satisfying customer needs, for example

- Developing custom products for targeted microsegments
- Focusing marketing campaigns for specific audiences
- Bundling services into meaningful packages to meet the needs of specific customers
- Providing customer care at a level commensurate with the value to the company

Table 4.1 Customer Care Maturity Model

CRITERIA	INFANCY ATTRIBUTES	MATURITY ATTRIBUTES
Customer	Transactional view; disparate knowledge	Strategic view; knowledge of preferences, propensities, values
Competition	Reactive; internally driven priorities	Proactive; customer/market-driven priorities
Organization	Product/function structure, skills, culture, and rewards	Customer-focused executive; relationship/satisfaction rewards
Process	Ad hoc; product/function-focused; inconsistent metrics	Flexible; customer-focused; metrics linked to external measures
Technology	Functional applications; information is not integrated	Systems synchronized across all touchpoints, fed to decision support

In order to remain competitive and become more customer focused, telecommunications providers will spend heavily over the next several years building and managing customer relationships.

4.2.1 Customer Analysis and Acquisition

Typically, market segments are differentiated as major accounts, corporate accounts, small/medium businesses, and residential subscribers (see Figure 4.2). The pyramid in Figure 4.2 characterizes the expected relative volumes for each market segment. Figure 4.2 gives some rough estimates for the size of each segment related to the total number of customers interested in one or more services of the provider.

Each of the market segments should be addressed differently. The principal considerations for each segment are as follows:

- Major accounts
  - Importance of service providers to the business
  - Choice
- Corporate accounts
  - Increasing cost focus
  - Expectation of account management/significant contact
- Small/medium accounts
  - Diverse customer profile

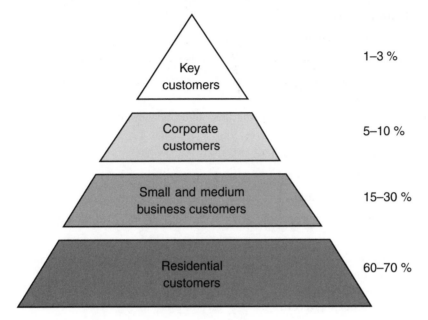

Figure 4.2 Differentiation of market segments.

- ■ Importance of reliable solutions
- ■ Significant cost awareness
- ■ Expectation of better service/more responsive process
- ■ Residential subscribers
  - ■ Distinct segments
  - ■ Price perception
  - ■ Assumption of reliability
  - ■ Directories/repair/billing service issues

The customer database is key for each kind of analysis. Usually, service providers maintain many customer databases without any synchronization. They might be similar to each other, but their attributes don't match each other. A customer profile, as usually maintained in a relational database, includes the following items

- ■ Basics (name, address, market profile, etc.)
- ■ A unique identifier for each customer
- ■ Legal, billing, and bill copy addresses
- ■ Record linkages between invoice records, discount records, and reporting records
- ■ Service profiles (service offerings, rate plans, products, and promotions)

- Rating and discounting attributes
- Equipment inventory
- Network services profile (telephone number, intelligent features, trunk groups, etc.)
- Customer preferences (bill cycle, bill frequencies, bill presentment, currencies, languages, etc.)
- Sales ledger profile (payments, adjustments, account balance, collection status, credit classification, etc.)
- Contracts and subcontracts
- Typical volumes by service
- History of complaints
- Other information, depending on the service provider and on the support system used

Depending on the needs and the agreement between service providers and customers, customer structures can be tailored to the external customer. Multiple levels can be created for customers and then linked to the applicable bill record, discounting record, and reporting record.

In practical use, multiple relational databases are combined to create specific links, such as

- Multiple services to one customer
- Multiple services to one account
- Multiple service classes to a service location
- Multiple usage types of a cellular class of service
- Multiple guiding parameters to a usage type (e.g., telephone number, calling card number, IP address)
- Multiple services to one contract

Similar links can be built using the same or separate relational databases to support marketing and sales.

4.2.2 Customer Relationship Management

An intensified customer focus can facilitate more effective and efficient customer care, which in turn can reduce churn, recruit new customers, increase revenue per subscriber, and provide growth in high-value segments.

Historically, the communications industry has focused its investments on services, networks, and internal operational efficiency. In a regulated environment where the goal was universal access and the ability to serve all customers equally well, the industry naturally focused its resources and attention on building efficient infrastructure and systems rather than understanding and forging relationships with various customer segments. Three trends are pushing service providers to focus on customers and develop deeper customer relationship management (CRM) capabilities to take a more effective and profitable approach to reaching these customers.

First, continued deregulation is opening previously protected local and global markets, providing new opportunities and new challenges. In truly competitive segments, such as long distance and wireless, market shares for incumbents have dropped 40 percent or more in a relatively short period of time.

Second, technology-driven markets provide opportunities for communications companies to expand their offerings, but they also give consumers alternatives. For example, Internet telephony is emerging as a long-term potential competitive threat to service providers' core competency. Many customers are giving up their local phone connections in favor of wireless—a trend that is maturing in many parts of the world.

Finally, recent surveys from market research companies show that local, long-distance, cable, and cellular/PCS providers are falling below customers' expectations on pricing, simplicity of pricing structures, and customer service.

Tangible projects such as billing offer, in contrast to customer relationship management, instant gratification. Although CRM leads to less churn and increased revenue, it is difficult to quantify in the short term. CRM helps to focus resources on high-value, high-potential customers and treat customers that may be of less future value to the provider appropriately as well, by not bombarding them with marketing messages and perhaps by taking a more passive approach to retention. It is important to realize that CRM is not a product but a strategy that needs products to become successful. It is neither one nor a set of application products. It is very important that service providers understand that they cannot buy CRM in a box.

Many initiatives are undertaken based on experience and intuition rather than reliable financial data. What is more, customers interact with companies in many ways, and CRM depends on a number of specific capabilities within marketing, sales, and service. For top management trying to allocate resources, the broad array of CRM capabilities presents a bewildering range of options. In short, service provider executives face a basic challenge: They need to invest in CRM capabilities, but they do not know where to invest to get the highest return or how to justify those investments.

Determining the business drivers for CRM implementation is an important first step, and they can include churn reduction, geographical expansion and market share exploitation. Beyond classifying customers, data can be used for detailed analysis, including the following:

- Customer profiling
    - Descriptive segmentation and tracking
    - Residential customers: geographic, demographics, lifestyles
    - Business customers: industry code, total revenues, head count
- Advanced analysis
    - Behavioral/predictive elements
    - Segmentation and tracking
    - Time series, regression, induction trees, and modeling tools

- Guided and ad hoc analysis
  - Dynamic assessment and tracking

Most of these techniques use on-the-fly aggregation, rotation, filtering, ranking, and custom calculation with a graphical, easy-to-use interface.

Carriers who rely solely on their billing systems for CRM are missing an opportunity to use publicly available demographics information. The second area of neglect is credit and risk management. For instance, customers may be high value from a marketing and upsell perspective, but a tremendous credit risk. Carriers are also missing loyalty program opportunities and the direct customer response that comes with it. Using billing data gives service providers a purely transactional view of the customer, and customers are not transactions. Customers are living, breathing people who might have service problems and questions and preferred buying patterns and to whom providers can upsell or cross-sell or deter from churning, but not by using just billing data. And this is the reason that billing applications vendors are aggressively trying to position themselves upstream of or as value added relative to billing. Billing is about bits and bytes, time stamps, and receivables. A customer relationship is about listening, understanding, changing, and responding appropriately. Billing data are narrow and capture only a piece of the information needed to understand and appreciate the customer. Paying on time does not necessarily mean that customers and service providers have an optimal relationship.

One of the biggest challenges that can be observed with service providers is that their organizations are structured around business and network lines rather than customer support lines. The result is that customers end up dealing with monolithic network operations and business operations, especially at the incumbent carriers. They split the customer-facing responsibilities, so if customers experience technical disconnects, they call a network support desk; if the disconnect is due to nonpayment, customers are referred to business operations. Ultimately, they are left with a fragmented customer experience, from an organizational perspective.

Frequently, CRM is considered an additional cost. Benefits cannot be easily quantified. In the future, progress is expected in the areas of data warehouses and data-mining capabilities. Data-mining tools will offer the opportunity to conduct ad hoc analysis on special subscriber segments.

4.3 The Customer Interface Management Process

Customer interface management may be a distinct process or it may be performed as part of the individual customer care processes on an individual service or cross-service basis. This encompasses the processes of directly interacting with customers and translating customer requests and inquiries into appropriate events, such as the creation of an order or trouble ticket or the adjustment of a bill. This process logs customer contacts, directs inquiries to the appropriate party, and tracks the status to completion. In cases where customers are given direct access to service management systems, this process ensures consistency of image across systems, as well as security to prevent a customer from harming this network or those of other customers. The aim is to provide meaningful and timely customer contact experiences as frequently as the customer requires.

Principal functions include the following:

- Receive and record contacts
- Register customer requests
- Direct inquiries to appropriate processes
- Monitor and control status of inquiries, and escalate
- Ensure a consistent image and secure use of systems

Figure 4.3 shows the principal functions of the customer interface management process, as well its input and output connections to other processes and functions.

Table 4.2 identifies the information sources for this process. Table 4.3 shows the information output and the targeted processes.

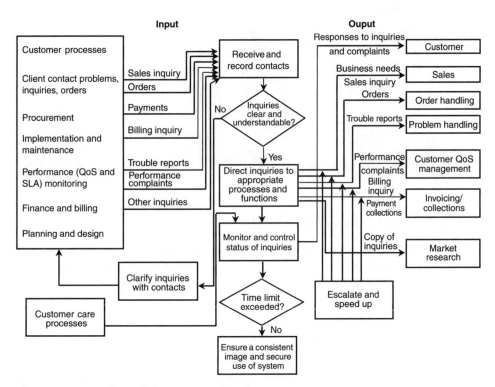

Figure 4.3 Functions of the customer interface management process.

Table 4.2 Information Input for the Customer Interface Management Process

SOURCE OF INFORMATION	INFORMATION
Customer	Order, inquiries, complaints about bills, reporting problems
Procurement	Actual status
Network maintenance and restoration	Progress on problem elimination
Billing	Payments
Customer QoS management	Performance problems
Network planning and development	Solution alternatives for performance problems
Providers	Responses for inquiries

Table 4.3 Information Output for the Customer Interface Management Process

INFORMATION	TARGETED PROCESSES
Responses for inquiries	Customer
Business needs	Sales
Orders	Order handling
Trouble ticket	Service problem resolution
Performance complaints	Customer QoS management
Inquiries about bills	Billing
Payment status	Payment collection
Actual status	Market research

4.3.1 Receive and Record Contacts

If a common customer interface management process is going to be selected, this function represents a *single point of contact* (SPOC) for all customer processes and for other support processes as well.

This function receives input (see Table 4.2) directly from customers about problems, inquiries, and orders; performance metrics from the performance-monitoring function; payment confirmation from invoicing; and feedback from other service providers.

Supported and recommended communication alternatives are phone, fax, and e-mail; Web access; and functional interfaces such as file transfer, remote procedure call (RPC), electronic bonding, and middleware.

4.3.2 Register Customer Requests

Registration is usually combined with tools implemented to support multiple areas. Examples are automated call distributors (ACDs) and trouble-ticketing products.

4.3.3 Direct Inquiries to Appropriate Processes

The customer interface is actually a broker function. After receiving and recording contacts, this broker function interprets input, checks for clarity, and, depending on the content, it refers inquiries to the targeted processes and functions (see Table 4.3). This function is executed in a loop, with the final results to be sent to the customer.

Supported and recommended communication alternatives are phone, fax, and e-mail; Web access; and functional interfaces such as file transfer, RPC, electronic bonding, and middleware.

4.3.4 Monitor and Control Status of Inquiries, and Escalate

Expected input should be provided with priorities. To each priority, a reasonable time frame for answers should be defined. Priorities may be grouped in terms of severity, criticality, importance, or other criteria. For each category, escalation procedures should also be deployed that contain provisions for time frames, targeted persons, and the preferred communication facilities.

4.3.5 Ensure a Consistent Image and Secure Use of Systems

Whatever method of communication is selected to operate between the functions, processes, and customers, mutual protection is important. Recent developments suggest the dominant use of IP technology, including intranets for internal use by the service provider and extranets for external use between service providers and their customers. This technology offers state-of-the-art protection technologies, based on firewalls. By carefully architecting extranets, maximal protection can be guaranteed to both contracting parties by defining demilitarized zones (DMZs) that house all critical servers. DMZs are separated from both communicating parties by firewalls (see Figure 4.4). Due to the diversity of managed objects in DMZs, the degree of administration, performance surveillance, and reporting needed must not be underestimated.

4.4 The Sales Process

This process encompasses learning about the needs of each customer and educating the customer about the communications services that are available to meet those needs. It includes working to create a match between the customer's expectations and

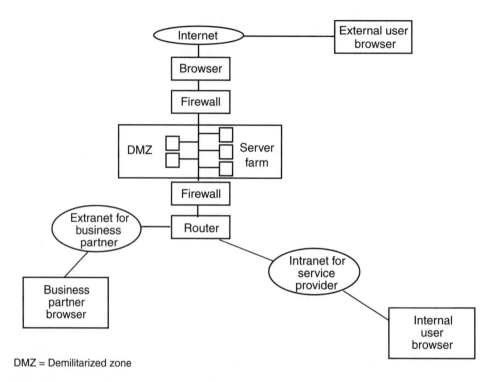

DMZ = Demilitarized zone

Figure 4.4 Use of a DMZ to separate intranets and extranets.

the service provider's ability to deliver. Depending on the service provider process, it can be pure selling or it can include various levels of support. The sales process may include preorder work and interfaces. The aim is to sell the correct service to suit the customer's need and to set an appropriate level of expectations with the customer. SLA negotiation, request for proposal (RFP) management, and negotiation are led from this process.

Principal functions include the following

- Learn about customer needs
- Educate customers about services
- Match expectations to offerings and products
- Arrange for appropriate options
- Forecast service demand
- Manage SLA and RFP negotiations

Figure 4.5 shows the principal functions of the sales process, as well as its input and output connections to other processes and functions.

Table 4.4 identifies the information sources for this process. Table 4.5 shows the information output and the targeted processes.

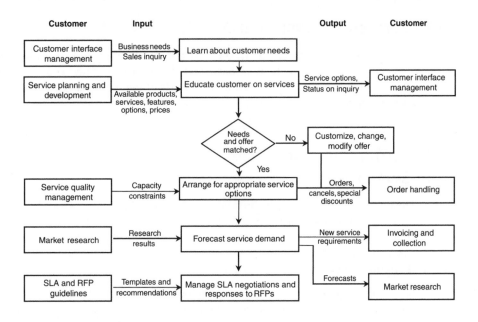

SLA = service-level agreement
RFP = request for proposal

Figure 4.5 Functions of the sales process.

Table 4.4 Information Input for the Sales Process

SOURCE OF INFORMATION	INFORMATION
Customer interface management	Business needs, sales inquiry
Service planning and development	Available services, features, prices, and options
Service quality management	Capacity constraints

Table 4.5 Information Output for the Sales Process

INFORMATION	TARGETED PROCESSES
Service options, status of inquiry	Customer interface management
Orders, cancels, special discounts	Order handling
New service requirements	Service planning and development
Forecasts	Service planning and development
Forecasts	Service quality management

4.4.1 Learn about Customer Needs

This function is never ending. Market research, postbilling, and customer satisfaction analysis should provide the necessary data about the changing needs of customers. Deregulation has been completed in most parts of the world, leaving a lot of playgrounds open to competition. In order to avoid customer churn, service providers must listen carefully to their customers.

4.4.2 Educate Customer about Services

The best customer is the educated customer. Product planning should update sales on the portfolio changes early enough. Basic input arrives indirectly from the service creation, planning, and development process. Time to market is decreasing for all service providers. The real differentiation is the way the message about new and changing services is sent to the customer.

Education may be supported by various tools, such as white papers, service description flyers, advertisements, sales and technical presentations, and Web pages. Successful sales organizations use a combination of all of these.

4.4.3 Match Expectations to Offerings and Products

Both parties should be satisfied with a service agreement. Service providers are expected to honestly approach the customer demands and try to meet these demands as closely as possible. Vaporware will not help to promote the customer relationship, nor will it prevent customer churn.

The portfolio and the customer database must be accessible to the customer sales representatives anytime they want to review the current status. Web access is absolutely necessary when intranets are in use at the service provider.

4.4.4 Arrange for Appropriate Options

Service providers maintain a basic portfolio of products and services. In addition, they may offer optional products and services. The strategies of service providers may differ in that some are very customer oriented, maintaining the core and a large number of options, and others are moderately customer oriented, emphasizing core products and services only. The right choice depends on the market position of the service provider and the strength of competitors. Also, the strategic choice is dynamic—it may change rapidly when service providers recognize the need for a change.

4.4.5 Forecast Service Demand

Service providers must live within their own capacity limits. Bandwidth is getting less expensive altogether, but service providers must plan and make provision for this bandwidth. In this respect, there are at least two parallel functions to be executed

- Forecast-driven planning based on global market research that is not related to any particular customer

- Customer-driven planning based on the aggregated service demand expected for certain geographic areas that is not related to any particular customer but to a cluster of customers

The sales or capacity planning organization must be continuously in contact. If necessary, they must honestly discuss capacity limits for certain customers.

4.4.6 Manage SLA and RFP Negotiations

In a competitive environment, the sales organization must be prepared to deal with requests for information (RFIs) and requests for proposals (RFPs). It is obvious that both are driven these days by QoS, SLAs, and price. The sales organization should be able to act quickly, using templates for both. Due to the competitive environment, they must not violate deadlines or compliance statements.

4.5 The Problem-Handling Process

The problem-handling process is responsible for receiving service complaints from customers, resolving them to the customer's satisfaction, and providing meaningful status reports on repair or restoration activity. This process is also responsible for awareness of any service-affecting problems, including notifying customers in the event of a disruption, whether reported by the customer or not; resolving the problem to the customer's satisfaction; and providing meaningful status reports on repair or restoration activity.

This type of proactive management also includes planned maintenance outages. The aim is to have the largest percentage of a problem proactively identified and communicated to the customer, to provide a meaningful status report, and to resolve the problem in the shortest time frame.

Principal tasks include the following

- Receive trouble notification

- Determine cause, resolve, or refer

- Track progress of resolution

- Initiate action to reconfigure if needed

- Generate trouble tickets for suppliers

- Confirm trouble cleared and notify customer

- Schedule with and notify customer of planned maintenance

There is a central support desk that is responsible for being the single point of contact for service problems. This support desk guarantees the availability of subject-matter experts for each potential problem area. The support desk keeps customers' information about the status and progress of problem resolution. Figure 4.6 shows the principal functions of the problem-handling process, as well as its input and output connections to other processes and functions.

Table 4.6 identifies the information sources for this process. Table 4.7 shows the information output and the targeted processes.

When a problem is reported by the customer, a trouble report may be sent to the service problem resolution function for correction. When a problem is identified by service problem resolution, then the problem handling function is notified in order to inform the customer about the problem.

4.5.1 Receive Trouble Notification

Service-related problems should be directed to an SPOC entity. Communication forms are manyfold and include phone and fax, e-mail, internal communication options of trouble-ticketing applications, service monitoring support systems, and element managers that are able to generate service alarms.

After receiving the notification about a service problem, incoming information is registered; confirmation is sent back to the initiator of such a service complaint.

4.5.2 Determine Cause, Resolve, or Refer

Depending on the priorities, the service desk may spend a certain amount of time to determine the cause of a service problem. Steps involved in this activity may include service problem detection, service problem isolation, and service problem determination.

Usually, this entity is expected to isolate the majority of service problems by highlighting workarounds to ensure service—even at the risk of restricted performance. Service problem determination is an option and depends on staffing and the skill levels of support personnel. If they are unable to determine and diagnose service problems, they refer them to other processes and functions.

Supported and recommended communication alternatives are phone, fax, and e-mail; Web access; and functional interfaces such as file transfer, RPC, electronic bonding, and middleware.

4.5.3 Track Progress of Resolution

In order to support SLAs, service providers are expected to be aware of the status of service problem resolution. It is a complex process that first of all includes service problem resolution and other providers. In collaboration with marketing, joint Web pages may be defined, maintained, and integrated into the workflow.

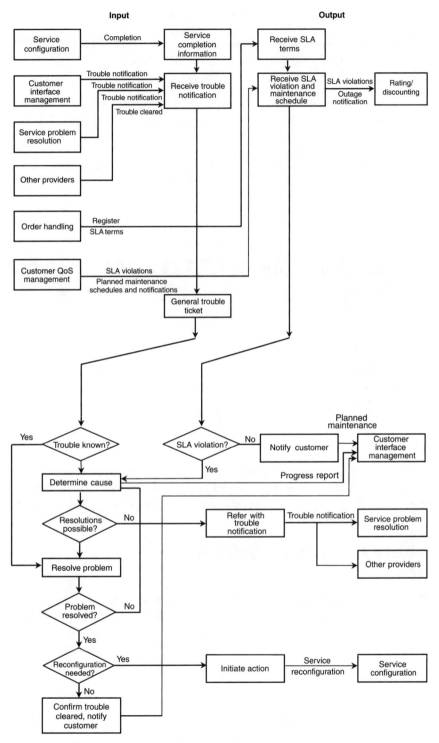

Figure 4.6 Function of the problem-handling process.

Table 4.6 Information Input for the Problem-Handling Process

SOURCE OF INFORMATION	INFORMATION
Customer interface management	Trouble notification
Order handling	Register SLA terms
Service configuration	Completion notification and service details
Other providers	Trouble notification, trouble clearance
Service problem resolution	Trouble notification, trouble clearance
Customer QoS management	SLA violations; planned maintenance scheduling and notification

Table 4.7 Information Output for the Problem-Handling Process

INFORMATION	TARGETED PROCESSES
Trouble reports, status reports, resolution notification	Customer interface management
Problem reports	Customer QoS management
Service reconfiguration	Service configuration
Trouble notification	Other providers
Trouble notification	Service problem resolution
SLA violations, outage notification	Rating and discounting

Workflow is applicable in supporting the relationship between customers and service providers, and between multiple service providers. In most cases, workflow and trouble-ticketing products support this as part of their original functionality.

4.5.4 Initiate Action to Reconfigure if Needed

This function may issue change requests, if the nature of the service problem is severe. Usually templates are available and are filled in by this function automatically. It assumes that both service problem determination and diagnosis have been completed by other processes, and the results of this have been sent back to this function. Change requests will be sent to the service configuration process for approval and deployment.

Supported and recommended communication alternatives are phone, fax, and e-mail; Web access; and functional interfaces such as file transfer, RPC, electronic bonding, and middleware.

4.5.5 Generate Trouble Tickets for Suppliers

For expediting service problem resolution by other suppliers, trouble tickets are the most widely used form of information exchange. This process can be supported by a best-of-breed trouble-ticketing application or as part of the workflow, connecting multiple service providers to each other. Independently of Web and workflow applications, service providers may be connected with each other using electronic bonding. In all cases, electronic communication is preferred and recommended.

4.5.6 Confirm Trouble Cleared and Notify Customer

The problem-handling process is the receiver of trouble reports from other providers to be processed within the jurisdiction of the service provider. At the same time, other service providers respond with confirmation of cleared problems. This confirmation may include the usual trouble-ticket entries, such as time stamps, initiating symptoms, service problem cause, and resolution steps.

After notifying customers about cleared problems, cleared trouble tickets should enter a database for further processing and maintenance. They will be helpful in solving future service problems using case-based reasoning.

Due to nonavailability of service to certain customers, SLAs may be impacted as well. In such cases, the rating and discounting process must also be notified.

4.5.7 Schedule with and Notify Customer of Planned Maintenance

Preventive maintenance helps to maintain a very high quality level for provided services. This function is responsible for identifying how low-traffic periods at network facilities and equipment can have as little impact on customers and operations as possible. This information must be correlated with workforce management to accomplish optimal schedules for technical staff. The results should be distributed to other processes and to the customer.

Supported and recommended communication alternatives are phone, fax, and e-mail; Web access; and functional interfaces such as file transfer, RPC, electronic bonding, and middleware.

Rules-based coordination and approval are necessary for scheduled network penetration. This forces risk assessments to be made on the processes such as the quantities, locations, and types of maintenance activities.

4.6 Customer QoS Management Process

This process encompasses monitoring, managing, and reporting on quality of service as defined in service descriptions, service-level agreements, and other service-related documents. It includes network performance, but also performance across all service parameters, such as orders completed on time. Output from this process is either standard (predefined) or an exception report, including but not limited to dashboards, performance of a service against an SLA, reports of any developing capacity problems, and reports of customer usage patterns. In addition, this process responds to performance inquiries from the customer. For SLA violations, the process supports notifying problem handling and for QoS violations, notifying service quality management. The aim is to provide effective monitoring. Monitoring and reporting must provide SP management and customers meaningful and timely performance information across the parameters of the services provided. The aim is also to manage service levels that meet specific SLA commitments and standard service commitments.

Principal tasks include the following

- Schedule customer reports
- Receive performance data
- Establish reports to be generated
- Compile and deliver customer reports
- Manage SLA performance
- Determine and deliver QoS and SLA violation information

Figure 4.7 shows the principal functions of the customer QoS management process, as well as its input and output connections to other processes and functions.

Table 4.8 identifies the information sources for this process. Table 4.9 shows the information output and the targeted processes.

4.6.1 Schedule Customer Reports

Reports traditionally use different ways of distributing performance-related metrics to customers and to other service providers. Scheduling means the determination of distribution frequency. Recently, new presentment forms have been added to standard reporting.

The practice of populating Web pages with performance-related information is going to replace traditional reporting. Web pages may be accessed and relevant information may be downloaded at the customer's convenience.

If scheduled reports are still preferred, standard daily, weekly, monthly, and quarterly reports are recommended, using 3-D presentation forms and colors to increase the ease of readability. Electronic distribution is preferred in every case.

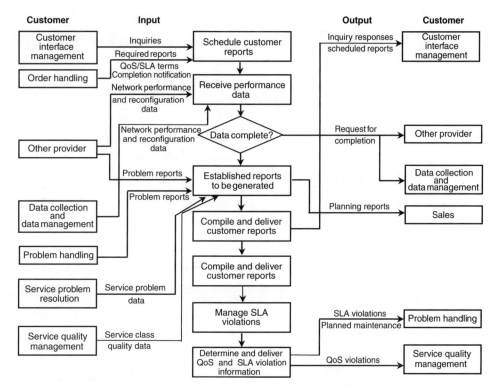

Figure 4.7 Functions of the customer QoS management process.

4.6.2 Receive Performance Data

This function is considered the central place to receive, interpret, process, and distribute performance-related information. Performance data are being sent by several other processes (problem handling, service quality management, network data collection and management) and by other service providers.

Quality-of-service metrics are the basis for service-level agreements between service providers, operators, and customers. The quality of the service is characterized and defined by the recommended metrics, broken down by the principal service assurance processes. But not all metrics can be applied, maintained, and reported at reasonable costs. Only those metrics that are understood and accepted by all parties and that can be applied, maintained, and reported at reasonable costs should be considered for SLAs.

4.6.3 Establish Reports to Be Generated

This function deals with developing reports and/or Web pages. In each case, both the content and the presentation forms are very important. Considerations are what reports need to be generated and how they should be presented.

Table 4.8 Information Input for the Customer QoS Management Process

SOURCE OF INFORMATION	INFORMATION
Customer interface management	Inquiries
Order handling	Required reports, QoS/SLA terms, completion notification
Other providers	Problem reports
Problem handling	Problem reports
Service problem resolution	Service problem data
Service quality management	Service class quality data
Other providers	Network performance and configuration data
Network data management	Network performance and configuration data

Table 4.9 Information Output for the Customer QoS Management Process

INFORMATION	TARGETED PROCESSES
Inquiry responses, scheduled reports	Customer interface management
Planning reports	Sales
SLA violations and planned maintenance	Problem handling
QoS violations	Service quality management

Site Design Considerations

The following considerations should be accounted for when designing a Web site.

Site Navigation

There are two points to consider when constructing the navigation layout for a Web site—namely, the structure of the information and how access to that information will be provided. The layout of the site is usually the most difficult part of the site design process, particularly if a lot of information will be accessible from the site. Adequate time must be put into designing the structure of the information to allow easy access for all users. Navigation tools must also be clear and easy to use, as well as functional within all types of browsers that will be used by the target audience. Navigational design must consider the same factors as many other GUI interfaces. Since movement within a Web site is typically nonlinear, navigational menus should be planned to allow users quick access to any part of the site.

Content Organization by Menus

The ability of users to move through a Web site and find the information or functions they are searching for plays an important role in determining how successful a site will be. Menus and submenus are powerful tools in the design of a Web site. In the same way that menus are used in traditional Windows-based design, HTML menus can be used to subdivide and group relevant content to allow users to be guided to their topics of interest gradually. The use of more than four levels of menus forces users to work too hard to find the information they are looking for. Using too few levels may be equally difficult to navigate, in particular when the information volume grows. Generally, three to four levels should provide appropriate depth and guidance for users. However, because of the varying content of sites, this is a flexible guideline. It is important to know that the menu structure for the site should be continually evaluated and improved as the site grows.

Interaction Models

There are many ways to organize the information contained within a Web site. The term *interaction model* refers to the structure that is implemented to allow the user access to the various pages within a site. The model best suited to a particular page will depend on the content and complexity of the information that the page presents. There are a number of interaction models in use. These models may be used independently or in combination throughout a site. These models are as follows:

Table of contents. This approach is taken from printed books. Users can easily find the headings they are looking for, and then hyperlink directly to that page. This type of access is useful for sites that provide textual or encyclopedic information.

Image map. These are graphics that use an embedded linkage map that relates hot spots on the graphic to URLs within the Web site. In this way, the user can view the graphic and point and click to move to different locations on the site.

Graphic menus. These provide the same visual approach to site navigation as image maps, without incurring the disadvantages of employing one single, large graphic, mapped with links. They employ smaller, simpler graphics, strategically placed to provide visual impact.

Search. Web site searches provide a useful means of allowing a user to access information contained on a particular Web site. Some form of search facility is usually a requirement for larger sites.

Indexing. This provides functionality similar to that of book indexes. It allows a user to rapidly locate information pertaining to a specific keyword or topic. It may be used in combination with search.

Page Design Considerations

The actual layout of a Web page is highly dependent on the type of information that is being presented. This segment provides some fundamentals of good page design.

Header

The header provides a user with access to commonly used functions within the companywide intranet and clearly differentiates intranet content from Internet content. The standard header provides links for navigation to common functions via the following graphics:

Company logo. Links to the company home page.

Directory. Links to the company's intranet directory Web site.

Services. Links to the company's intranet service page.

Search. Links to the company's search Web site.

Help. Links to the company's intranet help Web site.

Pre-imaged, mapped versions of the company's header are available on the intranet development and support site.

Footer

The footer gives the user important information about the page and provides consistency within the company's intranet. The standard footer usually contains the following

- A standard horizontal rule as a separator
- Copyright statement
- Statement regarding content ownership with an optional e-mail link to the designated page maintainer, which should not be the name of an individual
- Date of the last revision

Page Size

Page size must be designed with the actual usable space of the browser window in mind. Typically, this would be the lowest amount of usable space for the standard browser configuration in a 640×480 video monitor resolution. When designing a Web page, designers want to limit horizontal scrolling as much as possible. Keeping the width of Web sites less than 600 pixels (using tables) makes it much easier for users to navigate information. In some cases, horizontal scrolling is normal and acceptable.

The acceptable size for an intranet page is 100,000 bytes or less. This limit includes all of the images that are embedded on this page. This size will keep performance within acceptable limits for LAN, WAN, and dialup users with 28.8-Kbps modems.

Home Page

The layout and design of the home page of any Web site are extremely important. Besides being the first things a user sees upon entering a site, they define the organizational structure and tone for the entire site. Some essential elements for every home page include

- Visually appealing design
- Overview of site content
- Links to contents of the site
- Company/organization identifying information

Page Layout

HTML does not provide graphic designers the flexibility they are accustomed to in existing page layout and editing programs (e.g., MS Word, Adobe PageMaker). However, this does not mean that complex and functional applications cannot be created using HTML. Rather, one must realize that when used inconsistently the graphic and typographic controls of HTML can result in inconsistent designs.

To avoid the haphazard look of documents, designers should take care in how graphics are placed and organized. A consistent style will also allow for a consistent conversion from non-HTML documents. It is better to use simple icons and images rather than complex ones. Navigation tools should be kept in a consistent place.

Text Style

Text needs to be short and to the point, and should be organized in sections or paragraphs. When browsing, visitors tend to scan rather than read. They are usually searching for information and appreciate when sections are arranged in logical order. Similar ideas or facts should be presented in a consistent way, with the same components presented in the same way and in the same order. Consistency is a very important consideration in Web design.

Graphics

Graphic images should be used where appropriate to help users navigate and find information more quickly. Graphics also provide a look to the site that will help users identify where they are. Graphics should not be overused for internal publishing applications. Whereas external marketing Web sites often are graphically intense to catch attention, use of graphics in internal Web sites should be based on ease of navigation and usage. The type, size, and location of graphics throughout a site should be presented in a consistent manner; items of similar importance should have the same size and type of graphic. If a larger-than-normal graphic is employed, users are likely to assume that there is some additional significance. Often, the visibility and intended use of the site will dictate the level of graphics required for the site.

Graphic images should be designed for 256-color resolution. A common mistake that professional graphic designers make is designing with higher resolution and greater color depth than the deployment environment. The color scheme that was designed in 16-bit color may look bad in 256-color or even worse in 16-color environments. Design should follow the requirements of the target environment.

Most images are between 10K and 30K. The exception would be image maps on navigational pages or photographic images, which should be around 50K. One of the drawbacks with using images on a network is the time it takes to download very large files. Images must be kept as small as possible and must fit within the size of the browser's viewable space.

For images, it is best to use file formats. Graphics Interchange Format (GIF) and Joint Photographic Experts Group (JPEG) are both compressed formats. The GIF format is better for smaller graphic or line art images.

Local Navigation Elements

Each Web site should include a sitemap, showing a detailed layout of the site, with links to all possible sections and documents. Each page within a Web site should include a link to the sitemap page. Users may link to a Web site or Web page from a number of different places (navigation page, search results page, hyperlinks, etc.). The sitemap page gives users a quick and easy way to locate the information they need. On long pages, users may want to quickly go to the top of the page to view the table of contents or other introductory information. The Top of the Page icon helps users more quickly navigate to the top of the current page.

Links

While many Web sites incorporate graphics to support navigation, text links still play an important role in ensuring the usability of a site. Working with text in HTML is easy. In general, because it is easy to create links and change font types, several mistakes are commonly made. Some guidelines that aid in ensuring a site's readability and usability are listed as follows:

- Design for scanners, not for readers.
- Explain the page's benefit above the fold.
- A bold typeface will draw attention to a particular section.
- Avoid typing in all caps—it is more difficult to read.
- Links must be underlined in addition to being in color to assist users who may be color-blind or using black-and-white monitors.
- Avoid blinking text because it is difficult to read and annoying to users.

A typical Web page provides both informational text and links to more specific information. Most people are looking for visual clues to whether a page is useful or interesting enough to be worth reading. If they don't find what they want quickly, they will move to another site. One of the difficulties in using text for navigational purposes is the wording of the links. Proper wording of the text allows users to jump to a new topic or continue reading without losing their place.

All links to default pages should be set with a trailing "/." This eliminates the problem of DNS names turning into IP addresses. By default, the Web browser converts any hyperlink that does not include a Web page (such as a link to a home page) to the default page for the server. However, depending on the browser, this may convert the DNS name into the physical IP address of the hosting server. If the DNS name is converted to an IP address and users add the page to their favorites, the URL will be stored with the IP address. If the IP address of the site changes, the bookmark will no longer work. To eliminate this problem, simply include a trailing "/" on any link that does not include a page file name.

Abstracts and summaries are very helpful for large pages or large graphics. Whenever possible, users should have the opportunity of linking to further information if desired. Very large files or files that are not in a usable browser format (ZIP files, BMP files, etc.) should have links that allow users to download the files to their local PCs.

Other Graphic Elements

Separators are graphic, or possibly textual, elements that are used to break up or visually divide the contents of a single Web page. A separator can be as simple as a horizontal line to a shadowed line graphic or an actual image file. Use of separators helps to visually vary the subject matter on the page. Although separators can be effective, it is important to remember that they should not distract users from the page content; rather, their purpose is to divide the information into logical groupings.

HTML provides tags for standard information-gathering controls such as radio buttons, drop-down menus, and exit boxes. In general, guidelines created for traditional GUI-based development apply to Web page design. Following are some important considerations:

- In most countries people read from left to right, so text literals should be left-aligned.
- Exit boxes should be similarly sized and also left-aligned.
- Tabs should move the user downward through the page.
- Controls should be evenly spaced and aligned when possible.
- A default button should be provided.
- Mixed-case text should always be used.

Bullets are used in HTML in the same manner in which they are used in traditional word processing, to define a list of items. Although textual bullets are fine for use on Web pages, there are also many graphical bullets available that will add just a touch of color to an ordinary Web page.

Background and Text Colors

The use of appealing backgrounds and text colors can add an artistic look to Web sites, but the way colors are used also affects the usability of the site. Designers must be wary of improperly using color, as colors may have different meanings to different people and some users may be unable to distinguish some colors clearly.

Following are some user interface guidelines that are applicable to Web sites:

- Color is second only to movement in attracting attention.
- Three colors are sufficient for a color scheme.
- Certain colors should be used carefully.
- Shades of red attract attention, while the retina responds fastest to yellow.
- Blue is more difficult to focus on, making unsaturated blue a good choice for backgrounds.
- Avoid gaudy, unpleasant colors and combinations of red/green, blue/yellow, green/blue, and red/blue.
- If backgrounds are going to be used, they should be either a light-colored pattern or a solid color.

Printing

When the nature of a site is documentation, users must have the ability to print individual Web pages or an entire site's content. This can easily be accomplished by adding a link to a printable form of the entire document. Documents may also be provided in multiple formats, such as Microsoft Office formats, to accommodate the maximum number of users.

4.6.4 Compile and Deliver Customer Reports

This function populates reports and distributes them to the targeted destination, such as customers and sales. It also populates the Web pages to be accessed by authorized users.

4.6.5 Manage SLA Performance

Quality of Service metrics and SLAs are defined by this function. Metrics are classified as being either service independent or service dependent.

Service-Independent Metrics

The following are the service-independent metrics used to manage SLA performance.

- Availability for
  - Service access points
  - Applications
  - Devices
  - Transmission facilities
- Mean time to service restoration
  - Service access points
  - Applications
  - Devices
  - Transmission facilities
- Mean time between failures
  - Service access points
  - Applications
  - Devices
  - Transmission facilities
- Mean time to repair
  - Service access points
  - Applications
  - Devices
  - Transmission facilities

- Mean time of repair
  - Service access points
  - Applications
  - Devices
  - Transmission facilities
- Relationship: proactive and reactive problem detection
  - Service access points
  - Applications
  - Devices
  - Transmission facilities
- Relationship: preventive and reactive problem detection
  - Service access points
  - Applications
  - Devices
  - Transmission facilitie
- Relationship: number of referred problems to all detected problems
  - Service access points
  - Applications
  - Devices
  - Transmission facilities
- Meeting escalation guidelines
  - Service access points
  - Applications
  - Devices
  - Transmission facilities
- Number of chronic problems to all detected problems
  - Service access points
  - Applications
  - Devices
  - Transmission facilities
- Help-desk performance
  - Receiving notification
  - Solving trivial problems
  - Performance during first, second, and third shifts
  - Performance on weekends
  - Performance on holidays

- Number of outages
  - Service access points
  - Applications
  - Devices
  - Transmission facilities
- Average number of outages
  - Service access points
  - Applications
  - Devices
  - Transmission facilities

Service-Dependent metrics

The following are the service-dependent metrics used to measure SLA performance.

- Resource utilization
  - Service access points
  - Applications
  - Devices
  - Transmission facilities
- Leased lines
  - Bit error rate
  - Nonavailable seconds
  - Severely errored seconds
  - Block error ratio
- Plesiochronous digital hierarchy (PDH) devices
  - Number of problems
  - Average duration of problem restoration
- Synchronous digital hierarchy (SDH) devices
  - Number of problems
  - Average duration of problem restoration
- Frame relay service
  - Network delay
  - Committed information rate (CIR)
  - CRC errors
  - Discarded frames
  - Effective permanent virtual circuit (PVC) throughput

- ATM service
  - Available bit rate (ABR)
  - Constant bit rate (CBR)
  - Unspecified bit rate (UBR)
  - Variable bit rate (VBR)
  - Network delay
  - Errored cell rate
  - Effective PVC throughput
- xDSL service
  - Number of problems
  - Average duration of problem restoration
- Cable networks
  - Number of problems
  - Average duration of problem restoration
- Packet switching service
  - Throughput rate
  - Relationship: discarded packets to all packets
- IP services
  - Packet delay in one direction
  - Packet delay in both directions
  - Packet loss in one direction
  - Packet loss in both directions
  - Transmission throughput

Managing SLAs means the maintenance of QoS metrics, adding and deleting metrics, classifying metrics for various SLAs, and allocating SLAs to customer contracts.

The SLA is more than just a list of service metrics—it lays out the ongoing monitoring, reporting, and response process. The SLA should clearly define the responsibilities of both parties. For each function that is defined, the person responsible for controlling that function as it is performed needs to be identified by position.

A *service level agreement* is a formal negotiated agreement between two parties. It is a contract that exists between the service provider and the customer or between multiple service providers or between service providers and network operators. It is designed to create a common understanding about services, priorities, and responsibilities.

An SLA should also cover corrective actions—that is, the steps to be taken in the event that a service-level objective is not met. This should define who resolves the problem of each service deficiency, as well as consequences for not resolving the problem. Consequences can appear in the form of penalty clauses or, alternatively, a bonus clause for meeting the objectives. The end result will be the same.

An SLA can cover many aspects of the relationship between the customer and the service provider, such as quality and performance of services, customer care, billing, and provisioning. Performance reporting uses the SLA as a reference and does not address the other parameters known to exist, but those parameters are part of the SLA.

SLAs are an excellent tool for customer and service provider management. A well-crafted SLA sets and manages expectations for all elements of the service to which it refers. It assists the service provider in forcing operational change, improving internal measurement and reporting, assessing trends, and improving customer relationships and it provides a vehicle for potential differentiation from natural competitors.

Every SLA is different, although there are a few common threads that should be part of each one. Some common components are listed as follows (BLAC00):

Parties to the agreement. All parties to the agreement should be listed, especially when there are multiple service providers and/or client groups.

Terms of the agreement. The period of time that the agreement will be in place should be specified carefully. A typical length is between two and three years.

Services included. Each service that is included in the agreement should be identified. For each service, service-level metrics should be defined individually. The SLA should describe how the indicator is measured and who is responsible for performing the measurement.

Optional services. All optional services that the service provider is willing to supply on request should be listed, in addition to those listed in the current agreement.

Reporting and reviews. Reports that are supported by the monitoring tools should be defined and created. Also, the frequency of reporting, access to reports, and availability of real-time reporting, as well as periodic reports, should be defined. In many cases, Web access to these reports is required by customers.

Modifications. The process for changing the SLA, if necessary, should be defined and persons who are authorized for changes should be identified.

Refinements. Technology may require refinement of the SLA and a redefinition of the commitment. For example, new equipment may be added, and the client may therefore have increased performance expectations.

Tracking changes. Changes in the client organization (e.g., an increase in size or an acquisition) can place unexpected traffic on the network, resulting in poorer response time. Introduction of new applications can also change QoS and the cost of delivering it. Changes must be documented, and parties must take into account the impact of these changes.

Nonperformance. An SLA also defines nonperformance, or what is to be done when the indicators do not meet the levels specified. However, some consideration has to be given to the amount of deviation. For example, instead of requesting a 2-second response time, it is more realistic to request a response time of 2 seconds for 90 percent of transactions, and 5 seconds for 99 percent of transactions.

Payment regulations. Collection alternatives are agreed on here. Basically, there are two: flat rates for each month or usage-based payments.

The success of using SLAs depends on the following factors:

- The services covered by the agreements must be realistic and the providers must be able to meet them.
- QoS metrics must be understood and accepted by all contracting parties.
- Expected service levels must be measurable. When a service metric cannot be applied, it cannot become part of an SLA.

4.6.6 Determine and Deliver QoS and SLA Violation Information

As a result of comparing SLAs and QoS commitments with actual monitoring results, this function is responsible for informing the problem-handling and service quality management processes about violations. Indirectly, SLA violations may influence the rating and invoicing processes. Electronic information exchange with other processes and functions is preferred.

4.7 The Call-Rating and Discounting Process

The rating and discounting process encompasses the following functional areas

- Applying the correct rating rules to usage data on a customer-by-customer basis, as required
- Applying any discounts agreed to as part of the ordering process
- Applying promotional discounts and charges
- Applying outage credits
- Applying rebates due because SLAs were not met
- Resolving unidentified usage

The aim is to correctly rate usage and to correctly apply discounts, promotions, and credits.

Flat-rate accounting with IP-based services will not survive. In order to implement usage-based accounting, multiple data sources should be considered that include security servers, routers, applications, and all other components that have something to do with IP packets. This process determines the rates, depending on the application and on the resource. In many cases, this process is embedded into mediation solutions.

Principal functions are as follows

- Apply service rates to usage
- Apply negotiated discounts
- Apply rebates
- Process incomplete CDRs

■ Observe customer behavior

■ Identify fraud

■ Select mediation solutions

Figure 4.8 shows the principal functions of the rating and discounting process, as well as its input and output connections to other processes and functions.

Table 4.10 identifies the information sources for this process. Table 4.11 shows the information output and the targeted processes.

4.7.1 Apply Service Rates to Usage

Once the customer record has been populated and the service activated, information about calls, events, or, in general terms, usage must be collected and billed. An event can be a usage-sensitive call or any customer-generated activity that must have a charge applied to it. A processing module with or without a mediation device is used to collect and format the information and apply an initial rate to each activity. The rated event is then guided to the correct service offering within the customer record.

Calls that are collected by the call-processing module are rated according to the type of call. Usage calls are rated according to a user-defined initial charge table. They are later rerated at the time of billing according to the customer's rate plan. Event calls such as access to online services or custom calling events are rated according to a user-defined table and may be rated at time of billing according to a service offering rate table.

The network operator can establish unique rating plans based on conditions within the call detail records (CDRs). Plans can be created to target, for example, geographic areas, specific call types, or specific calling patterns. Optional calling plans can then

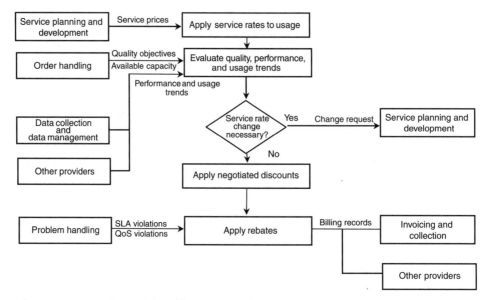

Figure 4.8 Functions of the call-rating and discounting process.

Table 4.10 Information Input for the Call Rating and Discounting Process

SOURCE OF INFORMATION	INFORMATION
Order handling	Customer record details, discounts
Service planning and development	Service prices
Problem handling	SLA violations, QoS violations
Other providers	Usage information
Network data management	Usage information

Table 4.11 Information Output for the Call Rating and Discounting Process

INFORMATION	TARGETED PROCESSES
Billing records	Invoicing and collection
Billing records	Other providers
Credit violations	Service quality management

be developed that specify charges or discounts that may apply to one or many master rate plans. The master rate plan is linked to the applicable optional plans and the message-processing module uses all the rating criteria to calculate the initial charge for the customer. The following steps are used to create single call-rating plans.

1. The network operator will assign a product code (a user-defined description) for the plan that the customer can subscribe to. For example, one plan may be created for domestic calling and another for international.

2. The network operator will populate the following tables to specify the call types that are to be included in the plan and how those calls should be initially rated.

Tables must be created to link all number codes and combinations to the carrier and serving area tables. The following rating alternatives are likely (SAVI98).

Event Rating

Customer-generated activities can be processed by the event-rating module. A client-defined table is utilized to apply a charge to the record. The table is message type specific; therefore, different record types can be uniquely rated.

Usage-Sensitive Rating

Instead of being distance or serving area sensitive, wireless or data products have traditionally been rated on a usage-sensitive basis. The usage-rating module is designed to accumulate calls that were generated during a billing period and to rate the calls based on client-defined criteria. This method of rating has been used for cellular, packet data, PCS, and satellite voice usage.

The customer structure should enable multiple service offerings for a single service user. Each service offering can be associated with its own set of rate plans, options, and promotions. When users populate the customer structure, they are presented with the product catalog that is specific to the service offering. A customer's call details are rated according to the rate plan and the details are stored with the applicable service offering. When billing generates the customer's bill, the call details are presented in order of service offering.

The attributes within the rate plan presentation specify the charging instructions for the accumulated traffic at time of billing. Usage limits are the conditions that the customer must satisfy in order to qualify for the discount levels. Customers can also specify whether the rate should be applied incrementally to the usage levels or retroactively to the usage. In a convergence system the network operator utilizes the same master file concept to establish rates for rate plans, billing options, equipment products, or promotions. If they select a rate plan as a product type, they are presented with the usage-rating presentation.

Usage Rating

The usage master file stores specifics on how to rerate accumulated usage at time of billing. Usually applications can support the following

- Rerating of usage for volume-sensitive plans
- Tapered pricing
- Threshold-level pricing
- Application of price overrides
- Calculation according to contract terms and monitoring against compliance
- Term commitment
- Volume commitment
- Combination of term and volume

Service Rating

The offering master file stores specifics on how to calculate charges for services. The offering types are rate plans, options (including different kinds of managed objects such as facilities and equipment), promotions, and service bundles. Rate plans can be single call-rating plans whereby a charge is applied to the individual call or a usage plan whereby the accumulated traffic is rated at time of billing. Usually applications can support the following

- Applying weekly, monthly, quarterly, or annual charges to a service
- Applying the charge at time of billing or calculating the prorated charges back to the activation, modification, or deactivation date
- Applying nonrecurring charges

- Applying discount attributes to the rate plan, for example, a plan utilizing direct dialed plan A for direct dialing, packet data plan B for packet data usage, and discount plan C to discount the usage based on total spent

- Including or excluding certain usage or call types from the discount plan, for example, a discount plan excluding calling cards during the discount process

Table 4.12 shows an example for a master rate table.

Service providers can create optional tables that define additional charging or discounting criteria that should be applied to the call at the time of rating. Any number

Table 4.12 Example for Master Rate Table

CALL PLAN ATTRIBUTES	DESCRIPTION	EXAMPLE OF VARIABLES	REQUIRED DATA ELEMENT ON THE CALL RECORD
Carrier	Network operator	ABC company	Carrier ID
Serving area	Originating geographical area	Country number ID code	Originating number
Destination	Terminating geographical area	Country number ID code	Terminating number
Products and services	Types of calls that should be included in the plan	Direct dialing, charge card, operator assisted	Call type (a unique identifier within the call record that can link the call to the product type)
Charge period	Time periods the plan is in effect	Day of week, start time, end time	Connect time Connect time
Mileage	Mileage bands that are used to assign call rates if the plan is to be distance sensitive	Miles, kilometers	Terminating numbers
Rates	Charge that should be assessed for the call	Initial increment length, initial increment charge, additional increment length, additional increment charge	Duration
Minimum charge	Criteria for assessing a minimum charge for a minimum duration for calls	Minimum duration, minimum currency amount, round up/ down flag, rounding threshold	Duration

of variations can be created for an attribute, and a specific rating criterion can be assigned to each variation. Optional labels can then be linked to the master rate plan. The design approach reduces keystrokes for service representatives as they select the master rate plan from an online catalog and do not have to select the optional plans.

Table 4.13 shows an example for an optional rate table.

Table 4.13 Example for Optional Rate Table

CALL PLAN ATTRIBUTES	DESCRIPTION	EXAMPLE OF VARIABLES	REQUIRED DATA ELEMENT ON THE CALL RECORD
Connect fees	Criteria for assessing a charge for the call connection.	Call type, connection amount, connection percent	Call type
Setup fees	Criteria for assessing a charge for setup.	Call type, setup charge, setup amount	Call type
Discount	The discount that should be applied to calls made during a specific time period.	Day of week, start time, end time, discount percent	Connect date, connect time
Holiday	The discount that should be applied to calls made on a specific date; the holiday table overrides any time of day discounts that are in effect.	Holiday code, date, start time, end time, discount percent	Connect date, connect time
Other line setup	The surcharge that should be applied to calls to a specific destination.	Holiday code, date, start time, end time, discount percent	Terminating number
Surcharge	The surcharge that should be applied to specific call type.	Surcharge code, setup amount, setup percent	Call type
International rating	The rate table that should be used to rate overseas calls; the terminating overrides can be used if the overseas calls are to be rated according to a third-party carriers table(s).	Terminating countries, terminating overrides	Terminating number

4.7.2 Apply Negotiated Discounts

One of the main benefits of a convergent customer care and billing system is that it allows cross-service discounting. This can be a useful marketing tool for service providers as they seek new customers and increased usage of individual and bundled services. There are many discounting options, including the following:

Time-of-day discount. This type of discount permits users to establish discounts based on the time period in which an event occurs.

Holiday discounts. This allows special discounts for usage on holidays (Christmas Day, Easter Sunday, Thanksgiving, etc.).

Rate plans and promotions. This can be associated with volume discount attributes that will be applied at time of billing.

Promotions. Customers can also receive proportions of their recurring charges in the form of whole or partial credits.

Enhanced holiday discounting. A separate holiday discount file can accommodate usage-based rating to complement or take the place of the generic-rating holiday discounts.

Longevity discount promotion. The network operator may reward long-term customers by offering discounted or free usage during, for example, their nth month of service.

Free/discounted usage promotions. Billing systems handle the application of discounts that provide free or distributed usage to specific areas. This is not a volume-based discount that should be assigned to customers via a promotion service offering. For example, this type of discount could provide clients with the ability to offer 60 free minutes or 20 calls at a specific discount to a specific area.

Frequent calling discounts. This enables network operators to offer plans that will provide discounts to frequently called areas, such as certain country or city codes.

Free terminating numbers. This file enables users to establish terminating numbers that can be rated as free.

Enhanced volume discounting permits service providers to offer discounts based on user-defined thresholds. Plans can be established to discount customers based on length of contract term or charge categories (weekly charge, monthly charge, non-recurring charge, cellular usage, packet data, etc.).

In order to take advantage of volume discounts, customers are expected to meet certain criteria, which include total amount spent, total minutes of use, total number of events, length of contract, and type of usage (cellular, 30 percent; fixed wire, 10 percent; etc.)

Tiered volume discounting is also possible with most billing applications. This type of discounting is now becoming increasingly popular as service providers look for methods to increase usage. The flexible discounting capabilities of billing applications ensure that operators will have sufficient system fluidity to consider change requests due to market demands and competitive advances.

4.7.3 Apply Rebates

Rebates may be granted when SLAs are not met. The problem-handling process provides the actual data on SLA status. SLAs are expected to include paragraphs on penalties for noncompliance. These paragraphs must be interpreted and quantified by this function. Results are forwarded to the invoicing and collection process.

4.7.4 Process Incomplete Call Detail Records (CDRs)

Error management will create cases based on parameters defined by users. Gap identification can be defined by both time points and sequence numbers. Duplicate call and duplicate batch identification can also be carried out by client-defined criteria. According to client-defined parameters at the validation, guiding, and rating stage, detail records that are in error can be dropped or put into a warning file. After a set number of recycle days, uncorrected detail records enter special procedures with an allocated error code for investigation and action, which can invoke manual adjustments or resubmission of the detail record. A fraud file is also contained in the error management module. Should a match be detected on any of the numbers involved or specified, the CDRs are automatically routed for special investigation. Figure 4.9 shows this process in some detail.

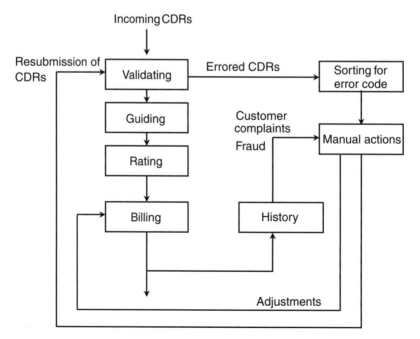

Figure 4.9   Process of error management.

4.7.5 Observe Customer Behavior

Raw data for the invoicing process can be utilized to observe customer behavior. This is usually not a real-time activity. In certain cases, raw data are transferred to data warehouses for further processing. Invoicing is the most obvious use, but also market research, sales, and marketing can take advantage of these raw data. Observations may include

- Changing usage patterns for customers
- Shifting usage between different services
- Usage patterns in correlation with time windows
- Usage patterns in correlation with the demography
- Traffic impacts of the growing number of teleworkers
- Openness toward new service deployments
- Acceptance of combined packages with other industries, such as airlines, car rentals, and hotels
- Impact of marketing actions on usage patterns

Traditional observations in the voice environment will be significantly extended by observing customer behavior in a multimedia environment. In such an environment, eCommerce targets include Web page visits, duration of visits, visits that complete business transactions, visits that break down, and statistics on the popularity of Web pages and Web sites.

The more eCommerce observations are targeted, the more observations and their evaluation move into near real time.

4.7.6 Identification of Fraud

The trend toward subscription fraud is one of the biggest concerns for carriers today. Although many carriers consider this type of fraud a form of bad debt, it is actually a form of fraudulent activity in which service is taken with no intention of ever making payment. The fraud applications that most telecom companies use are most often focused on the product sets from which the provider faces the most liability, such as calling cards and cellular services. With these services, the carrier assumes liability, releasing the end user from financial responsibility, which is similar to the liability a credit card company faces when fraud is discovered.

Fraud systems are, for the most part, driven by CDRs (MARS98). This basic informational billing component is the keystone of every known fraud system. What differentiates one fraud system from another is the speed of CDR delivery, analytical capability, alarm presentation, and analyst acceptance and action. Fraud systems have placed priority on the near-real-time detection of fraud events. They have begun to incorporate SS7 signaling, where available, to assist in the evaluation of calling records and to create a fraud alarm that activates as soon as possible. Some systems have initiated, as the launchpad from which to begin evaluation, profiling or signature alarms based on deviations from customer behavior patterns using CDRs. Fraud applications such as these are inadequate in two respects: They base evaluations on 12-hour time frames or less, and traffic must first flow across the network. In both instances, the fraud applications are reactive; a call event must first occur. Because most carriers take only a reactive approach to fraudulent activity, the picture is incomplete. Most fraud systems are phone number based. All evaluations occur in the testing of one number, whether it is a calling card number or a billing number. The systems do not take into account a wider customer base. To take a proactive approach to fraud, carriers also must make use of the information they acquire simply to bill a customer for a service or services. The following entries may be considered in fraud management

- Name and address
- Billing phone number
- Additional phone numbers (wireline and wireless)
- Promotional or plan codes
- Service types (card, pager, dial tone, personal 800, call forwarding/conferencing capabilities)

This is only a partial list. Service providers may also consider the information CDRs provide that could be used to fight fraud. For example, when the customer is evaluated at the point of installation, billing components can provide information on potentially fraudulent accounts well before call records are ever produced.

A fraud system is not just what service providers assume; it is more than a quick-and-run activity or a process based on information derived from call detail analysis and modeling. Although the dollar impact can be quite high if the service providers lose sight of the objective, their investigative talents must be expanded into other areas of the business. Fraudulent users perform their own testing to determine the thresholds within any real-time fraud system. This testing allows them the ability to surf just under the alarm thresholds and continue their fraudulent activity.

One method for detecting fraud includes expanding the time frames of CDR evaluation. Call accumulation over daily or weekly time frames can identify fraudulent trends that do not trip alarms in the real-time fraud systems.

Billing data consolidation allows fraud analysts to have a complete picture of a customer's traffic pattern in all types of services for all phone numbers and an average usage amount. These can be leading indicators for fraud that a real-time system would miss. But the problem with accumulated calls is that the volume of customers who might trigger alarms could quickly exceed the capacity to review the patterns. Another method is to incorporate product functionality and installation promotional practices into an evaluation process that can pinpoint potential fraud prior to service turn-up, calling card mailings, or check cutting. Sharing ideas prior to product or promotion release can identify shortcomings and provide the opportunity to either fix the problem, build a solution, or accept the inevitable, but at least everyone is aware of the problem prior to the release. The true benefit from all these methods is the expansion of communication between customer care department and customer.

Signal System 7 can also be utilized as a fraud management tool. An SS7 CDR is generated from messages flowing between originating and terminating switches. The monitoring system CDR generator reads call data, including call duration and called numbers, and produces a CDR. Alternatively, the CDR generator can provide information such as the type of call (ISDN, pay phone, etc.), the originating carrier, and whether a call was billed to a different number. To reduce link loading and increase the reliability of the SS7 network, the CDR generator must collect and correlate CDRs while relevant messages are being routed through the network. This means that all the call data needed to build a CDR may not reside at the same signaling transport point (STP) site. Consequently, STP site cross-triggering, filtering, and searching/matching must be integrated into the CDR generator.

Figure 4.10 shows an example of an SS7-based system for fraud management (BLAC99). The system shown is a rule-based system that looks for suspicious calling patterns and generates prioritized fraud alerts when a match is detected.

The CDR generator can be programmed to build call records for suspicious calls to known or high-risk destinations or from a particular calling number. Its programmability enables fraud center managers to detect new types of fraud or changing fraud patterns.

The CDRs are passed to a programmable detection and analysis engine, which matches the calls against known suspicious calling patterns to generate fraud alerts. The detection function is based on comparing the CDRs with a variety of lists and thresholds. The lists are dynamic and are usually maintained by the system adminis-

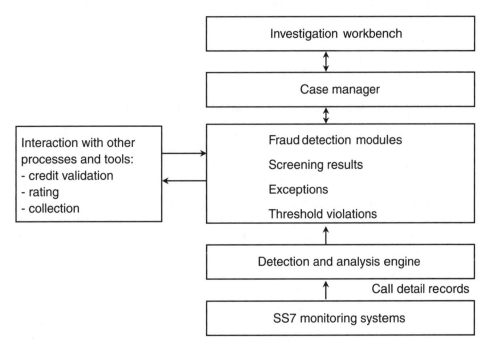

Figure 4.10 SS7-based fraud management system.

trator or fraud center manager. These could include lists for hot destinations, high-risk accounts and hot numbers. In addition, the lists could be used to separate customers into profiled groups. For example, a list could monitor all subscribers who have rented their houses to students; another could monitor all new subscribers during their first month of service. An important list is the exception list, which rejects CDRs from customers who have legitimate reasons for making calls to suspicious destinations. Since calling numbers on this list will never produce alerts, it is important that this list be well managed and kept up to date. Each list has an associated set of thresholds based on call volume or duration. Typically, the thresholds will include factors such as single call duration, aggregate call duration, and number of calls within a specified time period. When a CDR passes one of the thresholds on the list, an alert is generated.

The modules for generating, detecting, and analyzing CDRs are programmed by the fraud detection modules, which are customized for particular types of fraud—for example, direct-dial fraud or pay phone fraud. One advantage of this approach is that new fraud modules can be added as different types of fraud emerge, without changing the system's underlying architecture.

The alerts are supplied to the case manager, who allocates a value to each alert. This value is based on parameters configurable for each different type of call (long-distance, international, etc.). Each alert is attached to a case based on a key such as the calling number. If a case does not exist, then a new one is automatically created. Each case is assigned a value based on the aggregate values of the individual alerts, an approach that furnishes fraud investigators with a prioritized list of cases. All of the cases, case alerts, and call details are stored in a relational database.

In a typical fraud center, the fraud investigators usually begin by using filters in the investigation workbench to look for new cases or cases with new alerts. An investigator will use the data provided by the system, which is normally supplemented by information delivered from other business systems, to determine whether the case warrants further investigation. Many times the investigator will use the search capability of the system to look for similar active or closed cases.

On other occasions, the fraud manager will talk to customers and check whether they have made a certain number of calls within a certain period of time that accumulate high bills. If the likelihood is high that the customer doesn't intend to pay the bill, services should be terminated quickly before losses accumulate.

For organized call-sell types of fraud, the job is to collect as much information and evidence as possible on the call-sell operation. This will usually involve working closely with law enforcement agencies to close down the operation and prosecute the criminal act.

When service providers start to use real-time alerts, they have to examine the other procedures and processes around real-time fraud management. This usually involves working with other groups in the company to ensure that the time advantage gained from a real-time system is not lost elsewhere in the process. In some cases, business processes may be absent or confused, so consulting and business process establishment or reengineering may be required.

Although there is no ultimate solution for fraud, using a real-time, SS7-based fraud management system offers a number of significant advantages over systems that use billing records, including the following:

- Suspicious calls are reported while in progress.
- Fraud alarms and call history are available in real time.
- Information is taken directly from the call control protocol.
- The SS7 protocol is standardized and independent of switch type.
- The SS7 network is resistant to hacking.

These advantages can help operators significantly reduce their fraud losses and increase customer satisfaction and retention, which benefits their performance and profitability.

4.7.7 Selection of Mediation Solutions

Mediation is straightforward in circuit switched voice environments. The switches generate CDRs that are periodically provided by the switches for processing. With packet switched services, and first of all with IP applications, mediation is getting more complex. The mediation application is expected to correlate multiple information sources to generate an IP detail record (IPDR) that may be completely different from the CDRs. In these particular cases, mediation is a great help in offloading both the data collection and rating functions. Scalability is much better when the right mediation application is deployed.

There are multiple alternatives:

- The mediation application concentrates on data collection and formatting; in the case of IP, it also concentrates on the correlation of collected data, but does not offer rating and billing functions.
- In addition to the first alternative, the mediation application does support rating, but no billing features.
- The mediation application is expected to offer full functionality, from data collection through correlation, from rating to billing.

The ultimate decision may depend on factors such as how many different voice switches have been deployed, how many different IP-related data sources exist, and whether the service provider owns a customizable billing application.

4.8 The Invoicing and Collection Process

This process encompasses sending invoices to customers, processing their payments, and performing payment collections. In addition, this process handles customer inquiries about bills and is responsible for resolving billing problems to the customer's satisfaction. The aim is to provide a correct bill and, if there is a billing problem, resolve it quickly, with an appropriate status report to the customer. An additional aim is to collect money due to the service provider in a professional and customer-supportive manner. Some providers offer invoicing and collection functions for other providers as a service.

In order to analyze customers, customer data and billing data should be combined. Trends can be recognized that help to make decisions about future services and telecommunication products. The main goal is to avoid customer churn. If the requirements are determined by market segment—such as private households; tele-workers; small, medium, and large business customers—new customers can be acquired rather than losing existing ones. The analysis is complex and includes customer expectations, product portfolios, pricing, and willingness to pay.

The actual billing database has four principal segments:

- *Product/service data.* Products, packages, usage, and purchase date
- *Customer data.* Address, gender, payment type, customer spending, start data, and credit rating
- *Historical data.* Payment history, products ordered, products canceled, and term of contract
- *Call detail records.* Time of call, call destination, call origin, length of call, and number of calls

This process coordinates all the functions responsible for updating the data. This is not a trivial task, because several different organizations are in charge of these data.

The principal functions include the following:

- Creation and distribution of invoices
- Bill presentment
- Collection of payments
- Handling of customer account inquiries
- Debt management
- Wholesale and retail billing
- Billing on behalf of other providers
- Analysis of customer behavior
- Relationship management

Figure 4.11 shows the principal functions of the invoicing and collection process, as well as its input and output connections to other processes and functions.

Table 4.14 identifies the information sources for this process. Table 4.15 shows the information output and the targeted processes.

4.8.1 Create and Distribute Invoices

Invoice format applications are usually custom designed to meet customer-specific marketing preferences as well as regulatory requirements. Also, in-country and in-

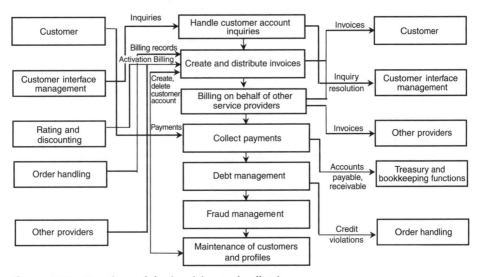

Figure 4.11 Functions of the invoicing and collection process.

state regulations can be considered for representing the invoice as a legal document. At a minimum, the invoice should support the following

- A system-generated invoice number
- A summary or legal remittance page in the legal language of the country
- A remittance stub to enable account payments to be made at a bank or by check

Table 4.14 Information Input for the Invoicing and Collection Process

SOURCE OF INFORMATION	INFORMATION
Customer	Payments
Customer interface management	Inquiries
Order handling	Create, delete customer accounts; establish desired bill data; activate billing
Other providers	Billing records
Rating and discounting	Billing records

Table 4.15 Information Output for the Invoicing and Collection Process

INFORMATION	TARGETED PROCESSES
Invoices	Customer
Inquiry resolution	Customer interface management
Accounts payable, receivable	Other providers
Accounts payable, receivable	Treasury and other financial functions

- Numbers to call for customer service
- Invoice messages at the summary level and at the current account detail level that supply the customer with supplementary information
- A breakdown of taxes
- A list of account payments
- A list of account and service location adjustments
- A summary of charges for each service location, detailing the usage, recurring and nonrecurring charges, and adjustments for each service (packet data, switched data, frame relay, others)
- A statement of charges if the customer's preferred method of payment is credit card or bank debit, which will be stamped "do not pay, the amount due will be transferred to your credit card or bank account"
- Page n of n numbering to aid in customer contracts
- Item numbers assigned to each call detail

Printed call details, if required and paid for, should include the following

- Date and time
- Called number
- Calling number
- Call type (direct dialed, calling card, etc.)
- IP address if VoIP
- Duration
- Method of rating (minutes, distance, number of pulses, etc.)
- Discounted amount
- Net charge for the call
- Call detail subtotals for each telephone or IP number that is linked to a service offering
- Optional call details for packet data, frame relay, ISDN, xDSL, and other services

A facility to tailor printed call details as governed by data protection requirements should also be considered and implemented. Usually, billing verification is likewise expected to be supported. Such an application has built-in edits and checks to ensure the accuracy of the invoice. This includes autobalancing routines as well as online data control and bill images that can be verified prior to the printing step of the billing process. There are separate routines to ensure that the billing inquiry screens, the account balance screens, and the printed bills are in balance. This application also ensures that the general ledger reports are in balance with the charge fee.

Billing packages are expected to collect CDRs from multiple switch formats. Data modeling can be performed specific to switches. The collection method and frequency are negotiated on a per-client basis. Usually, the following options are under consideration

- Real-time data transport
- Tape/cartridge transport
- Client-defined transport frequency
- Transmission type identification
- Immediate notification to verify receipt of transmission
- Gap identification (time points, sequence numbers)
- Duplicate call identification within batch
- Duplicate batch identification
- Data element editing and error identification

During mediation, original CDRs are converted into the format of the billing application. After editing, the original record and the converted record are stored in special processing files. User-defined data elements may be extracted and stored in special files to assist service representatives in responding to customer queries. The raw data may be used to generate traffic analysis reports.

Billing data may be useful for many areas besides billing. For instance, billing reports may summarize the following items

- Accounts receivable
- Revenue by rate plan
- Taxes by jurisdiction
- Trend analysis
- Account activity
- Activity by service
- In/out collect
- Cycle comparison

Not only batch, but also ad hoc reports may be extremely useful. These reports may include

- Account status
- Equipment inventory
- Network performance analysis
- Payments overview
- Staff productivity
- Sales activity
- Prepaid summaries

- Aged unbilled call detail records
- Number of adjustments made
- Pending orders due to incomplete provisioning
- Marketing analysis

Technically oriented reports are also useful for trunk and route analysis, including traffic volume summaries, volume by directions, blocked routes, and the identification of underutilized facilities and equipment.

For service providers that cover large geographical areas and multiple tax jurisdictions, assigning correct tax jurisdictions is very important in determining the right rates and correctly reporting and disbursing tax revenues. Postal code identification is a good start, but up-to-date tax rates by jurisdiction are also necessary. The customer database is the right place to maintain this information. Taxation may become an area with great savings potential for both service providers and customers, especially in the United States and Europe.

4.8.2 Bill Presentment

Billing applications should guarantee invoice information according to customer-preferred media. As an enhancement, the customer can choose to receive the invoice in a medium other than the traditional paper offering (for example: diskette, CD-ROM, EDI, EDIfact, or eCommerce). The customer will always receive at least the summary (remittance) page of the invoice on paper.

The output of the process is defined according to the customer's specific requirements. Typical billing options are as follows:

- Generate a paper invoice along with optional telemanagement reports.
- Copy billing data to tape, cartridge, or CD-ROM.
- Transmit billing data to a fulfillment or clearinghouse.
- Transmit billing data to a customer-defined database.
- Produce invoices in the language of choice.

Billing applications are also expected to support the creation of a customer bill on demand. The customer defines the business rules for generating an on-demand bill (e.g., immediately after the service has been finalized, when the customer exceeds a predefined credit limit, or at user request). The customer will be linked to the next available billing cycle and the invoice generated as part of that bill run.

A special billing cycle is also available to run on a daily basis if the customer does not wish to have these accounts included in standard bill runs or if a billing run is not scheduled. This billing cycle will only process accounts in the on-demand request file. The unbilled call details are available online at the conclusion of the message-processing run. Therefore, the current account balance of the customer, including unbilled calls can be compared to the credit limit.

Electronic bill presentment and payment (EBPP) is becoming an important marketing tool. Increasingly, service providers and billing managers are realizing the powerful

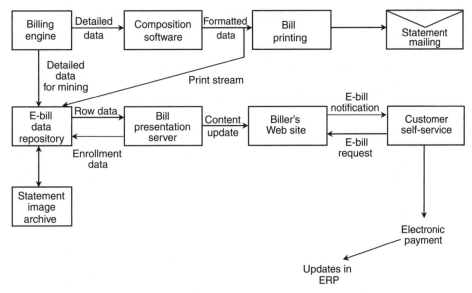

Figure 4.12 Electronic bill presentment and payment process.

role electronic bill presentment and payment may play. Before deciding about a product, service providers are expected to answer the following questions:

- What capabilities are the most important to the business plan?
- What do customers expect?
- Which software products offer the functionality and the flexibility to address these needs?
- What are the selection criteria—platform, features, price, licensing policy, etc.?

Figure 4.12 shows the process for EBPP. EBPP is the practice of delivering bills electronically and getting paid the same way. In most cases, EBPP is employed as a replacement for more traditional paper-based billing and the Internet is utilized as the distribution channel.

The process has several distinct steps. The first step is to enroll payees, which generally works like any other online enrollment or registration process. Systems must notify enrolled payees of bills, present the bills themselves, and process the payments. Behind the scenes, however, products must first extract the billing data for enrolled payees from existing accounting systems and provide tools to design the online presentation of bills. It is a complex process, and no single tool supports all the necessary steps.

EBPP has great potential to save costs and generate revenue. However, two major obstacles must be overcome first: Bill payers will have to change their behavior and organizations will have to make the investment required to bring EBPP services to market. Organizations contemplating an EBPP implementation should be aware that there are a number of potential benefits. The following are the most significant (FLYN99).

Savings on paper and postage. Billers can save as much as $1 per bill by converting a paper-based transaction to electronic. For companies with customer bases that range in the hundreds of thousands or even millions, the potential for savings is significant. But these savings are not likely to offset the initial investment for a long time. It takes time until a substantial number of customers accept this way of presentment and payment.

Improved customer care. Studies indicate that Internet users tend to have higher education levels, higher income, and higher levels of discretionary spending. Consequently, people likely to use EBPP services are profitable customers. With consumers increasingly able to choose providers as a result of deregulation in the utility and telecommunications industries, companies have been looking for ways to improve customer service, find other revenue-generating activities, and reduce customer churn. EBPP is very helpful in these areas. For business customers, EBPP can add a great deal of value by providing online analysis results. Bills can be segmented by department for bill-back purposes, which is very important for B2B applications. An EBPP site can also enhance customer service by providing related functionality such as fraud detection and analysis, provisioning, and dispute resolution.

Better cash management. Many customers think EBPP would negatively impact cash flow because it enables bill payers to hold onto a payment until the very last minute. Actual experience contradicts this, indicating that bill payers pay, on average, a few days sooner than with paper-based bills. Online billers can also offer customers the option to automatically schedule payments for a recurring bill. An e-mail can notify the customer that a billed amount will be automatically debited from their checking account or credit card on a specific date, which is similar to a direct debit. To make this more acceptable to the customer, the e-mail notification could contain a hyperlink to a Web site where the customer could view bill details, reschedule the payment, or cancel it altogether. Because the customer is never more than a click away from full control over the payment process, it is much more acceptable than a direct debit. For the biller, cash flow is improved because scheduled payments are almost never changed.

Faster and cleaner remittances. Electronic payments replace the error-prone process of inputting, processing, and reconciling paper-based payment transactions. Electronic payment transactions can be aggregated by an EBPP server and processed by the biller's bank at low costs. Many EBPP systems can also generate credit card payments via third-party service providers. Note, however, that third parties charge for initial deployment and for the transactions executed. And billers can still expect charges from their own bank when credits arrive at their account. It is easy to implement, but transaction fees can be as high as 3 percent of the value of the transaction.

Cross-selling and upselling revenue. EBPP can be a revenue-generating opportunity. EBPP can enable the kind of interactive one-to-one marketing that is not possible with paper bills. The bill itself contains information that can be used for targeted promotions. The bill amount and the customer profile may be matched, and a special advertisement may be included into the attachment with the bill.

Service providers and customers should be critical in selecting their EBPP solution. Important questions to ask or include into RFIs and RFPs are (FLYN99):

- Where can a live EBPP site be found?

- Do customers actually receive and pay their bills via this site?

- How is enrollment and registration handled?

- How are payments handled?

- Does it support Account Clearing House (ACH) and credit card transactions?

- Does it let customers schedule automatic payments?

- Is e-mail notification supported? If yes, what trigger is used?

- How does the system interface with other systems?

- Does it support Open Financial Exchange (OFX) for integrating with consolidator services?

- Does the system convert existing billing streams to HTML or XML? If so, is this conversion static or can the bill be dynamically reformatted depending on the user's profile, preferences, or some other parameters?

EBPP is an emerging area, about which both service providers and their customers should be patient. EBPP is usually embedded into interactive customer care (ICC) solutions.

4.8.3 Collection and Revenue Assurance

Credit verification applications assign each customer a credit classification when the account is created. Based on the account receivable amount and the credit class parameters, bill collection applications will automatically determine whether the account should be assigned to a credit controller. The applications will then populate the credit controller/collector work queue with specific account details.

Each customer is assigned a credit classification when the account is created. The credit classification master file stores the client preferences regarding collection action for each risk category. Typical values in the master file are:

- Should this credit class go to collections/credit control?

- What credit limit and credit days should this account be assigned?

- How many days after the account is in the collector queue should the supervisor be notified?

- Should the application automatically upgrade and downgrade the amount based on payment habits?

- What credit control steps should the system process and how many days should elapse between steps? The valid steps are phone call, letters, suspend service, deactivate service, apply security deposit, assign to a collection agency, write off account.

Based on the account receivable amount and the credit class parameters, the application automatically determines whether the amount should be assigned to a collector and if so, which one. The application will then populate the collector work queue with account details. The collector can view the collection history, account/service details, the payment history including postdated checks, current or previous promises to pay, the current collection/credit control status, and future steps that the application would carry out for account credit control and the timing of each step.

The collector then interacts with the customer and carries out the appropriate actions, including modifying the type of step and timing of steps that the application should take in the future. Supervisors have their own queue that is used to review the work of collectors within their workgroup. The collection application is entirely user maintained and provides clients with a valuable work tool to ensure that customer segments are treated correctly, that bad debt is controlled, and that the cost of collections is minimized. A sample list of collection application functions might include the following items

- Automated assignment, credit control, and dialing of accounts based on account profiles
- Automated letter generation for overdue accounts
- Setup of minimum values per credit classification for collection steps to be initiated
- Amendment of a credit limit for an individual account
- Suspension and reset of collection steps and timing
- Ability to enter promises to pay with automatic resumption of collections if payment is not received
- Automated account notation for overdue accounts
- Automated calculation of interest charges
- Automated assignment of accounts to collection agencies
- Automated write-off of account balances based on user-defined criteria
- Automated and manual escalation of exception items
- Reporting of overdue accounts by collector, agency, and managers
- Reporting of day's sales outstanding
- Automatic disconnect or suspension, direct connect to collection agency, or automatic reconnection if the service activation module is in use
- Online function to amend collections letter text
- Online function to alter collections and timing for each credit classification

Usually, invoice formatting, invoice presentment, and collection are supported by the same billing application.

Prepaid services are becoming popular in many countries. This simple process is as follows:

1. Customer payment is confirmed in various forms by the service provider.

2. Service is activated by using tokens or other forms of confirmation.

3. The service may be used until the payment limit is reached.

These cycles may be repeated as many times as the customer is interested in using the existing services.

Customer administration may be handled by using names or without using names. Both alternatives have benefits and disadvantages. In the case of nameless customers, proof of payment is by phone card or token. Service providers don't need to maintain customer data, and there is no risk of a negative balance. However, there is likewise no information about the customer, making marketing and new service creation very difficult. Another drawback is that customer satisfaction may be severely impacted by theft. Web access can be helpful for inquiries about actual balances and about services.

When customers are identified, valuable customer data can be maintained. Losses due to theft may be reduced as well. However, customer account data must be maintained in the customer database. Also, authentication is expected to be supported, and, in addition, more payment alternatives should be offered to customers. Web access can be useful for token activation, to get detailed billing data, and to activate payments.

Figure 4.13 shows a simple structure for supporting prepaid services, in which the customer database and the billing application are connected to each other. The billing application is supposed to give permission for use, activate and deactivate services, feed data to the interactive voice response to communicate with the customer, exchange information with the token administration system, process billing records in real time, and provide billing information for Web access. An additional service

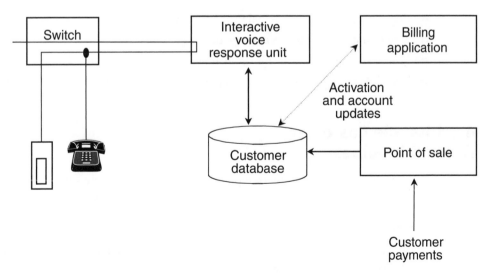

Figure 4.13 Prepaid services.

management module (not shown) may be separated from the billing application and be responsible for authentication and permission management on the basis of actual account status.

Providers of prepaid services distinguish themselves and their products by the flexibility they have in enhancing and changing services. This manifests itself in the actual scripting of the call, where private branding, promotional messages, access to other services, and voice mail may be used to distinguish one type of card from another. In addition, the call-rating database must allow for special rating methods, card activation and expiration schemes, recurring charges, restricted calling times and numbers, service access codes, and call-routing capabilities. These capabilities pay back the initial investment many times over. The prepaid centralized database should be able to rate calls coming from any switch location in real time, which is very important when prepaid customers are entitled to use multiple services. If prepaid administration is centralized, fraud management is easier to implement.

In summary, prepaid solutions have the following benefits:

- Service providers don't need to bother with payment collection.
- Customer administration is simple.
- Selling tokens can be handled by collaborating with other industries, such as banks, gas stations, or certain shops.
- Rating and pricing of services is simple.
- Besides Web access, actual billing data can be reported using various report generation packages.

However, the following requirements must be met by prepaid systems:

- Tight integration between the billing and the technical system supporting prepaid services
- Real-time processing of actual usage and billing data
- Safe technology for token management
- Proper security solutions for protecting customers and their tokens
- Life-cycle management of tokens (new, distributed for sales, activated, deactivated)

4.8.4 Handle Customer Account Inquiries

As a result of invoices and invoice presentment, customers may submit inquiries. This function is in charge of handling these inquiries, which are usually manyfold and include questioning items on the invoice, challenging items on the invoice, and communicating a demand for changes on the invoice.

Simple questions can be answered easily. Complaints about items on the invoice may by necessity involve technical areas that initiate an in-depth investigation that would include checking the original CDRs, looking for gaps in the CDRs, looking for healing errored records, looking for switch problems for the time frame relevant to the complaint, and checking on fraud for the numbers under investigation.

Service providers are expected to act fast and professionally. The actual number of pending complaints is an important benchmark.

4.8.5 Debt Management

Debt management is a financial function that is not necessarily integrated into this process. It assumes a tight connection with enterprise resource planning (ERP) applications. In most organizations, debt overviews are electronically forwarded to treasury processes to initiate further steps.

Billing data are useful for revenue assurance as well. Revenue assurance tools can handle the following functions:

- Verify new rating and charging plans.
- Perform comprehensive call audits.
- Summarize error reports by cause, such as rejects, unguided usage, unbillable calls.
- Analyze trends by customer segments and cycles.
- Verify bills before presentment.

Revenue assurance can be further supported by the following:

- Identifying, containing, and correcting billing errors.
- Ensuring accuracy, validity, and completeness of revenue transactions.
- Ensuring that all revenues are identified, reported, and understood in real time.
- Providing a trustworthy bill to the customers.

When done properly, debt management handles fewer events.

4.8.6 Wholesale and Retail Billing

Using the same billing application for both wholesale and retail billing can present a challenge. The software system must support differing business needs, business drivers, and network architectures. In addition, it must balance different invoice formats, account structures, customer access, reports, taxation, usage guiding, collection capabilities, rate plans, reconciliation methods, and so on (DANC99).

Consumer demographics and expectations for wholesale and retail services vary greatly. A wholesaler may have 40 to 50 large customers, while a retailer's customer base may encompass thousands of consumers. Moreover, while the charges are in the low hundreds for a retailer's customers, they may reach thousands of dollars for a wholesaler's customers. These different service expectations and functionalities must somehow be considered in the billing applications. To illustrate, existing retailers entering the wholesale market may assume that they can simply use their traditional retail applications to support their new business. However, while traditional retail applications may very well generate the wholesale invoices and enable customer service representatives (CSRs) to answer simple customer inquiries, they may not efficiently or cost-effectively meet the service provider's actual wholesale business objectives.

Specifically, most traditional retail billing applications support charge amounts with only two decimal digits. But database services may require rates that contain up to four decimal places. The wholesaler that maintains a caller name database and offers that service to other service providers must have a billing application that can define and maintain this service. Additionally, typical wholesalers use individual-case-basis pricing for a large percentage of their customers, so their billing applications must be able to efficiently support special pricing for each customer. While a retailer probably places more emphasis on an application that supports global, mass pricing updates, a wholesaler needs a simple and rapid way to make individual customer care updates. This is critical in many situations in order to avoid customer churn. For a retail service provider, the ability to offer promotions, such as "buy one, get one free" or "purchase local and long-distance service and get Internet access free," is critical. This type of packaging is not crucial for wholesalers, but the ability to provide tiered and stepped volume and contract-based discounts is. A wholesaler must be able to discount based on term of contract and committed usage (revenue, minutes of use, packets, and so on), and to discount not simply on the current month's activity, but also on aggregate usage over months and even years.

On the financial side of the business, retail applications typically have more demanding requirements. Wholesalers usually do not need automated credit checks and credit scoring to support their business, but these features are very critical to a retail provider. Additionally, since most wholesalers use account teams to support their customers, they have less of a demand for sophisticated collection modules. However, the wholesaler's application will need to be able to create standard financial, aging, and collection reports. Similarly, many billing and customer care applications offer a wide variety of payment options, such as credit card, bank draft, Web, and lockbox. Although this range of options is often very attractive for retailers, wholesale service providers may not necessarily need such a wide range, and if they are not careful, they could overpay for functionality they don't necessarily need.

The invoice is the service provider's principal mechanism for communicating with its customers. For wholesale customers, however, the invoice and its associated reports are vital for managing their business. The invoice is their single opportunity for reconciliation and network cost management. For example, in a wholesale environment, customers may be reselling service from a single source or from multiple service providers (DANC99). Whatever the case, these customers have to manage and reconcile the amounts they are charged with the amounts billed to their end customers. The analysis involved in this mission-critical function can be very complex, and an effective wholesale billing application is one that enables the process for the wholesaler's customers. Therefore, wholesale invoice information must allow customers to easily and accurately compare invoice information to financial records. In most cases, this means providing the information electronically and allowing customers to manipulate the data and customize it into layouts that match their own record formats and billing system outputs. For example, the billing application may produce reports or invoices that sort all communication services by product/service type. While this approach is certainly acceptable and logical, customers may record financial or billing information by customer or service ID. To simplify this customer reconciliation and analysis process, an invoice format is needed that allows the resorting of information on the basis of unique requirements. Another key item in the wholesale reconciliation process is allowing customers to tie the amount they are being charged for a given service or product to the amount they are billing their end users—or, more basically, enabling them to easily ensure that they are actually billing end users for all services and products for which they themselves are being billed. Doing this requires the creation of a common identifier that can quickly and easily tie the services together.

4.8.7 Bill on Behalf of Other Providers

Service providers may outsource billing functions to each other. In particular, competitive local-exchange carriers (CLECs) take advantage of this option. Considerations in this process are that the parties involved must share a customer database that includes sensitive information, they must use electronic data exchange, there must be mutual trust between the parties, they must charge a fair price for the service, and the processing of the bills for multiple service providers must be partitioned.

4.8.8 Analysis of Customer Behavior

Billing data are usually used by decision support systems to analyze customer behavior and usage trends. On the basis of these data, forecasts can be made and service providers can react properly to market trends. Determining seasonal and market trends helps to improve capacity planning. The analysis of contract status changes helps to avoid customer churn. Based on the analysis of usage volume and revenue generated by individual rate plans and service packages, the service portfolio can be fine-tuned. Major tasks include the following:

- Determine seasonal and market trends.
- Create or modify service packages and channel sales efforts toward the most profitable rate plans and service packages.
- Increase marketing efficiency and reduce maintenance time and costs by identifying obsolete or infrequently used rate plans and service packages.
- Quickly determine revenue distribution and evaluate trends.
- Analyze the effectiveness of marketing activities and sales campaigns.

Through usage reports, service providers can quickly determine patterns of usage for roaming partners. The results are backed with in-depth information on volume and trends, so service providers can negotiate better roaming agreements with certain key partners. Geographical areas can be identified for which roaming agreements still need to be signed in order to increase coverage in particular areas. Also, frequent roamers can be identified and special marketing programs developed for them.

On the basis of call data analysis, service providers can quickly react to network deficiencies and execute the following tasks:

- Refine network checks on a daily or weekly basis to address network errors in a timely manner.

- Help keep customers satisfied and improve customer retention; customer relationship management can be warned of problems early on and can be better prepared to deal with customer inquiries.

- Track volume for each customer switch.

- List numbers of completed and dropped calls per cell (wireless) and per customer.

Analysis applications may be structured by two criteria: level of data aggregation (high and low) and time nature of data (real-time and non–real-time).

When the level of data aggregation is low and is combined with real-time analysis, fraud management, quality of service, fault management, personalization, prepaid and upselling applications can be supported. When low-level data aggregation is combined with non–real-time analysis, capacity planning, customer profitability, lifetime value, intelligent debt collection, and campaign management applications can be supported. And finally, when high-level data aggregation is combined with non–real-time analysis, product profitability and customer segmentation applications can be successfully supported.

4.8.9 Relationship Management

Billing data can be successfully used for contract analysis, which is an important part of relationship management. By analyzing contracts and customer data, service providers can analyze customer behavior, make better forecasts, and be proactive about customer retention. Major tasks include the following:

- Determine which customers bring the most revenues.

- Quickly obtain an overview of the number of activations, deactivations, and other contract status types. If many contracts are in a pending state, for example, further research can be initiated to determine the reason, allowing a quick response before major bottlenecks occur.

- Determine the reasons behind a contract status change and create reports or charts on a regular basis for tracking purposes.

- Analyze what lies behind various changes and develop necessary measures to address specific issues and to improve company planning.

The analysis of contract deactivations includes quantifying and weighting such factors as nonpayment of bills, low usage, relocation, takeover, lost or stolen equipment, a switch to competition, coverage in the area, service affordability, roaming problems, number change, failure to locate customer, equipment damage, dissatisfaction with relationship management, end of trial, and dissatisfaction with equipment.

Beyond the financial aspects, electronic billing lets service providers use a strategy of iterative adoption for its online services and buys the provider time to sort out confusion about where all the different online customer care solutions fit. Companies are beginning to encourage customers to go online rather than sticking with paper-based bills and phone-based account service. They are concentrating on improving billing-related customer care immediately, gaining the added benefit of looking like Internet-savvy providers that are capable of attracting better customers, and, most important, they precondition their customers for the advantages of broader Internet customer care. Then when adoptions increase and the company is ready, the online billing solution can be extended into an integrated customer care (ICC) solution that starts out with a strong and enthusiastic customer base.

4.9 IP Billing Challenges and Solutions

IP billing is an unresolved issue at this point in time. Providers usually bill on the basis of flat rates, reserved bandwidth, or access speed to services. Corporate users like IP billing because it is not usage based. Overall, IP billing is not fair to users. Basically, IP networks are capable of offering secure, QoS-based service suitable for on-demand voice, video, application hosting, fax, secure remote access, content distribution, or just about any digital applications.

In the emerging Internet billing (IB) industry, a single industry standard has not established dominance as quickly as some industry players might have hoped. Billers, banks, IB service providers, and technology vendors have had to deal with several emerging standards. Open Financial eXchange (OFX) and Integrion Gold have surfaced, quickly followed by Interactive Financial eXchange (IFX). IFX is actually the convergence of OFX and Gold.

OFX formats the transaction and billing data in SGML. For IFX, the specification will be implemented entirely in XML. XML defines customized markup languages for many classes of documents, such as bills, purchase orders, and product catalogs. It can do this because it is written in SGML, the international standard metalanguage for markup languages. It is designed to solve many problems in existing Internet applications, most specifically the standardized description and interchange of data. It is intended to provide a single technical standard for describing documents such as bills. It can provide accurate description of billing data, such as subtotal, tax, and total, apart from defining how the bill looks. Such separation gives users a much more powerful and accurate way to search for information inside documents on the Internet or on intranets. Metadata also makes it possible for a document to be directed to and used by different workflow applications. A *document type definition* (DTD) specifies the contents for a particular XML document type, such as a phone or IP bill. In addition, metadata is useful in defining standard protocols for data exchange, as used in electronic commerce. The common denominator of future billing standards is expected to be based on XML.

One of the most important and fundamental concepts that anyone who wants to get into the business of delivering value-added services and content must understand is that there are many ways of structuring or rating consumption charges. Generally, rating schemes can be broken down into the following four categories:

Flat rate. This is currently the most common approach for generic Internet access, as well as paid content sites. Users pay a flat fee on a monthly or annual basis and get authorization to use the service or download as much content as they like. Flat-rate pricing has been used as a market share capture strategy, since it can be very attractive to customers. However, content and service providers realize that over the long term, such pricing can inhibit profitability. Users have no incentive to restrain their consumption, so the service provider's costs get driven higher and higher. Undifferentiated pricing also makes it easier for customers to compare service providers, leading to high churn rates.

Usage based. The most common alternative to flat-rate pricing is to bill customers based on usage. Usage may be defined in terms of time (as with a voice service) or traffic volume (as with site hosting services). Usage billing can also be done on a per-unit basis (i.e., every minute has a certain cost), a combination of flat rate and per unit (as with cellular service), a tiered basis (x cents per megabyte for the first 500 megabytes, y cents per megabyte thereafter), or any one of several other rating schemes.

Session based. This approach is more logical for streaming media and/or special net events. Rather than being charged for a given amount of time or volume, the customer is charged for a single session that may vary in length and volume depending on the particular content stream. Depending on the content provider's business model, customers may be able to buy several sessions for a single price, and then purchase additional individual sessions for another price. Several executions of the same net event may not incur additional charges for a specified duration.

Per incident. With this type of billing, the customer is charged based on the occurrence of a specific incident or user action, such as clicking on a particular hyperlink. This approach is particularly applicable to content purchases such as MP3s or e-books. It may also be applied by caching services to the hosting service provider clientele (i.e., per-hit pricing). Again, customers may be offered multiple incidents for one flat rate, with additional incidents at an additional charge, or they may be offered discounts on their nth incident. This approach is also used for measuring clicks per million for advertising.

There are many other parameters that can affect a content or service ratings scheme. It may be that a premium level of service is available for a certain price or for users of other linked services. Sometimes special pricing may apply to users who sign up by a certain date, while those who sign up later pay a different price. Sometimes geography may enter into the equation. Sometimes an individual user's affiliation with a corporation or other organization may affect pricing.

Anyone with a strong marketing background can appreciate how flexible such rating schemes have to be. Marketers often need to develop and offer new value packages to customers for promotional purposes—and they often have to do it very quickly. In other words, to effectively support their business objectives, marketers need a service-rating system that is highly dynamic and that allows new rating schemes to be implemented in near real time. The ability to rapidly activate and deactivate ratings schemes is a crucial capability for anyone who wants to successfully and aggressively market Web-based content or services.

4.9.1 Structure of a Billing System

Figure 4.14 shows a billing system structure with the rater in the middle. The rater operates at the core of the billing system. It accepts network transactions from the usage collection subsystem, assigns a price, and provides the rated transaction to the billing database. From there, account balances are adjusted and the records are stored for later use by the invoicing, reporting, accounting, and customer care systems.

There are two different types of billing. Selective or hierarchical schemes let ISPs bill back to specific users, departments, and individuals. One corporate account, for example, might have a virtual private network (VPN) billable to the IT department at headquarters, Internet access billed on a per-site basis, and Web hosting billed to individual divisions and departments.

Rate-based billing makes it possible to charge different rates for different IP services on a single invoice. Rates can also differ within a single service. Thus, guaranteed Internet access would cost more than best-attempt service. As long as a billing system can tap into the requisite sources of usage data, it should be able to deliver rate-based billing without much customization.

The difficult part for billing is to be able to offer information in real time to different ISPs and carriers. The Web can be useful by offering browser access to billing data.

4.9.2 IP Call Detail Records

There are no standards yet for IP usage-based billing. In voice environments, creating a bill means obtaining a log file of CDRs maintained in a Bellcore (now Telcordia)

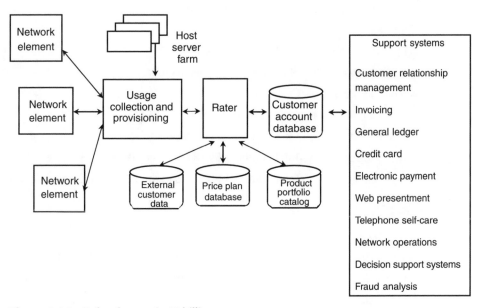

Figure 4.14 Role of raters in IP billing.

standard format on voice switches. The billing system reformats this data for use in invoices.

Table 4.16 summarizes data fields that may be required for usage-based billing for IP-based services.

Why can't it be done (yet) for IP?

For starters, voice calls are circuit switched; IP is a connectionless, packet-oriented protocol. This makes it more difficult to track traffic. And billing systems of service providers have to deal with only one type of service; ISPs want to charge different rates for a range of different applications. There is no IP CDR yet, which means billing packages cannot request usage data from network switches and be certain they will always get it in the same format. This is a serious problem, since Internet data are typically handled by several providers' networks. Without some uniform way to track traffic, there is no way for ISPs to exchange billing data or charge for carrying competitors' traffic. They can only charge customers a flat-rate admission fee at network entry points.

Table 4.16 Typical Usage Fields in an IP Voice Call

DATA FIELD	DESCRIPTION
Call ID	Unique call identifier
Call initiation date time	Time stamp of session initialization
Start date time	Time stamp when the session is connected
Duration	Duration of the session
Direction	Direction of the session
From IP address	IP address of the caller
To IP address	IP address of the destination
Incoming circuit ID	Calling phone number
Dialed number	Called phone number
Packets sent	Total number of packets sent
Packets received	Total number of packets received
Packets in error	Total number of packets in error (late, incomplete, corrupted, or otherwise useless)
Bytes sent	Total number of bytes sent
Bytes received	Total number of bytes received
Average delay	Average latency of all packets associated with the session
Delay variation	Peak transmission latency
Media type	Designates the service delivered

Making next generation, multiservices IP network a reality requires advances in IP security, quality of services, access technologies, and usage-based accounting, as well as an increase in bandwidth. Besides advances in technology, the commercial success of IP-based services requires robust and cost-effective business, operation, and network support systems (LUCA99A). Without them, the service providers cannot bill for application usage, content provided, or network resources consumed; quickly detect fraud; authenticate and authorize service usage; provision a voice, video, or SLA-based data service; support sophisticated credit structures such as prepayment and direct debit; or make profits.

IP-based services are expected to be priced by usage in order to be managed profitably. As such, bringing these services to market will require user-sensitive applications for provisioning, data collection, billing, reporting, and network management. Developing support systems optimized for advanced IP services is a considerable challenge. However, many suppliers of management applications address these issues. In particular, network elements and mediation systems can generate high-resolution usage information on a per-transaction basis. Likewise, network management and provisioning systems can configure the network in real time. Finally, billing, reporting, and other business support systems that can be optimized for IP-based services are beginning to appear on the market. The remaining challenge is, however, to develop and deploy interfaces between these various systems and applications in such a way that they can easily exchange usage, provisioning, and control information among themselves. In most networks, the fundamental unit of data exchange is the usage record, called a CDR (call detail record) by circuit switched service providers. But there are no CDRs yet available for packet switched services. Because an open, standard IP usage record does not exist, IP network elements and support systems cannot communicate cost effectively, thus creating a barrier to bringing next generation services to market.

Without a standard IP usage detail record, network elements and support systems are forced to develop proprietary interfaces and mechanisms to collect usage data. Considering a large number of IP applications and suppliers, there are certain serious challenges involved in individually and independently providing usage parameters (LUCA99A), as follows:

Inconsistent metrics. Network elements and mediation systems capture inconsistent usage characteristics for a given application or service. For example, in the case of IP telephony, one gateway or gatekeeper might record only basic information such as duration, called number, and calling number, whereas other gateways or gatekeepers might include time of day, codec used, and quality of service provisioned, as well as characterizing the network service delivered (e.g., in terms of drop rates, delay, and delay variation). Further, even if the same two network elements collect the same data, the meaning might not be the same. For example, does amount of data exchanged between parties include retransmission, protocol, or other overhead?

Proprietary access. Data structures that encapsulate the usage metrics are distinct for each network element and service type. Thus, a special filter needs to be written to interpret each usage type and network element type. Likewise, special interfaces will be needed, since each network element might have a different access protocol and handle security differently. Furthermore, each network element might capture usage information in real time or batch the data. This affects the degree of synchronization between the support and mediation systems and actual usage, as well as how long a given system might retain usage data without forwarding them to further processing or presentment.

Inconsistent provisioning. Each service provider defines service differently, so each has different provisioning requirements. For example, with SLAs or QoS-based services, a carrier might or might not guarantee availability, mean time to repair, drop rates, throughput, or network delay. Regardless of how a given SLA is defined, the network elements and management systems must be able to provision, collect, and represent the data consistently. Otherwise, a carrier will be bound to a given vendor and unable to mix and match network elements based on price, functionality, and performance.

The current proprietary environment requires that each support system develop, at considerable expense, interfaces to each network element as well as interpret the meaning of the metrics provided. Likewise, vendors and mediation systems must use their best judgment as to what usage data to collect, based on their vision of what providers might want to bill or report on. Given the complexity of the Internet services and the diversity of OSS/BSS/MSS requirements, such guesswork is not economical. In fact, many vendors distinguish themselves on these proprietary interfaces alone for competitive advantage in the market. A closed proprietary interface is not the answer. The IP industry needs a standard definition of IP-based services and related usage metrics that can be a common reference model for billing and other BSS systems, service provisioning, reporting, and usage collection. This common standard would eliminate the need to build costly interfaces to each network element or mediation system or between support systems, provide standard usage metrics for vendors to collect and export for a given service, specify the precise meaning of each usage metric, specify how long network elements need to retain usage information, facilitate provisioning, and allow billing systems to expose usage metrics in their rating interface consistently.

Characterizing the usage metrics for IP service is a difficult effort. Even the most basic IP service, e-mail, has a number of meaningful cost components for each transaction (size, distance, time of day, delivery options, disk storage for queued mail, and POP3 queries). Real-time services such as voice and video substantially increase the difficulty, as they require a far more complex set of metrics to characterize the service and the quality delivered.

The purpose of the IP detail record (IPDR) initiative is to define the essential elements of data exchange between network elements and operation support systems. It will provide the foundation for open, carrier-grade IP support systems that enable next generation IP networks to operate efficiently and cost effectively. Following are the specific goals of this effort:

- Define an open, flexible record format (the IPDR record) for exchanging usage information between network elements or network management systems and mediation, operations support, billing, or other business support systems required by an IP-based service provider.

- Define essential parameters for any IP transaction.
- Provide an extension mechanism so network elements and support systems can exchange optional usage metrics for a particular service.
- Provide a repository for defined IDPR formats.

Work is under way to define prototype IPDR formats for common service and represent the usage in state-of-the-art encapsulation techniques such as XML. After the preliminary work is complete, the IPDR formats will be taken public in an industry-wide effort to reach consensus on IP service definitions, core usage metrics, and optional usage metrics. The IPDR formats will be published in a repository and evolved over time as needed.

4.9.3 Information Sources for IP Billing

Since there are no IP CDRs, all vendors cobble together usage data from a variety of sources, including remote monitoring (RMON) probes, Radius servers, Web server log files, and router software agents.

Data sources that may be used in collecting customer utilization of Web-based services for billing purposes include the following.

URLs and Site Logs

Any company that wants to implement pay-to-play content or services will rely heavily on the visitor activity data captured by their site. These clicks are already used extensively for assessing the effectiveness of site design, as well as for other business purposes such as advertising and referral fees. However, the simple capture of URL data is insufficient for effective Web billing. That's because the different elements of a URL can have very different meanings in a billing/business context. Data sources include the following:

Domain names. This first rung in the URL ladder is obviously critical in determining that a user has accessed a given site. For Web hosting services, the domain name indicates which hosted customer's meter is now running. Some eBusiness sites also create separate domain names for individual services or content areas.

File names and extensions. In contrast to domain names, file names and extensions allow providers to bill for specific content or types of content, such as video streams, MP3s, or PDF files. Each file type may carry a different price tag. Individual files of the same type may even be processed differently from each other.

Variables. Many sites give users the ability to enter some type of variable as part of their service or content request. A site offering information about various geographic areas, for example, might have "city" as one of its variables. Each time a new city is entered, another click on the billing meter might be required. Or users might be allowed to check several cities for one price. Or they might be allowed to search cities in their own state for free and be charged only for cities outside the state. Regardless of how the charges are specifically structured, such a variable is a distinct element in the utilization and billing formulas.

URI substrings. When the domain name, file name and extension, and any variables from a URL are eliminated, the *universal resource indicator* (URI) is still available. This substring may also help define what type of content or service a user has accessed. Again, this URI may be important to a hosting service that is billing a customer separately for different content/service areas. Or it may be used by the site's owner to differentiate a premium server or other value-added feature.

Infrastructure Instrumentation

Networked infrastructures are built with a variety of devices, such as routers, switches, firewalls, or load balancers. In addition to performing operational/transport functions, these devices also generate highly valuable site activity data. Such data sources include the following:

- NetFlow records network and application resource utilization.
- Radius log files provide access information on a continuous basis.
- RMON data adapters provide utilization data for various network layers.
- Proprietary and/or device-specific protocols may be used.

These data are extremely useful in determining who accessed what, and for how long and/or how much of it they accessed. Many device vendors and third-party developers are introducing powerful application-aware monitoring tools that can help value-added content and service providers more accurately track the consumption of infrastructure resources. An effective rating system must be able to tap into all of these various data types and flexibly translate them into the specific types of utilization parameters that each particular rating formula requires.

Network-Level Data

This type of data is most often used by *network service providers* (NSPs) and hosting, although it may also be applied to a variety of Web business models. NSPs use network utilization, such as 95th percentile, for rating. In addition, a given network service may be running on a specific UDP port number, or a certain protocol may have a specific utilization charge attached to it. In such cases, basic network-level data will also have to be captured and incorporated into the service-rating formula.

In order to support a particular business objective, these diverse activity metrics may have to be aggregated with great flexibility, precision, and speed.

With so many different information sources available, it is essential to know the source of a billing system's data. For instance, since Radius servers track who accessed a particular Web host and for how long, their log files can be valuable for billing—especially when tallying charges for Web server space. But Radius servers disclose only a portion of the picture; they can track access to Web servers, but cannot report on network utilization—how much bandwidth on a given IP connection was consumed by a particular application or end user. This sort of information is becoming important to providers as they start selling multiple IP services.

Network probes and monitors are another excellent source of utilization data. RMON1 and RMON2 probes can be stand-alone, embedded hardware, or software. These probes continuously measure LAN segments and bandwidth utilization by end user and by applications. They can report metrics on layer 2, layer 3, or even higher. Usually, the large amount of captured data causes problems for processing, as do the bandwidth requirements to transfer data from probes to the centrally located processing facility.

Web servers maintain logs that may be utilized to get applications and end-user-related metrics. Examples of such metrics are identification of the visitors, duration of the visits, frequency of the visits, and resource demand from the visits. Most of these metrics can be utilized as a basis for IP billing.

Routers and switches are also valuable sources of accounting information. Routers and switches from Cisco Systems, for instance, run NetFlow, a proprietary flow-monitoring utility that keeps tabs on packet activity. Most billing vendors can tap directly into NetFlow—module under IOS—data. Vendors of IP billing packages should consider other vendors as well. The principle of data gathering will be the same, but API support on behalf of the vendor is necessary.

In addition, the following techniques can be utilized to capture billing and performance data.

Diagnostic packets. This technique relies on dedicated devices that send probe packets along the same network path as the session traffic. A remote device reflects the probe packets back to the source, thus traveling a reverse network path. Assuming that the probe and session packets are treated equally by the network, the session's drop rate, delay, and delay parameters can be inferred based on the performance measured for the probe packets.

Device reporting. Many real-time applications rely on the Real Time Control Protocol (RTCP) to exchange observed network performance information between the source and destination. That is, the source and destination exchange the observed network drop rate, delay, and delay variation using RTCP. This allows the stations to adapt to changing network conditions. End-system data are accurate, but not always feasible to collect. For example, a provider might not be able to interface with the end system or gateway unless it owns the device. Likewise, it is difficult to manage the large number of interfaces required to collect such information.

RTCP analysis. Instead of integrating with the source and destination system, another approach is to monitor the network capturing RTCP messages. This method yields the same levels of granularity and accuracy as the device reporting approach, but does not require any special interfaces.

Probing. The probe approach uses special devices to watch every message that traverses the network. Thus, by locating probes at the ingress and egress points in the network, probes can measure with a high degree of accuracy and isolate drop rate, delay, and delay variation for a given session across the network under consideration. This approach is also called *semantic traffic analysis* (STA).

4.9.4 Internet Billing

The public, circuit switched voice network is not optimized to carry bursty data traffic, but rather predictable voice traffic. Voice calls, by nature, are best served by circuit switched architectures, as they are today. Voice call holding times are three or four minutes on average with predictable busy periods, and the voice network was designed with this in mind. The problem intensifies because Internet calls are an entirely different type of traffic; Internet calls, via dialup modems, last about 20 minutes on average, and connect times of an hour or more are common because users don't pay any additional cost for long Internet sessions.

There are different architectural approaches (FINEB98). These approaches involve detecting Internet traffic and routing it to a packet network via a network element, loosely referred to as an *access server* (AS), which connects the PSTN to an Internet transport facility or backbone. Several of the architectures use SS7 to control call detection and routing, and thus require a type of SS7 node called an *internet call routing* (ICR) node. This could be a stand-alone, add-on device, or an existing STP running ICR software. The key is that SS7, an existing voice network resource, lends itself to the type of detection and rerouting necessary to make these fixes work.

There are two basic alternatives. *Postswitch* architectures are most appropriate in situations where congestion occurs in trunk groups and terminating switches. *Preswitch* is best for cases where the ingress switch is itself overloaded.

The key to success for any of these architectures is detecting an Internet call, as opposed to a regular voice call. The first alternative involves intelligent network triggers. This means essentially that a database could be used to keep track of all ISP numbers so that when a subscriber dials in, the network can check the dialed number against the database, recognize the call as intended for an ISP, and route it onto a packet network for delivery to that ISP. An IN single number service could be used in a similar fashion, or perhaps a special service code, much like 800 or 900 numbers, could be created to designate ISP numbers. Any of these methods can be implemented, but today the IN trigger model is most widely used. The first three architectural alternatives offer solutions for postswitch, each relaying on an ingress switch to detect and reroute Internet traffic. The first alternative is relatively simple (see Figure 4.15; FINE98A). In this case, the ingress switch detects an Internet call, possibly using any of the proposed methods, and automatically routes it to an access server over a normal voice line or primary rate ISDN interface (PRI), and out to a public packet network or dedicated transport facility. Line interfaces, however, are rather expensive, are difficult to manage, and do not allow for detailed traffic monitoring. PRI interfaces can be managed, but it is unlikely that the PSTN could support such interfaces on a broad scale.

The second and third alternatives are more complex (see Figures 4.16 and 4.17; FINE98A). These architectures take advantage of the SS7 network by using an ICR node to provide the access server with signaling capability. Access servers actually act as modem banks and are basically not capable of SS7 signaling on their own. The ICR node, communicating with the SS7 network, informs the access server on which circuit a detected Internet call is coming in from the switch. Using an SS7 trunk interface

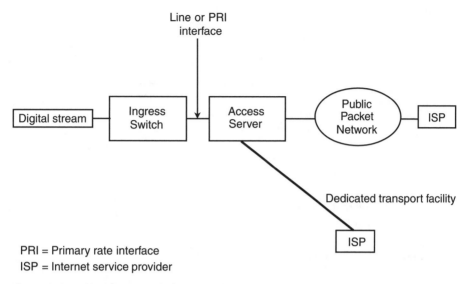

PRI = Primary rate interface
ISP = Internet service provider

Figure 4.15 Simple postswitch separation.

to the switch rather than a line or PRI, the access server can then grab that call and route it to the proper transport facility. An SS7 trunk interface is manageable, lends itself to detailed traffic monitoring, and should not create any problems if deployed on a large scale.

The third alternative could create a revenue opportunity for voice network operators. Because the access server provides modem functions, it is possible for a carrier to lease ports on the access server to ISPs. The ISP would then be freed from having to

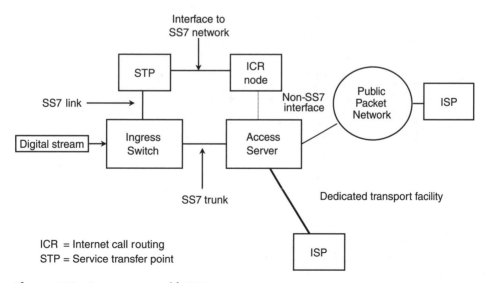

ICR = Internet call routing
STP = Service transfer point

Figure 4.16 Access server with SS7.

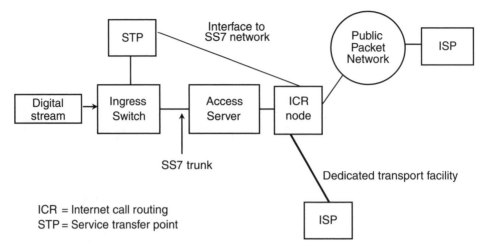

Figure 4.17 Intelligent access server with SS7.

maintain a modem pool and could lease a virtual presence in disparate areas without having to maintain a physical presence. It would also allow local exchange carriers (LECs) to monitor Internet traffic closely.

Preswitch architectures look basically the same as the postswitch solution (see Figure 4.18; FINE98A), except for one essential difference. In a preswitch architecture, a data switch is installed in front of a voice switch. Access nodes may be deployed for scenarios where ingress switches are being overloaded. In this scenario, an IN trigger in the ingress switch detects Internet calls and signals the preswitch to reroute them before they reach the ingress voice circuits. With this method, Internet calls never

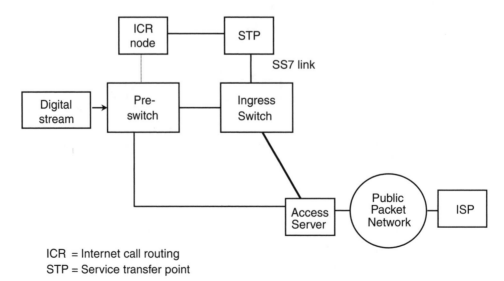

Figure 4.18 Simple preswitch architecture.

touch the PSTN. The problem with this approach is that installing the preswitch is extremely complicated and costly.

4.9.5 IP Billing Reconciliation

Today the majority of PSTN, private line, and Internet access traffic flows over multiple carrier networks. Intercarrier billing and bill reconciliation are based on time of voice usage or flat-rate private line leasing charges. CLEC reconciliation issues are typically with a single Regional Bell Operating Company (RBOC); international interexchange carriers (IXCs) reconcile with a single post, telegraph, and telephone (PTT) per country; and wireless carriers normally interconnect with a single incumbent local exchange carrier (ILEC) or IXC. Despite today's simplicity, rarely is there an intercarrier bill that is not challenged for accuracy. In a new IP area, carriers will be dealing with a large number of QoS metrics for multiple applications, hosting content, balancing bandwidth, distributing load, and so forth, which will require every IP packet processing session to be rated differently. If an IP carrier doesn't have a strategy for dealing with the complexity of IP carrier reconciliation, it will suffer business losses.

Public Internet services do not offer service-level agreements because carriers cannot guarantee quality of service to end users. In a new IP world, customers and carriers will want SLAs. Worse for the IP revolution, carriers cannot deliver on an SLA if they cannot measure QoS. Measuring QoS by a carrier will not mean that much to an end user if the carrier cannot validate what the user received. Users expect a service-level validation solution. This solution is complex and most likely expensive, because transparent measurement tools are required, some of them on the premises of the customer. Carriers will need compatible probes or agents in their own network, as well as their supplier's IP carrier network. Otherwise, how can a supplier support an SLA based on QoS if the carrier's customer cannot validate the QoS itself (LUCA99B).

In the IP-centric network future, users will have dozens, if not hundreds, of different kinds of IP carrier players and network services to choose from. Users and applications will have different QoS requirements, so some IP carriers will offer high-level QoS for enterprise, while VPNs and others will offer low-level QoS for inexpensive VoIP. Intercarrier bill reconciliation is something that happens months after the end-user billable event occurs. Furthermore, the data logged by the originating billing carrier is collected months before the billed terminating carrier receives it. For example, it takes approximately three months of ILEC switch access data to reconcile one month of actual usage. A carrier cannot go back and gather data for billing and rating after the fact. All kinds of new IP applications will be created on IP networks—but without an end-user billing and intercarrier settlement arrangement and an understanding by all of what data must be collected beforehand, these new applications will be just a hobby.

Revenue assurance practices for IP are either inadequate (looking for peaks in usage), too time consuming (overpayment to a carrier that is now in financial difficulties), or incapable of taking on next-generation fraud. The IP world is and will remain complicated, not only in terms of technology, but also in terms of regulation. For international service providers, this situation is even more complicated. This international environment is controlled by the World Trade Organization (WTO).

4.9.6 Micropayments

With emerging Internet services, service providers and merchants must deal with the question of charging small amounts to customer accounts. Individual billing for certain services, such as MP3 file downloading, directory assistance, listening to music, and purchasing scientific articles, is not economical. In such cases, the small amounts are aggregated for later billing. The basic model may be the same as with traditional billing solutions, in which delayed billing flags can be added to certain IP detail records. There are differences, however, when micropayment solutions include real-time customer identification, authentication, and credit limit surveillance.

Figure 4.19 shows a generic architecture for micropayment. The steps in the process are as follows:

1. The merchant activates the service.

2. A customer requests the service.

3. The customer is identified, and authentication and a credit limit check (optional) take place.

4. The customer is approved or rejected.

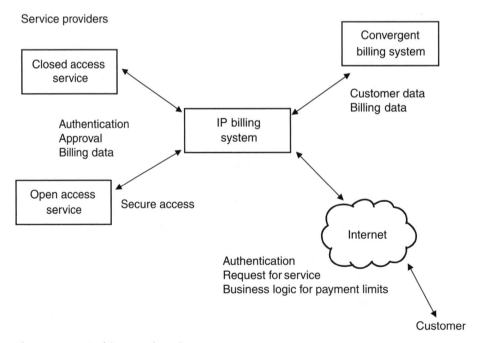

Figure 4.19 Architecture for micropayment.

5. Service fulfillment takes place.

6. A transaction record is generated.

7. The record is forwarded to the billing system.

8. The service is rated.

9. Account status is updated for the customer.

10. The customer is billed for the service.

The responsibilities are distributed to the IP billing systems, to the convergent billing system, and to the service provider merchant systems. Provider systems may open or closed; if open, additional access security solutions are required. Customers should be known to the service provider. If third-party systems are being offered, then customer information should be shared between the service providers and the merchants. Customer databases will most likely be maintained by the billing application of the service provider.

The IP billing system is expected to be responsible for downloading customer information from the master billing system, maintaining credit limit information on customers, maintaining service portfolios, documenting which customer is using what types of services, and approving or rejecting service requests issued by customers. The IP billing system can present customer bills via Web access. Consolidated billing records should be sent to the master billing application.

Service providers or merchant systems are expected to identify and authenticate the customer; forward this information to the IP billing system; create, activate, and provide the service as requested; and forward usage information to the IP billing system.

4.10 The Role of SS7 in Accounting

The FCC's rules provide several paths of entry into competition, and rulings have focused on terms and conditions within the following areas (BRYD97):

- Transport and termination of traffic exchanged by telephone networks
- Purchase of unbundled elements from existing local telephone networks by competitors
- Resale of existing retail telephone services

The rulings have generally benefited new competitors in the local telephone marketplace, including cable operators, CLECs, and long-distance carriers. Wireless providers, including cellular carriers and PCS providers, have also benefited significantly as their interconnection costs fall.

The main implications of these FCC rulings have been felt within the ILECs, particularly in the area of carrier access billing (CAB) systems. Most LEC billing systems were designed for an earlier, noncompetitive environment and require a major overhaul. They generally are not capable of accounting for the new ways the network is being accessed. So operators frequently impose flat-rate charges for wholesale interconnection and for enhanced services. They can't yet bill on a "pay for what you use" basis, which is fundamental to providing interconnection to network facilities and databases. Industry representatives are left to ask how they can gain compensation for competitive access, how they can account and bill for unbundled network components, and how they should charge for usage associated with resold lines. While these challenges will occupy the industry for some time to come, some important lessons can be learned from those who have tackled the issues head-on.

To access a complete customer base, all carriers must interconnect directly or indirectly with other carriers. As the dominant local loop provider, all ILECs must provide interconnection at any technically feasible point to other carriers requesting transmission of telephone exchange service and exchange access.

An area causing a lot of debate in the wake of the Telecommunications Act has been interconnection compensation. At stake is the level of charges competing carriers must pay the local phone companies to terminate calls on their monopoly networks. Debate over the financial model to be used for interconnection has ranged from "bill and keep"—an arrangement where no terminating charges are made—to full usage-based mechanisms calculated on a minutes-of-use basis. ILECs have been opposing this concept of "bill and keep," arguing that reciprocal-based usage charges were the fairest method because traffic was not in balance across network interconnections. ILECs have found that implementing effective usage-based charges for competitive interconnection has its own challenges. Traditionally, network elements have provided *automatic message accounting* (AMA; TERP98) data, which forms the input to downstream retail and wholesale billing systems. But many existing network elements were never designed to enable the recording of terminated usage on incoming and transit traffic. Even in situations where appropriate recording capabilities are available, enabling them to collect data on interconnect usage across a switch could overload an already stressed downstream AMA collecting and billing infrastructure.

Many operators have turned to alternative recording mechanisms in search of a solution for this key business challenge. The most widely adopted approach has been to use recordings based on the signaling message flow traveling along SS7 links between interconnected networks. The SS7 messages are fundamental to setting up calls in a modern digital network and controlling the key aspects of communication between switches. SS7 messages can be processed and aggregated by a link-monitoring system to produce a call detail record. The CDR contains all the information required to bill a customer or interconnecting operator.

Increasing use of the SS7 network as the foundation for Advanced Intelligent Network (AIN), local number portability (LPN), and mobility is creating a drive toward proper accounting and cost recovery. This becomes crucial with the realization that in a competitive world an operator's SS7 network can be used to carry messages as part of a service setup, but the resultant call and associated CDR could bypass that carrier's network. With the imminent introduction of LNP, cost recovery has been a high priority for many incumbents. In particular, requirements have emerged for usage-based charges for untranslated calls arriving into the network and third-party access to ILEC LNP databases. To understand actual SS7 usage and collect information as the basis for determining tariff levels, many LECs are implementing link-monitoring-based solutions to account for SS7 network usage between interconnecting networks. Figure 4.20 shows how the signaling transfer point can be utilized to collect usage data for accounting purposes.

Using SS7 as a billing data source for carriers offers the following benefits:

Ability to meet tight implementation schedules. To meet the requirements of recent legislation, vendors have developed and successfully deployed solutions within months.

Vendor independence. By its very nature, an SS7 link-monitoring approach to gathering usage billing data is independent of the underlying network elements. Therefore, there is no impact on SS7 network performance and, more crucially, no reliance on multivendor support for successful solutions.

New revenue streams. The opportunity to bill for new services on a usage basis, which is not feasible today, would become possible, such as use of the SS7 network itself by non-ILEC carriers.

Trouble-free integration with downstream billing and accounting systems. This is accomplished with support for industry-standard formats such as AMA and standardized transport mechanisms.

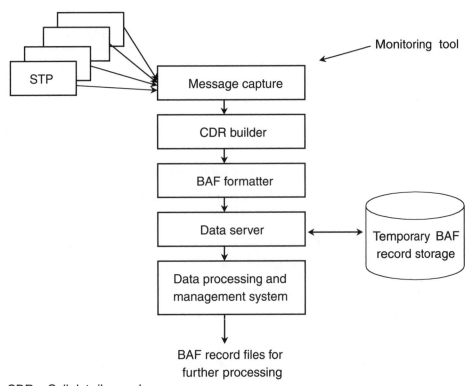

CDR = Call detail record

Figure 4.20 Use of SS7 as information source for CDRs.

4.11 Convergence in Billing

The strategy behind convergent billing is to move from electronic stapling to the most advanced platform and present the customer with a seamless transition between systems. The bill provides the only reflection of how effectively a company manages this transition. No matter the true extent of actual system convergence, the bill must be consolidated and the process appear convergent to the customer. Regardless of the method employed, diligence must be applied to generate complete, accurate, and timely information to customers. Customers will not accept any level of service that does not have these attributes, even when a single, convergent bill can be generated.

Creating the convergent bill starts by reviewing all the individual components that go into the final output. An inventory must first be taken of each product and feature to ensure that every platform's unique characteristics and requirements are covered. Business rules must be applied to develop convergent bills. Each product, the respective rating structure, and the discounting methodology must be clearly defined. Additionally, the sequence of products within the bill may depend on how the business rules define their common or distinct structures or components. Products and services may be combined, depending on the results of market research.

Starting with the very first page of the bill (the remittance page) and proceeding through every section, all dissimilar pieces of information (lockbox address, accounts receivable, etc.) that were once accurate under separate billing platforms must now be brought together as a single entity without loss of integrity. One way to ensure a solid product is to bring together subject-matter experts from various departments (such as marketing, finance, revenue assurance, information technology), who are familiar with all aspects of the separate billing components and product-related data. This approach requires putting a team in a room with the commitment to work together until the billing presentation rules are complete. Those involved must be prepared to devote several days to this effort.

The following phases of convergent billing can be distinguished (ELLI99).

The first stage consists of multiple OSS applications processing simultaneously in silos, each producing independent discount files or bills. The objective is to produce a single bill for convergent customers. These separate bills or discounted files are fed into a billing mediation/aggregation engine, which generates an electronically stapled bill, commonly referred to as a *convergent bill.* This provides the appearance of convergent billing to the customer, until the customer requests cross-product discounts, credits applied to multiple products, or rerated call details with the discounts applied.

The advantages of this phase of integration are as follows:

- It is the least expensive to implement.
- It provides the look and feel of paper convergence.
- It is the easiest and fastest to implement, because minimal customization is required.
- It executes a first attempt to meet the ultimate goal of true convergence.

- It is the first step toward cross-product discounting.
- It is the most timely to implement.

The disadvantages of this phase of integration are as follows:

- It offers limited cross-product discounts.
- It has limited rerating capability.
- It requires multiple customer database/product access.
- It involves multiple order management applications.
- It employs multiple business processes for similar functions.
- It needs a large staff to maintain and operate it.
- It requires manual intervention from end to end.
- It lacks completeness in bundling and unbundling product, rate structures, and discounting.
- It lacks a true product inventory database.
- It requires the retention of multiple platforms of source information for resolution of billing inquiries.
- It lacks the potential for a single point of contact in cases of multiple service providers for customer care.
- It lacks a convergent receivables system.

The second step consists of multiple billing applications that simultaneously process through the product-rating function. This separate rated data is fed into a discount aggregator, which in turn feeds a consolidated billing application. This phase is the first move toward automated convergence. It presents a bill to the customer that includes all or most of the products and services consumed. Often this phase is manually very intensive.

The advantages of this second phase of integration are as follows:

- It enables cross-product discounts.
- It involves only moderate complexity to implement.
- It is relatively timely to implement.
- It provides the first system look and feel of convergence.
- It may provide a review of current bill limitations and the need for enhancements.
- It improves on rating accuracy via complete universe forms for auditing.
- It assists in internal and competitor best-price rating.
- It helps to minimize customer churn.
- It minimizes the number of bill cycles.

The disadvantages of this second phase of integration are as follows:

- It has only limited rerating capabilities.
- It depends on multiple customer databases.

- It involves multiple order management applications.
- It may still require manual intervention, especially in call collection.
- It still lacks completeness in bundling and unbundling products and structures.
- It lacks a true inventory product database.
- It requires multiple platforms of source information for billing inquiries.
- It lacks true receivables convergence.

The third stage consists of multiple call collection and mediation applications feeding a rating aggregator, which feeds a single discounting engine and consolidated billing application. Combining different rating engines into one convergent engine is a significant challenge. The big question is whether this effort is worth the benefit. Each company needs to answer that question for itself, and in doing so also answer the question of what level of convergence does the company really need to meet its goals and mission statement. For true convergence, rating integration is required, but this will be the most complex and difficult part to deploy. It is very important that all existing and planned rating components be included in the design phase. Every company is expected to walk through this phase just once.

The advantages of this third phase of integration are as follows:

- It needs no human intervention to bring about convergence.
- It greatly improves marketplace competitiveness.
- It provides for inventory of event call types.
- It should minimize duplication of cross-product billed event records.
- It is a solid basis in product and rating structures.
- It provides for true cross-product discounting with rerating capability.

The disadvantages of this third phase of integration are as follows:

- It entails a significant cost and effort for integrating rating engines.
- It lacks true receivable convergence.
- It may reduce customer attention and contact, which can hurt customer satisfaction.

The final stage of billing integration consists of multiple networks or some combined network elements feeding a single billing platform, which collects, mediates, rates, discounts, credits and debits, and generates a convergent bill. If the other stages have been completed, then the focus of this phase is on integrating the remaining OSS areas to bring about complete system convergence. If a company is starting from the beginning, each of the previous stages must be incorporated into the overall design, project plan, and budget.

Assuming the work order is complete, this phase targets convergence in the areas of accounts receivable, accounts payable, general ledger, customer-facing systems, and data warehousing. These areas are affected because the total financial impact of a convergent bill must be shared with the rest of the business. This includes having convergent debits and credits applied to a convergent customer database and convergent accounting database, taxes applied and paid from a convergent point of view, and all market and trending data stored and accessible from one source. Once integration of data, interfaces, access mechanisms, and functional areas is complete, the stage of full-scale convergent billing has been reached.

The advantages of this final phase of integration are as follows:

- It virtually eliminates manual intervention to bring about convergent billing.
- It can help identify and introduce new products into the marketplace.
- It opens up new markets previously unavailable or unknown.
- It is an extremely competitive tool.
- It provides for true integration of all product components and data.
- It reduces a service provider's platform dependency.
- It meets all needs of end-to-end customer ordering and provisioning.
- It provides for one-stop shopping.
- It provides for receivables convergence.
- It creates one set of bill cycles to manage.

The disadvantages of this final phase of integration are as follows:

- It is very expensive to develop, maintain, and operate.
- It is very complex to operate and fix.
- It involves very large and expensive data storage and backup provision.
- A billing problem means no bill for any services until problem restoration.
- It must have sound front-end customer processes to provide fast account setup due to volume and complexity.

Convergent billing is a very complex target. Service providers are advised to consult with their customers, first about the degree of expected convergence.

Convergent billing continues to be a key challenge for wireless carriers. Most of the customers are opting for a convergent bill. Their reasons are that it provides for unified customer service for voice and data; customer-centric ordering, allowing both wireless and IP services to be ordered via the same platform; rating that combines all service offerings, such as for voice and data, a capability that takes on greater prominence as bills are presented in real time over wireless devices; strong back-office support required for large-scale operations in billing, accounts receivable, auditing, and customer service; and simplified systems implementation and management.

4.12 The Economics of Billing

Cost management for telecommunications service providers includes an evaluation of the true cost of billing. The expenses of billing should be quantified across two key dimensions (SHAW98): operational costs and functional scope. It is recommended for use in the categories of software, implementation, bill processing, data center, software maintenance and enhancements, and network applications.

Table 4.17 describes these six generic categories and some fundamental cost drivers and cost trends within each category, and models the life cycle of billing applications for six years.

Although the cost of raw processing power is falling, the requirements for processing power and data storage are rising rapidly. At best, it appears that computing costs per subscriber will remain constant. Billing costs must consider the rapidly increasing requirements to support processing-intensive, revenue-enhancing capabilities, such as near-real-time rating within the wireless segment, bill presentment, Web access, and marketing/data warehousing applications. The increase in processing per subscriber can only accelerate, as service providers and their customers realize the wealth of competitive data embedded in their billing systems.

While modern billing systems offer rapidly improving functionality and flexibility, the support required to maintain parameter tables in an environment of rapidly changing products will continue to increase. In addition, the revenue assurance function has often been understaffed or not staffed at all, and the increase in product offerings with inherently fragile processing will reemphasize the need for increased revenue assurance staffing. Vendor management will become an increasingly important factor in billing systems cost control. The logistics of coordinating a large number of different pieces of application software increases the complexity and cost of managing the system environments, including release and change control.

Costs are generally quantifiable and can be estimated with some accuracy in most cases. However, estimating the benefit side of the value equation is more complicated. Benefits can be generally grouped into revenue benefits and process efficiency benefits. To maximize billing value, service providers must develop a core competency in estimating these benefits, using approaches such as test marketing, customer research, and process root cause analysis. It is important to ensure that the process of making investment decisions encompasses the billing cost, process efficiency, and revenue areas, in order to generate a single assessment of the net value of a billing investment.

In order to ensure a safe position in a very competitive environment, service providers must base every major billing system investment decision on a detailed and accurate economic analysis.

4.13 Process of Consulting and Support (Professional Services)

The main goal is of this process is to reach a high level of collaboration between providers and customers. This collaboration should include establishing a special team of consultants for customers, arranging periodic status and planning meetings, and clearly defining the interfaces between provider and customer. The principal functions are:

Table 4.17 Analysis of Billing Costs

COST CATEGORY	HIGH-LEVEL COST COMPONENTS	COST DRIVERS	GENERAL COST TRENDS
Software	Initial license fees, base software, annual license fees, customization	Negotiated price, schedule slippage, degree of customization required, extent of subscriber base	Significant cost early in the life cycle; decreasing over time; costs in years 1 and 2 can be 6 times higher than those in years 3 to 6
Implementation	Testing tools, conversion, integration, installation and configuration management, training, transition costs	System complexity, schedule slippage, management ability, hardware costs, software quality	Significant cost early in the life cycle; costs in years 1 and 2 can be 6 times higher than those in years 3 to 6
Bill processing	Staff (employees and contractors), output processing, subscriber fees, revenue assurance	Extent and growth of subscriber base, economics of scale, SLAs, hardware, raw material, postage	New operations need significant investments early in the life cycle; existing operations need minimal additional resources; increase over time as subscribers increase
Data center	Client hardware, server hardware, systems software	Capacity of existing hardware, technological advances, growth of subscriber base, performance requirements, SLAs, economies of scale	New operations need significant investments early in the life cycle; cost per subscriber will fall more slowly than hardware costs because of increased demand of processing
Software maintenance and enhancements	Software releases, ongoing software customization, table management	Systems complexity, schedule slippage, regulatory requirements	Minimal during early stages of life cycle; increasing over time; by year 6, costs may be greater than initial software costs in year 1

Continues

Table 4.17 Analysis of Billing Costs *(Continued)*

COST CATEGORY	HIGH-LEVEL COST COMPONENTS	COST DRIVERS	GENERAL COST TRENDS
Network	Network maintenance, network enhancements	Growth of subscriber base, network capacity	New operations need significant investments early in life cycle, existing operations need minimal additional resources

- Estimation of consulting demand on behalf of customers
- Customer support
- Security consulting
- Training and education for customers
- Periodic and ad hoc consultation with customers

4.14 Summary

Customer care is gaining in importance as service providers recognize how much they can lose in customer churn and how much they can gain by retaining their existing customers. Offering Web access to information on quality of service, service levels, product portfolios, and billing, customers and service providers are developing a closer relationship. Consumers and businesses can also be provided with the ability to both view and pay bills via the Internet using the guidelines and recommendations of electronic bill presentment and payment (EBPP). This new service allows billers to cut paper processing costs and garner customer loyalty and Web site hits. Financial institutions, bill consolidators, Internet portals, and makers of personal financial manager (PFM) software products are expecting a fair market share. Customers and service providers together can successfully demonstrate the progress of B2B and B2C in an eCommerce environment. As part of this alliance, the separation between front-office and back-office business applications is going to disappear.

CHAPTER 5

Provisioning and Order Processing

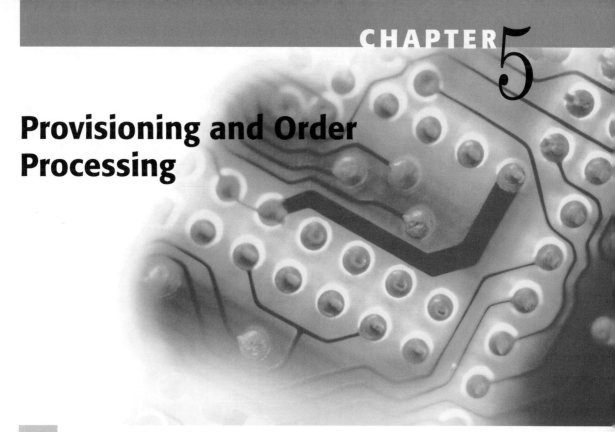

5.1 Introduction

In order to operate to serve customers, service providers are expected to create, design, and deploy telecommunication products and services. This example of a fulfillment process shows a possible sequence of activities to support a customer inquiry, subsequent order for service, the configuration of the service, the installation, and completion of the request (Figure 5.1). Depending on the service provider process, orders can be placed through the sales process and/or directly through the order management process. For a specific service provider, some customers may be supported by a specific sales team that places some or all orders for the customer and tracks them to completion. These dual-trigger process interfaces and follow-ups are shown as 3/3A and 20/20A.

Information exchanges in Figure 5.1 are numbered as follows:

1. Selling
2. Selling
3. Order

    3A   Order status and completion
4. Service request
5. Assignment request
6. Network configuration request

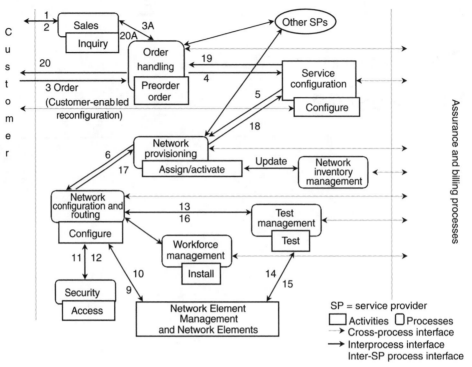

Figure 5.1 Fulfillment process example.

7. Installation request and completion

8. Installation request and completion

9. Element configuration complete

10. Element configuration complete

11. Network access check and complete

12. Network access check and complete

13. Test request

14. Perform test and test data

15. Perform test and test data

16. Test complete

17. Network configuration complete

18. Assignment complete

19. Service complete

20. Order status and completion

    20A Order status and completion

The complete fulfillment flow-through may not actually be required every time for some simple services that have preassigned service capacity. For example, the flow for an instance of a service setup could be bypassed at network provisioning, when configured and tested facilities have been preprovisioned. This depends on a particular provider's operational process and policy. It will also impact the timing of interactions with network inventory management, hence the interface sequence number has been omitted. Interfaces may be required with other service providers or network operators when the service offered to a customer is one of many different kinds of joint service arrangements.

Figure 5.1 also shows cross-domain interfaces to service assurance, customer care, and billing processes. The accurate grouping of business processes may differ. The same business process may become part of both fulfillment and service assurance process groups. Good examples for these cross-boundary processes are inventory, security, and network data management.

5.2 The Inventory Management Process

This process encompasses anything to do with physical equipment and the administration of this equipment. The process is involved not only in the installation and acceptance of equipment and with the physical configuration of the network, but also with the handling of spare parts and the repair process. Software upgrades are also a responsibility of this process.

In implementing IP-based services, the number of managed objects is going to grow. Physical assets also include servers, access servers, gateways, gatekeepers, routers, and new connections. These new components are usually identified by sites, ports, and type. They are connected to each other during the provisioning process. Logical asset management includes domains, addresses, and also other identification alternatives. Critical success factors are completeness of data, actuality of data, synchronization between multiple databases, and aligning assets between inventory databases and the actual network. The principal tasks of this process are as follows

- Installation and administration of the physical network
- Performing work in the network
- Managing the repair activities
- Aligning inventory with network
- Managing spare parts
- Managing faulty parts

Table 5.1 identifies the information sources to this process. Table 5.2 shows the information output and the targeted processes.

Figure 5.2 shows the functions of the network inventory management process. It clearly identifies input information and allocates it to functions that are ordered in the right sequence. Also, information output is defined that helps to identify the links to other functions.

Table 5.1   Information Input for the Inventory Management Process

SOURCE OF INFORMATION	INFORMATION
Service configuration	Adds/changes/deletes
Network maintenance and restoration	Work order, work cancel, work stop
Network planning and development	Work orders
Network provisioning	Work orders
Element management	Change notification
Supplier	New/spare/repair part available, equipment problems, and updates

Table 5.2   Information Output for the Inventory Management Process

INFORMATION	TARGETED PROCESSES
Maintenance scheduled/complete	Network maintenance and restoration
Network capacity available	Network provisioning
Order request	Network planning and development
Notifications/orders/returns	Supplier

5.2.1 Network Inventory Data Model ITU M3100

One of the key areas in supporting telecommunications service suppliers is assets—in other words, *inventory management.* Many terms are used to describe the same thing: *technical inventory, physical inventory, cable management, asset management.* All imply a very detailed level of identifying and maintaining attributes of facilities and equipment.

In certain cases, managers start with cable management and then move to equipment and to more logical views of networks and systems. Depending on the need, various attributes of managed objects can be maintained.

Inventory offerings range from reporting/query capability against existing MIB contents to comprehensive inventory systems built around special products such as PowerBuilder. Inventory offerings require professional services customization and may include systems integration.

An *inventory* is a concentrated maintenance of attributes of managed objects in the environment of service providers. Practically speaking, there are no logical limits to the objects that should and should not be included.

Attributes store reportable information about physical and logical items. Also, external sources provided by suppliers and customers may be included. Customization permits the system to accept customer required input and to provide required out-

Input   Output

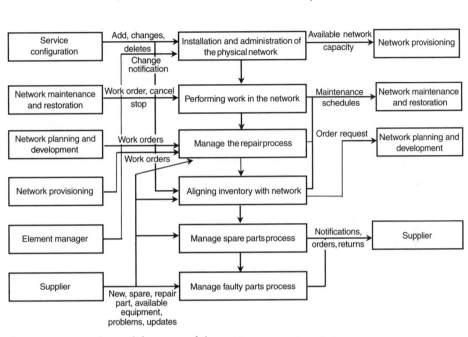

Figure 5.2 Functions of the network inventory management process.

puts and reports. Examples of items that can be included in the network inventory after customization include off-net resources and customer-promised equipment. Additional attributes can be added to enhance the network inventory's tracking abilities. For example, attributes can track equipment that is reserved, returned, broken, assigned, or installed. This would allow reporting on assigned but not yet installed equipment.

Customer rules could be created to compare inventory levels of equipment against minimum levels determined by the service provider. These rules could generate requirements for orders. For example, applicable equipment would have attributes of quantity in inventory and a minimum acceptable inventory. From a user interface, items can be removed from inventory, activating a rule that decreases inventory quantity by the user-input amount. The resulting inventory would be compared to a minimum acceptable inventory. If the inventory level fell below this, a message could indicate the need to order more items for the given inventory class.

The intent of network inventory is to give the service provider the ability to model the actual network as closely as possible. This network inventory should be automatically updated with feedback from the actual network by using operations, business support, and management systems.

Inventory management is a very complex area and is defined differently by various customers. Many types of data must be stored and maintained to make an inventory, including the following items

- Physical inventory
- Inside-plant physical inventory (network elements and their attributes, jacks, etc.)
- Outside-plant physical inventory (e.g., cables and fiber)
- Logical inventory (e.g., capacity, time slots, and circuits)
- Business inventory, including principal applications
- Customer inventory (e.g., customers, contacts, and orders)
- Supplier inventory (e.g., service providers, contacts, contracts, initial and recurrent charges, off-network resources)
- Engineering and planning inventory (e.g., GIS information, build-out plans)
- Parts inventory (e.g., spares, parts on order, parts in repair)

Based on the types of data to be stored and the uses of this data, there are different types of inventory systems that can be built. For example, a facility inventory system maps circuits to inside-plant inventory, bandwidth, and off-net resources. Inventory systems are integrated with the functionality of operations support systems to provide service management solutions. For example, after building a facility inventory system, a service provider may want to have the system perform provisioning as well. Another service provider might want to determine which customers are affected by a network outage—effectively merging logical inventory, physical inventory, and business inventory with fault management.

Most service providers understand their business information needs and each will request a network inventory system. However, each service provider's definition will differ based on its selections and definitions of the preceding inventory items and their required functionality.

Physical network management begins with proper documentation. However, generating and maintaining network documentation in the past was usually a difficult task. Information needed was very often spread throughout the organization in architectural drawings, schematic diagrams, paper files, equipment documentation, circuit lists, or in the heads of network management personnel. With such a diversity of information sources, contributors, and owners, standardization is almost impossible. Consequently, during the troubleshooting process, network management staff must spend unnecessary time searching documentation, sometimes finding the information to be obsolete and inaccurate.

The main objective of documentation systems is to provide a mechanism to logically document a network in a central repository with easy update and retrieval facilities and a mechanism to enforce drawing standards. The most powerful packages consist of a graphical system, typically a mixture of CAD and a GUI, linked to a relational database and complemented with standard reporting and querying tools. The key user interface in these applications is the graphical representation of the network. Graphical views and intelligent symbols allow network managers to visually navigate their physical infrastructure, quickly adding or locating equipment and connections. Like logical network management maps, physical views can be linked hierarchically to child views. The top view can be used as the entry, representing an enterprise topological map. Step by step, more detailed views can be easily generated.

Usually, in these packages, elements of the communication infrastructure—devices and cabling—are represented by user-defined symbols, which are linked to corresponding objects in the relational database. Inventory packages usually let users create their own objects to supplement a library of predefined ones. Activating the symbol may query the database for attribute information, such as configuration or warranty data. Using such inventory systems, network managers can track cabling and devices on a detailed level. This detail can generate circuit traces, which is very useful in troubleshooting.

The significant investment of time required to populate a database concerns users, and they may decide against a product. Vendors have recognized this problem and responded with commitments to leverage existing data by providing import facilities from other databases and other discovery routines. After capturing information into the database, most applications can automatically generate a graphic representation of the network, including asset and connectivity information.

Unlike logical inventory systems, physical applications track an extensive level of detail in the database. For example, while a usual network management system views a client/server transaction as one connection, a physical inventory system would view the end-to-end connection as a system of multiple components. In a 10BaseT setup, it would probably track a client/server transaction as follows: the end node to the adapter cable, wall plate, RJ-45 jack, house cable run, punch-down block, punch-down termination, cross-connect to the patch panel, patch panel port, patch cable run, hub port, hub card, to the hub. Most of the applications can delve into the most minute operations, tracking cables at the pair, or even at the wire, level.

Some physical inventory tools can also help users design networks. For example, some products contain a feature called *automatic circuit build,* or *route recommender.* This feature allows a telecommunications operator to request connectivity between two endpoints, such as a Windows client and a Unix database server. The design application, using predefined cable types, its knowledge of existing structure, and its analytical abilities, will suggest circuit routes and cross-connects. The application makes its recommendations based on cable-length requirements, data link protocol specifications, and capacities of patch panels, PBXs, and hubs. This feature is very useful in voice networks, where the number of cross-connects far exceeds that in data networking and where detailed information is much more difficult to obtain. After recommending a circuit route, most products can then issue work orders with corresponding detailed installation instructions. Products that support wide area networks can provide circuit-building suggestions across multiple sites while considering available bandwidth.

A rules-based expert system provides an excellent foundation for automating the processes of network moves, adds, and changes. Change management functions allow a telecommunications operator to graphically move users and equipment through single drag-and-drop operations. Upon operator confirmation, the system performs all associated disconnects and reconnects and inserts the relevant zone-related attributes. Products that have expert system engines will allow these operations to be performed by operators who do not have in-depth knowledge of network capacity planning. The system will insert all of the change information into a pending move record and generate the work orders needed for the technician to start the physical installation. Once the technician completes the job, the operator declares the change request completed, and the necessary database modifications are made permanent.

Figure 5.3 shows an inventory data model on the basis of ITU M3100. This figure gives examples of managed objects and of the interfaces to domain managers and to the network inventory server. Obviously, not all elements and services are indicated in this figure.

Basic requirements toward inventory systems include the following

- Support of ITU M3100 model and containment tree
  - Equipment
  - Termination point
  - Circuit
- MIB containing all network elements
- Automated design and assignment
- Support of CORBA interfaces and services
- Linked to fault MIB for auto discovery
- Support of Java application servers
- Support of C++ database access

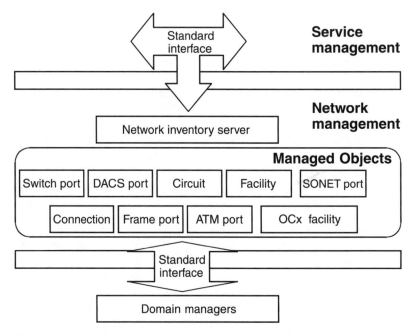

Figure 5.3 Network inventory data model (ITU M3100).

- Support for CMIP methods with IDL (Get, Set, Create, and Delete)
- Linked with CAD for creating network drawings

5.2.2 Typical Managed Objects

Circuit switched and packet switched networks support different networking philosophies, but they may share many physical managed objects. But there are typical managed objects for each.

Circuit switched solutions are typical for voice services. Also, certain data services are built and provisioned using this traditional but highly redundant and reliable structure. Figure 5.4 shows a typical structure, indicating the major managed objects, all of which are part of equipment inventory. Inventory examples are as follows:

1. *Subscriber (customer).* Information is summarized here about persons or an organization that purchases services, including pertinent contacts, billing information, sites associated with customers, and more, comprising the customer object class. More than one customer may be associated with a site, and a single customer may be associated with multiple sites.

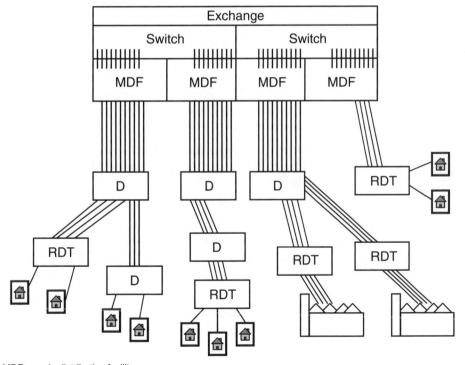

MDF = main distribution facility
D   = distributor
RDT = remote digital terminal

Figure 5.4 Typical structure of a circuit switched hierarchy.

2. *Site.* It is any location that houses equipment or where circuits are terminated. Site information includes the site name, site type, site address, contact person, site phone/fax number, and any access restrictions, such as mandatory early notice prior to arrival. Other information unique to a particular site may be defined in a site record as well. Sites must be defined before associated equipment can be created. A piece of equipment will always be associated with a site. Customers/subscribers may also be associated with a site in a many-to-many relationship.

3. *Generic equipment.* A piece of equipment is associated with a physical location in the network and uses a generic "site-aisle-duck-slot-card-port" hierarchy. Unique naming of equipment should be enforced within a site to prevent dual assignments of any port to more than one circuit. Equipment can be either of two types: shelves or containers. *Containers* are equipment elements that contain other equipment, such as bays and cabinets. *Shelves* are pieces of equipment that house slots in which cards are placed. Also, the capacity should be maintained to support the provisioning process.

4. *Exchange.* A building housing one or more switches and main distribution facilities.

5. *Switch.* The link from a network branch to the rest of the network. Switches handle the routing of calls from the caller to the number called.

6. *Main distribution facility.* A special instance of a distributor that serves as the final node in the network before a switch.

7. *Distributor.* A node in the network. In the general sense of the term, all nodes in the network are distributors. At a more detailed level, there are different kinds of distributors.

8. *Serving terminal.* A special instance of a distributor; a node serving as an access point to the network, linking the customer's installation to the telephone network. Each address in the tree directory is assigned to a serving terminal as its access point to the telephone network.

Figure 5.4 is an example of the logical layout of equipment in the physical network. Further details are absolutely necessary to constitute a working network. Other components include the following:

Cable. A data entity representing a group of wire pairs that originates from a group of sequential clips in a distributor and ends in a group of sequential clips in another distributor farther down in the network hierarchy.

Clip. A data entity representing a clip in a distributor. One clip can connect one wire pair to the distributor.

Wire pair. Physical connection between subscribers and serving terminals and between serving terminals and distributors, respectively. A circuit segment between two equipment ports.

Duct. Physical construct for pipes.

Vault. Physical construct to accommodate cables.

Pipe. Physical construct to embed cables and fibers.

Manhole. Access point to the ducts and pipes.

Further logical components are circuit or connection paths that are used to describe an end-to-end sequence of equipment ports, circuit segments, cables, and wire pairs. Figure 5.5 shows how a PCM connection is defined across multiple equipment. The relationship between cabling and connection is extremely important, as shown in Figure 5.6.

It is expected that the inventory database—relational or object-oriented—maintains both logical and physical equipment and facilities.

Packet switched solutions are predominantly for data services. But this boundary is disappearing by offering VoIP (voice over IP), voice over frame relay, and FoIP (fax over IP). This structure is no longer hierarchical; it could be meshed, partially meshed, or peer-to-peer. Figure 5.7 shows a typical structure indicating the major managed objects, all of which are expected to be part of the equipment inventory. All generic definitions about customers, sites, and equipment are applicable here.

Typical inventory items include the following:

Routers. They are responsible for directing the traffic within the IP packet switched network.

Layer 2/layer 3 switches. They provide switching services with varying intelligence to increase transmission efficiency.

Servers. Computing devices dedicated to certain tasks (communication, data management, Web page hosting, printing, etc.)

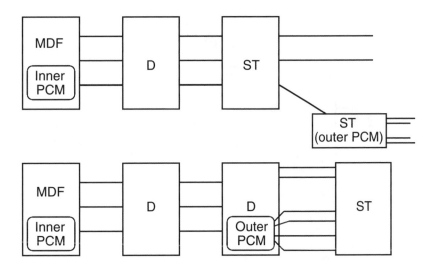

ST = serving terminal
D   = distributor
MDF = main distribution facility

Figure 5.5 Configuring a PCM connection.

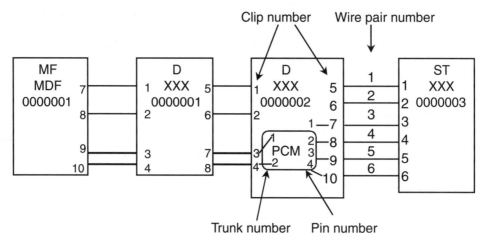

Figure 5.6 Registration of a PCM line connection.

Firewalls. They are in charge of protecting sensitive information of service providers or enterprises. Actually, they work as a software filter to investigate each input and output package. In doing so, performance may be impacted.

Load balancers. Processors designed to understand load profiles and distribute the load to communication channels and to servers depending on the actual utilization metrics.

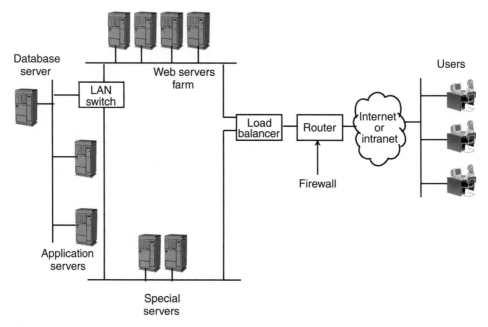

Figure 5.7 Intranet as a packet switched example.

LANs. Local area networks are in charge of connecting local devices with high bandwidth at reasonable costs.

Local cabling may change as new technologies emerge. xDSL enables service providers to offer high-speed data or mixed voice and data services, as shown in Figure 5.8.

Similar changes are expected when cable modems are implemented to combine video, voice, and data services, as shown in Figure 5.9

In all previously mentioned cases, mandatory and optional attributes of managed objects must be defined and maintained in an inventory database. Certain equipment in both circuit and packet switched areas offers a management information base (MIB) that can be considered the core of an inventory database.

Table 5.3 gives a few examples of MIBs of principal managed objects. Table 5.4 shows a few examples of attributes applied to circuits.

5.2.3 CAD/CAM and GIS Solutions

Voice, data, and video networks cover a physical area, and their components (e.g., equipment and facilities) exist in relation to a geographical reality. In other words, the process of network registration consists not only of registering managed objects comprising the network, but also of registering the physical location of the components. This is the area where different geographical documentation systems are under consideration.

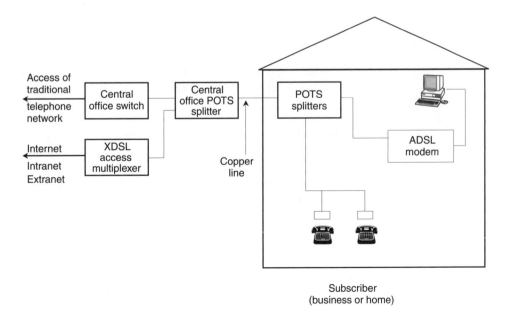

Figure 5.8 Use of xDSL technology in subscriber environments.

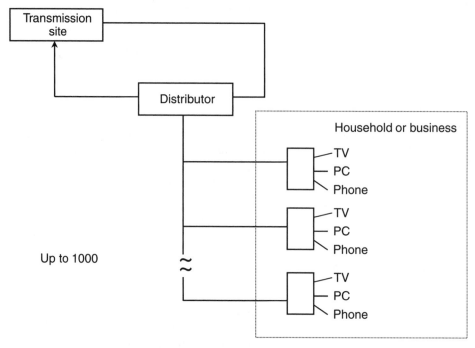

Figure 5.9 Use of cable technology in subscriber environments.

CAD/CAM technology is frequently used to prepare drawings of network maps. Geographic Information Systems (GIS) are becoming popular with service providers, utility companies, road construction companies, and local governments because they can precisely illustrate the physical layout, including all the necessary details about pipes, ducts, and communication shafts.

Within many telecommunications companies today, OSS environments comprise a number of legacy stand-alone systems designed to manage a relatively static environment. The engineering department is no exception to this, where traditionally CAD systems were selected to document the physical layout of the network infrastructure. CAD systems are limited in that they hold nothing more than drawings or pictures of the network and, as a result, do not build a continuous fully connected model of the plant infrastructure. In addition, often no attributes are stored relating to the graphics. Database access is supported, but the data is stored outside the drawing itself. CAD drawings are held in a proprietary data format without any means of accessing the data other than through translators. Drawbacks of CAD systems can be summarized as follows:

- They are simply islands of data.
- They have limited network modeling capabilities.
- They have fragmented network infrastructure drawings.
- No attribute data are stored relating to graphical features or, if so, they reside in an external database.

Table 5.3   MIB Examples for Leading-Edge Technologies

FRAME RELAY MIB

The `frDlcmiTable` contains 10 objects. Their purpose is to identify each physical port at the UNI, its IP address, the size of the DLCI header that is used on this interface, timers for invoking status and status inquiry messages, the maximum number of DLCIs supported at the interface, whether the interface uses multicasting, and some other miscellaneous operations.

The `frCircuitTable` contains 14 objects. Their purpose is to identify each PVC, its associated DLCI, whether the DLCI is active, the number of BECNs and FECNs received since the PVC was created, statistics on the number of frames and octets sent and received since the DLCI was created, the DLCI's Bc and Be, and some other miscellaneous operations.

The third table is the `frErrTable` containing four objects. Their purpose is to store information on the types of errors that have occurred at the DLCI (unknown or illegal) and the time the error was detected. One object contains the header of the frame that created the error.

ATM MIB

Each physical link (port) at the UNI has an MIB entry that is defined in the `atmfPortTable`. This table contains a unique value for each port, an address, the type of port (DS3, SONET, etc.), media type (coaxial cable, fiber, etc.), status of port (in service, etc.), and other miscellaneous objects.

The `atmfAtmLayerTable` contains information about the UNI's physical interface. The table contains the port ID, maximum number of VCCs, VPCs supported and configured on this UNI, active VCI/VPI bits on the UNI, and a description of public or private for the UNI.

The `atmVpcTable` and `atmVccTable` contain similar entries for the VPCs and VCCs, respectively, on the UNI. These tables contain the port ID, VPI or VCI values for each connection, operational status (up, down, etc.), traffic shaping and policing descriptors (to describe the type of traffic management applicable to the traffic), and any applicable QoS that is applicable to the VPI or VCI.

WIRELESS MIB

The mobile client Group contains information to be relayed from the remote workstation to a network management system on the attached network. This group stores information on mobile client name, description, location, phone number, power management configuration, connection hardware and software, client type (CPU, RAM, disk, video), system software, date, time, network adapter used, and configuration and statistics.

The mobile server group contains information to be relayed from the local network server to a network management system on the same network. This group stores information about the network server where remote connections can be originated, such as server's name, remote network hardware, slot and port number, server uptime, connection speed, service type, and traffic statistics.

The trap group describes SNMP trap types for remote workstations, such as mobile computer docked, undocked, suspended, resumed, pcmcia inserted, and a trap

Continues

Table 5.3 MIB Examples for Leading-Edge Technologies *(Continued)*

table. This is a table of alerts, which can be sent to the specified IP address using the specified protocol by setting the value of the `mobileTrapTrigger` object to the index of an entry in this table. Adapter group contains information about network adapters, including hardware information and type of connection.

Link group provides data about mobile network links, such as link status and link performance

CABLE MIB

The `docsDevBase` group extends the MIB-II system group with objects needed for cable device system management. It includes the device role, date and time, serial number, and reset conditions.

The `docsDevNmAccessGroup` provides a minimum level of SNMP access security to the device by network management stations. The access is also constrained by the community strings and any vendor-specific security. The management station should have read/write permission for the cable modems.

The `docsDevSoftware` group provides information for network downloadable software upgrades. It includes file identification, administration status, operational status, and current version.

The `docsDevServer` group provides information about the progress of the interaction between the CM and CMTS and various provisioning servers. It includes boot state, DHCP, server time, configuration file, and TFTP configuration parameters.

The `docsDevEvent` group provides control and logging for event reporting. This group offers fairly detailed information on control parameters, syslog details, throttle conditions, severity codes, and priorities. It also offers entries for vendor-specific data.

The `docsDevFilter` group configures filters at link layer and IP layer for bridges data traffic. This group consists of a link layer filter table, `docsDevFilter-LLCTable`, which is used to manage the processing and forwarding of non-IP traffic; an IP packet classifier table, `docsDevFilterIpTable`, which is used to map classes of packets or specific policy actions; and a policy table, `docsDevFilter-PolicyTable`, which maps zero or more policy action tables. At this time, the MIB specifies only one policy action table, `docsDevFilterTosTable`, which allows the manipulation of the type of services bits in an IP packet based on matching some criteria. The working group may add additional policy types and action tables in the future—for example, to allow quality of service (QoS) to modem service identifier assignment based on destination.

XDSL MIB

`xdlsDevIfStats` group provides statistics specific to the xDSL link. Statistics are collected on a per-port basis and on specific intervals. Hence such a table is indexed by the `xdsl DevifStatsIfIndex` and `xdslDevIfStatsInterval`. Also, statistics are grouped into remote and central statistics. *Remote* means that the statistics are collected by the device at the customer premises. *Central* means that the statistics are collected by the device located at the central office. The objects that are not grouped into these two groups are related to both ends of the xDSL link.

`xdslDevIfConfig` group provides configuration information specific to a xDSL device, or system. The table is indexed by an object that corresponds to ifIndex.

Table 5.3 *(Continued)*

These ifIndex entries themselves denote and identify specific xdsl interfaces on the board or module. Also, the configuration parameters are grouped into two broad categories: up and down. *Up* reflects the upstream direction (from customer premises to the central office). *Down* reflects the downstream direction (from the central office to the customer premises.
`xdslRemoteSys` group's description is identical with the mib-2 system MIB.
`xdslRemoteDTEStatus` group provides status information about the DTE port of the DSL RTUs.
`xdslDevMvlIfConfig` group provides configuration information specific to a xDSL (MVL) device or system. The table is indexed by an object that corresponds to ifIndex. These ifIndex entries themselves denote and identify specific xdsl(Mvl) interfaces on the board or module.
`xdslDevNAPCustomerAccount` group provides customer accounting information on each DSL port. Network access providers can accurately bill their end-station DSL customers by the amount of usage. The table is indexed by ifIndex and `xdslDev-NAPCsutomerAcocuntInterval`. The ifIndex identifies specific xdsl interface on the device and `xdslDevNAPCustomerAccountInterval` specifies the accounting information that is for the current day or for the previous day. Customer data excludes all traffic used for management purpose.
`xdslLinkUpDownInformation` group contains the reason that the DSL Link went down. This information is obtained when the DSL Link is coming up.
`xdslRemoteInjection` group identifies the processes at the remote site indicating injection types and various traps.

- Data can be extracted only via data translators.
- They have no spatial analysis capabilities.

Today's business climate puts a very different demand on the systems responsible for managing the dynamic and complex networks. As a result, a new generation of GIS technology is now available that provides an integrated approach. Typical uses are

- Design and documentation
- Capture of external plant information
- Production of construction drawings

Improvements in GIS technology have enabled an increased role within the scope of the engineering environment with the following features

- Complete asset inventory systems with end-to-end connectivity
- Capture of inside- and outside-plant information
- Maintenance of different states of the network
- Complete network model reflecting the physical network as it is in the real world

Table 5.4 Attributes of the Managed Object: Circuit

CLASS NAME: CIRCUIT
Class definitions: A logical point-to-point connection between two end pieces of equipment that traverses one or more facilities and possibly one or more intermediate pieces of equipment. Circuits may be simple or complex. A *simple circuit* is supported by two end pieces of equipment and an interconnecting facility.
A *complex circuit* is supported as well by intermediate equipment and additional facilities. In general, a complex circuit consists of an ordered sequence of less complex circuits of the same bandwidth and associated cross-connects within any intermediate equipment.
A parent/child relationship may also exist between circuits in that a circuit may share the bandwidth of another circuit.

Data elements:
    Circuit type
    Circuit ID
    Circuit status
    Circuit alias
    Circuit bandwidth
    Endpoints (= 2 equipment IDs)
    Facility IDs (1 or more)
    Parent circuit ID
    Child circuit IDs
    Component circuit IDs for complex circuits
    Circuit group ID
    Network ID
    Customer ID
    Service provider ID
    Service ID
    Effective time
    Element management system ID
    Contact IDs

- Integration of various support, documentation, and management tools at the spatial level

Usually, third-party vendors provide maps that can be applied to the physical layout of the networks operated by service providers. Figure 5.10 shows a very simple example indicating the physical addresses for each managed object. The prerequisite is that the addresses be up-to-date and well maintained. It is not a trivial task, considering frequent landscaping and constructions. Each address error may mean wasting workforce time.

It is strongly recommended to centrally maintain all maps. There are different kinds of maps, including

- Overview maps with only fair resolution

- Layer maps maintaining just the immediate surroundings of cables and fiber

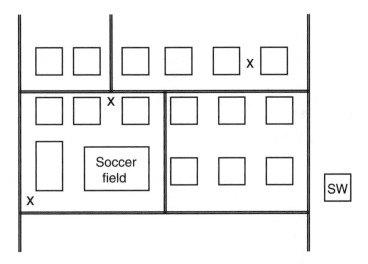

X = serving terminals (distributors) / remote digital terminals

☐ = switch (SW)

Figure 5.10 Simple GIS example.

- Schematic plans or drawings showing all components exactly without the physical positioning
- Key maps covering larger geographical areas with low resolution
- Detailed maps covering small geographic areas with the highest possible resolution

In summary, it is expected that the DEN initiative will also penetrate this area in the near future. Service providers must start by streamlining their existing directories in the following areas

- Site directories
- Streets, squares, avenues, and boulevards directories
- Map directories
- Equipment directories
- Organizational directories

Emphasis should be on eliminating redundancy as soon as possible.

5.2.4 Installation and Administration of the Physical Network

This function deals with reviewing work orders on the basis of logical configuration decisions and allocating these work orders to the proper workforce for implementation. In this respect, workforce optimization techniques must be considered and implemented.

It is assumed that ordered items have arrived, have been tagged, and have been checked for quality. In other words, these items are available for use in the network.

5.2.5 Performing Work in the Network

The responsibility of this function is the actual installation of physical components, including networking facilities and equipment. It assumes in-depth knowledge about sites and networking components.

The ultimate goal is to perform work without interrupting operations. If it is not possible for technical reasons, interruption intervals must be kept to a reasonable minimum.

5.2.6 Managing the Repair Activities

Certain components of facilities and equipment must be repaired rather than replaced. This process needs attention and a lot of coordination. In this case, workforce management plays a key role to optimize routes and minimize impacts on the productive network.

Workforce management should dispatch all the technical functions that may involve repair, replacement, first implementation, preventive maintenance, and inspection.

5.2.7 Aligning Inventory with Network

This is supposed to be a continuous activity. Persons in charge must know the inventory database very well and must have access to the operational network to discover active components on the network. A number of network management tools can help with their discovery and mapping functions—in particular, in SNMP environments.

Information on the exact quantity, location, and release version of network hardware and software is a must. New-generation networks require routine upgrades and patches. Knowledge of release and version codes is crucial in eliminating potential release incompatibilities.

The ultimate goal is to unify the inventory database and all databases supporting network operations. This trend is clear: the TMN architecture is helpful, and network element manager vendors are in favor. But it still needs considerable integration effort.

In most IP-based networks, management tools support a network discovery function. Network discovery checks active components operating on the network. This function is supported by the SNMP protocol only. Service providers are recommended to run this discovery function periodically.

5.2.8 Managing Spare Parts

After acceptance, parts are physically sent to storage areas. A central entity is expected to keep records of the physical location and volumes of parts. Parts not immediately assigned to networking facilities and equipment are considered spare parts. They are extremely important in helping with problem resolution if parts must be replaced. Issues addressed differently by various service providers are as follows

- Optimal volumes of spare parts
- What spare parts should be kept in storage areas
- Where they should be physically stored
- What the reservation policy is in real time
- How to avoid violations of internal procedures

Optimal solutions require accurate data and the use of operational research techniques. It is obvious that this function is closely connected to data warehouses and ERP solutions.

5.2.9 Managing Faulty Parts

Considering the large variety and volumes of parts of service providers' networks, the question is not whether, but when and where parts are going to break down. The network maintenance and restoration process is responsible for replacements. This function has to deal with repairing or eliminating faulty parts. Issues addressed differently by various service providers are as follows

- Criteria for eliminating (retiring) faulty parts
- Outsourcing or insourcing the repair work
- Where to store and repair faulty parts
- Feedback to suppliers if metrics are out of range (e.g., MTBF)
- Statistical analysis of parts' long-term performance

Optimal solutions require accurate data and the use of operational research techniques. It is obvious that this function is closely connected to data warehouses and ERP solutions.

5.2.10 TMN and GIS

The benefits of GIS could be applied to support business processes of telecommunications service providers. The benefits of use are obvious considering that telecommunications services are end-to-end-related and include a number of geographical domains and multiple providers with different networking infrastructures. Managing physical and logical infrastructures requires very accurate documentation. State-of-the-art documentation systems work with digital maps that can be acquired from third-party vendors.

Network management tasks can be defined and supported in various TMN layers. The level of detail and the type of information required differ by layer. The service and business management layers may be using three-dimensional applications that may not be required in the network and element management layers.

The applicability of GIS will be evaluated for three TMN layers.

Network Management Layer

The graphical presentation and documentation of physical networks belong to the traditional tasks of CAD/CAM applications. Principal documents include cables (earth and air), cable ducts, vaults and shafts, telco buildings, location of equipment, and allocation of ports to wire pairs and wire pairs to cables, respectively; in addition, other technical attributes of components have to be maintained. Details of component attributes are expected to be maintained in the network management layer.

GIS applications are extremely important for wireless communication networks, such as mobile phones systems, URH, and satellite, and in analyzing wave diffusion models. Models also include area of coverage and geography of selected areas. Inventory items are part of static configuration management.

Basically, there are two types of configuration management solutions. *Dynamic configuration management* means on-demand configuring of routes on the basis of real-time status and performance data of facilities and equipment. It is obvious that GIS applications cannot support this management function by its capabilities of three-dimensional presentation services. *Static configuration management* includes the logical configuring and changing of routes, equipment configurations, or both; maintaining types and location of equipment; and maintaining both physical and symbolic names and addresses. Other attributes may also be maintained and information displayed. In the case of relative stability of configuration parameters, GIS applications may be successfully used for displaying logical and physical routes of the network on top of various digital maps.

GIS applications contribute to the improvement of performance, fault, and security management. Performance metrics, load profiles, eventual faults, and outages or security violations can be positioned and displayed on top of accurate digital maps. This kind of presentation helps to estimate and quantify impacts on customers and on service areas in real time, resulting in expedited problem resolution, load balancing, and security protection.

A geographic information system is also a great help in preventive and reactive maintenance functions. GIS can pinpoint the location of faults with high accuracy, can highlight the optimal route for workforce to the site, and can search for and assemble the appropriate support documentation.

Service Management Layer

Managing services requires accurate data on service configuration, customer-level quality metrics, and actual metrics agreed to in service level agreements (SLAs). GIS can assist in quickly retrieving information on load profiles, fault summaries, network extensions, and visualization of service areas, also the correlation of this information with subscribers, contracts, subcontracts, service level agreements, bills, and bill presentation can be done in near real time. This results in improved customer care and increased customer satisfaction.

Business Management Layer

Business management requires a number of strategic and tactical decisions on behalf of top management. This is the area where enterprise resource planning (ERP) can be utilized very effectively. In order to support decisions on complex and interrelated issues, visualization on the basis of GIS may help. Visualization examples may include the view of network segments, the position and size of existing service areas, peering with other service providers, income statistics by service areas, statistical background data to support marketing, demographic data by service areas, and expected level of consumption by regions. Most of these data are not available in traditional management and documentation systems. GIS and data warehousing in combination can offer significantly better support to top management of service providers and also of enterprises.

In summary, the meaningful collaboration between TMN, GIS, and ERP will ensure a higher quality of information exchange and presentation for service providers.

5.3 The Service Creation, Planning, and Development Process

This process is expected to be periodically executed. Triggers may come from customers or from the marketing departments of telecommunications providers. This process encompasses the following functional areas

- Designing technical capability to meet specified market need at desired cost

- Ensuring that the service (product) can be properly installed, monitored, controlled, and billed

- Initiating appropriate process and methods modifications, as well as changes to levels of operations personnel and training required

- Initiating any modifications to the underlying network or information systems to support the requirements

- Performing preservice testing to confirm that the technical capability works and that the operational support process and systems function properly

- Ensuring that sufficient capacity is available to meet forecast sales

Developing IP-based services, there is a shift toward applications. The difference can be clearly seen when e-mail and videoconferencing are compared with managed lines and ISDN. The trend is without any doubt toward software-based definitions of new services, resulting in very high change rates in networking infrastructures. Principal functions are as follows:

- Develop and implement technical solutions.
- Develop and implement procedures.
- Define and implement systems changes.
- Develop and implement training.
- Develop customer documentation.
- Plan rollout, test, start service, and manage project.
- Set product/service pricing.

Table 5.5 identifies the information sources to this process. Table 5.6 shows the information output and the targeted processes.

Figure 5.11 shows the principal flowchart for the sequence of functions supporting service creation, planning, and development.

Table 5.5   Information Input for the Service Creation, Planning, and Development Process

SOURCE OF INFORMATION	INFORMATION
Customer	Input, alpha, and beta tests
Customer care processes	Available servicing options
Sales	New service requirements
Market development	Needs and constraints
Service quality management	Recommendations for service modifications
Other providers	Capabilities, capacity
Network planning and development	Capabilities, capacity

Table 5.6   Information Output for the Service Creation, Planning, and Development Process

INFORMATION	TARGETED PROCESSES
Service details, training, testing, and project management details	All other processes
Service options	Sales
Service options	Order handling
Quality objectives	Service quality management
Service prices	Rating and discounting
Capacity plan, new service descriptions	Other providers
Capacity plan, new service descriptions	Network planning and development

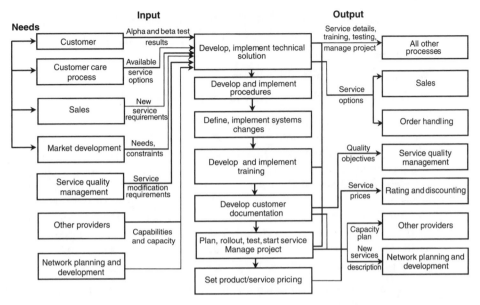

Figure 5.11 Functions of the service creation, planning, and development process.

5.3.1 Develop and Implement Technical Solutions

The portfolio of products and services can be subdivided into the following categories

- Voice-based services
- Data-based services
- Video-based services
- Cable-based services
- Internet-based services
- Applications-based services

Service providers (e.g., ILECs, CLECs, IXC, CAPs, ISPs, and ASPs) will need to connect their ordering and provisioning processes to participate in the service-offering value chain. Simple tasks such as accurate customer orders will need interconnection for the provisioning process. For example, providing basic telecommunications processes for voice and data will require the collaboration of local, long-distance, and ISP companies participating in the service mix in order to create the appropriate connections to provision the basic service offering. The convergent market also includes the combination of different services and technology offerings to the end user. How will these technology domains be crossed for the ordering and provisioning process? Some popular examples of service and technology offerings include the following (LEWI98A)

- Data service package with ISDN, frame relay, and xDSL
- Enhanced services such as caller ID, distinctive calling, call forwarding, and others
- User-defined bandwidth on demand
- Usual, well-established Plain Old Telephone Service (POTS)

In order to successfully fulfill customer orders and provision the required services to the customer, cross-technology processes (e.g., telecommunication and data communication) will need to be implemented on the same platform or on open platforms using common and standard applications. In the telephony world, a customer order is processed and almost always issued. The purchase order number becomes the focus of all activities in the ordering and provisioning process within the service provider's organization. Primary customer information (name, address, service type, credit, etc.) is attached to the customer service order (CSO), extended by applicable tariff rates, and assigned a telephone number. The circuit paths are then provisioned to the physical location of the customer.

Service providers may go a step further by bundling services. Examples are as follows (KEWI98A)

- One single number for cell phone, pager, office, and home with rollover to voice mail
- Combined local and long-distance service
- Data communication services together
- Any combination of these service bundles

Matters become even more complicated when we consider local number portability (LNP). This enables customers of telecommunications services to retain their current telephone number even if they move to a different geographical area of a local access transport area (LATA) or change service providers. Ultimately, customers are able to use single numbers for services, including business, home wireline, wireless, and pager service. One number will search for the customer through all of their subscribed services and could finally roll into a personalized voice mail. A couple of organizations (e.g., TeleManagement Forum) are actively working to define implementation guidelines that address the issues of and requirements for fulfillment, assurance, and billing that will enable service providers to support LNP and other bundled services

Local number portability is required by the Federal Communications Commission (FCC). It will lead to significant changes in billing systems at incumbent local-exchange carriers (ILECs), competitive local-exchange carriers (CLECs), and wireless service providers. Due to the complexity and added cost of implementing these changes, new or smaller providers would most likely outsource billing to a service bureau.

LNP software applications are generally implemented in two ways. In the first instance, the location routing number (LRN) information is stored in the larger, more robust SCP database, which can handle the LRN information in addition to a variety of other customer account process information. The other alternative is to implement just the LRN lookup information in the SS7 with its reduced database capacity. The SCP-based solution allows much more flexibility in integrating LNP information with LRN databases. The drawback is that each LNP query to the SCP database increases traffic on the SS7 link between the STP and the SCP. The stripped-down STP solution allows LRN lookups to take the place of the STP without further burdening the SS7 network. Regardless of whether it is implemented using traditional SS7 circuit technology or IP data networking connectivity, LNP applications will require an enormous increase in SS7 traffic due to the increased use of the SCP databases. But the increases in SCP access won't stress the SS7 network as much as the traffic going from the SS7 signaling transfer point STP to the SCP database. This potential bottleneck exists because traditional SS7 network architecture caps out at a maximum of thirty-two 56-Kbps link sets using standard SS7 T1-based links for transport. By extending just the LRN database lookup functions from SCP to the limited database capacity of the STP, response time can be significantly reduced.

Based on market research results and customer requirements, this function concentrates on the technical solutions of products and services. It designs the technical capability to meet specified customer needs with optimal resources at reasonable costs. New, improved, and changed services can be planned and developed only for existing and planned networking resources. This information is provided by the network planning and development process. It is always preferable to use the real network for capacity verification rather than just resource availability records in databases.

The other basic information is the present products and services portfolio of the service provider. In the early stage of this function, designers should classify the service requests in one of three ways:

1. New service request.

2. Service improvement request.

3. Changed service request.

In the first case, the new request should be properly positioned in the portfolio. Functions and features must be carefully evaluated for duplications with existing services. In the case of improvement and change, the request should be carefully evaluated, the feasibility checked, and the available resource capacity validated.

In the case of a new service creation, many items must be considered prior to a go-no-go decision

- Time to market

- Demand on networking resources

- Human resources demand

- Position to competition

- Expected short-range and long-range revenue

- Expected breakeven point

- Addressing generic and specific need by the new service
- Feasibility of QoS expectations from the service

Many service providers are ambitious to maintain a very large services portfolio with a number of very similar services. In most cases, these portfolios are not economical over the long range.

5.3.2 Develop and Implement Procedures

It is assumed that procedures are in place for existing services. This means that the templates can be reused for new, improved, and changed services. Procedures include

- Flow of activities to support the service
- Allocation of responsibilities to human resources
- Escalation steps for problem handling
- Definition of metrics for service assurance

5.3.3 Define and Implement Systems Changes

In order to support new, improved, or changed services, hardware and software changes in facilities and equipment are usually required. This function defines those change requests. The prerequisite is that the mutual dependency between services and underlying resources is well known. This is a question of the accuracy of the inventory database in which services and their relations to hardware and software components are maintained. Good examples are with VPNs and CNMs.

IP-Based Virtual Private Networks (VPNs)

As a VPN delivery transport, the Internet is the low-cost leader. But, many service providers also offer VPN services over their private IP backbones. While these VPNs may be limited in scope to subscribers of the service provider network, they offer more predictable and controllable performance than is available from the Internet. The public Internet offers ubiquitous access and low cost. Private IP backbones can provide VPNs with levels of quality of service (QoS). With the appropriate mix of services, enterprise network managers can develop an outsourced WAN strategy that meets a range of cost and performance needs.

Three VPN tunneling protocols are currently in line to become industry standards:

1. *Point-to-Point Tunneling Protocol (PPTP).* This protocol is a tunneling protocol designed to encapsulate dialup Point-to-Point Protocol (PPP) traffic within a secure PPTP tunnel. It is similar to IPSec in that it does not support any inherent method of access control once a tunnel has been built.

2. *Layer 2 Transmission Protocol (L2TP).* This is an extension to PPP that authenticates dialup users and provides a routed connection to a network-based server. L2TP is the successor of PPTP. It is a combination of the Layer 2 Forwarding (L2F) Protocol proposed by Cisco and PPTP proposed by Microsoft. This protocol is designed to tunnel the link level of higher-level protocols over the Internet.

3. *IP Security Protocol (IPSec).* This is the standard proposed for IP security. It defines a set of standard security protocols that authenticate TCP/IP connections, add data confidentiality and integrity to TCP/IP packets, and are transparent to the application and the underlying network infrastructure. It offers LAN-to-LAN and client-to-LAN encryption and authentication methods for IP-based traffic. This effort is supported by a wide variety of vendors and is being implemented in the IPv6 version of the protocol. It specifies encryption and authentication, but does not include any method of access control other than packet filtering.

In summary, IPSec is the best IP VPN solution for IP environments, as it includes strong security measures, notably encryption, authentication, and key management, in its standard set. PPTP and L2TP are suitable for multiprotocol non-IP environments.

Here are some of the issues to resolve and decisions to make in order to implement IP VPNs.

1. Some industry problems have been settled, some are being mastered, and some are the subject of standards debates and the lengthy standards process.

2. Security is a critical component of a VPN implementation, especially for those implemented over the public Internet. Encryption delivers the "private" in virtual private networking, but it is very process-intensive. Because of this, hardware-based VPN products deliver the best performance. The Internet was not initially designed with high security in mind, which means that for corporations to entrust it with their most sensitive data, some additional work must be done to ensure that the right people are accessing the networks (*authentication*) and that the data itself cannot be used by outsiders (*encryption*).

3. The Internet was not designed to deliver performance guarantees. Applications designed to work with a guaranteed network latency may not perform adequately on the Internet.

4. IP VPNs must include tools for the network manager and service providers to manage security, performance, and costs. Both managers must be able to manage the following

   ■ Installing and provisioning equipment in a secure fashion

   ■ Scaling the VPN when the requirements grow beyond its current capabilities

   ■ Tracking problems beyond their own borders (for the network manager this means across the outsourced WAN, and for the service provider this means across multiple subscriber networks)

   ■ Establishing extranet relationships with a range of business partners, some highly trusted and some not

Customer Network Management

Customer network management (CNM) has been a long time coming for several reasons. First, it is difficult to measure how much customer network management benefits the bottom line. CNM generally falls into the cost-saving side which is very hard to sell to management. Selling is easier when the CNM user is actually a value-added provider, which makes CNM a critical component of the value-added service.

Second, when it comes to CNM, many network managers simply do not know what services to require from the supplier. Third, some network managers have serious security concerns about letting an outsider get a detailed look at mission-critical data. Others are afraid that CNM is an attempt by the carrier to lock the customer into a long-term relationship. And yet others worry that CNM is the first step toward outsourcing.

Fourth, CNM is very complex to implement. Enabling customers to perform both read and write operations on the internal operations support systems of the telecommunications providers places considerable stress on those OSSs. Most OSSs are not designed for the extra transaction handling and security imposed by CNM. Further, integrating a CNM interface with the network management system of the customer is a difficult task.

Corporate networks must be able to perform various management tasks. In particular, the following tasks should be supported

- Fault management, including fault detection, analysis and reporting, tracking, and resolution

- Performance and quality-of-service management

- Configuration management, including inventory management, service control, service ordering, and tracking

- Security management, including the protection of the network and its management from both outside and within

- Accounting management, including invoicing, maintaining user and usage profiles, scenario analysis, trend reporting, and exception reporting

Most of these tasks must be duplicated for equipment and services of the providers. This redundancy can lead to serious inconsistencies between the provider, the corporation, and reality due to the lack of synchronization between inventory files and databases. Moreover, without near-real-time information about the provider's network, it is difficult to establish and maintain coherent, end-to-end views of the network, its services, and its performance.

Corporations that buy services from multiple providers find that their problems multiply as the number of interfaces to the service provider rises: operational, fault reporting, inventory, service modification, accounting, and so on. However, even when these interfaces were unified into a one-stop-shopping concept at the provider end, integration with the corporation's internal management systems remains a problem. There are a number of issues to be resolved:

1. *Accounting management.* If a customer wants to receive billing information from the provider in near real time (end of shift or end of day) to update an accounting system, some form of electronic interface between customer and provider is needed. Alternatives like e-mail or sending a tape via courier are not the best solutions.

2. *Bandwidth management.* Without integrated CNM and enterprise network management, customers that want to change the bandwidth of a service or add more channels to voice and data have to contact the provider through its interface. After confirmation, which may take some time, the customer can start to reconfigure its routers and other network devices. Ideally, using a CNM system would require a single application that would accept the request for additional bandwidth. A component of this application would wait for notification that the change has been made and then initiate reconfiguration of the customer network.

3. *Quality of service.* Many customers use their own network management systems to verify that the provider is meeting contracted quality-of-service commitments. Doing this properly involves a significant amount of resources. The provider on the other end is probably collecting the same data for the same purpose. It would be best if both parties were working from the same view of the service.

4. *Fault management.* Customers will likely perform initial detection and diagnosis of fault using their own network management and monitoring systems. Without CNM, they then must relay this data via phone or fax to the provider and track the progress of fault rectification using the same medium. Assuming the high level of sophistication on both ends, this is not the most efficient way to solve problems.

5.3.4 Develop and Implement Training

Readiness and preparedness require that training be completed for all human resources that are scheduled to be involved in supporting the new, improved, and changed services. Principal tasks are as follows

- Develop training documentation
- Determine who has to be trained
- Schedule training classes
- Complete training
- Evaluate training experiences—in particular, results during stress tests

5.3.5 Develop Customer Documentation

Prior to launching a new, improved, or changed service, customer documentation must be completed. Documentation must—at a minimum—contain the following

- Description of service functions and features
- Procedures to order the service

- Procedures to cancel the service
- Procedures to change the service
- Procedures to get more information about the service
- Summary of benefits using this service
- Guidelines for pricing the service
- Recommendations for cases in which the service offers the greatest benefits to customer
- Performance expectations, including QoS metrics that may be added to SLAs
- Sample SLAs
- Methods for service assurance
- Contact numbers for problem notification with the service

5.3.6 Plan Rollout, Test, Start Service, and Project-Manage

Service launches must be carefully prepared. Various service tests must be completed prior to starting the service. Prior to launching any services, assessment of completeness and readiness is required. Assessment of completeness includes, but is not limited to

- Attainment of launch objectives
- Availability of resources
    - Network elements (hubs, switches, routers, multiplexers)
    - Signaling solution
    - Facilities
    - Support systems for customer care, order handling, provisioning, operational management and billing
    - Human resources (key positions staffed)
- Completeness of documentation
- Evaluation of testing results
    - Element tests
    - Integration tests
    - Interface tests
- Evaluation of training results

Readiness is usually tested by assessing three modes:

1. *Normal mode.* Testing and evaluation of systems, processes, network equipment, and facilities to verify that functional requirements are met and services can be supported at forecast levels of usage.

2. *Stress mode.* Testing and evaluation of systems, processes, network equipment, and facilities to verify that functional requirements are met and services can be supported at abnormally high levels of usage.

3. *Disaster mode.* Testing and evaluation of systems, processes, network equipment, and facilities when there is a loss of functionality or outage of some element for various levels of duration.

Evaluation reports may discover gaps in various areas. Those gaps should be grouped around priorities:

Priority 1. High severity level and high probability of occurrence.

Priority 2. High severity level and low probability of occurrence.

Priority 3. Low severity level and high probability of occurrence.

Priority 4. Low severity level and low probability of occurrence.

Rollout depends on the availability of facilities and equipment supporting the service. The feedback on this is expected from the network planning and development process.

5.3.7 Set Product/Service Pricing

This input is requested by the rating and discounting process. Service price depends on many factors

- Complexity of service
- Resource demand of the service
- Human resources demand
- Expected operating costs
- Degree of automation for provisioning and problem handling
- Price of comparable services offered by the competition

Usually, promotional prices are set first. After evaluating the operational and financial experiences, the service pricing may change.

5.4 The Network Planning and Development Process

This process encompasses development and acceptance of strategy, description of standard network configurations for operational use, and definition of rules for network planning, installation, and maintenance.

It is about the planning of boundary nodes, routes, and capacity. Considering IP-based services, multiple alternatives for the implementation are available. It depends on the technologies with which IP can collaborate. Popular solutions are as follows

- IP over ATM
- IP over frame relay or
- IP over SONET/SDH

After the topology of the networks has been determined, physical and logical connections are expected to be provisioned. Also, backup and reserve capacity are provisioned so that future customer demands can be met more rapidly.

Special modeling tools are very useful to predict future performance under various load conditions. These tools utilize what-if scenarios to emulate performance under various load conditions. These tools depend on the protocols used. Many providers work with multiple tools, and there are different tools for practically each service. This process is also responsible for selecting and deciding on measurability of SLA metrics.

In addition, this process deals with designing the network capability to meet a specified service need at the desired cost and for ensuring that the network can be properly installed, monitored, controlled, and billed. The process is also responsible for ensuring that enough network capacity will be available to meet the forecast demand and for supporting cases of nonforecast demand. Based on the required network capacity, orders are issued to suppliers or other network operators, and site preparation and installation orders are issued to the network inventory management or to a third-party network constructor. A design of the logical network configuration is provided to the network provisioning process. Principal functions are as follows:

- Develop and implement procedures.
- Set up framework agreements.
- Develop new methods and architectures.
- Plan required network capacity.
- Plan the mutation of network capacity.
- Issue orders to suppliers and other network operators.
- Plan the logical network configuration.
- Evaluate service metrics.

Table 5.7 identifies the information sources to this process. Table 5.8 shows the information output and the targeted processes.

Figure 5.12 shows the principal flowchart for the sequence of functions supporting network planning and development.

5.4.1 Develop and Implement Procedures

In order to support the service's portfolio of service providers, the underlying network should be built with optimal capacity at reasonable costs. This function concen-

Table 5.7 Information Input for the Network Planning and Development Process

SOURCE OF INFORMATION	INFORMATION
Service configuration	Additional capacity requests
Service planning and development	New service description and capacity plan
Network data management	Capacity request
Network provisioning	Capacity request
Network maintenance and restoration	Capacity request
Network inventory management	Capacity request
Supplier	New networking technology

Table 5.8 Information Output for the Network Planning and Development Process

INFORMATION	TARGETED PROCESSES
Preordered engineering assignments	Service configuration
Capabilities and capacity	Service planning and development
Configuration requirements	Network provisioning
Maintenance rules	Network maintenance and restoration
Work orders	Network inventory management
Performance goals	Network data management
Orders	Suppliers

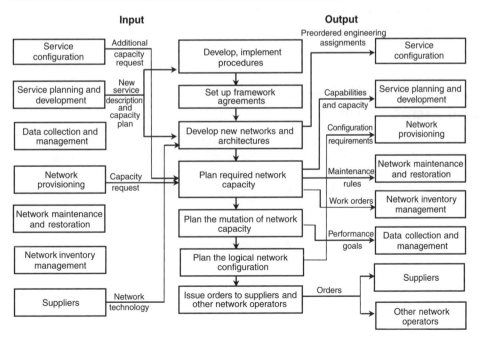

Figure 5.12 Functions of the network planning and development process.

trates on the development of procedures, forms, and templates to be used in the network planning and development process, including the following items

- Capacity request forms
- Description of capacity request for new services
- Templates for new technology scans

To some extent, the output side can be standardized

- Work-order forms
- Forms for configuration requirements
- Maintenance rules

If workflow products are in use, all of these forms and templates are offered automatically.

5.4.2 Set Up Framework Agreements

In advanced multimedia networks, most of the networking equipment incorporates considerable processing capacity. This function is in charge of evaluating hardware and software frameworks for those processors. Hardware is getting more and more interchangeable. Software frameworks are usually based on Unix, Windows NT, or Windows 2000.

Additional items to be decided by this function are

- Framework for database servers
- Framework for data warehouses
- Licensing agreements with third-party vendors

5.4.3 Develop New Methods and Architectures

Network convergence is the wave of the future. Most service providers are busy building new network infrastructures and offering new services to overlay on existing infrastructures. In particular, the IP service will completely change the way networks are planned, developed, and implemented. Two examples will demonstrate the power of this process.

Determination of the Optimal Lower Layers to Carry IP Traffic

The supporting lower-layer infrastructure (Figure 2.14) is going to be reassessed. Besides the traditional IP-ATM-SONET/SDH combination, other options are also under consideration. This alternative is conservative, least risky from the engineering point of view, and achievable now. It may, however, lead to low efficiency and high costs. Enhanced frame relay may substitute ATM everywhere, offering lower costs at good quality of service (QoS). But in certain areas there are no QoS standards available. ATM transport may eliminate the SONET/SDH layer offering ATM ring functions similar to distributed ATM switches. Only a few vendors consider this an option. ATM/IP hybrids based on SONET/SDH would reduce the number of routers and result in lower management expenses. This technology is in the test phase, still unproven. IP over SONET/SDH eliminates the ATM layer completely. If megarouters are at cost parity with ATM switches, this alternative would be the low-cost IP delivery solution. This technology is unproven; operating costs of megarouters are difficult to predict. Optical IP would be the lowest-cost delivery of IP services. In this case, IP is directly connected to the optical subnetwork of Layer 1, using neither ATM nor SONET/SDH. It is the least proven technology; there are serious concerns about fault management with this alternative. Table 5.9 shows the comparison of alternatives.

Table 5.9 Alternatives for Supporting IP Networking

APPROACH	SIGNIFICANT BENEFITS	PROBLEMS	LIKELY ADOPTERS
1. ATM + SDH/ SONET = B-ISDN	Most conservative, least risky engineering approach. Deployable now.	Stacked network elements lead to low efficiency and high cost.	PTTs. Many of them committed to this technology in the 1990s.
2. ATM Transport	Eliminates the entire SDH/SONET layer of network elements. Compliant with ITU recommendations 1.432. ATM ring functions as a distributed ATM switch.	Telco politics are barriers to acceptance. Few vendors for network elements.	Both incumbent and new entrants are interested.
3. Switched routing (ATM or FR + IP hybrids)	Eliminates Layer 2 switching (ATM or FR). Reduces the number of routers.	Unproven.	Most carriers are interested—if the approach actually is more cost-effective than megarouters.
4. IP over SHD/ SONET	Eliminates ATM layer of network elements. If megarouter is at cost parity with ATM switch, this approach will be low-cost IP delivery solution.	Unproven—assumes megarouters are more cost-effective than layer 2 and 3 hybrids or ATM switches.	ISPs. Telcos wholesaling capacity to ISPs.

Continues

Table 5.9 Alternatives for Supporting IP Networking *(Continued)*

APPROACH	SIGNIFICANT BENEFITS	PROBLEMS	LIKELY ADOPTERS
5. Optical IP	Eliminates ATM layer of network elements. If megarouter is at cost parity with ATM switch, this approach will be low-cost IP delivery solution. Most efficient for delivery of IP services.	Least proven. Convergence time after faults may be a problem while optical restoration is needed.	Internet backbone providers with ample rights of way (e.g., power utilities). Valid for IP-only markets.
6. Enhanced frame relay in place of ATM	Approximately 15% more link efficiency for IP traffic today. QoS would combine FR and ATM advantages. Voice trunking over FR works as well as ATM.	Will not support circuit emulation of DS1s. Inevitable evolution to larger packets will diminish efficiency advantage to perhaps 7 to 10%. QoS and high-speed links are not yet standardized.	Pure IP players (ISPs) get the greatest benefit from avoiding the ATM "cell tax."

Develop VoIP Solutions

Real-time voice traffic can be carried over IP networks in three different ways:

1. *Voice trunks* can replace the analog or digital circuits that are serving as voice trunks (e.g., private links between company-owned PBXs) or PSTN access trunks (links between a PBX and the carrier). Voice packets are transferred between pre-defined IP addresses, thereby eliminating the need for phone number to IP address conversions. Fallback to the PSTN or other private voice circuits is always an option in this scenario.

2. *PC-to-PC voice* can be provided for multimedia PCs (microphone and sound support) operating over an IP-based network without connecting to the PSTN. PC applications and IP-enabled telephones can communicate using point-to-point or multipoint sessions.

3. *Telephony* (any phone to any other phone) communications appear as a normal telephone to the caller, but may actually consist of various forms of voice over packet network, all interconnected to the PSTN. Gateway functionality is required when interconnecting to the PSTN or when interfacing the standard telephones to a data network. In the future, IP-enabled telephones will connect directly. For true universality, standards for VoIP must be adopted and applied.

Future VoIP network will include IP-based PBXs, which will emulate the functions of a traditional PBX. Design and development challenges for product development arise in five specific areas:

1. Voice quality should be comparable to what is available using the PSTN, even over networks having variable levels of QoS.

2. The underlying IP network must meet strict performance criteria, including minimizing call refusals, network latency, packet loss, and disconnects. This is required even during congestion conditions or when multiple users must share network resources.

3. Call control (signaling) must make the telephone calling process transparent; the callers need not know what technology is actually implementing the service.

4. PSTN/VoIP service interworking involves gateways between the voice and data network envisionment.

5. System management, security, addressing (directories and dial plans), and accounting must be provided and preferably consolidated with the PSTN operation support systems

The race to create VoIP products that suit a wide range of user configurations has now begun. Standards must be adopted and implemented; gateways providing high-volume IP and PSTN interfaces must be deployed; existing networks need to be QoS-enabled; and global public services need to be established. Also, adoption of VoIP must remain economically viable even if PSTN prices decrease.

Providing a level of quality that at least equals the PSTN is viewed as a basic requirement, although some experts argue that a cost-versus-function-versus-quality trade-off should be applied. Although QoS usually refers to the fidelity of the transmitted voice and facsimile documents, it can also be applied to network availability (e.g., call capacity or level of call blocking), telephone feature availability (conferencing, calling number display, etc.), and scalability (any-to-any, universal, expandable).

The quality of sound reproduction over a telephone network is fundamentally subjective, although standardized measures have been developed by the ITU. Three factors can profoundly impact the quality of the service:

1. *Delay.* Two problems that result from high end-to-end delay in a voice network are *echo* and *talker overlap.* Echo becomes a problem when the round-trip delay is more than 50 ms. Since echo is perceived as a significant quality problem, VoIP systems must address the need for echo control and implement some means of echo cancellation. Talker overlap becomes significant if the one-way delay becomes greater than 250 ms. The end-to-end delay budget is therefore the major constraint and driving requirement for reducing delay through a packet network.

2. *Jitter (delay variability).* Jitter is the variation in interpacket arrival time as introduced by the variable transmission delay over the network. Removing jitter requires collecting packets and holding them long enough to allow the slowest packets to arrive in time to be played in the correct sequence, which causes additional delay. The jitter buffers add delay, which is used to remove the packet delay variation that each packet is subjected to as it travels the packet network.

3. *Packet loss.* IP networks cannot provide a guarantee that packets will be delivered at all, much less in order. Packets will be dropped under peak loads and during periods of congestion (caused, for example, by link failures or inadequate capacity). Due to the time sensitivity of voice transmissions, however, the normal TCP-based retransmission schemes are not suitable. Approaches used to compensate for packet loss include interpolation of speech by replaying the last packet and sending of redundant information. Packet losses greater than 10 percent are generally not tolerable.

Maintenance of acceptable voice-quality levels despite inevitable variations in network performance (such as congestion or link failures) is achieved using such techniques as compression, silence suppression, and QoS-enabled transport networks. Several development results, most notably advances in digital signal processor (DSP) technology, high-powered network switches, and QoS-based protocols, have combined to enable and encourage the implementation of voice over data networks. Low-cost, high-performance DSPs can process the compression and echo cancellation algorithms efficiently.

Software preprocessing of voice conversations can also be used to further optimize voice quality. One technique, called *silence suppression,* detects whenever there is a gap in the speech and suppresses the transfer of things like pauses, breaths, and other periods of silence. This can amount to 50 to 60 percent of the time of a call, resulting in considerable bandwidth conservation. Since the lack of packets is interpreted as complete silence at the output, another function is needed at the receiving end to add "comfort noise" to the output.

Also, echo cancellation can be helpful. As was noted earlier, echo becomes a problem wherever the end-to-end delay for a call is greater than 50 ms. Sources of delay in a packet voice call include the collection of voice samples (called *accumulation delay*), encoding/decoding and packetizing time, jitter buffer delays, and network transit delay. G.168 from ITU defines the performance requirements that are currently required for echo cancelers.

Engineering a VoIP network and the equipment used to build it involves trade-offs among the quality of the delivered speech, the reliability of the system, and the delays inherent in the system. Minimizing the end-to-end delay budget is one of the key challenges in VoIP systems. Ensuring reliability in a best-effort environment is another. Equipment manufacturers offering the flexibility to configure their systems to fit the environment and thereby optimize the quality of the voice produced will have a competitive advantage.

Most of today's typical data network equipment (e.g., routers, LAN switches, ATM switches, network interface cards, and PBXs) will need to be able to support facsimile traffic. Furthermore, VoIP-specific equipment will either have to be integrated into these devices or work compatibly with them. VoIP equipment must also accommodate environments ranging from private, well-planned corporate intranets to the less predictable Internet. The following techniques may contribute to improving quality:

Providing a controlled networking environment. In this environment, capacity can be preplanned and adequate performance can be assumed. This would generally be the case with a private IP network—an intranet—that is owned and operated by a single organization.

Using management tools. These are used to configure the network nodes, monitor performance, and manage capacity and flow on a dynamic basis. Most internet-working devices include a variety of mechanisms that can be useful in supporting voice. For example, traffic can be prioritized by location, by protocol, or by application types, thereby allowing real-time traffic to be given precedence over noncritical traffic. Queuing mechanisms can also be manipulated to minimize delays for real-time flows. More recent developments, such as tag switching and flow switching, can also improve performance and reduce delays.

Adding control protocols. This helps to avoid or alleviate the problems inherent in IP networks. Protocols such as Real Time Protocol (RTP) and Resource Reservation Protocol (RSVP) are also being used to provide greater assurances of controlled QoS within the network. Other mechanisms such as admission controls and traffic shaping may also be used to avoid overloading a network, which may cause busy signals on the phone.

VoIP equipment, which can be categorized into client, access/gateway, and carrier class/infrastructure segments, should be configurable to capitalize on these different techniques, but it must also be sufficiently flexible to add new techniques as they become available. Manufacturers of embedded software should focus on how best to utilize the functions instead of focusing on the problems associated with implementing and testing the objects themselves.

5.4.4 Plan Required Network Capacity

Sizing resources is supported by analytical models and by simulation tools. Prior to using these tools, capacity demand must be aggregated by

- Communication forms, such as voice, data, and video
- Networking sites
- Service offers
- Access networks
- Transport networks
- A combination of all of the preceding

Computing the required network capacity is not an exact science. Modeling and simulation tools allow evaluation of multiple alternatives regarding data input and configuration. After a finite number of iterations, capacity planners know the limits of their proposed physical configuration.

Sizing resources is part of a process that consists of the following steps:

1. The first step is to define accurate requirements that the network must satisfy. This involves collecting information on anticipated traffic loads, traffic types, and sources and destination of traffic This information is used in turn to estimate the network capacity needed.

2. The design process includes various design techniques and algorithms to evaluate and quantify various network topologies. It also includes link and node placements, traffic routing paths, and equipment sizing.

3. After a candidate network solution is developed, it must be analyzed to determine its cost, reliability, and delay characteristics. This step is called *performance analysis.* After this step, the first design iteration is finished.

The entire process may be repeated with revised input data and/or using a new design approach. The basic idea of this iterative process is to produce a variety of networks from which to choose. For most realistic design and sizing problems, it is not possible from a mathematical point of view to know what the optimal network should look like. To compensate for this inability to derive an analytically perfect sizing solution, the network designer must use a trial-and-error technique to determine best options. After surveying a variety of designs, the designer can select the one that appears to provide the best performance at the lowest cost.

Because network design and sizing involve exploring as many alternatives as possible, automated heuristic design tools are often used to produce quick, approximate solutions. Once the overall topology and major design aspects have been decided, it may be appropriate to use additional, more exact solution techniques to refine the details of the network design.

5.4.5 Plan the Mutation of Network Capacity

During the growth phases of the network, it helps to know when assigned capacity should be augmented and groomed to allow for more effective use of available bandwidth and a more robust architecture, perhaps implying redundancy and alternate routing.

This function may use the same modeling and simulation tools as the planning function does.

5.4.6 Issue Orders to Suppliers and Other Network Operators

In order to guarantee the high quality of requested services, orders are issued for networking facilities and equipment. Depending on the service provider, ordering can also be supported by the network inventory management process.

Orders to suppliers and other network operators (ONOs) are expected to be in electronic form; EDI, eCommerce, or extranets could be viable choices.

5.4.7 Plan the Logical Network Configuration

After completing the design and planning for the physical network, the logical network configuration is the next target. This function is gaining importance as packet switching technology takes over. Here are some of the key disciplines to be supported by this function

- Definition of physical and virtual circuits

- Filling in routing tables

- Parameter setting for multiplexers

- Introducing addressing and identification schemes

- Ensuring local number portability

- Deploying control and congestion management

- Using multiprotocol label switching to emulate circuit switching in a packet switched environment

- Deciding about the implementation of policy-based networking (PBN)

5.4.8 Evaluate Service Metrics

Based on the list of service metrics defined and explained in Chapter 4, Section 4.6.5 as part of the customer QoS management process, this function selects the appropriate metrics for the network under consideration. The results of evaluation and selection may look like the following

- Frame relay network
  - Network delay
  - Committed information rate (CIR)
  - CRC errors
  - Discarded frames
  - Effective PVC throughput
- ATM network
  - Available bit rate (ABR)
  - Constant bit rate (CBR)
  - Unspecified bit rate (UBR)
  - Variable bit rate (VBR)
  - Network delay
  - Errored cell rate
  - Effective PVC throughput

Mixed solutions are typical; good detailed metrics for the element and network management layers are available. There are frame relay and ATM monitoring devices available in the industry that are providing all these metrics. The final selection of tools depends on the management frameworks and element management systems in use. The monitoring devices are expected to work with both of them.

5.5 The Network Provisioning Process

This process encompasses the configuration of the network to ensure that network capacity is ready for provisioning of services. It carries out network provisioning as required to fulfill specific service requests and configuration changes to address network problems. The process must assign and administer identifiers for provisioned resources and make them available to other processes. Note that the routine provisioning of specific instances of a customer service—in particular, simple services such as POTS—may not normally involve network provisioning, but may be handled directly by service provisioning from a preconfigured set.

Provisioning IP-based services involves a large number of nodes and servers that are completely unknown in a voice environment. Provisioning requires experienced subject matter experts. Provisioning volumes of today can be managed. Future requests must be satisfied by automated provisioning procedures, leaving only unusual provisioning requests to human operators. Workflow is considered the glue that connects multiple processes to each other. Principal functions of this process are

- (Re)configuration of the network; installation of initial configuration and reconfiguration due to capacity problems
- Administration of the logical network so it is ready for service
- Connection management
- Testing the network

Table 5.10 identifies the information sources to this process. Table 5.11 shows the information output and the targeted processes.

Table 5.10 Information Input for the Network Provisioning Process

SOURCE OF INFORMATION	INFORMATION
Service configuration	Preservice assignment and provisioning requests
Network planning and development	Configuration requirements
Network maintenance and restoration	Configuration request
Network inventory management	Available capacity
Element management	Change events, command confirmations, test results

Table 5.11 Information Output for the Network Provisioning Process

INFORMATION	TARGETED PROCESSES
Assignment and configuration ready	Service configuration
Capacity requests	Network planning and development
Start monitoring	Network data management
Work orders	Network inventory management
Start/stop usage/performance data, configuration commands, test	Element management commands

Figure 5.13 shows the principal flowchart for the sequence of functions supporting network provisioning.

5.5.1 (Re)configuration of the Network: Installation of Initial Configuration and Reconfiguration due to Capacity Problems

Based on the input from various other processes, this function executes initial configuration and reconfiguration of the network. It is assumed that capacity of facilities and equipment is available.

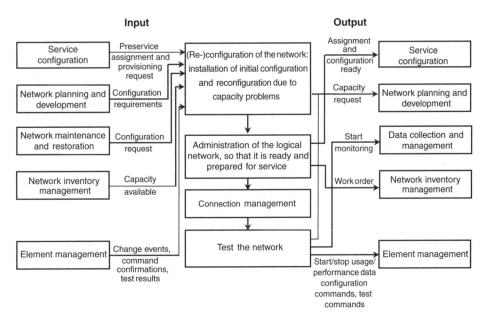

Figure 5.13 Functions of the network provisioning process.

Some of the tasks can be jointly implemented by planning the logical configuration from the network planning and development process. Prior to administration, all new resources should be provided with names and addresses that are maintained in the network inventory database.

BOND

In order to speed up xDSL deployment, vendors aim to tightly integrate the most crucial functions of their OSSs. These are the areas where the most false configurations happen. The Back Office Network Development (BOND) initiative is supported by a number of vendors, enabling the consortium to deliver a rich functionality. BOND is also responsible for linking the critical physical layer management to OSS. Without physical loop management systems integrated with the OSS, there is no way to ensure that a particular type of xDSL will work as promised.

The following suppliers are offering the following contributions:

- Cygent Inc.—prequalification and ordering xDSL services.
- NightFire Software—automating prequalification, loop pre-ordering, and ordering between wholesale service providers.
- Syndesis—provisioning across multiple networks.
- Vitria Technology Inc.—customizing the xDSL deployment and management process.
- BusinessEdge Solutions, Cap Gemini, and Ernst & Young—system integration ensuring interoperability with key OSS vendors.

Further partners are included for fault management, customer care, billing, and for more advanced order management.

MSPP

Integrated multiservice networks will use Multi Service Provisioning Platforms (MSPP) to provide connectivity across hardware and protocol layers in use and for future networking enhancements (BELL00). MSPPs enable service providers to offer customers new bundled services at the transport, switching, and routing layers of the network. These platforms reduce the provisioning time demand while improving the flexibility of adding, migrating, or removing customers.

These provisioning platforms allow service providers to simplify their edge networks by consolidating the number of separate boxes needed to provide intelligent optical access. They significantly improve the efficiency of SONET/SDH networks for transporting multiservice traffic. These platforms also reduce the number of network management systems needed, and decrease the resources needed to install, provision, and maintain the network. But these platforms are very complex systems, involving a variety of hardware and software technologies, millions of lines of code, and a range of functionality. The approaches to problem-solving depend on the vendor. Focus should be on the following items:

- *Physical interfaces.* Because MSPPs are close to the customer, they must interface with a variety of customer premises equipment and handle a range of physical interfaces. Most vendors support telephony interfaces (DS-1, DS-3), optical interfaces (OC-3, OC-12), and Ethernet interfaces (10/100BaseT). DSL and Gigabit Ethernet may also be offered by some vendors.

- *Protocol processing.* MSPPs have significantly increased the intelligence at the network edge due to the increased amount of higher-layer protocol processing. MSPPs can break open diverse types of traffic streams, and aggregate switch or route traffic to its proper destination. MSPPs targeting the metropolitan core usually focus on Layer 1 time division multiplexer and selected Layer 2 (ATM) processing. Those closer to the edge will target additional services such as frame relay and edge routing.

- *Optical transport.* The optical transport capabilities of MSPPs vary. MSPPs targeting the metropolitan core will typically have backplane speeds in the 240 to 400Gbps range, starting with OC-48 and scaling to OC-192 and DWDM. Conversely, MSPPs targeting the metropolitan edge will typically be in the 6 to 50 Gbps range, starting with OC-3/OC-12 and scaling to OC-48 with DWDM in the future.

- *Integrated digital cross-connect switching.* This is an optional functionality. It enables carriers to do much of the cross-connect function at the edge of the network, and avoid backhauling traffic to the central office for cross connecting. This can free transport bandwidth as well as extensible digital cross-connect ports in the central office.

- *Provisioning and network management.* The flexibility in which an MSPP can be provisioned and managed is largely a result of the management architecture. Network architectures with combined physical interfaces and protocol processing require a separate card for each protocol and interface combination. Suppliers that have separated physical interfaces from protocol processing can provide multiple choices for protocol-port connections. This increases significantly the flexibility for service providers to offer remote provisioning options to their customers.

It is expected that MSPP capabilities will be integrated into existing OSSs offering order processing and provisioning.

5.5.2 Administration of the Logical Network to Prepare for Service

During network and circuit installation, services are coming up automatically, triggered by provisioning applications. Also, testing can be switched on during this phase. Upon activation, this includes sending completion messages to provisioning and billing systems.

New installation performance monitoring is important to start the administration. Rules inhibit alarming in the time frame between circuit activation and customer-promised equipment installation; also, alarm activation is based on first detection of signal or time-based triggers.

5.5.3 Connection Management

It is a special test about connectivity. Its importance is very high, when connectivity is required with a number of other service providers.

5.5.4 Test the Network

One of the key functions of this process is to test the network in the necessary depth. It involves testing under the following conditions:

Normal conditions. Testing and evaluating systems, processes, and network equipment to verify that functional requirements are met and services can be supported at forecast levels of usage.

Peak conditions. Testing and evaluation of systems, processes, and network equipment to verify that functional requirements are met and services can be supported at abnormally high levels of usage.

Stress conditions. Testing and evaluation of systems, processes, and network equipment to verify that functional requirements are met and services can be supported at artificially increased usage level that may represent the ultimate scalability toward the service.

Disaster conditions. Testing and evaluation of systems, processes, and network equipment when there is a loss of functionality or outage of some elements for varying time periods.

For facilities and equipment, component tests are followed by integration tests. The new installation monitoring function records the testing conditions and results. This kind of testing prior to launching a service is usually conducted by external consulting companies that are absolutely unbiased. They are requested to summarize the findings in a gap analysis report, highlighting the results in the following clusters:

Priority 1. High severity level and high probability of occurrence.

Priority 2. High severity level and low probability of occurrence.

Priority 3. Low severity level and high probability of occurrence.

Priority 4. Low severity level and low probability of occurrence.

Test documentation must be completed at the time of launching the service.

5.6 The Service Ordering Process

The service ordering process includes all the functions of accepting a customer's order for service, tracking the progress of the order, and notifying the customer when the order is complete. Orders can include new, change, and disconnect orders for all or part of a customer's service, as well as cancellations and modifications to orders. Preorder activity that can be tracked is included in this process. The development of an order plan may be necessary when service installation is to be phased in, and the need for preliminary feasibility requests and/or pricing estimates may be part of this process when certain services are ordered. The aim is to order the service the customer requested, to support changes when necessary, and to keep the customer informed with meaningful progress of the order, including its successful completion. Principal functions of this process are

- Accept orders
- Determine preorder feasibility
- Prepare price estimates and SLA terms
- Develop order plan
- Perform credit check
- Request customer deposit
- Reserve resources
- Initiate service installation
- Complete orders and notify customers
- Initiate billing process

Table 5.12 identifies the information sources to this process. Table 5.13 shows the information output and the targeted processes.

Figure 5.14 shows the principal flowchart for the sequence of functions supporting service order processing.

Service orders to other providers can be generated by the ordering process or by the service configuration process depending on the nature of the service ordered by the customer. They can also be generated from network and systems management processes when part of network infrastructure.

A customer is identified as a person or company who is responsible for the purchase and consumption of the telecommunications products and services. Each customer has a unique identification number in operations support systems. The logical entity,

Table 5.12 Information Input for the Service Order Provisioning Process

SOURCE OF INFORMATION	INFORMATION
Customer interface management	Orders/cancels, change requests, status inquiries, desired due date
Sales	Orders/cancels, change requests, status inquiries, desired due date
Credit bureau	Credit check response
Other providers	Service order and status
Service planning and development	Options and prices
Service configuration	Feasibility, due date, completion
Network planning and development	Preorder engineering, assignments
Network provisioning	Preorder engineering, assignments

Table 5.13 Information Output for the Service Order Provisioning Process

INFORMATION	TARGETED PROCESSES
Estimated due date, estimated price, confirmed due date, order status, completion notification	Customer interface management
Register QoS and SLA terms, profiles	Problem handling
Required reports, QoS and SLA terms, completion notification	Customer QoS management
Service order and status	Other providers
New/changed service notification and activation	Invoicing/collection
Preservice feasibility request, activate service	Service configuration
Special discounts, customer record details	Rating and discounting
Credit check/request	Credit bureau

customer, can represent a wide variety of actual entities, from a private person in a single-family home to a company with many offices spread across the country. The entity, customer, has several related subentries, which provide a means of further organizing the various types of data related to the broad spectrum of customers served by a service provider.

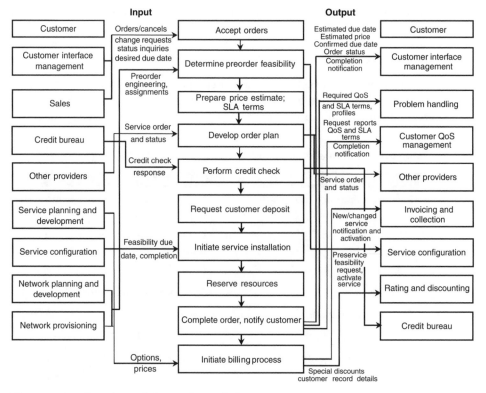

Figure 5.14 Functions of the service ordering process.

5.6.1 Accept Orders

This function deals with the registration of service orders from customers. It includes the registration of new customers as well as changes to customer data for existing customers. The customer service order deals with registration of orders of services from customers. The order is registered through workflow process steps and is processed on the basis of information on network capacity available from the network inventory management process. Data stemming from the order is passed on to the billing system so that the products and services included into the customer service order appear as charges on the customer bills. The maintenance of products and services is handled in the service creation, planning, and development process.

One of the primary tasks of operations support systems is to administer the resources of the telephone network in order to facilitate the allocation of resources to customers. In order to handle the ordering of telephone lines, the responsible order subsystem must have access to information concerning the resources available in the network. Thus, in order to understand the way the ordering process works, it is necessary to understand the way the operations support systems use data on customers and information on the network to manage process of resource allocation.

Figure 5.15 shows a concrete example from a service provider for the customer service ordering process.

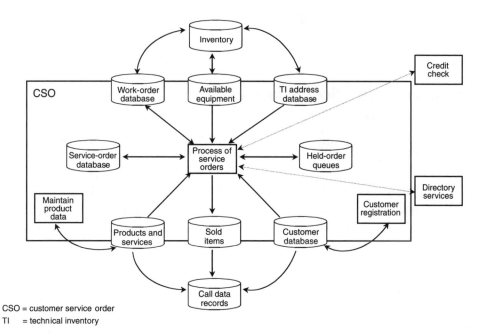

CSO = customer service order
TI = technical inventory

Figure 5.15 Customer service orders process.

5.6.2 Determine Preorder Feasibility

Based on information input from the other processes, the customer service representative (CSR) or his or her workstation is always aware of the actual changes in available capacity. This input may come from any of the following sources

- Sales
- Service creation, planning, and development
- Service configuration
- Network planning and development
- Network provisioning

The planning function includes demand evaluation for certain geographic areas for fulfilling future orders. When a person approaches the service provider and expresses interest in receiving a telephone line (or other services), two processes are initiated. First, information about the person or entity (e.g., name and address) is entered into the operations support system. Through this process, the person becomes registered as a customer in the system. The second process involves inquiries about the telephone line (or other services) the customer wants. This information includes the address at which the line should be installed and any special requirements for the line. This process is called *creating a request.*

When a line request is created, the operations support system automatically checks whether a line is available in the geographical area in which the line is to be installed. If there is, the request can be processed immediately. In other words, the request can be fulfilled. When a line request is fulfilled, two processes take place automatically:

1. The operations support system reserves the line so that it won't be used to fulfill line requests from other customers.
2. A letter, known as the *contract proposal,* is generated and sent to the customer.

5.6.3 Prepare Price Estimates and SLA Terms

The contract proposal contains price estimates for the products and services ordered from the service provider. Depending on the service order, the alternatives for SLAs are expected to be included into the contract proposal. There is obviously an interdependency between SLAs, products and services, and pricing.

It is further assumed that the machine or human CSR has real-time access to multiple databases that contain the information necessary to include in the contract proposal.

5.6.4 Develop Order Plan

If a request cannot be fulfilled at the time it is created, it is placed on a waiting list, known in many telco environments as the *hold-order queue.* Operations support systems poll the hold-order queue periodically, ensuring that all the requests are fulfilled as soon as resource capacity is available in the network. The customer receives two letters in connection with requests in the queue. The first letter, called the *hold-order confirmation,* is generated and sent at the time the request is placed into the queue; the second letter, the *contract proposal,* is generated and sent to the customer at the time the resource (e.g., the line) becomes available to fulfill the request.

5.6.5 Perform Credit Check

The credit validation function interfaces with an external agency to acquire a credit score for a prospect or customer record. Interfacing in real time with the client-defined agency, this function provides one of the following responses

- A credit score
- A listing of similar names
- A not-found message

The credit class master file is associated with a credit score range and identifies the conditions of service that the customer must satisfy (deposit, prepayment, restricted dialing authorities, etc.). Manual override is allowed by authorized users, who are required to provide an override reason code.

This function updates a listing of credit verifications with the following information

- Name of customer
- Phone/fax number of customer
- E-mail address of customer
- Service number for customer
- Credit check date
- Status found
- External score
- Associated credit class
- Override history
- Override reason code
- Service-denied reason code

Full sort and search capability is available on all columns. Each prospect or customer record is automatically updated with the relevant information from the listing. Usual reports are

- Customers with approved credit
- Customers with denied credit
- Customers with credit overrides
- Customers with acceptable risks
- Customers with nonacceptable risks

5.6.6 Request Customer Deposit

Depending on the results of the credit validation, the customer may be asked for an advance payment. In such a case, the process is on hold until the receipt of the payment to the credit bureau or directly to the service provider.

5.6.7 Reserve Resources

This happens when the ordered product/service is available. Timewise, it may happen during the registration step or later after the resources will have been provisioned.

5.6.8 Initiate Service Installation

The customer signs and returns the contract proposal to formally accept the service. At this point, the CSR signals the operations support system to use the information in the request to generate an order for a product. The order for the request takes effect after it has been approved by the CSR or his or her deputy. When an order has been approved, the operations support system generates a *work order* (a document containing instructions for a technician to carry out the work so that the ordered service becomes operational). Additionally, an optional order confirmation letter may be sent to the customer.

5.6.9 Complete Orders and Notify Customers

When the technician has completed the work, the order is considered completed. The line is now operational, the customer may be billed for the service, and the order process is complete.

5.6.10 Initiate Billing Process

When a customer purchases a product, two types of records must usually be kept. The first is a record of the customer order, including information such as the order number and the date the order was placed. The other type of record is the purchase record, which serves as input to the billing process.

Figure 5.16 shows the link between the customer service order and the billing process. The numbers within the graphic show the following information:

1. Signals that a new order is registered.
2. Shows that two types of data are created: *order* and *billing* data (divided into subscription data and one-time data).
3. Shows billing data as input for generating bills.
4. Indicates how bills are generated (they contain charges for the products included in customer order; a record of the data billed is also created).

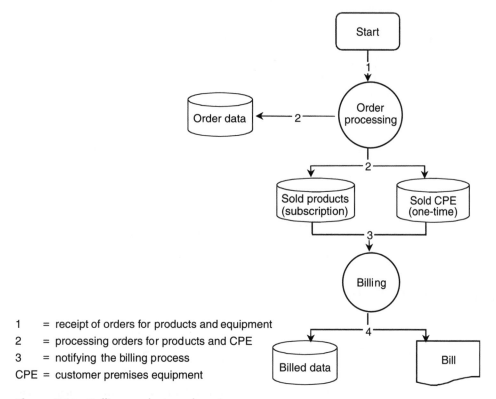

1 = receipt of orders for products and equipment
2 = processing orders for products and CPE
3 = notifying the billing process
CPE = customer premises equipment

Figure 5.16 Selling products and services.

When a customer purchases equipment, he or she is charged a one-time purchase price, which is so defined in billing applications. When a customer subscribes to a service, he or she is generally charged a subscription price at regular intervals. In addition, the customer may also be charged a one-time fee for provisioning the service. Figure 5.17 illustrates how an operations support system handles data for various situations. In the example, the customer is subscribing to a telephone line and number and, in addition, purchasing two items—a handset and a fax machine.

Billing data for subscriptions revolves around the idea that the billing application must keep a permanent record of the subscription while keeping track of the date through which the customer has been billed for the subscription. When a bill is generated for a subscription for a phone line for a certain month, then the billing application updates the database so that the next bill it is going to generate will target the next month. Charges for one-time purchases work differently. When the billing application generates a bill for a one-time product, it deletes the record from the table containing billable data, ensuring that the customer is not billed twice for the same item. One-time fees associated with subscriptions are handled the same manner.

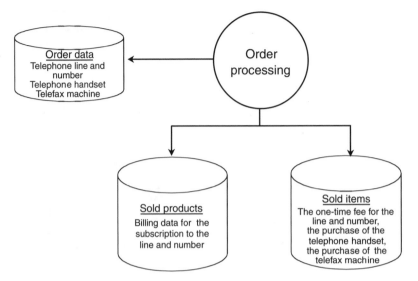

Figure 5.17 Example for a subscription and sold items.

5.7 The Service Configuration Process

This process encompasses the installation and/or configuration of services for specific customers, including the installation/configuration of customer premises equipment. It also supports the reconfiguration of service (due to either customer demand or problem resolution) after the initial service installation. The aim is to correctly provide service configuration within the time frame required to meet ever decreasing intervals.

Offering IP-based services, additional functions must be considered. In particular, firewalls and application services such as e-mail, Web hosting, and their configurations are important. Also, setting parameters to support QoS and SLA requirements is important. The more that can be automated, the better it is for service providers in the competitive market.

Principal functions include the following

- Design solution (preorder)
- Assign capacity (preorder)
- Configure network and customer premises equipment (CPE)
- Update customer configuration record
- Initiate/accept configuration requests to/from other providers
- Initiate installation work
- Activate/deactivate service

■ Report service implementation completion.

Table 5.14 identifies the information sources to this process. Table 5.15 shows the information output and the targeted processes.

Figure 5.18 shows the principal flowchart for the sequence of functions supporting service configuration. The functions discussed in this section are based on a variety of requests, including the following:

■ Changing the network configuration

■ Configuring a service on the basis of customer service orders

■ Activating/deactivating a service

■ Expanding the capacity of resources

Table 5.14 Information Input for the Service Configuration Process

SOURCE OF INFORMATION	INFORMATION
Customer interface management	Request for reconfigure
Order handling	Configure service, activate service, preorder feasibility
Problem handling	Request for reconfigure
Service problem resolution	Request for reconfigure
Service quality management	Additional capacity requirements
Other providers	Request results, available capacity
Network provisioning	Request results, available capacity

Table 5.15 Information Output for the Service Configuration Process

INFORMATION	TARGETED PROCESSES
Completion notification	Customer interface management
Completion notification	Order handling
Completion notification	Problem handling
Completion notification	Service problem resolution
Adds, changes, deletes	Other providers
Adds, changes, deletes	Network inventory management
Preservice requests, provisioning requests	Other providers
Preservice requests, provisioning requests	Network provisioning
Additional capacity requirements	Other providers
Additional capacity requirements	Network planning and development

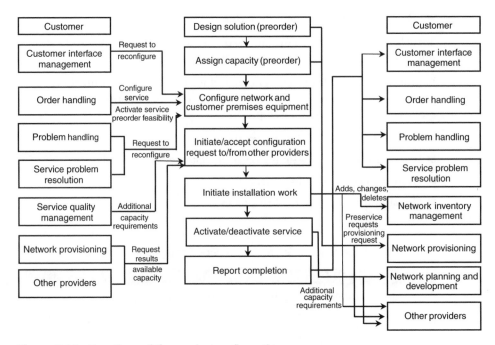

Figure 5.18 Functions of the service configuration process.

5.7.1 Design Solution: Preorder

Depending on the service provider's environment, this function can be supported here or by the network planning and development process. A reasonable split can be made with logical and physical design, leaving modeling and logical design to the network planning and development process. This function is not related to a specific customer service order, but assumes (similarly to planning) future orders by products and services. It is a preconfiguration function of likely orders for predicted products and services in certain geographic areas. Marketing input is extremely important to ensure a very high hit rate.

5.7.2 Assign Capacity: Preorder

Assignments are still independent from actual customer service orders. The decision is based on predictions provided by market research and order handling. Based on these predictions, capacity may be assigned first by products/service.

5.7.3 Configure Network and Customer Premises Equipment

This function is event-driven from customer service order handling. It means the necessary extensions are being made in switches, distributors, routers, serving terminals, and so forth to accommodate the new customer service order. Depending on the service provider, customer premises equipment (CPE) could also be included when order handling supports this type of managed objects.

5.7.4 Update Customer Configuration Record

All adds, changes, and deletes are sent to inventory management to update the appropriate database entries. The configuration process cannot be considered completed until these updates will have been confirmed.

5.7.5 Initiate/Accept Configuration Requests to/from Other Providers

Each service provider has multiple peers. It becomes a very serious administration to keep track of all incoming and outgoing requests and service order completion. Depending on the service providers, these requests can be handled as customer service requests, or specially expedited functions may be deployed to promote high-priority orders.

5.7.6 Initiate Installation Work

As part of workforce management, work orders are issued for execution by teams of technicians. They may reside centrally or both centrally and decentrally. The support documentation is included into the workflow that glues single functions into a complete process.

5.7.7 Activate/Deactivate Service

The actual deployment of work orders is handled by this function. Figure 5.19 shows an example of activating a connection. Figure 5.20 shows the opposite case: deactivating an existing connection as requested by the customer. The flow of treating the work order is very similar to the workflow for activating a connection. The difference is the status that has to be set on the wire-pair assignments of the involved connection paths, which should be set to disconnecting instead of connecting when issuing the work order and to free instead of operating when completing the work order.

5.7.8 Report on Service Implementation Completion

As indicated in Figure 5.18, other processes, providers, and customers receive confirmed messages about the activated or deactivated services.

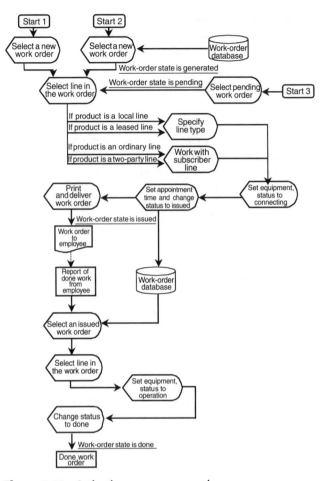

Figure 5.19 Activation process example.

5.7.9 Change Management

Change management should follow a well-proven and established procedure within the service provider's organization. This procedure includes the following phases: planning, approval, execution, and documentation of changes. Submission of change requests can follow the same path as other customer service orders do.

The customer service representative should be able to evaluate the requests and categorize them on the basis of the following information

- Change coordinator segment
  - Identification of change
  - Change number
  - Date of request

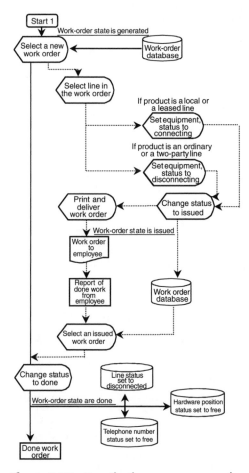

Figure 5.20 Deactivation process example.

- Requester segment
  - Requester name and affiliation
  - Location
  - Change description
  - Components involved by inventory identification
- Network and system components affected by change
  - Major change—change is most likely disruptive
  - Medium change—change can be disruptive
  - Minor change—change is not disruptive
- Due date
- Priority of change
- Reason for change

- Personnel involved in executing the change
- Fallback procedure when change fails
- Approval segment

  Date of approval

  Signature
- Evaluation segment

  Result of change

  Downtime caused by the change

  Date of actual implementation

  Cancellation or postponement

This categorization helps to approve, schedule, and execute the changes on time. In most cases, change management applications are available that need little customization prior to deployment.

Cutovers are always very critical to service providers. The cutover process can usually be limited to a combination of the following two events:

- Merging of one or more existing serving terminals into a new serving terminal that always implies a new networking segment from the serving terminal to the main distribution facility.
- Number change that indicates a change from one switch to another without changing networking segments.

The first cutover action (Figure 5.21a) illustrates that a new network is constructed all the way from the main distribution facility to a new serving terminal. The operations support system supports the planning of such cutover actions.

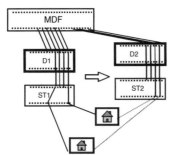

Figure 5.21a   First cutover action with a new distributor and serving terminal.

The second cutover action (Figure 5.21b) illustrates that a new network is constructed with a cable going directly from the main distribution facility to a new serving terminal. The operations support system supports the planning of such cutover actions.

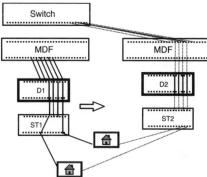

Figure 5.21b Second cutover action with a new serving terminal.

The third cutover action (Figure 5.21c) illustrates that a new network is constructed all the way from a different main distribution facility to a new serving terminal. The operations support system supports the planning of such cutover actions. But planning does not include the network between the switches and the main distribution facilities.

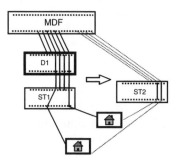

Figure 5.21c Third cutover action with a new main distribution facility.

The fourth cutover action (Figure 5.21d) illustrates that one number interval is changed to a new number interval. The operations support system is expected to support such a cutover action. There are no limitations on whether the new number interval is on the same or on a new switch. But the new number interval may not be assigned to another switch (e.g., it is not possible to assign a number interval that is assigned to an existing switch to a new switch).

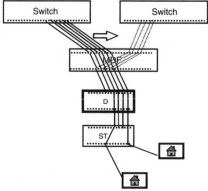

Figure 5.21d Fourth cutover action with number interval changes.

The assignment of phone numbers will depend on whether the last cutover action (where numbers are going to be changed) is combined with other cutover actions in which a new serving terminal is inserted into the network.

If a number change is specified and not combined with any cutover action relating to a serving terminal, then the assignments of numbers will be specified. That means the first phone number in the old phone number interval will be exchanged with the first phone number in the new phone number interval and so forth.

If a number change is specified and combined with any cutover action relating to a serving terminal, then the assignments of numbers will be done only for those phone numbers that are attached to lines affected by the cutover on the specified serving terminal. That means all phone numbers that are not attached to any line affected by the cutover will not be changed.

Special rules must be written with an upgrade procedure that will monitor specific key performance indicators before, during, and after change implementation. There are always instances where compatibility or configuration issues are overlooked or unknown. This focused monitoring alerts management of performance issues that the upgrades may cause so that back-out processes may be launched.

5.7.10 The Evolution of Service Provisioning

Depending on the size and maturity level of service providers, there are many ways to implement the service provisioning process. ILECs have accumulated a lot of experience with provisioning; some CLECs are just starting to learn. For relatively small service providers, manual solutions are acceptable. In this environment, separate terminals are attached to each network element or domain to complete service provisioning, and technicians must be colocated with equipment to respond to alarms or to conduct repairs. Figure 5.22 (MORT98) shows an example of this alternative. After the customer agent receives a call from the customer, the dispatcher is notified via telephone to send a technician to the customer site. E-mail, phone, or fax alerts the technician on the terminal at the network element if work is required. All testing is also performed manually.

Equipment usage analysis and capacity planning remain manual. Usually, the network is overengineered. The next step occurs when the service provider wants to centralize its workforce. By making use of remote terminals connected to the equipment, a smaller number of technicians can perform more of the manual operations functions. Some provisioning and diagnostics activities can be centralized, but technicians must be dispatched to the various sites to execute physical labor. People remain the main interface between machines, as shown in Figure 5.23 (MORT98). The only difference in service provisioning in a centralized versus a manual environment is that the technicians are centrally located, with their terminals connected to the network equipment by an internal data network. As such, they are able to log on to all the equipment from one location instead of having to be physically located with the equipment. Fewer people can perform more work than before.

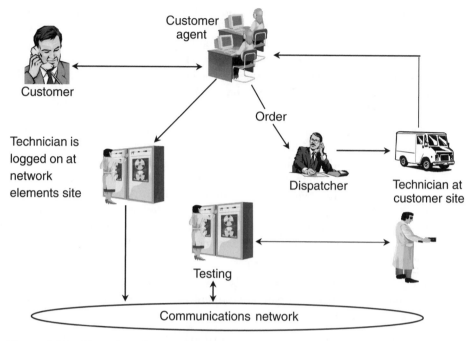

Figure 5.22 Manual service provisioning.

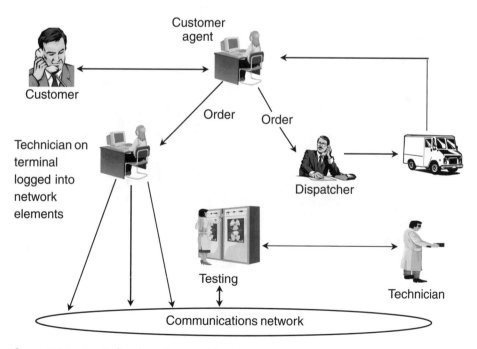

Figure 5.23 Centralized service provisioning.

With this solution, basic usage data off the trunks and switches is available in support of resource provisioning. While inventory is centralized, it resides on a main database that is not accessible remotely. It is assumed that customer care and billing is provided by a service bureau. When the network and service portfolio grow, service providers need more people to operate the network. But it is difficult to find, hire, and train the right people. In this phase, service providers are looking to mechanize their operations.

While the billing function is still with a service bureau, service providers start using billing data management. They deliver detailed records in a more timely and efficient manner. As a result, customer billing is becoming more accurate. Work and order management software that provides customer inventory and trouble tracking now coordinates all critical work items as shown in Figure 5.24 (MORT98). In this mechanized environment, service provisioning is mediated by the work and work-order management operations support system. After the customer agent enters the order information, the system takes over and coordinates and tracks all critical items performed by the workforce.

A mechanized engineering system is needed to allocate resources. While this is a significant improvement compared to the centralized operation stage, it is still a stand-alone inventory system that is not yet accessible remotely.

By introducing automation, a large portion of the manual work can be turned over to computers. Automation can be overkill for small service providers, but it is a must for larger ones. In order to give service providers greater control over their service commitment processes, an integrated customer care system is added to the

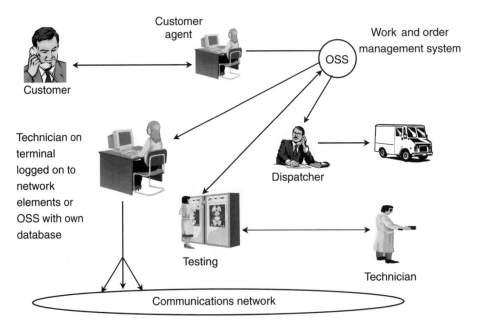

Figure 5.24 Mechanized service provisioning.

core order handling and provisioning functionality to effectively reduce the layers of internal handoffs. Deploying operations support systems significantly improves the ability of service providers to define, capture, manage, and automate workflow in support of maintenance and provisioning functions. In addition, by connecting the order management system to network configuration and trouble management systems, service providers can achieve flow-through operations, as displayed in Figure 5.25 (MORT98). As in the mechanized environment, the customer is still talking to a customer agent linked to an operation support system. The difference is that instead of having a technician logged on to the network elements, a configuration management function handles this task automatically. Because the software now includes an automated dispatch system, the need for a dispatcher is eliminated as well. It should be noted that this system does far more than just assign jobs. This automated solution constantly optimizes the dispatching process by assigning technicians to specific jobs based on their qualifications or locations in relation to customer sites.

In order to demonstrate to customers that they are very valuable to the service provider, on-demand service provisioning may be considered. Figure 5.26 shows such a case (MORT98). On-demand service means that it is activated automatically while the customer is speaking with the customer service representative. With an operations support system that is strong on configuration management, there is no need to dispatch a technician. However, this assumes that the facilities are in place (i.e., have been preprovisioned) to support instant service activation.

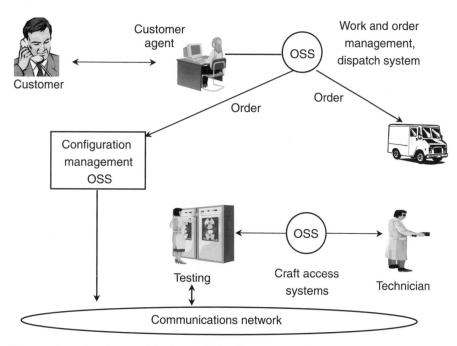

Figure 5.25 Service provisioning activities for automated operations.

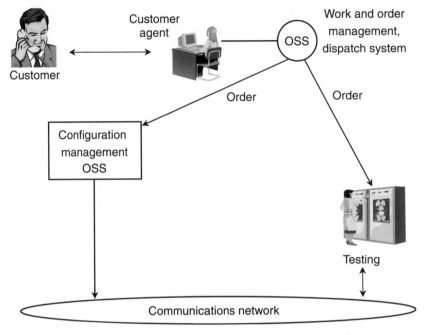

Figure 5.26 Service provisioning activities for on-demand services.

In summary, high-speed provisioning needs powerful workforce and workflow management.

Customer-performed provisioning is also becoming popular. A secured access enables customers to order and assign services via their own interface to their service and network management systems. This may be considered an advanced version of customer network management.

5.7.11 Workflow Concept Implementation

Telecommunications service providers are operating a number of business processes in the areas of customer care, order processing, provisioning, and operational management. With most providers, these processes have been designed, implemented, and operated individually. There are interfaces between these processes, but, particularly with legacy processes, the interfaces are manual.

Workflow is focused on handling business processes in an integrated manner. Innovative service providers are increasingly relying on workflow-based end-to-end business processes (e.g., flow-through service provisioning) to provide the best possible services, in spite of the internal and different structure of business processes.

Workflow can spread across company boundaries to anywhere in the world on the Internet or on intranets. This opens up a completely new way of doing business through home work, mobile work, and virtual enterprises.

Handling business processes well is fundamental to modern service providers. Done well, it increases productivity, improves quality, reduces the time needed for customer service, and enhances operational control. Workflow offers the opportunity to automate business processes and to provide continuity between a customer requiring service and the production of those services.

Representation of Procedures and Processes

The central feature of a workflow engine is the representation of the procedure that a business process must follow. It is this representation that is interpreted by the workflow engine to assign activities to participants according to the state of each process in progress and to move the process forward from one activity to the next. This ensures that the activity will be executed by the participant who has the proper expertise and authority. The process representation is made graphically, and some engines can display it on the participant screen to show the state of a process. For example, a customer who placed an order through an Internet electronic commerce application could monitor the steps leading to delivery.

Through the Internet, intranets, and extranets, participants will be assigned their work automatically and dynamically according to each specific case. The work queues of each worker can be centrally monitored and adjusted as required.

Most workflow activities invoke existing applications. The workflow engine transfers the necessary information to and from those applications. A workflow engine is a tool to integrate, as part of a long-term transaction, several existing applications. A key component of workflow engines is the worklist handler, which gives the participant a list of activities assigned to him or her and which helps to set priorities for the participant's list of activities. On the Internet, intranets, and extranets, this could be implemented with HTML or XML forms, with Java-based handlers, or with both. The essential feature is that any workstation with a universal browser can access the workflow engine and participate in the automated processes.

Workflow engines are able to define deadlines for each process and monitor them. They are able to deal with missed deadlines through a variety of actions such as alerting a supervisor, changing priorities, or even changing the path to be followed inside the procedure. This is an essential feature in an Internet, intranet, or extranet environment where workflow participants are not colocated and can be members of different organizations.

Workflow engines log every single event with a time stamp. They provide statistics from that log on each class of business processes—for example, average duration of the process, average duration of each activity, and average waiting time for a process. These statistics can be used to monitor the activity of remote participants like mobile and home workers. They can also be used as the foundation of virtual enterprise management to check the performance of every partner against a negotiated service contract.

Benefits of Workflow Applications

The following benefits can be observed with workflow applications.

Increased Security

In a workflow application, each participant sees only those tasks assigned to him or her by the workflow engine. Participants' access is controlled by defining rules of assignment for each activity within each procedure.

Enhanced Reactivity

By eliminating manual actions between the end of one activity and the next, one workflow can reduce the time between the start of a business process and its successful completion.

Clear Progress Reports

Workflow applications provide detailed progress reports, including activities in progress, their status and the persons involved and responsible, and a view of the remaining activities to be carried out—all in a matter of seconds. Clients as well as members of the organization can be given exact information on the status of a business process.

Improved Productivity

By taking charge of activity planning and assignment, workflow eliminates most supervisory tasks. With workflow, the user sees a list of activities to be completed. Once he or she chooses an activity, all the documents and forms attached to that activity appear at the workstation automatically. When it is completed, the information created during its execution is automatically filed in its proper place.

Better Quality and Cost Control

A workflow application maintains a diary of all the events it controls, including date and time, the tasks concerned, and the name of the participant. Information from the diary includes reports on the costs and progress of each activity and on performance of the procedures themselves.

Workflow Implementation

Benefits can be summarized as follows.

Company Benefits

Workflow increases control over the productivity of information-related tasks. While reinforcing confidentiality and access-control measures, workflow brings factory methods for managing and controlling processes.

Client Benefits

Clients benefit from improved service quality, better response time, clear information about the status of their request, and more accessible company agents.

Company Agent Benefits

Agents sees lists of activities they have to carry out individually and thus can organize their own work accordingly. The context of each activity can be presented. Workflow offers agents flexibility in their work and speed of execution plus a high level of control.

Manager Benefits

Workflow systems present managers with decisions to be made at the appropriate time and with enough information to enable them to intervene effectively. They can act sooner, more rapidly, and with greater fairness. Workflow gives constant access to the status of each case, and a monitoring system allows managers to keep processes under control. Workflow can revolutionize the supervisory function, bringing it much closer to its industrial counterpart.

Organization Analyst Benefits

With workload-assisted procedures, organization analysts have every kind of statistic necessary to analyze workloads, costs, peak periods, and many other aspects of the company's operations. They can use simulation tools to model procedural refinements at an unprecedented level of detail and accuracy, and the logged data is available at marginal cost.

Concrete workflow implementation examples with telecommunications service providers are Oracle Workflow and BusinessWare from Vitria Technology.

Whichever decision is made, the workflow engine selected is expected to work together with other integration concepts (e.g., CORBA, DCOM, MQSeries) that are used frequently for infrastructure integration.

5.8 The Security Management Process

Due to the fact of opening networks, connecting partners, and using a public domain such as the Internet, security risks increase considerably. Virtual private networks are one solution to providing existing infrastructure with acceptable protection. Security expectations may be different in various industries, but the generic security management procedures are identical, or at least very similar. Security management enables intranet managers to protect sensitive information in the following ways

- By limiting access to Web servers and network devices by users both inside and outside of enterprises
- By notifying the security manager of attempted or actual violations of security

Security management is in charge of protecting all systems solutions. This process includes a planning and controlling function. In particular, three basic threats are considered:

1. Loss of availability of services.

2. Loss of integrity.

3. Loss of privacy.

This process includes the following main functions

- Identification of information to be protected

- Analysis of access options to protected information

- Selection and implementation of solutions for protection

- Periodic reassessment of security solutions

Table 5.16 identifies the information sources to this process. Table 5.17 shows the information output and the targeted processes.

Figure 5.27 shows the principal flowchart for the sequence of functions supporting security management.

5.8.1 Identifying Information to Be Protected

Sensitive information is any data an organization wants to secure, such as that pertaining to customer accounts, price lists, research and development data, payroll, addresses, bill-of-material processors, acquisition and marketing plans, product announcements schedules—the possibilities are almost limitless.

The identification is a team effort in which practically every department or business unit participates. After agreeing on the sensitive information, the team is expected to

Table 5.16 Information Input for the Security Management Process

SOURCE OF INFORMATION	INFORMATION
Customer	Definition of sensitive information
Network inventory management	List of network and system components
Element manager	Technical capabilities

Table 5.17 Information Output for the Security Management Process

INFORMATION	TARGETED PROCESSES
Periodic reports	Customer
Inquiries about technical choices	Consulting and support
Security decisions	Element manager
Security decisions	Network maintenance and restoration
Security extensions in system and network components	Network inventory management

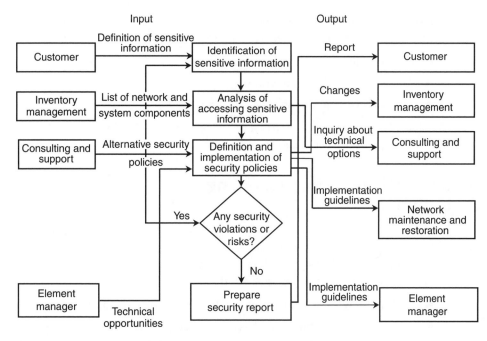

Input   Output

Figure 5.27   Functions of the service management process.

determine the most likely location in which to keep this information. It could become a relatively long list due to the distributed nature of LANs. Most likely locations are the mainframe, which may play the role of a big server, or the database engine and all the servers in the interconnected LANs. Occasionally, even workstations maintain important information that should be protected.

Identifying sensitive information means classifying that information. Most organizations have well-defined policies regarding which information qualifies as sensitive; often it includes financial, accounting, engineering, and employee information. In addition, a particular environment can have sensitive information that is unique to it. The main purpose of intranets is to improve the internal documentation and communication within enterprises. Web servers are the focal point of information maintenance. Obviously, not everything is for everyone. Depending on the individual responsibilities, access rights to information sources can be relatively easily structured and implemented. In summary, sensitive information is on the home pages with particular content residing on Web servers.

5.8.2 Accessing Sensitive Information

Once the Webmaster and network managers identify sensitive information and know where it is located, they must determine how users can access it. This time-consuming process will usually require that Webmasters and network managers examine each piece of hardware and software that offers a service to users. In this respect, intranets are no different from any other complex network. Generic sensitive access points (see Figure 5.28) are as follows

- End-user devices such as browsers
- Access and backbone networks
- Web servers maintaining sensitive information

Table 5.18 shows a threat matrix for service providers that indicates the severity of threats against networks and systems owned and operated by the service provider.

5.8.3 Selecting and Implementing Protection

The next step in security management is to apply the necessary security techniques. The sensitive access points dictate how the protection should be deployed, using a combination of policies, procedures, and tools. In this respect, the following levels of security techniques must be considered

- End-user devices, such as universal browsers (use of chip cards or chip keys)
- Access and backbone networks (use of encryption, authentication, and firewalls)
- Web servers (use of server protection, operating systems protection, special tools, and virus protection)

Security procedures include the following:

1. *Entity authentication.* This mechanism verifies the identity by comparing identification information provided by the entity to the content of a known and trusted

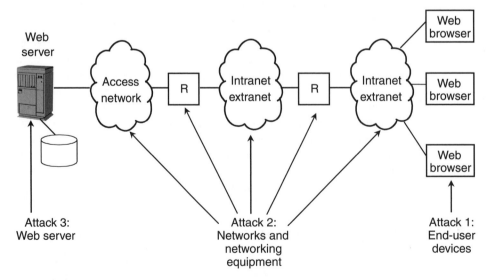

R = Router

Figure 5.28 Access points with security risks.

Table 5.18 Threat Matrix for Service Providers

Threats	Passive threats: Listening to connections, data exchange, and traffic flow analysis*	Repetition Modification Insertion	Congesting networks	Faking false identity and denial of communication	Unintentional operating problems
Targets					
Access networks	H	H	M	M	L
Copper	L	L	L	M	L
Fiber	H	H	L	M	L
Wireless equipment	M	M	L	M	M
Transport networks	H	H	H	L	L
Copper	L	L	L	L	L
Fiber	H	H	L	L	L
Wireless equipment	M	M	L	L	M
Switches	L	L	L	M	M
Management systems	L	L	M	H	L
Support systems	L	L	M	H	L
Documentation systems	L	L	L	M	L
Customer equipment	H	H	H	H	M
Customer network components	H	H	H	H	M

* Severity of threats: H = high, M = medium, L = low.

information repository. This information may take the form of something the user knows, something the user has, or something the user is. For stronger verification, more than one of these characteristics may be required.

2. *Access control lists and security labels.* Access control lists are information repositories that contain data relative to the rights and permissions of access granted to each authenticated identity known to the system. Security labeling provides a mechanism to enhance or refine the levels of control imposed on a resource or entity. This is done by defining specific controls on the label tag itself.

3. *Encipherment/decipherment.* Cryptography is the mechanism used to provide confidential service. It is also used quite frequently in complementing other mechanisms to provide total security solutions. Encipherment and decipherment essentially deal with the transformation of data and/or information from an intelligible format to an unintelligible format and back to an intelligible format. This is basically a mathematical process employing the use of keys and algorithms that apply the key values against the data in a predetermined fashion.

4. *Modification detection codes and message authentication codes.* Data integrity is supported by the use of some sort of checking code. Three methods of calculating the checking code are in common use: cyclic redundancy check (CRC), modification detection codes (MDC), and message authentication codes (MAC). A CRC is relatively easy to compute and has typically been used to recognize hardware failures. It is a weak check for detecting attacks. An MDC is computed using cryptography, but no secret key is used. As a result, MDC is a much stronger check than CRC, for it is very difficult to find a second message with the same MDC as the legitimate one. However, an MDC has the same delivery requirements as a CRC in that a CRC or an MDC may be delivered with data by encrypting it via a secret key shared by the sender and recipient. The MAC is cryptographically delivered using a secret key shared by the sender and recipient, so it may be delivered with the data being protected without further trouble.

5. *Digital signature.* In addition to data integrity, nonrepudiation services such as digital signatures are becoming more important to many customers. Digital signatures provide proof of data origin and/or proof of delivery. The first provides the recipient with proof of who the data sender was. The second provides the sender with a receipt for the delivery of data to the intended party.

6. *Authentication by special equipment.* Recently, new solutions have been introduced to identify a user to his or her workstation or browsers. The use of chipcards and chip keys is based on a personalized set of information hard-coded into the chip. Loss of the card or key may still lead to unauthorized use.

7. *Authentication by personal attributes.* In very sensitive areas, personal attributes (keystroke dynamics, signature dynamics, voice, color of eyes, hand scans, fingerprints, etc.) may be used as the basis for identification. The cost of these techniques, however, can be very high.

8. *Improving data integrity.* This technique deals with solutions based on a checksum computation. The results are used to expand the message that will be sent to the destination address. The techniques are expected to be sophisticated enough not to be broken easily. The original message and the checksum are encrypted together. Also, time stamps and message identification have to be added to help reconstruct the message. Those additional flags may be encrypted as well.

9. *Prevention of traffic flow analysis using fillers.* Fillers may be used to fill time gaps between real data transmissions. If both communications can be encrypted together, the intruder can't recognize any rationale or trend or any random, periodic, or other pattern by listening to the traffic. On the other hand, the use of fillers is not unlimited. It may become very expensive, and communication facilities of intranets may be temporarily overloaded, resulting in performance bottlenecks.

Firewalls play a significant role in security management of intranets. A *firewall* (Figure 5.29) is a device that controls the flow of communication between internal and external networks (e.g., the Internet). A firewall serves several functions. First, it acts as a filter for inbound Internet traffic to the servers of enterprises. As a filter, the firewall prevents unnecessary network packets from reaching Web and application servers. Second, it provides proxy outbound connections to the Internet maintaining authentication of the internal Internet users. Third, the firewall also logs traffic, providing an audit trail for usage reports and various planning purposes.

Firewalls are not without risks. Many companies assume that once they have installed a firewall, they have reduced all their network security risks. Typically, firewalls are difficult to penetrate, but when they are broken, the internal network is practically open to the intruder.

Furthermore, a firewall does not address internal network compromise. Approximately 70 percent of all network security breaches occur from within the corporation (i.e., by persons already inside the firewall). A dialup modem established by the company or by an engineer for remote access is one easy way past a firewall. Also, misconfigured firewalls may cause problems. Firewalls are highly susceptible to human error. In a dynamically changing environment, system managers routinely reconfigure firewalls without regard to security implications. Access control lists on a firewall can be numerous and confusing. Intranet managers should be sure that firewalls have

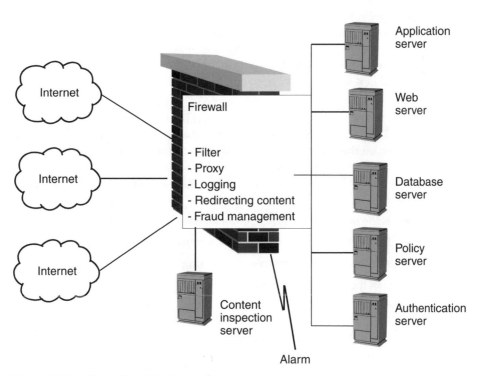

Figure 5.29   Firewall architecture.

been set up correctly and that they are performing well. At least seven risks have been observed with firewalls:

1. *Source porting.* Filter rules are based on source and destination port addresses. A TCP/IP-enabled machine has 65,535 possible virtual ports, some of which are defined for certain services; for example, e-mail is port 25. When one machine FTPs to another and wants to transfer a file back from the FTP server, typically the server opens source port 20 to connect to the FTP client and transfer data. Therefore, many firewalls allow source port 20 into a network. An intruder can modify telnet to make the connections come from source port 20, thereby penetrating the firewall. A security auditing tool can check to see if source port 20 is allowed to connect to the network.

2. *Source routing.* It represents an IP option that allows users to define how packets are routed. When source routing is on, many firewall filter rules are bypassed. Many router-based firewalls allow source-routed packets to pass. Many Unix hosts have source routing built into the kernel and do not allow it to be turned off. A security auditing tool is needed to check whether source-routed packets can make a pass through the firewall and connect to various services.

3. *Socks.* Socks is a library of proxy application firewalls designed to allow certain services through and keep intruders out. The fundamental problem with Socks is the same as with many security tools: they are often misconfigured. Often the administrator establishes rules to allow certain services through the firewall, but the rules necessary for denying access to intruders are never implemented. Consequently, services seemingly work fine with the firewall, but the firewall's inability to keep intruders out is not recognized until an intruder breaks through. Even then, the cause of the problem may never be recognized. A security auditing tool can attempt to connect to important services through the Socks port, to see whether filter rules have been configured properly.

4. *TCP sequence prediction.* TCP sequence prediction or spoofing tries to trick a host that trusts another host. For example, if host A and host B are in a corporate network, and host A is trusted by host B, then host A is allowed to log on to host B based on this trust, without a password. An intruder who can make his or her host C look like host A will also be able to log on to host B. A security auditing tool should be used to test the following issues regarding TCP sequence prediction.

   ■ Is the host TCP sequence predictable?

   ■ Does the firewall or router block spoofed packets from the internal network?

   ■ Are the exploited services rsh and rlogin running?

   ■ Can the machine be exploited?

5. *Direct RPC scan.* The port mapper is a service that allows users to identify the ports on which the remote procedure calls (RPCs) reside. Many filter-based firewalls may block the port mapper on port 111. The RPC commands themselves remain in place on various machine ports. It usually is hard to determine where the services are if the port mapper is blocked. However, if an intruder scans directly for the RPC services, the intruder could bypass this type of security.

6. *Stealth scanning.* In stealth scanning, an intruder does not attempt to establish a connection, but rather uses packets at a low level with the interface. These low-level packets elicit different responses depending on whether a port is active. This technique allows TCP port scanning many times faster than a regular connect routine on Unix and does not trigger alarms built into many Satan detectors and tcp wrappers. While many firewalls block particular packets that would establish a connection, stealth scanning packets do not attempt to establish a connection; therefore, they can bypass firewall security and identify services running on an internal network.

7. *Connectionless protocols.* Firewalls find it difficult to track packets used for services that don't require established connections, such as the User Datagram Protocol.

For intranets, a network-based intrusion-detection system is required to protect the perimeter network from hacker attack. Network-based intrusion-detection systems may be deployed as probes or agents running on servers. Probes are the most effective method of providing network-based intrusion detection. This probe minimizes the impact to existing systems because it is a passive listener reporting back to a centralized console without interruption. Intrusion detection will perform the following functions at the network-device level:

■ It will inspect data streams as they pass through the network, identify the signatures of unauthorized activity, and act.

■ An alarm will be generated immediately upon detection of the event.

■ The alarm will notify the appropriate security personnel and trigger an automated response to the several issues to be considered.

In addition to intrusion detection, a TCP proxy aggregator may be considered. This will tighten security through the firewall by limiting the exposed ports. It also provides an offload for session/connection management and a more robust technical implementation in terms of port permutations supported.

Tunneling and encryption provide data integrity and confidentiality to networks that need to appear as point-to-point networks but that actually consist of various routes to an endpoint. Usually, tunneling protocols, such as Layer 2 Tunneling Protocol (L2TP), Point-to-Point Tunneling Protocol (PPTP), and IPSec (Internet Protocol Security), and encryption standards, such as DES, MD5, Triple DES, and others, are used.

Mobile code programs such as Java and ActiveX pose an increasing security threat. Content inspection software should do the following:

■ Provide full control over Java, ActiveX, and other mobile code activity in the corporation

■ Prevent undetected, costly mobile code attacks, such as industrial espionage and data modification

■ Enable safe Internet/intranet/extranet surfing while taking full advantage of Java and ActiveX technologies

A content inspection server will accept mobile contents redirected from a firewall in order to scan for attack signatures. If the scan detects vulnerability, the contents will be blocked and the client prevented from downloading the mobile code. This denial will alert an appropriate administrator and notify the requesting client. If the scan does not detect any vulnerability, the mobile code is redirected to the firewall for routing to the client.

In summary, security management challenges increase in intranets due to many access points in the network. Combinations of new techniques and new tools are required to combat the problem.

5.8.4 Periodic Security Audits

The last step in effectively securing access points in intranets is maintenance. The key to maintenance is locating potential or actual security breaches. It requires an ongoing effort of stress-testing intranets, assigning tasks to outside professional security companies, reviewing case studies of security violations, and evaluating new security management techniques and tools.

Network management systems must know the current operating system and application configuration at all times. Network attacks will cause changes to one or more of the standard configurations, be they physical or logical changes. In addition, normal operating performance indicators will change (e.g., utilization increases or decreases, source and destination address changes, service request type and volume changes). The systems must have the ability to know the baseline performance and then at periodic intervals to perform comparisons and cause alerts for predefined discrepancies.

5.8.5 Public Key Infrastructure

The concept of a public key infrastructure (PKI) is relatively simple, but actually setting up a PKI can be complex (MCKI00). The basic idea is to protect sensitive data through encryption. Each end-user device is equipped with encryption software and two keys: a public key for distribution to other users and a private key that is kept and protected by the owner.

A user encrypts the message using the receiver's public key. When the message is received, the user will decrypt it with his or her private key. Users may have multiple key pairs to conduct communications and data exchange with different other users. With an increasing number of key pairs, it is important to implement a method of administering the keys and their usage. PKI enables the centralized creation, distribution, tracking, and revocation of keys.

The first step in setting up a PKI is establishing a system for authentication in order to positively identify users before receiving communication rights. Digital signature is the preferred authentication method for PKI. Each certificate contains specific identifying information about a user, including his or her name, public key, and a unique digital signature that binds the user to the certificate. To get a certificate, a user sends a request to a designated registration authority, which verifies the user's identity and tells the certification authority to issue the certificate. The certificate itself is a digital document that is generally stored and administered in a central directory. The certificate is transmitted automatically when needed without interrupting the ongoing work of the user. The certificate authority verifies a certificate's authenticity for the receiver. Again, for the user, this is generally transparent.

Certificates should not last forever. Each certificate is issued with an expiration date and sometimes will need to be revoked early (e.g., when an employee quits). A certificate authority can revoke a certificate before its expiration date by identifying it in a regularly published certificate revocation report. As with key pairs, there is a need to coordinate the issuing and revoking of certificates. That is another function of a PKI, acting as a comprehensive architecture encompassing key management, the registration authority, certificate authority, and various administrative tool sets. PKI tools are available from various vendors. Generally, a central directory is also implemented as part of a PKI; this is a place to store and look up certificates along with other relevant information.

Another element of a PKI is the certificate policy, which outlines rules for the use of a PKI and certificate services. For example, if a user mistakenly shares his or her private key, it might be expected to notify the security staff or the certificate authority. The rules are summarized in a certificate practice statement (CPS). The rules are written in consultation with IT, various user groups, and legal experts. The CPS provides a detailed explanation of how the certificate authority manages the certificates it issues, along with associated services such as key management. The CPS also acts as a contract between the certificate authority and users, describing the commitments and legal limitations and setting the foundation for future audits. PKI vendors can provide samples and templates for the contracting parties.

Staff is needed to set up, administer, fix, and manage a PKI. In the first step, a security officer is needed who will become responsible for setting and administering the security policy of the service provider. This person does not need to be part of IT, but must understand the issues and will probably need a security bond. In the second step, a PKI architect is needed who will become responsible for examining requirements and designing the customized PKI. This person may also support implementation as project coordinator. In the third step, a PKI security administrator is needed. This individual will use certificate authority management tools to add, enable, and revoke users and their certificates. All these activities are important for ongoing operations. The last step requires a directory administrator and someone to act as a registration authority. However, it is possible to set up an automated registration authority to handle user requests made through their Web browsers. In that case, current staff may be used, such as database administrators who can help to set up and maintain the automated registration authority service.

5.8.6 Securing Support, Documentation, and Management Systems

Operations, business, and marketing support systems are crucial to the ability to order, activate, bill, and maintain services. In addition, today's corporations have become critically dependent on e-mail and Web-based tools to manage all aspects of their businesses. As with network and customer protection, a service provider must be able to detect and eliminate any attacks that would cause a loss of functionality in business systems.

In the IP world, the probability of forwarding viruses and forged packets to and from customers is high. As a communications services provider, one of the single most costly risks, in terms of both revenues and reputation, is infecting customers' networks. The ability to detect, block, then tackle known and new forms of viruses is critical. Livelihood in this market is solely dependent on a reputation as a secure network service provider.

5.9 Summary

Service fulfillment processes are complex and rely heavily on legacy structures. With a few exceptions, they are not customer-oriented at this point of time, but concentrate on rapid execution of back-office processes. Workflow is the glue between various processes, with the ultimate goal of automated flow-through provisioning. In this sense, provisioning represents the completion of many processes and indicates the availability of services for use. Service providers should look for an efficient workflow tool that may help to streamline functions and automate as many functions as possible. ECommerce requirements may push service providers to open their service fulfillment processes to their customers. They are hesitant to do so because customers may access sensitive information and capacity-manage valuable resources. Definitively, enterprises with a CNM relationship with service providers are at an advantage. New entrants who don't have any legacy resources and processes will more quickly agree to collaborate with customers. Security management is extremely important in all cases, but from different perspectives: Service providers must protect their valuable resources against intruders; they should prove to their customers that the underlying networking infrastructure of services is well protected and available according to the terms of their service-level agreements; finally, they should prove that dedicated customer resources and customer-related sensitive information are protected.

Some of the processes and functions are subject to Web-based access using the intranets of service providers. It assumes up-to-date information on all employees involved in service fulfillment processes and functions.

CHAPTER 6

Network Operational Management

6.1 Introduction

Most service providers are driving their service assurance processes to become proactive, meaning they are triggered by automation rather than by the customer. This is important for improving service quality, customer perception of service, and lowering overall costs. Customer care processes have been basically reactive in the past. The extreme pressure on cost, customer demand for more control, and customer demand for more proactive service support are driving a major shift to proactive support through automation. With the advent of Internet access, the goal for processes and automation is now interactive support, including giving the customer the ability to see and act on service performance.

Service assurance processes are interlinked. Figure 6.1 shows a possible sequence of activities in response to a network-detected problem. The figure shows two ways a potential service-affecting problem could be identified—either by an alarm event or by synthesis of network data through network data management. Neither is exclusive. Network data management logically collects and processes both performance and traffic data as well as usage data. The usage data is used as a logical part of the billing process.

Information exchanges are numbered as follows:

1. Network data, alarm data, events.
2. Report degradation.

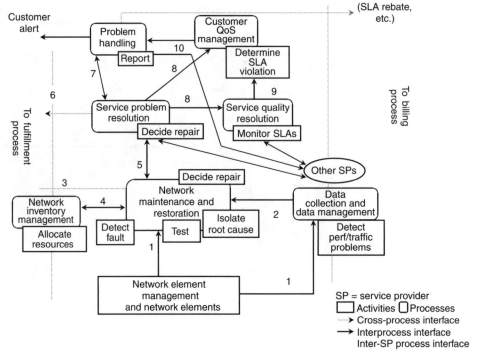

Figure 6.1 Service assurance process example.

3. Network reconfiguration or change.

4. Work order.

5. Notify problem/fix.

6. Service reconfiguration or change.

7. Trouble report or ticket.

8. Report problem data.

9. Service level agreement (SLA) impact.

10. Service impact.

6.2 The Service Problem Resolution Process

This process encompasses isolating the root cause of service-affecting and non–service-affecting failures and acting to resolve them. Typically, failures reported to this process affect multiple customers. Actions may include immediate reconfiguration or other corrective actions. Longer-term modifications to the service design or to the network components associated with the service may also be required. The aim is to understand the causes impacting service performance, implement immediate fixes, or initiate quality improvement efforts. The principal tasks include

- Isolate and resolve service problems
- Identify chronic failures
- Provide performance data
- Recommend service redesign, if appropriate
- Initiate escalation procedures
- Analyze service quality
- Generate reports about services

Table 6.1 identifies the information sources for this process. Table 6.2 shows the information output and the targeted processes.

The service problem resolution process has multiple steps. Trouble reports are received from the problem handling process indicating service-impacting irregularities. Service problems are usually caused by network facilities and equipment and are the entry point to further problem determination, problem diagnosis, and restoration

Table 6.1 Information Input for the Service Resolution Process

SOURCE OF INFORMATION	INFORMATION
Problem handling	Trouble report
Service configuration	Reconfiguration is complete
Other providers	Service-affecting faults, test results, planned maintenance scheduling, and notification
Network maintenance and restoration	Service-affecting faults, test results, planned maintenance scheduling, and notification

Table 6.2 Information Output for the Service Resolution Process

INFORMATION	TARGETED PROCESSES
Problem data, planned maintenance schedule	Customer QoS management
Problem data, planned maintenance schedule	Service quality management
Reconfiguration requests	Service configuration
Trouble report, trouble cleared, planned maintenance schedule	Other providers
Trouble report, trouble cleared, planned maintenance schedule	Problem handling
Negotiate/report service design changes	Service planning and development
Service problem indication, test requests	Network maintenance and restoration

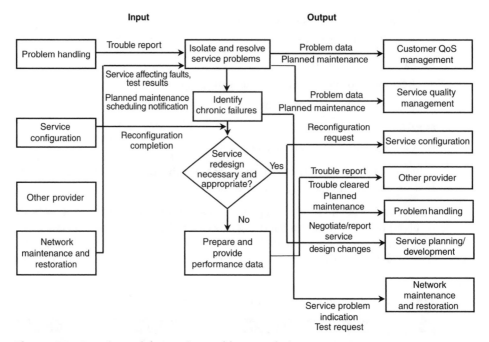

Figure 6.2 Functions of the service problem resolution process.

of the service. Management and support tools have been recently expanded to recognize and report on service problems first. Figure 6.2 shows the flow of functions for this process. All input and output information flows are displayed as well.

6.2.1 Isolate and Resolve Service Problems

There are three basic alternatives within this function:

1. Reactive fault management.
2. Proactive fault management.
3. Preventive fault management.

In most cases, reactive service problem restoration is implemented. This function is driven by customers over the problem handling process. Fault correlation to service is required by the tools implemented. It means that upon detection of network degradation, information is automatically presented on the services and customers impacted. Automatic generation of customer trouble tickets and proactive customer notification is included.

When multiple troubles of a service are reported by customers, a report may be sent from problem handling to service problem resolution for correction. When a trouble is identified by the service problem resolution process, then service problem resolution notifies problem handling.

In the first case, the trouble report outlines the detected problem that must be isolated and restored. This function continues with problem determination, problem diagnosis, and finally, with restoration. Principal tasks include:

Detecting and locating problems. Network infrastructure components generate a number of messages, events, and alarms. Meaningful filtering, combined with user input, helps to detect abnormal operations. Management platforms and their management applications are usually able to determine the location of faults. This phase indicates that something is wrong.

Determining the cause of the problem. Based upon information generated by element managers or correlation results provided by management platforms, the cause of the problem is determined. This phase indicates what is wrong.

Diagnosing the root cause of the problem. In-depth measurements, tests, and further correlating messages, events, and alarms will help to determine the root cause of problems. This phase indicates why the problem happened.

Correcting the problem. Through the use of various hardware and software techniques, managed objects are repaired or replaced, and operations can return to normal. This phase indicates that the problem has been resolved.

Figure 6.3 shows these simple steps in a flowchart. A voice-related example for circuit switched applications is shown in Figure 6.4.

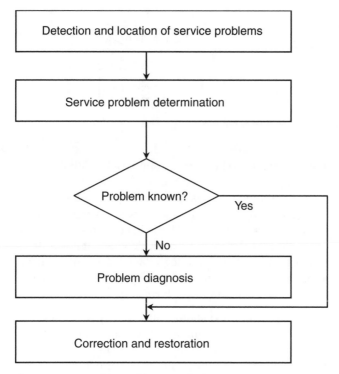

Figure 6.3 Service problem resolution steps.

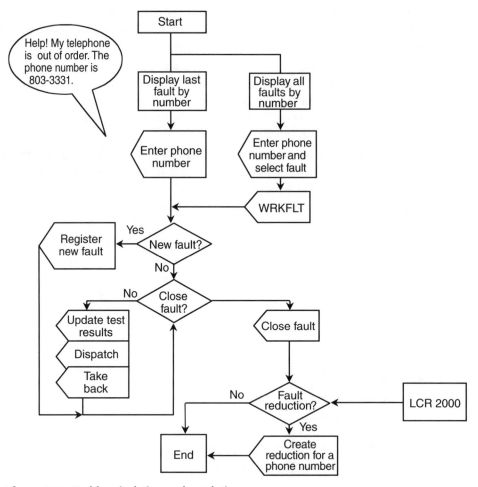

Figure 6.4 Problem isolation and resolution.

Proactive service problem resolution shows many similarities with the reactive case in terms of problem determination, diagnosis, and restoration. However, the problem detection case is completely different. In this case, monitoring at the network and network element level can quickly detect performance anomalies and alarm the network maintenance and restoration process to initiate remedial or corrective activities. Fault correlation to network facilities and elements are needed here. It means the ability to automatically diagnose network outages and degradation, then filter out all sympathetic alerts—presenting only the root-cause defect. Figure 6.5 shows an example of problem escalation to customers using multiple layers.

The problem handling process is notified about status; it is up to the severity of the proactively detected problem whether the impacted customers are notified about potential service impacts. Partitioning is extremely important when distributing views on network status. It allows views to be presented for network operations center staff, allowing for separation based on organization, customers, customer network

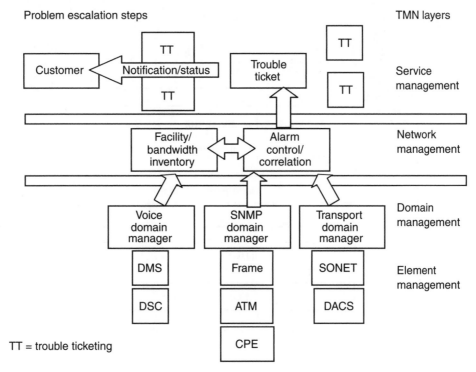

Figure 6.5 Problem escalation to customers.

managements (CNMs), virtual private networks (VPNs), or skill sets. Other groupings are also supported, for example, geographic, network layer, network element,
service type, high-profile customers, newly activated services, and so on. In a collaborative environment, the actual status may be presented and continuously updated in
Web pages. These pages can be accessed by all authorized customers.

Preventive service problem resolution goes one step further, and offers modeling
capabilities. In this case, based upon a simplified model of the networking infrastructure of the service provider, what-if scenarios are evaluated in real time. The results
help to decide about the right recommendation for configuration changes.

6.2.2 Identify Chronic Failures

This function concentrates on the statistical evaluation of chronic service failures.
This function connects to various data sources to collect history data on service outages. Figure 6.6 shows an example of how data can be collected and processed for
chronic service failure analysis.

Principal tasks include sorting service outages by severity, by duration of service
impacts, and by outage frequencies. After these sorts, service providers may set the
priorities to tackle chronic service outages. The highest priority will be assigned to
cases with severe service impacts and high frequencies.

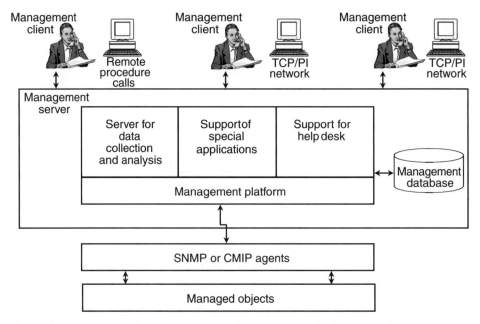

Figure 6.6 Data collection and processing for chronic service failure analysis.

High-priority items are referred to the network maintenance and restoration process for root-cause analysis. This analysis tries to correlate service failures with network level and network element level failures and troubles. As an ultimate result, critical network elements and their suppliers are clearly identified. This information is copied for order processing.

6.2.3 Provide Performance Data

Similar to the previous function, performance data are evaluated for various layers of the Telecommunication Management Network (TMN) architecture. In particular, the service, network, and element management layers are the targets. In the physical network, service providers implement the ability to cause alerts based on support infrastructure (power, environmental, etc.), optical sheath degradation, optical levels, modal dispersion, and bit error rate performance. In IP and switching networks, the ability to monitor and cause alerts is based on utilization, latency, jitter, and congestion.

If performance bottlenecks or degradation is identified at the service management layer (SML), this function concentrates on correlating service performance data with network facilities and equipment for the network and network elements layers. Performance data are accessed in a data warehouse or in performance databases maintained by the network data collection and management process. Figure 6.7 shows how performance data are accessed, processed, and distributed.

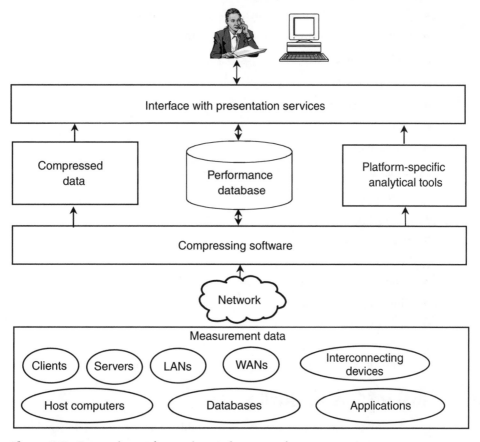

Figure 6.7   Processing and reporting performance data.

6.2.4 Recommend Service Redesign, If Appropriate

This function takes all internal input from the previous processes and evaluates whether services must be redesigned for performance reasons. Service models could be helpful. In these what-if scenarios, alternatives are evaluated for various services. If such models are applicable, actual recommendations are supported by modeling results. Also, testing certain service alternatives may be initiated by this function.

6.2.5 Initiate Escalation Procedures

Escalation procedures for service-related problems must be prepared prior to launching services. Escalation involves multiple dimensions, such as

- Service metrics that are measured and continuously evaluated for unusual conditions
- Determination of severity levels for service-related problems

- Clarification of the management hierarchy to determine the notification route
- Setting time limits for the restoration within each severity class

Examples for severity levels are

- Important
- Very important
- Critical
- Very critical

Examples for a potential management hierarchy are

- Shift supervisor
- Manager of duty
- Site manager
- Vendor liaison manager
- Vendor or service provider
- Chief operations officer
- Chief executive officer

Table 6.3 is an example of a complete escalation procedure including service problems, time limits, notification paths, and recommendations for rectification.

6.2.6 Analyze Service Quality

Service providers commit themselves to quality of service (QoS) by signing service level agreements (SLAs). On the basis of data collected for service metrics (see Chapter 4), service providers analyze the trends of service quality. Doing so, they set internal thresholds for quality alarms that are stronger than those offered to and agreed upon with customers in SLAs. This function deals with large data volumes, whereby data warehouses or datamarts can be very helpful.

6.2.7 Generate Reports about Services

Performance reporting means the automatic generation of business reports depicting network, service, and process performance. Customer views and online access to performance by customers must be supported. This opportunity enables customers to manage their purchased services, providing information on network availability, service availability, and maintenance SLAs and performance.

6.3 The Service Quality Management Process

This process supports monitoring service or product quality on a service class basis in order to determine whether

Table 6.3 Escalation Procedure for Service Level Agreements

	ESCALATION STEPS			
SEVERITY	**0**	**1**	**2**	**3**
Critical problems				
Duration for the escalation step	0.5 H	1.5 H	2 H	24 H
Responsible for problem restoration	HD	Operator	Service provider	Crisis manager
Information is provided for	Customer Operators NO	Customer Operators NP	Customer Operators Service provider NP	Customer Operators Service provider NP
Recommendations	Identify impacts	Workaround	Expedited fixes	Expedited analysis
Major problems				
Duration for the escalation step	2 H	3 H	4 H	
Responsible for problem restoration	HD	Operator	Service provider	
Information is provided for	Customer	Customer Operators	Customer Service provider	
Recommendations	Identify impacts	Workaround	Root-cause analysis	
Minor problems				
Duration for the escalation step	4 H	8 H	18 H	
Responsible for problem restoration	HD	Operator	Service provider	
Information is provided for	Customer	Customer Operators	Customer Service provider	
Recommendations	Identify impacts	Workaround	Root-cause analysis	

NCC   Network control center
HD   Help-desk
NP   Network planning
NO   Network operations

- Service levels are being met consistently
- There are any general problems with the service or product
- The sale and use of the service is tracking to forecasts

This process also encompasses taking appropriate action to keep service levels within agreed targets for each service class and to either keep ahead of demand or alert the sales process to slow sales. The aim is to provide effective service-specific monitoring and to provide management and customers meaningful and timely performance information across the parameters of the specific service. The aim is also to manage service levels to meet SLA commitments and standard commitments for the specific service.

There have been quality metrics for voice services for a long time. For IP-based services, the term *quality* is relatively new. The whole philosophy behind IP-based services is to offer best effort quality depending on the capacity constraints of networking infrastructures—but there are no guarantees, even for that. This level of quality cannot be tolerated by business users. There are two alternatives with IP-based services:

1. *IntServ (integrated services).* This alternative supports Reservation Protocol (RSVP) and as a result, bandwidth is guaranteed for application network ingress and egress points.
2. *DiffServ (differentiated services).* This alternative analyzes the ToS header (type of service) of IPv4 and assigns priorities depending on the ToS entries.

Priority setting in IP nodes is controlled by policy-based networking (PBN). The principal tasks include

- Manage life cycle of service/product portfolios
- Monitor overall delivered quality of a service class
- Maintain SLAs
- Monitor available capacity/usage against forecasted sales
- Initiate service improvements
- Inform sales on constraints

Table 6.4 identifies the information sources to this process. Table 6.5 shows the information output and the targeted processes.

Figure 6.8 shows the flow of functions for this process. All input and output information flows are displayed as well.

6.3.1 Manage Life Cycle of Service/Product Portfolios

This function continuously evaluates the viability of products and services. It is very complex because multiple data sources must be interpreted and correlated to each other (see Table 6.4). This function does not focus, however, on the financial evalua-

Table 6.4 Information Input

SOURCE OF INFORMATION	INFORMATION
Sales	Forecasts
Service planning and development	Quality objectives, available capacity
Service problem resolution	Service problem data
Customer QoS management	QoS violations
Other providers	Performance and usage trends
Network data management	Performance and usage trends
Other providers	Problem trends, maintenance activity, and progress
Network maintenance and restoration	Problem trends, maintenance activity, and progress

Table 6.5 Information Output

INFORMATION	TARGETED PROCESSES
Constraints on capacity	Sales
Service class quality data	Customer QoS management
Service modification recommendations	Service planning and development
Additional capacity requirements	Other service providers
Additional capacity requirements	Service configuration
Performance and usage requests	Network data management

tion of products and services. It offers a continuous technical evaluation of products and services with recommendations for improvements, such as

- Modification of products and services
- Adding capacity for better service quality

If this function concludes that products and services are no longer feasible for technical reasons, it communicates this message to the sales process.

6.3.2 Monitor Overall Delivered Quality of a Service Class

This function aggregates input for service quality. It evaluates a number of QoS metrics for voice, data, and video services. In order to differentiate, multiple service classes may be formed. Service providers may offer platinum, gold, and silver services—similar to other industries—primarily to their business customers. This differentiation clearly dictates various thresholds of service metrics. All measurable service

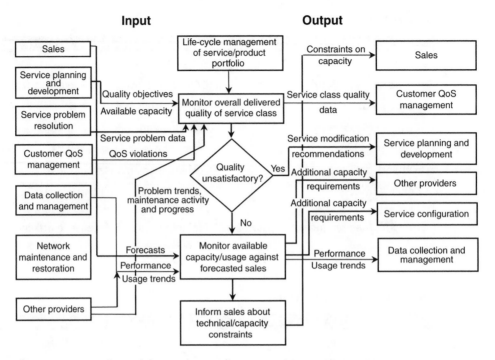

Figure 6.8 Functions of the service quality management process.

metrics are part of service level agreements. Monitoring results are expected to be sent to the customer QoS management process.

6.3.3 Maintain Service Level Agreements

Surveys of market research companies show clearly where the interests are on behalf of customers. This interest should be taken seriously by service providers and network operators. Customers are interested first of all in service-oriented metrics that are technology independent. It means that technology-dependent metrics need not be included in SLAs. However, they are important in computing technology-independent metrics.

The priority sequence of metrics from the perspective of customers is the following:

- Availability of all components (devices and transmission links) connected to the network
- Availability of application on the network (accessing applications)
- Availability of servers
- Network round-trip time or network delay
- Application response time during peak periods

- Availability of clients
- Server delay
- Mean application response time
- Client delay
- Median application response time
- Percentage of transactions completed within defined performance levels

Service availability (SA) as a percentage (SA%) to indicate the time during which the contracted service at the respective service access point (SAP) is operational. *Operational* means that the customer has the ability to use the service as specified in the SLA.

An event affecting the service at the SAP can be defined as an *outage*. The duration of this specific event is the *outage interval*. Ordinarily, this concept is used for the unavailability percentage (UA%) and service availability percentage (SA%) calculations as follows

- SA% = 100% – UA%
- UA% = (sum of outage intervals/activity time) × 100%

Service availability always has three dimensions (SCHL00):

1. Time dimension (see Figure 6.9).
2. Site dimension (see Figure 6.10).
3. Functional dimension (see Figure 6.11).

Consolidating all three results into one, Figure 6.12 shows the three-dimensional representation of service availability and unavailability. In most SLAs, contracting parties concentrate on the time dimension only. By defining SLAs, locations are mentioned, but more in the sense of networking boundaries and less in the sense of including or excluding sites. The functional dimension brings in the application layer that is most important for customers.

Until now, service providers were not forced to sign complex SLAs. In the past, they had given certain service guarantees for facilities and equipment, but hardly for services. Due to liberalization, this is changing dramatically.

An additional issue for SLA management is to determine whether an event affecting the service at the service access point (SAP) is causing a complete service outage (service fully unavailable) or a partial service outage (service degraded available).

Critical success factors for measuring and computing availability are

- Trouble tickets
- Proactive tools
- Workforce with dispatch capabilities
- Efficient help-desk
- Skills and experiences of subject matter experts

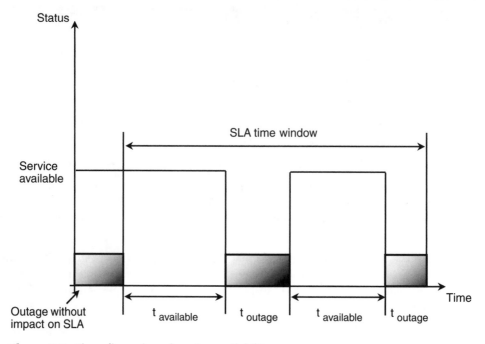

Figure 6.9 Time dimension of service availability.

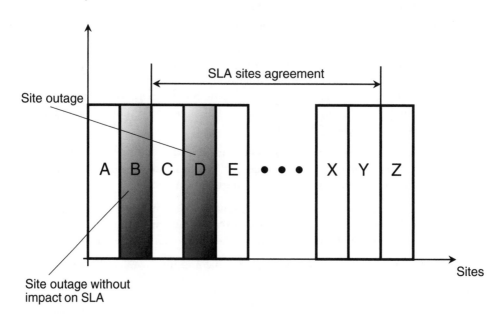

Comments:
- weight of sites may be different
- minimal number of available sites may be determined

Figure 6.10 Site dimension of service availability.

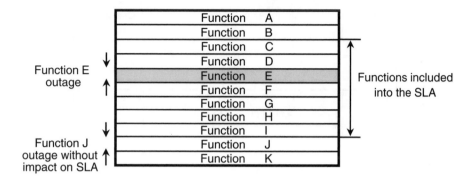

Comments:
- functions are with different weights

Figure 6.11   Functional dimension of service availability.

Response time is one of the key metrics in all SLAs. Its definition varies, but usually users consider the duration between sending the inquiry and receiving the full answer as response time (see Figure 6.13). This figure displays the differences between two alternatives:

1. Time up to the first character of the response on the screen of the user.
2. Time up to the last character of the response on the screen of the user.

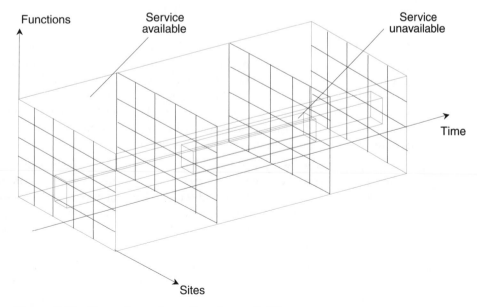

Figure 6.12   Three dimensions of service availability.

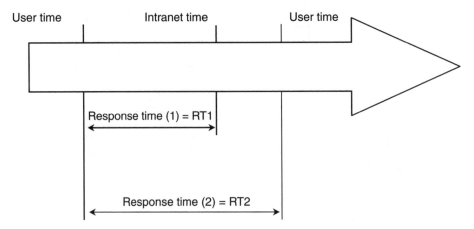

Figure 6.13 Response time definitions.

The second definition is a better-suited definition for the working cycle of users. The difference between RT2 and RT1 depends on many factors, such as the throughput of the backbone and access networks, servers in these networks, number of hops, and the hardware/software capabilities of the client's workstation or browser. Present measurement technology offers the following alternatives:

Monitors and packet analyzers. They filter and interpret packets and draw inferences about application response times based on these results. These monitors passively listen to the network traffic and calculate the time it takes specific packets to get from source to destination. They can read the content of packages revealing eventual application errors and inefficiency. But they cannot measure response time end-to-end.

Synthetic workload tools. They issue live traffic to get a consistent measurement of response time on a particular connection in the intranet or for a given application. These tools are installed on servers, desktops, or on both. They typically send Transmission Control Protocol (TCP) messages or Structured Query Language (SQL) queries to servers and measure the time of the reply. Results from multiple sources are correlated to give a more detailed view about intranet response times. They are very accurate to the end-to-end response time.

Application agents. They work within or alongside applications, using software that monitors keystrokes and commands to track down how long a specific transaction takes. They can run at both the client and server. They clock specific portions of the application at the server or at the workstation. The use of agents needs customization and the correlation of many measurements in order to give users a performance estimate about their intranet.

User of ARM MIBs. Application response monitoring (ARM) defines application program interfaces (APIs) that allow programmers to write agents into an application so that network managers and Webmasters can monitor it for a range of performance metrics, including response time. It is a complete offer to application management, but it requires rewrite of existing code that many companies are unwilling to do.

Figure 6.14 shows the locations of these tools and agents.

When evaluating products, many components must be factored in. These factors are

- Customization needs
- Maintenance requirements
- Deployment of code
- Overhead of transmitting measurement data
- Load increase due to synthetic workload
- Reporting capabilities
- Capabilities to solve complex performance problems
- Capabilities to conduct root-cause analysis
- Combination with modeling tools
- Price of the tools

Critical success factors for measuring and reporting response time are

- Measurement procedures
- Availability of application management information bases (MIBs)

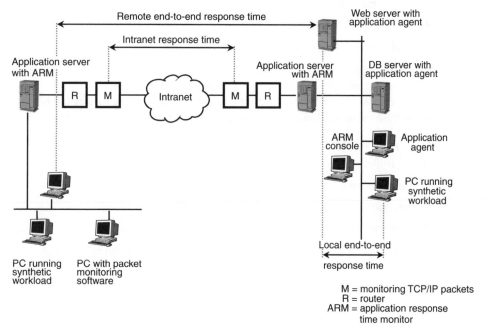

Figure 6.14 Positioning response time measuring tools.

- Proactive tools
- Workforce with dispatch capabilities
- Efficient help-desk
- Skills and experiences of subject matter experts

The pressure on service providers and network operators is increasing. Some guidance for metrics have been recently published by them. Examples are

minimal network delay	70 to 100 ms
minimal packet loss	1 %
network availability	99 to 100 %

Also, compensation policies are published. Examples include

- 1 day free-of-charge services
- 3 days of free-of-charge services

Figure 6.15 shows a high-level overview about the principal activities of service level management (SLM).

SLM requires that multiple metrics are continuously supervised and measured. Depending on the contract, several reports are generated and distributed. Data sources include

- Trouble tickets
- Alarms [Simple Network Management Protocol (SNMP) traps or alarms from other sources]
- Alarm and security logs
- Performance metrics that have been measured by various tools

All collected data must be formatted in order to guarantee a unified format (see Figure 6.16). No complicated processing is expected in this phase. The results are summarized in a table format including a number of events that are going to be used to evaluate service level violations. Typical events are

- Type of event
- Identification of event
- Time stamp
- Severity
- Importance

Another table is prepared containing customer master data including the list of all services agreed upon with the service provider and network operator

- Customer ID
- Service ID (A)
- Service ID (B)
- Service ID (N)

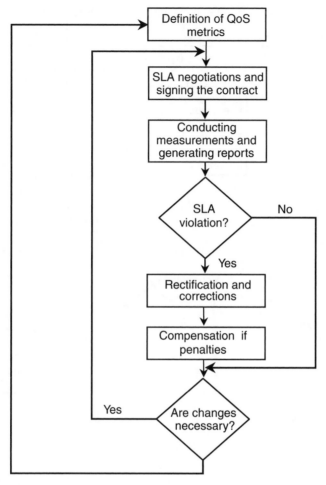

Figure 6.15 Service-level management process.

The service portfolio is expected to be maintained in another table, together with their typical service metrics

- Service ID (A)
- Attributes (A)
- Service ID (B)
- Attributes (B)
- Service ID (N)
- Attributes (N)

The SLAs—as far as possible standardized—are maintained in a separate database. In the best interest of service providers and network operators, the number of different SLAs should be kept to a reasonable minimum. When reports are expected to be generated, the following is used to identify reports and their periodicity

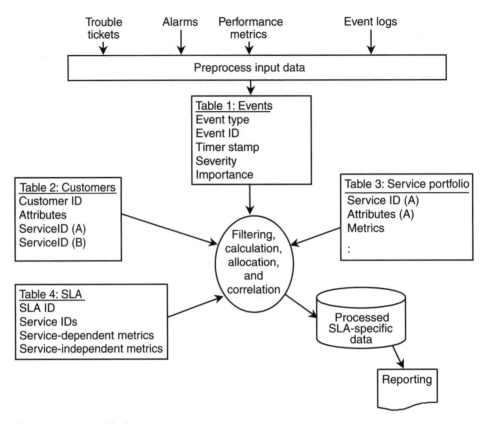

Figure 6.16 Detailed SLM process.

- SLA ID (A)

  Services in A

  Metrics in A
- SLA ID (B)

  Services in B

  Metrics in B
- SLA ID (N)

  Services in N

  Metrics in N

One of the big obstacles in implementing SLAs is the inability to create a solid base-line of data to quantify the historical performance of the service provider with various customers. Without a complete body of historical data, it is difficult to create a meaningful and realistic SLA, and expectations may be set unrealistically high. Also, not all tools will capture all of the components of the network, and the metrics will be incomplete. SLAs of the past have failed due to their lack of accurate measurement data. Data were manually recorded and were often unreliable. New monitoring tools have increased the quality and quantity of data available for SLA evaluation.

As competition is progressively introduced into all service provision markets, and customers become increasingly discerning, service providers are realizing the need to differentiate their products through value-added services. Additionally, industry deregulation is transforming a traditionally monopolistic marketplace into an extremely competitive one. One prime mechanism to combat this is the provision of an off-the-shell SLA document that clearly sets out the obligations of both the service providers and the customer.

Critical success factors for maintaining SLAs are

- Clear understanding of QoS metrics
- Powerful data collection and correlation capabilities
- Support of both real-time and historical reporting
- Low overhead of tools for the network, systems, and applications

6.3.4 Monitor Available Capacity/Usage against Forecasted Sales

Besides monitoring status of managed objects, the monitoring of their usage level is also important. Available capacity should be compared to forecasted capacity; if there is a shortage, planning for additional capacity should be initiated. Forecasted capacity at the sales level should be broken down into networking facilities and equipment. The service configuration process is then responsible to order capacity extensions.

6.3.5 Initiate Service Improvements

If the QoS is not satisfactory, but the life cycle for a certain product or service is not yet over, service improvements should be under consideration. This function is expected to evaluate

- Performance by products and services using QoS metrics
- Alternatives of tuning and improvements
- Technical and economical feasibility of options for improvement

Figure 6.17 shows a typical flowchart for the service improvement function. This function initiates service improvements, but other processes and functions are responsible for the execution of improvements.

The process starts with detailing the requests and objectives of service improvements. In some cases, the problems of service degradation might be known. If yes, network managers know what to do, what to change, and how to make the necessary changes. In most cases, however, managers and analysts are facing new problems. Subject-

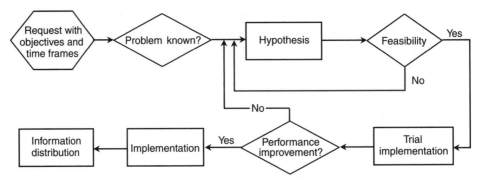

Figure 6.17 Example of service improvements.

matter experts are responsible for the hypothesis of service improvements. Usually, technically-oriented experts brainstorm excellent ideas that are feasible in technical terms, but lack financial feasibility. If this is the case, experts should return the hypothesis until they can cost justify the technical solution. Trial implementation of the service follows with a number of measurements to prove whether the changes guarantee an improved service performance. If yes, final deployment can be signed up; if not, experts should start again with another hypothesis. Usually, network managers limit the number of traveling the loops.

6.3.6 Inform Sales on Constraints

This function is extremely important for the sales process in order not to oversell certain services when the lower-layer capacity of facilities and equipment is not available.

It is recommended to present the results as a time function; in doing so, sales can offer the services for the right time when completeness and readiness can be guaranteed. Figure 6.18 shows an example.

This figure makes sales aware that launching services A, B, and C depends on the available bandwidth in access networks in certain geographic areas. Building or expanding the bandwidth may depend on other subcontractors that lay cables or change the media of cables. Those construction processes cannot be accelerated too much.

6.4 The Network Maintenance and Restoration Process

This process encompasses maintaining the operational quality of the network in accordance with required network performance goals. Network maintenance activities can be preventative—such as scheduled routine maintenance—or corrective. Corrective maintenance can be in response to faults or to indications that problems may

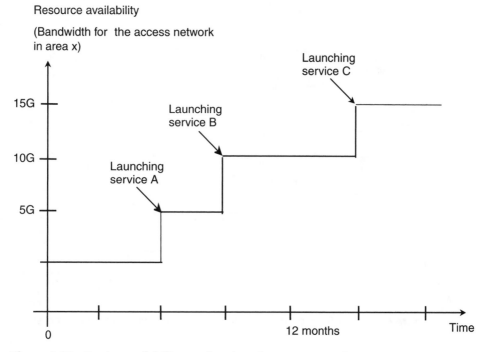

Figure 6.18 Service availability as a function of resource capacity.

be developing (proactive). This process responds to problems, initiates tests, does analysis to determine the cause and impact of problems, and notifies service management of possible effects on quality. The process issues requests for corrective actions.

Supervisory functions should be extended for IP-based services. In most cases, distributed monitoring capabilities must be implemented. Voice networks use Transaction Language 1 (TL1), Common Management Information Protocol (CMIP), and Telecommunication Management Network (TMN) as the basis of supervising status and resource utilization. The IP world brings Simple Network Management Protocol (SNMP) and Remote MONitoring (RMON) into the supervisory scenario. Powerful filters and correlation engines are required for the reduction of the total amount of data generated by the supervisory function.

Principal tasks include

- Problem analysis, including testing
- Proactive recognition of problem trends
- Network quality maintenance and restoration
- Maintenance of historic data of network problems and performance

Figure 6.19 shows the flow of functions for this process. All input and output information flows are displayed as well.

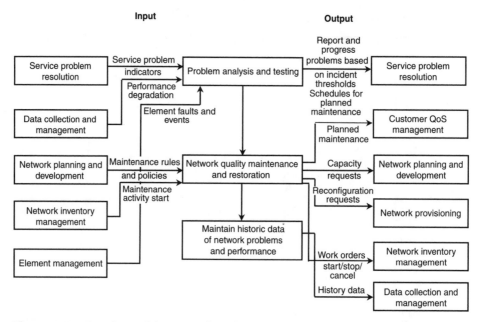

Figure 6.19 Functions of the network maintenance and restoration process.

Table 6.6 identifies the information sources for this process. Table 6.7 shows the information output and the targeted processes.

6.4.1 Problem Analysis, Including Testing

Root-cause analysis is important to prevent future problems. This function receives all the necessary input about problems, symptoms, and impacted customers. History records may be very helpful as well. They are available out of trouble tickets or from SolutionPacks from equipment suppliers. It requires very deep knowledge and skills on behalf of personnel.

An *expert system* is a computer program that has incorporated knowledge of a specific area of expertise, which it uses to solve problems at a high level of performance, similar to a human subject matter expert. The ultimate performance depends on the knowledge base and on combining principles.

For solving complex problems, the number of possible alternatives—using conventional applications—is very large. Expert systems accumulate a base of necessary facts and inference rules. By applying the inference rules to the facts to develop new facts, or chaining them together, expert systems generate the necessary pieces of the system.

Expert systems are designed by a knowledge engineer, who is responsible for converting the rules of problem solving for the domain expert, who is an expert in the field in which the expert system is implemented. The architecture of expert systems consists of four principal components (see Figure 6.20):

Table 6.6 Information Input for the Network Maintenance and Restoration Process

SOURCE OF INFORMATION	INFORMATION
Service problem resolution	Service problem indicators
Network planning and development	Maintenance rules and policies
Network data management	Performance degradation
Network inventory management	Maintenance activity start ready
Element manager	Element event or fault

Table 6.7 Information Output for the Network Maintenance and Restoration Process

INFORMATION	TARGETED PROCESSES
Report and progress problems based on incident thresholds, etc. Schedule and notify of planned maintenance	Service problem resolution
Planned maintenance	Customer QoS management
Capacity request	Network planning and development
Reconfiguration request	Network provisioning
Work order, start/stop/cancel	Network inventory management

1. *Knowledge base.* Problem specific and contains knowledge structures and production rules. It is created by the domain expert.

2. *Inference engine.* Problem independent. It is specific to the knowledge structures and is built by the knowledge engineer.

3. *Working memory.* Keeps track of all data presented and the conclusions deduced in dealing with the particular problem.

4. *User interface.* Designed to allow natural dialogues.

Production rules are a popular way of representing knowledge. They are generally of the form—if condition, then action. If all the conditions are true according to the current state of the working memory, the actions are taken. There are two fundamental directions of inference that control how the production steps are chained together. Using forward chaining, the production starts with the available data and moves forward from condition to action. This allows for data- or event-driven reasoning. Backward chaining starts with a hypothesis and moves backward to find productions that satisfy the antecedent of the goal.

There are, however, limitations for designing expert systems. The design may be justified where:

■ Human subject matter experts are not available in the numbers needed.

■ It is difficult to educate new subject matter experts.

■ There is an absolute demand for this expertise.

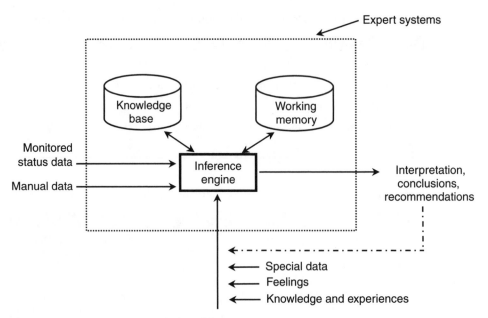

Figure 6.20 Expert systems (ES) architecture.

- The problem can be well defined and must have a solution.
- Problems are complex and not easy to solve quickly.
- Mistakes are very costly.

In this respect, operations and maintenance of service providers meets these requirements. Operations and maintenance is the principal target for the implementation of expert systems.

Service providers are frequently using trouble-ticketing systems. They represent a valuable source of information for solving new problems. Trouble tickets can be sorted and processed after resolving problems and closing trouble tickets. In a history database of trouble tickets—it may become part of a data warehouse or a datamart—all relevant data are available

- Symptoms of a problem
- Time stamps of problem resolution (detection, notification, diagnosis, repair, test)
- Explanation of diagnosis
- Identification of the cause of the problem
- Recommendations for solving the problems

Using case-based reasoning, symptoms of new problems can be entered, and the application will search for identical or at least similar cases from the past. The subject-matter expert is presented with those cases that might be helpful to solve the present problem.

6.4.2 Proactive Recognition of Problem Trends

Management of services, networks, and network elements does include monitoring capabilities. Assuming that operational areas of managed objects are known by baselining, network managers can evaluate performance and usage trends. Trends may be applied to utilization profiles and to frequency of problem occurrences. They can then be referenced to any of the TMN layers.

Deteriorating performance of facilities and equipment is an early warning sign about potential problems. The prerequisite of proactive problem recognition is the right use of the right tools. Tools include trouble-ticketing systems, systems and network monitors, datamarts, and data warehouses.

Neural networks may play a significant role in this operational domain. This technology is able to take a large number of samples from various networking components. These samples are processed in real time and the results are compared with expected profiles of the networks determined by baselining or by other monitoring activities. When the samples match the profiles, no further action is taken; if not, deviations are highlighted, interpreted, and reported to network operational persons in charge.

6.4.3 Network Quality Maintenance and Restoration

QoS metrics are expected to be continuously supervised by network operations. There are no industry standards for the metrics, but service providers are experienced on what metrics to monitor. Principal metrics include

- Service-independent metrics:
    - Availability
    - Mean time to service restoration
    - Mean time between failures
    - Mean time to repair
    - Mean time of repair
- Service-dependent metrics:
    - Resource utilization
    - Voice metrics
    - Managed lines service metrics
    - Frame relay metrics
    - Asynchronous Transfer Mode (ATM) service metrics
    - Digital subscriber line (xDSL) service metrics
    - Cable network service metrics
    - Packet switching service metrics

- Mobile service metrics
- Video service metrics
- IP service metrics

More details on these metrics can be found in Chapter 4, Section 4.6.5.

It is important to use the right tools for quality maintenance. In voice networks, the usual indicators of traffic management may be used. In IP-based networks, the metrics are different, but measurable as well. Chapter 7 gives more details on measurement and reporting tools.

If deviations are reported by monitors, this function is in charge of analyzing the causes and restoring service as soon as possible. Restoration may mean configuration changes, capacity extensions, and repair of networking components.

6.4.4 Maintenance of the Historic Data of Network Problems and Performance

Trouble tickets and all other records on tuning and optimization should be registered. These records may be maintained on their own—with smaller service providers—or may populate data warehouses in case of larger service providers. History data are very important to solve future problems and performance bottlenecks. The data source is the same as with the network data management process. In many cases, they use the same database or database segments, maintained in the data warehouse.

Testing scenarios may be maintained with this function as well. This function is also responsible to issue work orders to other processes, such as to network inventory management.

6.5 The Data Collection and Data Management Process

This process encompasses the collection of usage data and events for the purpose of network performance and traffic analysis. This data may also be an input to billing (rating and discounting) processes at the SML, depending on the service and its architecture.

The process must provide sufficient and relevant information to verify compliance/ noncompliance to SLAs. The SLAs themselves are not known at the network management layer (NML). The process must provide sufficient usage information for rating and billing.

This process must ensure that the network performance goals are tracked, and that notification is provided when they are not met (threshold exceeded, performance degradation). This also includes thresholds and specific requirements for billing. This includes information on capacity, utilization, traffic, and usage collection. In some cases, changes in traffic conditions may trigger changes to the network for the purpose of traffic control. Reduced levels of network capacity can result in requests to network planning for more resources.

In voice environments, switches and central office (CO) switches are the principal sources of data. Mediation devices collect data, process them, and distribute them to the rating and billing processes. The variety of data sources in IP environments is much higher. Routers, security servers, and firewalls may serve as data sources. Also, higher protocol layers, such as the application layer (e.g., use of RMON2 probes) may serve as a data source. All other processes are provided with raw data by this process. It is mandatory to have powerful and efficient database or data warehousing solutions.

Principal tasks include

- Collection of usage data via call detail records (CDRs) and IP detail records (IPDRs)
- Mediation on collected data
- Use of Signaling System 7 (SS7) in collecting data
- Data warehousing for maintaining data
- Baselining and generating performance metrics for reporting
- Maintaining trouble tickets in a database
- Providing notification on performance
- Initiating traffic metrics collection

Figure 6.21 shows the flow of functions for this process. All input and output information flows are displayed as well.

Table 6.8 identifies the information sources to this process. Table 6.9 shows the information output and the targeted processes.

6.5.1 Collection of Usage Data via CDRs and IPDRs

There is a standardized way to keep track of internal activities of switches. Switches—independent of their sizes—generate logs called call detail records (CDRs). Switches deal differently with CDRs. In every case, they assemble CDRs into automatic message accounting (AMA) files. This standardization has been proposed by Bellcore (now Telcordia).

New network services and comprehensive measurement strategies are creating a need for enhanced tools to manage this data. In addition to new data generating network elements, new applications are also being developed which require access to this data (e.g., marketing, customer care). The value given to this data also varies widely, requiring the capability to treat different AMA data in different manners.

The increasing complexity of network services and the sophistication of customer needs are multiplying the degree of flexibility required of accounting management.

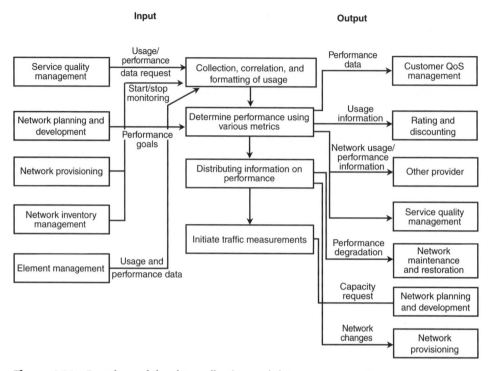

Figure 6.21   Functions of the data collection and data management process.

Table 6.8   Information Input for the Data Collection and Data Management Process

SOURCE OF INFORMATION	INFORMATION
Service quality management	Usage/performance data request
Network planning and development	Performance goals
Network provisioning	Start/stop monitoring
Network inventory management	Start/stop monitoring
Element management	Usage/performance data

Table 6.9   Information Output for the Data Collection and Data Management Process

INFORMATION	TARGETED PROCESSES
Performance data	Customer QoS management
Usage information	Rating and discounting
Network usage/performance information	Service quality management
Network usage/performance information	Other providers
Performance degradation	Network maintenance and restoration
Capacity request	Network planning and development
Network changes	Network provisioning

The concept of billing data is changing as the network and operations systems infrastructures are enhanced to support increasingly complex products and services.

There is a definite need to streamline the CDR collection process. Switches have a limited number of ports where data can be exchanged with external devices. Both vendors and operators are careful about access rights to these ports. In other words, everybody wants to limit the number of access entries. Element managers, maintenance personnel, vendors themselves, and CDR collectors are competing for the access to these ports. The best way is to use mediation systems that fully control input and output data streams to and from switches.

There are different types of CDRs, such as

- Outgoing
- Incoming
- Billing
- Intelligent networks (IN)

Figure 6.22 shows CDRs generated in a very unsophisticated switching environment.

CDR types include

5	outgoing
6	incoming
12	billing
15	IN

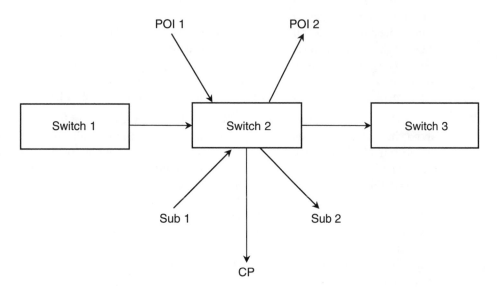

Figure 6.22 Generation of CDRs.

The legend for the Figure 6.22:

POI   point of interconnect

Sub   subscriber

CP   central provider

RT   record type

(x)   removed from billing stream

*   missing RT generated

The CDRs are

FROM	TO	DESCRIPTION	CDRs/RT
Sub1	Sub2	Local (on-switch)	12
Sub1	POI2	Outgoing (external)	5, 12
Sub1	Switch3	Outgoing (internal)	(5), 12
Sub1	CP	IN (on-switch)	15*
POI1	Sub2	Incoming (external)	6
POI1	POI2	Transmit (off-net/off-net)	5, 6
POI1	Switch3	Transmit (off-net/on-net)	(5), 6
POI1	CP	IN (external)	(6), 15
Switch1	Sub2	Incoming (internal)	(6)
Switch1	POI2	Transit (on-net/off-net)	5, (6)
Switch1	Switch3	Transit (on-net)	(5), (6)
Switch1	CP	IN (internal)	(6), 15

CDRs and the AMA standard are successfully covering the voice and the circuit switching environment altogether. However, the IP and packet switching environment needs standardization of IP detail records. In this respect, the IPDR initiative may help. The IPDR initiative has made progress creating a standard record format for IP service usage. The group has already addressed a number of topics, including terminology, syntax, and transport procedures. Member companies are now working on prototyping experiments, which they hope to demonstrate to several service providers.

Each phone connection generates a CDR, which contains important information about the transmission such as start and end times, duration of call, and originating and terminating number. CDRs for circuit switched voice are nothing new, and the service providers have their own method of storage and maintenance. While traditional CDRs are growing rapidly, many providers are also experiencing the need for IP-based services also referencing IPDRs. Currently, IP services are generally billed at a flat rate rather than by usage. IP services such as voice and video could be billed on a whole set of parameters other than simply duration and distance of the call. And the real-time nature of billing for IP-based services introduces a number of new challenges besides collection-usage data. One of these challenges is forwarding raw data for mediation (KARV99).

During the process of collecting data from switches, moving it through operations support systems, and ultimately storing it, a number of issues and concerns often come up as volumes increase. These include problems with redundancy of data. Because a number of back-end support systems rely on CDR information, there is a tendency to create multiple copies of these networks. Not only does this add to the data bottleneck, but it can also be confusing when it comes time to figure out which customer used what types of services.

Another issue is scalability (KARV99). Some larger service providers are handling millions of call records daily, the volume of which in many cases, is reaching the tera-byte level, and they need to develop storage solutions to accommodate this amount of data. For other service providers, the concern regarding IP services is not so much how to extract the CDRs from a switch or router, but how to do it quickly and with-out losing data along the way to the mediation device. In the case of regular, PSTN-based phone calls, CDRs might accumulate on a carrier's switch before being moved in batches at predefined intervals to a database and then to the rating and billing applications. Traditional switches usually have a lot of RAM as well as local storage space. Therefore, they can record all relevant metrics and then dump the data into storage. Once the switch reaches a predefined threshold, it either pushes the data out in batches to the mediation device or billing application, or holds onto the informa-tion until a mediation application pulls it out.

The batch method is not as effective in an Internet or intranet model, mostly because CDRs for IP services stay on a switch or router for a only few seconds and, therefore, need to be quickly captured. Instead of batching, service providers need to continually collect the raw data from a router and bring it into their system without dropping it dur-ing the process. In most cases, the data are pushed from the router when a session ends and goes to some kind of local data store. Not much processing is required; the empha-sis is on not losing data in this phase. After raw IPDRs are captured by the local data storing application, they usually go immediately to the mediation platform. Typically, the data are only rudimentary. They could contain detailed metrics such as duration, byte count, number of packets, and so on. But since most customers will use dynami-cally allocated IP addresses, the raw CDR may not contain information about the user. To find out which user had access to a particular IP address and at what time, the medi-ation application would have to communicate with the authentication server or other databases. It could then link up that information to the metrics about the session. The end result of this processing is billable data records that can be sent to the billing system.

After CDRs are collected, rated, and billed, the archived data can be used to reconcile accounts and is indispensable to many of a carrier's customer relationship manage-ment strategies. Also, regulation may require keeping these records for several years. The challenge of making these data useful for many purposes lies in setting up an application to not only store the CDRs, but also to make them easily accessible in a format that is meaningful. While they are extracting and processing CDRs, service providers also have to think about managing them as efficiently as possible. Storage area networks (SANs) may be helpful to connect and maintain data storage.

Another method of archive management for CDRs is to use a data warehouse. Larger service providers are completing millions of phone calls each day, resulting in multiple terabytes of data that need to be stored. After CDRs are processed, the task of managing those records is very complex. Many service providers use relational databases to handle the task of storing CDRs because they can provide access to large amounts of data and the intelligence to sort data according to the user's preference. However, they sometimes fall short when applied to a very specific task such as managing millions of such CDRs. Databases are helpful to reduce the total storage demand and can offer accessibility, analysis, and also reporting. Performance is always a problem with relational databases, particularly in cases with complex relationships and large data volumes. Another drawback is that many larger service providers are using multiple relational databases to store CDRs. Then they need a metadatabase or an excellent data dictionary to find the right database with the data they are looking for.

Service providers need to streamline the process of loading data into the data warehouse. One way to load CDRs, especially ones based on IP-services, is directly from a mediation device. Once IPDRs go through the billing application, they are generally in a format that is optimized for billing, but not for other uses. Instead, after IP call detail information has been processed by the mediation application to include not just the raw metrics, but also the correlation to the customer, some service providers are pushing those records directly to a data warehouse. The data will be needed by different departments, and not only for billing purposes. By sending information directly from mediation, the billing system is not overloaded because they take data out of the records for billing purposes only. Using the mediation platform for supporting data warehouse entries means that customers draw information from as close as possible to the source, instead of waiting until further downstream when it will become more difficult to reformat or retrieve information.

Using the data warehouse to accommodate CDRs and IPDRs may generate a scalability problem. Even a few months of data can easily add up to multiple terabytes, requiring very powerful processing of data within the data warehouse. For older detail levels of data, external data storage solutions must be considered.

IP usage data may be utilized by a number of front- and back-end systems. Billing is considered the most important and most widely used application, but other applications may also be beneficial to service providers (KARV00):

Reporting. A service provider could get information such as aggregate volume per time period, the type of traffic, and the source of traffic coming from other service providers. Rather than relying on sampling, since mediation systems look at all traffic data and process it, the carrier can produce accurate reports based on this data. This type of information can be invaluable to management personnel because they can view the actual load and utilization situation in their networks.

Analysis and profiling. IP mediation data would allow the service provider to see customer by customer, ISP by ISP, VPN by VPN, how much of a service is actually being used. In a multilayered service model, this information could help move customers into service packages that might benefit them more. With this proactive customer care, the carrier can reduce the likelihood of the user leaving the service. In some cases, where customers are moved to a premium package to save them money, the carrier might actually guarantee itself additional revenue from the highest-priced plan.

Avoiding customer churn. IP mediation data can be used by churn management software as well. Besides acquisitions, actual churn rates are very important. It is less expensive to keep customers than to acquire new ones. Usage data coming from IP mediation systems may be utilized to recognize trends about customer behavior. Also, customers can be identified that are likely to discontinue with services.

Capacity planning. Because the usage data are complete (they contain information about traffic origins, destinations and routes, when peak usage times are, and the types of traffic carried in the network), they can be used to ensure the service provider's infrastructure is sufficient for the traffic load.

6.5.2 Mediation and Mediation Systems

Mediation refers to those systems that collect data from network elements and pass it on to downstream back- and front-office applications, such as billing, customer care, fraud management, and decision support. In addition to data collection and routing, mediation systems perform functions such as usage data verification, network event reconstruction, filtering, and data format translation. Figure 6.23 shows an unsophisticated example for a generic mediation system.

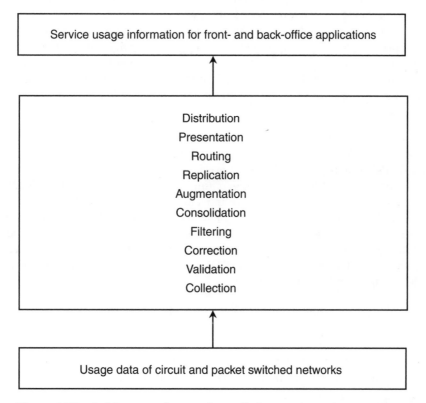

Figure 6.23 Architecture of a generic mediation system.

Customers usually don't understand exactly what mediation means or what mediation systems can accomplish. The traditional view of mediation systems is that they are a replacement for magnetic tapes in the billing process—in other words, a little more than automated data collectors and transporters. This view only applies to the first generation of mediation systems. While the first generation collected raw data and transported it to specific systems, current systems are able to operate in complex, multivendor network environments, perform postcollection processing, make intelligent routing decisions, and are read-write capable to refine data before transport to downstream systems (FINE98B).

An important aspect of a good mediation system is its ability to reconstruct complex network events out of data delivered from multivendor, multitechnology networks. The barriers between wireline, wireless, voice, and data networks are falling. It is conceivable that a customer could use a wireless modem on a laptop PC to place a roaming PCS call to an Internet service provider (ISP) roaming number. The customer could then browse for items he or she wants to consider buying. In case of a purchase, the transaction will include funds transfer or debit or credit card charge. This mix of services might be billed through a single provider, but actually delivered by multiple carriers with interconnect agreement. The transaction in this example needs to be accounted and billed for, but just as important is the service provider's ability to reconstruct the events of this transaction to develop a customer profile for marketing, and perhaps also for fraud protection. Modern mediation systems are designed to provide event reconstruction by correlating various CDRs, partial CDRs or other bits of usage data, translating the multiple data formats into data appropriate to a carrier's specific downstream applications, and performing data verification to avoid duplicates and support revenue assurance. Because data will come from multiple carriers that supply the underlying network services, a mediation system must be able to support carrier interconnection, both for intercarrier settlement purposes and for event reconstruction.

In voice environments, it is straightforward to walk through the procedure indicated in Figure 6.23. Telecommunication service providers have been collecting experiences with CDRs for many years. Mediation needs customization in terms of switch vendors, geography, real-time processing, optimal use of bandwidth and minimizing inquiries toward switches on behalf of mediation systems. Figure 6.24 shows a practical example with three different kinds of switches. It is typical that service providers work with different vendors. In this case, concentration is by switch vendor, not by geography. It is assumed that there is a data communication network (DCN) carrying internal data only. These data include CDRs, mediation output, inquiries toward switches, commands, and returns.

A mediation system should support the following functions:

- Support of various collection protocols
    - Transport, such as X.25, BX.25, TCP/IP, OSI
    - Other protocols, such as AMATPS, XFER, RCF, MTP, FTAM
    - Sequence and integrity checks

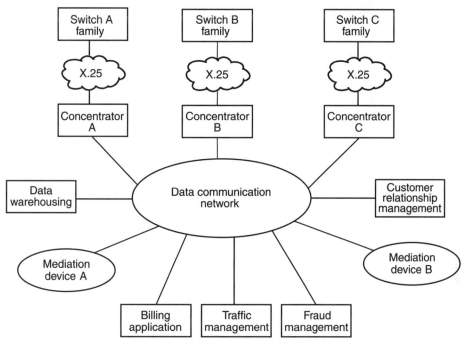

Figure 6.24 Mediation solution for various switches.

- Data formats
  - Fixed and variable lengths
  - Self-identifying subrecords, such as AMA
  - Self-identifying fields
  - Tagged data, such as ASN.1
- Data encoding
  - Binary, BCD, TBCD, ASCII, EBCDIC
  - Word, byte, and nibble swapping
  - Alignment, padding, termination
- Data content
  - File headers and trailers
  - Block headers and trailers
  - Data fields
- Data streaming
  - Record selection for output data streams

- Data mapping
  - From input to output
  - Filling in the gaps
- Transfer protocol
  - Batching
  - Formatting, such as CSV
  - Sequence and integrity checks

Business requirements for mediation solutions are

- Routing by call scenario, for example, outgoing calls, premium rate services
- Preparing records for billing, for example, derived information
- Removing nonbilling information, for example, time change
- Paralleling operation of old and new billing systems until cutover
- Migrating workload to new billing systems
- Supporting revenue assurance
- Protecting downstream applications from network changes
- Aggregating duration calls
- Adding missing area codes
- Merging fields
- Supporting truncated numbers
- Stripping nonbilling information, for example, number portability prefix
- Detecting duplicate records
- Bulking meters
- Processing operator-assisted calls, including dropped calls
- Archiving network data

Error management as part of mediation is extremely important. Many service providers have been registering considerable business losses due to errored CDRs that cannot be processed and billed. Some details about this function may be found in Chapter 4, Section 4.7.4.

Mediation systems vendors often stress test real-time capabilities of their solutions. The problems are that there isn't a true definition for the term and there is some question as to the usefulness of real-time capabilities, especially in billing. The most practical applications for real-time functionality seem to come in prepaid billing and fraud detection and management. For fraud, the reasons are simple. The faster they can be detected, the faster they can be stopped. A common mediation system function is data delivery to fraud management applications. Prepaid billing is dependent on real-time information to debit customer accounts.

Although mediation systems have grown in functionality and versatility, most of the products on the market are not yet designed to work in a packet world. Some systems do support ATM and frame relay equipment, but most only include interfaces to major circuit and wireless switches. Some are designed with an open architecture and can be customized to accommodate virtually any type of network equipment that produces usage data, but this is rarely a simple task. Similarly, there are products designed specifically for IP networks, but these generally do not support circuit switched or wireless environments. Because the market probably cannot wait for an all-encompassing solution, it is important to select vendors that will provide continuing support and upgrades for their implemented systems and have the experience and resources to deliver integrated solutions.

Internet Protocol (IP) provides a means for service providers and enterprise operations to provision service at the network layer of the OSI model of computing. The big potential for new, IP-based services has resulted in the rapid development and deployment of diverse new services by carriers, Internet service providers (ISPs), applications service providers (ASPs), and enterprises. In delivering these services, there is a fundamental need to automate the process of service provisioning, account of network costs, and generate revenue accordingly—by billing customers on the basis of service usage. To meet these business requirements, IP operations increasingly rely on hardware and software that has been specially developed to support real-time provisioning and billing processes unique to IP infrastructures.

These front- and back-office innovations challenge service providers how they are able to create the IP equivalent of call detail records (CDRs) using a manageable framework to rate and bill for services. Without such CDRs, successful emerging revenue models for IP network services cannot be implemented. Mediation provides a process for integrating and efficiently managing real-time data streams between network elements and back-office applications. Therefore, as ISPs, carriers, ASPs, and enterprises decide on service expansions, there is a growing need for an IP-related mediation solution to be implemented with IP-related provisioning and billing applications.

IP mediation software helps glue together network usage data collected from heterogeneous network elements such as servers, probes, routers, and so on, in a manageable fashion that facilitates the support of rating and billing processes defined according to business policy requirements. With mediation software made specifically for the IP service marketplace, carriers, ISPs, ASPs, and enterprises have the ability to efficiently coordinate CDR data between the heterogeneous hardware and software elements used to create and deploy new services. Figure 6.25 shows an example for IP mediation.

The largest obstacle is that the IP protocol suites were not originally designed to provide feedback concerning network or application usage, or service-level performance. Instead, the intelligence and management operations were handled by end systems (e.g., TCP). The result is that usage information is collected by the various network and service elements and stored in log files. One mediation design approach is to read and analyze log files for particular usage data, and then forward them to the business support systems, such as billing applications. For example, when the user dials into an IP network, the access server collects a user ID and password. The log-in information is then authenticated at a Radius server, which logs the event. At the end of the billing period, the amount of time the user spends on the network can be deter-

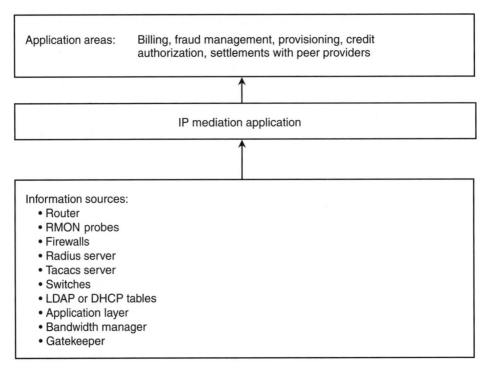

Application areas: Billing, fraud management, provisioning, credit
authorization, settlements with peer providers

IP mediation application

Information sources:
- Router
- RMON probes
- Firewalls
- Radius server
- Tacacs server
- Switches
- LDAP or DHCP tables
- Application layer
- Bandwidth manager
- Gatekeeper

Figure 6.25 Example of IP mediation.

mined by evaluating the log files. The same approach is used to account for e-mail or
for Web page visits (LUCA99B).

The new generation of mediation systems will have to handle a large number of different network elements—over 100 types. Service providers will see the level of complexity increasing with multiple elements like gateways, routers, switches, log files, counters, database information, and complicated IP flows. Mediation systems will need to collect information from several sources in the IP network, filter large amounts of data, correlate information, and aggregate information, and everything must happen in real time. In this new world of mediation, performance, flexibility, and fault tolerance are key success factors for suppliers of mediation solutions.

6.5.3 Role of SS7 in Mediation

Billing continues to play a key role as local number portability (LNP), advanced intelligent network (AIN) services, and interconnection issues intensify. Incumbent local-exchange carriers (ILECs) must be able to track usage on their networks, both voice and SS7, to a level of detail never seen before so they can bill competitive local-exchange carriers (CLECs) for specific network usage.

Usage sensitive data collection is possible in end office, central office, and tandem switches, assuming new additional software can be installed and maintained. All data needed for usage-sensitive billing are available on the network. One way to collect these data would be to upgrade every end office and access tandem switch with additional measurement software. This would require a major reengineering effort. Relatively new technology, however, can enable the necessary data collection at a much lower cost, using SS7 link monitors. An SS7 link monitor takes call data off the SS7 network at the signal transfer point (STP), thus monitoring each SS7 link between switches (FINE97).

An SS7 link monitor is essentially an information collection system. As SS7 packets pass through a signaling transfer point (STP), their data are replicated and filtered by customized hardware and software attached to the STP before being transported to a centralized system based in, for example, a network control center. The ideal method for managing SS7 data is to extract it from the links and process it as rapidly possible and as locally as possible with the result that what is transported back across the network is a very high level of information. The wrong way to do it is to transfer all of the information back to the central location. It would mean to replicate what the signaling system is doing. The platform in the network control center could be a management framework with a number of device-dependent and device-independent management applications.

SS7 packets carry specific messages regarding every call made on the network. Everything in an SS7 packet is essential. Within the packets, there are originating point codes that identify the switches involved. There is furthermore an initial address message which can give the called number and the calling number. SS7 packets can carry information about the AIN service activated for every call. Because these data are accessible, it is possible to track call origin, destination, the route and number of switches involved, session length, any special services used and exactly how those services were provided. It is possible to track how much extra SS7 capacity or time was used for database dips and/or any extra messaging. All these data can be correlated to construct a complete view of every call, allowing an ILEC to measure exactly how much of its SS7 resources are being used by a competitor's customers, and enabling gathering of a level and type of billing detail that would otherwise be impossible. The SS7 network can therefore become not only a means of signaling and service providing, but also a genuine source of revenue.

Link monitoring technology may fundamentally change the way carriers look at billing. Billing traditionally has been a switch-centric science, but not anymore. An SS7 link monitor can collect billing data more efficiently than switches because it requires fewer collection sites and is based on a central platform. A centralized platform also means that any necessary software changes or upgrades can be made at one location, rather than multiple switch sites. A link monitor can also provide more software flexibility.

As SS7 networks are built out, the call for new STPs will grow, but those STPs need to be designed with the postderegulation marketplace in mind. Embedding link monitoring functions in STPs is a matter of product differentiation. Technically, from a pure data collection perspective, it doesn't matter if the monitor is built in or added on. From a budgetary perspective, however, the more functions hardware can provide, the more monetarily attractive it becomes. There is, however, one major concern: the processing burden. There are significant capacity issues associated with interfering with the SS7 network and being able to filter out and capture all of the information that users need to capture. A mixture of embedded and add-on technology will arise depending on the situation. In a high-traffic area, it might be a better idea to handle monitoring on a separate platform so that the STP just handles switching and is not overloaded. In this scenario, the add-on hardware pays for itself due to the traffic volume. In a lower-traffic area, embedding the software is more economical because the capacity concerns are not as serious, and expenses are lowered because extra hardware is not required.

SS7 will provide the bridge between the circuit and packet worlds to make the vision of a seamless hybrid network a reality. It will take more than routers with SS7 stacks, however, to make it happen. Interconnection and internetworking standards must be developed and a number of issues, such as security and interconnect billing, must be addressed before services can be offered.

An IP-to-PSTN gateway is responsible for converting traditional voice signals into IP packets and vice versa. Multiple gateways are often connected to a gatekeeper that then communicates to the outside world. The gatekeeper is likely to be responsible for converting from an IP standard, such as H.323, to SS7 and thus providing signaling functionality out to the public switched telephone network (PSTN). As networks become more and more interconnected and the divisions between them disappear, more and more services provided by many carriers on a variety of networks will be delivered in single sessions. This means settlements or interconnect billing at a higher level of complexity. SS7 can play a role in this advanced settlements process because of the data on network activity that it contains.

There are several issues to be solved before circuit and packet networks are no longer considered separate entities. Now service providers are in just the very early stages, laying the foundation for the communications options of the future. Packet technologies may someday replace the circuit switched network entirely, but not without a long coexistence. If IP-based services are going to achieve carrier-grade status, they will have to take advantage of the feature-reach signaling protocol, SS7, that makes the PSTN work.

6.5.4 Data Warehousing for Maintaining Data

A *data warehouse* is a database created specifically for the purpose of business analysis, in contrast to online transaction processing systems, established for automating business operations.

The data warehouse contains data extracted from various support, documentation, financial, marketing, and management systems of telecommunications service providers. Data can be moved and altered, or transformed, to make it consistent and accessible for analysis by end users. It can be used by service providers of all sizes, with all types of hardware, software, and networking infrastructure.

Figure 6.26 shows the generic structure of a data warehouse solution with a telecommunications service provider.

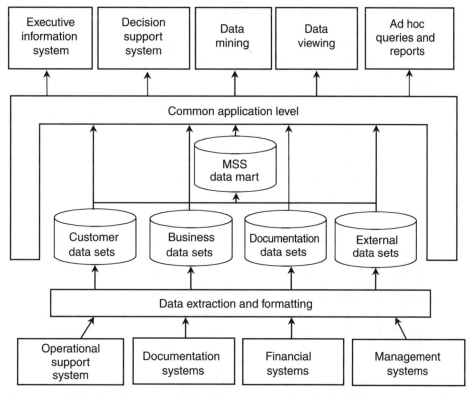

Figure 6.26 Architecture of a data warehouse of a telecommunication service provider.

Data are extracted from support, documentation, marketing, financial, and management systems. After proper formatting, various data sets can be partitioned. These data sets feed data to a marketing support system (MSS) datamart, and also to a common application interface, to serve various end-user applications, such as

- Consolidation of many data sources into one database
- Marketing research and support
- Maintenance of product portfolios
- Consolidation of knowledge packs to support reactive fault management
- Maintenance of history trouble tickets

The data warehouse is integrated, containing data from diverse legacy applications. It is historical, and it comprises both summary and detailed data. Information in the warehouse is subject-oriented, time-variant and nonvolatile. Subject-oriented means that the data warehouse is designed and organized by the major subjects of the corporation, such as customer, vendor, and activity. In contrast, the legacy environment is organized by functional applications. The data warehouse is integrated because it contains data that have been transformed into a state of uniformity. For instance, gender can be considered as a data element. One application may encode gender as male/female, another 1/0, and a third x/y. As data are placed in the data warehouse, they are converted to a uniform stage; that is, gender would be encoded in only one way. As a data element passes onto the warehouse from applications where it is not encoded in this way, it is converted to create consistency.

But internally coding data is only one aspect of integration. The representation of data should also be considered. In one application, a data element is measured in yards, but in another application, it may be measured in inches or centimeters. As this data element is placed in the data warehouse, it is converted into a single uniform state of representation. A third characteristic of a data warehouse is time-variance. Each unit of data can be considered a snapshot of data, and each snapshot has one moment of time at which the snapshot was made. The values of the data are said to be time-variant, that is, dependent on the time of the snapshot. Unlike time-variant warehouse data, operational data are updated as business conditions change. Operational data represent values that are updated any time the real-world objects they represent change. In the data warehouse, each time a change occurs, a new snapshot is created to mark that change. The time-variant characteristic of the data warehouse is what allows so much data to be stored there.

Finally, the data warehouse is nonvolatile; it is generally a load-and-access environment. After the data have been transformed and integrated, they are loaded en masse into the warehouse, from which they are accessed by end users. In contrast, data in the operational environment are updated on a record-by-record basis. This volatility requires considerable overhead to ensure the integrity and consistency of the database for such database activities as rollback, recovery, commits, and locking. The basic technology for the data warehouse does not require the underlying integrity component of the transaction-oriented database management system. Because of its nonvolatility, the data warehouse permits design practices that are in many ways unacceptable in the operational environment, and vice versa. Figure 6.27 shows a typical structure of a data warehouse.

The data warehouse commonly has a four-level structure. The bulk of the data resides at the current level of detail, where it is accessed by end-user analysts. From this level, a lightly summarized level of detail is created, which serves midlevel management. Next comes the highly summarized level of data, for the benefit of top management. Beneath these three levels lies the older level of detail data that are at least 2 or 3 years old.

There is a predictable flow of data into and through the data warehouse. Data enter into the current level of detail of the warehouse from the integration and transformation processes, which, in turn, have been provided with data by the legacy-type applications.

The data then flow into the older level of detail as they age. As the data are summarized, they flow into the lightly summarized level of data, and then again into the highly summarized level. Finally, perhaps the most important component in the data warehouse architecture is the metadata.

End users cannot efficiently access the data in the warehouse unless they have a way of knowing what data are stored there and where they are located. *Metadata* are data about data, a catalog of what data are in the warehouse and pointers to the data.

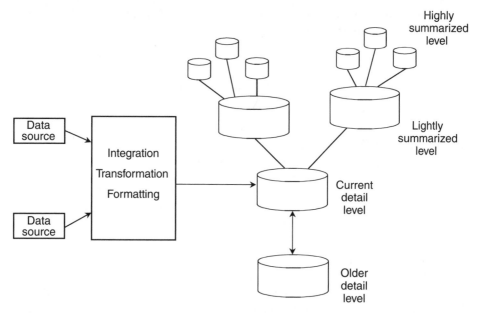

Figure 6.27 Structure of the data warehouse.

Users must not only be able to locate data in the warehouse, they must also be able to manage the data. For this reason, the metadata not only needs to describe the structure of the data in the warehouse, but it must contain data modeling information, including data extraction and transformation histories and data summarization algorithms. This information is essential, so end users can trace the data back to operational sources. The metadata may also contain data usage statistics. The availability and increasing maturity of extraction and transformation tools, combined with powerful features for creating and managing metadata, are key drivers behind the rapidly increasing number of data warehouse implementations.

A data warehouse can reside on a variety of platforms, depending on the data level of detail and summarization. Frequently, the data warehouse is physically distributed, but logically unified. Typical solutions are

- Highly summarized data usually reside on PC workstations
- Lightly summarized data usually reside on client/service structures
- Current data usually reside on mainframes or on client/server structures
- Older detail level data are expected to reside on bulk storage devices

State-of-the-art data warehouses offer Web access with the following benefits:

Infrastructure. Using Web access shifts the burden of platform compatibility to the browser and presentation vendors.

Access. Both internal and external users can easily have access via the Internet, eliminating the need to extend the corporate network.

Cost. Web browsers are a fraction of the cost of OLAP and other client tools. They also have shorter learning curves.

Leverage. The Web browser can be used in every application that provides a Web gateway.

Control. Maintenance can be isolated to a centralized point.

Independence. Web access allows a wide choice in hardware and operating systems.

6.5.5 Baselining and Generating Performance Metrics for Reporting

Each service provider should determine the optimal operational areas. Due to differences in infrastructures, customers, traffic patterns, and load distribution techniques, service providers are recommended to interpret QoS metrics for their own environment first. This phase is called *baselining.*

The results of baselining are realistic thresholding that may help to better control operations and optimize performance. This function is responsible to populate all service layer, network layer, and element layer metrics for the complete product portfolio of the service provider. This function distributes the formatted and preprocessed information to a large number of other processes. To a certain extent, this function prepares decisions as well. This refers first of all to requesting network changes and capacity extensions.

6.5.6 Maintaining Trouble Tickets in a Database

Trouble tickets offer a very rich set of information for multiple use. Most of the performance metrics are computed from this information source. Each trouble registered is provided with time stamps. Most likely they are in the following order:

Time reported	T0
Time received by the responsible group	T1
Time network service restored	T2
Time vendor notified	T3
Time vendor responded	T4
Time vendor restored	T5

Using these time stamps, statistics may be calculated for

Total vendor time	T5–T3
Total user nonavailability	T2–T0
Total service outage	T5–T0

Other entries in trouble tickets can be linked to case-based reasoning by identifying the symptoms and their resolution. Also, expert systems may profit from the cases maintained in this database.

During the process of benchmarking service providers, this trouble-ticket database may play a key role by providing history data about the internal performance of the service provider.

6.5.7 Providing Notification on Performance

This function is expected to evaluate collected metrics with baselined thresholds. If performance degradation is obvious, the network maintenance and restoration process must be notified.

This type of notification is not necessarily an SLA violation, but an early warning. Reasons can be quickly found prior to customers experiencing any service degradation. In this responsibility, there are connections to service problem resolution processes, particularly to proactive fault management, as well.

6.5.8 Initiating Traffic Management

Traffic management has emerged as a strategic tool to keep pace with increasing competition between service providers. In today's environment, it is essential to offer excellent communication services with optimized resources.

The term *traffic* describes the flow of messages through a communications network, whether voice, data, or video, analog or digital. Traffic characteristics for any segment, or in total within the communication network, are influenced by many traffic metrics. Traffic may be of two basic types: nonrandom and random. Nonrandom traffic has a predictable arrival rate and holding time. It is rarely, if ever, encountered in voice traffic engineering, but may be encountered on a limited basis in time-of-day file transfers or batch applications in the data environment. Videoconferencing set up for time-of-day would represent this category as well. Random traffic, on the other hand, exhibits, over a period of time and from moment to moment, fluctuations from an anticipated average value or measure, such as the number of calls or attempts arriving during a specified time interval. Since random traffic is what the business/financial planner will be dealing with in the voice, data, and video environment, traffic metrics should be defined very carefully.

In today's voice environments, the only constant is change. In mature markets, competition is causing market fragmentation and spawning new kinds of voice services and service providers. In emerging markets, the demand for the installation of new lines is causing growth at unprecedented rates. In all markets, grade of service (GoS) levels must be maintained and even increased using the same or fewer resources.

Basics of Voice Traffic Metrics

Traffic engineering is not an exact science, even for trained voice traffic engineers. Theories and assumptions are used to engineer the many components of the voice switching network, including the transport facilities, based on acceptable levels of service and the economics of revenue gain or loss versus the investment to capture that revenue. Within each local-exchange carrier (LEC), and even many nontelecommunications service providers, there are established guidelines or standards for service levels for each network component. In addition, these service levels may change from time to time based on usage trends, revenue projections, and overall economic conditions.

The voice traffic engineer has a great variety of statistical measurements that are used in determining the engineering probabilities and projections with a high degree of accuracy. However, with a basic understanding of traffic engineering principles, facility and equipment requirements can be made with sufficient accuracy.

Data input for voice traffic engineering include

- Call minutes per month (CMM)
- Call message volume (CMV)
- Average call length (ACL)
- Working days per month (WDM)
- Busy hour percentage (BH%)
- Call processing time (CPT)

These inputs are used to determine the traffic load in the busy hour. This traffic load (i.e., the demand for the use of the network trunks in the busy hour) is the fundamental basis for engineering the number of network trunks or facilities. The following metrics should be calculated

- Busy hour messages (BHM)
- Average call holding time (ACHT)
- Busy hour CCS (BHCCS)
- Grade of service (GoS)

Call minutes per month (CMM) are the total conversation minutes expected to take place over that period of time on the facilities that are to be engineered. A monthly time period provides an acceptable period in which to receive a statistical cross section of volume. This volume can be used to determine averages, and it provides a higher confidence level than looking at an hour or a day. CMM are obtained from historical data, such as toll or per-message billing, station message detail recording, or other sources where call lengths are available. All call lengths totaled for the month, 24×7 will be used. If the historical data being used are in paper format and of great volume, sampling the CMM may save some time. However, toll bills can be segregated by time, location called, or other factors. The samples must be representative before being increased to 100 percent. If such data are not available, the total CMM may be estimated as the call message volume (CMV) times the estimated average call length (ACL). CMM is also a critical element for determining costs or prices in financial spreadsheets.

Call message volume (CMV) is the number of telephone calls that will be carried over the designed trunks or facilities. The calls could be incoming, outgoing, and/or both, depending on how the facilities are or will be configured. Messages or calls should include all calls over a 30-day period, including nights and weekends. The primary source for obtaining CMV is historical data. If historical data are not available, the planner is required to estimate the CMV.

Average call length (ACL) is determined by dividing the CMM by the CMV. This result is the average conversation time per call or average call length. If historical data are not available or the planner has not estimated the CMM and CMV, the ACL needs to be estimated. The nature of the proposed business operation determines the ACL estimate. The average business call is approximately 4 to 5 minutes. However, businesses that operate incoming call sales centers may have ACLs of 2.5 minutes or less. Help line services, customer service centers, and outgoing solicitation operations may have ACLs of 6.5 minutes or greater. Automated call distributors (ACDs) are an excellent source of information for ACL.

Working days per month (WDM) are the normal number of operational days per month of the business or business element under study. If the business focus involves half days or other fractional amounts, they should be considered as well. Most organizations use either 21, 22, or 23 working days as an average month. This is based on the usual Monday through Friday workweek. If the business is operational 7 days a week, 30/31 working days must be implemented for the month.

Busy hour percentage (BH%) can be determined directly by inspection of historical call record data, if available. If the planner is working without historical data, however, an estimate of the percentage of total calls that occur in the busiest hour may be used. Most businesses experience a period of time during a given day, week, or month in which more volume occurs than in other periods of time. This, of course, may be dependent upon a number of factors including the type of business, business hours of operation, and the time zone(s) in which the particular business is located. Usually, business activities find the busy hour to be between 10:00 A.M. and noon and between 2:00 and 4:00 P.M. It is possible that during these periods of time, traffic is fairly and evenly distributed over each of the 4 hours. In the absence of measured data, a reasonable estimate of busy hour traffic would be about 20 percent of the total traffic volume in one day. Twenty percent of a day's calls is expected to occur in the busiest 1-hour period.

With virtually every type of switching equipment, whether private branch exchange (PBX), key system, or central office (CO), a facility will be seized longer than the actual talk time or call length. Call processing time is the time required for the various network elements to process a telephone call, and as this processing is taking place, the trunk is not available for conversation or to handle other calls. While this time may not show up on the billing, it is an important factor in determining the number of facilities required. In order to compute the average call holding time (ACHT), CPT is added to ACL. By using new signaling technologies, such as SS7, call processing time is minimal and server availability is not affected by the process. Call processing time will depend on such factors as the type of customer equipment, type of LEC serving central office and connectivity plans, interexchange carrier (IXC) network connectivity, and far end-office type. An average of 3 to 6 seconds per call for CPT appears to be applicable for most cases.

Busy hour messages (BHM) are the quantity of calls that occur during the busiest hour of the working day. This is normally an input required from the planner, as BMH is calculated by using the input of dividing the monthly call message volume (CMV) by the number of working days per month (WDM) and multiplying the result by the busy hour percentage (BH%). If CMV and BH% are not input from historical data, then BMH is an estimated direct input from the planner.

Average call holding time (ACHT) is equal to the ACL plus the CPT, and expressed in 100 call seconds (CCS). Since one CCS is equal to 100 seconds of trunk usage, each trunk is, therefore, theoretically able to carry 36 CCS in a one-hour period of time. AHCT is computed on the basis of input by service providers and equipment manufacturers.

Busy hour CCS (BHCCS) is the result of multiplying the BHM times the ACHP. The formula for this metric contains an adjustment factor for various forms of uncompleted calls. These uncompleted calls add overall holding time to the busy hour, increasing the BHCCS.

Grade of service (GoS) is the proposed, or objective, level of anticipated call blocking that may occur on the engineered facilities. In other words, GoS designates the expected percentage of offered, or attempted, calls that will be blocked in the busy hour.

The Traffic Management Process

The majority of voice networks are based on fixed hierarchical routing (FHR). Switches are connected to each other in a routing hierarchy. Local switches (end-office switches) have direct connections to subscriber equipment such as telephone and PBX. End offices typically have direct connections to other end offices in the same geographic area. Tandem switches have connections to other switches, not to customer premises.

Switching is done hierarchically to provide alternate routing for traffic overloads and facility failures. Each switch is given a class designation depending on its location in the hierarchy. In the case of failure or overload, lower class switches can route calls to higher class switches. A typical routing hierarchy is shown in detail in Figure 6.28. Traffic between two local switches is normally routed through a high usage (HU) trunk group. High usage trunk groups are engineered so that some traffic during the busy hours will overflow to an intermediate high usage (IHU) trunk group. Traffic from IHU trunk groups overflow to alternate final (AF) trunk groups. Overflow traffic from AF trunk groups goes to a "no circuits available" announcement. In practice, networks, switches, and routing appear in many configurations. For example, some switches perform both tandem and end-office functions, and some networks do not have any end offices or tandem switches at all.

A telephone network is a dynamic entity. Traffic volumes, calling patterns, and the introduction of new services all create the need to constantly reengineer the network. The ultimate goal of traffic engineering and planning is to cost-effectively provide customers with a target GoS. Simply put, GoS is expressed as the percentage of unsuccessful call attempts because of insufficient network capacity. Many service

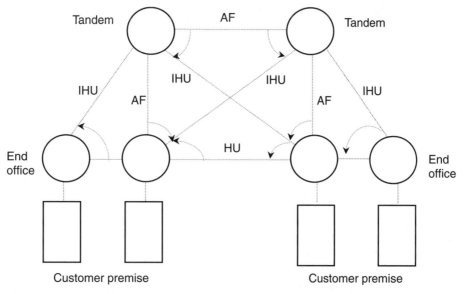

Figure 6.28 Typical alternate routing hierarchy.

providers engineer their network for a certain GoS level measured during the busy hour. The busy hour is that hour of day in which there is the greatest amount of traffic. A GoS of 2 percent means that during the busy hour, no more than 2 call attempts out of 100 will be unsuccessful because all circuits are occupied.

Network engineers analyze facility usage and performance statistics to ensure that current network resources are appropriately allocated and functioning correctly. Network planners use the same data to allocate new resources for projected growth. In order to engineer the network, several factors are taken into consideration, including previous growth, planned introduction of new services, and projected customer growth.

The goals of real-time traffic management are to ensure maximum use of all equipment and facilities at all times and to complete as many calls/messages as possible. Network events, such as mass callings, equipment failures, and focused overloads, can seriously affect customer service levels and operating revenues. In situations of extreme network overload, real-time traffic management maximizes network resource usage and protects vital network services. In cases of localized network overload, traffic can be routed to those parts of the network having resources available. Some examples of network problems include:

- *General network overload.* When the entire network is saturated with calls. For instance, this can happen on a national holiday.

- *Focused overload.* When an unusually high number of calls are directed at a single telephone number or location. Examples of this include radio show call-ins and ticket sales.

■ *Equipment failures.* Including minor failure of equipment, such as a line card or multiplexer, or events as serious as one or more switches failing to operate.

In order to maximize call completion and preserve network resources, the following principles apply when considering network management actions

■ Keep all circuits filled with messages

■ Use all available circuits

■ Give priority to single-link connections, when all available trunks are exhausted

■ Inhibit switching congestion

The most effective way to respond to network events is through the use of network management controls. There are two major categories:

1. *Protective controls.* They limit the amount of traffic that can come into the network. Traffic offered to a switch may need to be limited if that switch is receiving traffic beyond its capacity. When a network is overloaded, not all traffic can complete, so preference should be given to traffic with the highest chance of completing.

2. *Expansive controls.* They reroute traffic from those areas of the network experiencing overload to areas with capacity available. Network overload may occur because of above-average calling levels or network equipment failures.

By using reroutes, a network manager can take advantage of time-zone and busy-hour differences. On a peak-traffic day, all circuits are often fully occupied and network managers can take advantage of calling patterns that are time sensitive.

Traffic analysis is a broad category concerned with the analysis of traffic and network problems. These may include intermittent traffic problems, equipment-related problems, or volatile traffic patterns. This function is often performed in conjunction with other groups, such as facility or transmission management. Traffic analysis requires diverse network information that allows network managers to track the source of network problems. Often, traffic data may reveal that a problem exists. However, transmission alarms or facility information may be needed to determine the root cause of the problem. The network analysis group must be able to generate ad hoc reports and analyze network information interactively to determine patterns and recognize unusual network events.

Traffic Characteristics

Random traffic may be characterized as one of the following three types:

1. *Poisson-distributed traffic.* If during the busy hour, there is no specific or precisely defined trend in the traffic, it is said to be Poisson-distributed traffic. In other words, if a call arrives at a specific point during some time interval, then it is just as likely to arrive at any other point in that time interval. Mathematically, this is characterized by a variance-to-mean ratio equal to 1.0.

2. *Peaked traffic.* Random traffic that does not exhibit the Poisson characteristics may be either peaked or smooth. This does not mean that such traffic has a strict schedule or that it is predictable, but merely that it is non-Poisson. The character-

istics of peaked traffic may show more simultaneous calls, no calls, many calls of less-than-average call holding time, many calls greater-than-average call holding time, or any combination of these or other conditions. Peaked traffic conditions are normally associated with trunk capacity groups that are linked with each other in a first choice, alternate route, high usage, and/or final route traffic engineering scenario. Mathematically, peaked traffic is characterized by a variance-to-mean ratio greater than 1.0.

3. *Smooth traffic.* Unlike peaked traffic, where there is a great variance, either high or low, from Poisson distributed traffic, random traffic that is smooth varies only slightly from the Poisson traffic and is constant (i.e., call arrival times and the number of calls at the average call holding time are more consistent and predictable). Mathematically, this is characterized by a variance-to-mean ratio less than 1.0.

Basically, there are three traffic capacity models widely used in engineering voice circuits:

1. *Poisson traffic capacity model.* It assumes that all end users of a given system have access to all the trunks in a given trunk group, that call duration is generally at or near the average call holding time, and that attempted calls that encounter an all trunk busy (ATB) condition will be redialed after waiting for a period of time, approximately the average call holding time. This model is best suited for engineering PBX and key systems that have one-way trunk groups or two-way trunk groups that have limited access to only the users of that system.

2. *Erlang B traffic capacity model.* It is used when there are many trunk groups available to end users and those trunk groups are routed together so that every call offered to those trunk groups are completed or immediately denied service. Traffic engineers generally use this model for engineering components within the telephone network and some types of interswitch trunk groups.

3. *Erlang C traffic capacity model.* It is used when there are many trunk groups available to end users and those trunk groups are routed together so that every call offered to those trunk groups either finds a trunk in which to complete the call immediately, or is delayed (i.e. held or queued within the system until a trunk becomes available). Traffic engineers generally use this model for engineering various service circuits within the network complex.

Tools for Voice Traffic Management

There are two different units in general use for measuring traffic intensity or traffic load. They are CCS and the erlang. CCS is an abbreviation for centa call seconds, or 100 call seconds. Since there are 3,600 seconds in an hour, there are a maximum of 36 CCS in an hour (i.e., each trunk can carry a theoretical maximum of 36 CCS in an hour). Facility sizing is based on the busy hour traffic. For example, if there are 100 calls during the busy hour with an average call holding time of 4 minutes (240 s), each call would represent 2.4 CCS, resulting in a total traffic load of 240 CCS in the busy hour. One erlang is equal to 1 hour (3,600 s) of traffic (i.e., 36 CCS). Therefore, to convert CCS to erlangs, one has to divide the number of CCS by 36. Using the example shown previously, the same busy hour traffic load represents 6.67 erlangs.

There are various tools available to successfully manage traffic. In general, the following tool categories are important to traffic engineering.

Traffic engineering and planning functions require tools that can collect traffic-related statistics and produce reports in both detailed and summary formats. Because the data collected are so varied, as shown in Table 6.10, tools must be both flexible and easy to use.

In order to diagnose and respond to traffic problems in real time, network managers need the following

- Access to real-time traffic statistics
- Easy-to-use applications for issuing controls to any switches in the network
- Applications that enable predefining and applying groups of controls, called control preplans
- Traffic statistics that help to diagnose problems; trunk group statistics are obtained from switches in 5 or 15 minute intervals
- Definition and implementation of thresholds

Switching controls are the most effective method for responding to network events. In order to be effective, a network management system should provide methods for rapid implementation of network controls. It also should insulate the user from differences between switch models and the effects of software load changes. Controls should be tracked in real time so the traffic manager always knows what controls are in effect.

Traffic analysis requires a flexible set of tools that allows a user to detect and analyze network traffic trends and problems. Questions faced include:

Table 6.10 Sample Data Requirements for Traffic Engineering and Planning

NETWORK ELEMENT	PARAMETER	DETAIL LEVEL
Switch	Call completions	Busy hour Daily
Remote switching unit	Call failures by reason Projected call increase	Weekly Monthly Yearly
Trunk group	Usage Overflows Attempts Answer-to-seizure ratio	Busy hour Daily Weekly Monthly Yearly
Network	Call completions Call failures by reason	Busy hour Daily Weekly Monthly Yearly

- Why are calls lost on trunk group A in the middle of the night?

- Why is traffic decreasing in certain parts of the network?

- What is the cause of a severe drop in GoS levels in the western region last week?

- Did service provider A receive the amount of traffic from service provider B that was estimated?

In order to determine the cause of problems in the network, a traffic manager needs access to detailed and summary traffic data, switch configuration data, and other network alarm information. The ability to interactively generate ad hoc reports and queries is essential for determining the source of problems in the network. Calls can be lost because of sudden increases in traffic, faulty trunk groups, or incorrect configuration within the switch itself. As networks increase in complexity, access to information becomes more and more important for analysis of network problems. Tables 6.11 and 6.12 show traffic reporting examples.

Basics of IP Traffic Management

IP traffic management can be considered at various layers of the Internet Protocol stack. Lower-layer solutions concentrate on the transmission of traffic from source to destination not considering applications and their priorities. Traffic shaping and load balancing are not very efficient at low layers. Moving up in the layers and considering applications, or in other words content to be transmitted to destinations, more intelligent decisions can be made at the network edge. Web switching is the new generic term for solutions that use Uniform Resource Locator (URL) load balancing, network address translation, and embedded Domain Name Service (DNS) intelligence capabilities to speed up Web traffic. All decisions about resource allocation should be based on content.

Content-Driven Traffic Management

Web traffic poses a significant number of challenges to existing Internet and intranet infrastructures. Most Web sessions are short-lived. As such, they have fewer TCP packets compared to batch mode operations such as file transfer. In addition, HTTP traffic tends to spike and fall radically. This creates instant demand for hot content that in turn causes network and server congestion. When Web technology is used to support systems and network management, transport paths are shared between productive traffic and management traffic. Management traffic is even more sensitive against bottlenecks. Web site traffic is highly mobile in that a unique event on a particular Web site could trigger a significantly high hit rate within a very short period of time. This would be typical in cases with periodic management report distribution and major systems and network outages.

Web traffic behavior is significantly different from today's client/server paradigm. It has the following unique characteristics:

- The amount of data sent from a server is significantly larger (5:1) than the amount of data sent from a client to a server. This suggests that optimization of server-to-client traffic has more significant impact to the intranet and that client request

Table 6.11 Monthly Trunk Group Exception Report

Report Generated on: May 3, 2000	Monthly Trunk Group Exception Report Switch: West	Report Interval: April 2000

TRUNK GROUP	DATE	HOUR	CIRCUITS	USAGE	% OVERFLOW	% UTILIZATION
TrkGrp1	April 4	18:00	112	95	5	98
TrkGrp2	April 12	21:30	188	95	0	90
TrkGrp10	April 3	17:00	103	92	5	85
TrkGrp34	April 28	19:30	155	72	0	92

Table 6.12 Quality of Service Report

Report Generated on: May 3, 2000	Weekly Quality of Service Report Switch: East	Report Interval: April 1, 2000 to April 30, 2000

WEEK	APRIL 1–7, 2000	APRIL 8–14, 2000	APRIL 15–21, 2000	APRIL 22–28, 2000
Number of attempts	1,234,456	1,398,294	1,345,091	1,422,782
Call breakdown in percent				
1. Call connections	97.6	98.6	98.5	98.2
2. Ext. tech. irregularity	0.56	0.98	0.86	0.97
3. Unanswered calls	10.2	11.1	10.7	10.8
4. Subscriber busy	22.4	23.1	22.6	22.3
5. ATB destination busy	0.56	0.79	0.81	0.62
6. ATB home exchange	0.21	0.34	0.23	0.27
7. Call to non-working number	0.02	0.04	0.03	0.04
8. Int. tech. irregularity	1.07	0.98	0.80	0.81
9. Call loss (2 + 5 + 8)	2.19	2.75	2.47	2.40

redirection to the best-fit server could have significant performance advantages for Web traffic flows.

- The median transfer size for Web server documents is small (e.g., 5 KB). This implies that Web flows are mostly short-lived flows. They are more likely to create instantaneous congestion due to their bursty nature. This suggests a resource management model must deal appropriately with short-lived flows. Even though HTTP supports persistent connections, due to interoperability issues with existing network caches, it is unclear how widespread deployment will be, or how soon.

- The top 10 percent of Web server files are accessed 90 percent of the time and are accountable for 90 percent of the bytes transferred. This suggests that Web server selection, caching, and content replication schemes that focus on this top 10 percent will yield the greatest gain.

- A significant percentage (e.g., 15 to 40%) of the files and bytes accessed are accessed only once. That is, some small number of large files often consumes a disproportionate amount of total server and network bandwidth. In addition, servers suffer performance degradation when subject to significant job size variation. This is due primarily to memory fragmentation, which occurs when buffering variable size data in fixed length blocks. Furthermore, subjecting servers to workloads consisting of both hot and one-time requests will result in lower performance due to frequent cache invalidation of the hot objects. Therefore, a server selection strategy that takes into account content, job size, and server cache coherency can significantly improve network and server resource allocation and performance. In addition, requests for large files may be good candidates for redirection to a server that has a shorter round-trip time to the client.

- Hosts on many networks access Web servers, but 10 percent of the networks are responsible for over 75 percent of this usage. This suggests that resource management strategies that focus on specific client populations may yield positive results in some cases.

Real-time traffic is becoming an increasingly significant proportion of Web traffic. Web site resource management strategies must take into account an increasing demand for support of real-time applications such as voice, distance learning, and streaming media. To deal with both legacy and Web traffic as well as real-time Web traffic, these strategies will need to include admission control as well as bandwidth and buffer allocation components.

The hardware of Web servers is practically the same as with other servers. The software is divided in most cases between Unix and NT; industry analysts expect a clear shift towards NT for price reasons in the future. Web server sizing should not only follow generic guidelines, but also detailed criteria specified by analyzing Web traffic patterns. If resource demand is higher than server capacity, multiple servers can be put together into server farms. This solution may satisfy the resource demand criteria, but requires careful attention of allocation and flow control.

While Web server performance improvements are part of the performance optimization solution, they must be accompanied by improvements in network and content management technology to have a true impact on WWW scaling and performance. Specifically, developments in the following three areas are critically important:

1. *Content distribution and replication.* By pushing content closer to the access points where users are located, backbone bandwidth requirements can be reduced and response time to the user can be improved. Content can be proactively replicated in the network under operator control or dynamically replicated by network elements. Caching servers are an example of network elements that can facilitate the dynamic replication of content. Other devices and models are likely to emerge over time.

2. *Content request distribution.* When multiple instances of content exist in a network, the network elements must cooperate to direct a content request to the best-fit server at any moment in time. This requires an increasing level of content intelligence in the network elements themselves.

3. *Content driven Web farm resource measurement.* A server or cache in a server farm ultimately services a specific content request. Local server, switching, and uplink bandwidth are precious resources that need to be carefully managed to provide appropriate service levels for Web traffic.

Content-Smart Quality of Service and Resource Management

In a typical Web site, the top 10 percent of Web server files are accessed 90 percent of the time and are accountable for 90 percent of the bytes transferred. Therefore, techniques that optimize performance for these files will have the most significant impact on total Web site performance. This requires that the network itself be aware of which content is hot and which servers can provide it. Since content can be hot one instant and cold the next, content-smart switches must learn about hot content by tracking content-access history as it processes content requests and responses.

To effectively manage Web site servers, network, and bandwidth resources, something must also be known about the content size and quality of service requirements. These content attributes can be gleaned through the processing of active flows, through proactively probing servers, or through administrative definitions. In addition, it is important to track server performance relative to specific pieces of content. All of this information can be maintained in a content database that provides an analogous function to a routing table in a router or switch. Content-smart switches make a content routing decision based on the information contained in the database, connecting a client to a best-fit server in either a local or remote server farm. This enables the emergence of a business model based on replicating content in distributed data centers, with overflow content delivery capacity and backup in case of a partial communications failure. Additionally, overflow content capacity intelligence minimizes the need to build out to handle flash crowds for highly requested content.

Content-Smart Flow Admission Control

Two factors often contribute to congestion in a server farm. One is that servers are not up to the task of handling the amount of incoming traffic. The other is that the link bandwidth from servers to the Internet is overwhelmed by the combination of inbound and outbound traffic; this is complicated by the fact that the amount of outbound traffic from servers is on average about five times that of the inbound. As a result, a TCP/HTTP connection could be successfully made only to find out that the server could not be allocated the necessary bandwidth to deliver the requested content. To make matters worse, some server implementations come to a grinding halt when presented with an excessive number of TCP/HTTP connections—sometimes requiring a hard reboot.

Load Distribution and Balancing

In order to satisfy the high performance expectations of site visitors, bandwidth in backbone and in access networks should be managed effectively. Usually, servers are consolidated into server farms that are using the infrastructure of local area networks (LANs). It is very unlikely that this LAN causes any bottlenecks. Larger enterprises may use multiple server farms deployed at various locations. In order to optimize content allocations, traffic and page references should be monitored and evaluated. At different locations in the network, hardware and software are expected to be installed that intelligently analyzes the requests and directs the traffic to the right destination. The right destination could be threefold:

1. Server farm destination with the requested content.

2. Server farm destination with the lightest load.

3. Server farm destination with the closest location to the visitor.

There cannot be any compromise on item 1, but there could be a trade-off between 2 and 3, depending on the networking traffic.

The emergence of Web computing and Web traffic over the Internet or intranets has created some unique new problems. It is estimated that over 80 percent of Internet traffic is related to Web-based HTTP traffic. Even applications, such as FTP and RealAudio, which run over TCP and UDP respectively, typically use HTTP to set up the transfer. Since HTTP is an application protocol that runs over TCP, LAN switches and routers, which run Layer 2, 3, and 4, have very limited ability to influence Web traffic behavior. This burden is left to Web servers, which take on the function of TCP/HTTP connection management and, in some cases, the responsibility to distribute HTTP requests to servers within a server farm. This creates inevitable scaling problems as Web sites grow.

The current Internet can be described using a model where local bandwidth is plentiful in the premise LAN located at the edge of the Internet. However, the uplink from LAN or remote user to the Internet is often severely bandwidth constrained by orders of magnitude. Although congestion can occur anywhere in the Internet path between a client and a server, the most frequent culprits are the wide area network (WAN) connection between the client and the Internet and the WAN connection between the Web farm and the Internet. Actions taken to ensure that this bandwidth is not over committed will help improve end-to-end performance.

Instantaneous bandwidth mismatches can occur for a network device that functions as a demarcation point between the public Internet and the Web farm. Examples are:

■ The incoming link of the traffic is a faster media type (e.g., Fast Ethernet), and the outgoing link is a slower type (e.g., T1 or T3).

- The instantaneous fan-in (i.e., the number of flows being sent at the same time to the same output port) can vary dynamically from one instant to the next.

- A number of traffic sources (e.g., outbound server traffic) may be sharing the bandwidth of a 45 Mbps T3 pipe in a bursty manner over a very high speed switching fabric (e.g., 10 Gbps). This creates a need to regulate flow admission into a slower pipe from multiple higher-speed traffic sources.

Information about the use of Web pages, their users, the frequency of access, resource utilization and traffic volumes can also be collected in the network or at the interfaces of the network. In many cases, the borders between tools and techniques in the server and networking segments are not clear. Tools are different from each other; the differentiators are data collection technologies, performance metrics used, and reports offered.

In the Internet and intranet area, effective bandwidth management is a critical success factor. The role of network planners is going to be redefined. Real-time and near–real-time bandwidth allocation definitions are needed. Network managers agree that load balancers are needed.

There is little progress in standardizing load distribution performance metrics, but the following few metrics can be successfully used

- Number of referrals to server farms

- Number of lost requests due to load situations

- Number of requests with unacceptable response time

- Number of broken connections due to network problems

Content-Smart Link Management

This technique can ensure that more flows are not admitted than can be handled through the switch or on the uplinks on average. It is still critical, however, to deal appropriately with traffic bursts and temporary congestion on these links to ensure that Web flows get the appropriate quality of service. Priority queuing provides a way to prioritize requests based on their type precedence. Fair queuing and weighted queuing methods improve over the priority queuing scheme by addressing the low priority traffic starvation problem with a scheme that separates traffic into well-identified flows so that each receives a fair or weighted fair share of transmission bandwidth.

Class-based queuing (CBQ) was developed by the Network Research Group at Lawrence Berkeley Laboratory as an improvement upon these existing bandwidth management techniques. It proposes a model in which traffic is categorized in hierarchical classes. Flows inherit their flow characteristics from their parent flow class tree and can have local characteristics of their own. Flows are identified based on the IP address and the inner attributes within the IP header and payload. CBQ provides more granular control of transmission bandwidth and distributes it to member flow classes in accordance with their allocation policies. The model itself is independent of the scheduling techniques that run underneath it, therefore implementation details will vary based on the target architecture.

Content-smart link management borrows concepts from CBQ. However, where CBQ is a model that operates on a packet-by-packet basis based on Layer 3 and 4 classification techniques, content-smart link management classifies flows at admission time based upon the content requested, its attributes, and configured policies. These policies support the enterprise and service provider service models described in an earlier section of this chapter. This facilitates the classification of flows in a two-level hierarchy that includes owners (or customers) and content. Actual scheduling of flows is managed by a hardware-based flow scheduler that supports guaranteed bandwidth flows, prioritized/weighted flows, and best effort flows. Hardware-based scheduling is critical in order to scale the Web farm.

Content-Smart Load Balancing

Simple load balancing techniques such as round-robin, weighted round-robin, and least connections are inadequate for Web traffic. For example, Web traffic load balancers must support sticky connections, which allow a particular server to be selected regardless of server load due to content locality or transaction integrity. Because of the disproportional ratio of hot content files to total content (1:10), it is highly desirable to support a content replication model that does not require that content be equally and fully mirrored amongst servers in a server farm. This means a load balancing technique must be intelligent enough to recognize if content is available on a particular server before making the selection decision.

Content-smart load balancing takes into account several factors that have a significant impact on the overall performance and cost of a Web server farm:

Server cache hit rate. By directing requests for hot content to a server that has recently serviced that content, this technique ensures that cache hit rate, reducing disk access latency for the most frequently accessed content. Since a significant percentage (15–40%) of the files are accessed only once and 90 percent of the files are accessed only once or not accessed at all, it is important to keep those infrequently accessed files from thrashing a server cache. That is, an infrequently accessed file should be invalidated in server cache promptly to increase the chances that a more frequently accessed file can remain in cache.

Burst distribution. Short-lived, bursty flows can best be handled by distributing them among eligible servers so long as the servers have been performing below a defined threshold for a period of time.

Web flow duration. Most Web flows are short lived. However, a relatively small number of infrequent, long-lived flows have a far significant impact on overall bandwidth and server resource consumption. For that reason, long-lived flows should be separated from short-lived flows from a load balancing perspective and short-lived flows of similar QoS requirements should be aggregated to increase TCP flow intensity and reduce per-flow resource allocation overheads.

Content-biased server performance measurement. Current server loading can best be measured by examining the request/response time interval of a server as it handles requests. This measurement is most accurate when the connection between the switch and the server is direct. In addition, server performance is not uniform across all content. For example, computer-intensive applications may perform better on one server than another. Other servers may perform better for other types of content. Server performance information needs to be qualified by content.

In the Internet and intranet area, effective bandwidth management is a critical success factor. The role of network planners is going to be redefined. Real-time and near–real-time bandwidth allocation definitions are needed. Network managers agree that load balancers are needed. The questions are whether

- Hardware- or software-based load balancers are better
- Embedded or stand-alone solutions should be preferred
- Use of the combination of both would be optimal

In the first case, considering high-traffic volumes, hardware solutions should be preferred. Software solutions in critical load situations may slow down processes and risk performance. At this time, there are no accurate guidelines for tolerable workload, but a range up to 5 percent seems to be reasonable.

Switches, routers, and firewalls are almost everywhere in Internet access networks and in intranets. To embed traffic control and sharing functions would save extra components, but also would—as stated earlier—generate additional load and may impair the principal functions. The embedded solution may also include the use of RMON capabilities for real-time load profiling. The stand-alone solution is sensitive against single point of failure, but would offer an overhead-free traffic and load management. The following attributes may play an important role when evaluating alternatives (ROBE98).

Use of Load Balancing Switches

BENEFITS

- Load balancing is performed in a device that is needed anyway in the network.
- Centralized management.
- Good opportunity to control and guarantee quality of service.

DISADVANTAGES

- Performance may be impacted by management functions.
- Single point of failure for both switch and management functions.

Use of Load Balancing Firewalls

BENEFITS

- Load balancing is performed in a device that is needed anyway in most networks.
- Centralized management.
- Includes special functions and services, such as traffic management and application-based load balancing.

DISADVANTAGES

- Switches are still needed.
- Single point of failure for both firewall and management functions.
- Performance depends on hardware and operating system configuration.

Use of Load Balancing Traffic Shapers

BENEFITS

- Load balancing is performed by a device most likely present in the networks anyway.
- Centralized management.
- Offers traffic shaping and balancing for Internet or intranet access in addition to server access.

DISADVANTAGES

- In most cases, switches and firewalls are needed in addition to these devices.
- Single point of failure for both traffic shaping and load balancing.
- Little experiences yet with performance and scalability.

Issues of Data Collection

Architecture of a product answers the question whether it can support a distributed architecture. Distribution may mean that collecting, processing, reporting, and distributing data can be supported in various processors and at different locations. Figure 6.29 shows these functions with a distributed solution.

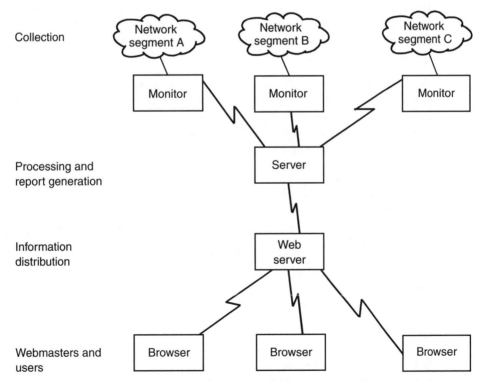

Figure 6.29 Generic product architecture for processing traffic measurements data.

The monitors are passively measuring the traffic in the network segments. They are actually microcomputers with ever increasing intelligence. Their operating systems are either proprietary or based on Unix or more likely on NT. Usually, they are programmed to interpret many protocols. TCP/IP, UDP/IP, and HTTP are high on the priority list of vendors.

The data-capturing technique is essential with traffic measurement tools. The measurement probes are attached to the digital interface of the communication channels. They can reside directly on the network (stand-alone probes) or colocated with networking equipment. In this case, the probe is used as a plug-in. Even software probes can be used and implemented into networking components or into end-user devices. The hardware or software probes usually include event scheduling. It means determining polling cycles and time periods when downloading measurement data is intended. Transmission should be scheduled for low-traffic periods. Probes are expected to deal with large data volumes. These volumes depend—to a large degree—on visitor's traffic in networking segments. Probes have limited storage capabilities; implementation examples show capabilities up to 24 hours. When this limit is exceeded, measurement data are overwritten by new data. Usually, measurement data are downloaded for further processing. It is important to know how downloads are organized and how rapidly they can be executed. If wide area networks (WANs) are involved, they may show bandwidth limitations. The bandwidth is usually shared with other applications with the result of potential traffic congestion. Bandwidth-on-demand solutions are rare with measurement probes. When transmission is arranged for low-traffic periods, the actuality of measurement results may suffer. In such cases, local storage requirements increase, and processing, report generation, and information distribution are delayed by several hours or even by days.

Two solutions may help. The first is using intelligent filtering during and shortly after data collection. Redundant data are removed from captured packets during collection. Data volumes decrease, local storage requirements decrease as well, but processing requirements of the probes increase. The second solution may use data compression or data compaction with the same results and impacts as with the first solution.

Overhead is a very critical issue with large data volumes. Data capturing is expected not to introduce any overhead in case of hardware-based probes. Overhead is minimal with software-based probes. It is assumed that measurement data are stored away immediately after collection. If local processing is taking place, overhead must be critically quantified. If resource demand is high, probes must be upgraded properly. Data transmission overhead can be heavy, when everything is transmitted to the site where processing takes place. Dedicated bandwidth would be too expensive for measurement and management purposes only. If bandwidth is shared with other applications, priorities must be set higher for business applications than for transmitting measurement data.

It is absolutely necessary that all data are captured that are necessary to conduct a detailed Web-site analysis of visitors or groups of visitors.

- Who is the visitor?

- What is the purpose of the visit?

- Where is the visitor coming from?

- When has the visit taken place?

- What key words have brought the visitor to the site?

- What search machines helped to access the site?

- How long was the visit?

Data losses cannot be completely avoided. Probes, monitors, log files, networking devices, user workstations, or transmission equipment may fail; in such cases, there will be gaps in the sequence of events. Backup capabilities may be investigated, but information technology (IT) budgets won't usually allow to spend too much for backing up large volumes of log file data. In the worst case, certain time windows are missing in reporting and in statistics. Those gaps may be filled with extrapolated data.

Due to considerable data volumes in particular with Web log file analyzers, databases should be under consideration to maintain raw and/or processed data. Database managers would then offer a number of built-in features to maintain data. Clustering visitors may be deployed from various perspectives, such as geography, common applications, common interests on home pages, date and time of visits. Automatic log cycling can also be supported here by the database managers. Open database connectivity (ODBC) support helps to exchange data between different databases and to correlate data from various databases. Besides measurement data, other data sources can also be maintained in the same data warehouse. Besides routine log files analysis with concrete targeted reports, special analysis may also occasionally be conducted. This special analysis, called data mining, can discover traffic patterns and user/visitor behavior. Both are important in sizing systems and networking resources.

One of the most important questions is how measurement data analysis performs when data volumes increase. Volume increase can be caused by offering more pages on more Web servers, more visitors, longer visits, and extensive use of page links. In any case, collection and processing capabilities must be estimated and quantified prior to deciding on procedures and products.

In order to reduce processing and transmission load of measurement data, redundant data should be filtered out as near as possible to the data capturing locations. Filters can help to avoid storing redundant data. Filters can also be very useful in the report generation process. Again, unnecessary data must not be processed for reports. Powerful filters help streamline reporting.

Not everything can be automated with analyzing measurement data. The user interface is still one of the most important selection criteria for products. Graphical user interfaces are likely, but simple products are still working with textual interfaces. When measurement data are integrated with management platforms, this request is automatically met by management platforms.

Reporting is the tool to distribute the results of analysis. Predefined reports and report elements as well as templates help to speed up the report design and generation process. Periodic reports can be automatically generated and distributed for both single Web servers and Web server farms. In the case of many Web servers, report generation must be carefully synchronized and scheduled. Flexible formatting helps customize reports to special user needs.

Output alternatives of reports are many. The most frequently used solutions include Word, Excel, HTML, and ASCII. Also, the distribution of reports offers multiple choices. Reports can be

- Stored on Web servers to be accessed by authorized users who are equipped with universal browsers
- Uploaded into special servers or even pushed to selected users
- Distributed as attachments to e-mail messages
- Generated at remote sites; this alternative may save bandwidth when pre-processed data instead of completely formatted reports are sent to certain remote locations

Documentation may have various forms. For immediate answers, an integrated online manual would be very helpful. Paper-based manuals are still useful for detailed answers and analysis. This role, however, will be taken over by Web-based documentation systems. In critical cases, a hot line can help with operational problems.

Measurement data analysis is actually another management application. If management platforms are used, this application can be integrated into the management platform. There are many ways to integrate; most likely a command-line interface (CLI) will be deployed.

Load balancers are only successful when policy profiles can be implemented and used. Policy profiles are most likely based on supporting various transmission priorities. Priorities may be set by applications, by users, or by a combination of both. The technology for solution may differ from case-to-case and product-to-product, but most frequently the TCP flow is intercepted.

Load balancers are expected to support a number of services, such as quality control, resource management, flow control, link management, and actual load balancing. Advanced products support all these services, dependent of page content. It requires more work to gather the necessary information about content, but it offers better services for high-priority content.

Functions in a narrower sense include traffic shaping, load balancing, monitoring, and baselining. Baselining means to find the optimal operational conditions for a certain environment. It may be expressed by a few parameters, such as resource utilization, availability, and response time. Load balancers should monitor these few metrics and act on them. Traffic shaping and load balancing help to get back to normal conditions by splitting traffic, redirecting traffic to replicated servers, delaying payload transport, and so on.

One of the most important questions is how load balancing performs when data volumes increase. Volume increase can be caused by offering more pages on more Web servers, more visitors, longer visits, extensive use of page links. In any case, collection and processing capabilities must be estimated prior to deciding for procedures and products.

Load balancing products can be managed by SNMP or WBEM agents. They are handled by managers like any other kind of managed objects.

Managing load balancers out of a management platform offers integration at the management applications level. Baselining and monitoring may even be supported by other applications. When using management intranets, universal browsers may be used to view, extract, process, and distribute management information. The only prerequisite is that WBEM agents have been implemented and that CIM is supported for information exchange.

IP Traffic Optimization

In order to help IT managers track IP performance and optimize bandwidth usage across WANs, several new vendors offer hardware- and software-based load balancing products. Load balancers typically reside at the edges of corporate networks and decide upon traffic priorities. They apply a policy that defines different traffic types and determine what happens to each. A very simple policy may call for priorities for a specific sender. Other criteria may be TCP port numbers, URLs, and also DNS. Traffic shaping may be supported by queuing or via TCP rate control. There are products available for both categories.

Optimization is accomplished by controlling enterprise traffic flows at the boundary between the LANs and the WAN. Because these products give priority to traffic according to application type or even individual users, they will let IT managers take the first steps toward policy-based QoS in their networks. These products are a logical evolution from the passive probes that gave users a certain level of visibility for fault operations monitoring but no actual control over traffic. These products go further and can manipulate traffic. IT managers expect that this new class of traffic-shaping tools will ease the contention for bandwidth without forcing them to purchase more and larger physical transmission lines.

Bandwidth management is rapidly becoming a must for Internet service providers as well as corporations running their own global intranets. The reasons for bandwidth management are the following

- Trend to Internet/intranet-based business
- Need for guaranteed bandwidth
- SLAs
- Need for granularity

Corporate networks are rapidly evolving from a classic client/server paradigm towards an intranet-based model, based on information-sharing and Web navigation. The result is the demand for significantly more bandwidth. Adding more channels and more bandwidth to each channel will not guarantee availability and performance where it is needed most. An intranet-based model implies the following factors:

- *Changing patterns of network use and unpredictable demands for bandwidth.* Global users access the network 24 hours a day, 7 days a week. As information appears and disappears on Web sites, access patterns change, and saturation moves around the network.

- *Demand for increased amounts of bandwidth.* People may stay on the link for extended periods of time and download large amounts of data.

- *Demand for guaranteed QoS in terms of bandwidth and minimum delay.* Emerging Internet applications are both bandwidth intensive and time sensitive, often requiring support for voice, video, and multimedia applications across the network infrastructure.

- *Lack of control by IT staff.* Workgroups and departments generally create their Web sites without IT approvals, generating increased traffic without necessarily having the infrastructure to handle it. This often results in excessive traffic at the fringes of the network where Web sites are situated, generating traffic precisely where there is least provision.

- *A change in user attitude.* Users expect instant access to information without delays or restrictions, especially if that information is critical to their work.

Current networking technology has two major limitations:

1. The bandwidth available on a link at any given moment cannot be predicted in terms of quantity or quality. Bandwidth management is needed to allow applications that require a specific quality of service in terms of bandwidth and delay (such as desktop video conferencing) to reserve the bandwidth quality of service they need.

2. It is difficult to control which applications or users get a share of the available bandwidth. In some circumstances, an application or a user can take control of all the available bandwidth, preventing other applications or users from using the network. To solve this problem, the user can either add extra capacity at additional costs, resulting in an over-provisioned network that still does not guarantee equal access, or the user can introduce bandwidth allocation.

Virtual private networks (VPNs) are a popular value-added Internet service that corporations are increasingly moving toward. Enterprise customers seeking a VPN provider are more likely to sign with an ISP who can offer a contractual SLA—one that guarantees quality of service.

Although service level agreements cannot guarantee end-to-end service across the public Internet, they can be implemented for transport over a single-vendor network, or for Internet server hosting. In these areas, an SLA is an important differentiator for an ISP.

Generally, the customer subscribes to a particular class of service, and signs an SLA accordingly. Packet throughput is monitored as part of the agreement. ISPs who want to get a piece of this additional business, clearly need to implement bandwidth management in order to meet SLAs that guarantee quality of service toward customers. Only efficient bandwidth management can enable them to tune network behavior so that customers receive the quality of service they are charged for.

The new network service paradigm is a service-driven network. This is a responsive, reliable, modular infrastructure, based on the latest generation of management technology and built on dynamic, flexible management services. To respond to today's business needs, ISPs and large enterprises must deploy the service-driven network. It delivers innovative services, such as unified roaming, push browsers, multicast, online shopping, and so on, to customers faster and at a lower cost than ever before.

Bandwidth allocation based simply on filtering by protocol is not sufficient to meet bandwidth management needs. One of the key issues in this area is the extensive and increasing use of HTML/HTTP systems for online transaction processing (OLTP). Within the next few years, the volume of HTTP-based OLTP traffic is expected to exceed the volume of traditional OLTP traffic. A fine level of granularity is needed for bandwidth management to take into account more than just the protocol when assessing the relative importance of network traffic. Bandwidth management must base allocation not only on protocol type, but also on the application and users involved.

Along with this is the concept of increasing the value of the data being collected and mediated. Usually, it means to extend network-centric statistics by application-centric statistics. SLA monitoring tools offer two alternatives: real-time or historical. Real-time monitoring of SLAs is very important for proactive fault management by recognizing service problems before they escalate. They may give service providers an opportunity to address a problem before the terms of the agreement are violated. Historical trend analysis lets service providers verify service levels over time, as well as identify trends that may lead to future violations of service levels.

Web application requirements have gone from zero to mission-critical within a very short period of time. The available tools have not kept up with this speed. In a business environment where connections failed means the same thing as closed for business, IS/IT professionals are left to struggle with the challenges of building a highly available, high-performance intranet infrastructure.

There are many problems that interact with each other:

- The majority of Web sites, both Internet and intranet, use single Unix or NT servers. Like mainframe solutions of the past, these centralized servers have become single points of failure. Even minor system upgrades become major service problems for demanding users.

- As the demand of interactivity grows, the cost of WAN bandwidth becomes a major factor. System configurations that force all user access out across the WAN for each request stretch out retrieval times, and raise users' frustration levels.

- The increasing complexity of Web applications add even more overhead. Electronic commerce and multitier content architectures that build pages on the fly out of applications and databases make high reliability an even more important—and more costly—goal.

The severe problem in addition to all of these is that the Web technology base is narrow. In other words, solutions that can be applied to these problems are expensive and not very effective. Adding WAN bandwidth and a bigger server is just the first step in a never ending circle. Adding mirrored, distributed servers increases server costs significantly as well as the complexities and costs of content distribution. Hiring more Webmasters and Web administrators to reboot downed Web applications and servers is not the ultimate solution. And in a world of increasingly dynamic content and transactions, how effective will server caches and load balancing tools really be?

When evaluating products, many components must be factored in. These factors are

- Customization needs
- Maintenance requirements
- Deployment of code
- Overhead of transmitting measurement data
- Load increase due to synthetic workload
- Reporting capabilities
- Capabilities to solve complex performance problems
- Capabilities to conduct root-cause analysis
- Combination with modeling tools
- Price of the tools

End-to-end service-level monitoring is getting extremely popular with Web-based applications. Monitoring is targeting availability and response time measurements. Element-centric management platforms look down and manage elements. Response time monitoring tools look through the infrastructure from one end to the other.

Application-related measurements can also be done with RMON probes. The way to do this, is to track an application on its entire path across the enterprise. To support that approach, the remote monitoring vendor is able to collect and report traffic statistics, which IT managers use to measure how quickly an application makes its round-trip run.

Typical look-through products work on the principle of Java applets in combination with C++ scripts. The code is distributed to various selected endpoints in the network. These agents generate synthetic transactions against targeted applications, such as databases or intranet Web pages. Response time for these scripted transactions—including the response times over each individual hop along the route—are logged on a management server, which assembles and organizes the collected data. The data are then available to users through a client-side Java interface.

The new type of network instrumentation closely mimics the end users' actual experience since it measures the end-to-end responsiveness of an application from one or more outlying LAN nodes to the application server and back again. By doing so, it delivers a metric that accurately reflects application and service performance levels on the network. Trying to gauge the end-to-end performance level of an application over the network by monitoring each distinct element along the service delivery path has proven unsuccessful. Element-specific monitoring is still essential for troubleshooting and maintenance, but network managers have to start looking at some new kinds of instrumentation if they want to view the environment from the end-user's point of view.

6.6 Summary

Network operational management is responsible for the ongoing operations of the networking infrastructure. These processes are transparent to customers until SLAs are met. Service providers spend a lot of money maintaining a high quality of service. The key is the right tool set to monitor components, collect data, correlate multiple information sources for root-cause analysis, and finally to rectify problems at various levels of the TMN architecture. Information exchange with customers is expected on the SML only. Processes and functions serving the network and element management layers remain hidden to customers.

Service assurance is also responsible to proactively recognize trends that may cause outages or performance bottlenecks. Implementing capacity extensions or changing obsolete components may avoid service quality degradation. Data warehousing helps maintain data about service and traffic metrics, capacity utilization, and trouble tickets. All are important for service reconfigurations.

Service providers must deal with large data volumes because both legacy and emerging IP networks must be properly monitored. Tool sets are completely different at this time. Converging the circuit and packet switching management domains may take many years. State-of-the-art tools, such as expert systems, neural networks, knowledge conservation instruments, case-based reasoning along with data mining techniques help automate network operations. As a result, subject matter experts are off-loaded from routine work and can concentrate on more challenging operational tasks, such as root-cause analysis, Web load balancing and content caching, and content-based resource allocation in IP-based services.

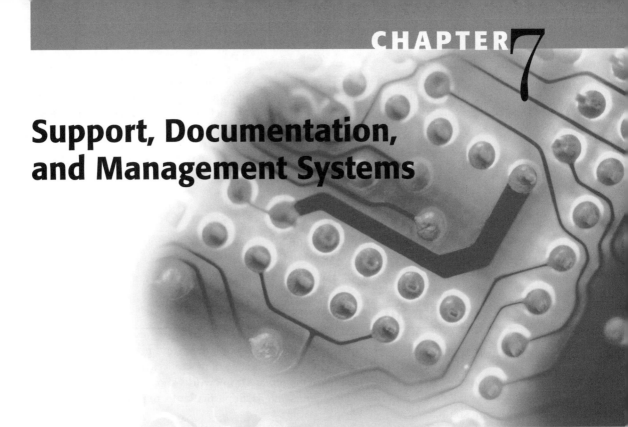

Support, Documentation, and Management Systems

7.1 Introduction

Principal processes of customer care, billing, order processing, provisioning, and operational management cannot be implemented and supported without appropriate tools. This chapter is devoted to support, documentation, and management tools. It starts with management frameworks that are considered the foundation for integrated management solutions. Besides basic structures, management services and applications are also introduced. In order to help service providers, a few best of suite framework products are analyzed.

Customer care and billing tools start with design considerations of a new billing system, followed by the evaluation of a few products addressing traditional and new billing needs. Flow-through is the typical feature of order processing and provisioning support systems. Two best-of-breed solutions are shown in greater detail. Integrated management is the ultimate goal of many service providers. In addition to frameworks, four practical approaches are discussed that are provided by device manufacturers and independent software vendors.

Service level agreements (SLAs) are critical for the relationship between service providers and their customers. In order to support SLAs with metrics, a couple of state-of-the-art tools are introduced that may be deployed by both contracting parties.

Special attention is on the tools supporting eCommerce by mediating usage data for B2B and B2C applications. Mediated data may then be used for utilization trending and billing.

And finally, interoperability issues are addressed with the assumption that multiple support, documentation, and management applications should work with each other. Besides products, concepts like management intranets and spatial integration are also addressed.

Suppliers of solutions are

- Framework suppliers (OSI, Telcordia, Micromuse)
- Consulting companies (Andersen, AMS)
- Computer manufacturers (IBM, Compaq, HP, Sun)
- Equipment manufacturers (Lucent, Ericsson, Siemens, Nortel)
- Outsourcers (EDS, INS)

7.2 Management Frameworks

Management frameworks consist of an application's platform and management applications. The application platform consists of management services and the computing hardware and operating system. Management frameworks show unique features that differentiate them from management systems, in particular from proprietary management solutions.

Actually, there is no scientific definition of a management framework. In order to decide whether certain products qualify as a framework, an elaborated list of attributes is going to be addressed first. When products are able to support the basic framework attributes, they are qualified as *frameworks.* The advanced attributes may serve then as differentiators between frameworks. Figure 7.1 shows the basic architecture of management frameworks. It consists of a run-time environment, development tools, and APIs. The run-time environment is subdivided into management applications, management services, and the basic infrastructure (GHET97). Management services can further be subdivided into basic and advanced services differentiating management frameworks from each other. Between the run-time environment, development tools, and the implementation, there are application program interfaces (APIs) for interconnecting pieces with each other.

7.2.1 Basic Infrastructure

Basic infrastructure concentrates on the hardware and software features of the management frameworks. The most important attributes are listed in the following sections.

Hardware and Software Platforms

Hardware platform is characterized by a wide variety of hardware including Intel 386/486, Pentium, HP 9000, RS/6000, Sun Sparc, Tandem, Alpha, Systes/88, and eventually others. Backup support should be addressed here as well. In terms of the

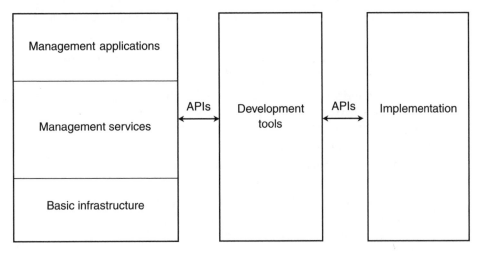

Figure 7.1 Architecture of management frameworks.

software, Unix and Windows NT dominate. In the future, Java, Jini, and Linux should be considered with some market penetration.

Directory Services

Management frameworks deal with a great variety of entities and a great number of resources. The service of allocating human-readable names to each managed resource (object) is the goal of *directory services*. Directory services are based on commonly agreed standards that model the naming paradigm, provide naming notations, allocate identifiable names to managed resources, translate names into physical addresses of resources, and ultimately provide location transparency of the resource in the system. All these considerations are valid for network and systems management frameworks. Framework management services and management applications use naming information from the directory services in order to perform their functions in relationship with managed resources and other management frameworks. The principal directory service requirements are (GHET97)

- Global information directory service and universal access to directory information

- Separation between the names of managed objects and the underlying physical networks

- Translation capabilities between various directory systems

- Translation between logical addresses and network addresses or routing addresses

- Storage of directory information and access to directory information, including metadata

- APIs in order to easily incorporate directory services into applications

Considering directory service capabilities, the following components are used as examples (GHET97):

Directory services users. People, management applications, electronic messaging, routers/servers, other management framework services.

Resources requiring naming. People, organizations, computers, processes, files, mailboxes, network devices, printers, object class abstractions, object instances, management applications, management services, management agents.

Directory system types. Centralized, distributed, standard, proprietary; interpersonal communications directory (human), intersystem communications directory (computers and software systems).

Directory service generic operations. Query (read, list, search, compare), modification (add/remove entry, modify entry, modify naming space, quit), binding/unbinding (security authentication).

Directory enabled networking (Chapter 2) and the use of LDAP (Chapter 3) show the first concrete implementation examples for directory services.

Time Services

In distributed systems and network environments, where processes and applications are running on different machines, it might happen that time differences occur between systems. The time difference becomes critical when correct time stamps determine sequencing of events, job scheduling, measurements timing, and reporting intervals. A consistent use of time services is imperative when dealing with global networks that span multiple time zones.

In most cases, Internet Network Time Protocol (NTP) is used. Its primary reference time source is the absolute Universal Time Clock (UTC) or sources directly derived from UTC.

Software Distribution

In complex environments, management systems are usually distributed. They consist of servers, clients, and the communication paths between them. In order to keep them in sync, software versions or releases running on servers and clients must be compatible to each other. Manual software distribution is too slow and not reliable enough. Electronic software distribution offers two popular alternatives: push and pull. Distributing software by push offers easier scheduling, better automation, and does not require the physical presence of administrators. But receiver servers and clients should be prepared for the distribution. Distributing by pull offers better control by administrators, allowing changes during distribution at a price of low automation. Scheduling is flexible and depends solely on human decisions. At this time, pull is privileged in Web environments.

Security Services

Open distributed network environments consist of an increasing number of interconnected computing resources, networks, and users. The networks are no longer closed networks but mixtures of private and public networks. The networks include heterogeneous components and this has a bearing on security services as well. Security of a network depends on the security of adjacent networks or other trusted partners. Frequent changes, like adding new resources and new users, bring additional concerns regarding security. *Security* can be seen as the security management functional feature built into certain management applications, namely security management applications. Since management frameworks control resources, security becomes an issue, as other framework services have to operate securely in order to make the whole system secure. Security is often embedded in framework services such as communications, database management, and object manipulation services, which perform management operations.

7.2.2 Management Services

Management services address more specific items towards management applications. The most important features are listed in the following.

Communication Services

Network architectures. The targeted networks to be managed are very different. Many products are expected to manage legacy networks and more open networks at the same time. The most widely used protocols supporting network architectures include DECnet, IPX/SPX, OSI, SNA, DSA, APPN, TCP/IP, Guardian, and eventually others. Capabilities of managing SNA and TCP/IP are the highest priority.

Network management protocols. The products are expected to support at least SNMP. It is an additional advantage when they can do more. SNMP support may include the capabilities of working with proxy agents with the capability of converting non-SNMP into SNMP. Protocols to be supported include CMIP, CMOT, LNMP, NMVT, RMON, SNMPv1, SNMPv2, and eventually DMI to manage desktops.

The management platform provides SNMP support in several ways. First and foremost is the ability to poll SNMP devices and receive SNMP traps, as described previously. However, in order to configure polls on MIB variables of various devices, one must first know what those variables are. Management platforms provide MIB browsers for this purpose. An MIB browser queries user-selected SNMP network devices and displays their MIB values. In addition, most platforms can display line or bar graphs of those MIB values, provided they are in numeric form (counters, etc.).

MIB browsers are crude tools at best, displaying raw and often cryptic, low-level device information. For this reason, platforms also provide MIB application builders that allow users to quickly create applications for displaying information on MIB objects in a more meaningful way. MIB applications may include graphing real-time information on selected network nodes. However, even MIB applications builders are limited in supporting high-level analysis that is more open, provided by third-party applications.

MIB compilers allow users to bring in third-party, device-specific MIBs (also called private or extended MIBs) and register them with the management platform. While most platforms ship with a number of third-party MIBs, they do not include all possible MIBs from all vendors. An MIB compiler is necessary for adding support for third-parties whose MIBs are not shipped as part of the standard platform.

. Some MIB compilers are more robust than others. Some MIB compilers will fail or abort processing if there is an error in the MIB being compiled. Unfortunately, errors in third-party MIBs are not rare. Therefore, it is desirable to have an MIB compiler that can flag errors and recover, rather than stop dead.

Also, HTTP agents should be supported by the framework. A number of manufacturers embed Web agent capabilities into their devices in order to make maintenance and configuration easier. At the same time, these agents can play the role of data collectors for device status. Certain manufacturers work with a double stack, including SNMP and HTTP.

Core Management Services

The management framework is expected to offer core services and interfaces to other applications. The basic management applications to be provided are discovery/mapping, alarm management, and platform protection.

Discovery and Mapping

Device discovery/network mapping discovery refers to the network management system's ability to automatically learn the identity and type of devices currently active on the network. At minimum, a management platform should be capable of discovery active IP devices by retrieving data from a router's IP tables and Address Resolution Protocol (ARP) tables.

However, even this capability does not guarantee that all IP devices on a given network will be detected. For example, relying solely on routing tables is inadequate in purely bridged networks where there are no routers. Thus, a more comprehensive discovery facility should also include other mechanisms such as broadcast messages (PING and others) that can reach out to any IP device and retrieve its address and other identifying information.

On the other hand, discovery mechanisms that rely completely on broadcasting (e.g., PING) will incur a tremendous amount of overhead in finding devices out on the network. Ideally, a management platform should support a combination of ARP data retrieval and broadcasting.

Furthermore, a complete network discovery facility should be capable of detecting legacy system nodes, such as DECnet and SNA. Currently, most platforms rely on third-party applications or traffic monitoring applications to supply discovery data on non-TCP/IP devices.

Another desirable feature is the ability to run automatic or scheduled dynamic discovery processes after the initial discovery, to discern any changes made to the network after the initial discovery took place. In large networks especially, overhead and consumed bandwidth for running a dynamic discovery process continually in background mode may be too great; therefore, the ability to schedule discovery at off-peak hours is important.

It is also important for the user to have the ability to set limits on the initial network discovery. Many corporate networks are now linked to the Internet, and without predefined limits, a discovery application may cross corporate boundaries and begin discovering everything on the global Internet. Some management platforms allow users to run discovery on a segment-by-segment basis. This can help the discovery process from getting out of hand too fast.

Many management frameworks are capable of automatically producing a topological map from the data collected during device discovery. However, these automatically generated maps rarely result in a graphical representation that is useful for humans. Particularly, when there are hundreds of devices, the resulting map can look very cluttered—enough to be of little use.

Even when the discovery process operates on a limited or segment-by-segment basis, there is eventually going to come a time when the operator must edit the automatically generated network map to create a visual picture that is easier for human beings to relate to. Therefore, the ability to group objects on the map and move them around in groups or perform other types of collective actions, can be a real time-saving feature.

Alarm Capabilities

Management frameworks act as a clearinghouse for critical status messages obtained from various devices and applications across the network. Messages arrive in the form of SNMP traps, alerts, or event reports when polling results indicate that thresholds have been exceeded.

The management framework supports setting thresholds on any SNMP MIB variable. Typically, management platforms poll for device status by sending SNMP requests to devices with SNMP agents, or Internet Control Message Protocol (ICMP) echo requests (pings) to any TCP/IP device.

The process of setting thresholds may be supported by third-party applications or by the management platform. Some frameworks allow operators to configure polls on classes of devices; most require operators to configure a poll for each device individually.

Most frameworks support some degree of alarm filtering. Rudimentary filtering allows operators to assign classifications to individual alarms triggered when thresholds are exceeded, such as informational, warning, or critical. Once classifications are assigned, the user can specify that only critical alarms are displayed on the screen while all other alarms are logged, for example.

More sophisticated alarm facilities support conditional alarms. An example of a conditional threshold may be "errors on incoming packets from device B > 800 for more than 5 times in 25 minutes." Conditional alarms can account for periodic spikes in traffic or daily busy periods.

Finally, the framework should support the ability to automatically trigger scripts when specific alarms are received.

User Interface Services

Graphical User Interface's (GUI's) basic job is to provide a color-coded display of management information, multiple windows into different core or management applications, and an iconic or menu-driven user interface. By providing a standardized interface between the user and the underlying tools, the GUI simplifies what a user needs to learn and provides a standard tool for application developers.

Most management operations are available from a menu bar; others are from context menus. Point-and-click operations are standard features, as is context-sensitive help. Most frameworks allow some degree of customization of maps and icons.

While most framework GUIs are the same, there can be a few subtle differences. Some GUIs have larger icons than others. While this makes it easier to read information on the icon and distinguish status changes more quickly, a screen can quickly become cluttered with just a few large icons. Icon size is strictly a matter of user preference. The most widely used GUIs are Motif, OpenLook, OS/2 Presentation Manager, and Windows.

Web access to the framework from universal browsers is absolutely necessary. It gives the opportunity of remotely operating the framework from any operator location. It may decrease operational expenses by replacing some of the expensive workstations by universal browsers. The prerequisite is that the framework is able to present all data in HTML or XML formats.

Database Services

The database is the focal point for key data created and used by the management applications. They include MIB data, inventories, trouble tickets, configuration files, and performance data.

Most frameworks maintain event logs in flat-file ASCII format for performance reasons. However, this format limits the network manager's ability to search for information and manipulate the data. Therefore, links to relational database management systems (RDBMSs) are now important aspects of the framework architecture.

An RDBMS is essential for manipulating raw data and turning it into useful information. Users can obtain information from an RDBMS by writing requests, or queries, in Structured Query Language (SQL), a universally standard language for relational database communication.

While most management frameworks also supply report writer facilities, these tools are generally not the most sophisticated ones. However, most higher quality third-party reporting applications can extract data from an RDBMS using SQL.

Conversion capabilities into HTML/XML formats are gaining importance. Most likely, a Common Gateway Interface (CGI) of the framework will convert HTML/XML into SQL and vice versa.

Object Manipulation Services

Object-oriented and object-based technologies are helpful in relation to user inter-faces, protocols, and databases. The use of object request brokers (ORB), CORBA, DCOM, COM+, or other middleware provides a glue needed to accomplish interop-erability between heterogeneous systems. These services provide support for infor-mation exchange between objects as abstractions of physical and logical resources ranging from network devices, computing systems resources, to applications and management services. It includes operations on MIBs, object support services provid-ing location transparency for objects exchanging requests and responses, persistent storage for MIBs, and support for object-oriented applications development.

Network Modeling Services

Network modeling is an artificial intelligence capability that can assist in automated fault isolation and diagnosis as well as performance and configuration management. Modeling allows a management system to infer status of one object from the status of other objects.

Network modeling is facilitated by object-oriented programming techniques and lan-guages such as C++. The goal of modeling is to simplify the representation of com-plex networks, creating a layer of abstraction that shields management applications from underlying details.

The building block of this technology is the *model* that describes a network element, such as a router. A model consists of data (attributes) describing the element as well as their relationships with other elements. Abstract elements such as organizations and protocols can also be modeled, as can nonintelligent devices such as cables. A model may use information from other models to determine its own state; modeling can reduce the complexity of management data and highlight the most important information. In this way, fault isolation and diagnosis can be automated. In addition, models can be used to depict traffic patterns, trends, topologies, or distributions to assist in performance and configuration management.

7.2.3 Management Applications

APIs and developer's toolkits framework vendors encourage third-party applications by providing published application programming interfaces (APIs), toolkits that include libraries of software routines, and documentation to assist applications developers. Another aspect to this effort is the partners programs—the marketing angle of encouraging third-party applications development.

An API shields applications developers from the details of the management platform's underlying data implementation and functional architecture. Management framework vendors generally include in their developer's kits several coded examples of how APIs can be used as well as the APIs themselves.

In most cases, when an application takes advantage of platform APIs, it must be recompiled with the platform code—resulting in a tightly integrated end product. Many independent software vendors (ISVs) and other third-party developers lack resources necessary to pursue this level of integration. Or perhaps a more accurate way of stating this is that ISVs aren't convinced that putting out the extra effort to fully integrate their applications with all leading management platforms will result in a proportionally larger revenue stream. ISVs and other third-party developers face a choice: tightly integrate their products with one management platform vendor, or loosely integrate them with all leading platform providers. Most third parties have chosen the latter route, as they are unwilling to turn off prospective customers who may have chosen a different platform vendor as their strategic management provider.

As a result, at least 80 percent of the third-party applications available today are only loosely integrated with the underlying management platform—at the menu bar—and completely ignore APIs and other environment libraries. This is expected to change as the market matures and as platform vendors begin to offer high-level APIs that make porting applications from one management platform to another into an almost trivial exercise.

Integration may also be supported by XML and CIM, using the concept of management intranets. In this case, the independence of management applications remains, but they can access each other's data and transfer them if necessary using Web protocols.

In summary, published APIs and libraries make it possible for independent software vendors (ISVs) and other third parties to write applications that take advantage of other basic services provided by the management platform. To date, few third parties have taken full advantage of platform APIs, although this is expected to change over the next few years. Frameworks are powerless without management applications. They are provided by equipment vendors or by ISVs and serve various purposes.

Device-Dependent Applications

Equipment vendors develop and deploy management applications in order to promote sales of their equipment. Today, it is not possible to sell networking gear without element management systems—in other words, without management applications. These applications are offered and sold at reasonable prices. Equipment vendors don't make much revenue with these element management systems because they must support multiple frameworks. Web-based management will bring relief by offering a unified interface to management applications. This interface is to be supported by all framework vendors.

Device-Independent Applications

They are designed, developed, and deployed to work in different environments. Usually, they address the following management areas

- Trouble ticketing
- Performance analysis and reporting
- Security management
- Modeling and capacity planning
- Workforce management
- Data warehousing

Also, these management applications can be integrated into frameworks using Web-based technology. The big benefit is that management applications can be loosely coupled with the framework and with each other.

7.2.4 Management Operations Support Services

Any management framework consists of framework services and management applications. The services are implemented as a set of related processes, databases, and file sets. The basic thrust of management implies collection and processing of management-related information. The coordination of all the framework processes, including those that are part of the development environment, is done through additional framework components commonly called management operations support services. These services are also responsible for application integration with framework services, and for multiple national language systems support.

Management frameworks are basically a set of interconnected software programs that run on one or more computing platforms. Management operations support services provide supervision, coordination, maintenance, and management of processes, applications, and databases that are part of the management framework. The requirements of management operations support services are (GHET97)

- Facilitating interactions between framework services
- Allowing overall coordination and supervision of background processes
- Supporting integration between management services
- Allowing configuration and customization of framework services and associated processes
- Supporting registration of management applications that run on management platforms
- Providing easy integration of management applications with framework services
- Supporting multiple national language systems

- Facilitating incorporation of management information models into frameworks
- Supporting installation of framework services and management applications
- Supporting MIB loading, backup, and clean-up facilities
- Supporting distribution of management frameworks services and associated databases
- Supporting Internet technologies

This list of requirements indicates that management operations support services play a critical role in monitoring, administration, and management of the management framework itself.

The structure of management operations support services is characterized by a layered architecture. The upper layer consists of management processes, data structures, and management applications (GHET97). The middle layer presents important support functions, such as supervision and synchronization of management processes, configuration of processes and databases, access to databases and files, and integration between framework services and management applications. The lowest layer consists of tools, supporting installation, MIB loading, backups, and other usual housekeeping functions. Figure 7.2 shows these layers.

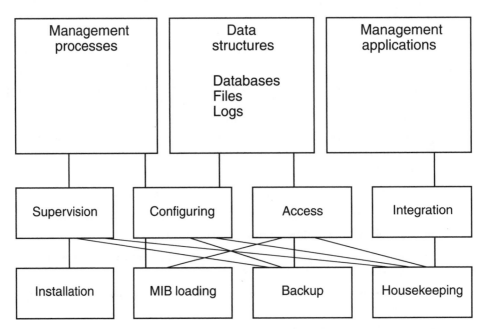

Figure 7.2 Overview of management operations support services.

7.3 Best of Suite Framework Products for Support Systems

Frameworks help to target integrated solutions. Each of the product suites introduced in this segment represent a number of successful implementations in various network infrastructures. But, in all cases, there is room for additional applications, in particular, in the field of eCommerce. Frameworks are considered enablers of integration.

7.3.1 NetExpert Product Family from Objective Systems Integrators

OSI's integrated service and network management solutions for fault, configuration, accounting, and performance management can be used to control, coordinate, and automate processes—from service requests down through the network and element or device levels that implement those requests. By unifying these service delivery, assurance, and usage processes, service providers can offer superior services at a competitive price.

NetExpert Virtual Service Management (VSM) is the foundation of OSI's NetEx Unified Management Architecture (UMA), a flexible business model for open service and network management that improves customer service, controls costs, and gets services to market faster. VSM provides the enabling technology for creating integrated service and network management systems that adapt easily to change in converging wireless, wireline, and IP networks. Based on the TMN model, VSM empowers service providers to unify customer-facing and network management systems, thanks to the benefits of object-oriented design, open interfaces, and management gateways. Main features include

- Support of SNMPv1, SNMPv2, and SNMPv3
- Support of CORBA, CMIP/Q3, ASCII/legacy, TCP/IP, and X.25
- WebOperator provides a Java-based operator workstation
- High availability minimizes downtime
- Peer-to-peer data sharing among NetExpert systems
- CORBA Access eases application integration and development of user interfaces
- NXRI simplifies integration with Remedy's Action Request System
- VisualAgent enables graphical modeling
- Common Class Library supports integration and interoperability of cross-domain applications

The NetExel solution series offers service providers an integrated set of fault, configuration, accounting, and performance management applications for automating service delivery, assurance, and usage monitoring processes. The applications' ability to share and compare data among these processes enables higher-value functions than single purpose OSSs can provide—such as SLA compliance, flow-through provisioning, and automated usage adjustment. The NetExel series covers:

Service delivery. CM Exel enables service providers to introduce and manage communications services such as order entry and subscriber provisioning through automated control and coordination of system and network functions.

Service assurance. FM Exel and PM Exel enable service providers to monitor and manage the quality of service provided, for maximum customer satisfaction.

Service usage. AM Exel collects, processes, and manages critical billing data for added revenue and competitive advantage.

The NetExec system series. CircuitExec, mobileExec, and virtual Exec customize NetExel applications for the specific needs of wireline, wireless, and IP service providers, providing market- and vendor-specific interfaces that enable them to focus on differentiating services instead of integrating incompatible systems and technologies.

NetExperts' key value lies in its ability to automate the exchange of information between diverse manual and computerized systems and processes, reducing the steps and costs involved. This flexible suite of unified applications can be deployed incrementally as service providers' needs change and as their customer bases grow. Figure 7.3 shows the Unified Management Architecture from OSI.

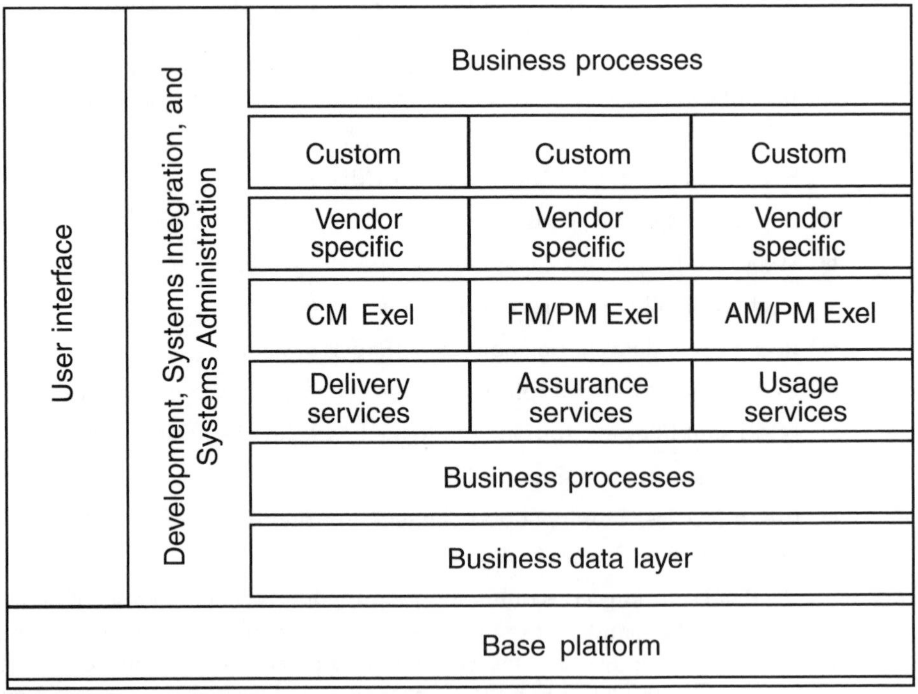

Figure 7.3 Unified Management Architecture from OSI.

NetExel applications can be integrated for a unified view of network resources. The components are

CM Exel. It controls and automates service activation across networks and manages requests to completion, reducing the cost of service delivery.

FM Exel. It manages faults automatically so network managers can identify and resolve problems rapidly, enabling service providers to assure service availability and increase SLA fulfillment rates.

PM Exel. It automates performance management, providing historical and real-time network data, to assure high quality services and reduce customer churn.

AM Exel. It automates the collection of usage data from any network element and lets service providers analyze and enhance the data for added revenue and competitive advantage.

NetExpert Virtual Process Manager (VPM) makes business processes visual and systems and resources accessible, so service providers can quickly automate and change service delivery, assurance, and usage workflow with ease. Figure 7.4 illustrates how end-to-end service management can be supported by VPM.

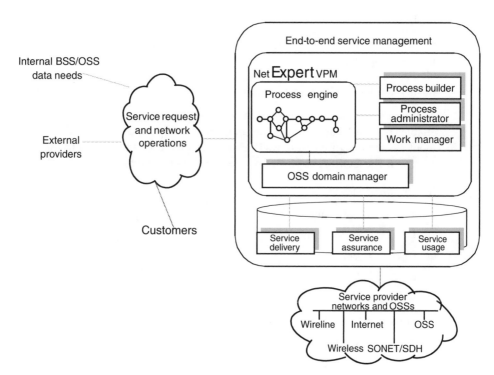

Figure 7.4 End-to-end service management by VPM.

The technical attributes of VPM are:

Work manager. Web-enabled forms to allocate and complete work items; starts, suspends, aborts, and tracks business processes and initiates new ones; distributes work throughout the organization of service providers.

Process and task builders. A point-and-click interface to develop, introduce, and update tasks and processes.

OSS domain manager. NetExpert VSM's protocol-independent manager of transactions for the NetExpert MIB and other OSSs.

Service delivery is a continuous process. NetExpert VPM gives service providers the flexibility to enhance service delivery and management processes as providers gain experience and market share. By capturing successful processes in NetExpert VPM, service providers can leverage them in building new processes for future service offerings. Version control, at the task and process level, and historical analysis improve delivery time frame and determine where operational inefficiencies lie.

Virtual Business Management (VBM) will help with collecting, processing, and distributing usage-related data for (see Figure 7.5)

- Customer care
- Marketing
- Billing
- Network operations center
- Network planning

In such a role, VBM is also a mediation solution.

NetExpert is taking advantage of the current progress with CORBA. CORBA Access enables communication with other operations support, documentation, and management systems. Figure 7.6 shows the basic architecture of these communication connections. The CORBA application is responsible for the following

- Obtain alerts
    - Get all open alerts
    - Get alert definitions
- Update alerts
    - Clear alerts
    - Acknowledge alerts
- Subscribe to alert change notifications
    - Alert created or acknowledged
    - Alert assigned or cleared
    - Alert severity or count changes

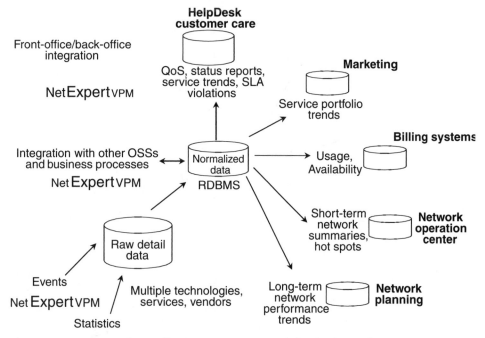

Figure 7.5 Business data collection, processing, and distribution architecture.

- Managed object instances
  - Create managed object (MO)
  - Delete managed objects
- Managed object attribute updates
  - Set specific MOs attribute(s)
  - Set group of MOs attribute(s)
- Managed object queries
  - Obtain attributes for specific MO
  - Obtain MOs based on attribute values
  - Obtain MOs based on relationships
- Subscribe to MO change notifications
  - Specific MO created or deleted
  - Specific attributes change to specific value
- Generate events
  - Start specific event in intelligent dynamic event analysis subsystem (IDEAS)
  - Optional wait for completion
- Generate confirmed events

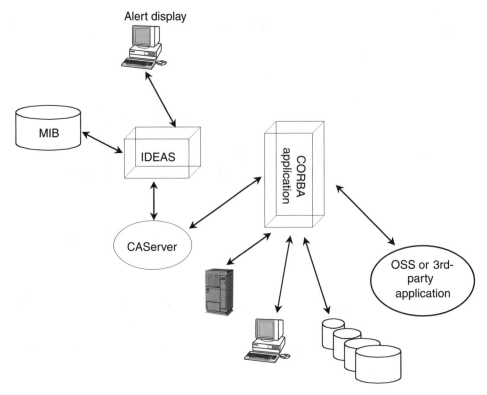

Figure 7.6 The architecture of CORBA Access.

Using CORBA as the choice for interoperating other systems puts NetExpert into a strategic role for all service providers and network operators who want to integrate their front-office and back-office systems.

7.3.2 TeMIP from Compaq

At the highest level, TeMIP consists of (1) a management information repository (MIR) for storage of data structures, functions, and management information, (2) an executive kernel responsible for supporting all the interactions between components, and (3) a set of interfaces to all the management modules belonging to the framework. Figure 7.7 shows the TeMIP architecture.

Three types of management modules interface the kernel:

1. *Access modules.* Provide access to various agents attached to real management entities such as physical network elements or systems logical resources.

2. *Presentation modules.* Provide the user interfaces.

3. *Functional modules.* Provide the actual management services such as event management, object manipulation, and management operation support services.

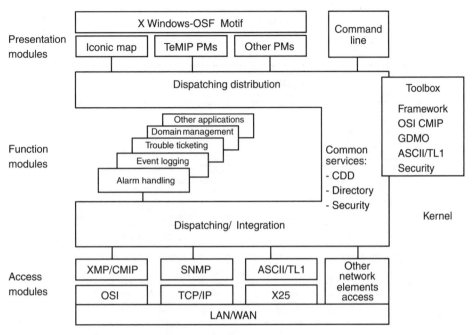

Figure 7.7 TeMIP architecture from Compaq.

These management modules are a set of cooperative processes rather than independent modules. Compaq/Digital has been adding access and functional modules over the last couple of years, such as SNMP, OSI CMIP, ASCII/TL1, and TMN support. A more detailed view of the framework can be seen in Figure 7.8 (GHET97).

An important emphasis is placed on the TeMIP distributed framework, which allows any of the constituent modules to run on physically distributed systems. Each of these systems is considered peer directors. Among directors, some play the role of servers, others play the role of clients. Direct communications and management information exchange is provided only between director servers. The implementation of the TeMIP architecture can range from stand-alone centralized management systems to hierarchical or cooperative networks of managers topologies.

The TeMIP GUI is based on OSF/Motif and X Windows systems and provides a common view of all the managed resources. The icon map PM provides presentation and language localization to the alarm handling, event logging, and trouble ticket FMs. The icon map provides map windows, a navigation box, graph windows, and a toolbox for customization. Forms and command-line interfaces are also available.

The platform provides many generic functional modules. The alarm handling and the event logging FMs are based on ISO standards. A log panel window allows the user to customize the logging environment. The trouble ticket FM is based on the recommendations of the TeleManagement Forum. The performance analyzer FM provides normalized and statistical data for TCP/IP hosts, RMON probes, and DECnet nodes. It collects information about DECnet/OSI end systems, data links, intermediate systems,

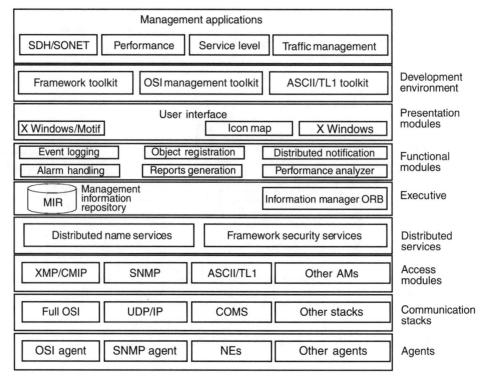

Figure 7.8   TeMIP framework in detail.

routing ports and routing circuits, circuits, nodes, and protocols. The statistics collected include throughput rates, counts, averages, overhead percents, and utilization metrics.

The information manager is the platform's object request broker and is similar but not compatible with CORBA from OMG. It receives requests from clients along with their arguments. Then, acting as a client, the information manager connects through an RPC binding to the appropriate server. Location transparency is achieved through distributed name services, which provides a global directory service.

Security services consist of access control (access control filters, user profiles, access control management), logging of operator commands (storage of prefiltered commands entered by users), and a security development toolkit.

The TeMIP framework provides access to managed resources through access modules. All of the relevant network protocols are supported by the framework. The SNMP AM supports the MIB II management information base. In addition, an MIB compiler is provided to check the concise MIB syntax and to support loading of the MIB into MIR. The SNMP AM allows get and set operations on the agents and can test reachability of an object at the IP level by using the ICMP PING protocol.

The TeMIP applications map is shown in Figure 7.9. This map includes three major groupings for external management applications:

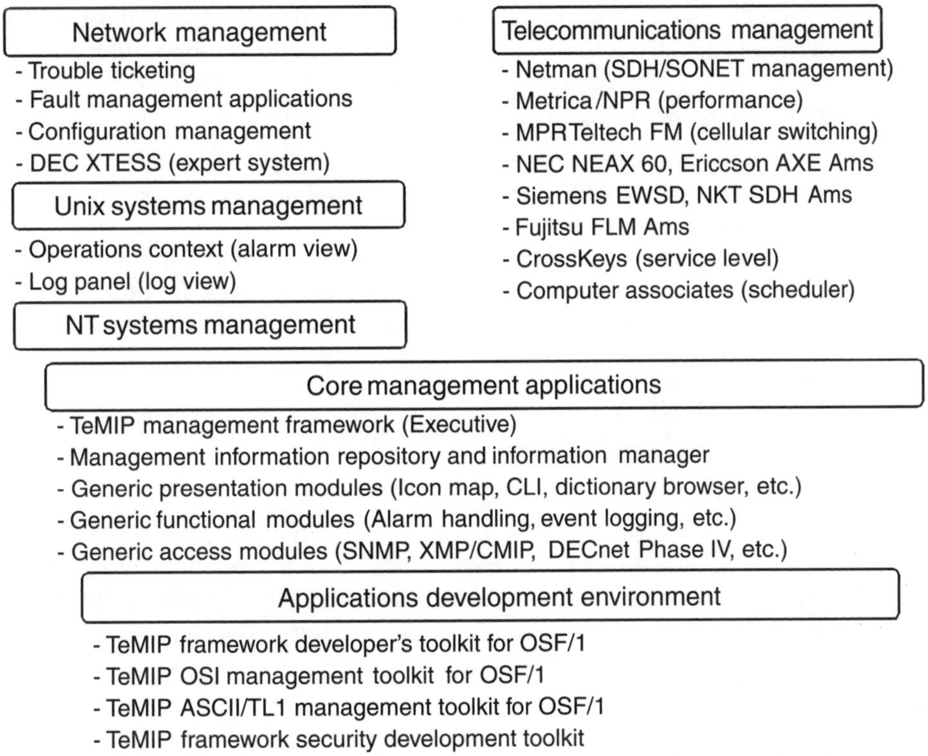

```
┌─────────────────────────────────┐      ┌─────────────────────────────────────┐
│     Network management          │      │   Telecommunications management     │
└─────────────────────────────────┘      └─────────────────────────────────────┘
- Trouble ticketing                       - Netman (SDH/SONET management)
- Fault management applications           - Metrica /NPR (performance)
- Configuration management                - MPRTeltech FM (cellular switching)
- DEC XTESS (expert system)               - NEC NEAX 60, Ericcson AXE Ams
┌─────────────────────────────────┐      - Siemens EWSD, NKT SDH Ams
│     Unix systems management     │      - Fujitsu FLM Ams
└─────────────────────────────────┘      - CrossKeys (service level)
- Operations context (alarm view)         - Computer associates (scheduler)
- Log panel (log view)
┌─────────────────────────────────┐
│     NT systems management       │
└─────────────────────────────────┘
```

```
┌──────────────────────────────────────────────────────────────────┐
│              Core management applications                        │
└──────────────────────────────────────────────────────────────────┘
```
- TeMIP management framework (Executive)
- Management information repository and information manager
- Generic presentation modules (Icon map, CLI, dictionary browser, etc.)
- Generic functional modules (Alarm handling, event logging, etc.)
- Generic access modules (SNMP, XMP/CMIP, DECnet Phase IV, etc.)

```
┌──────────────────────────────────────────────────────────────────┐
│              Applications development environment                │
└──────────────────────────────────────────────────────────────────┘
```
- TeMIP framework developer's toolkit for OSF/1
- TeMIP OSI management toolkit for OSF/1
- TeMIP ASCII/TL1 management toolkit for OSF/1
- TeMIP framework security development toolkit

Figure 7.9 Applications map of TeMIP.

1. Network management.

2. Telecommunications management.

3. Unix systems management.

7.3.3 Telcordia Solutions

Telcordia is known for legacy systems. Its greatest challenge is overcoming this image. To its credit, it is a legacy support systems provider and still serves most of the major incumbent service providers in the United States. More recently, its focus has shifted towards next generation network support and custom-off-the-shelf-system (COTS) development with its Media Vantage product suite, that covers everything from element to network to service management excluding billing and customer care. Telcordia encourages its customers to migrate to COTS. Telcordia uses a migration approach consisting of surround, supplement, and supplant. The first step is to surround older support systems with more modern interfaces, using browser and Java technology, and system-to-system integration where possible using CORBA interfaces. The second step is to identify systems that perform well but are limited in scope, such as older copper loop provisioning systems, and supplement them with adjunct applications that can support new services and network technologies. The third step is to replace old systems that simply cannot cut it anymore. Telcordia provides an example where it replaces the old LMOS workforce management system from Lucent with a new MediaAdvantage Force product.

From a software perspective, the partnerships of Telcordia are designed to fill gaps, which means that most of them are best-of-breed players because the Telcordia product portfolio is wide ranging. One example is Astracon, which develops connection management solutions. This solution supports real-time configuration, provisioning, and end-to-end session control of hybrid network services. Telcordia has incorporated this product into its NCON network configuration system.

7.3.4 Product Suites from Lucent Technologies

Lucent Technologies has been completing its product suite to address all principal areas of service providers. Lucent has started with the NetCare service in the area of outsourcing. Step-by-step they have been adding new products and features to this service. In addition, Lucent can reengineer their legacy systems in the area of order management, provisioning, and traffic management. The most important products are described in the following.

Connectvu APX

This product is a multivendor switch configuration manager for various North American and international switches. It is built on top of a scalable platform that can grow with the network. It uses a relational Informix database and user-friendly graphical user interfaces. The core offer is for service activation of lines and trunks. It focuses on services for line provisioning, (e.g., POTS and Centrex), end-users trunk provisioning (e.g., PBX) and Centrex Common Block. Optional modules are available to provide provisioning flexibility for customized solutions required by today's competitive service providers. The task toolkit option is a task-based programmable tool that increases provisioning efficiency by providing a high-level GUI that allows users to work at high-level tasks by masking many of the lower-level details associated with switch recent change. It spans across the network management and element management layers of TMN. Flow-through of upstream tasks or business-level service requests are accomplished through CORBA-IDL, which translates the service requests into switch-specific commands to query or update the switch database. Downstream switch interfaces are supported depending on switch type. Building on the end-customer visible service activation portion, it offers infrastructure provisioning for those customers who desire a robust configuration management solution. Resource provisioning (e.g., charging, rate center, line class code) and network provisioning (e.g., message trunks, intermachine trunks) comprise the infrastructure provisioning capabilities.

It employs a unique switch coupler to create and maintain an isomorphic copy of the switches known as the shadow database that provides centralized access of switch network data. The system utilizes this virtual copy of the network switch database to provision the network. Both line-side shadow and/or infrastructure shadow database capabilities are offered. This combination of core and optional features provides a strong foundation for both stand-alone product solutions as well as an integrated flow-through provisioning solution.

Actiview

Actiview Service Management solution integrates complex business and operations processes for service provisioning, maintenance, workforce management, and customer care. In addition, the workflow design and architecture provides the critical link between the business, service, network, and element management layers of the TMN architecture to provide true integrated customer and network management. It can help to streamline work processes from initial order to billing—even when customer and market needs are changing. It can be deployed either as a stand-alone product or as a module integrated with other systems.

It enables total work process flow-through across multiple business locations, organizational structures, technologies, and network services. Lucent is designing packages of Actiview modules that are proven support tools for singular or convergent environments, including:

Wireline. It supports the delivery of voice and data services—regardless of the network technologies involved.

Wireless. It supports the delivery of subscriber services for CDMA or TDMA, including GSM.

Workforce management. It supports the assignment, dispatch, service scheduling of technician and field installation and repair processes.

Actiview can include the following modules:

Order manager. It manages and enables automation of service activation and order processing. Also available to give service providers additional functionality, such as:

■ **Order creation.** It provides GUI-based order entry and validation for downstream network activation. An optional customer record database stores account, service, and product data for billing and provisioning.

■ **Living unit data administration.** It determines network availability by validating the subscriber service address and retrieving routing information.

Trouble manager. It controls the maintenance process with integrated support network problems, customer-reported problems, and scheduled or routine maintenance.

Dispatch manager. It controls and manages service technician assignments to ensure that the right technician is in the right place at the right time.

Field access manager. It manages and controls work-related information to and from field technicians, helping ensure data integrity.

The Actiview solution delivers precise, automated process handling from basic voice messaging to more sophisticated convergent combinations. The modular solution has the flexibility to anticipate and respond to changing market and business needs in the following ways:

- With the order creation and provisioning platform, service providers can define, manage, and automate complex service offerings better.

- With its maintenance software, service providers can proactively manage outages, integrate network troubles, and improve technical support.

- Database managers let service providers track individual customer and location information, and verify service availability and network data.

- Actiview solution uses the simple Java software, CORBA-based application programming interfaces, and object-oriented methodologies.

- It runs on Unix system-based commercial hardware platforms and industry standard relational database management systems.

- The graphical user interface provides a browser look-and-feel, with customizable menus for easy multitasking.

Billdats

Network usage data affords a rich set of customer information that in addition to providing billing input, can offer service providers significant opportunities when processed by downstream applications. With the right billing data management software, service providers can generate new revenues, deploy services faster, manage fraud better, and adapt more quickly to the new opportunities afforded by deregulation. The Billdats data manager, a comprehensive data collection, distribution, and management solution, can capture, store, and process usage data in near-real time for distribution to other critical applications. It integrates the polling, file handling, administration, and distribution tasks into existing networks of service providers. It can access multiple network elements of dedicated data facilities, packet networks, dialed links, or local/wide area networks.

Lucent has installed Billdats solutions in wireline networks, data networks, and wireless networks for service providers of all sizes. After the acquisition of Kenan products, Lucent is expected to offer more in the area of convergent billing, Web access to billing data, postbilling analysis and support for customer relationship management (CRM).

Switched Access Remote Test System (SARTS)

SARTS provides service providers a centralized and straightforward way to test special services and analog circuits by integrating with the test remote and access equipment of the customer's choice. This can be accomplished by the open interfaces of the product. Because the auto test features of SARTS emulate the logic of humans, they perform similar to the way an efficient, expert tester would. Furthermore, its unique algorithms are adaptive in nature and can determine the appropriate tests to be run in nearly any given situation. The results of these tests are then presented in plain English. The product is also capable of being integrated into a total work flow-through environment so service providers can help provide a high level of customer service while, at the same time, reduce operations costs even further. Imagine having new special services tested and results reported to a work management system prior to turning up the customer service—all without any human intervention. Similarly, service providers can have trouble tickets tracked from entry through dispatch to the repair technician without human assistance.

With the test automation, work flow-through and open interface features, Lucent provides a single system to integrate testing for all service types. In order to further facilitate the handling of SARTS, the service assurance GUI is extended by a Web-based toolkit of both automated and manual tests for special circuits. Tests are spanning end-to-end circuit analysis and diagnostics. In addition, macropackages are offered that bundle common test sequences for rapid troubleshooting over segments of a circuit.

NetMinder

NetMinder is a very powerful performance management system, being able to collect more than 50,000 measurements per minute and track 20,000 simultaneous active controls to manage traffic in the world's largest public switched networks. In addition, the NetMinder system provides scalable performance management solutions for wireless, intelligent, signaling, and data networks. Its software automatically alerts network managers to serious, difficult-to-find, network-wide problems, and then delivers the appropriate tools to help them recover operations quickly. Increasing network complexity and customer demands for improved QoS are just some of the factors that are causing operators around the world to select this solution. The following modules are available:

Network capacity engineering (NCE) feature set. Provides voice and signaling traffic data collection and analysis for network equipment engineering. By analyzing and validating traffic data, network operators can effectively deploy network facilities to improve the efficiency of equipment use. NCE can help operators maximize their network resources (switches and facilities) to cost-effectively provide end users optimal service.

Network traffic management (NTM) feature set. Supports near real-time management of traffic in public switched networks and associated signaling networks. With this module, network operations managers can optimize traffic flow during periods of network stress caused by traffic overloads or equipment failures. NTM supports the management of traffic carried by national, regional, local, and intelligent networks. It provides surveillance and analysis of traffic carried by circuit switched networks. It also monitors the traffic on circuit groups and signaling links as well as the status of exchanges, signal transfer points, and service control points.

Network trouble patterning (NTP) feature set. Collects and correlates call irregularity messages generated by network elements during call set-up failures to deduce the status of voice and SS7 networks through extensive statistical and patterning analysis. The analysis process automatically determines network trouble patterns and produces near real-time alerts. NTP provides surveillance capability at the network architecture level and allows for a comprehensive view of affected customers or services across multiple network elements. While other operations systems detect malfunctioning or out-of-service network elements or facilities, NTP can also detect logical problems within elements that are not themselves reporting trouble. Through analysis of statistical patterns in call irregularity data compared with standard network architecture and routing schemes, NTP can also sectionalize the fault.

Packet traffic management (PTM) feature set. Measures and monitors performance and provides congestion management in both the core and access portions of the data packet network. As complex data networks grow and converge with voice networks, network traffic management becomes more important and more complex and network congestion can impact service. The first step towards avoiding network congestion is to monitor and manage data packet traffic in real time. It is the only way to handle unanticipated packet volumes across multiple service layers (data and voice) and maintain quality of service during unusual network events. Specifically positioned for multivendor SNMP-based IP and ATM networks, including voice over packet, the PTM module is designed to enhance performance and improve service reliability. The PTM feature set offers technically advanced tools for monitoring, measurement, analysis, and visualization of performance data and immediate identification of network congestion.

ITM Network Analyzer

The element management systems that control transport networks also store valuable configuration, performance, maintenance, and usage data—information that can help service providers to improve network service and contain costs. The Network Analyzer enables service providers to review and evaluate complex transport networks. Its software collects and consolidates data generated throughout the networks. High accuracy can be achieved due to the use of the Dynamic Network Operations (DNO) process that has been patented by Bell Laboratories.

A number of graphical analysis reports are available that include:

Network impact analysis reports. Help service providers to assess operations' effectiveness, evaluate overall network performance, as well as perform preventive maintenance.

Circuit quality assurance reports. Help service providers evaluate circuit quality, detect recurring outages, and identify candidates for circuit rearrangement. Individual customer reports may also be created to facilitate service-level agreement reporting via the Web.

Network asset analysis reports. Help service providers track network resources, optimize network usage, and plan capacity expansions.

Customized reports. Help to quickly address specific needs with a few simple commands.

The Dynamic Network Analyzer software supports all the diverse, multidomain networks that Lucent's ITM element management systems were designed to handle (e.g., SDH/SONET, DWDM, and DCS). A Windows-based interface provides secure, immediate access to all transport network data, no matter how configured or managed. The Analyzer even provides secure remote access via laptop computers or Web browsers with the result that network personnel can query, report, and analyze consolidated data from anywhere, at anytime.

OneVision Integrated Network Controller

A single system might be needed for multivendor SDH/SONET, DWDM, and DCS management. OneVision Integrated Network Controller can provide such an integrated solution by giving service providers the power to manage their transport networks and optionally partition such networks into well-defined secure segments.

This product provides SPs with end-to-end circuit-level operations, including configuration, fault, and performance management. For example, it provides scheduled, on-demand circuit reconfiguration, real-time alarm surveillance, and circuit tracing. It also effectively manages services that traverse add/drop multiplexers, digital cross-connect systems, and subscriber loop carriers. With support for multiple technologies, multiple vendors, and integrated element, network, and service management, this product lets SPs manage a network of one to 1,000 network elements with a simple and powerful Web-enabled GUI.

Service-Level Management Tools—NetCare VitalSuite

This product is used by service providers to offer customers concrete reports showing compliance to SLAs. It is also used by customers to keep tabs on their providers. VitalSuite continuously monitors both data networking and application performance, both from the end-user and internal operations perspectives. It provides end-to-end monitoring of applications, networks, and service performance. Users can get a high-level overview of performance or use heat charts to drill down for more granular information. The solution consists of three components:

1. *VitalAgent.* The foundation of the product family—a powerful agent that resides on desktops throughout the enterprise, monitoring user transactions, and recording everything from response times and delays to bottlenecks and failures. The data are analyzed, condensed, and forwarded to centralized server-based products, where they are aggregated with other VitalAgent data to provide an overview of network and application performance.

2. *VitalAnalysis.* It uses VitalAgent data to create heat charts that show how clients, the network, servers, and applications are performing as a unit. Heat charts let customers gauge the system's relative health through color-coded displays that grow increasingly brighter to warn of impending problems. Clicking on a heat chart cell lets customers drill down to view virtually any aspect of network or application performance in detail, telling customers exactly what has happened over the past day, week, or month. By providing reports that summarize network

and application performance over time, VitalAnalysis proves indispensable for monitoring and verifying service-level agreements.

3. *VitalHelp.* It is a real-time fault detection and troubleshooting tool that lets customers fix problems quickly—before users are aware they exist. VisualAgent reports problems directly to the VitalHelp server, providing an instant analysis of the event. For problems that occur outside corporate boundaries, VitalHelp Remote extends the reach, letting customers run diagnostic tests on the desktops of telecommuters and other mobile users. By providing advance warning of user problems, VitalHelp keeps support phones on the hook.

Performance Management Service

Analysis, reporting, and trending are very useful functions to support performance tuning and capacity planning. But service level management (SLM) may need reports delivered in real time. Most of the products introduced earlier offer this capability. For the company interested in this kind of reporting who does not want to establish such a service, Enterprise Pro from International Network Services (INS) may be an interesting alternative. It differentiates itself from other products with so-called QoS alert capabilities. It immediately notifies network managers when network traffic exceeds a predetermined threshold. And with server monitoring, it helps get to the root cause of problems. Reports can be viewed through e-mail or via Web browsers or from OpenView consoles since INS has integrated Enterprise Pro with the OpenView management platform.

Enterprise Pro is installed on a server connected to the LAN as shown in Figure 7.10 (REAR98). Network managers can set performance thresholds per device, per group of devices, or per segment through a GUI. Using SNMP, the software gathers information from MIBs embedded in routers, switches, bridges, and hubs. It also can collect bandwidth-utilization data from RMON1 (Remote Monitoring) and RMON2 probes throughout the network. As soon as a threshold is exceeded, Enterprise Pro generates a report to the management console or to a browser.

Enterprise Pro can collect data from NT, Novell, and Unix servers. It collects statistics on CPU load, memory utilization, and disk space utilization—information that helps to isolate and resolve problems. Instant updates help corporate networkers start problem resolution before users notice faults or performance degradations. And all that means they have a better chance of meeting service level agreements they have signed with various external and internal users.

Enterprise Pro offers information in various levels of detail. Operators, administrators, and network managers can drill down for reports of the latest alarms, results of the last 5-minute poll, or a combination of these. It is also possible to customize reports to present information for various sites or groups of devices. Reports can, for instance, be tailored to show activity on the LAN, or on all hubs, or on all routers in a specific geographical area.

Using Enterprise Pro means that certain performance management functions are outsourced to INS. Price/performance ratio is worth considering with this type of outsourcing.

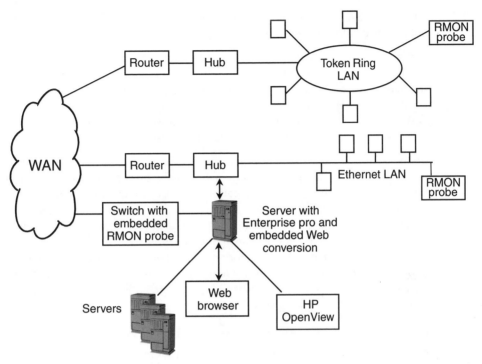

Figure 7.10 Architecture of Enterprise Pro service architecture from Lucent Technologies.

7.4 Best of Suite Products for Customer Care and Billing

Customer care and billing processes are facing customers. General requirements of products are the availability of certain data in real-time, extremely user-friendly interfaces, capabilities of self-care using Web technology, and the ability of supporting customer relationship management.

7.4.1 Design of a New Billing System

The migration from one billing system to another involves four principal steps:

1. Extraction of data from the existing database.
2. Translation to a new database structure.
3. Importation of the data to the new database.
4. Running applications against the new database.

There are a number of reasons that conversions are so difficult. In the simple model of billing systems' conversion, the existing database is accurate, complete, and auditable. This is usually not the case. Even more severe is the fact that basic billing data are used almost everywhere within the organization of the service provider.

Setting up a project management task force responsible across the whole organization for the implementation of the new billing system is an important step in recognizing the magnitude of the conversion. The new billing system will impact every department in the organization, and at the same time, will generally be resisted by everybody. The task force is charged with assessing the impact of the changes and ensuring that the organization is ready for the new billing system.

Many existing databases are not clean anymore due to years of add-on, patchwork development and maintenance. In the worst cases, this only becomes apparent when the conversion is on its way. The creation of a new billing system with a fresh database is an opportunity to establish a clean system with data that are reconcilable and auditable. This opportunity is lost if the old data are forced into the new billing system. In an ideal world, data cleanse operations would run continuously through the lifetime of a system. It is essential for any conversion process to undertake an initial cleanse of the existing data. This is a lengthy process but it could be run in parallel with system development and testing. Typically, the following data should be included for the new billing system

- Subscribers (names, addresses, payment information, etc.)
- Contracts (dates, services, process, discounts, etc.)
- Phone numbers
- Accounts receivable transactions
- History of customer with the service provider
- Billed usage
- Unbilled usage
- Customer contract history including usage patterns

Software tools can be used or developed to carry out basic checks such as testing the validity of address formats or reconciling billing system data on services and phone numbers maintained in the system. Data cleansing involves a multifunctional team comprising systems experts and business function owners and users. The time and money spent in this phase will be saved many times over during the actual conversion.

An important aspect of the development process is the early identification of priorities. While these vary between implementations, an example priority list is as follows (NORR98):

Network interfaces. These interfaces allow service providers to perform the critical tasks of activating customers, provisioning services, and collecting usage data. Without these clearly defined interfaces, service providers cannot provide services to customers and cannot collect revenue. The new system is going to interact with the network in a new way and typically the creation of these interfaces falls on the critical path, due to their complexity.

Customer facing interfaces. Billing systems development and deployment of call centers are carried out in many cases in parallel. This dual development requires careful management to maintain transparency to external customers during the conversion phase. This means ensuring that customer service representatives always have access to necessary information.

Business interfaces. These include the interfaces with banks, credit card companies, credit bureaus, print shops, and other external agencies. They are required for the collection of revenue and the printing of bills amongst other things and are clearly of great importance. They rank lower in the priority list only because they are less complex and the effect of their absence is not felt immediately in terms of customer service. But these interfaces have to be careful with early planning because these agencies are driven by the same business goals as service providers. They may not be so responsive when problems are detected with these interfaces. eCommerce will help with the standardization of these interfaces.

Financial interfaces. These interfaces to internal financial systems ensure that the billing system is integrated into the corporate accounting and management control processes of the organization. Priority should be given to adequacy of reporting and auditability of the system. Many of these interfaces can be handled manually if necessary for a short period.

It is essential that the bulk of testing use copies of live data from the old system. Final tests should be carried out using copies of full-size databases, if possible. It is the unexpected data gaps or inaccuracies that will cause problems, and these are the occurrences that cannot be replicated to simulated data.

In order to minimize risks with the ultimate conversion, there are three approaches: trials, pilots, and parallel runs. *Trials* are the extension of the testing process and are very valuable. A trial using friendly or test customers is often the first time the new billing system's operations resemble a normal business environment. If the development process has been well managed, a trial provides the opportunity to fine-tune the billing system and ensure that it supports the underlying business processes. A trial may uncover serious problems, while a delay to implementation is still possible even though undesirable. An effective trial should be as realistic as possible, testing out business scenarios from end to end of the billing process. For example, customers should be activated, provisioned, use various services, have usage rated and billed. Bills should be generated, printed, and distributed. Payments should be processed, financial ledgers updated, and customers should be allowed to query bills and other information. Unless unavoidable, none of the above should be simulated. This approach may seem too ambitious, but too many stories of billing implementations that have failed are due to inattention to these details.

Pilots involve a limited live implementation of the full system. A pilot is appropriate only when such a limitation can be applied sensibly, such as geographical area or portfolio segment. To be useful, the pilot must exercise the same functionality as the full rollout. Pilots can be effective, especially when the old billing system consists of a number of discrete but similar databases such as defined by geographical areas. In these cases, lessons learned from the pilot conversion and implementation can be utilized in subsequent conversions.

Parallel runs are recommended as a fail-safe approach to conversion. The theory that the old billing system should be fully maintained until the new system has been fully proven is an appealing and plausible idea. But parallel runs are always expensive and typically unworkable (NORR98). They are unworkable because new billing systems usually require less support persons, and sometimes the staffing changes are made before the ultimate conversion. An effective parallel run generally requires an increase in resources, needed both to maintain the existing system and gain familiarity with the new one. Parallel runs require the maintenance of two business processes as well. If accepted, parallel runs should be seen as a short-term measure.

In addition, training should be planned through the life cycle of the development process. An excellent way to train and build confidence in the new billing system is to identify key users within each functional area of business processes. These key users should be involved in the design stages of the new billing system, particularly in the testing and trials.

In summary, the basic process of conversion may be very simple, but the actual execution of a conversion is complex due to the interdependencies of billing systems with other business processes of service providers.

7.4.2 Convergent Billing Platform (CBP) from ADC-Saville Systems

Convergent Billing Platform (CBP) was designed to provide comprehensive billing and customer care solutions from a single integrated platform. This system is a valuable solution to those companies who wish to provide customer service in a competitive environment. The internal benefit of CBP is the rich repository of corporate data on all aspects of the customer relationship. Query tools enable service providers to design management information reports across all applications and to interface with corporate decision databases. This product enables network operators to create customer value, to quickly respond to the future marketing challenges in current markets, and to capitalize on new markets as regulatory changes break down traditional barriers. Figure 7.11 shows the CBP system, the modules it supports, and the interfaces/outputs that interact with the core modules.

Modules of CBP address the business needs of service providers and include

- Prospect management
- Credit verification
- Inventory, equipment, and workforce management
- Customer profile maintenance
- Marketing and maintenance of product portfolios
- Order processing
- Usage collection, processing, validation, rating, and bill preparation
- Billing, including formatting, verification, and on-demand billing
- Sales ledger

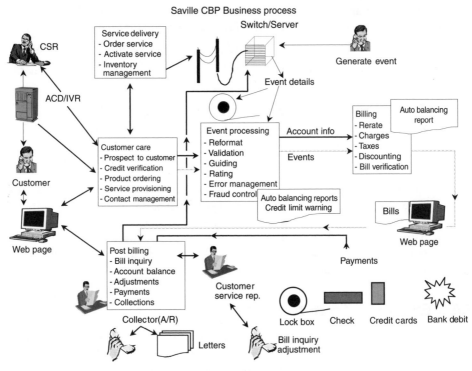

Figure 7.11 Business processes supported by CBP.

- General ledger interface and reporting
- Customer care, including customer inquiries, contact logs, relation management, and customer management
- Collection of payments
- Management information

Using this convergent billing platform, service providers and network operators may benefit in the following ways

- Maintaining comprehensive customer information and service profiles
- Recording customer interactions in a contact log and forwarding action items to departments or users
- Delivering service to the customer in near real time
- Creating trouble tickets and dispatching them to the correct workforce for resolution
- Billing, discounting, and providing supplementary information according to the preference of the individual customer
- Enabling service providers and network operators to modify prices and introduce products that are specific to customer segments

- Discounting customers according to their value to the corporation and according to the margins associated with product lines and offerings

- Generating accurate invoices and providing critical revenue information

- Providing effective management information on the network, customer base, and financial performance

- Accurately reflecting and managing customer receivables

- Providing work management tools to match the load to the available customer care workforce

- Providing presentation and work tools to maximize user efficiency

CBP enables service representatives to communicate with and respond to customers from a single integrated system that goes far beyond the capabilities of traditional billing solutions. Because business processes are integrated within a relational database, service providers and network operators will have access to the critical customer, network, marketing, and financial data necessary to become and remain a leading telecommunication service provider.

7.4.3 Ensemble from Amdocs

The Ensemble suite of products supports customer care, billing, and ordering activities in voice, data, and IP environments. Ensemble supports the full range of convergent multiservice operations, including local, cellular, data, paging, long-distance, international, broadband, Internet, and IP services. The scope of the application includes T-CRM, with front-end navigator and business management applications, billing and rating functionality, and comprehensive marketing applications. Ensemble helps with convergence in competitive markets while providing a strategic platform for supporting the next generation of telecom products, services, and technologies.

Principal features of the application include:

Use of advanced technology. Ensemble applies and optimizes the benefits of object-oriented design, rule-based applications, Web-enabling, client/server and a three-tiered architecture. The advanced and robust system design provides for high-powered performance throughput, economy of operation, enhanced user productivity and cost-effective growth. The use of industry-standard system software and development tools facilitates integration with third-party products.

Modularity. It allows the carrier to choose only the modules and applications it requires to meet its current business needs. The platform includes both shared modules that support cross-network and cross-service functionality, as well as specified components to support the particular needs of each network environment. Platform modularity allows the configuration of solutions to match each carrier's business model, including multiservice and one-stop-shopping business environments as well as single service environments.

Scalability. System scalability supports virtually unlimited growth without having to modify the software architecture. Ensemble is based on standard built-in Unix operation system features, enabling cost-effective expansion through the progressive addition of hardware components rather than through quantum leaps. In addition, Ensemble uses parallel and multithread processing to optimize system scalability.

Flexibility. A rule-based, table-driven architecture ensures flexibility in the definition of switch inputs, new services, price plans, rating rules, discount schemes, and bill formats. The system architecture is specifically designed to simplify and accelerate the introduction of new and complex services and packages. The online table facility enables frequently changing business variables, such as rate per unit and sales commissions, to be modified and applied immediately.

Figure 7.12 shows the principal components of Ensemble. Each of these components will be described in some detail.

Order Management

It consists of two modules: service negotiation and delivery control.

1. *Service negotiation.* Enables process-flow-driven negotiation and order capture in one dialog session. The module provides immediate information about product offerings, product availability, price plans, and sales support tools, enabling the service negotiation process to be conducted and completed in real time. It allows service representatives to view the customer's current orders and services to detect interdependencies or conflicts. It can be used to reserve network resources and

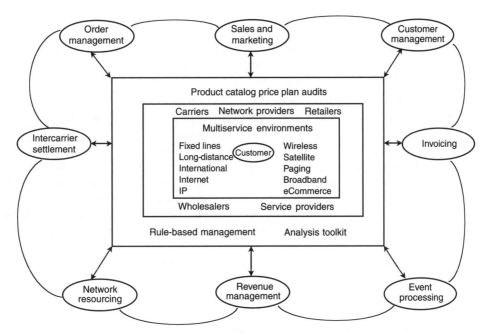

Figure 7.12 Components of Ensemble from Amdocs.

propose service and price quotes. This module provides a single point-of-sale, eliminating the need for multiple, separate systems for different lines of business. The system can accommodate cross-product packages and price plans. It incorporates the latest GUI technology and can be configured in a user-friendly manner.

2. *Delivery control.* Enables flow-through provisioning and order tracking. Equipped with a workflow engine, it communicates ordering tasks to provisioning facilities at the service provider. Negotiation, provisioning, and order flow are mapped out for each product offering. Delivery control features a mediation layer to ease integration with the service provider's operations support system (OSS), such as network, billing, and directories. This layer facilitates the dispatch of ordering tasks and the exchange of information between order management and the service provider's other systems. The product architecture provides for smooth integration of the order management system with multiple telecommunications infrastructures.

Customer Management

There are three modules for this component: customer service, hierarchies management, and self-service.

1. *Customer service.* Based on a comprehensive and consolidated view of customer profile information, customer service enables a single representative to handle calls related to account management, billing inquiries, adjustments, payments, deposits, collection, and complaints. Representatives have access to all customer data (e.g., hierarchy, payments, collection history, adjustments, credits, bill images, and usage), allowing efficient one-call customer service.

2. *Hierarchies management.* Facilitates the management of complex customers, such as large corporations, by supporting an unlimited number of hierarchy levels. It enables different types of concurrent hierarchical representation, including billing, legal, or discount hierarchies, while providing a consolidated view of customer information maintained in one or more systems.

3. *The www.self.service module.* Enables service providers to provide customer care and ordering services to their customers through the Internet on a 24-hours-a-day basis. This module provides customers with secure access to their own personal information, usage history, and billing data, as well as ordering options, using their standard Internet browser. This module is built around a cohesive security architecture that protects the system and the internal network of the service provider. Equally important, it reduces the number of customer calls, enabling carriers to achieve efficiencies in customer care and ordering operations. This module's robust infrastructure accommodates a large number of customers simultaneously and provides rapid online data retrieval.

Sales and Marketing

Ensemble supports five modules, including commission management, churn management, campaign planning, retail management and customer behavior analysis.

1. *Commission management.* Used to support sales activities performed by the service provider through telemarketing, dealers, and other channels. This module is used to define and maintain the agreements between the service provider and various external sales organizations, as well as support the calculation of dealer compensation, sales commissions, adjustments, and other financial activities.

2. *Churn management.* Designed to help the service provider identify high-value customers with a high probability of churn based on usage patterns, customer data, and sociodemographic information found in the marketing database or in a data warehouse. Using advanced data mining techniques, churn management offers an environment for analyzing and understanding the causes of churn, predicting the probability of customers to churn, designing incentives for retention, defining focused retention campaigns, and evaluating retention effectiveness and return on investment.

3. *Campaign planning.* Uses data mining and data warehouse techniques to facilitate effective planning of sales campaigns. The application defines campaign parameters, prioritizes products offered to the customer, optimizes communication channels and allocates sales resources.

4. *Retail management.* Supports the complete management of the retail stores of the service provider. It supports all the standard point-of-sale and cash management functions with special emphasis on the unique features of the telecom market. This module supports one streamlined session with the customer, including subscription registration, immediate provisioning of handset access, equipment sales and rental, repairs, and returns. Retail management also supports all the back-office activities of equipment inventory control in the retail stores and regional warehouses.

5. *Customer behavior analysis (CBA).* Provides an in-depth look at customer usage trends. This product uses a graphic display to depict analysis of usage, including, for example, the breakdown between voice and data, impact of new price plans, usage of specific services, call and data transmission destinations, historical comparisons of usage behaviors, and day and night usage. CBA uses 3-D visualization techniques to map data attributes into visual dimensions and present a clear picture of customer behavior. The results of the analysis are forwarded into the T-CRM Navigator and Customer Service modules, so that this information is available to the service provider's representatives managing each customer contact.

Network Resourcing

This group of functions is supported by four modules including number management, SIM card management, wireless provisioning, and IP provisioning.

1. *Number management.* Maintains a record of all the changes in a telephone number throughout its life cycle. It supports all number inventory maintenance activities, such as load and assignment, and builds and maintains all relevant number information.

2. *SIM card management in the GSM environment.* Facilitates inventory management of SIM card numbers and MSISDN numbers. The SIM card management module supports tracking of IMSIs used by the operator and the allocation scheme used by the operator for different HLRs.

3. *Wireless provisioning.* This module manages all provisioning to the network elements, which may include HLRs, voice mail machines, intelligent network (IN) computers and other auxiliary devices. This module reformats service transactions to the required switch protocols and forwards each transaction to its appropriate network element. Wireless provisioning ensures consistency between the service provider's customer data and the data maintained in the switches.

4. *IP provisioning.* A flexible, powerful interface that has the ability to connect and provision a variety of Internet application servers, such as mail servers, network authentication servers, and Web servers. IP provisioning facilitates rapid, real-time connection to IP network elements.

Intercarrier Settlement

This group of functions is supported by four modules, including partner agreement management, usage processing, invoicing, and settlement management.

1. *Partner agreement management.* Covers the full range of intercarrier business agreements—interconnect, roaming, international traffic, and wholesale. This module manages comprehensive information about business partners and agreements, including rates, traffic types, discounts, currencies, payment terms, and conditions. The module details partners' physical interconnections and their impact on partner agreements. Partner agreement tracks all information required to perform rating, invoicing, and reconciliation.

2. *Usage processing.* Responsible for the ongoing processing of usage records, according to the appropriate operator and service information. It utilizes Ensemble's advanced acquisition, formatting, and error management technologies, with flexible guiding and rating functionality dedicated to intercarrier usage events.

3. *Invoicing.* Provides the main communication channel between the operator and its partners. Invoices and reconciliation reports are created for various settlement periods. Investigative tools check for discrepancies and errors, dramatically improving the accuracy of intercarrier invoicing.

4. *Settlement management.* Manages the partners' accounting activities, including the issue and receipt of payments, bidirectional disputes, issuing and recording debit and credit notes, and interfacing to other financial management systems. This automated process streamlines the settlement activities into a standardized business process, with comprehensive auditing of revenues and expenses.

Event Processing

This component consists of four modules, including acquisition and formatting, guiding and rating, error management, and fraud management.

1. *Acquisition and formatting.* This module mediates between the event processing modules and the network elements. Using rule-based technology, this module is responsible for the receipt, validation, and reformatting of usage event data from various networks and service platforms, such as wireline, cellular, IP, and prepaid. In addition, it merges event records generated by various network elements into one event record as required, and distributes the reformatted event records to downstream systems.

2. *Guiding and rating.* Based on a multiservice rating engine that is used to rate network and nonnetwork generated events. This module is designed to rate any defined event, including data services transactions, phone calls, network feature activation and deactivation, service orders, and value-added services. These events are rated in accordance with flexible defined price, promotion, and discount plans, including cross-service sales packages. The guiding process identifies the customer, service provider, and services associated with a given usage event, while the rating process calculates the charge for each record accordingly. Usage events are rated immediately and applied directly to the customer's account.

3. *Error management.* Analyzes and corrects errors detected in event processing. It is a highly sophisticated table-driven tool, with capabilities for handling both single and mass errors using batch and online procedures. By automating the handling of groups of errors and by improving the rate of error resolution, it helps to reduce costs and increase revenue.

4. *Fraud management.* Detects potential fraud, issues alerts, gathers evidence of fraud, and facilitates the work of fraud investigators. It offers a broad spectrum of fraud protection for direct-dialed calls and specialized functionality for alternate-billed services, such as calling card, collect, and bill to third party. These systems use multiple technologies from diverse disciplines such as expert systems, artificial intelligence, statistics, visualization, and other information theory techniques to ensure a high likelihood of success in fraud detection.

Revenue Management

This group concentrates on two modules: accounts receivable and collection.

1. *Accounts receivable.* This module supports posting and maintenance of charges, invoice receipts, payment receipt from various sources, cash application, and financial reporting. It supports all aspects of complex fixed-mobile convergence by maintaining charges at a very detailed level, including line of business, service provider, product type, charge type, and subscription number. Interfaces to external financial systems, such as general ledger and accounts payable, are also supported.

2. *Collection.* This module automates collection procedures for delinquent accounts in accordance with company policy, manages customer accounts with outstanding debts and provides flexible, easy-to-define collection paths for different customer types. The collection workflow is defined in tables based on each service provider's specific collection policy.

Invoicing

This function consists of two modules: billing and flexible bill formatter.

1. *Billing.* Complies, generates, and summarizes all the elements that are to appear on the consolidated bill. These include recurring charges, usage charges, one-time charges, credits, and adjustments, from one or more lines of business. Billing also performs product-specific tax calculations. The system allows service providers to produce a single bill for customers subscribing to different services, such as local, long-distance, cellular, and IP. Based on the customer hierarchies, multiple bills are consolidated and a discount engine calculates the consolidated discount. Bill quality is ensured through bill sampling and auditing procedures.

2. *Flexible bill formatter.* Facilitates the flexible design of new or personalized bill formats, utilizing a table-driven, rule-based architecture. The bill format design is performed online using an intuitive, user-friendly interface, while the run-time code for bill production is generated automatically. It includes a high-performance utility for mass production of customer bills, supporting color graphics, customized bills, logos, fonts, and two-sided printing. Output files are produced for printing as well as electronic transmissions.

Internet Administration Framework

The Solect division of Amdocs is dealing with IP-based services and accounting offered by Internet Administration Framework (IAF). It provides many opportunities for service providers who want to introduce innovative new business models, increase the number of subscribers, reduce churn, and offer differentiated services. It was built and designed to take advantage of new services and new distribution channels such as the hosting application. It empowers service providers to rapidly launch distinctive offerings for any IP service.

Features and functions can be summarized as follows:

Service management module. Provides the most flexible platform for defining and registering new services, using a dynamic attributes model and the provisioning data collectors (PDCs). The dynamic model manages all customer attributes that can be set up, such as account, contract, and services. This allows service providers to differentiate service offerings when targeting market segments, such as retail, wholesale, hosted ISPs, and packaged applications.

PDC. Operates like a plug-in, offering service providers the opportunity to add new services without costly coding delays or system downtime, which enables new services to be configured rapidly allowing for quick time-to-market and substantial cost savings.

Product console. Allows the service provider's marketing managers to create product offerings, pricing, and bundles quickly and easily through a Web-based graphical user interface.

Rule-based rating engine. Allows service providers to develop complex rating rules in a simple, logical manner.

Customer care module. Includes a highly customizable HTML interface application for customer service representatives and for self-care.

The architecture is well suited to meet the competitive pressures inherent in the explosive growth opportunities of the Internet. The key is to provide value-added features and truly differentiate services. IAF Horizon can meet all the requirements of speed, reliability, and unlimited access.

NetFlow usage-based billing for broadband services allows network operators and service providers to create, manage, and bill usage-based offerings. In the world of the Internet, it extends beyond the concept of purely measuring and rating units such as seconds or bytes. The usage metric is becoming a rich combination of bytes, bandwidth used, time-of-day, QoS, level of service, application, source, and destination information. This allows service providers to differentiate offerings, influence user behavior, and extract the value from the network. Through the use of NetFlow as a collector of flows of data traffic in an IP network, IAF Horizon can rate and bill for actual usage through a dedicated network connection.

NetFlow switching is a high-performance network layer path that captures traffic statistics, including per-user, per-protocol, per-port, and per-type of service statistics. NetFlow FlowCollectors provide fast, scalable, and economic data collection from multiple routers exporting NetFlow data records. It collects data and reduces data volume through filtering and aggregation. A *network flow* is defined as a unidirectional sequence of packets between given source and destination endpoints. Flows are highly granular—flow endpoints are identified both by IP address as well as port numbers of the transport layer application, for example WWW and FTP. Practically any usage can be billed.

The IAF Rater uses rule-based rating to maximize flexibility and performance. Rating options include

- Specific unit prices.
- Quantity-based rating and discount.
- Fixed-price and percentage-off discounting.
- Time-of-day or time-of-week filtered rating and discounting.
- Stop and tier discount plans.
- Pricing according to source and destination IP address.
- Prorating subscription on fees.
- Tiered pricing may be established separately for Internet, intranet, or extranet.

Mobile data services introduced with GPRS represent new revenue opportunities for mobile service providers (MSP) through differentiated product offerings. With IAF support, MSPs can rapidly and cost-efficiently offer mobile IP services that can be bundled with traditional GSM services. IAF provides the tools for effective service management, customer care and rating, allowing MSPs to provision, collect and bill for GPRS services. The customer care and billing software can improve existing GSM solutions in this field through seamless integration with GPRS solutions from wireless vendors.

IAF offers a seamless interface and workflow for system users by integrating with legacy GSM systems. Integrating with existing GSM components such as the Home Location Register (HLR) and workflow systems ensures consistent customer information for both GSM and GPRS services. IAF empowers existing billing systems by enabling bundling of traditional mobile services and new data services available with GPRS.

Product Console helps MSPs attract new customers and/or incremental revenues by bundling new services such as GPRS Access Service, Internet, intranet, e-mail, and WAP applications with traditional GSM services. It has a carrier-grade billing system, which uses a rule-based rating engine that supports rating on any service attribute, including data volumes and value of content. It can support pricing plans for roaming subscribers when roaming agreements are in place. Billing supports postpaid and prepaid services for both corporate and consumer offerings.

The IAF infrastructure is distributed, and capable of supporting a very large number of subscribers. It consists of three main components (Figure 7.13):

1. IAF server.

2. IAF database.

3. IAF provisioning data collectors (PDC).

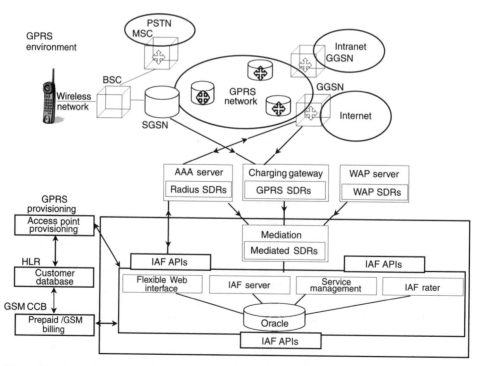

Figure 7.13 Components of the IAF infrastructure.

The Charging Gateway within the GPRS network consolidates event records from network elements, such as the Radius server and WAP server. IAF collects event records via PDCs, providing a layer of business mediation for complex rating schemes such as split billing. IAF is designed to support IP services available today as well as future IP services that will be offered by UTMS.

Customer care offers WAP-based self-care, allowing mobile users to manage their own accounts by providing access to personal information directly from their mobile terminal. WAP self-care includes changing passwords, viewing transactions, and bundling invoices. Self-care results in higher customer satisfaction while reducing MSP costs. There is also less churn, especially when customers are offered a variety of invoice options, such as paper, e-mail, HTML, and WAP. MSPs can manage customer acquisition through autoregistration, a cost-effective approach that allows mobile subscribers to sign up for services and offerings without the assistance of a customer service representative.

The reporting feature includes key reports on revenue, subscriber growth, churns, fraud, and receivables aging. Reporting on third-party revenue and roaming agreements allows service providers to effectively manage important partnerships. Services can be grouped for profitability. Reporting allows other key systems to access critical financial and subscriber data as required.

A variety of business models may be supported, including:

Sponsored services. MSPs can set up a service to be sponsored by a third-party sponsor.

Revenue sharing. MSPs can utilize the services of a value-added service provider to offer its mobile users a wide range of services and applications.

Virtual mobile service provider. MSPs can set up discrete services for a virtual MSP. Third-party organizations may wish to offer their customers mobile services. The virtual MSP has complete control over their respective services and can support multiple virtual MSPs.

7.4.4 Infranet from Portal Software, Inc.

Infranet delivers a totally integrated real-time solution that enables users to rapidly develop, price, and provision as many new services as users need to take advantage of the multitude of possible revenue opportunities. In addition, Infranet's sophisticated rating engine and flexible account administration facilities enable users to more effectively manage customer usage and billing as users can stay one step ahead of customers' evolving needs and expectations.

Real-Time Capabilities

Infranet delivers all the real-time functionality needed to be successful in today's market—features simply not available with batch-oriented or quasi–real-time fast batch systems. Its comprehensive real-time architecture means that every business operation is performed as an end-to-end transaction—from data input to final storage in the database—in real time. This enables Infranet to provide a complete range of powerful, integrated capabilities for providers of IP-based services, including the creation and management of customer accounts, development and provisioning of service offerings, and customer activity tracking, rating, and analysis. In the final analysis, a real-time system's most important feature is that it translates directly into satisfied customers. And a satisfied customer is a loyal customer. With Infranet, users can increase revenues and decrease costs while improving customer satisfaction.

Principal Attributes

The use of this product enables businesses to maximize their revenues by the following attributes:

Real-time account creation and provisioning. With Infranet, users can activate services as soon as registration is complete and start capturing revenue from customer usage immediately.

Real-time marketing. The real-time capabilities allow users to make targeted offers to customers while they are online using either demographic data collected during registration or information gleaned from their online activities. Because Infranet provides up-to-date second data for real-time analysis and the ability to immediately add or modify pricing plans and promotions, users can launch a promotion and begin to evaluate its effectiveness immediately.

Real-time integrated financials. Infranet tracks all account activity in real time enabling real-time integration with financial systems. This includes posting event charges to unbilled account receivables, real-time update of general ledger accounts for instant reporting, and real-time billing on demand.

Real-time rating and volume discounting. With the rating engine, events are rated as transactions, in real time, enabling the cost of each event to influence the cost of other events occurring simultaneously. This allows users to implement a multitude of business models including true transaction-based real-time support for prepaid accounts, cross-service real-time volume discounts, credit/debit of nonmonetary resources, and more.

Reduce costs and improve customer satisfaction. Infranet's real-time capabilities can increase customer satisfaction while reducing the costs associated with running the Internet and intranet businesses.

Real-time data validation and credit checking. Infranet reduces the costs of data correction and dealing with customer issues arising from erroneous information by validating customer data for accuracy and completeness as soon as it's entered.

Real-time authorization of service use. Infranet prevents fraud by analyzing account behavior in real time every time service access is attempted. This includes real-time checks for simultaneous usage or blocked services. It also performs real-time credit-limit checking, including real-time availability of prepaid resources.

This provides full support for prepaid business models and helps eliminate the high costs of collecting on bad debt.

Real-time usage rating. Infranet provides immediate revenue assurance by rating usage immediately and ensuring that customers' account balances are always updated in real time. As a result, revenue leakage through the stages of batch processing is eliminated, and cumbersome and costly revenue recovery procedures are no longer needed.

Real-time customer service. Infranet reduces the costs associated with customer service calls by enabling 24×7 customer self-service via the Web. These customers can review their real-time account and balance information at any time and take advantage of special offers. Even when a customer inquiry is directed to a customer service representative (CSR), the CSR always has real-time information available to handle the call most efficiently.

Collaboration with Other Products

The open architecture includes open, documented APIs that allow users to customize standard features and integrate other Internet and enterprise applications such as customer care, call centers, and general ledger accounting systems. Portal offers a suite of modules that integrate Infranet with terminal server hardware, e-mail, IP-telephony gateways, Cisco NetFlow, and Internet applications suites such as Microsoft's Commercial Internet System (MCIS). Through Infranet's APIs and integration tools, service providers can integrate virtually any other application server, network device, or mediation system to support any type of service.

Support for New and Emerging Markets

Infranet fully supports rapidly emerging market opportunities, of which private branding, application hosting, and online content publishing represent some of the more potentially lucrative offerings. Private branding allows users to leverage the outsourcing business model to enable customers to become virtual IP service providers, or branded service providers—offering IP products or services under their own corporate identity without having to build the necessary in-house infrastructure to manage and support them. Infranet's branding wizard enables users to quickly and easily provide private branding capabilities across all service offerings of users. Its comprehensive real-time capabilities enable users to provide customers with a full range of hosted customer management and billing services—account creation, pricing, rating, billing, customer management, and invoicing—all managed within a single Infranet installation. Infranet ensures absolute brand security for customer data, price plans, invoices, and reports, and provides secure, real-time developer access.

Application service providers (ASP) also extend their infrastructure to corporate customers to host access to high-end business applications such as enterprise resource planning (ERP), sales force automation, Web hosting, and eCommerce. Application hosting opens new markets for the service provider and software vendor while enabling small and midsized businesses access to software they could not otherwise afford. ASPs require a next generation customer management and billing system, like Infranet, that is flexible enough to address changing business needs while allowing providers to provision, interact with customers, remit to third parties, and bill for services in real time.

Online content providers and publishers have similar requirements. With Infranet, users can provide real-time access to content based on account privilege and status, charge for content at different service levels, and manage both free and fee-based services. Infranet also integrates with existing applications and systems for digital rights management.

7.5 Best of Suite Products for Order Processing and Provisioning

Best-of-suite products are expected to combine multiple processes into a chain using workflow principles. Usually, products embed existing workflow concepts, for example from Oracle, HP, or Vitria, and implement their order processing and provisioning applications around them.

7.5.1 Telecom Business Solution from MetaSolve

Telecom Business Solution (TBS) is composed of a set of subsystems integrated by a common data and process repository. Each subsystem supports a critical aspect of the customer service provisioning process. Telecom Business Solution is built on MetaSolve's Integrated Telecommunications Information Architecture that addresses enterprise data information management. Figure 7.14 shows each of the subsystems. The subsystems can be described as follows:

Network design. This subsystem brings together the geographical, physical, and logical dimensions of the network into a single, cohesive view supported by a set of integrated equipment administration and network design modules. The equipment administration modules track the installation and configuration of the equipment that forms the hardware platforms of the network. Each of the individual network design modules implements functions that support the management of specific network technologies exhibiting unique design characteristics. A core principle implemented in each of these modules is the support for the logical view of the network. When a design is ready to physically implement, the network management gateways enable the logical network design to be provisioned or to be put into service at the network element level.

Service provisioning. This subsystem utilizes the service request worksheet function, enabling the provisioning engineer to design how to deliver a service in terms of on-net and off-net facilities, as well as future facilities. integration of the service provisioning subsystem with the order management and network design subsys-

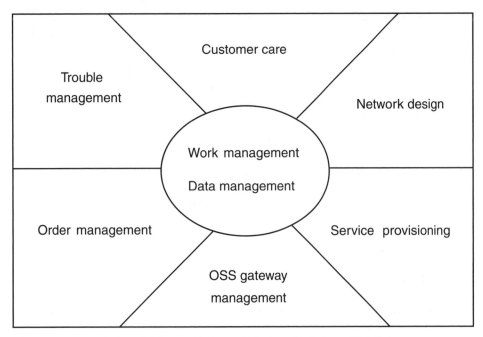

Figure 7.14 Modules of Telecom Business Solution (TBS) from MetaSolve.

tems provides an accurate view of what the customer ordered and what the network can support. When a service design is ready to physically implement, the network management gateways enable flow-through provisioning of the design details to the physical network element level that is addressed by OSS external to TBS.

Order management. This subsystem enables the creation and management of multiple types of orders or transactions within the organization and with other service or network providers as necessary. The work management subsystem coordinates the completion of tasks across work plans for related service requests, by providing a comprehensive look at the status of a given customer's request for service.

Trouble management. This subsystem is integrated with order management, service provisioning, and network design, enabling one comprehensive, consistent view of customer details, what services are provided to them, and how those services are provided. It captures and manages service assurance activities, including trouble tickets originating from customers and from system alarms that are provided by other fault management systems.

Customer care. Customer care is a concept designed to provide the integrated view of customer and network data to internal resources. It is made possible through the integrated telecom information architecture. TBS is dependent on other systems or manual modules for inputting customer details through the order management and trouble management modules or through other external systems for order entry and trouble ticketing.

Work management. This subsystem brings all the pieces together, enabling work to flow electronically across a service provider's organization, giving visibility to processes and resource utilization.

Data management. The Integrated Telecom Information Architecture expresses the business objects, the business relationships between them, and business rules in the form of a relational data model. This architecture promotes data sharing and high levels of data integrity across a service provider's organization.

OSS gateway management. The OSS gateway architecture supports the exchange of information between the TBS software and other systems or external organizations. MetaSolve uses software partners to provide the necessary interconnection support for the access service request (ASR), local service request (LSR), and related electronic bonding functions between carriers.

The TBS software is a three-tier architecture with the following composition:

- The client requires Pentium processor workstations with minimum of 32 MB RAM running Windows 95/98 NT.

- The database server is Oracle 7.3 or higher.

- Operating system is everything compatible with Oracle including Unix, Sun Solaris, HP-UX, IBM Risk 6000, AIX, and NT using personal Oracle.

- Application layer is Windows NT, though MetaSolve is exploring the need to support the server side with Unix.

- All external APIs are CORBA-based, though work is underway to also write each in Microsoft COM. Typically, when a new API is needed, it is first written in CORBA and then in COM. All internal APIs between subsystem modules are written in COM.

7.5.2 Service Fulfillment Products Suite from Nortel/Architel

The Architect OSS product portfolio provides a variety of service fulfillment capabilities including order management, inventory management, design/assign, service activation, and OSS interconnection.

Figure 7.15 represents a summary-level overview of the product suite. Dependencies include third-party applications for customer care and billing, along with fault, performance, traffic, and SLA management functions in support of service assurance. The service fulfillment products include the Objectel Design, Assign and Inventory system, Order Management System, the Automatic Service Activation Program, and InterGate. These products are dependent upon third applications to address the complete service fulfillment and service assurance processes. The functional modules are design, assign, and inventory management.

Objectel is the name of this suite that enables total inventory management for facilities-based service providers. It is a circuit design and network inventory system that allows carriers to automate the network capacity management function and new service

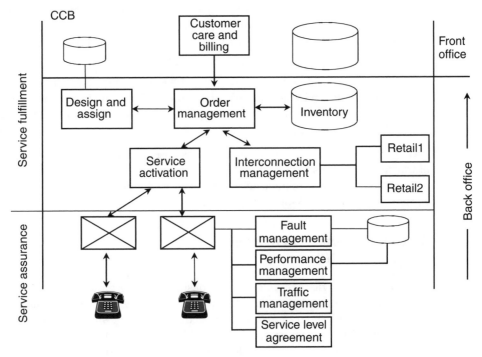

Figure 7.15 Service delivery functional application architecture.

design process to improve service response times and leverage network equipment investment. The physical network inventory is a hierarchical model for both physical facilities and designed circuits. Objectel provides connectivity information and site data using graphical network topology maps and equipment layout displays. This allows a service provider to maintain an accurate inventory of all equipment in the network. Objectel also is focused on the equipment located within a controlled environment rather than the cables and pass-through devices associated with the outside plant environment.

This product supports physical and logical views of the network inventory. It has dependencies upon customer facing systems for collecting customer-related configuration data.

Objectel supports various network domains such as circuit-based technologies, such as DS0, DS1, DS3, and other topologies including ATM, SONET/SDH, frame relay, and IP. The Objectel design manager provides an end-to-end view of assigned physical facilities.

Order Management

OMS is a workflow engine. It addresses the process management needs associated with its service provisioning and activation applications. OMS interfaces with other customer-facing and network-facing systems used in the service fulfillment process. OMS contains several business process templates that represent the service provisioning and service activation needs for a variety of network-based services.

OMS facilitates the exchange of information between a third-party customer care system and network-facing applications such as Objectel Design, Assign and Inventory system, the ASAP service activation system and the InterGate interconnection gateway. OMS contains a number of business process templates optimized to address the service fulfillment function.

OMS provides standard procedural as well as object-oriented interfaces over a variety of transport protocols to permit rapid integration with legacy and contemporary systems. OMS is designed to interface with a heterogeneous environment and provide support to multiple back-office applications.

Automatic Service Activation Program (ASAP)

ASAP is a multiservice activation engine designed to coordinate and perform all needed element activation tasks within a specific service, network domain, or across multiple domains. The transaction-based activation engine supports a variety of wireline, wireless, and transport elements. ASAP service activation engine decomposes a service request into multiple components as needed to address customer services involving one or more network elements. It is dependent on other customer- and network-facing systems to supply a completed service request, for example all customer and network inventory assignment details are defined so that these configuration details can be communicated to the affected network elements.

ASAP interfaces with service provider networks that contain one or more network elements as well as a variety of element management systems. ASAP supports multiple technical interfaces and network management protocols, including Q3, DCE RPC, TL1, TCP/IP (Telnet and Socket), Asynchronous Serial, Dial-Up, SNMP, X.25, X.29, and FTP.

Interconnection Gateway

InterGate is an interconnection gateway that allows service providers to securely exchange and track interconnection requests. InterGate, shown in Figure 7.16, has the ability to support various interconnection message types defined by standards bodies such as the ORB, ECIC, and TMN. InterGate supports the PIC/CARE, LSR, ASR, and trouble-ticketing processes across a variety of protocols including EDI, CMIP, CORBA, and e-mail.

The InterGate OSS interconnection gateway supports the data mapping, protocol translation, and transaction-processing functions for a number of interconnection processes.

Architel has established its products to address several of the scalability issues that are a regular concern for the service provider community. Objectel, OMS, ASAP, and

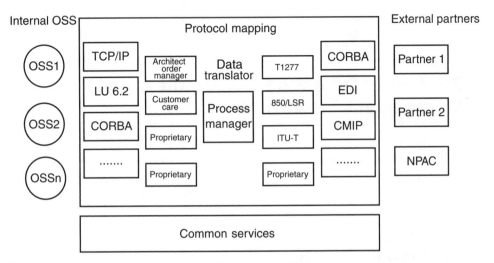

Figure 7.16 Functional architecture of the InterGate OSS.

InterGate applications each provide CORBA-based interfaces. Some applications such as OMS and InterGate also use CORBA internally. This product suite supports a wide variety of scalability needs, as the architecture for each has been designed to address a number of scalability techniques including:

Multithreaded. Multiple simultaneous connections between an application like ASAP and the network elements it communicates with are critical for optimized response time and throughput volumes.

Multiprocess. It allows multiple servers to address specific throughput requirements. This is important for the large number of transaction requests that traverse between ASAP and the many network elements it supports in a large service provider environment.

Distributable. It allows a service provider to run multiple machines and to distribute multiple servers over each machine to address specific functional needs.

Multi-CPU. It supports one or more applications running on multiple CPUs within the same machine or multiple machines according to customer throughput requirements.

Multi-instance. It addresses the need for supporting multiple instances of an application running on one or more machines. This is especially important for addressing transaction-processing needs associated with clustering and for supporting high availability requirements.

With a significant number of customer implementations, Architel understands the scalability concerns of larger carriers.

The product suite addresses a number of technical standards, especially those in support of open communications such as CORBA and CMIP. Architel is actively participating in standard bodies, such as Ordering and Billing Forum (OBF), the Workflow Management Coalition (WfMC), and the TeleManagement Forum (TMF).

7.6 Best of Suite Products for Integrated Management Systems

Integrated management is always the ultimate goal. Besides robust framework solutions, other opportunities also exist. Solutions introduced in this segment usually start with a core product and grow into a higher level of integration by communicating with other management applications using standardized middleware solutions.

7.6.1 Product Suite from Hewlett-Packard

HP is one of the few vendors who offers many solutions to service providers. The OpenView family is well known as a platform for integrating enterprise management applications. HP has been implementing specific applications for telecommunications service providers. A few interesting offers are presented in this segment.

Changengine

In the area of service delivery, HP has key products such as HP Changengine, partnerships with vertical market solution vendors, and a large and experienced delivery channel with HP consulting. Service delivery is about the creation, selling, installation, provisioning, and billing of a service, product, or collection of products to customers. The customer could be a private or a business customer including other service providers. In particular, solutions are valuable for xDSL and IP/VPN service offers. They bring the following benefits

- Get services to the market faster
- Have a quicker rollout of services
- Significantly reduce service delivery times to the customer
- Enable self-provisioning of services
- Potentially reduce human resources demand
- Be able to measure service and delivery levels
- Be able to leverage existing technologies and infrastructures

Service delivery crosses a range of departmental, application, and network equipment boundaries. It affects both OSSs, such as network activation, and BSSs, such as order management. By crossing these technological and departmental boundaries, it still needs manual intervention for tasks such as installation. Changengine is a powerful workflow management system that integrates automated and manual processes. It includes

- Service order handling
- Service configuration
- Network provisioning
- Network configuration

By integrating these individual processes, this product takes advantage of the guidelines of Enterprise Application Integration (EAI). At a very high level an EAI product provides the ability to abstract application functionality as reuseable business services. It will then provide infrastructure components to use these services and pass data and business events through to other business services. Depending on the product, other functionality such as business-level reporting, data transformation, and high-level business modeling tools may be available.

Processes are graphically created and modified and are then managed and run by HP Changengine. The processes themselves map directly how a service provider delivers services to their customers. The product controls the processes and delivers work to users or interfaces with the business application using the application integration technology. With the diversity of BSS and OSS applications, a flexible and robust application integration environment is required. ActiveWorks Integration System from Active Software is an integration environment that already has over 50 adapters to different applications and provides the architecture on which to create further integration points. The tight integration with HP Changengine enables Changengine to manage the service delivery processes, metrics, and user community and can direct ActiveWorks to interface with OSS and BSS applications where required.

HP WebQoS

HP WebQoS allows service providers strong business-oriented service-level agreements by maintaining consistent response time and high reliability, even under extreme loading conditions. Customers can use the combined strength of HP OpenView VantagePoint and Keynote Perspective to identify Web site slowdowns while using the integration of HP WebQoS to systematically control and resolve instances where Web site demand is above capacity.

Managing Converged Voice and Data Networks

HP's OpenView Communications SNMP Management Integration (OVC/SMI) facilitates the management of converged voice and data networks. It is available across the complete Communications Service Assurance solution suite. OVC/SMI simplifies the process of integrating SNMP topology and alarm data with telecommunications-related data on HP Service Assurance products. It enables service providers to quickly and easily create an integrated graphical view of voice and data network topologies and alarms on a common user interface.

The OVC/SMI software collects SNMP vendor MIBs and SNMP topology and trap data from HP's OpenView Network Node Manager (NNM). The customer uses these data and OVC/SMI configuration tools to create configuration files that define the topology and trap mapping. Once the configuration files are in place, the OVC/SMI's SNMP Adapter maps the incoming SNMP alarm data to X.733 format and passes them to the OVO/Assurance. There, they are processed, correlated with events from network elements and element management systems, and displayed by the OVC fault management system.

This solution includes a selection of default configuration choices for common SNMP environments. Use of these defaults simplifies and speeds up OVC/SMI deployment, and leads to rapid development of an integrated IP and Telco Assurance System.

OVC/SMI integrates the assurance products with NNM. Any number of NNM's can be connected, so long as the aggregate of SNMP objects and Telecom objects does not exceed the OVC/Assurance managed object and event rate limits.

The OVC/SMI architecture is shown in Figure 7.17. It achieves SNMP integration by adding modular components to OVC/Assurance so that topology uploads and traps can flow from NNM into the fault management platform (FMP). The added components create configuration files that store the mapping information for both trap and topology data for the SNMP objects. The added components also upload the SNMP configuration data to the OVC/SMI fault management platform.

The SNMP configurator (1) loads relevant SNMP MIBs and NNM trap and symbol configuration files. The customer chooses the subset of elements and traps to be included in the OVC/Assurance fault management process. The configurator is used to create SNMP trap-to-X.733 mappings based on the selected NNM configuration

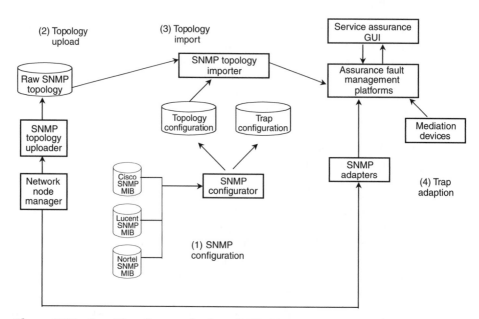

Figure 7.17 OpenView Communications SNMP Management Integration.

files. Finally, the configurator validates consistency with upper-level OVC/Assurance models.

The SNMP topology uploader (2) uses SNMP protocol (trap/get) to upload the NNM topology subset chosen during the configuration step (1). The uploader creates a raw data file of SNMP objects with related information and attributes. The uploader recognizes data from NNM, and also from SNMP manager written by other companies.

The SNMP topology importer (3) translates the raw SNMP topology data into OVC/Assurance SNMP topology object data and passes the translated data to the OVC/Assurance fault management platform. Both the raw data and translated data files are ASCII and can be easily edited. Also, the topology map Perl script used in the translation can be edited. OVC/SMI provides full access to the ASCII-based configuration files and allows for customization of the SNMP trap mapping and topology data mapping.

The importer and uploader can be rerun periodically to update the topology with auto-discovered SNMP objects, provided the MIBs and trap configurations for such objects were included in the configuration step.

The SNMP adapter (4) uses trap configuration files from the SNMP configurator and topology object data from the topology importer to correctly map incoming SNMP trap data into X.733 alarm format and send them to the OVC/Assurance fault management platform. The translated SNMP topology and trap data are then integrated with the telco topology and alarm information in the OVC/Assurance display.

This solution provides a powerful set of integrated service management functions, including a consolidated view of network resources, comprehensive monitoring, and control of heterogeneous network elements. Combined with the NNM functionality, which automatically discovers SNMP network devices and provides a map to display and monitor the ongoing status of the data network, HP OVC simplifies the management of converged networks. The result is an automated solution that provides a single view of voice and data networks, accelerating the delivery of services to market and providing a distinct competitive advantage for service providers.

Smart Internet Usage from Hewlett-Packard

SIU collects, aggregates, and correlates usage data from across networks and IP services infrastructure. It collects usage data from a full range of routers, switches, probes, gateways, and applications including Cisco's NetFlow technology. It presents the data in an open, user-configurable format. This allows users to implement usage-based billing systems, manage capacity, and analyze subscriber's needs and behavior to develop strategic marketing programs and profitable value-added services. Key features are highlighted in the following text.

Distributed DataStore (DDS) Architecture

SIU's architecture includes Distributed DataStore, a unique technology that enables data collection at or close to the source and user-configurable distribution of collector hierarchies. This provides virtually unlimited scalability for large networks. Industry standard CORBA technology is leveraged to ensure robust communications between remote components. SIU's highly modular design provides very flexible configuration control and load balancing for a very wide diversity of service provider applications.

Flexibility of Output

With the internet data record (IDR), SIU features completely configurable output formats, without having to write any code. Users can configure SIU to output its results as HTML, XML, ASCII-delimited records, ASCII-fixed field reports, binary records, or as an SQL database schema. The choice of attributes that are mapped into various fields are totally up to the user.

Scalability

SIU has been designed for scalability from the ground up. SIU can be easily scaled across multiple networks, across multiple geographic locations, and to millions of subscribers.

Carrier-Grade High Availability

SIU has been designed for scalability. SIU can be configured to ensure no single point of failure causes a loss of critical accounting data or the data mediation to be interrupted.

Multiple Platforms

SIU is available on HP-UX, Microsoft Windows NT, and Sun Solaris. Since SIU was developed in Java, it can easily be ported to additional platforms.

Configurable Aggregation Schemes

Without having to write any code, users can specify multiple, simultaneous aggregation and correlation schemes using a rich tool set provided with SIU. These can be tailored to feed multiple, simultaneous different usage applications for real-time policy-driven data correlation.

User-Defined Attributes

SIU provides extensive capability for systems integrators to specify new adornment attributes for new data sources or new applications.

Metering/Billing Options

- Time of day
- Source or destination location
- Megabytes of traffic used
- Service or end-application accessed
- Quality of service (QoS) levels
- Subscriber class membership
- Nontraffic resources

Data Sources

SIU collects usage data from four major types of data sources, which include

- *Networks.* Routers, switches, gateways
- *Access services.* Radius, session managers
- *IP services.* Web hosts, VPN, e-mail, application servers
- *Systems applications.* Resource utilization, disk usage

To deliver the SIU billing solution, HP has encouraged broad industry participation to enable service providers to confidently select billing applications and system integration partners suited to their usage-management requirements. HP will work with billing partners to ensure integration between the IDR and the billing application. HP will also provide comprehensive training on SIU to maximize success with usage management and to help partners more successfully deliver usage-management solutions.

7.6.2 Netcool Suite from Micromuse

The Netcool suite is considered a valuable service-level management application. Netcool creates an environment for viewing the availability of network services in real time. The suite includes client/server configurable applications that collect events, customize views of IT services, and generate reports on the network compliance with SLAs.

Due to the client/server technology, application software can be distributed across the network. The application software collects fault information and filters noise from across the network. Its primary advantages are that it installs rapidly and allows individual operators to customize views of service by responding to simple onscreen prompts. SNMP and non-SNMP management systems become strategic management elements. It is commonly used as the core management desktop since it consolidates data from various network management consoles, transmission infrastructures, telephony devices, data networks, LANs, WANs, and applications.

It has five basic architectural elements: Probes, ObjectServers, Desktops, Filters, and Gateways (see Figure 7.18). In short, Probes bring data into the system; the Object-Server performs all processing; the Desktops allow operators to view, manipulate, and act on the data; the Filters allow operators to design personalized views of events and services; Gateways pass information to other external applications.

Table 7.1 displays the most important components of Netcool.

The Netcool suite has four basic qualities service providers are demanding:

1. *Adaptable.* Netcool integrates seamlessly with the existing infrastructure and is capable of rapidly adapting to change. The server portion of the system runs on all the major Unix operating systems, while the client portion adapts to 50 different environments off the shell. From a user perspective, the system is easy to configure, administer over time, delivering a low cost of ownership. It supports

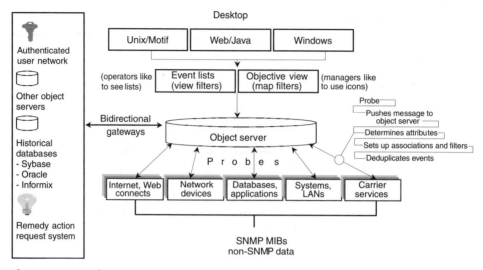

Figure 7.18 Architecture of Netcool.

adaptable empowering operators and developers with flexible tools of collecting, filtering, correlating, and displaying information in a highly customized fashion.

2. *Customizable.* Netcool is customizable on two levels. First, it easily accommodates any network environment by collecting fault data from over 100 different management environments. Second, it allows each operator to custom-build personal views of event data and service availability information using a drag-and-drop set of SQL-like filters.

3. *High performance.* For Netcool, there is a memory-resident active database that stores events and services as object-based data. It also provides features that allow services to be defined and event management to be carried out in real time in extremely high–event-load networks.

4. *Scalable.* At a technical level, management products face a problem of scale. It is possible to predict an event rate in a network. A small network may generate a large number of events, while a large network may generate proportionally fewer events per element. To scale to any environment, the management applications input system nodes to be extremely fast and scalable. Netcool's client/server architecture enables maximum scalability.

The Netcool suite of service-level management applications provides real-time updates on network service and application availability for operators in the network operations centers of service providers and corporate enterprises. In addition to real-time event analysis, history reports are also required. These reports allow management of service providers to review historical summaries on network availability and underlying events. This allows them to make informed planning decisions and to determine if availability, service, and cost-containment goals are being met. Netcool

Table 7.1 Components of Netcool

COMPONENTS	DESCRIPTION
Probe	Passive supersets of code that collect events from more than 100 management data sources, which are stored, viewed, and manipulated in the ObjectServer.
ObjectServer	An in-memory active database, optimized for collecting events and designing filters and views, which provides the core processing functions for Netcool.
Desktops	It is a suite of graphical operator tools, running under Windows, NT, or Java, that provide the front-end customizing filters and service views.
EventObject	The single object entity status and event becomes when stored in ObjectServer, allowing advanced filtering and viewing manipulators (as compared to flat database records).
EventList	Spreadsheet-like interfaces into ObjectServer event data and color-coded events according to severity, and provide information useful for troubleshooting each event.
EventList Console	Object-based screen interface showing the status of enterprise-wide services using color-coded lamps representing a summary of event severity within each service.
ObjectiveView	Object-based topographical front-end tool set, which allows operators to build clickable maps, icons, and other graphical interfaces to ObjectServer data and EventLists.
FilterBuilder	Desktop interface based on Boolean correlation tools, which allows operators to associate collected event data with the availability of business services.
ViewBuilder	Desktop utility that allows operators to design personalized views of events and services by selecting user-interface preferences.
Gateways	Bidirectional interfaces that allow ObjectServer data to be shared with other ObjectServers, RDBMS archives, or trouble-ticketing applications.
ReportServer	Java-based data engine for Netcool Reporter that formats, processes, and schedules reports on service object availability, which can match the metrics in service level agreements.
Internet Service Monitors	Suite of active monitors that determine availability and response times of key Internet protocols and services: HTML, FTP, DNS, SMTP, POP-3, NNTP, and Radius.

Reporter is a query and reporting tool that provides interaction with Netcool data archived in various databases. The multithreaded Java-based application allows management to analyze key historical information over the Web using standard Web browsers. In addition, it allows the rapid creation of a wide variety of charts, graphs, or text-based reports.

The product can also be successfully used by Internet service providers. Netcool provides real-time monitoring of all elements that make up an ISPs network and all services that are affected by outages of those elements. Netcool/Impact helps Netcool EventList operators answer three fundamental questions when faced with a critical event:

1. What specific processes, applications, and people are affected (impact analysis)?

2. How should the operator prioritize work to handle the most critical tasks first (response and prioritization)?

3. Who is responsible at this moment in time for this problem, and what policy do they follow to fix it as rapidly as possible (policy-based fault management)?

Netcool/Impact provides impact analysis and facilitates policy-based management of real-time events and operator-initiated queries by leveraging data from different data sources and using them to define and enforce policies.

The primary technical advantage of Netcool/Impact is that it automates the time-consuming process of resolving events. Operators typically respond to events manually or by searching corporate data structures for resolution policy and procedure information. It accelerates the time to respond to events and ensures that the response is successful by leveraging existing institutional knowledge and incorporating it into the operational environment. Operators can concentrate on other tasks instead of just troubleshooting problems. It augments the problem resolution capabilities of the ObjectServer, helping to maintain availability of applications and services. As a Netcool suite application, it deploys quickly and provides a rapid return on investment. It builds a bridge between real-time network event feeds and relevant information stored throughout the service provider's network that can be used to determine how specific events will affect business processes, services, and customers.

It accesses existing institutional knowledge in external databases and utilizes their inherit relationships. It can pinpoint the effect of a single event or generate how types of events affect services and users. In addition, Netcool/Impact can also automatically warn users about a pending problem before they notice a disruption in service. It helps organizations more efficiently resolve problems by automatically assigning incoming faults and events to particular support technicians and establishes the event status so technicians can prioritize their work. It also facilitates policy management by letting operators define resolution procedures for particular events. It supports event escalation by keeping track of the time it takes for technicians or administrators to acknowledge an event and resolve the problem. If the event remains outstanding for a designated time period, it escalates the event up the chain of responsibility.

7.6.3 SmallWorld from SmallWorld Communications

This product provides an integrated business and operations support solution for the network operator, delivering benefits by unlocking the value of the spatial data building integrating solutions that link

- Customer and network domains
- Inside and outside plants
- Physical plants and logical circuits
- Engineering design and network operations

Significantly, the solutions play a vital role in automating key business processes such as planning, network design and engineering, service provisioning, network maintenance and restoration, and by doing so provide

- Increased operational efficiency
- Higher customer service levels
- Capability to rapidly deploy new technologies and services
- Data and application sharing
- Analysis and presentation of data
- Continuous process flow-through

Figure 7.19 shows the model of the product. It is capable of displaying the total network—combining data from network operations, planning, maintenance, and circuit analysis, with the actual data from the physical network inventory. Adherence to open systems standards has resulted in the development of applications that integrate with existing systems while handling most types of corporate data used in communications, thereby avoiding time-consuming translation processes. The product family consists of five independent, but integrated applications.

Circ.it

It enables circuit assignment, bandwidth allocation, and capacity planning. It helps customers to develop and manage an accurate model of the assignable elements in

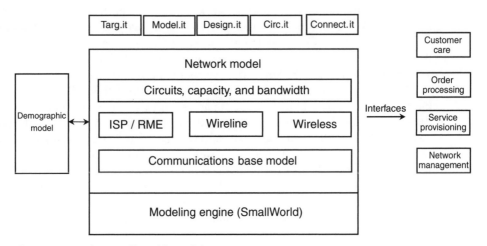

Figure 7.19 The SmallWorld model.

the network, including facilities, the physical path of a communication signal, the bandwidth across a facility, the data rate and the protocol riding on the facility. In addition, it provides manual and semiautomated circuit routing, including preference, avoidance, and least cost routing, as well as path protection and diversity. It is part of an integrated network engineering/network management operations support system environment, building on top of model.it. It presents a unified view of circuit infrastructure, showing the complete utilization picture—viewing facilities, connections and circuits throughout the network, all in a single, data-driven system.

Targ.it

It analyzes the business data of customers to help achieve maximum return of investment (ROI) for new build or leasing lines. It enables service providers to interrogate all business data by offering integration of geographical data with strategic datasets in the particular environment. This set of software tools provides a structured approach to market analysts by taking users through the process, from defining catchment areas for products and services to analyzing and visualizing these in the form of maps, reports, and graphs. In addition, the open environment enables integration with other business tools such as churn, fraud, and billing systems. It provides key applications for:

- *Prebuild analysis.* Targeting new build to maximize penetration against cost.

- *Postbuild analysis.* Analyzing revenue, penetration, and churn values against predicted models.

- *Operational support.* Targeting direct marketing campaigns, analyzing sales performance.

Model.it

It provides the fundamental building blocks to meet the network management challenges that lie ahead. It helps service providers to develop and manage an accurate, maintainable, end-to-end model of physical network components, from the switch to the subscriber locations, to help service providers more efficiently engineer and manage wireline networks. The application supports input of data either by translation, capture from paper records, or from data in the field, and allows different states of the network to be maintained, including an as-built view of the network. So up-to-date information is stored representing both the inside plant rack-mounted equipment and the outside plant fiber, coax, and copper components. It can also model the cable and equipment layout inside office and residential buildings, and generate schematic representations to provide the different views of the network required by different users. The familiar Windows-based interface enables fast and easy access to data while reducing overall costs. Physical network data are stored in a standards-compliant relational database that enables easy integration with other corporate operations support systems.

Design.it

As regulator build rates increase the pressure on service providers to achieve network construction, design.it provides a powerful set of tools for automating design processes, significantly reducing the time and cost of this operation. Automated routing and design tools are provided for fast and accurate layout of the fiber, copper, and coax networks. Cables with associated equipment can be routed through underground trenches or on overhead structures, and designs can then be costed, producing bill of material reports. In addition, it provides tools for managing duct space records. Complex cross-sectional views of the trenches and ducts can be built automatically, during routine operations to manage duct capacity and utilization.

Connect.it

It links network inventory with operations. SmallWorld solutions provide open systems interoperability of applications and operational systems, achieving integration in order to streamline business processes. This is key to providing continuous process flow-through in the BSS and OSS environment. There are a number of key processes, such as service provisioning, network restoration and maintenance, and customer care. To offer complete solutions for these processes, connect.it integrates with other key business systems, such as

- Network management
- Workorder and asset management
- Order handling
- Billing
- Subscriber management
- Trouble ticketing

Integration with these systems is achieved using standard mechanisms, including CORBA, OLE/COM, and ODBC. The system architecture of the SmallWorld product family enables work with multiple management platforms, including products from Compaq, Hewlett-Packard, Oracle, Objective Systems Integrators, SAP, and Telcordia. The architecture of SmallWorld is displayed in Figure 7.20.

7.6.4 Cisco Solution Center

Cisco content networking delivers the intelligent network services required to drive the next generation Internet business model. Through the dynamic recognition of Internet business applications, such as eCommerce, supply chain management, and workforce optimization, network services are engaged to achieve end-to-end performance, availability, and security. Content networking architecture has three components:

1. Intelligent traffic classification and network services delivered through Cisco's operating system.

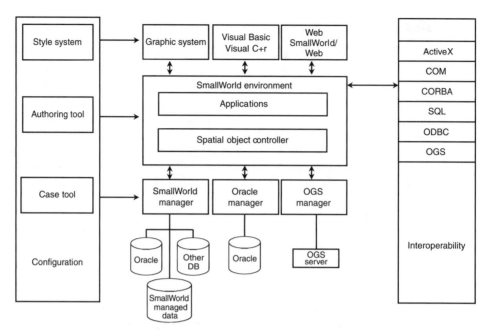

Figure 7.20 The SmallWorld architecture.

2. Intelligent network devices that integrate Internet business applications with network services.

3. Intelligent policy management framework for configuration, monitoring, and accounting.

Before the proliferation of an eCommerce business model, the services offered by service providers were founded on Layer 2 and Layer 3 technologies. These services included the migration from a shared Layer 2 environment to a switched environment as well as routing services from a Layer 3 perspective. Typical tasks were IP address management, any-to-any connectivity for both Layer 2 and Layer 3, routing protocol maintenance, and in some cases quality of service (QoS) guarantees for specific applications. These tasks were typically performed under a specific service-level agreement, assuring uptime. This framework can be considered an internetworking environment, as the emphasis is on the any-to-any connectivity of end users over specific networks to servers on other networks. Other offerings in this internetworking model were transparent LAN services for simple Layer 2 connectivity or virtual private networks (VPNs) across a shared network.

Content networking builds upon internetworking and, in fact, assumes that internetworking is guaranteeing maximum uptime with any-to-any connectivity using the intelligence of routing and the speed of switching. The driver for content networking is the need to provide intelligent wire-speed Layer 4 through Layer 7 services in new eCommerce environments. Because the fast adoption rate of the Internet is a key to business growth, market and competitive pressures are increasingly being put on service providers to deliver secure and reliable Web and application hosting services. The final result is that service providers—whether commercial or internal to the enterprise—must now be aware of host and content availability. The same service-level agreements that were put in place for simple connectivity will now be expected for Layer 4 and Layer 7 services. ContentFlow is the framework that will allow service providers to offer these services in a reliable, scalable, and manageable manner.

Cisco is playing a key role of creating, deploying, and implementing IP-based services. Besides providing equipment and element management systems, Cisco assists service providers to

- Select management frameworks
- Integrate management applications
- Support QoS-based SLAs
- Partner with companies who provide supplementary solutions

Figure 7.21 shows the structure of the solution center. InfoCenter is the closest to the operational management of service providers. The core product is NetCool that is being customized for interfacing other managers and peering other centers. InfoCenter is working with a number of products offering usage-based billing and performance trending. Infranet from Portal and IMS from Belle Systems are the closest to InfoCenter. In both cases, NetFlow from Cisco is the key information source.

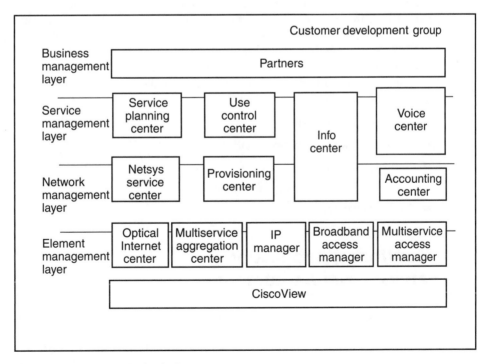

Figure 7.21 Structure of solution center.

NetFlow collects a rich set of traffic statistics from its routers and switches. These statistics include user, protocol, port, and type of service requested and delivered. Unlike conventional switching where incoming information packets go through access list checks, accounting data collection, and switching one by one, only the first packet in a flow goes through the whole process with NetFlow collection. All subsequent packets are processed on a connection-oriented basis. Network flows are defined as a unidirectional sequence of packets between given source and destination endpoints within a given time frame. Flow endpoints are identified by their IP addresses, as well as by transport layer application port numbers, such as WWW, e-mail, and so on.

For successful operations, NetFlow should be configured in routers properly, including

- Product initial item code
- Product periodic item code
- Incoming bytes for net groups
- Outgoing bytes for net groups
- Internet item code
- Phone item code

Cisco has developed a phased plan for delivering policy-based management tools for enterprise VPNs that also leverage the features of Cisco Powered Networks deployed by service providers. In the initial phases, VPN features are integrated into the Cisco-Works 2000 product family, enabling Web-based, end-to-end management of Cisco networks. Through CiscoWorks 2000 enhancements, network managers can manage security and QoS parameters of VPNs. In the final phases, policy-based management of VPN features and security parameters are added and extended to include DEN management. Furthermore, Cisco provides tools for measuring and monitoring service provider performance against service-level agreement commitments. In particular, the following tools are included:

- Response time reporter
- Internetwork performance monitor
- Security manager
- Access control list management tools
- QoS policy manager

7.7 Monitoring Applications for Service Level Agreements

Quality of service in SLAs cannot be managed without the necessary support by measurement and reporting tools. This segment is devoted to state-of-the art product examples. Most likely, service providers need multiple tools in combination to meet all the requirements in their SLAs signed with their customers or with other providers.

7.7.1 Health Monitor
from Concord Communications

Technology managers face increasing pressure from both budget-conscious corporate managers and technology-dependent end users to document the quality and consistency of information technology services. Provision of regular, meaningful service-level metrics forms the basis of effective service level agreements between IT providers and IT customers. Today, the process of collecting, analyzing, presenting, and distributing service-level information represents an enormous investment of time and expertise, yet still leaves senior management demanding more frequent, reliable, and meaningful documentation of service levels.

Network Health Service Level Reports automate the collection, analysis, presentation, and distribution of service-level information. They consist of three reports:

1. *Executive report.* A single-page summary of service-level performance across the enterprise. Executives can review the previous period's activity with respect to their own service-level definitions. The report also summarizes the monthly activity of the organization's most important business units, giving managers the relative effect of how their business units are affecting IT service.

2. *IT manager report.* An immediate summary report on service levels across the IT environment, from clear visibility of long-term trends at the enterprise level, to general service-level performance by business units, down to detailed service-level metrics on a device-by-device basis. IT managers can customize the report by selecting devices and service-level metrics, as well as a specific time frame for inclusion in the report.

3. *Service customer report.* A single-page, site-specific, monthly summary of service-level information for service customers. This report identifies long-term service trends, provides a customer-wide service-level trend, as measured by exception totals, and details service level for each of the customer's IT devices.

While supporting automated service-level calculation and reporting at an aggregate level, the service-level reports maintain the ability to deliver information on individual IT elements, such as routers, WAN lines, frame relay circuits, or servers. Through custom element tables, the reports calculate and report on service level, measured by availability, latency, bandwidth distribution, among other metrics, on individual network or server devices. Management information provided include the following metrics:

Availability. Measures how often IT resources are available to IT customers; it is one of the most important metrics for evaluating IT effectiveness.

Latency. Measures how fast the network moves information, a critical indicator of service level for technology end users.

Bandwidth distribution. Provides a key measurement of IT service levels, as high-bandwidth utilization is closely linked to poor IT service.

Network volume. Measures network traffic trends by enterprise or region; a key indicator of overall usage trends of IT resources.

Exception trends. Sums and trends the volume of network health exceptions over time. By defining thresholds to trigger exceptions at a breach of service level, IT managers can manage overall service level by tracking the total number of exceptions.

Health index. Measures service level enterprise-wide or by individual IT elements, identifying the relative contributors to poor service.

Technology-specific metrics. Measure service level by monitoring critical performance metrics on network and systems hardware such as errors, faults, collisions, buffer utilization, and discards.

The company has started early to offer information and all types of reports via the Web. After completing the analysis, report content is converted into HTML pages and housed on Web servers. Besides service-level reports, the following additional reports are available:

LAN/WAN reports. Analyze the traffic on network infrastructures, reporting on the performance of individual segments, rings, and WAN circuits.

Frame relay reports. Extend the scope of LAN/WAN reports, and help to manage cost-effectiveness on frame relay investments.

Router/switch reports. Analyze how efficiently internetworking devices are managing the network load, and help to pinpoint specific devices causing problems.

Server reports. Measure the availability of servers on which key applications reside. They also report on key server performance metrics including CPU, memory, disk, and communication utilization.

ATM reports. Help to maximize ATM deployment with quality of service measurements and usage information.

Traffic accountant reports. Look at RMON2 and application-layer data to identify users, groups, and applications driving traffic.

Network Health understands the information IT managers need and automatically collects, analyzes, and distills the information down to key points. Without visibility across different vendors' devices and technologies, it is difficult to make informed, enterprise-wide capacity planning and investment decisions. Network Health delivers automation on three levels.

Automation of Device Discovery and Configuration

It automatically discovers network devices and configurations itself. It supports standards like SNMP, MIB II, RMON1, and RMON2, coupled with an extensive library of supported devices, saves operations team time and resources. And, with new devices constantly being added to the Network Health list of supported equipment, managers are assured that Network Health will grow with them and continue to support deployment of new technologies as networks expand.

Automatic Trend Analysis

It collects and applies key metrics to condense data into only the critical information needed to optimize network performance. Network managers eliminate hours typically spent in writing programs to access and collect key data as well as time often spent to further analyze and present the information to management. Its colorful, easy-to-understand formats enable network managers to easily assess the status of their network, identify potential problems, and recognize their trends.

Automatic Report Distribution

It allows the IT or network management organization to tailor the content, distribution, and presentation of valuable information to fit the requirements of just about any internal process. Service-level reports are usually delivered via the Web. Managers responsible for specific regions or devices receive daily reports that highlight exceptions and trends based upon their existing business processes and customized to the needs of their specific environments. Service providers can send out reports to their customers, tailored to the customer's resources and service-level goals.

The Web interface gives an immediate access to performance reports across the whole enterprise and automates the process of distributing reports to consumers across the organization. Clicking on the actual reports on the desktop gives users additional details on specific network elements, down to the port and interface card level. The Web interface also features online help and makes it easy to drill down for additional detail and correlation of trends across technologies.

Network Health includes a powerful, integrated relational database and a graphical console. The database stores the collected data, while the analysis engine analyzes historical resource requirements and trends as well as forecasts future resource requirements. Network Health is running on SunSparc and HP 9000 under Solaris and HP/UX. It also runs on Intel P2 under NT 4.00 SP 3 and 4.

7.7.2 VistaView from InfoVista

This product is a Web-based distributed solution, capable of scaling to large organizations with multiple branch offices. Its architecture permits scheduled, on-demand, or real-time reports of service-level compliance or violation for network equipment and facilities. Also, end-to-end application performance can be reported.

The InfoVista engine collects data from a variety of sources, calculates the metrics, and stores the results for long-term analysis. The InfoVista Workshop is a GUI tool that allows easy creation of new metrics and definition of business-relevant indicators and expressions. VistaViews are ready-to-use sets of reports that target specific problems, such as WAN, LAN, applications, and so on, giving immediate visibility on service delivery of the IT infrastructure. They were all created using the workshop and come with comprehensive documentation that explains how to interpret each report and how to act based on its content. VistaViews collect data from networked infrastructures and provide graphical reports in hourly, daily, weekly, or monthly format. All reports can also be monitored in real time for troubleshooting and fine-tuning. Each VistaView application offers three types of reports:

1. Detailed reports enable IT operations staff to quickly troubleshoot performance problems.

2. Exception reports provide immediate information on exceptional situations and are targeted at network and IT managers.

3. Executive reports offer a synopsis of service levels and trends over a designated period and are targeted at CIO/network managers to help them make strategic decisions.

The following reports are available

- VistaView for routers
- VistaView for Ethernet switches
- VistaView for LAN segments
- VistaView for network service levels
- VistaView for WAN circuits
- VistaView for frame relay
- VistaView for ATM switches
- VistaView for remote access servers
- VistaView for BMC patrol agents
- VistaView for Compaq insight agents
- VistaView for Internet applications
- VistaView for enterprise servers
- VistaView for help-desk

The VistaMart product line is a telco-class software that combines real-time management with powerful business process analysis, offering a repository that can integrate with help-desks and proprietary metrics, as well as corporate information; back-office features such as data analysis/mining; central management; and the ability to combine multisourced quality of service measurements with trouble ticketing systems, application monitoring, and so on, providing a complete picture of quality of service.

7.7.3 SiteScope from Freshwater Software

The quality of Web sites is a mirror for the company. Public Web sites tell visitors how the Web site owners appreciate time and interest of visitors. Internal Web sites connected by intranets tell how Web site owners appreciate productivity of the company employees.

Web servers fail—an event obvious to all types of network and system management tools. Web applications fail for a lot of reasons that are not so obvious. There may be network failures, modem and dialing problems, excessive firewall controls, invalid page links, application bugs, DNS failures, resources overloaded due to a surge in traffic, poor back-end database performance, or other events preventing Web application availability.

To discover these problems, react to them rapidly, and prevent their recurrence by root-cause analysis, Webmasters need to monitor the Web server, network devices on both sides of the firewall, and application services such as e-mail and databases. Webmasters and Web administrators need to constantly test the application for response time and accuracy. Discovering that the application does not return the correct answer in a reasonable time and reporting that information to the responsible staff, are the first steps in improving application availability. But in order to decide what actions to take, Webmasters need enough information to pinpoint the cause of the problem. For that reason, Webmasters need monitors that can be specialized to supervise Web applications and monitors that can observe from both sides of the firewall. Webmasters want to improve notification by connecting Web site monitoring to traditional systems and network management consoles. In addition, more ambitious Webmasters want a solution that can automatically take corrective actions.

General Description

SiteScope is a suite of software tools for monitoring simple and complex eBusiness Web sites. It tests Web applications by simulating a user's transaction and verifying that the transaction completes swiftly. SiteScope can be used to monitor multiple servers and devices in single or multiple locations, on both sides of the firewall. SiteScope responds to events by sending notification or taking investigative or corrective action. Finally, SiteScope provides management reports on the service level of the Web application. Figure 7.22 shows the oversimplified configuration of SiteScope.

SiteScope provides the following features (ALDR99)

- Browser access
- Default configuration
- Comprehensive monitoring
- Customizable monitors and groups
- Automated event response
- SNMP integration with enterprise management
- Support for NT, SGI/IRIX, and Sun/Solaris platforms

SiteScope is a Java-server application comprising monitors, the SiteScope framework, a browser-based dashboard, and tools for diagnosis. The browser enables administrators to control and configure SiteScope from any Internet connection. Webmasters use Web site's security mechanisms to control who can do what with SiteScope monitoring and information. SiteScope incorporates the Java Runtime Environment from Sun Microsystems, Java SNMP software from Advent Network Management Group, Java Generic Library from Object Space, Java PerfTools from ORO, and the XML Parser in Java from Microsoft.

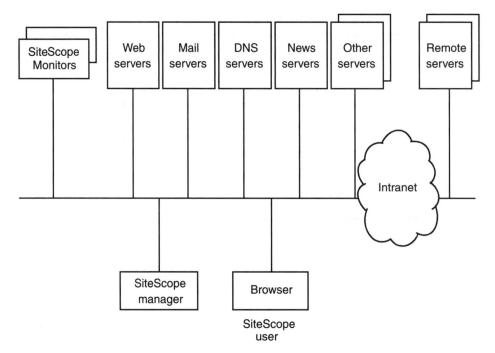

Figure 7.22 Configuration of SiteScope.

SiteScope Monitors

The following monitors are available with the product:

URL monitor. It verifies availability and access time for specified URLs to ensure that Web pages are always available in an acceptable time frame. The URL monitor can detect the availability of back-end databases as well as the proper functioning of CGI scripts. String matching capabilities allow users to verify monitored page's content. Proxy servers are supported to allow Webmasters to see outside their firewall. Leveraging integrated support on the NT platform, SiteScope on NT supports monitoring secure https URLs.

Disk space monitor. It reports the percentage of disk space currently in use so that Webmasters can act before they run out of disk space. Administrators can customize both warning and error thresholds.

Service monitor. It verifies that specified processes are running, including Web, Mail, FTP, News, Gopher, and Telnet.

Ping monitor. It verifies that specified hosts are available via the network to ensure continuous availability of critical connections (e.g., routers and ISP connections).

CPU monitor. It reports the percentages of CPU currently in use to ensure that administrators and Webmasters know when the CPU is being overloaded.

DNS monitor. It verifies that a DNS server is working and that host names can be resolved.

FTP monitor. It connects to an FTP server and verifies that a file can be retrieved.

News monitor. It connects to a news (NNTP) server and verifies that groups can be retrieved.

Port monitor. It determines whether a service on a port can be connected to.

Memory monitor. This monitor measures virtual memory usage and notifies Web administrators before problems occur. Web administrators or Webmasters can set the warning and threshold limits.

Web server monitor. It reads the Web server log and reports data on hits, bytes, errors, hits per minute, and bytes per minute.

Mail monitor. It verifies that the mail server is accepting requests, and that messages can be sent and retrieved.

Directory monitor. It checks directory file count and the total size of all files in the directory to help Webmasters to detect unauthorized changes to the Web directory.

SNMP monitor. This monitor returns the value of an SNMP get.

Link check monitor. It checks all the internal and external links on a Web site and returns an error if a link cannot be reached.

URL list monitor. This monitor checks a large list of URLs. This is very helpful for ISPs who want to check URLs for their customers.

URL transaction monitor. This monitor verifies that an online transaction can be performed by checking returned page content.

File monitor. It watches the size and age of a file and reports any unauthorized changes. It can even run a script to automatically copy a backup file to return a file to its proper state if it finds that a file has been changed.

Log file monitor. This monitor can read through an application's log file looking for specific error messages. If it finds an error or other specified message, it can send out notification.

Other monitors. New monitors are added frequently. SiteScope monitors are always listed on the company's home page.

A monitor is a Java-based program. Monitoring can be performed on the Web server to get tighter control of the Web application, outside the Web server, or beyond the firewall to get a clearer view of the user's end-to-end experience. The monitors provide both broad, general monitoring, such as Web server health as represented by page-retrieval time for a URL. They can also provide very specific monitoring, such as server memory usage or file size and age, useful in tracking down application problems. Administrators can build monitors and scripts for site-specific events using the templates and tools provided with SiteScope.

With SiteScope, Web administrators can

- Monitor the availability of http and https URLs and proper functioning of CGI scripts
- Remotely monitor NT servers from a primary NT server

- Track status of multiple Web servers from one central panel
- Verify the availability of critical connections (e.g., ISP's router)
- Watch for low disk space and overloaded CPU
- Ensure that important processes are running
- Generate management reports showing Web server performance
- Forward SNMP traps to an enterprise SNMP platform
- Execute automated recovery scripts

SiteScope helps Web administrators keep their sites operational using real-time performance monitoring. When shared resources become constrained or components fail, SiteScope alerts the Web administrator via e-mail or pager in real time. SiteScope can also initiate automatic error-handling by restarting hung processes and executing automated recovery scripts.

Immediately after installation, SiteScope automatically begins to collect data by verifying that the Internet/intranet connection is working correctly, checking on CPU and disk space usage, and scanning the Web server log for hit information. Over 20 standard monitors and the power to create site-specific custom monitors enable Web administrators to customize the SiteScope monitoring environment. Using Java API, Webmasters can incorporate their own site-specific monitoring scripts into SiteScope, allowing them to retain any homegrown scripts they need for their site and still take advantage of the alert and reporting features built into SiteScope.

Reports are by default generated on a daily and weekly basis, although the viewing of ad hoc reports is also available. Because many of the tests run by monitors represent service-level measurements, the reports reflect this information and are therefore easy to map to the end user's experience. For example, showing the average response time of a URL is a direct measurement of the user's experience waiting for a page to load in their browser. Peak service-level measurements are also important, especially if a high variability in service levels is unacceptable. The daily average for retrieval of a Web page may be less than 3 seconds, but if there are times when the response time increases to 15 seconds or more, then there are users for whom the desired service level is not being met.

The most frequent uses of reports are for identifying trends and for comparison. Trend data allows the anticipation of additional resource needs, such as memory or disk space. Trends can also identify time-dependent problems. One real example was a system where URL retrieval times always peaked or timed out at the top of every hour. Random manual checking would probably not have uncovered this trend, but it turned out that a scheduled background process was running periodically on a Web server, slowing the server down significantly. Comparison of historical data is of great benefit in identifying causes of problems. If URL retrieval time slows at the same time as the Web server's memory paging is quite high, the chances are that additional memory might alleviate the problem. However, if during the same slow URL retrieval, the Web server's statistics (CPU, memory, etc.) were normal, the correlation with various network connection monitors might uncover delays in the network as the cause of slowdown.

7.7.4 VeriServ from Response Networks

It is designed for both enterprise IT organizations and application service providers. By measuring the quality of application delivery to the end user directly through active, real-time testing, VeriServ verifies the performance of mission-critical client/server, intranet, and extranet applications such as resource planning, decision support, groupware, team collaboration, and eCommerce. The product is targeted for administrators, operations staff, help-desk, and management who need to understand the application service levels of the business units and end customers they support.

With the VeriServ explorer, an operator defines the types of applications to be monitored and the end-user locations from which to measure. The operator might also define specific alarm thresholds for response time and throughput. The VeriServ domain controller then instructs the VeriServ agents to begin testing the applications.

The agents execute their tasks and compile statistical summaries, periodically uploading consolidated results to the VeriServ domain controllers. A single VeriServ agent can perform hundreds of real-time transactions to any application that VeriServ supports, or to any IP-addressable entity on the network. VeriServ can also execute custom test scripts running between pairs of agents.

When a task exceeds an alert threshold, the VeriServ explorer displays an alarm. Besides providing this real-time heads-up of service quality, the program also summarizes all results and stores them in the VeriServ controller's database for historical reporting. This feature provides managers with the means to guarantee application service levels, and to enforce them through verified service level agreements.

The system overhead of a VeriServ installation is very low, unless it is being used deliberately for stress testing. It represents no more strain on the environment than a real user. A typical VeriServ agent installation needs only 48 KB of disk space and uses less than 0.1 percent of system resources at the workstation.

VeriServ simulates an end user, sending real traffic to actual applications, and reporting on the applications' availability and performance. It provides a new class of data not available with traditional management platforms. Reports on performance are available on demand, either from the VeriServ explorer or through a Web browser. Typical reports might include a graphical representation of response time by location, application, organization, and time of day. Other reports could include, for example

- Select reports by response time, throughput, or both
- Custom reports criteria through a Web-based interface
- By percent of goal reached or by absolute performance
- Application performance from remote locations

VeriServ reports on percent of goal achieved, a simple way of viewing service quality against service goals. VeriServ delivers critical application response time and throughput data in a variety of useful forms.

Users can monitor response time of mission-critical applications continuously as seen by end users in various locations. This lets users anticipate and avoid end-user frustration caused by application problems and other service degradations—whatever the source of the problem. It also helps users to establish and enforce service-level agreements with business unit managers and external customers.

VeriServ is also valuable as a diagnostic tool for application, network, and system troubleshooting. When it detects an emerging service problem, VeriServ will highlight which service components are affected and whether it is a response time or an availability issue. Users can then tap VeriServ's real-time monitoring data to review problems at a high level. It can also help to diagnose problems through historical trends and patterns.

It can stress test components or entire systems by simulating end-user traffic. VeriServ can also stress test components or entire systems by simulating end-user generated traffic. It can also be used to evaluate what-if scenarios involving geographic distribution of users, new applications, new servers, and new network configurations. It can be used to reverify the whole application delivery environment after a planned or unplanned environment outage, for example a network or system upgrade. For example, users can use this product to determine whether the environment can support thousands of concurrent application sessions, simply by escalating the appropriate traffic volumes of individual tasks. Network and IT managers can see exactly how their entire system performs, end-to-end, using the same data that they use to monitor performance in their day-to-day environment.

VeriServ can monitor the response time of mission-critical applications continuously as end users see them around the network. Managers can anticipate and prevent application brownouts and service degradation—regardless of the source of the problem. They can also implement and verify service-level agreements with client business units and external customers. Thresholds can be set for specific services, with alarms displayed when performance falls out of limits. Not only does VeriServ provide a true early warning of end-user application service problems, it also provides true measurements of the service from the end user's perspective, so that managers can discuss the situation constructively, rather than struggling to understand their complaints.

This product measures application response time, availability, and throughput directly. A VeriServ component, the VS agent, interacts with the application exactly as an end user would, and measures the application's response. Periodically, the VS agent reports its results to another VeriServ component, the VS domain controller, which stores the results in a database. Operators control VeriServ and view reports through a third component, called the VeriServ explorer.

Using VeriServ to perform high-level troubleshooting, users can deploy personnel and specialized test equipment efficiently to solve problems. Since all VeriServ components share the same view of service performance throughout an environment, field service technicians can work closely with operations and support personnel while restoring service. As a service is being restored, managers can use VeriServ to monitor progress and ensure that the fix has brought the environment back to specified production levels.

The VeriServ operational view shows tasks running from the same VeriServ agent and indicates in color the alarm state of each task:

Good	Green	Currently meeting goals
Transitional	Yellow or orange	Exceeding goals briefly
Failed	Red	Exceeding goals for an extended period

Users and operators can create views simply by clicking and dragging tasks onto the view from a menu.

A minimum configuration includes one VeriServ explorer, one controller, and one agent. The actual number of each of the components depends on the requirements of a particular installation. There are no constraints on the maximum numbers of Veri-Serv software components. All three components can easily run the same worksta-tion, with little effect on the performance of other applications. Components may also be distributed throughout the network.

VeriServ can be extended to test any client/server application running on a TCP/IP network. The initial release tests the major Internet services, such as HTTP, Telnet, FTP, DNS, POP3, SMTP, and NNTP, and any SQL database application through ODBC. For Web-based applications, VeriServ can download a header or a page, and can check for the presence of specific text. SQL tests can check and log into an SQL database and execute actual SQL commands. Application modules include major commercial applications such as SAP R/3, PeopleSoft, Oracle, Lotus Notes, Baan, and Microsoft Exchange Server.

All VeriServ components run under Windows NT or Windows 95. The product ships with a Paradox database for smaller installations. For larger implementations, a Microsoft SQL server can be used as a database manager. VeriServ agents run on a certain number of representative client stations within an enterprise. These agents conserve bandwidth between themselves and the VeriServ controller by compressing results data statistically before transmitting them to the database, eliminating the net-work burden that would result from uploading unprocessed results.

The VsWeb report engine is installed on a Windows NT machine that controls the database of response time and availability information gathered by VeriServ agents throughout a networked environment. The report engine automatically generates a Web site for viewing reports, and automatically updates that Web site each time it runs. In addition, the report engine builds and administers a library of response time and availability reports for viewing and analysis.

Everybody responsible for guaranteeing the performance of network infrastructures can benefit from VeriServ. It helps improve the quality of service for internal and external end users in the following three areas:

1. *Improved network and server response speeds application delivery.* VeriServ gives man-agers the ability to baseline performance and set goals for response time and availability throughout the application delivery environment. It monitors the response of all network devices and servers in real time, helps troubleshoot faults and bottlenecks, and via its VsWeb report engine, generates Web-based reports

automatically for quick viewing and analysis. The result is improved application delivery end-to-end.

2. *Enhanced database and application response improves quality of service (QoS).* VeriServ enables managers to baseline application delivery and database availability, and work proactively to improve quality of service. It monitors end-to-end performance even in the most extensive environments—including extranets, VPNs, and outsourced infrastructures. VeriServ helps troubleshoot, and in many cases prevent, outages, including intermittent and difficult-to-diagnose problems with applications. The VsWeb report engine delivers real-time and historical reports on an automatically generated Web site.

3. *Higher quality service levels guarantee customer satisfaction.* VeriServ is designed to help accomplish some of the most demanding management goals, demonstrating the actual quality of service being delivered, and documenting response time and availability to verify service level agreements. With this product, IT organizations and service providers can manage internal and external customer expectations better, and the VsWeb report engine makes it simple to deliver detailed reports—showing how well the systems and networking environment is supporting end users.

7.7.5 Resolve from CrossKeys

Using Resolve, service providers can quickly deploy differentiated services and assure service delivery. It is specifically designed as a service-level management solution. Resolve retrieves data from each endpoint and link that together make up a delivered service, allowing Resolve to produce flexible reports quickly against service level agreements. Resolve includes

- SLA management
- Flexible reporting of end-to-end service performance
- Network interfaces that retrieve network events, synchronize service objects, and import network statistics and trouble tickets from external systems
- Measurement of performance for frame relay, ATM, and TDM access-based services
- Service modeling capability through Universal Service Components (USC)
- Mixed technology service management
- Support for quality of service (QoS) parameters
- Multiple thresholds for QoS parameters
- Web access to reports

Resolve helps service providers increase customer satisfaction through a simple, automatic tracking and reporting system for customer QoS commitments. Resolve service performance reports track services from a customer's point of view. Resolve reports automatically relate network data to customer data, making reports suitable for use by all departments in a service provider's organization, including network operations, marketing, customer service, senior management, and sales.

Resolve is built around the Resolve server. It is scalable to suit the requirements of carrier-class service providers. Resolve client workstations run the client applications, Resolve reporter and Resolve configurator. The Resolve server maintains network service information while client applications add reporting and administrative functionality. Resolve clients access a service-level management object model on the central Resolve server. Its network interfaces provide connections to network management systems and Resolve interfaces to other operating systems, expanding the range of information collected from external sources. Services that contain mixed vendor types produce as many different data types as there are technologies. To ensure that accurate and meaningful reports are produced for mixed vendor services, Resolve normalizes all data received from network elements into a vendor-neutral format prior to performing report calculations. Figure 7.23 shows the architecture of Resolve, including the server and the clients.

Resolve Clients

The distributed architecture allows client workstations to be remotely located from the Resolve server. The ability to separate the server geographically from client applications allows service providers to manage large, complex networks from a central location.

Resolve Reporter

It enables service providers to generate preconfigured reports based on customer and service information. Service providers are able to modify preconfigured Resolve reports to suit specific customer reporting requirements. With the reporter, critical business information can be retrieved and managed directly from the desktop. Standard reports can be produced simply by clicking a button. Users can generate and reformat standard reports and build ad hoc queries. Users can customize the reporter by adding new report buttons to the graphical data model interface providing easy access to new ad hoc reports. Users can save and log new queries and reports for use by other Resolve users.

Standard reports display network data in tabular and graphical form. Users can design new reports to summarize query results in either format. Advanced users can create cross-tabular calculations to view relationships between multiple sets of data in a single report. Resolve reporter allows users to present customer facing data in a wide variety of chart and table formats. Resolve reporter's chart and table formats are flexible, as users decide how best to illustrate the performance of delivered services.

Reports in table format organize network data vertically and horizontally, displaying data in more than one category, or dimension, at a time. Reports in chart format present network data graphically using pie, bar, line, and area charts for both standard reports and custom queries. To make Resolve reports more useful and appealing to end customers, users can fully format reports by reorganizing report contents, changing fonts, adding corporate logos, clip art, and borders, or by adding color to text and graphics.

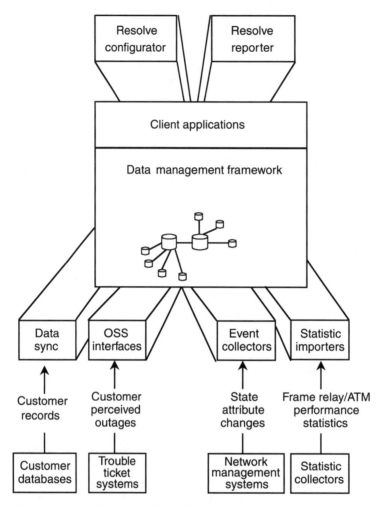

Figure 7.23 Architecture of Resolve.

Reports can be distributed to internal staff or customers on screen, in print, by e-mail, or by file. Service providers may also make reports available to customers in HTML or XML. Users can upload files to a Web server, where the report and the associated data can be downloaded by end customers. Report contents can be exported to a variety of applications including word processors and spreadsheets. To simplify the process of reporting subscribed service performance to end customers, service providers can place multiple reports on the same page using the enhanced reporting features. System administrators can control user access to specific reports in Resolve reporter. System administrators are able to designate internal parties who receive service performance reports and can maintain central control of the data model.

Resolve Configurator

It can be used to control customer, service, and contract data. System administrators create SLAs to associate customer and network components to a service and committed QoS. With Resolve configurator, system administrators can create

- A customer object for each organization that purchases services
- A contract object with performance thresholds for each SLA signed with a customer
- A service profile object with performance thresholds for each service offering

It can also be used to record changes in network and service offerings. For example, system administrators can use it to create new associations when customers purchase new services, when new network links are connected using a network management system, or when new customers are won. It also provides administrative functions that allow service providers to define specific roles to Resolve users.

Resolve Server

It is a single integration point to the network management system. Its clients do not need to be reengineered when new network interfaces are added to the server. Resolve represents data using a vendor-neutral approach, normalizing statistics in the data warehouse. It employs a data warehouse architecture to store and summarize the large amounts of information required to effectively and efficiently manage delivered services. Resolve processes network events in real time to provide network operations staff with the ability to react to network trouble spots immediately. Resolve processes network statistics in the background and summarizes data daily and monthly in the data warehouse for reporting purposes. This framework includes

- Service management information base (SMIB)
- Historical information base (HIB)
- Summarized information base (SIB)
- Archived information base (AIB)

The SMIB is the central storage repository for customer and service information and associated SLA information. The SMIB updates information in the HIB and SIB, and is the primary access point to information on current attribute and state values of service objects for Resolve reporter and Resolve configurator.

To ensure full database restoration in the event of a system failure, the SMIB supports full transaction logging. Transaction logging prevents the loss of critical SMIB contract and customer information.

The HIB stores detailed, long-term performance and availability data. Using Resolve reporter, service providers can access HIB data to perform detailed historical analysis of delivered services based on trends identified from the analysis of SIB data. Data is forwarded to the HIB from the SMIB or is directly collected from a network interface. The HIB is optimized for high-speed inserts to handle the large volumes of service performance data produced by the network. Resolve reporter accesses the HIB when raw, detailed data for specific time intervals are requested.

The SIB stores data forwarded from the SMIB and HIB. The SIB aggregates network data and provides summaries to Resolve reporter for use in overview and trend reports. The SIB can be customized to provide specific summaries based on service provider requirements. Resolve reporter uses SIB summaries for high-speed reporting. The SIB stores summaries of historical events (i.e., circuit attributes, state changes) service object states, frame relay PVC, UNI, and ATM PVC service performance data. Availability, performance, and inventory reports are generated by Resolve reporter using these summaries. SIB summaries also provide the potential for long-term service performance trend analysis. The AIB is used to store SMIB, HIB, and SIB data. The AIB can be archived to tape or disk to prevent data loss and to restore historical data from past months for detailed analysis.

7.7.6 NextPoint S3 Performance Monitoring Software from NextPoint Networks

Network device availability is one of the key metrics of service management. This product uses a PointCast-like interface with specific channels to drill down on equipment availability and application response time statistics. NextPoint is extending the product's reach to give IT managers more options for measuring application response time. S3 incorporates a new intelligent agent that records production transaction response times. The same agent also tracks response times of synthetic transactions—a capability bundled with the initial version of the product. That duality gives IT managers the option to customize specific applications so that they can track response time in live production conditions or to simulate IP, Oracle, and SAP, as well as other transactions. In order to program applications for live-mode response time monitoring, they must be somewhat reworked. That is a task that commercial application vendors are still resisting, internal application developers dread, and IT management fears may actually slow down transaction times.

NextPoint offers an API specification, a developer's agent, and agent certification testing. Synthetic transaction monitoring lets IT managers simulate Web, e-mail, Domain Name Service, Dynamic Host Configuration Protocol, Oracle, SAP, and other application activity to estimate round-trip response times.

Although the product measures basic response times, it doesn't have the level of sophistication IT officers may be looking for in the future to aggregate response time information and turn it into a broader measure of productivity.

The product integrates two complementary and important perspectives of the network: the business user and the network administrator. In doing so, S3 answers two important questions: Did the network meet business service expectations, and how can service be improved?

Lightweight intelligent agents track business-centric metrics such as response time and availability from strategic locations around the network. Synthetic transactions technology proactively derives end-to-end response time at the application and network levels. The optional agents supplement RMON and SNMP data sources with a more accurate measure of transaction response time from the end-user perspective. NextPoint S3 complements the business-centric perspective with comprehensive operational management of the multivendor infrastructure, including real-time alerts, drill-down navigation, and IP services management. It automates real-time fault isolation with policy-based analysis to reduce false alarms. IP services (e.g., DNS, DHCP) represent an increasingly important part of the end-to-end network infrastructure. S3 discovers IP services and monitors their availability and performance. S3 also automatically identifies duplicate and stale IP addresses.

Networks evolve greatly over time, with new users, new applications, and topology changes. Even in their daily traffic variance, however, most networks display remarkable consistency, reflecting the cyclic nature of most business applications. These dynamic patterns may be the result of normal end-user and application events such as routine backups and employee work shifts. Traffic signatures technology surpasses standard trend analysis to understand network traffic variance and uncover hidden patterns of response time and utilization.

Web technology is used to distribute information to users. Push technology lets users quickly identify and select information organized by channels of interest, such as service management, exceptions, and applications. Channels are further segmented along resource type, application, reports, maps, and so on, so no extraneous information is presented to cloud the message. Users can customize the channels. Information can be accessed from anywhere that is convenient to users. Security mechanisms prevent unauthorized access.

NextPoint S3 provides reports to highlight application and network performance issues, stability problems, and other events on both a real-time and historical basis. The reports also demonstrate when network service expectations have been met, and important objectives of business-centric management have been met. Each S3 user can create and access reports tailored to their needs. The Web interface allows this from the convenience of the user's desktop. In addition to the predefined reports, the standard database interface means that any generic reporting package may be used instead.

The architecture of NextPoint S3 architecture consists of a robust infrastructure of servers and lightweight intelligent agents to provide scalability and manage complexity. At the same time, the Web interface isolates the user from the complexity with push technology. Figure 7.24 shows the components of the S3 architecture.

The components are:

Distributed server. Provides engine for real-time and historical analysis, alarm/event handling, and other tasks. The automated task director manages automation routines such as the router configuration management task. Features a modular, object-oriented design for scalability.

NextPoint S3 server   NextPoint S3 Web clients

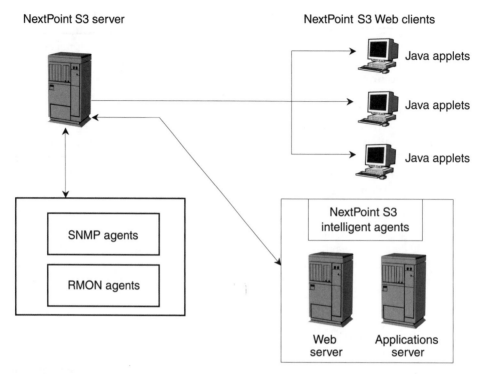

Figure 7.24   Architecture of NextPoint S3.

Intelligent agents. They provide the user perspective by residing on strategic resources throughout the enterprise—application servers, workstations, network hubs, and so on. Built to be lightweight to avoid burdening production systems with management overhead.

Database. An ODBC-compliant API layer isolates NextPoint S3 system tasks from proprietary databases. S3 works with multiple databases, such as Oracle and MS Access.

Web interface. The full-function Java interface features push technology that provides dynamic information distribution, flexible access, and ease of administration. User authentication ensures system integrity.

Plug-in modules. Modular options allow users to tailor S3 to specific environments. Frame relay, LAN, and WAN are some of the available options.

In summary, S3 benefits include the following

■ Enhances quality of service

■ Tracks impact of network infrastructure on business user (application availability, response time, etc.)

■ Complements business-user perspective with operational details of network performance

- Measures and demonstrates network service with meaningful reports
- Monitors network service levels against business-centric objectives
- Improves operation staff productivity
- Enhances information distribution using fully Web-based push technology
- Automates real-time fault isolation
- Automates routine IP services operations (e.g., address management)
- Tracks enterprise-wide router configuration changes automatically
- Reduces network cost-of-ownership
- Optimizes fault detection to reduce downtime
- Enables network tuning to minimize costly network slowdown

7.8 Support Systems for eCommerce

Many service providers should reposition themselves and offer IP-based services in their portfolio. There are three key factors in this process: first, deploy the new infrastructure; second, create and sell new services; and third, bill for those services based on usage. This segment introduces solutions that are dealing with collecting, mediating, and reporting data that may be used for IP usage-based billing.

7.8.1 NetCountant from Apogee Networks

NetCountant satisfies a unique problem within a distributed network environment—it provides an effective mechanism to enable the billing of network services on a usage basis. The application allows an organization to furnish users with monthly billing information that reflects their actual consumption of the network infrastructure. It provides a methodology for implementing the same metering services used in the power, water, and telephone industries and allows the organization to run the network operation as a business process.

Most large organizations struggle with managing the constantly escalating bandwidth expenses of their corporate network infrastructure. NetCountant provides a solution for managing and controlling the consumption of network resources—that is, it allows users to manage the amount of network dollars spent relative to the business needs of the firm.

Components of the Product

NetCountant consists of three main components: the billing and management subsystem (BMSS), which handles tariff calculation and reporting functions; the collector subsystem (CSS), which gathers utilization data; and the administration and user interface, which runs as Java applets.

General features include

- Support of multiple network protocols, such as IP, IPX
- Support of multiple application protocols, such as HTTP, FTP
- Time-sensitive metering
- Dynamic tariff generation algorithms
- Multiple fixed- and variable-cost components
- Subnet and host-sensitive accounting rules
- RMON2, NetFlow, and SNMP MIB support
- Rich billing and traffic reporting functions
- User-defined subscription plans
- Leverages Web/Java

NetCountant permits enterprise and service provider users to control cost and impact the usage behavior of their internal subscribers. In addition to its main purpose—managing the high costs of providing network services—NetCountant has the ability to influence the way internal users make use of the infrastructure, a function critical for delivering a well-managed end-to-end quality of service. It accomplishes this goal by pushing consumption accountability out to each end user or department. The application possesses features designed to meet the complex requirements of the large corporate user as well as those of public Internet service providers.

Operating Environment

NetCountant is designed to run on the following operating systems

- Microsoft Windows NT
- Sun Solaris

It leverages Java technology extensively, and its graphical user interface (GUI) can be launched from a Web browser. The Java GUI allows the user to interact with all functions of the system in a highly intuitive manner. It is designed to operate with the following browsers

- Microsoft Internet Explorer
- Netscape Navigator

NetCountant is highly valuable for Internet service providers and other online businesses. As the Internet moves from flat-rate to a usage-based model for subscriber services, NetCountant is a valuable solution for tracking and invoicing subscribers based on actual services rendered. It can also be used to monitor interconnection agreements with other ISPs. Figure 7.25 shows the architecture of NetCountant.

FlowCollect is designed to aggregate and analyze network traffic flow gathered from Cisco routers and switches. It then translates the data in RMON2 groups. By rationalizing NetFlow data into RMON2 format, the system enables third-party network management applications to leverage NetFlow's information and instrumentation.

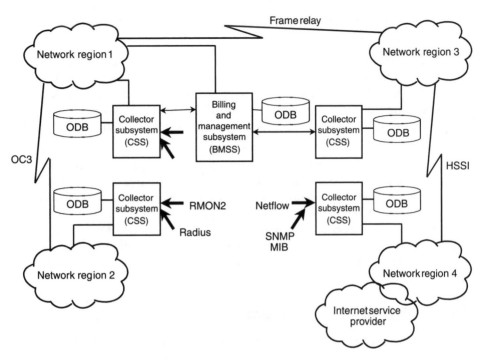

Figure 7.25 Usage-based accounting and billing with NetCountant.

The NetCountant/SP collection and processing framework consists of multiple collection systems that collect usage information from data sources like RMON2 probes, NetFlow collectors, Radius servers, address management systems, load balancing devices, content delivery systems, packet shapers, e-mail servers, and firewalls. In particular with Web switches, Content Flow Messaging Protocol (CFMP) is used to collect information. CFMP is a streaming push interface with a bidirectional control channel for retrieval of any source of data into FlowCollect. This protocol provides several benefits in that it is solely targeted towards data that capture content and the acts of usage. The transport mechanisms designed here provide scaleability, robustness, resilience, reliability, extensibility, push and pull mechanisms, and asynchronous and synchronous support.

The processing system consolidates the raw content and usage records in a local data store. After the consolidation, the records are processed and correlated. For example, information from the address management servers is correlated with information from RMON2 probes to determine the specific dynamic host who used a specific IP address during a specific interval of time. This correlation accurately enables content and usage consumption to be attributed to a specific entity. Similar correlations are performed for dial-in usage from Radius servers. Specialized algorithms are used in order to perform identification and elimination of duplicate content and usage records. In a meshed network, it is possible for different network elements to record the same usage information as it passes along locations and networks. The specific algorithms developed by Apogee are used for duplicate elimination, which enable the processing module to avoid assigning duplicate consumption to a given source or destination entity.

The processing system reads and applies billing policy rules that are available through downstream billing and rating applications. Therefore, the behavior and the nature of the processing depend on the billing rules and policies available to the processing module. It is important to note that this solution is able to adapt the mediation system based on the billing policy rules provided by the processing system.

The final conceptual processing step is the resolution of business and organizational entities that have contributed to the usage/consumption. This resolution is done based on the business, network customers, and organizational structure information available to the processing system. Threshold algorithms are used in conjunction with the billing rules to enable special processing of certain content and usage information. These processed Internet content data records (iCDR) are stored in an open repository. These records are available for use by multiple applications, such as billing, monitoring, capacity planning, cost optimization, and market intelligence applications.

7.8.2 IMS from Belle Systems

IMS offers a rich feature set that can be tailored to suit the provider's individual business and technology needs. This includes the ability to create accounts and associated profiles, and to authenticate users, whether accessing a service provider's network or corporate VPN. Via advanced mediation capabilities, all network activities can be tracked in minute detail, before being rated and consolidated into a single invoice or detailed departmental account. Service providers can use the HelpDesk and service management functionality within IMS to offer superior assistance to their customers, whilst comprehensive reporting facilities add further value. Advanced self-service functionality allows customers to self-manage many aspects of their own accounts, from initial registration through to purchasing new services and online payment, reducing the support overhead for service providers. Figure 7.26 displays the architecture of IMS.

Core Functionality

IMS incorporates comprehensive functionality, ranging from interface with core network elements—via its deployment and mediation functions—through to billing and customer self-care. The product is able to configure and manage a broad range of network technologies, including dial access servers, routers, and voice gateways, as well as many core technologies from Cisco Systems. Integration with software from companies such as Atlantech Technologies and Orchesteam offers a universal interface for the configuration and management at the network element level. IMS is built around a highly reliable Radius server for full control and management of user authentication. Powerful mediation functions enable the collection of statistical and call detail records (CDR) information from multiple sources around the network. IMS then correlates this information before filtering and sorting records for rating and billing processes. With its inherent flexibility, IMS can deploy complex rating schemes to

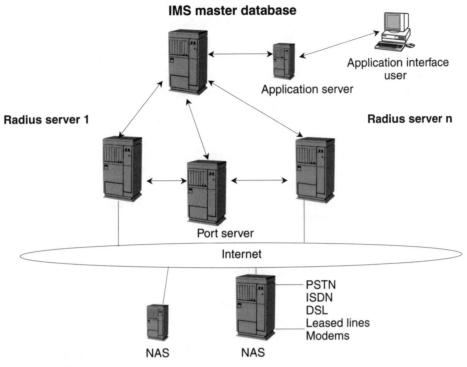

IMS master database

Application interface user

Application server

Radius server 1

Radius server n

Port server

Internet

PSTN
ISDN
DSL
Leased lines
Modems

NAS

NAS

Figure 7.26 Architecture of IMS.

users and profiles, covering aspects such as discounts for groups of users, by profile type or usage pattern. IMS takes the rated data and passes this to an external general ledger system. Users can access the system to view and settle online bills, request new services, and change their service profiles.

Service Enhancements

This product supports a number of emerging applications, including:

eCommerce. The MicroPayment Server functionality within IMS is able to support the growth in eCommerce deployment with a fully functioning e-merchant solution that service providers can use to attract eCommerce customers. As well as providing a platform for rapid entry into this market without massive infrastructure costs, IMS facilitates secure, efficient eCommerce transactions and consolidated billing within a single system.

VoIP. By offering Radius authentication functionality for the access servers, and by taking Radius accounting records from voice gatekeepers, IMS is able to manage the access onto the network for VoIP users and rate, bill, and provide self-service functionality accordingly. Additional functionality includes two-way interaction with the IVR capabilities of the Cisco product set, allowing end users to gain access to account information via a standard telephone. Facilities, such as remaining time or credit, can be read out to the user by the IVR facilities under instruction from IMS. With full support for these VoIP gatekeepers, together with direct end-user control of the access servers, service providers can take advantage of the inherent facilities within IMS to offer wholesale voice dial services to resellers.

Voice integration. Unlike many competing products, the service management capabilities within IMS are not restricted to one particular traffic type. As well as handling IP data traffic and VoIP, IMS is able to integrate traditional voice traffic into its service provisioning, rating, and accounting functionality, via its interface to Priority Call Management's Oryx application and Cisco's VCO switches. Further interfacing to products such as Cisco's Selsius Call Manager can offer comprehensive voice call management to enterprise levels. Additionally, IMS has been designed to support the industry standard Open Settlement Protocol that will allow IMS-based providers to apply and account for complex interconnect settlement on traditional voice traffic and to consolidate this into a single account or invoice if required by the customer.

Roaming. With full global roaming, functionality, and an interface to international roaming associations such as GRIC and i-Pass, IMS enables dialup users to access their service even when they are calling from outside the provider's geographical infrastructure. With this functionality, service providers can easily configure and manage roaming agreements and service parameters—limiting the number of simultaneous roamed sessions per operator, customer, or region, for example. From this roaming setup information, IMS is also able to handle all accounting and traffic management processes, aggregating this data into a single invoice if appropriate.

IMS is based on the Oracle 8 platform and operates on leading Unix hardware systems from Hewlett-Packard and Sun Microsystems. It has been developed using industry standard technology and open standards, such as C++ and Java. IMS also includes CORBA-based business logic interfaces that enable third-party applications to be easily integrated.

7.8.3 XACCTusage from Xacct

XACCTusage is a multisource, multilayer network usage metering and mediation solution that gives network service providers (NSPs) including enterprise intranet providers, the intelligence to right-price IP services. With this product, service providers can generate usage-based billing and implement utilization-based charge-back models. It derives IP session and transaction information, collected in real time, from a multitude of network components. XACCTusage gathers, correlates, and transforms data from routers, switches, firewalls, authentication servers, LDAP, Web hosts, DNS, and other devices to create comprehensive usage and billing records.

XACCTusage transforms raw transaction data from network devices into useful billing records though policy-based filtering, aggregation, and merging. The result is a set of XACCT detail records (XDR), similar in concept to the CDRs of the telephony industry. XDRs can be easily integrated with existing customer care and billing systems.

In addition to billing data, XDRs enable NSPs to deploy new services based on documented usage trends, plan network resource provisioning, and audit service usage. XACCTusage provides a clear picture of user-level network service utilization by tracking a variety of metrics such as actual session quality of service (QoS), traffic routes, and end-user application transactions. Figure 7.27 shows the IP mediation architecture of Xacct.

XACCTusage is based on a modular, distributed, highly scalable architecture capable of running on multiple platforms. Data collection and management is designed for optimal efficiency to minimize impact on the network and system resources. Principal components are

Information source modules. They are modular, abstract interfaces that are designed to be platform-neutral. They act as interfaces or translators, sending IP session data, in real time, from network elements to gatherers. Each module is designed for a specific type of network data source. They are packaged separately, allowing users to customize configurations to meet the specific requirements of networks. System reliability is enhanced through on-the-fly dynamic reconfiguration, allowing users to add or remove modules without disrupting ongoing operations.

Gatherers. They are multithreaded, lightweight, smart agents that run on nondedicated hosts, as a normal user application on Windows NT or Unix, as a background process, or daemon. Gatherers can easily be installed on the same network segment as the source device, such as a router and switch, or on the application server itself, to minimize the data traffic impact on the network. Gatherers logically can interconnect multiple information source modules.

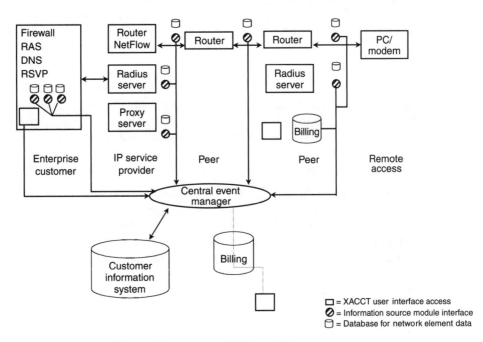

Figure 7.27 Sample use of Xacct IP mediation architecture.

Gatherers perform flexible, policy-based data aggregation. They filter out unneeded data and retain only the necessary information. Distributed data filtering and aggregation eliminates capacity bottlenecks, improving the scalability and efficiency by reducing the volume of data sent on the network to the central event manager. Typically, data collected from a single source do not contain all the information needed for billing and accounting, such as user name and organization. By combining IP session data from multiple sources, such as authentication servers, DHCP, and Domain Name Systems (DNS), XACCTusage creates meaningful session records tailored to specific user needs.

Central event manager. It is the central nervous system of the Xacct system, providing centralized, efficient management and control of all Xacct modules. Its functions include

- Coordinating data collection
- Merging records from multiple gatherers
- Performing database maintenance, integrity checking, and recovery
- Managing upgrade and licensing administration
- Providing data security for intermodule network communications

As each IP session may generate multiple transaction records, during the merge process the central event manager employs intelligent algorithms to identify and discard duplications, enhancing the efficiency of the data repository.

Central database. It is responsible for maintaining date and billing records. It stores the XDRs in a RDBMS-managed repository such as Oracle, Sybase, and Microsoft SQL, and is fully compatible with other ODBC-compliant RDBMS implementations. Optionally, XACCTusage is available with an integrated (Oracle, Microsoft, or Sybase) database.

XDRs can either be fed directly to the billing system or stored in the central database. Users can modify the central database to suit their needs; they can add, delete, edit, or index fields and age data. On-demand access is enabled through database queries and reports. The product provides extensive built-in reporting features accessible through the browser user interface. The scheduler allows for automatic report generation at regular predefined intervals. In addition, users may use any off-the-shelf ODBC-compliant reporting package to generate customized graphs and charts.

User interface server. It is responsible for presentation services toward users. The Web-based user interface allows off-the-shelf browsers to access the system on-demand locally or remotely. It provides remote and local access, and access control. Using a Java-enabled Web browser, network administrators can manage the entire XACCTusage system. Secure password protection ensures that only authorized personnel may log in to the system from anywhere on the network. XACCTusage monitoring feature adds an extra dimension to the existing network management tools, providing

- Raw input data rate
- Postfiltering data rate

- Postaggregation data rate at all junctions
- Exceptions

Customized reporting with built-in report generation helps to visualize billing data. Comprehensive network security features allow secure communication between system components and multiple levels of restricted access. Billing records, maintained in XDR formats, can be processed by any billing applications.

7.8.4 eCare Product Suite from Daleen Technologies

eCare is an innovative, Web-based product suite that presents customers, partners, and suppliers with an engaging, personalized, and intuitive environment for performing comprehensive and personalized self-care. It establishes a unified, customer-centric, and process-oriented enterprise portal. This media-rich portal enables users to explore and research products and services; engage in online purchasing, ordering, and status tracking; receive service outage notifications and reports; resolve service problems; view bills; and perform bill usage analysis. All users have the ability to conduct business directly and receive immediate interactive assistance, 24 hours a day, 7 days a week, while at all times being insulated from the complexities of a service provider's operations. Service providers gain the ability to profile all customers in order to cross-sell and up-sell products and services; provide customer personalization; and integrate with internal enterprise resource planning (ERP) and operations support systems (OSSs), as well as other business systems. Active customers, trading partners, and supplier participation in service fulfillment, delivery, and problem solving are major factors in achieving customer loyalty, strong business relationships, and operational efficiencies.

Components of the Product Suite

The product suite consists of the following components:

Self-care. eCare provides a Web-centric customer self-care portal for all customer segments, ranging from consumer to commercial. It has been designed for service providers that intend to offer a high level of interactive customer self-care. The functionality includes

- Unified account management
- Online service modification and enhancement through self-ordering capability
- Service trouble records and dispute resolution
- Customer self-registration
- Interactive customer care with live agent
- QoS and SLA support

Electronic bill presentment and payment (EBPP). eCare provides flexible EBPP for business-to-business and business-to-customer environments with convergence of billing services. It has been designed for service providers that wish to take current billing and payment processes to the Internet. The functionality includes

- Electronic bill presentment over the Internet
- Usage and rate analysis
- Online dispute claims and resolution
- Internet-enabled reverse caller lookup for name and address
- Bill and usage consolidation and flexible interfaces to multiple billing systems
- Electronic bill payment
- Customer account and service portfolio viewing

eCatalog. eCare provides a rich content management environment to develop a Web-based product and service catalog. Customers may research and purchase products and services over the Web through eCatalog. It has been designed for service providers who want to initiate a Web-based business model over the Internet. This product includes the following functionality:

- eCatalog editor for defining Web-enabled products and services
- Rule-based engine for customers to access products and services
- Online ordering with shopping cart, intelligent order entry, order tracking, and integrated order fulfillment
- Customer account and service portfolio viewing
- QoS and SLA support

Internet marketing. eCare provides the ability to conduct customer-specific and personalized marketing over the Internet. This product is offered for service providers that wish to transition outbound call center activities, as well as customer interaction and traditional marketing onto the Internet. The functionality includes

- Customer profiling
- Personalization
- Service upsell and cross-sell
- Internet and network analysis
- Customer account and service portfolio viewing
- QoS and SLA support

eCare Architecture

Optimal performance and high-end scalability are achieved through a multithreaded, multiprocess distributed object architecture, designed with advanced Web and transaction server technologies. eCare is a robust and scalable product with high-grade security and universal access.

eCare leverages, integrates, and automates back-office infrastructure with a front-end, Web-based solution that captures customer information and provides service fulfillment. It uses an open, cross-platform architecture that reaches external gateways to communicate with partners and suppliers to complete provisioning requests. By integrating easily with legacy systems and effectively interfacing with partners and suppliers, it ensures a continuous flow of information. It transforms separate, compartmentalized OSS software into dynamic systems based upon business rules and processes.

There are two architectural layers supporting the eCare customer applications: the eCare Application Framework and the eBusiness Framework. Additionally, a user-friendly environment is provided for system administration and configuration. Figure 7.28 shows the architecture.

eCare Application Framework. It supports the eCare applications utilizing state-of-the-art Internet and eCommerce technologies, including XML, intelligent Java-Beans and supporting servlets and applets, and platform-independent Internet scripting languages such as Java Server Pages (JSP). The multithreading and multiprocess architecture provides the capability to support the high-traffic volumes typically associated with Internet portals.

eBusiness Framework. It facilitates the seamless integration of electronic business applications into operational environments, supporting both legacy and emerging technologies. This CORBA-based framework enables the service provider to graphically define the complex business processes that are typically required by advanced eCommerce activities, including self-service ordering and customer self-registration. This architecture provides the flexibility required to natively support

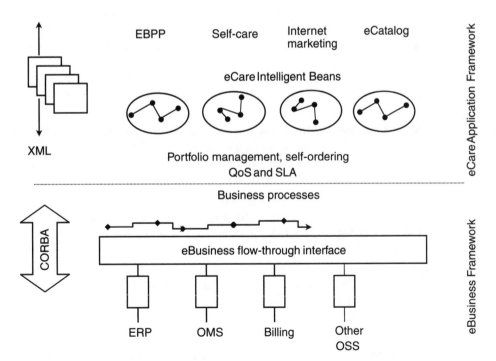

Figure 7.28 eCare system building blocks.

additional business applications such as ERP, order management systems, billing and customer care, and OSSs, or to support these interface requirements via prepackaged enterprise application interface (EAI) vendor plug-ins or connectors.

eCare System Building Blocks. They represent the functionality that is combined to create all products in the eCare suite. They include

eCare Intelligent Beans. The eCare Application Framework utilizes a state-of-the art, component-based JavaBean technology used to facilitate the eCare functional building blocks.

XML. Based upon the benefits achieved by the hierarchy provided within XML, eCare makes extensive use of self-describing XML to represent complex requests within the application framework in areas such as online ordering, customer dispute, and trouble reporting.

CORBA. eCare utilizes the advanced distributed architecture provided by the CORBA standard to enable eCommerce back-office applications.

Business Processes. Within the eBusiness Framework, eCare provides support for Web-enabled collaborative and flow-through business process integration, incorporating XML requests.

eCare Features

The most important features of this product suite are

eCommerce security. eCare security ensures customer confidence over the Internet, extranets, and corporate intranets by applying authentication and encryption technologies to all information exchanged. eCare encryption is enabled through the use of advanced digital certificates. By utilizing proven technologies such as Secure Socket Layer (SSL) and Public Key Infrastructure (PKI), these digital certificates provide the utmost security for information exchanged between customers and service providers over eCare.

Extended and flexible business process integration. The eCare workflow technology incorporates processes from the customer's premises to the service provider, and may extend to suppliers' sites. eCare provides powerful workflow design tools for business process definition.

Flexible electronic bonding to partners. eCare, through its electronic bonding technology, allows rapid turn-up of trading partners, suppliers, and resellers into an extended enterprise, enabling partners to conduct electronic business directly with the service provider.

Open OSS mediation. eCare's workflow process steps can be quickly integrated with existing business and operations support systems through an open OSS mediation layer. The mediation layer supports synchronous and asynchronous, stream and object-oriented communications, using technologies such as CORBA, XML, and TCP/IP.

Scalable distributed architecture. eCare is architected for a scalable number of users and transactions over the Internet. eCare's optimized performance and high-end scalability are achieved through a multithreaded, multiprocess distributed architecture, designed with advanced Web and transaction server technologies.

Personalized Multimedia content. eCare utilizes the extensive multimedia capabilities of WWW to provide compelling content and to engage customers in an interactive dialog.

eCare Advantages

The advantages of using this product suite can be summarized as follows:

Customer self-care. eCare presents customers with an engaging, personalized, and intuitive environment to explore and purchase products and services, manage their accounts and service portfolios, report service problems, and receive immediate interactive assistance.

Comprehensive eCommerce functionality. eCare incorporates comprehensive and advanced eCommerce functionality including portfolio management, self-ordering, and QoS/SLA in all product offerings.

Unified customer view and service management. eCare provides service providers with a simple and unified method for handling their varied portfolios of products and services. Its OSS mediation technology provides a convergent platform, enabling simplified service presentment and management across all product categories and organizational divisions.

Care for all customer segments. eCare enables service providers to empower all of their customers, whether business or residential. Residential customers are provided with the ability to manage products and services for their residence and home-based business in one account. Business customers are provided with the ability to manage large service portfolios across diverse geographic locations and accounting centers.

Powerful usability and simplicity. eCare runs on any Web browser and delivers intuitive and powerful customer interaction. The Web pages are designed to guide customers through all processes, and deliver immediate and personalized interaction.

7.9 Interoperability Solutions

Several approaches to interoperability have been taken into consideration over the last couple of years. One example is the use of TMN for application interface design and network management protocols. TMN is extremely helpful as a guideline to structure processes, functions, and tools. Transaction processing and message-oriented middleware also have been applied to integration projects, but these technologies seem to be applicable for short ranges only. Service providers are looking for a flexible technology with little future risks. Object approaches are promising. They can be based on different ORB technologies. For shallow integration, management intranets may be utilized. Based on CIM and XML, a certain level of standardized information exchange between Webified support, documentation, and management systems may be accomplished. Spatial network management systems combined with enterprise application integration can help solve both the internal and external integration issues around support, documentation, and management systems.

7.9.1 ActiveOSS from Microsoft

Microsoft maintains the opinion that current support systems cannot keep up with the requirements to support new network services, self-provisioning capabilities, and direct access to service-level agreement monitoring systems. Service providers are interested in commercial information technologies for improved integration, adaptability, and price/performance. ActiveOSS is based on Windows DNA architecture, NT server technology, and COM—all technologies in use outside the service provider's world. The overall architecture also incorporates Smart TMN and related work by TINA. Figure 7.29 shows the ActiveOSS architecture (FINE98C).

At the heart of the product is a transaction server running COM or DCOM. Basically, COM is an integration infrastructure designed to facilitate communication between software components operating on the same host, or with DCOM, on multiple networked hosts. COM was originally developed to create interoperability between components, potentially within the same application. Despite its complexity, COM is the most widely deployed component object model with a broad base of development tools and vendor support. ActiveOSS, using COM and data translation services (DTS) technology, acts as a centralized management and translation point for a network of various support systems. Conceptually, applications ride on top of the frame-

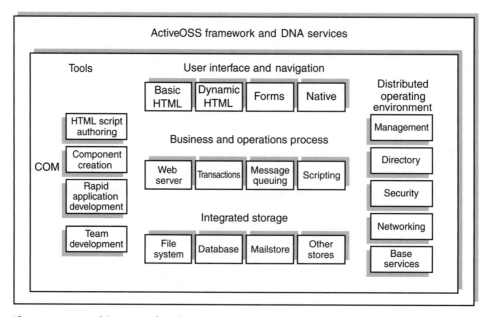

Figure 7.29 Architecture of ActiveOSS.

work but communicate through it. COM abstracts various application interfaces into objects, basically mapping the functions of the application into a common model that can be stored in a database. This common model allows the various applications to communicate in a uniform manner within the platform or across multiple networked platforms. By abstracting interfaces into software objects, applications can be upgraded and/or changed without impacting surrounding systems because integration is based upon independent software components that communicate, not applications that are heavily customized to work together. In this sense, changing or upgrading an application generally means mapping a new interface into the framework, or modifying an existing one, with tools provided with the product.

The platform also provides basic application services, such as security and data persistence, which can be managed from a central point. Interfaces and application services tend to be buried in application source code and differ from vendor to vendor. Inconsistency among vendors can make application management difficult because each application's attributes and performance are unique. This framework is intended to create uniformity among application services without any modifications to source code. Application services are built and managed by the framework. One main focus is provisioning, as opposed to ordering. It helps to speed up activations and reduce the time to market of services. Microsoft leverages its broad base of Internet technologies to be reimplemented for customer self-service.

7.9.2 ObjectSwitch from Kabira Inc.

It is conceptually similar to ActiveOSS, but uses different technology and is marketed from a different perspective. ObjectSwitch is using CORBA for its component integration technology. CORBA has matured more slowly than COM, following a more traditional standardization process, and has lost some early adopters as a result. CORBA is becoming widely accepted now in many industries. Because CORBA has been developed by a wide range of companies, some of the specifications have been left open, which has led to several versions. Because the technology was designed specifically for distributed computing, however, it is implemented more than COM for enterprise-level integration.

CORBA not only supports more languages than COM, but also is supported on more Microsoft platforms than COM. This approach tries to change the way service providers look at and architect their support systems. In the traditional way, companies that are building applications for a service provider are looking at the application and user requirements at a certain point of time. Typically, they must make trade-offs and implement their business processes with the technology already in place. With this product, business processes and application services are uniformly defined on the platform, not buried in application code, and thus become more flexible. Figure 7.30 shows the architecture of the product (FINE98C).

Using this approach, a service provider can offer online provisioning to a customer, but tie the new application into an existing provisioning process without any disruption to the other applications. Once a new interface is established, CORBA handles the integration, thus shielding applications from changes in each other. The established application services and business processes shield the developer from worrying about the implementation details. The developer should be able to focus on the application, while the platform deals with, for example, communication between Oracle and Sybase databases, or conversion of SS7 TCAP messages into readable data for a service management application.

ObjectSwitch is not only an application platform, but also an intelligent mediation system. It can be used as a gateway between support systems or a data collection and conversion, or a billing mediation system.

7.9.3 Management Intranets

This is the first time in the industry that a common method of describing management information has been agreed upon and followed through with implementation. Other efforts have failed because of the lack of industry support. Because the model is implementation independent, it does not provide sufficient information for product development. It is the specific product areas—applications, system, network, database, and devices—and their product-specific extensions that produced workable solutions.

CIM will take advantage of emerging object-based management technologies and ensure that the new model can be populated by DMI and other management data suppliers including SNMP and CMIP. The CIM is being designed to enable imple-

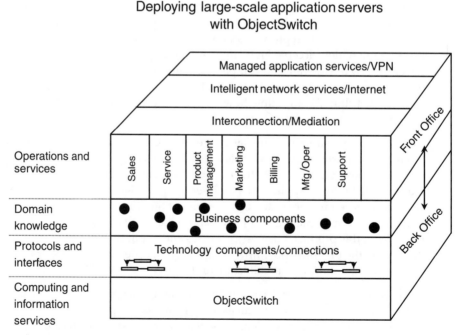

Figure 7.30 Architecture of ObjectSwitch.

mentations in multiple, object-based execution models such as CORBA and COM, and object-based management technologies such as JMAPI.

With CIM data encoded in XML, it is possible to access the data using simple HTTP, allowing management solutions to be platform independent and distributed across the enterprise.

Recently, the DMTF has announced that it is incorporating the directory enabled networks (DEN) initiative into CIM. CIM will be extended to support directory information. In this way, there will be a consistent and interoperable way of modeling network elements and services in heterogeneous networks that is consistent in directories and management databases.

The beauty of this approach to tool integration is that it allows each vendor to use its own agents and information collection infrastructures as demanded by its own particular functional and device coverage needs. The dependencies among different management software vendors are reduced, while still allowing particular pairs of vendors the freedom to exploit each other's services and infrastructure as part of strategic partnerships. For independent software vendors, this strategy for tool integration will significantly reduce the resources spent on compatibility testing and porting. Only one user interface needs to be supported—the browser—and the basic points of integration with other tools and frameworks are potentially limited to standards defined by WBEM/DMTF. This means that more resources can be spent on enhanced functionality and exploring ways to use advanced Web technologies such as Java, XML, and multicasting, or to take advantage of advanced Internet standards and services such as the Lightweight Directory Access Protocol (LDAP) standard. Figure 7.31 shows the basics of Web-based support systems integration.

For users, this means a quick, simple, task-level integration that allows network operators to shift rapidly from tool to tool, for example troubleshooting a network problem highlighted in the alarm manager of the management framework. Solving the system and service management challenges of the Web era demands a new generation of network management systems featuring tighter linkage between network, system, and application-level management information. Effective allocation of network resources requires that network elements understand the different performance and business criticality profiles of the applications and users riding the network. Management information for computing and network elements and resources, whether for purposes of configuration, troubleshooting, or performance management, resides in enterprise management applications that will be able to share this information using CIM and XML. However, information describing users and binding them to applications services and computing resources is more often the province of enterprise directory systems. Directories already hold some of this kind of data because of the role that they play in locating systems, mailboxes, Web pages, and application processes.

7.9.4 Spatial Integration

Service providers are now beginning to support the integration of the physical, logical, and spatial data from TMN and legacy systems. The challenges are increased data velocity, a service-based and event-driven architecture, and being scaleable to sup-

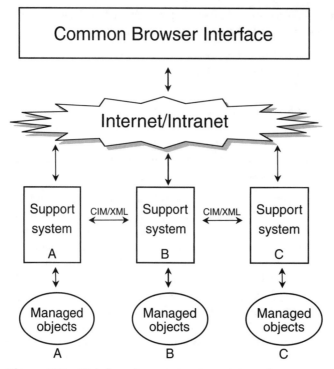

Figure 7.31 Web-based support systems integration.

port growth and future service offerings that are yet to be defined. *Spatial integration* means the use of special tools for spatial views of network resources and their support, documentation, and management systems. Network elements, major paths, wiring centers, and network access points are all visible on an overlay on an actual map. The granularity of the map can be different; it could be a state, county, city, or even a few streets. Service providers may visualize, for example, on a regional map all wireless elements, transmission elements, access elements, gateways, and access points to other service providers. The location of the mobile repair workforce is visible as well. Simply looking at the screen with the map, managers can dispatch the closest repair team to the point of failure. Additional overlays may include data overlay networks for Internet, corporate virtual network services, and point of presence of ISPs. With this ability, the full-service network is manageable from end-to-end, including all communication forms supported by the provider. End-to-end views visualize logical connections in the network, helping to troubleshoot customer-related problems.

In a more granular view, wiring centers can be displayed floor-by-floor, providing the ability to select specific rack, shelf, and card views. By combining element managers with spatial tools, network elements can be visualized, helping to repair or replace components of the network element. Spatial view can be downloaded from a central repository to the local workforce.

To further enhance the value of the spatial solution set, demographic maps could be added to aid market studies showing customer and neighborhood profiles. School, hospital, and industry locations could be easily viewed for business and technical planning. Network engineers can increase planning accuracy in enhancing or expanding networks based on in-place resources as they compare to changing market conditions.

7.10 Summary

Based on various networks and their network management disciplines, various front-office and back-office business applications may be built and implemented. The processes and functions are the same as indicated in Chapter 1, but their allocation to front- and back-office is new.

Figure 7.32 shows this new allocation. Also, this figure shows the changing paradigm for service providers as they put more emphasis on customer relationships. The results are

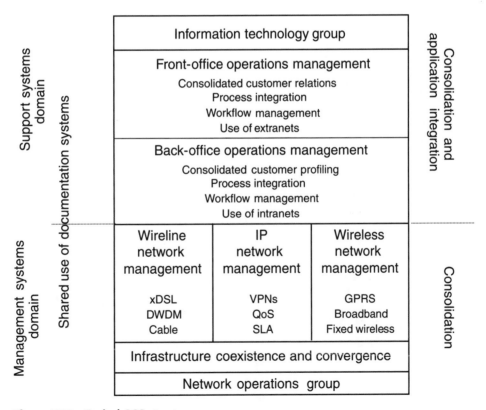

Figure 7.32 Typical OSS structure.

- Communications companies move from a network-centric model to a customer-centric model if they wish to compete.

- Incumbents must retain their high-margin business clients.

- Local incumbents must move into the long-distance marketplace to offset lost revenues in local competition.

- Emerging carriers in both local and wireless must steal the high-margin business clients that incumbents so desperately want to keep.

- The customer is central to the process.

- Sales, marketing, and customer-care efforts are designed to gain, and retain, a communications company's best customers.

- The practical implementation of a structure like this happens in multiple steps and may come from multiple vendors. Modules are expected to be connected to each other using state-of-the-art middleware solutions.

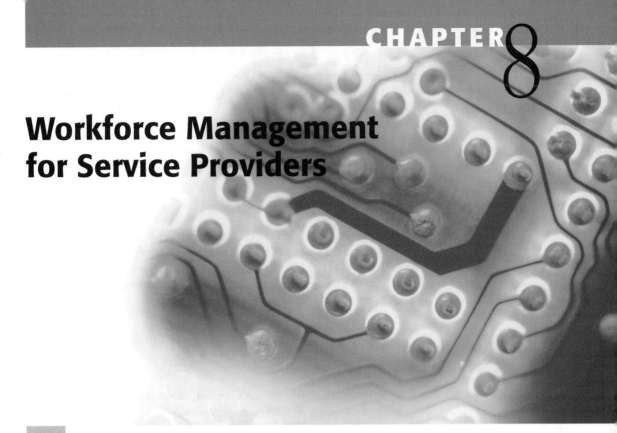

CHAPTER 8

Workforce Management for Service Providers

8.1 Introduction

Workforce is one of the critical success factors in building, deploying, maintaining, and operating communication networks. Motivated people are the differentiating factor between a well-run and a badly-run business in the service provider area. This chapter focuses on human resources and their management by introducing a sample organization. Human resources (HR) are assigned to principal business processes and support tools of the service provider. Sample job profiles help the HR department of the service provider to upgrade profiles, post jobs, and hire the right people. Enabling technologies such as document, knowledge, and workflow management help to increase the efficiency of the service provider's organization. Workforce dispatch is not addressed here; dispatching is included into the business processes discussed in Chapters 4, 5, and 6. The process and most likely results of benchmarks are shown. Benchmarks help to compare the performance of service providers with each other, with industry averages, and with best practices.

8.2 Sample Organizational Structure

Figure 1.6 in Chapter 1 shows a simple structure with lean management. Depending on the size of the service provider, both centralized and decentralized structures can be observed. Operations, administration, and maintenance is a distributed organization with many regional managers. Central control should be combined with decentralized dispatch. Sales and marketing and all customer-facing activities should be distributed as well. Other organizational units may be organized centrally. Using state-of-the-art communication technologies, the physical presence of certain functions is not relevant anymore. Up to a certain point, teleworking may be supported as well.

8.2.1 Assigning Subject Matter Experts to Processes

Table 8.1 shows a high-level allocation matrix of principal support processes of service providers to organizational units. Service providers are expected to break down this matrix further and allocate each function to subject matter experts. By doing so, redundancies in responsibilities, including finger-pointing in cases of emergencies, can be avoided.

8.2.2 Assigning Subject Matter Experts to Support Systems

Table 8.2 shows a high-level allocation matrix of principal support systems of service providers to organizational units. Service providers are expected to break down this matrix further and identify the individual ownership for support systems. By doing so, redundancies in responsibilities (e.g., procurements, customization, and integration) can be avoided.

8.3 Building the Teams

The allocation of business processes and support tools to people complicate the hiring process by making it very difficult to write job descriptions and analyze candidates' background materials. The following is a list of recommended criteria when hiring network management staff.

Identify team members. Section 8.2 gave an overview of principal network management functions. Depending on the size of the network, the human resources demand may be computed. After subtracting the available staff from the total demand for each functional area, the demand for new hires can be quantified.

Recruit candidates. Advertisements, conferences, headhunters, and individual contacts to colleges, universities, and other companies help to find candidates to be interviewed.

Establish interview criteria. Guidelines and evaluation criteria have to be set prior to starting the interviews. In order to keep investment for both parties low, written applications must be filtered carefully. Occasional phone conversations may fill existing gaps. Invitations to personal interviews should be sent out to candidates whose applications are matching the expectations.

Hire properly qualified candidates. Hiring has to be for mutual benefit and not just to fill the job. Future turnover can be avoided this way.

Assign and/or reassign responsibilities. Static job descriptions should serve as a guideline only. Within this framework, more dynamic descriptions with rotation in mind are necessary.

Institute performance evaluations. Periodic reviews are most widely used. If possible, upward performance appraisals should be agreed upon as early as possible in the team-building phase.

Promote openness and handle complaints. In order to emphasize team spirit, opinions and even complaints must be encouraged on behalf of network management supervisors. The employees must have the feeling that their comments and suggestions are handled at the earliest convenience of managers.

Resolve personnel problems quickly. In order to avoid tensions within the network management organization, problems must be resolved for mutual benefit as quickly as possible. The reward system must provide opportunities to do so. Often, visibility of how the reward system works resolves problems almost automatically.

Institute systematic training and development programs. Systematic education should include training for network management functions, network management instruments, and personal skills. A curriculum in coordination with vendors and educational institutes would guarantee high quality and employee satisfaction.

Regularly interface network management staff with users. In order to promote mutual understanding of working conditions and problems, both parties should exchange views and opinions. The level of formality may vary from very informal to very formal; in the second case, written service-level agreements are evaluated.

Evaluate new technologies. As part of the motivation process, network management renovation opportunities must be evaluated continuously. This process includes new management platforms, new technologies of distribution, feasibility of new and existing solutions, new monitors, changes in de facto and open standards, simplification of management processes, changes in the offerings of leading manufacturers, and monitoring the needs of users. Thus, enrichment of lower-level jobs may easily be accomplished.

8.4 Keeping the Teams

In order to keep the network management team together, expectations of employers and employees must match to a certain degree. Table 8.3 shows a sample of expectations on both sides. The contract between the individual and the organization is often psychological because much of it unwritten and unspoken. There are several reasons for this:

- Both parties may not be entirely clear about their expectations and how they wish them to be met. They may not want to define the contract until they have a better feel for what they want.

Table 8.1 Allocation Matrix for Support Processes

ORGANIZATIONAL UNITS / Processes	FINANCE	SALES AND MARKETING	HUMAN RESOURCES	OPERATIONS, ADMINISTRATION AND MAINTENANCE	STRATEGIC PLANNING	LOGISTICS AND FACILITY MANAGEMENT	INFORMATION TECHNOLOGY
Customer care and billing							
Customer interface management		X		X			
Sales		X					
Problem handling				X			
Customer QoS management				X			
Call rating and discounting	X						
Invoicing and collection	X						
Consulting and support		X	X	X	X		X
Provisioning and order processing						X	
Inventory management	X	X					

522

Service creation, planning, and development	X		X
Network planning and development			X
Network provisioning		X	
Service ordering	X	X	
Service configuration		X	
Security management		X	
Network operational management			
Service problem resolution	X	X	
Service quality management	X	X	
Network maintenance and resolution		X	
Data collection and data management		X	X

Table 8.2 Allocation Matrix for Support Systems

ORGANIZATIONAL UNITS	FINANCE	SALES AND MARKETING	HUMAN RESOURCES	OPERATIONS, ADMINISTRATION AND MAINTENANCE	STRATEGIC PLANNING	LOGISTICS AND FACILITY MANAGEMENT	INFORMATION TECHNOLOGY
Support tools							
Management frameworks				X			X
Operation support systems	X	X		X			X
Business support systems	X	X				X	X
Marketing support systems		X					X
Documentation systems	X	X	X	X	X	X	X
Management systems				X			X
SLA surveillance instruments		X		X			

	Col 1	Col 2	Col 3	Col 4	Col 5	Col 6	Col 7
Customer relationship management tools						X	
Billing applications						X	
eCare tools				X		X	
Modeling applications	X			X			
Knowledge tools	X		X	X			
Geographical information systems				X			
Enterprise resource planning tools		X			X		X

Table 8.3 Expectations in the Employer/Employee Relationship

EXPECTATIONS OF THE INDIVIDUAL	EXPECTATIONS OF THE EMPLOYER
1. Compensation	1. An honest day's work
2. Personal development opportunities	2. Loyalty to organization
3. Recognition and approval for good work	3. Initiative
4. Security through fringe benefits	4. Conformity to organizational norms
5. Friendly, supportive environment	5. Job effectiveness
6. Fair treatment	6. Flexibility and willingness to learn and develop
7. Meaningful or purposeful job	7. No security violations

- Neither of the parties are aware of their expectations. For example, organizations are hardly able to define the term *loyalty*.

- Some expectations may be perceived as so natural and basic that they are taken for granted (e.g., expectations of not stealing and an honest day's work for a day's pay).

- Cultural norms may inhibit verbalization, which is particularly important with multinational companies hiring employees in various countries.

At any given time, there will be some relatively fulfilled and unfulfilled expectations; however, each party has to have a minimum level of fulfillment. If either party concludes that the fulfillment of its needs is below this minimum level, it will view the contract as having been violated.

Turnover in the organizational units of service providers can be very disadvantageous for maintaining service levels to end users. Corporate and business unit management should try to avoid above average turnover by implementing rewards to satisfy employees. Creating satisfaction with the rewards given is not a simple matter. It is a function of several factors that organizations must learn to manage.

The individual's satisfaction with rewards is in part related to what's expected and how much is received. Feelings of satisfaction or dissatisfaction arise when individuals compare their input (knowledge, skills, experience) to output (mix of rewards) they receive.

Employee satisfaction is also affected by comparisons to other people in similar jobs and organizations. People vary considerably in how they weight various inputs and outputs in that comparison. They tend to weight their strong points (e.g., certain skills or a recent performance peak) more heavily than their weak ones. Individuals also tend to correlate their own performance to the rating they receive from their supervisors. The problem of unrealistic self-ratings exists partly because supervisors in most organizations do not communicate a candid evaluation of their subordinates' performance to them.

Employees often misperceive the rewards of others; their misperception can cause the employees to become dissatisfied. Evidence shows that individuals tend to overestimate the pay of colleagues doing similar jobs and underestimate their colleagues' performance.

Finally, overall satisfaction results from a mix of rewards rather than from any single reward. Rewards fall into two principal categories: extrinsic and intrinsic. *Extrinsic rewards* come from the employer as compensation, benefits, job security, training, promotions, effective network management instruments, and recognition. *Intrinsic rewards* come from performing the task itself and may include job satisfaction, sense of influence, quality of environment, and quality of assignment. The priority of extrinsic and intrinsic rewards depends on the individual person. The following list gives a frequently seen priority sequence to keep the support teams together.

Compensation. Pay is still the most important motivation factor. Organizations try to use a number of person-based or skill-based compensation techniques combined with the dependence of sales revenues of the larger organization, if applicable. Pay is a matter of perception and values that often generates conflict.

Benefits. Benefits take special forms, depending on the employer's business (e.g., company car, life insurance, lower interest rates, housing). The cost of benefits at companies can be as high as 35 to 45 percent of pay.

Job security. Seniority is a very valuable management practice, particularly when the economy is stressed. Job security policies include retirement plans, options for early retirement, and nonlayoff agreements. Job security packages are more advanced in Europe and Japan than in the United States.

Recognition. Recognition may come from the organization or from other employees. One periodic form of recognition is the performance appraisal conducted by the supervisor. A relatively new form, the so-called upward appraisal, is considered a form of subordinates' recognition. It is difficult because most managers do not want to be evaluated by their subordinates. For the subordinates, it is the forum for communicating ideas for improvement.

Career path and creation of dual ladders. In order to keep motivation high, managerial and technical assignments must be compensated equally. Promoting technically interested persons into managerial positions may not have the desired results; these persons are usually high in affiliation motivation and low in power motivation. Helpful activities include career counseling and exploration, increasing company career opportunity information, improving career feedback, enhancing linear career, slowing early-career advancement, and enriching lower-level jobs with more challenges.

Effective training. This type of motivation helps to keep the specific and generic knowledge of the employees at the most advanced level. Three to six weeks' training and education annually is considered adequate in the dynamically changing network management environment.

Quality of assignments. Job descriptions are expected to give the framework for expectations. But dynamic job descriptions may help to avoid monotony and promote job rotation. The client contact point, systems administration, and change control may be rotated periodically.

Use of adequate tools. Better-instrumented networking environments facilitate the jobs of the network management staff, increase the service quality to users, and improve the image of the network management organization. At the same time, persons working with advanced tools are proud of their special knowledge and of their employer. They are highly motivated to continue with the company.

Realistic performance goals. As part of dynamic job descriptions and job rotation, realistic performance expectations may help to stabilize the position of the network management team. Management must find the balance between quantifiable and nonquantifiable goals. Average time spent on trouble calls, response time to problems, time of repair, and end-user satisfaction or dissatisfaction are examples for both types of goals.

Quality of environment. This is more or less a generic term expressing the mix of network management–related instruments, pleasant working atmosphere, comfortable furniture, adequate legroom, easy access to filing cabinets or to hypermedia, acceptance of opinions on shortcomings, and team spirit.

Employee control. Despite high team spirit, individuals need certain levels of control that can be determined only by managerial skills. Depending on the person, positive motivation, negative motivation, or a combination of both may work best.

The preceding list has concentrated on key motivation alternatives only. There are many more. In order to find the optimal combination for individual installations, a human resources management audit is recommended.

8.5 Job Profiles and Responsibilities

Successful operations require a well-educated management team with adequate skill levels. In order to make hiring and cross-education easier, the most important profiles for the teams should be well prepared and well maintained. These job descriptions serve as a basis to evaluate the completeness of existing descriptions and of existing documents on both managers and subject matter experts of the service provider.

Job profiles should include the following items

- Responsibilities
- External job contacts
- Qualifying experiences
- Required education
- Personal attributes
- Salary range

In order to help service provider to prepare job profiles, a few examples are shown.

PROFILE OF NETWORK OPERATIONS MANAGER

Responsibilities

1. Supervises and monitors the quality of network management.
2. Estimates cost and resource requirements.
3. Reviews and approves processes and instruments.

4. Performs planning and scheduling of products' implementation.

5. Develops, implements, and enforces procedural and security standards.

6. Evaluates performance of processes, instruments, and people; reports results to management.

7. Plans and directs acquisitions, training, and development projects.

8. Creates and supervises SLAs.

9. Defines and selects QoS metrics.

External job contacts

1. Other managers within information systems.

2. Some users.

3. Some vendors.

4. External consulting companies.

Qualifying experience and attributes

1. Prior experience in statistics, mathematics, accounting, computer science, telecommunications, or equivalent.

2. Training in advanced practices, skills and concepts, administrative management, supervisory techniques, resource management, budgeting and planning.

3. Excellent communication skills.

4. Excellent negotiation skills.

5. Excellent managerial skills.

PROFILE OF INVENTORY MANAGER

Responsibilities

1. Manages the online configuration application, including establishment of requirements for this area.

2. Maintains the network configuration.

3. Maintains vendor information.

4. Knows status of program and access methods used by the system.

5. Maintains security of inventory control records.

6. Tracks the delivery and installation of new equipment.

7. Implements coordination.

External job contacts

1. Technical support.

2. Network operation, change, and problem coordinators.

3. Call center.

4. Customers.

5. Service and problem manager.

6. Vendors.

Qualifying experience and attributes

1. Has knowledge of communications facilities and offerings.

2. Has some knowledge of systems programming and database structure.

3. Has inventory-control skills.

4. Is familiar with conversion procedures and general project management.

PROFILE OF SERVICE AND PROBLEM MANAGER

Responsibilities

1. Ensures that problems are routed to proper person or function for resolution.

2. Monitors status of outstanding problems via open trouble tickets.

3. Enforces priorities and schedules of problem resolution.

4. Maintains up-to-date problem records that contain problem descriptions, priority, and status.

5. Schedules critical situation meetings with appropriate parties.

6. Fulfills administrative reporting requirements.

7. Cross-organizes resources if required.

8. Assumes responsibility for total communication network.

9. Provides input to experience files.

10. Provides input to what-if catalogs.

11. Evaluates security logs.

12. Evaluates SLA violations.

External job contacts

1. Vendor representatives.

2. Technical support.

3. Call center.

4. Change manager.

5. System and application programmers.

6. Network operations manager.

Qualifying experience and attributes

1. Has broad knowledge of QoS metrics.

2. Has broad information system and teleprocessing background.

3. Has good aptitude in communication and coordination.

PROFILE OF CALL CENTER OPERATOR

Responsibilities

1. Network supervision.

   - Implements first-level problem-determination procedures

   - Maintains documentation to assist customer in terminal operation

2. Problem logging.

   ■ Uses procedure guide for opening trouble tickets

   ■ Reviews change activities log

3. Problem delegation.

   ■ Determines problem area

   ■ Assigns priorities

   ■ Information distribution

4. Additional duties when call center activity is low.

   ■ Data entry for configuration and inventory

   ■ Summary of active problems for problem coordinator

   ■ Entering change information for change coordinator

   ■ Monitoring of security

   ■ Generating management and technical reports

5. Recommends modification to procedures.

External job contacts

1. Customers.

2. Vendor representatives.

3. Problem and change managers.

4. Network operation and technical support.

5. Network administrator for trouble tickets.

6. QoS and SLA managers.

Qualifying experience and attributes

1. Familiarity with functional applications and terminal equipment.

2. Training in personal relationships.

3. Clerical rather than technical.

   ■ Data-entry skills

   ■ Problem-determination know-how

4. Sensitivity to customers.

   ■ Understanding of their business needs

   ■ Pleasant telephone voice

   ■ Language know-how

PROFILE OF NETWORK INFRASTRUCTURE OPERATOR

Responsibilities

1. Observes ongoing operations and performance to identify problems.

2. Initiates corrective action where required within the scope of knowledge and authority.

3. Interprets console messages from network software or applications programs and performs required actions.

4. Assists with network-oriented problem determination.

5. Implements backup procedures.

6. Implements bypass and recovery procedures for system/network problems.

7. Fulfills administrative reporting requirements on network problems.

8. Maintains communications with systems control.

9. Monitors all network activities.

10. Uses and invokes network diagnostic aids and tools.

11. Uses and provides input to database for problem and inventory control.

12. Does second-level problem determination.

13. Does network start-up and shutdown.

14. Schedules network activities such as testing and maintenance.

External job contacts

1. Technical support staff.

2. Configuration and inventory function.

3. Problem and change coordinators of network administration.

4. Customer education and customer support desk.

5. Vendor representatives.

6. Network administration.

Qualifying experience and attributes

1. Training in concepts of network infrastructure operations.

2. At least one year of network experience with the following:

   - Access and transport networks

   - Lines, clusters, and terminal types

   - Service levels

   - Distribution schedules

3. Alert, intelligent, strives for efficiency.

4. Can execute bypass/recovery procedures.

5. Can perform authorized network alterations.

6. Understands the following:

   - Escalation procedures

   - Operating of problem and change management

   - Reporting requirements and procedures

7. Has communication skills.

8. Can use various tools, depending on the availability of such tools.

PROFILE OF SERVICE TECHNICIAN

Responsibilities

1. Provides in-depth (third-level) problem determination as necessary.

2. Provides technical interface with vendors as necessary.

3. Designs and maintains up-to-date problem determination, bypass, and recovery procedures.

4. Provides technical interface as necessary with application and system programmers.

5. Uses inventory-control database.

6. Ensures valid run procedures.

7. Assists with network configuration/reconfiguration.

8. Reads dumps from network equipment.

9. Starts and evaluates special-purpose diagnostics.

10. Evaluates QoS metrics.

External job contacts

1. Change manager.

2. Problem manager.

3. Call center operator.

4. Vendor technical personnel.

5. Application and system programmers.

6. Network infrastructure operator.

7. Inventory manager.

Qualifying experience and attributes

1. Several years' experience with a broad range of communication equipment and the tools and aids necessary to maintain the network, including the following:

   - Network operation
   - Network-control programs
   - Access and transport networks
   - Network equipment
   - Configuration/reconfiguration procedures

2. Good aptitude for communicating with people.

3. Can use diagnostic tools.

4. Understands vendor standards and procedures.

5. Has patience in pursuing problems.

PROFILE OF SERVICE-LEVEL MANAGER

Responsibilities

1. Assumes responsibility for all access and transport networks.
2. Negotiates service levels.
3. Evaluates service-oriented parameters.
4. Provides feedback to capacity planning
5. Designs and generates service reports.
6. Costs service levels and negotiates charge-back.
7. Assumes responsibility for QoS management.
8. Executes baselining.
9. Measures QoS metrics.

External job contacts

1. Capacity planning and design.
2. Operations support.
3. Performance monitoring and tuning.
4. Customers.

Qualifying experience and attributes

1. Has excellent communication skills.
2. Has overview on communication networks.
3. Understands the relationship between service level, costs, and resources utilization.
4. Has knowledge of TMN.

PROFILE OF BUSINESS PLANNER

Responsibilities

1. Pursues business plans of the service provider.
2. Creates portfolios.
3. Characterizes and represents present networking workload.
4. Projects networking workload.
5. Develops installation and migration plans.
6. Assigns due dates for installations.
7. Supervises pilot installations.
8. Prepares network design alternatives that will meet future needs.
9. Produces fallback plan.
10. Selects modeling tools.
11. Executes benchmarks.

External job contacts

1. Business planners of the larger organization.

2. Network performance analysts.

3. Vendors of projection tools.

4. Modeling coordinator.

5. Application systems developers.

Qualifying experience and attributes

1. Communication skills.

2. Knowledge of the business of the larger organization.

3. Some experience in networking technologies.

4. In-depth knowledge of projection techniques.

5. Political skills.

6. Planning and scheduling skills.

7. Communication skills in working with vendors.

8. Detailed knowledge of fallback procedures.

PROFILE OF TECHNOLOGY ANALYST

Responsibilities

1. Prepares feasibility studies for network planning and for network changes.

2. Evaluates technologies, architectures, and protocols.

3. Makes and evaluates reference visits.

4. Evaluates utilization and service level.

5. Accomplishes comparative lab measurements.

6. Performs hardware and software selection.

External job contacts

1. Application systems developers.

2. Service-level manager.

3. Communication providers.

4. Vendors.

5. Inventory and assets coordinator.

6. Other users.

Qualifying experience and attributes

1. Communication skills.

2. Overview on communication forms, services, and networks.

3. In-depth knowledge of service level.

4. In-depth knowledge of networking facilities and equipment.

PROFILE OF SECURITY ANALYST

Responsibilities

1. Defines monitoring and surveillance functions.

2. Evaluates and selects security management services.

3. Evaluates the performance impacts of security techniques.

4. Constructs threat matrix.

5. Recommends instruments to be selected.

6. Supervises installation of instruments.

7. Customizes passwords and access authorization.

8. Programs instruments.

9. Establishes procedures for securing the network management systems.

External job contacts

1. Security officer.

2. Vendors.

3. Security auditor.

4. Other internal users.

Qualifying experience and attributes

1. Has superior personal record.

2. In-depth knowledge of security management services and tools.

3. Has technical skills to customize products.

4. Has some communication skills toward vendors.

8.6 Filling the Jobs

Let us assume, job descriptions are clear; there are enough candidates to select from; hiring managers are in place, hiring guidelines have been prepared and budget for human resources is available.

Two more important questions must be answered next: How many resources individual processes need and how skill requirements may be met.

8.6.1 Head Count Example

Little information is available in the telecommunications industry about the proper size of the team supporting principal business, marketing, and operational processes of the service provider. In many cases, head counts are broken down in terms of fault, configuration, accounting, performance, and security management (FCAPS); in other cases, they are sized by the number of managed objects or by processes. This section provides a simple example that may be considered as a starting point. This example is based on the experiences of an outsourcer who is in charge of managing data networks from many customers with a broad range of infrastructures.

Table 8.4 shows the aggregated results for FCAPS, plus network design and planning.

The numbers in the table relate to one shift only. If more shifts must be supported, the numbers will increase. Depending on the services offered by the provider, a full occupation in the table may mean a certain number of hours to be staffed annually, as shown in Table 8.5.

An average person could work approximately 1600 hours a year, considering vacation, holidays, training, and sickness. In order to get the real number of human resources required to fill a certain position, the total hours required for the function should be divided by 1600. Considering the configuration management function for small networks, Table 8.4 indicates 3 FTEs for support. Assuming a 7 days $\times$ 8 hours activity, Table 8.5 indicates 2,920 annual hours for 1 FTE; the total request is $3 \times 2,920 = 8,760$ annual hours. Using 1,600 hours as an accepted basis for an average subject matter expert, the service provider needs 5.47 (rounded to 6) persons to support configuration management for small networks.

Considering the fault management function for medium-sized networks, Table 8.4 indicates 19 FTEs for support. Assuming a 7 days $\times$ 24 hours activity, Table 8.5 indicates 8,760 annual hours for 1 FTE; the total request is $19 \times 8,760 = 166,440$ annual

Table 8.4 Head Count Summary

NUMBER OF MANAGED OBJECTS (MO)	UP TO 5000	BETWEEN 5000 AND 15,000	BETWEEN 15,000 AND 50,000	BETWEEN 50,000 AND 250,000	OVER 250,000
Functions					
Fault management	4	9	19	29	45
Configuration management	3	5	10	17	25
Accounting management	2	4	8	11	14
Performance management	3	5	8	12	18
Security management	2	3	5	8	10
Network design and planning	2	5	10	13	16
Grand total of FTEs*	16	31	60	110	127

* FTE = full-time equivalent.

Table 8.5 Staff Hours Required

SERVICE AVAILABILITY		TOTAL ANNUAL HOURS
5 days × 8 hours	=	2,080
5 days × 16 hours	=	4,160
5 days × 24 hours	=	6,240
7 days × 8 hours	=	2,920
7 days × 16 hours	=	5,840
7 days × 24 hours	=	8,760

hours. Using 1,600 hours as an accepted basis for an average subject matter expert, the service provider needs 104 persons to support fault management for medium-sized networks.

Based on experiences of service providers and outsourcers, the total demand on human resources should be fine-tuned using the following weighting factors

- Complexity of managed objects
- Speed of technology change
- Technology and age of managed objects
- Geographical distribution of managed objects
- Number of trouble tickets generated for managed objects
- Educational level and skills of subject matter experts
- Quality of support, documentation, and management tools

Human resources are the dominating expense factor in operating communication networks. Hardware, software, and physical infrastructure cost relatively less than people.

8.6.2 Skill Matrices

In order to help service providers recruit employees, skill matrices have been prepared for each of the principal processes addressed in Chapters 4 through 6.

Besides identifying principal functions for each process, typical knowledge, experiences, and skills have been evaluated. Depending on the job posting, HR can assemble the proper mix of required skills for interviews, as delineated in Tables 8.6 to 8.23.

The process of building and expanding the network management team is complicated by a number of factors. Here are the most important ones:

- Scarce technical resources
- No standard job descriptions and responsibilities
- Few specific academic training programs
- Rapidly changing networking technology

Table 8.6 Customer Interface Management Process

PRINCIPAL FUNCTIONS	FUNCTIONAL KNOWLEDGE	TECHNOLOGY AND PORTFOLIO KNOW-HOW	KNOWLEDGE OF TOOLS	PROJECT ADMINISTRATION SKILLS	PERSONAL COMMUNICATION SKILLS
Receive and record contacts	X	X	X		X
Register customer requests	X		X		
Direct inquiries to appropriate processes	X				X
Monitor and control status of inquiries and escalate	X				
Ensure a consistent image and secure use of systems	X		X		

Table 8.7 The Sales Process

PRINCIPAL FUNCTIONS	FUNCTIONAL KNOWLEDGE	TECHNOLOGY AND PORTFOLIO KNOW-HOW	KNOWLEDGE OF TOOLS	PROJECT ADMINISTRATION SKILLS	PERSONAL COMMUNICATION SKILLS
Learn about customer needs	X	X			X
Educate customer on services	X				X
Match expectations to offerings and products	X	X			X
Arrange for appropriate options	X				
Forecast service demand	X	X	X		
Manage SLA and RPF negotiations	X			X	X

Table 8.8 The Problem-Handling Process

PRINCIPAL FUNCTIONS	FUNCTIONAL KNOWLEDGE	TECHNOLOGY AND PORTFOLIO KNOW-HOW	KNOWLEDGE OF TOOLS	PROJECT ADMINISTRATION SKILLS	PERSONAL COMMUNICATION SKILLS
Receive trouble notification	X	X	X		X
Determine cause, resolve, or refer	X			X	X
Track progress of resolution	X	X			X
Initiate action to reconfigure if needed	X			X	
Generate trouble tickets to suppliers	X		X		
Confirm trouble cleared and notify customer	X		X		X
Schedule with and notify customer of planned maintenance	X				X

Table 8.9 Customer QoS Management Process

PRINCIPAL FUNCTIONS	FUNCTIONAL KNOWLEDGE	TECHNOLOGY AND PORTFOLIO KNOW-HOW	KNOWLEDGE OF TOOLS	PROJECT ADMINISTRATION SKILLS	PERSONAL COMMUNICATION SKILLS
Schedule customer reports	X		X		
Receive performance data	X		X		
Establish reports to be generated	X				
Compile and deliver customer reports	X		X		
Manage SLA performance	X	X		X	X
Determine and deliver QoS and SLA violation information	X	X			

Table 8.10 The Call Rating and Discounting Process

PRINCIPAL FUNCTIONS	FUNCTIONAL KNOWLEDGE	TECHNOLOGY AND PORTFOLIO KNOW-HOW	KNOWLEDGE OF TOOLS	PROJECT ADMINISTRATION SKILLS	PERSONAL COMMUNICATION SKILLS
Apply service rates to usage	X				
Apply negotiated discounts	X				
Apply rebates	X				X
Process incomplete CDRs	X				X
Observe customer behavior	X				
Identification of fraud	X	X	X	X	
Selection of mediation solutions	X		X		

Table 8.11 The Invoicing and Collection Process

PRINCIPAL FUNCTIONS	FUNCTIONAL KNOWLEDGE	TECHNOLOGY AND PORTFOLIO KNOW-HOW	KNOWLEDGE OF TOOLS	PROJECT ADMINISTRATION SKILLS	PERSONAL COMMUNICATION SKILLS
Create and distribute invoices	X	X		X	
Bill presentment	X		X		X
Collect payments	X				X
Handle customer account inquiries	X	X			X
Debt management	X				X
Wholesale and retail billing	X	X			X
Bill on behalf of other providers	X	X			X
Analysis of customer behavior	X		X		X
Relationship management	X				X

Table 8.12 Process of Consulting and Support

PRINCIPAL FUNCTIONS	FUNCTIONAL KNOWLEDGE	TECHNOLOGY AND PORTFOLIO KNOW-HOW	KNOWLEDGE OF TOOLS	PROJECT ADMINISTRATION SKILLS	PERSONAL COMMUNICATION SKILLS
Estimation of consulting demand	X				X
Customer support	X	X			X
Security consulting	X		X	X	X
Training and education for the customer	X	X	X	X	X
Periodic and ad hoc consultation	X	X	X	X	X

Table 8.13 The Inventory Management Process

PRINCIPAL FUNCTIONS	FUNCTIONAL KNOWLEDGE	TECHNOLOGY AND PORTFOLIO KNOW-HOW	KNOWLEDGE OF TOOLS	PROJECT ADMINISTRATION SKILLS	PERSONAL COMMUNICATION SKILLS
Installation and administration of the physical network	X	X			X
Performing work in the network	X			X	
Manage the repair activities	X		X	X	
Aligning inventory with network	X		X		
Manage spare parts	X		X		
Manage faulty parts	X		X		

Table 8.14 The Service Creation, Planning, and Development Process

PRINCIPAL FUNCTIONS	FUNCTIONAL KNOWLEDGE	TECHNOLOGY AND PORTFOLIO KNOW-HOW	KNOWLEDGE OF TOOLS	PROJECT ADMINISTRATION SKILLS	PERSONAL COMMUNICATION SKILLS
Develop and implement technical solutions	X			X	X
Develop and implement procedures	X			X	X
Define and implement systems changes	X	X		X	X
Develop and implement training	X			X	X
Develop customer documentation	X			X	X
Plan rollout, test, start service, and project-manage	X			X	
Set product/ service pricing	X	X	X		

Table 8.15 The Network Planning and Development Process

PRINCIPAL FUNCTIONS	FUNCTIONAL KNOWLEDGE	TECHNOLOGY AND PORTFOLIO KNOW-HOW	KNOWLEDGE OF TOOLS	PROJECT ADMINISTRATION SKILLS	PERSONAL COMMUNICATION SKILLS
Develop and implement procedures	X				
Setup framework agreements	X				
Develop new methods and architectures	X				
Plan required network capacity	X		X		
Plan the mutation of network capacity	X		X		
Issue orders to suppliers and other network operators	X				X
Plan the logical network configuration	X		X		
Evaluate service metrics	X		X		

Table 8.16 The Network Provisioning Process

PRINCIPAL FUNCTIONS	FUNCTIONAL KNOWLEDGE	TECHNOLOGY AND PORTFOLIO KNOW-HOW	KNOWLEDGE OF TOOLS	PROJECT ADMINISTRATION SKILLS	PERSONAL COMMUNICATION SKILLS
(Re)-configuration of the network	X		X		
Administration of the logical network	X			X	X
Connection management	X				
Test the network	X	X	X		X

Table 8.17 The Service Ordering Process

PRINCIPAL FUNCTIONS	FUNCTIONAL KNOWLEDGE	TECHNOLOGY AND PORTFOLIO KNOW-HOW	KNOWLEDGE OF TOOLS	PROJECT ADMINISTRATION SKILLS	PERSONAL COMMUNICATION SKILLS
Accept orders	X				X
Determine preorder feasibility	X		X		
Prepare price estimates and SLA terms	X	X			
Develop order plan	X				
Perform credit check	X				X
Request customer deposit	X				X
Reserve resources	X	X	X		
Initiate service installation	X				
Complete orders and notify customers	X				X
Initiate billing process	X				

Table 8.18 The Service Configuration Process

PRINCIPAL FUNCTIONS	FUNCTIONAL KNOWLEDGE	TECHNOLOGY AND PORTFOLIO KNOW-HOW	KNOWLEDGE OF TOOLS	PROJECT ADMINISTRATION SKILLS	PERSONAL COMMUNICATION SKILLS
Design solution (preorder)	X	X			
Assign capacity (preorder)	X	X			
Configure network and CPE	X		X		
Update customer configuration record	X		X		
Initiate/accept configuration requests to/from other providers	X				X
Initiate installation work	X		X		
Activate/deactivate service	X		X		
Report about service implementation completion	X				X

Table 8.19 The Security Management Process

PRINCIPAL FUNCTIONS	FUNCTIONAL KNOWLEDGE	TECHNOLOGY AND PORTFOLIO KNOW-HOW	KNOWLEDGE OF TOOLS	PROJECT ADMINISTRATION SKILLS	PERSONAL COMMUNICATION SKILLS
Identification of information to be protected	X	X	X	X	X
Analysis of access options to protected information	X	X	X		
Selection and implementation of solutions for protection	X		X	X	X
Periodic reassessment of security solutions	X		X		X

Table 8.20 The Service Problem Resolution Process

PRINCIPAL FUNCTIONS	FUNCTIONAL KNOWLEDGE	TECHNOLOGY AND PORTFOLIO KNOW-HOW	KNOWLEDGE OF TOOLS	PROJECT ADMINISTRATION SKILLS	PERSONAL COMMUNICATION SKILLS
Isolate and resolve service problems	X	X	X	X	X
Identify chronic failures	X	X	X	X	
Provide performance data	X	X	X		
Recommend service redesign	X				
Initiating escalation procedures	X			X	
Analysis of service quality	X	X	X		
Generating reports about services	X		X	X	

Table 8.21   The Service Quality Management Process

PRINCIPAL FUNCTIONS	FUNCTIONAL KNOWLEDGE	TECHNOLOGY AND PORTFOLIO KNOW-HOW	KNOWLEDGE OF TOOLS	PROJECT ADMINISTRATION SKILLS	PERSONAL COMMUNICATION SKILLS
Life-cycle management of service/ product portfolios	X			X	
Monitor overall delivered quality of service	X	X	X	X	
Maintain SLAs	X	X	X		X
Monitor available capacity /usage against forecasted sales	X		X		
Initiate service improvements	X	X			
Inform sales on constraints	X	X			X

Table 8.22   The Network Maintenance and Restoration Process

PRINCIPAL FUNCTIONS	FUNCTIONAL KNOWLEDGE	TECHNOLOGY AND PORTFOLIO KNOW-HOW	KNOWLEDGE OF TOOLS	PROJECT ADMINISTRATION SKILLS	PERSONAL COMMUNICATION SKILLS
Problem analysis, including testing	X	X	X	X	X
Proactive recognition of problem trends	X	X	X		
Network quality maintenance and restoration	X	X	X	X	
Maintain historic data of network problems and performance	X	X	X		

Table 8.23 The Data Collection and Data Management Process

PRINCIPAL FUNCTIONS	FUNCTIONAL KNOWLEDGE	TECHNOLOGY AND PORTFOLIO KNOW-HOW	KNOWLEDGE OF TOOLS	PROJECT ADMINISTRATION SKILLS	PERSONAL COMMUNICATION SKILLS
Collection of usage data via CDRs and IPDRs	X	X	X	X	
Mediation on collected data	X	X	X		
Use of SS7 in collecting data	X	X	X		
Data warehousing for maintaining data	X		X	X	X
Baselining and generating performance metrics for reporting	X		X		X
Maintain trouble tickets in a database	X		X		X
Provide notification on performance	X		X		X
Initiate traffic metrics collection	X		X	X	

- Changes in network management instrumentation
- Shorter career paths
- Few upward mobility alternatives

8.7 Enabling Technologies for Workforce Management

These technologies enrich other applications covered in previous chapters. They are integrated with prerequisite systems—usually existing support, documentation, and management systems—to provide robust functionality. Document-, knowledge-, and workforce-related technologies are covered in this section. More details can be found in CISC98.

8.7.1 Document-Related Technology (DRT)

Document management has gained importance as it has left the isolation of being a niche and ad hoc solution for various processes of service providers. DRS is increasingly playing the role of an integration aid gluing together multiple documentation products. Document management is a set of technologies used to incorporate and manage existing and new documents within an enterprise for the purpose of wider distribution and easy access.

Each document is a file or part of a file, structured or unstructured and stored in a computer system, that can be considered an authentic and unambiguous unit and that can be retrieved at any point in time. A document is composed of a collection of information in any format (video, audio, text, Web pages, CD, paper, images, schematics, drawings, spreadsheets, etc.) located anywhere within the company. Such documents might or might not have any construct, but they are structured in the way they are captured or validated to be an enterprise document.

Due to the opportunity for modifying, adding, and changing data in computer systems, there are very severe requirements in regard to maintaining electronic documents. These requirements are centered around the following:

- Retrieval of status, composition, form, and content of documents at the point of their creation
- Maintenance of dynamic links between document units
- Automatic updates of documents
- Changes in relationships
- Structuring documents of individual components
- Dependency of formats and run-time environments
- Other guidelines of documents maintenance

The principal application areas of DRS include imaging, workflow, repository, and retrieval. The implementation frequency depends on the industry; service providers concentrate on all areas, with a slight emphasis on workflow. Each phase of the service cycle (Chapter 1, Figure 1.2) includes some form of DRS.

Document management helps to integrate various technological and organizational solutions for service providers. Figure 8.1 shows a simplified structure of this integration.

DRS today penetrates almost all areas of processes and functions supported by service providers. In particular, good practical examples are seen with ERP- and IP-related integration.

There are two types of documents:

1. *Collaboration documents.* These are short, unstructured documents, such as e-mails, notes, messages, postings, and memos. They help group work and are characterized as immediate posting, minimal audit, and history tracking or revi-

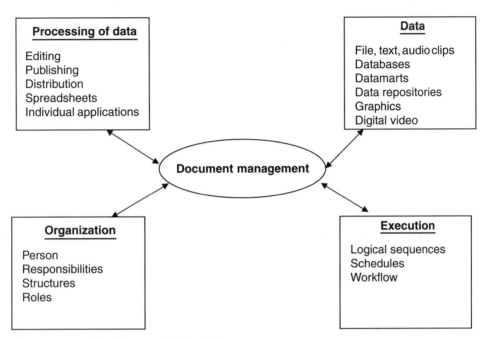

Figure 8.1   Integration capabilities of document management.

sion tracking. They do not need to be validated because the collaboration in which they appear is itself the validation process.

2. *Enterprise documents.* These help drive business operations. They include manufacturing procedures, product design specifications, marketing requirements of products, business transactions, and escalation procedures. They need to be validated, tracked, monitored, and widely distributed in order to support operations.

A document management systems (DMS) should ensure that the contents of the documents it contains are current, accurate, and approved. *Current* means that the document is in effect at the time of publishing. Often within organizations there are many revisions and changes to enterprise documents; knowing which one is current and approved is crucial to operations. *Accurate* means ensuring an enforced review for each document. The enforcement steps are up to the implementers and users of the system. Once defined, they provide accuracy to a document within the enterprise. *Approved* means that the document can be used. This feature is highly critical to marketing departments of service providers when services are vulnerable to constraints such as legal, contractual, ethical, moral, or just pure marketing positioning.

The following areas are currently considered the primary targets of DRS penetration:

- Internet, intranet, and extranet documentation

- Document, workflow, and knowledge management

- eCommerce and the use of digital signatures

- Document input, distribution, and storage

- OCR, ICR, and pattern recognition
- Databases, data warehouses, datamarts, and retrieval engines
- Imaging and multimedia
- Archival and records management
- Secure communication and unified messaging
- Groupware and office solutions
- Forms, templates, and output management
- Middleware and componentware
- Content management and content distribution

Using DMS offers several key benefits to service providers:

Manageable and scalable information. The instrumental benefit in using DMS is to control all existing enterprise documents for the purpose of tracking and reuse. Without such a system, it is extremely difficult for a service provider to fully understand its own intellectual property and operations. Furthermore, such information is often reused or reformatted as business changes. Estimates from industry experts claim that as much as 60 percent of employees' time is spent re-creating documents. The ability to reuse documents in a different format and context is a highly scalable competitive advantage.

Higher productivity. DMS helps all branches and groups within the organization know exactly what to do by providing them with current, accurate, and approved information to work on. This is the highest form of productivity tool short of the human effort itself.

Faster time to market. One of the results from this high-productivity tool is the ability for a company to run its operations as effectively as possible. The effect is faster time to market for products and services.

Accurate and effective execution. The goal of DMS is to ensure that information is current, accurate, and approved. The contents of DMS are usually procedures, processes, or operational flows of an organization, as well as other documents that detail how a corporation functions.

A professional DMS requires the following steps for proper deployment:

1. *Analyze the documents to be managed.* Not all documents of the service provider need to be managed in the DMS.

2. *Determine the purpose of management.* After step 1, a clear objective of such a system must be defined. For example, this objective could be the information exchange with other providers.

3. *Select the appropriate technology.* Since DMSs can offer a wide selection of technologies, users can narrow down the technology segment for quick and easy implementation and focus on project planning.

4. *Plan for implementation.* To effectively implement a DMS, several key players should buy in before the project can start. Because DMS is mainly designed for

enterprise documents, the support of senior management is necessary even before a feasibility study. DMS is more a cultural change than a technology change. While DMS utilizes the latest in network, security, distributed objects, and other enabling technologies, the true impact is on the operational process that all people must buy in to. Thus, not only must the implementation plan clearly detail the benefits of using such a system instead of the old filing cabinets, but it must also provide immediate benefits, because each of the three major milestones—capture, validate, and release—is accomplished to encourage wide usage and employee participation.

5. *Capture.* Documents are created by word processing software, imaging, graphics software, and spreadsheets. A key point in this phase is not only that new documents are created in a standard format that allows ease of scalable distribution and access, but also that existing legacy documents should be converted into the same standard. Most DMS vendors offer software that accepts documents in multiple formats and platforms into their information repository. Not only is integration of multiple formats important, but integration of multiple document identities is critical. Many documents are composed of other documents that are quite large. For example, users might need to capture or create a new document that is a structured composite of three other documents that might not be in the same physical storage or format. Such a system would then maintain a dynamic linkage throughout the life of a particular document to allow distribution of the document anywhere on the network without losing any integrity.

6. *Validate.* This phase includes several key operations. First, the document has to be verified for accuracy. Verification can be accomplished by having a work management technology to enforce review and approval steps before classifying a particular document as being accurate. Second, all revision control and management must be in place to ensure that the document is indeed the latest official information. Third, security and ownership rules are assigned so that document control and auditing can be accomplished.

7. *Release.* This step includes distribution, ownership, access, and archiving. Within each of these operations, a strong backbone network with security is required. Back-end archiving can be accomplished with information repository, with ownership, or with access rules, all of which are part of standard DMS software offerings from major vendors.

8.7.2 Knowledge Management

Knowledge management tools allow individuals to query the enterprise information base, thus enabling increased employee efficiencies through information sharing and reuse. The concept of knowledge management has been rapidly gaining momentum with service providers. The following areas are of prime interest:

Information sources. Creating information bases requires the use of several other point technologies, including database transactions, groupware, call-tracking systems, workflow, document management systems, and live collaboration.

Discovering information. Defined as the ability to effectively tap into information to gain true knowledge, this area includes search engines, publish/subscribe agents, data-mining tools, and collaborative context filtering.

Content management. Maintenance of an information store requires an effective storage and retrieval mechanism, including document management systems, push technologies, and other technologies already mentioned.

Service providers are very much interested in protecting information they have been collecting for a long time. There are two groups of information: *Explicit information* is made up of those elements that are actually documented in some fashion and exist in some physical form. *Implicit information* consists of everything else, including human experiences that can become valuable knowledge if known and applied. In terms of knowledge tools, there are four general categories:

1. *Expert tools.* Generally considered in technical support areas and include expert systems, case-based reasoning tools, and rules engines. These tools generally require some decision tree in order to gain their full potential, but when implemented, they can often replace human personnel to solve problems.

2. *Knowledgeware.* An ever growing category of tools that attempt to easily discover knowledge within an information repository. Examples of these products include search engines, indexing tools, natural language processors, and document summarization tools.

3. *Directory.* A structured method for discovering implicit information. It should contain all the roles and people that make up the enterprise, along with their projects and the classification of their knowledge. The directory is the tool used to find the experts in an organization.

4. *Collaboration.* The best way to extract knowledge from a subject matter expert in an accepted manner, collaboration tools can be in the form of audio-/video-/data-conferencing systems, groupware tools such as threaded discussions and databases, or meeting facilitation tools.

Service providers can benefit from knowledge tools in multiple areas. A few examples follow.

1. *Knowledge tools improve the information flow to customers and suppliers.* Providing the best and most timely information to customers through service providers is a key principle in eCommerce. For example, suppliers need product and parts forecasts. They also need to be aware of product specifications and changes. Customers, on the other hand, need exposure to new services, service availability, configuration and pricing, and order status. The general practice of knowledge management is key to all the requirements. The use of knowledge tools enables improvements in the supply chain process, such as the following:

   - Allowing customers to discover the product best suited to their needs
   - Allowing better exposure to changing market conditions
   - Adapting distribution plans to changing market conditions
   - Performing historical demand analysis for improved supply forecasting

2. *Knowledge tools reduce customer support expenditures.* Support personnel need to be able to quickly find the right answers to solve customer problems. Customers, on the other hand, could use direct and fast access to product support information in order to remain happy customers. To these ends, knowledge tools offer the following advantages:

   - Allowing technical support personnel to capture the knowledge of their peers in solving customer problems

   - Ensuring that the same answers are provided for the same problems

   - Allowing customers to resolve their own product support needs for timeliness and efficiency

3. *Knowledge tools improve the selling process.* By equipping the sales force with both the most up-to-date product knowledge and awareness of current customer and market conditions, a sales force has better opportunities to sell the company's products and services:

   - Providing product configuration to sales staff and customers

   - Knowing the customer environment and needs for more effective selling

   - Tracking competitors

   - Having a proactive awareness of the market conditions that the customer faces

   - Understanding customers' previous purchases for cross-selling

4. *Knowledge tools reduce overall employee cycle time.* This area relates to the supply chain and customer care areas, but has a perspective that is more internal to a company. Examples include the following:

   - Preventing employees from duplicating the work of others

   - Keeping staff abreast of new developments within the company or the market

   - Providing workgroups with leading practices as examples in their areas of work

   - Allowing employees to easily find answers to problems they have encountered

Successful implementation and use of knowledge management tools depends on motivated people, good processes, and the right technology choice. Due to heavy pressure on service providers to become better managed and leaner—particularly in legacy environments—service providers are rapidly deploying this technology.

8.7.3 Workflow Management

Workflow management is a combination of technologies that allow service providers to automate and control any of their business processes. Doing business means executing processes. Successful companies are able to execute crisply, allowing them to build consistency and quality throughout their operations. The most important aspect of successful process implementation is control. When service providers are able to control their principal processes, they can build in definability, repeatability, and accountability, which allows them to understand and adapt their processes to meet changing needs.

An important concept in understanding workflow management is the difference between a model of a process and an instance of a process.

Process model. A process model is a series of steps that outline the data for a process and the criteria for that data to move through the process (*change of state*). For example, a process model of a customer order is "unconfirmed" until the service provider changes this state into "confirmed by date."

Process instance. A process instance is an actual occurrence of the process that was defined by a process model. For example, the service order would be created as an "unconfirmed" instance when the customer actually orders it. This instance would remain in the workflow management system until confirmation of the order.

A workflow management system would require the following technologies:

Process modeling system. This tool allows service providers to break the process into discrete, repeatable tasks and assign them to users, rules, or systems. It also allows them to define the valid states of a process and the criteria for transition from one state to the next. Sophisticated versions of these tools can enable service providers to attach process metadata attributes to each task or role; process simulations can be run for time and cost analysis.

User or client applications. These applications allow users to create an instance of a process. Typically, all users interact with the instance by using an application to perform on-screen tasks such as approval, rejection, or rerouting. Applications can also perform task management functions, such as listing outstanding tasks or accepting or rejecting assigned tasks. The applications perform the functions, but the instance is maintained in the state management engine.

Workflow engine. This system, also known as *run-time environment,* is the core of the workflow management system. It is the repository in which user applications create and manipulate instances of a process as they flow through the states defined by the process model. Agents, or automated system processes, can also act against these instances to provide automatic escalation of stalled processes and exception situations.

Management system. This tool allows a system or process administrator to view, monitor, and administer both individual instances of a process and the overall performance of the engine itself.

Workflow revolves around processes—modeling them, controlling them, understanding them, and refining them. Although each process that service providers automate has its own specific benefits, the overall benefit is enhanced control over efficient processes. Following are some other benefits that the service provider may expect:

Reduced costs. With built-in escalation of stalled processes and immediate routing of tasks, processes can be simpler to perform or occur faster, so service providers' costs are lower. By automating processes that span all involved human resources, costs for control and quality can be reduced.

Reduced workforce. When a process is automated or simpler to perform, service providers need fewer workers for the same tasks.

Enhanced cash flow. Shorter turnaround time for a process usually results in faster time to market or more timely expense management.

Increased employee and customer satisfaction. When tasks are easier to complete and less frustrating, employee satisfaction increases. When processes are completed more rapidly or with better results, customer loyalty increases.

Additional revenue opportunities. Instead of managing inefficient processes or working on complex tasks, employees can focus on revenue initiatives.

Efficient workforce management cannot be accomplished without workflow management tools.

8.7.4 Web-Enabled Workforce Management

Workforce management of the service provider may be supported by Web-based applications. Information presentment and distribution may be supported by intranets. The following areas should serve as examples for implementation:

Job posting. Job openings may be posted on the Web. Service providers can expose new openings to internal users for a period of time prior to letting external candidates view them. By soliciting resume posting, costs of recruitment advertising may be saved.

Recruiting. Service providers can build a database of resumes that hiring managers can search via the Web. Using this database, hiring managers are more likely to find applicants who have submitted resumes.

Employee directory. Service providers can create a query screen that lets employees look up any other employee in the company by name, phone, e-mail, location, or department. The costs of publishing paper-based directories may thus be saved.

Employee education and training. Service providers can create an online development program, placing plans online to be reviewed and revised by counselors and employees in an interactive manner. By providing access to these programs, employees receive a message that the employer values them as individuals and fosters a spirit of growth among employees. Also, the productivity of employees is increased by this guided development.

Payroll. Service providers can enable nonexempt employees to enter their time cards via the Web. As a result, duplicate entry of time cards can be avoided, and they can be routed for approval as needed.

Personnel status changes. Service providers can let managers request personnel status changes such as promotion, salary change, and termination via the Web. As a result, automatic validation and routing of the forms is supported, errors are reduced, and the whole process is streamlined.

Employee compensation review. Managers and employees may be allowed to build performance reviews online. Managers can add their comments, and both employee and manager can approve them. Both employee productivity and procedure efficiency may be improved by this Web-based information exchange.

Workforce management can be improved significantly by using the capabilities of intranets.

8.8 Benchmarking

Budget pressures force service providers to improve the efficiency and effectiveness of their networking infrastructures. The key to improvement lies in processes, tools, standards, and in human resources of operations, administration, and maintenance. In most cases, however, service providers are not clearly aware of the value of their operation: Are they stronger or weaker than the industry average? Audits and benchmarks help to answer this question. Basically, benchmarks can be utilized for the following three purposes:

1. To highlight gaps in business processes, tools, standards, and human resources.
2. To compare industry averages or best practices.
3. To prepare outsourcing decisions.

In the first two cases, metrics are needed to quantify performance. Various data-collection techniques (e.g., forms) may be used to evaluate which business processes are supported; which tools are used; which management protocols have been implemented; how human resources are assigned to processes and support, documentation, and management tools; and what skill levels the management team has.

In order to get feedback about the networking environment, investments made, and process details, different questionnaires are used. They can be filled in prior to or during the benchmarking process. In order to quantify and compare performance of service providers, a number of benchmarking metrics are used, grouped around generic, organizational, process-specific, and cost indicators. The results may be used for individual service providers to identify areas of improvement or to compare performance with industry averages or best practices. Usually, service providers are interested in all of these.

The third target is the preparation of outsourcing decisions. There is a mutual interest for both parties—the service provider and the outsourcer—in quantifying the value of the network, its infrastructure, its management, and its human resources in the areas of operations, administration, and maintenance. Benchmarks can easily be incorporated into the "diligence" segment of the outsourcing process.

Thanks to the growing acceptance of audits and benchmarking, it is becoming increasingly common for service providers to get together and compare notes on how they solve problems and what the results are. Theoretically, these service providers are each coming away with a stronger sense of their operation's position relative to others in and out of their industry. The mediator role is usually supported by consulting companies.

Auditing and benchmarking help determine what accomplishments really exist or can be achieved and give companies the chance to match or exceed the best in the business. Now these activities are an integral part of the total quality management program, based in most cases on ISO 9000 or total quality management (TQM).

ISO 9000 offers practical guidelines for how to improve the quality of conducting businesses. It became a condition of doing business in Europe. TQM has similar goals in the United States.

The principal phases of network management audits and benchmarks are as follows:

- Data collection
- Documentation (analysis of topologies, managed objects, performance reports, network management instruments, closed trouble tickets)
- Interviews with various persons in the operations, administration, and mainte-nance organization (major problems, feasible solutions, job assignments, educa-tion, skill levels)
- Observation of operational efficiency (reaction to trouble calls; how to use sup-port, documentation and management tools; supporting quality on various shifts; shift-change processes and documentation)
- Comparing best practices and industry averages

This phase includes only the specific branch or cross-branch evaluation. Usually, cross-branch indicators are used first. Results are usually visualized and may indicate considerable differences in certain areas between industry and client results.

8.8.1 Gap Analysis

This phase provides real details and addresses the functions of all business processes of service providers for customer care, billing, order processing, provisioning, and network operations management. Also tools such as support, management and docu-mentation systems, monitors, analyzers, element management systems, integrators, and modeling tools are addressed in depth. In addition, the assignment of human resources to processes and tools is investigated in depth, and recommendations to avoid redundancies are included.

8.8.2 Elaborating the Recommendations

The gaps identified in the previous phase are the basis for improvements or for sup-porting the decision to outsource certain business processes. If insourcing, the tasks are setting priorities and time frames and estimating the demand for reengineering business processes, acquiring tools, and hiring or cross-educating human resources.

Benchmarking service providers is not a trivial exercise. Usually, the benchmarking team consists of two to five people. Two types of persons conduct benchmarks: senior consultants and analysts. Skill levels overlap in certain areas, but usually both types have specific areas of expertise. Benchmarking definitely requires teamwork. More details on benchmarking can be found in TERP95.

8.9 Summary

Service providers are living in a very competitive environment. Technology is used to reengineer business processes. As more processes are automated, the amount of repetitive, task-oriented work will decline. And as newer technology is adopted, existing technologies will be either replaced or wrapped into the new ones, which will result in eliminating the need for certain skills. Some jobs (e.g., order entry clerks, accounts payable clerks, legacy tools specialists) are at high risk. But as processes change, they create new roles and functions that did not exist previously. New jobs are created in business areas (e.g., production buyer, supply chain manager, content development manager) and technology areas (e.g., knowledge engineer, business analyst, rules developer). This trend comes from the shift to more business-to-business integration. But even within established job titles, the job content often changes.

A dynamic workforce is a great value for service providers because it offers increased employee retention and organizational flexibility.

CHAPTER 9

Trends for Service Providers

9.1 Introduction

Increasingly complex networks challenge the limits of existing support, documentation, and management systems and internal system resources. In an integrated environment, carriers will prosper or wane by their support systems strategies, their implementation, and their execution. One-stop shopping for communications may satisfy businesses and simplify consumers' ordering processes, but the integration of multiple, rapidly changing networks and their associated support systems push the limits of most internal IT departments. In particular, existing support systems and internal systems resources are inadequate to support today's rapid changes in customers, services, and technologies.

The diversification of service providers is continuously growing. It becomes very difficult to draw the line between service offers of various providers. In most cases, a vertical differentiation is worth a try. There are service providers who concentrate on the physical network infrastructure (ILEC, CLEC, NSP), on the logical infrastructure, including some value-added features of service integration (ILEC, CLEC, ISP, ICP), and finally, on the content (ISP, CSP, ASP). In most cases, however, more than one vertical layer is supported. In case of ASPs, actually, everything is offered in one package. In the horizontal display, service providers and their products build a value chain, starting with individual service modules and ending with a complete outsourced service offer.

9.2 Technology Trends

Service portfolios of the future will concentrate on IP by implementing IP on various underlying network infrastructures, such as ATM, frame relay, or directly on fiber. Applications may be funneled via IP as well. The result is that the effectiveness and efficiency of IP is critical to service providers. The full migration to packet-switched solutions from circuit-switched ones may take several years, particularly for incumbent service providers and legacy applications.

Service portfolios are going to be structured into wireline, wireless, and IP—embedding in all three cases voice, data, and video. Time to market is the critical success factor of the future for all service providers. In particular, in the area of IP-based services, service creation, provisioning, rating, and bill presentment are online, real-time processes. Traditional services are going to be supported by self-care, which will put more control into the hands of customers.

Using improved and automated workflow and workforce management technologies, provisioning efficiency will increase significantly. Today, approximately 40 percent of service orders need correction during or after the flow-through of provisioning steps. Among the many reasons for this are typing errors, service order omission, incorrect syntax, database crashes, address mismatches, invalid resource id-s, lack of documentation of customer requirements, missing fields in orders, invalid records, unknown physical facilities of customers, and incorrect dispatch.

Various middleware solutions and management protocols help to optimize and standardize the information exchange between various processes, functions, and support tools.

As service providers implement billable next-generation services and put in place the mechanisms necessary to analyze and bill activity associated with those services, fundamental changes in how NSPs, ISPs, and ASPs run their businesses are likely to happen. To date, the service provider's game has been about gaining market share—doing whatever is necessary to build a viable customer base and gain dominance in a particular region or market. The next phase of the evolution will involve building profitability and focus. This doesn't mean simply creating new, billable services. To achieve success in an increasingly sophisticated marketplace, next-generation service providers will have to be able to rapidly answer the questions that they have not had to ask up to this point:

- Which services are meeting profitability goals? Which ones are not?
- For what types of customers do these services deliver the best margins?
- How can loss leaders and high-margin services be bundled most effectively?
- Which business partners or even erstwhile competitors are helping service providers generate the most revenue?
- What should billing systems' statements look like?

Answering these questions requires a highly granular, highly flexible database of traffic activity and associated financial metrics. The first phase of fee-for-services deployment is likely to be characterized by experimentation and change. Marketing programs will be launched, the results analyzed, and any necessary corrective actions taken. Service providers will respond to internal financial metrics, customer feedback, and the actions of other competitors. In such a fluid environment, rapid access to accurate data will be essential. The issue of billing is a particularly interesting component of any cohesive marketing strategy. As service providers begin to charge for services on a more granular basis, their billing statements will also have to contain more granular information. But there are challenges:

- What type of information will service providers want to show to their customers?
- Will they be able to add value by delivering data on how the customer used the Internet (by application, destination, and time-of-day)?
- Will business customers see such data as a useful component of their security and/or network management practices?
- What types of electronic billing data will customers find most useful as they attempt to integrate billing data with their own enterprise management platforms?

The strategic importance of digital communications, especially over shared IP networks, is growing every day—and so are the costs. Service providers will have to become more financially accountable in response to this trend. Packets and headers will have to be translated into monetary units. The accounting tools employed by service providers will therefore become an inextricable component of how shared, multipurpose IP network infrastructures are used, sold, managed, and built.

Service providers will also need to link traffic/billing data to policies associated with service-level agreements. They may address how a variety of service parameters (number of outages, their duration, latency thresholds, etc.) will affect billing policies on a a priori and a posteriori basis. The first case is based on the predetermined fees in the service contract. Often, the exact same traffic from two different customers will have to be billed differently—despite the fact that there may be no actual difference in latency or application—because one has signed up for premium service. The latter is based on penalty provisions in the contract; if agreed-upon benchmarks are not achieved, deductions will have to be made from the base rate.

9.3 Telco in the Box

Chapters 4, 5, and 6 addressed principal processes and functions for service fulfillment, service assurance, and billing. In the future, service providers may need a further step of simplification. Figure 9.1 shows a compact solution, consisting of principal processes and various databases. The key success factors are as follows

- Accurate data in the customer, product portfolio, and inventory databases
- An efficient workflow engine gluing the processes and their support tools together
- A well-educated workforce with the necessary skills
- Meaningful service assurance metrics that may be measured, maintained, and reported on

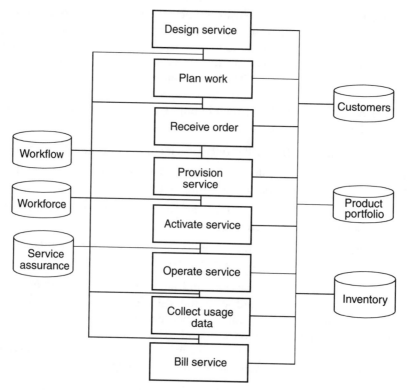

Figure 9.1 A simple view of service providers.

Particularly for smaller service providers, processes and databases may be preconfigured. The final customization of the application, "telco in the box," can then be made together with the service provider.

9.4 Trends with Support Systems

In order to support new technologies, new services, and each step of the support process, the expectations toward support systems are growing constantly. In general, the following attributes must become part of next-generation support systems:

Maximal scalability. Events, alarms, and management-related transaction volumes are not always predictable. Support systems are expected to support sudden changes of volumes and unpredictable increase of volumes within a short period of time due to unusual operating conditions, such as traffic reroutes, reconfiguration of the physical network, recovery, service launching, and unfiltered event storms.

Ultrareliability. Support systems and the data communication network are expected to be operational on 24 × 7 × 365 basis. High-availability features combined with high-reliability components are critical to achieve this goal.

Rapid integration into value chains. Operations and business support systems play an important role in the value chain, consisting of IP component suppliers, support systems' application suppliers, equipment suppliers, system integrators, network operators, service providers, and content providers. Being compliant to international and de facto standards, replacements in the supplier chain are easy, offering service providers best-of-breed solutions.

Excellent price/performance. Due to significant competition in this segment, service providers can hope for reasonable prices combined with excellent performance. This ratio can even further be improved when taking advantage of outsourced solutions for selected support functions such as billing.

Off-the-shelf technology. Time-to-market requirements of service portfolios don't allow lengthy design and implementation phases. It is recommended to take best-of-breed building blocks off the shelf and connect them to each other and to legacy applications using the integration capabilities of middleware and management frameworks and the concept of enterprise application integration (EAI). If service providers are developing an automated business process, they want to make use of existing systems and integrate these into the solution. For example, they might not have the time or resources to develop an entire solution from scratch, or they might not want to rely exclusively on one supplier's tools to provide the solution. Instead, they might want to have the flexibility of choosing the best application for each particular job (i.e., employ a best-of-breed approach). EAI helps to integrate applications from several sources.

Use of software engineers available on the market. Shortage in human resources may delay development and implementation projects for support systems. Powerful project and workforce management combined with state-of-the-art software technology may help to stabilize project progress and make deliverables more predictably.

Ability to cope with uncertainty and constant change. Support systems are expected to be equipped with innovative components such as fuzzy logic, expert systems, and neural networks. These algorithms assist service providers in dealing with uncertainty and setting up parameters to adopt to changes.

Support systems will be tackled in the mobile device arena soon. Mobile devices have made remarkable advances within a short period of time, even if mobile data network bandwidth is still too scarce in comparison to the fixed lines desktop Web experience. Implementation examples for using wireless access are many. They require client software to be loaded on the mobile device, but technology is moving in a direction where these applications will require only a Web browser. As enterprises and service providers build more Web-based access mechanisms, and perform the back-office integration to support them, mobile access becomes simpler. The trick is in content transformation technology and integrated microbrowsers. These microbrowsers are generally multiprotocol-enabled and able to read XML, WML, and other common mobile Web formats. In combination with transformation technology on the back-end, they can access any data that can be formatted to their requirements.

Once mobile providers are equipped for content transformation, they can offer more content transformation, they can offer more mobile data services across a range of verticals, including communications OSS applications. With technology this young, it must be deployed horizontally first to provide the backbone for vertical applications implementation. The mobile devices equipped with microbrowsers aren't asked to do much more than receive, display, capture and send text-based data—something they are anyhow optimized for. The key to moving forward is Web technology. With many OSS applications already being Web-enabled, a large piece of the development effort to mobilize these applications is already accomplished.

There are several OSS application areas where mobile technology can extend back-office functionality to the field, namely inventory management, workforce management, trouble ticketing and progress control, overall process management and business-to-business customer self-care. While there is no question that mobile data access to OSSs can extend their coverage and functionality range, the business case for them has not yet been validated. Workforce management looks like the first functional area to go mobile, but it is important to remember that the mobile device is only a front-end piece. To enable the mobile device, service providers must have a well integrated information infrastructure for the device to access. Present limitations in terms of bandwidth and area of coverage will be lifted in the near future.

A completely new type of support system—frequently referenced as eOSS—is needed for eCommerce. Service providers don't want to miss this opportunity, so they invest heavily in acquiring new OSSs or in reengineering existing ones. The presence of eOSS has a number of consequences:

1. *The flat rate–based IP service accounting is history.* The basic flat rate IP pricing model is not compatible with new IP-based solutions such as IP telephony, streaming audio and video, videoconferencing, and special push technologies, all of which place high demands on networks. Currently, competitive providers must support these and other premium services if they are to attract and maintain customers—regardless of economic risks. For the first time, new eCommerce support systems allow companies to bill based on actual usage of IP-based services and applications. Information can also be used for strategic planning and bandwidth allocation.

2. *Differentiation between premium and value-added applications.* Support systems for eCommerce make it possible to conduct a full application-based analysis of IP flows. Detailed analysis of IP traffic means that ISPs can charge premium rates for high-end, differentiated services. Some products perform a seven-layer traffic analysis, looking beyond the packet header to construct detailed information about the IP session in real time. As a result, it is possible for the IP or ICP to differentiate between value-added services, such as IP telephony and videoconferencing, and simple Internet access and to bill appropriately.

3. *QoS is becoming a business driver.* Looking forward, the implementation of next-generation support systems entirely changes the determination of quality. Where QoS is now determined by network performance, future QoS will be determined by the value of the content/application/service delivered. Over the next couple of years, money flows should be redirected to service providers of premium content. For example, funds generated by music delivered over the Internet should be redirected from the distributor to the artist.

4. *Real time service delivery.* Automated provisioning solutions allow service providers to gain significant competitive advantage by reducing lead times of days and weeks to minutes and hours—raising customer satisfaction and capturing revenue immediately.

5. *Optimization of routing.* Least-cost and time-of-day routing is possible. The right choice of communication services helps to reduce traffic costs.

6. *Dynamic bandwidth allocation.* Support systems for eCommerce manage the explosion in bandwidth demand by dynamically allocating bandwidth to guaranteed accounts. Bandwidth provisioning applications can be utilized to distribute bandwidth on a pay-per-use or subscription basis.

7. *Technical barriers to VoIP and FoIP are eliminated.* Not the quality, but the lack of proper support systems, represents the real barrier to VoIP and FoIP adoption. Most carriers delivering IP voice today are billing through prepaid models requiring callers to dial a personal identification number. New support systems enable carriers to save and make a profit by delivering voice call over the IP network. These new support systems also allow carriers to grow call volumes by eliminating PIN requirements. These solutions permit service providers to determine the costs/profits associated with relaying calls over PSTN. Several new support systems allow collaboration with clearinghouses. In a prepay example, balance information, along with the call's origination and destination, will allow the local gateway to tell the caller how many minutes he or she may speak.

8. *Various considerations of usage.* Support systems are expected to determine usage on number of bytes, duration, service level, and time of day. In addition, they can help to enhance network engineering strategies by tracking application type (Internet, e-mail, voice, video), distance (local, long distance, or international), and billable content (copyright royalties, audio/visual clips). Finally, future support systems should be able to analyze usage trends, discover abusive users or bandwidth hogs, and identify network problems and disconnects.

In summary, support systems for eCommerce help to accomplish the following

- Initiate new revenue-creating services
- Reduce network complexity
- Improve time to market

9.5 Interfaces and Integration

Support, documentation, and management systems are not isolated from other business systems of the service providers. Figure 9.2 shows their role in relation to each other, illustrating the shared role of frameworks at the core, supporting data maintenance, workflow, messaging, and workforce management. Also, frameworks are challenged for future applications. They are expected to add value by supporting the following attributes

- Flexibility to support new communication services, convergence networks, voice, and data

- Adaptability to implement to new pricing schemes (e.g., new services, bundles, new metrics, and thresholds)

- Interoperability with numerous best-of-breed OSS systems and, where applicable, existing legacy solutions

- Scalability to support rapid carrier growth

- Expediency to facilitate rapid time to market

The outside layer represents many other enabling processes and functions of service providers that have not been addressed explicitly in this book. These include (but are not limited to) the following:

Enterprise resource planning (ERP). This represents a well-known set of functions and services, including asset management, maintenance, general ledger, accounts payable, procurement and purchasing, bill verification, and commissions management.

Figure 9.2   High-level interfaces for service providers.

Customer relationship management (CRM). This offers emerging customer-facing services, including trouble management, account management, cross-selling, bill inquiry, and bill adjustment functions.

Sales force automation. This represents an emerging area of account, sales force, opportunity, contract, and contact management.

Business intelligence. A special area of providing tailored business rules for operations metrics, SLA management, data warehousing, product management, marketing, and CRM.

Decision support systems (DSS). Based on business intelligence, business rules are implemented for a higher level of automation, in particular to operate the underlying network infrastructure.

Support of eBusiness. This new and emerging area could play a significant, even a survival role for service providers. It includes Web-based order entry and returns, Web-based trouble reporting and status inquiries, electronic bill presentment and payment, and Web-based customer profile and product information. This is the basis for B2B and B2C on behalf of service providers.

Interconnection between multiple service providers. All the technologies implemented with enterprises, small businesses, and residential customers may be implemented between multiple providers, retailers, and wholesalers. Besides traditional techniques for supporting settlements, eCommerce techniques are also expected to be implemented.

Employee training and education. Besides powerful workforce solutions to support workforce dispatch optimization, training, education, and cross-education of all employees of the service provider are extremely important. It includes knowledge distribution about the service portfolio, sales techniques, support systems, documentation systems, management systems, basic financials, and the strategic position of the company among other competitors. State-of-the-art Internet-based technologies may help to increase educational efficiency.

There are a few practical recommendations to service providers to improve their support, documentation, and management systems.

FOR SUPPORT SYSTEMS

- No need to push new technologies into existing legacy OSSs, but use state-of-the-art support systems and interconnect them with legacy systems using middleware.

- Promote collaboration between multiple OSSs, MSSs, and BSSs using middleware, particularly CORBA.

- Continuously improve performance of these systems, because business success depends on good performance.

- Use special support systems that help to put B2B and B2C ideas into practice.

FOR DOCUMENTATION SYSTEMS

- Replace paper-based documents; convert them into digital forms and include them in the companywide document management system. If a technology has been chosen, complete conversion as rapidly as possible.

- Keep data in all the databases up-to-date; both support and management systems receive their actual data from documentation systems.

- Cleanse data; the quality of documentation is a great value in the hands of service providers. Data owners are expected to continuously clean data based on input from maintenance technicians and the provisioning workforce. Input may come also from management systems that are capable of discovering the network and its components in real time.

- Make documentation systems more dynamic by controlled integration with support and management systems. Integration is most likely using a middleware product in addition to CORBA.

- Connect documentation systems with design and planning tools by clearly defining the interfaces. Design and planning tools base their modeling and sizing on actual and live data provided by documentation systems. The result of the design and planning process should be fed back to documentation systems after approval and successful provisioning.

- Distribute information using state-of-the-art Internet technologies by granting access (view, extract, or report) to subject matter experts with proper authorization. The user of information should be made responsible for mining the right data from documentation systems. At the same time, protect the information maintained in documentation systems because it represents a very high value to the corporation.

In the case of new applications, choose off-the-shelf solutions instead of developing homegrown applications; time to market is shorter, maintenance is easier, knowledge transfer is practically unnecessary, and access to new features and releases are guaranteed by the supplier.

FOR MANAGEMENT SYSTEMS

- Implement solutions following the guidance of the emerging TMN standard.

- Filter and separate messages, events, and alarms by TMN layers; distribute information accordingly, following escalation hierarchies, customer care hierarchies, or a combination of both.

- Try to reduce the number of different-element management systems.

- Utilize the integration capabilities of existing management frameworks first, prior to implementing new ones.

- Reduce the number of management frameworks, but connect the existing ones via standardized protocols or middleware solutions.

- Streamline access to managed objects, such as switches, routers, gateways, firewalls, by using a mediation system with extended functionality. Support not only collecting usage and billing records, but also sending commands and inquiries to managed objects.

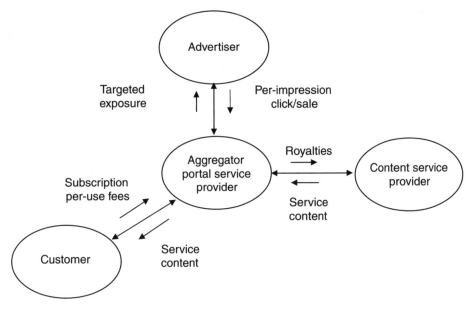

Figure 9.3 Positioning service providers.

9.6 Summary

Service providers should position themselves first. A large number of tempting portfolio opportunities exist. In particular, as part of new ecosystems and eCommerce, providers must have a plan about how far to penetrate new opportunities and service areas. New to telecommunications service providers are areas such as hosting, portal, and content services. Figure 9.3 shows a basic illustration for various services. Explicitly, content, portal, and advertisement services are shown; implicitly, network, application, hosting, Internet access, and security services might be included.

Independently from the service portfolio chosen, settlements are needed between peering service providers. The basis for accounting is very different; it could be the value of content, such as quality, timeliness, relevance, special events, usage, performance, or subscription for a flat rate. The technology to support each of them or a combination of them is available. In addition to accounting, innovative technologies for service creation and service activation are needed. Customers will play a more important role in those areas, helping service providers by communicating their future needs. Finally, powerful and properly equipped call centers with Web access will support customers with operational solutions in real time.

ADAM96　Adams, K. E., and K. J. Willets. *The Lean Communication Provider.* New York: McGraw-Hill, 1996.

ALLE00　Allen, D. "How to Get Ready for Voice over DSL?" *Network Magazine* (April 2000): 51–56.

AUST00　Aust, C. "Value Addition by Intelligent Network." *Datacom-Telecommunication.* (March 2000): 30–34.

BANG99　Banglesdorf, R. "10 Reasons CRM Waiting for Take-Off." *Billing World.* (November 1999): 60–65.

BLAC94　Black, U. *Emerging Communication Technologies.* Englewood Cliffs, NJ: Prentice Hall, 1994.

BLAC99　Black, J. "Real-Time Fraud Management Using SS7." *Billing World.* (July/August 1999): 56–58.

BLAC00　Blacharski, D. "The Changing Face of Service Level Agreements." *Network Magazine.* (February 2000): 94–97.

BOBR98　Bobrock, C. "Web Developers Follow Old Scripts." *Interactive Week.* (November 2, 1998): 29.

BRYD97　Bryden, S. "Carriers Look to SS7 Data for Solution to Usage Billing Dilemma." *Billing World.* (1997): 46–48.

CISC98　"Global Networked Business Approach and Architecture," White Paper, Santa Clara: Cisco Systems, 1998.

CLAR99　Clark, E. "Tweaking the Bandwidth Management Barometer." *Network Magazine.* (November 1999): 88–94.

DANC99　Dancy, B. "Billing for Wholesale Services—Just Like Retail—or Is It." *Billing World.* (October 1999): 47–50.

DORN00 Dornan, A. "Networking for Managers." *Network Magazine.* (January 2000): 52–55.

ELLI99 Ellingsworth, D., and D. Wile. "Choosing Your Path—From Electronic Stapling to True Convergence." *Billing World.* (October 1999): 36–42.

FINE97 Finegold, E. "SS7 Link Monitors." *Billing World.* (May 1997): 25–30.

FINE98A Finegold, E. "Easing Internet Traffic on the PSTN and Billing for It?" *Billing World.* (January 1999): 47–51.

FINE98B Finegold, E. "The Role of Mediation Systems in Changing Networks." *Billing World.* (September 1998): 32–36.

FINE98C Finegold, E. "Interoperability—New Integration Technologies." *Billing World.* (October 1998): 46–52.

FINE00 Finegold, E. "Network Service Management." *TelOSSource Magazine.* (January/February 2000): 20–22.

FLYN99 Flynn, J. "The Business Case for E-Billing." *INFORM Magazine,* Association for Information and Image Management International. (September/October 1999).

GHET97 Ghetie, I. G. "Networks and Systems Management—Platforms, Analysis, and Evaluations." *Kluwer Academic.* (1997).

GIAC00 Giacalone, S. "Label Switching Aids Scalability, QoS, Technology Update." *Network World.* (March 6, 2000).

HAMA00 Hamada, T., H. Kamata, and S. Hogg. *TINA, The Telecommunications Handbook.* Boca Raton: CRC Press, 2000.

HERM99 Herman, J. *Management Intranets.* Boston: Northeast Consulting, 1999.

HERO96 Hero, G. S. "Customer Based Management." *Billing World.* (November 1996): 32–34.

HOWE99 Howes, T. "LDAP: Use as Directed." *Data Communications.* (February 1999): 95–103.

KARV99 Karvé, A. "Strategies for Managing IP Data." *Billing World.* (December 1999): 60–66.

KARV00 Karvé, A. "IP Mediation Enters the Real World." *Billing World.* (January 2000): 58–62.

KRAS99 Kraskey, T. and J. McEachern. "Next-Generation Network Voice Services." *Network Magazine.* (December 1999): 96–102.

LEWI98A Lewis, K. "Ordering and Flow-through Provisioning in a Convergent Marketplace." *Billing World.* (April 1998): 54–60.

LEWI99 Lewis, K. H. "Corba Tutorial." *TelOSSource Magazine.* 2 (1999).

LIEB00 Liebmann, L. "Load Balancing: Where the Action Is." *Network Magazine.* (March 2000): 60–64.

LUCA98 Lucas, M. and L. Schweitzer. "Mediation in a Multi-Service IP Network." *Billing World.* (October 1998): 54–63.

LUCA99A Lucas, M. "The IP Detail Record Initiative." *Billing World.* (July/August 1999): 30–32.

LUCA99B Lucas, M. and O. Cohen. "Usage Collection and Analysis in an IP OSS." *Billing World.* (March 1999): 52–56.

LUCA99C Lucas, M. "Why Have an IP Carrier-to-Carrier Billing Reconciliation Strategy?" *Billing World.* (November 1999): 6–8.

MANN98 Mann-Rubinson, T. and K. Terplan. *Network Design—Management and Technical Perspectives.* Boca Raton: CRC Press, 1998.

MARS98   Marsh, J. "Fighting Fraud: Increased Uses for Billing Data." *Billing World.* (September 1998): 20–22.

MCK100   McKinley, B. "The ABCs of PKI." *Network World.* (January 17, 2000): 55–56.

MINO00   Minoli, D., E. Minoli, and L. Sookchand. "Video Communications." *The Telecommunications Handbook.* Boca Raton: CRC Press, 4-1–4-68.

MORT98   Mortensen, M. "Growing up with Operations Systems." *Billing World.* (May 1998): 58–63.

NOLL00   Nolle, T. "The Phone Bill of the Future." *Network Magazine.* (January 2000): 82–90.

NORR98   Norris, R. "Managing the Transition Period from Old to New Billing Systems." *Billing World.* (February 1998): 46–52.

POWE00   Powell, T. and J. Lima. "Wireless Web." *Network World.* (March 20, 2000): 81–83.

SCHL00   Scheupmann, R. "Realistic Service Availability." *Telecom Report.* Berlin: Computer Measurement Group, May 2000.

SAVI98   *Convergent Billing Platform, User's Guide.* Saville Corporation, 1998.

SHAW98   Shaw, V. and I. B. Blubaugh. "The Economics of Billing: Maximizing the Value Equation." *Billing World.* (June 1998): 74–80.

SNEL00   Snella, M. "Managing Networks in the 21st Century." *TeleOSSource Magazine.* (January/February 2000): 36–38.

STAL99   Stalling, W. *SNMP, SNMPv2, SNMPv3 and RMON.* Reading: Addison-Wesley Publishing Company, 1999.

TELO99A   *TelOSSource Magazine: Integration Tutorial.* September/October 1999.

TELO99B   *TelOSSource Magazine: Fusion: A Look at Objects as a Solution for Telecom Service & Operational Requirements.* November/December 1999.

TELO00A   *TelOSSource Magazine: The Convergence of Spatial Solutions and Enterprise Application Integration.* March 2000.

TELO00B   *TelOSSource Magazine: XML and the Collaborative Communications Industry.* June 2000.

TERP95   Terplan, K. *Benchmarking for Effective Network Management.* New York: McGraw-Hill, 1995.

TERP96   Terplan, K. *Effective Management of Local Area Networks.* New York: McGraw-Hill, 1996.

TERP98   Terplan, K. *Telecom Operations Management Solutions.* Boca Raton: CRC Press, 1998.

TERP99   Terplan, K. *Web-based Systems and Network Management.* Boca Raton: CRC Press, 1999.

TERP00   Terplan, K. *Intranet Performance Management.* Boca Raton: CRC Press, 2000.

ZORZ00   Zorzi, M. *Mobile and Wireless Telecommunications Networks, The Telecommunications Handbook.* Boca Raton: CRC Press, 2000, p. 2-40–2-65.

3SS	operations, business, and marketing support systems
ABR	available bit rate
ACD	automated call distributor
ACH	Account Clearing House
ACSE	association control service element
ADPCM	Adaptive Differential Pulse Code Modulation
AIN	advanced intelligent network
AMA	automatic message accounting
AMPS	advanced mobile phone service
API	application program interface
ARM	application response monitoring
ARP	Address Resolution Protocol
ASP	applications service provider
ATM	Asynchronous Transfer Mode
BML	business management layer
BSS	business support system
B-ISDN	Broadband ISDN
CAB	carrier access billing
CAD	computer-aided design
CAI	Common Air Interface
CAM	computer-aided manufacturing

CAP	competitive access provider
CAP	carrierless amplitude phase
CBR	constant bit rate
CBR	case-based reasoning
CBQ	class-based queuing
CCITT	International Telegraph and Telephone Consultative Committee
CCS	common channel signaling
CDDI	Copper Distributed Data Interface
CDF	Channel Definition Format
CDMA	code division multiple access
CDPD	cellular digital packet data
CDR	call detail record
CFMP	Content Flow Messaging Protocol
CGI	Common Gateway Interface
CI	component interface
CIM	Common Information Model
CIR	committed information rate
CLEC	competitive local-exchange carrier
CLI	command-line interface
CMIP	Common Management Information Protocol
CMISE	common management information service element
CMOL	Common Management Information Protocol over LLC
CNM	customer network management
CO	central office
COM	Common Object Model
COPS	common open policy service
CORBA	Common Object Request Broker Architecture
CPE	customer premises equipment
CPS	certificate practice statement
CRC	cyclic redundancy check
CRM	customer relationship management
CSO	customer service order
CSP	communications service provider
CSR	customer service representative
CSS	cascading style sheet
CSU	communication service unit
CT	cordless telephony
CTI	computer-telephone integration
DATM	distributed application transaction measurement
DCF	data communication function
DCN	data communication network
DCOM	Distributed Common Object Model
DECT	Digital European Cordless Telecommunication
DEN	directory enabled networks
DHCP	Dynamic Host Configuration Protocol
DIF	Directory Interoperability Forum

DiffServ	differentiated services
DII	Dynamic Invocation Interface
DMI	Desktop Management Interface
DMS	document management system
DMT	discrete multitone
DMZ	demilitarized zone
DNS	Domain Name Service
DOM	Document Object Model
DPE	distributed processing environment
DRT	document-related technology
DSL	digital subscriber line
DSML	Directory Services Markup Language
DSP	digital signal processor
DSS	Document Style Sheet
DSS	Decision Support System
DSSSL	Document Style and Semantics Specification Language
DSU	data service unit
DTD	document-type definition
DTMF	dial tone multifrequency
DTS	data translation services
DVD	Digital Versatile Disk
DWDM	dense wavelength division multiplexing
EAI	enterprise application integration
EBPP	electronic bill presentment and payment
EDI	electronic data interchange
EJB	Enterprise JavaBeans
EML	element management layer
ERP	enterprise resource planning
ESP	enterprise service provider
FCAPS	fault, configuration, accounting, performance and security management
FCC	Federal Communications Commission
FDDI	Fiber Distributed Data Interface
FDM	frequency division multiplexing
FDMA	frequency division multiple access
FHR	fixed hierarchical routing
FoIP	fax over IP
FPLMTS	future public land mobile telecommunications systems
FTP	File Transfer Protocol
GDMO	Guideline for the Definition of Managed Objects
GIF	Graphics Interchange Format
GIS	Geographic Information Systems
GoS	grade of service
GPRS	general packet radio service
GPS	global positioning system

GSLB	global server load balancing
GSM	global system for mobile communication
GUI	Graphical User Interface
HMMP	HyperMedia Management Protocol
HMMS	HyperMedia Management Schema
HMOM	HyperMedia Object Manager
HPPI	High Performance Parallel Interface
HTML	HyperText Markup Language
IB	Internet billing
ICC	interactive customer care
ICDR	Internet call detail record
ICMP	Internet Control Message Protocol
ICP	integrated communications provider
ICR	Internet call routing
IDL	Interface Definition Language
IEX	interexchange carrier
IFX	Interactive Financial eXchange
IIOP	Internet Inter-ORB Protocol
ILEC	incumbent local-exchange carrier
IM	instant messaging
IN	intelligent network
IntServ	integrated services
IOS	Internet operating system
IP	Internet Protocol
IPDR	IP detail record
IPMS	interpersonal messaging system
IPSec	IP Security Protocol
ISDN	Integrated Services Digital Network
ISP	Internet service provider
ISV	independent software vendor
ITU	International Telecommunication Union
IVR	interactive voice response
JaMAPI	Java Management Application Programming Interface
JPEG	Joint Photographic Experts Group
LAN	local area network
LATA	local access transport area
LCN	logical channel number
LDAP	Lightweight Directory Access Protocol
LDIF	LDAP data interchange format
LEC	local-exchange carrier
LIB	label information base
LMDS	local multipoint distribution service

LNP	local number portability
LRP	location routing number
LSR	label switch router
MAC	message authentication code
MDC	modification detection code
MDF	main distribution facility
MF	mediation function
MI	management interface
MIB	management information base
MIF	management information format
MMDS	multichannel multipoint distribution service
MOM	Management Object Model
MPLS	multiprotocol label switching
MS	message store
MSP	management services provider
MSS	marketing support system
MSS	mobile satellite system
MTBF	mean time between failures
MTOR	mean time of repair
MTS	Microsoft Transaction Server
MTSR	mean time of service restoration
MTTR	mean time to repair
NAT	network address translation
NEF	network element function
NEL	network element layer
NML	network management layer
NMVT	network management vector table
NOS	network operating system
NSP	network service provider
NTP	Network Time Protocol
ODBC	open database connection
ODL	Object Definition Language
ODMA	open distributed management architecture
ODP	open distributed processing
OFX	Open Financial eXchange
OLTP	online transaction processing
OMA	object management architecture
OMG	Object Management Group
ONO	other network operator
OO	object orientation
OOT	object-oriented technology
ORB	object request broker
OSF	Open Software Foundation

OSI	Open System Interconnection
OSI	Objective Systems Integrators
OSS	operations support system
PBN	policy-based networking
PCM	pulse code modulation
PCS	personal communications services
PDA	personal digital assistant
PDP	policy decision point
PDU	protocol data unit
PEP	policy enforcement point
PFDL	Policy Framework Definition Language
PIB	policy information base
PIN	personal identification number
PKI	public key infrastructure
PNP	private numbering plan
POP	point of presence
POTS	Plain Old Telephone Service
PPTP	Point-to-Point Tunneling Protocol
PRI	Primary Rate Interface
PSTN	public switched telephone network
PTT	Post, Telegraph, and Telephone
PVC	permanent virtual circuit
QAF	Q adapter function
QoS	quality of service
Radius	remote authentication dial-in user service
RBOC	Regional Bell Operating Company
RDBMS	relational database management system
RDF	Resource Definition Framework
RDT	request data translation
RFI	request for information
RFP	request for proposal
RMON	Remote MONitoring
ROSE	remote operations service element
RPC	remote procedure call
RSVP	*Resource* Reservation Protocol
RTP	Real Time Protocol
RTCP	Real Time Control Protocol
SAN	storage area network
SAP	service access point
SDH	synchronous digital hierarchy
SGML	Standardized General Markup Language
SIU	smart Internet usage
SLA	service-level agreement

SLM	service-level management
SMAE	system management application entities
SMASE	system management application service element
SMF	systems management facility
SMI	structured management information
SMIL	Synchronized Multimedia Integration Language
SML	service management layer
SMS	short message service
SMTP	Simple Mail Transfer Protocol
SNA	Systems Network Architecture
SNMP	Simple Network Management Protocol
SONET	synchronous optical network
SP	service provider
SPOC	single point of contact
SQL	Structured Query Language
SS7	Signaling System 7
SSP	service switching point
ST	serving terminals
STA	semantic traffic analysis
STDM	statistical time division multiplexing
STP	signaling transfer point
SVC	switched virtual circuit
TCP	Transmission Control Protocol
TDM	time division multiplexing
TDMA	time division multiple access
TINA	Telecommunication Information Network Architecture
TL1	Transaction Language 1
TMN	Telecommunication Management Network
ToS	type of service
UBR	unspecified bit rate
UDP	User Datagram Protocol
UM	unified messaging
UML	Unified Modeling Language
UPT	universal personal telecommunication
URL	Universal Resource Locator
UTC	Universal Time Clock
VBR	variable bit rate
VCI	virtual channel identifier
VCI	virtual circuit identifier
VIP	virtual IP address
VoIP	voice over IP
VPN	virtual private network
VXML	Voice XML

WAE	Wireless Application Environment
WAN	wide area network
WAP	Wireless Application Protocol
WBEM	Web Based Enterprise Management
WDP	WAP Datagram Protocol
WFQ	weighted fair queuing
WLL	wireless local loop
WML	Wireless Markup Language
WRED	weighted random early detection
WSF	workstation function
WSP	WAP Session Protocol
WTO	World Trade Organization
WWW	World Wide Web
XDR	XML Data Reduced
XHTML	Extended HTML
XLL	eXtensible Linking Language
XML	eXtensible Markup Language
XSL	eXtensible Style Language